# Instructor's Manual

and

# Test Bank

to Accompany

FUNDAMENTALS OF

# Multinational Finance

**MOFFETT STONEHILL EITEMAN**


Michael Moffett

Thunderbird – The American Graduate School of International Management

Curtis J. Bacon

Southern Oregon University

Boston San Francisco New York
London Toronto Sydney Tokyo Singapore Madrid
Mexico City Munich Paris Cape Town Hong Kong Montreal

Instructor's Manual and Test Bank to Accompany Moffett/Stonehill/Eiteman, *Fundamentals of Multinational Finance*



ISBN: 0-201-89281-2
1 2 3 4 5 6 7 8 9 10-DPC-0605040302

## INTRODUCTION

**Instructor's Manual/Test Bank**. The Instructor's Manual, prepared by the authors, contains complete answers to all end-of-chapter questions, problems, and chapter mini-cases, and includes selected spreadsheet solution images (spreadsheet solutions to all end-of-chapter problems are accessible on the instructor's portion of the book's Web site). The Test Bank, prepared by Curtis Bacon of Southern Oregon University, contains over 1,200 multiple-choice and short-essay questions. The multiple-choice questions are labeled by topic and by category – recognition, conceptual, and analytical types.

***In addition to this Instructor's Manual/Test Bank, a robust package of materials for both instructor and student accompanies the text to facilitate teaching and testing.***

**Computerized Test Bank**. The Test Bank is also available in Test Generator Software (Test-Gen-Eq with QuizMaster-EQ). Fully networkable, it is available for Windows and Macintosh. Test-Gen-Eq's graphical interface enables instructors to view, edit, and add questions; transfer questions to tests; and print different forms of tests. Search-and-sort features enable the instructor to locate questions quickly and arrange them in a preferred order. QuizMaster-EQ, working with your school's computer network, automatically grades the exams, stores the results on a disk, and allows the instructor to view and print a variety of reports.

**PowerPoint Presentation Slides**. Prepared by Shafiq Jadallah, the extensive set of PowerPoint slides provides lecture outlines and selected graphics from the text for each chapter.

**Study Guide**. Written by Timo Korkeamaki of Gonzaga University, the Study Guide enhances understanding and retention of concepts by providing detailed study outlines and helps students prepare for tests through a series of self-test questions, including true/false, multiple-choice, and short essay – all with answers.

**Instructor's Resource Disk**. This CD-ROM contains the Computerized Test Bank files, the Instructor's Manual files, and PowerPoint files.

**Web Site**. A dedicated Web site at <u>**www.aw.com/moffett**</u> contains the Web exercises from the book with wired links, electronic flashcards of glossary terms, and selected solutions and spreadsheets for end-of-chapter problems on the student's side, with Instructor's Manual, Test Bank, PowerPoint slides, and spreadsheet solutions for all end-of-chapter problems on the instructor's side.

## SELECTED SOLUTIONS AVAILABLE ON WEBSITE

The solutions to the following end-of-chapter problems, by chapter, are accessible by students from the book's website ( **www.aw.com/moffett**).

| Chapter | Problem |
|---|---|
| 1 | ---- |
| 2 | #2, #4 |
| 3 | #1 |
| 4 | #1, #4, #7, #10 |
| 5 | #1, #4 |
| 6 | #1, #4, #7 |
| 7 | #2, #5, #8 |
| 8 | #1, #4 |
| 9 | #2, #5 |
| 10 | #1, #4 |
| 11 | #2 |
| 12 | ---- |
| 13 | #1, #4, #7 |
| 14 | #2, #6 |
| 15 | ---- |
| 16 | #1, #4 |
| 17 | ---- |
| 18 | #2 |
| 19 | #1, #4 |
| 20 | #1, #3 |
| 21 | #1, #4 |
| 22 | #2, #4 |
| 23 | #1 |

# Instructor's Manual

## Test Bank

Follows page 287

## CHAPTER 1: THE GLOBALIZATION PROCESS

*Questions*

### 1-1. Trident's globalization

The difference in definitions for these three terms is subjective, with different writers using different terms at different times. No single definition can be considered definitive, although as a general matter the following probably reflect general usage.

*International* simply means that the company has some form of business interest in more than one country. That international business interest may be no more than exporting and importing, or it may include having branches or incorporated subsidiaries in other countries. International trade is usually the first step in becoming "international," but the term also encompasses foreign subsidiaries created for the single purpose of marketing, distribution, or financing. The term international is also used to encompass what are defined as multinational and global below.

*Multinational* is usually taken to mean a company that has operating subsidiaries and performs a full set of its major operations in a number of countries; i.e., in "many nations." "Operations" in this context includes both manufacturing and selling, as well as other corporate functions, and a multinational company is often presumed to operate in a greater number of countries than simply an international company. A multinational company is presumed to operate with each foreign unit "standing on its own" – although that term does not preclude specialization by country and/or supplying parts from one country operation to another.

*Global* is a newer term which essentially means about the same as "multinational;" i.e., operating around the globe. Global has tended to replace other terms because of its use in demonstrators at the international meetings ("global forums?") of the International Monetary Fund and World Bank that took place in Seattle in 1999 and Rome in 2001. Terrorist attacks on the World Trade Center and the Pentagon in 2001 led politicians to refer to the need to eliminate "global terrorism."

### 1-2. Trident, the MNE

Trident became a multinational enterprise (MNE) when it began to establish foreign sales and service subsidiaries, followed by creation of manufacturing operations abroad or by licensing foreign firms to produce and service Trident's products. This multinational phase usually follows the international phase, which involved the import and/or export of goods and/or services.

### 1-3. Trident's advantages

a. Entry into new markets, not currently served by the firm, which in turn allow the firm to grow and possibly to acquire economies of scale.
b. Acquisition of raw materials, not available elsewhere.
c. Achievement of greater efficiency, by producing in countries where one or more of the factors of production are underpriced relative to other locations.
d. Acquisition of knowledge and expertise centered primarily in the foreign location.
e. Location of the firms' foreign operations in countries deemed politically safe.

## 1-4. Trident's phases

a. *International trade.* Two advantages are finding out if the firms' products are desired in the foreign country and learning about the foreign market. Two disadvantages are lack of control over the final sale and service to final customer (many exports are to distributors or other types of firms that in turn resell to the final customer) and the possibility that costs and thus final customer sales prices will be greater than those of competitors that manufacture locally.

b. *Foreign sales and service offices.* The greatest advantage is that the firm has a physical presence in the country, allowing it great control over sales and service as well as allowing it to learn more about the local market. The disadvantage is the final local sales prices, based on home country plus transportation costs, may be greater than competitors that manufacture locally.

c. *Licensing a foreign firm to manufacture and sell.* The advantages are that product costs are based on local costs and that the local licensed firm has the knowledge and expertise to operate efficiently in the foreign country. The major disadvantages are that the firm might lose control of valuable proprietary technology and that the goals of the foreign partner might differ from those of the home country firm. Two common problems in the latter category are whether or not the foreign firm (that is manufacturing the product under license) is a shareholder wealth or corporate wealth maximizer, which in turn often leads to disagreements about reinvesting earning to achieve greater future growth versus making larger current dividends to owners and payments to other stakeholders.

d. *Part ownership of a foreign, incorporated, subsidiary; i.e., a joint venture.* The advantages and disadvantages are similar to those for licensing: Product costs are based on local costs and that the local joint owner presumably has the knowledge and expertise to operate efficiently in the foreign country. The major disadvantages are that the firm might lose control of valuable proprietary technology to its joint venture partner, and that the goals of the foreign owners might differ from those of the home country firm.

e. *Direct ownership of a foreign, incorporated, subsidiary.* If fully owned, the advantage is that the foreign operations may be fully integrated into the global activities of the parent firm, with products resold to other units in the global corporate family without questions as to fair transfer prices or too great specialization. (Example: the Ford transmission factory in Spain is of little use as a self-standing operation; it depends on its integration into Ford's European operations.) The disadvantage is that the firm may come to be identified as a "foreign exploiter" because politicians find it advantageous to attack foreign owned businesses.

## 1-5. Unique challenges

The major unique financial challenges are:

a. Operating costs and sales revenues occur in a variety of currencies.

b. Funds must frequently be moved from one currency and/or country to another currency or country.

c. Funds may be blocked in some countries, and firms must learn to operate efficiently when such blockages occur.

d. Analysis of credit risk for both suppliers and customers extends across national boundaries and thus is more difficult than domestic credit analysis.

e. Operating environments, including variations in the laws and rights associated with incorporation, differ from country to country.

f. Companies must deal with different tax structures, a task that is greater than simply coping with different tax rates. Companies need a unique set of skills to minimize the impact of taxes worldwide.

g. Companies must cope with nationalistic attitudes about the proper place of multinational/global firms within the domestic economy.
h. Local banks and capital markets may be needed, but their operating procedures and services may differ sharply from those of home country banks.
i. Unique risks exist that spring from the need to translate financial statements maintained in foreign currencies into the form and currency used by the parent firm to report its operations.
j. Uncertainty may exist as to how to achieve an optimal financial structure. Some may question if the concept of an optimal financial structure should exist.

**1-6. Corporate objectives**

*Labor union* representation required by statute is an example of governmental direction toward the corporate wealth maximization (CWM) model, in that such a requirement is intended to make the board responsive to stakeholders other than owners. Under the CWM model, such a statute would be viewed favorably, while under the SWM model such a statute would be viewed as undue interference in the right of owners to manage the assets into which they alone have invested money.

**1-7. Interlocking directorates**

Interlocking directorates allow firms, via intertwined management and governance, to *cooperate* and/or *collude*. A simple answer along corporate wealth maximization (CWM) or stockholder wealth maximization (SWM) lines is not so easy here. Many countries characterized by the CWM model, such as Germany and Japan, allow interlocking directorates so that "all stakeholders" will be represented. SWM countries, such as the United States, often prohibit interlocking directorates on the premise they may stifle unfettered competition because decision may be based on friendships, influence, or promises of reciprocity. "Crony capitalism" is a term often used to describe economic systems where decisions are frequently based on friendships, influence, or promises of reciprocity.

**1-8. Leveraged buyouts**

A leveraged buyout is perceived in a country that believes in corporate wealth maximization (CWM) as generally irresponsible. The liquidation of assets, often at market prices that do not reflect the value of the activity to workers and their communities, is not consistent with the CWM philosophy. Those believing in shareholder wealth maximization (SWM) argue that if the selling shareholders – the initial owners of the firm – are paid a price for their shares that is higher than the market as a result of the leveraged buyout, the market forces which are so important for competition and growth are allowed to work. Additionally the selling shareholders now have more capital to freely invest in other ventures, in turn creating more jobs and attendant benefits.

**1-9. High leverage**

High leverage increases both the risk of corporate bankruptcy and the possibility of a greater rate of return for shareholders. The corporate wealth maximization (CWM) model looks askance at higher leverage because any benefits will flow only to shareholders, while other stakeholders (such as labor) will bear the brunt of the risk should the company go bankrupt because of the fixed financial costs of disproportionately high debt. Under the shareholder wealth maximization (SWM) model, the decision on the degree of leverage resides with the owners as represented by the board, and the tradeoff between risk and return is presumably based on their risk-return preferences. Under modern financial theory, the risk-return attributes of a single company are meaningful only in the context of the contribution that company makes to a diversified portfolio.

### 1-10. Conglomerates

Conglomerates created to achieve diversification are presumably looked upon more favorably in countries tied to the *corporate wealth maximization* (CWM) model because the greater size of the conglomerate means the business entity in its entirety is larger; i.e., has greater wealth and is possibly less vulnerable to competition or takeover by another firm. Worker jobs are safer. An offsetting argument is that firms in CWM countries with interlocking directorates can act as if they were conglomerates, even though structurally they are not.

Under the *shareholder wealth maximization* (SWM) model, conglomerates created to achieve diversification are formed only when the owners alone believe that synergies will come about because of the consolidation. Critics of conglomerates in SWM countries point out that shareholders can achieve unique diversification in their own portfolios without conglomerate diversification being "forced" upon them. Additionally an argument is sometimes made that management skilled in one type of economic activity may be quite incapable in another type of activity, and that consequently conglomerates may perform less well overall than would a portfolio composed of the no-longer-existing separate constituent companies.

### 1-11. Risk

*Shareholder Wealth Maximization (SWM)* firms usually consider risk as a constraint on seeking to maximize current earnings. In an operational context for managers, *risk* is usually taken to be the expected variability for earnings over a period of future years. In a more specific portfolio sense for investors (as distinct from managers) , risk in SWM countries is the added systematic risk that the firm's shares bring to a diversified portfolio. *Unsystematic risk,* the risk of the individual security, can be eliminated through portfolio diversification by the investors. Thus *unsystematic risk* is not be a prime concern for management unless it increases the prospect of bankruptcy. *Systematic risk,* the risk of the market in general, cannot be eliminated.

*Corporate Wealth Maximization (CWM)* firms define risk in a much more qualitative sense. The term "patient capital" is sometimes used to imply that only performance over a very long term is of concern. In addition, the much greater array of stakeholders with divergent interests implies that some sort of consensus must be reached before a decision is made that might negatively impact one of the set of stakeholders – even if other sets of stakeholders gain.

### 1-12. Disenfranchising a shareholder

Certainly the two families gained in terms of maintaining their control of Roche. To the extent they can prevent an outsider with a significant investment from joining the board, they have a sinecure free from molestation by outsiders who might have new ideas. In the short run this promises stability for workers, venders, and local governments (which have tax receipts.) It will remain to be seen if, in the long run, the disenfranchisement of one significant stockholder keeps out the new ideas that might make the firm more competitive over a span of years.

**1-13. Stock options**

Stock options are used in Shareholder Wealth Maximizing firms to align the interests of managers with those of shareholders, in the belief that those managers will then make decisions which will enhance the wealth of all stockholders, including those executives. Of course, those executives are punished (financially) if the firm they manage fails to increase in market value.

Stock options to managers in Corporate Wealth Maximizing firms are unlikely, because they seek to cause managers to act to benefit the shareholders without, necessarily, benefitting the array of other stakeholders in the firm.

**1-14. Disgruntled shareholders**

Disgruntled shareholders may:

a. *Remain quietly disgruntled.* This puts no pressure on management to change its ways under both the Shareholder Wealth Maximization (SWM) model and the Corporate Wealth Maximization (CWM) model.
b. *Sell their shares.* Under the SWM model, this action (if undertaken by a significant number of shareholders) drives down share prices, making the firm an easier candidate for takeover and the probable loss of jobs among the former managers. Under the CWM model, management can more easily ignore any drop in share prices.
c. *Change management.* Under the one-share, one-vote procedures of the SWM model, a concerted group of shareholders can vote out existing board members if they fail to change management practices. This usually takes the form of the board firing the firm's president or chief operating officer. Cumulative voting, which is a common attribute of SWM firms, facilitates the placing of minority stockholder representation on the board. If, under the CWM model, different groups of shareholders have voting power greater than their proportionate ownership of the company, ousting of directors and managers is more difficult.
d. *Initiate a takeover.* Under the SWM model it is possible to accumulate sufficient shares to take control of a company. This is usually done by a firm seeking to acquire the target firm making a tender offer for a sufficient number of shares to acquire a majority position on the board of directors. Under the CWM model acquisition of sufficient shares to bring about a takeover is much more difficult, in part because non-shareholder stakeholder wishes are considered in any board action. (One can argue as to whether the long-run interests of non-shareholding stakeholders are served by near-term avoidance of unsettling actions.) Moreover, many firms have disproportionate voting rights because of multiple classes of stock, thus allowing entrenched management to remain.

**1-15. Dual classes versus a one-share-vote class of common stock**

A variety of arguments exist as to why Europeans allow this differential in voting rights. In some countries it is believed that "ordinary" individual shareholders are not qualified to influence business decisions. The average share-owning individual investor is presumed to be neither business-oriented nor knowledgeable about the business and prospects for the firm in which shares are owned. Hence they are not sufficiently informed to be trusted with influence of the selection of directors or other important corporate issues. Dual classes of stock allow one class (the "informed professional") to control the company while the second class (the "uninformed amateur") to provide capital and reap ownership rewards but not have a chance to "mess up the company" by having power over decisions.

A second reason for dual classes of stock is that takeover bids by other companies are made more difficult because the acquiring company would have to purchase the class of stock that has voting power, which class is usually held or controlled by existing management. Hence the job tenure of existing management is made more secure, even if they do not perform well and the value of shares in the market drops.

**1-16. Corporate governance**

*Corporate governance* is the control of the firm. It is a broad operation concerned with choosing the board of directors and with setting the long run objectives of the firm. This means managing the relationship between various stakeholders in the context of determining and controlling the strategic direction and performance of the organization. Corporate governance is the process of ensuring that managers make decision in line with the stated objectives of the firm.

*Management* of the firm concerns implementation of the stated objectives of the firm by professional managers employed by the firm. In theory managers are the employees of the shareholders, and can be hired or fired as the shareholders, acting through their elected board, may decide. *Ownership* of the firm is that group of individuals and institutions which own shares of stock and which elected the board of directors.

**1-17. Trident's goals**

Financial goals differ from strategic goals in that the former focus on money and wealth (such as the present value of expected future cash flows.). Strategic goals are more qualitative – operating objectives such as growth rates and/or share-of-market goals.

Trident's strategic goals are the setting of such objectives as degree of global scope and depth of operations. In what countries should the firm operate? What products should be made in each country? Should the firm integrate its international operations or have each foreign subsidiary operate more or less on its own? Should it manufacture abroad through wholly owned subsidiaries, through joint ventures, or through licensing other companies to make its products? Of course, successful implementation of these several strategic goals is undertaken as a means to benefit shareholders and/or other stakeholders.

Trident's financial goals are to maximize shareholder wealth relative to a risk constraint and in consideration of the long-term life of the firm and the long-term wealth of shareholders. I.e., wealth maximization does not mean short term pushing up share prices so executives can execute their options before the company crashes – a consideration that must be made in the light of the Enron scandals.

## MINI-CASE: CORPORATE GOVERNANCE AT BRASIL TELECOM

1. **What do you believe a government expects to gain from privatizing major sectors like telecommunications?**

Privatization is often conducted in pursuit of both political and economic goals. Politically, the recent trend globally has been toward market-based economies, in which government ownership is to be minimized. Economically, privatization is considered by many emerging market countries as a significant way of raising capital and building globally competitive institutions and industries.

In the case of Brasil and the telecommunications sector, the privatization auction raised an enormous amount of capital, as well as attracting foreign owners with world class experience in that specific industry. The hope was that owners like Telecom Italia would provide capital, technology, and managerial expertise to take the Brazilian telecom industry forward into the 21st century.

2. **Why would two major investors like CVC/Opportunity and Telecom Italia create a partnership to gain control of a firm and then be unable to agree on the firm's future strategy?**

As is often the case with joint ventures and strategic alliances, the initial motivations for the partnership are not the same as the long-term strategies of the individual players. Alone, either of the two parties could not have obtained the capital or political links necessary to take control. However, CVC/Opportunity is primarily interested in building the profitability of BT itself over time, whereas Telecom Italia sees BT as only one element of a much larger and complex strategy for telecommunications industry penetration in Latin America as a whole.

3. **If you were in management at Brasil Telecom, how would the fighting between your owners alter your ability to do your job? What could you do to 'manage your owners'?**

The tendency among most larger firms is for management to either make all major decisions or guide ownership's interest in those decisions. BT's management, if it were to focus its attention on a daily basis on the disagreements among its owners, would find itself standing still. 'Managing owners' is a difficult and dangerous process of management. In the case of Brasil Telecom, it appeared from the very beginning that Telecom Italia would not be a long-term owner, and most of management had therefore sided with CVC/Opportunity for expedient reasons.

Management will typically try to ignore it to whatever degree possible, and prevent ownership's divided input from entering daily management and leadership. Unfortunately, for major strategic and capital decisions such as the rate at which BT is to fulfill infrastructure obligations, the owners must be involved.

4. **If you were a minority investor in Brasil Telecom, holding some of the publicly-traded shares, what rights do you believe you should have in the ownership-control debate?**

Minority shareholder rights is a very controversial subject in global business today. Many countries have enacted complex laws to protect minority shareholders. (For example, in many countries like France a corporate raider may not acquire more than 30% ownership of the publicly traded shares without making a public tender offer to all remaining shareholders.) Most minority shareholders will realize that they will not have any real voice in the future direction of the firm. In this case, minority investors are increasingly passive owners. The debate, can, however, become increasingly complex as foreign ownership like Telecom Italia starts appearing to abuse the rights of domestic investors – minority investors and major investors – adding fuel to the fire of public debate.

## CHAPTER 2: HISTORY OF FOREIGN EXCHANGE RATES

*Questions*

### 2-1. Spot rate-interbank

Under normal conditions (no national holidays), your bank and Citibank would exchange funds (i.e., "settle") on the second business day after the trade.

### 2-2. Rules of the game

The gold standard required each country to set the rate at which its currency unit could be converted into gold and be willing to exchange gold for its currency or vice versa at that rate.

### 2-3. Role of the IMF

The IMF was established to render temporary assistance to member countries trying to defend the value of their currencies against cyclical, seasonal, or random occurrences. Additionally it was to assist countries having structural trade problems. More recently it has attempted to help countries, such as Russia, Brazil, Argentina, and Indonesia to resolve financial crises.

### 2-4. Classifying regimes

The following regimes would generally be classified as fixed exchange rate regimes:

a. Exchange arrangements with no separate legal tender.
b. Currency board arrangements
c. Other conventional fixed peg arrangements.
d. Pegged exchange rates within horizontal bands
e. Crawling pegs
f. Exchange rates within crawling pegs

The following regimes would generally be classified as floating rate regimes:

g. Managed floating with no pre-announced path for the exchange rate.
h. Independent floating.

### 2-5. Impossible Trinity

Countries with floating rate regimes can maintain monetary independence and financial integration but must sacrifice exchange rate stability.

Countries with tight control over capital inflows and outflows can retain their monetary independence and stable exchange rate, but surrender being integrated with the world's capital markets.

Countries that maintain exchange rate stability by having fixed rates give up the ability to have an independent monetary policy.

## 2-6. Emerging markets and currency regimes

Emerging market countries often try to fix their currencies with respect to their major trading partner's currency in order to reduce currency risk for importers, exporters, and investors.

## 2-7. Rupiah's softness

If the Indonesian rupiah is deemed "soft," it is expected to drop in value relative to major currencies deemed "hard." You are in the euro zone, and you may presume that soon it will take more rupiahs to buy euros than it does at present. Your action should be to exchange rupiahs for euros now, rather than later.

## 2-8. Hong Kong hardness

If you believe that the Hong Kong dollar is as hard as the dollar, you believe that a change from the current exchange rate will not take place. Hence you should be indifferent as to the currency in which you receive your rent.

However if you believed that weaknesses in the Hong Kong economy or the fact that it has now been absorbed into China (albeit as a special economic zone) will eventually force the government to devalue the Hong Kong dollar, that is the same as saying that you believe the U.S. dollar is harder than the Hong Kong dollar. In that case you would want to receive your rent in U.S. dollars, just to be safe.

## 2-9. Fixed rate regimes

In a current board arrangement, the country issues its own currency but that currency is backed 100% by foreign exchange holdings of a hard foreign currency – usually the U.S. dollar.

In dollarization, the country abolishes its own currency and uses a foreign currency, such as the U.S. dollar, for all domestic transactions.

## 2-10. Floating rate regimes

In a completely free floating rate regime, the treasury or central bank does not enter the foreign exchange market for the purpose of influencing the rate. (Treasuries or central banks in floating rate regimes do buy and sell foreign exchange for the operating purposes of their government.) The exchange rate is determined by the buying and selling of all independent parties. In some countries the treasury or central bank intervenes from time to time, usually without announcing it is doing so, to influence the exchange rate by its participation. This is sometimes referred to as a "dirty float," and is done to discourage speculators from pushing the value of the local currency substantially away from its fundamental value.

## 2-11. Trident's eurodollars

Do nothing! Your Eurodollars are in fact nothing more than a U.S. dollar denominated deposit in a bank that happens to be in London. Unless the bank fails (unlikely), your dollar purchasing power is intact. You have U.S. dollars; they are just residing in Europe.

### 2-12. Devaluing the dollar

Before the devaluation, the country's $200 million were equivalent to:

$$\frac{\$200,000,000}{\$20.67/oz} = 9,675,859 \text{ ounces of gold.}$$

After the devaluation, the country had a claim only to:

$$\frac{\$200,000,000}{\$35.00/oz} = 5,714,286 \text{ ounces of gold.}$$

By trusting the United States to remain on the old gold standard, the country lost 9,675,859 – 5,714,286 = 3,961,573 ounces of gold. This was equivalent to 40.9% of the gold value of its pre-devaluation foreign exchange reserves.

### 2-13. Why flexibility?

a. A country with internal economic problems, such as high unemployment or slow economic growth, might want to pursue economic policies that tend toward inflation as a stimulus for economic growth.
b. A country may not have the necessary foreign exchange reserves, or even want to hold sufficient foreign exchange reserves, to enable it to adhere to a fixed exchange rate policy.
c. Maintaining fixed exchange rates in the face of weak economic fundamentals, such as balance of payments deficits and greater inflation than its trading partners, may force the country to devalue its currency at some time in one big devaluation. Flexible exchange rates allow the currency to depreciate slowly and steadily, and speculators are not inclined to "bet" on the timing of the next big devaluation.

### 2-14. Monetary unification

Any group of countries seeking to establish a monetary union and a single currency for the group must have very similar inflation rates, interest rates, fiscal deficits, and degrees of government debt. The countries must also be willing to surrender to a central monetary authority control over monetary policy, including such decisions as issuing the common money and carrying out policies which would change the quantity of money in circulation. Cross-border transactions, both physical (commercial) and monetary must be free; i.e., the group of countries become a single market for all economic purposes.

### 2-15. Trident and the eurozone

The advantage to Trident from the advent of the euro is that it may operate throughout the euro zone without any risk of transaction exposure. As will be explained in Chapter 8, transaction risk is the risk of financial loss (or possibly gain) to a firm from a change in exchange rates between the time a financial obligation is entered into (say an account receivable or account payable) and the time it is settled by payment of the obligation.

In a broader context, integration of most European currencies into a single currency should allow the entire euro zone to prosper as it takes on attributes of a larger and more efficient "domestic" market. As the euro zone prospers, so will Trident.

**2-16. Argentina's currency collapse**

Argentina's currency board exchange regime of fixing the value of its peso on a one-to-one basis with the U.S. dollar ended for several reasons:

1. As the U.S. dollar strengthened against other major world currencies, including the euro, during the 1990s, Argentine export prices rose vis-à-vis the currencies of its major trading partners.
2. This problem was aggravated by the devaluation of the Brazilian real in the late 1990s.
3. These two problems, in turn, led to continued trade deficits and a loss of foreign exchange reserves by the Argentine central bank. (4) This problem, in turn, led Argentine residents to flee from the peso and into the dollar, further worsening Argentina's ability to maintain its one-to-one peg.

*PROBLEMS*

## 2-1. Frankfurt and New York

This question is posed in a way to confuse a partly informed reader. Because a foreign exchange rate is the price of one country's currency in units of another currency, the exchange rate between the dollar and the euro can be expressed in two ways, both of which are technically correct:

€1.0870/$, or $0.9200/€

Each of these is the reciprocal of the other (adjusted for rounding). Although both are technically correct, convention states the exchange rate as dollars per euro: $0.9200/€

| Problem 2.1 Frankfurt and New York | |
|---|---|
| **What is the exchange rate between the dollar and the euro?** | |
| | |
| **Assumptions** | **Values** |
| | |
| Buy a US dollar in Frankfurt for (in euros/$) | **1.0870** |
| Which is equivalent, the reciprocal, in $/euro | **$0.9200** |
| | |
| Buy a euro in NY for (in $/euros) | **$0.9200** |
| Which is equivalent, the reciprocal, in euros/$ | **1.0870** |

## 2-2. Peso exchange rate change

Although the Mexican peso is currently an independently floating currency, in 1994 the peso was pegged to the dollar. Otherwise the government could not have changed its value! Thus the drop in value of the peso from Ps3.2/$ to Ps5.5/$ was a devaluation.

| Problem 2.2 Peso exchange rate change | |
|---|---|
| Peso was "devalued" from 3.2 per dollar to 5.5 per dollar. | |
| Any time a government sets, or resets, the value of a currency, it is a managed or fixed exchange rate. A governmental decision to decrease a currency's value when it is a fixed exchange rate is termed a "devaluation." | |
| **Calculation of Percentage Change in Value** | **Values** |
| Initial exchange rate (peso/$) | 3.20 |
| Devalued exchange rate (peso/$) | 5.50 |
| **Percentage change in peso value** | -41.82% |
| (beginning rate - ending rate) / (ending rate) | |

## 2-3. Good as gold

The value of one currency in terms of the other was determined by the ratio of their respective prices of gold. This is because each currency was defined as equal to a certain amount of gold.

$$\frac{\$38.00}{£4.2474} = \$8.9466/£.$$

| Problem 2.3 Good as Gold | | |
|---|---|---|
| What if gold had cost $38.00 per ounce? | | |
| **Assumptions** | **Values** | **Values** |
| Price of an ounce of gold in US dollars | $20.67 | $38.00 |
| Price of an ounce of gold in British pounds | £4.2474 | £4.2474 |
| What is the implied US$/pound exchange rate? | $4.8665 | $8.9466 |
| (dollar price of an ounce / pound price of an ounce) | | |

## 2-4. Gold standard

As in the previous problem, the value of one currency in terms of the other is determined by the ratio of their respective prices of gold.

$$\frac{FF310}{\$20.67} = FF15.00/\$.$$

| Problem 2.4 Gold Standard | | |
|---|---|---|
| | | |
| What was the exchange rate between the FF and US$? | | |
| | | |
| Assumptions | | Values |
| Price of an ounce of gold in US dollars | | $20.67 |
| Price of an ounce of gold in French francs | | 310.00 |
| | | |
| What is the implied French franc/US$ exchange rate? | | 15.00 |
| (French franc price of an ounce / US$ price of an ounce) | | |

**2-5. Spot rate – customer**

You will pay $10504.20, to be settled on Wednesday:

$$\frac{\text{Ps}\,100{,}000}{\text{Ps}\,9.52/\$} = \$10{,}504.20.$$

| Problem 2.5 Spot Rate – Customer | |
|---|---|
| What must your company pay? | |
| | |
| **Assumptions** | **Values** |
| Spot rate on Mexican peso (pesos/US$) | 9.5200 |
| Your company buys this amount of pesos | 100,000.00 |
| | |
| **What is the cost in US$?** | $ 10,504.20 |
| (the peso amount divided by the spot exchange rate) | |

## 2-6. The ideal currency

If one-year interest rates in Spain are lowered, the general level of all interest rates in Spain will fall. Investors in Spain will then liquidate their investments, exchange pesetas for dollars, and invest in U.S. dollar securities in order to obtain two percentage points higher return. (The spread might differ for different types or maturities of securities, but it would be in the vicinity of two percentage points.)

This action by investors in Spain will cause the Spanish central bank to lose its dollar reserves as it tries to hold the fixed exchange rate in the face of a flight of capital. If the interest differential continues, Spain will run out of foreign exchange and no longer be able to sustain its exchange rate. The disappearance of foreign exchange reserves, if it continues, will cause Spain to do one of two things (or some combination):

a. Spain could devalue its currency so that more pesetas are needed to acquire dollars, thus breaking with its policy of maintaining a fixed exchange rate.
b. Spain could prevent its residents from exchanging pesetas for dollars, and thus stop the outflow of foreign exchange reserves. This would violate the "ideal" objective of free convertibility.

In summary, if Spain wants to maintain a fixed exchange rate and free convertibility of its currency, it cannot set its domestic interest rates at a level different from those in other countries.

## 2-7. Possible values of the euro

This is intended as a discussion question that has no fixed solution. The "present time" base period for discussion will depend on whatever date the class is discussing this issue. The intent of the question is to have students analyze the political effects of the first major international confrontation of the 21st century.

## MINI-CASE: TSAR ALEXANDER III'S RUSSIAN GOLD LOAN

1. **What is the value of the total bond as originally issued in French francs, German marks, British pounds, Dutch florins, and U.S. dollars?**

The total bond issue as described on the bond itself is 113,600,000 Gold roubles. Each individual bond is listed as having the following bond value and coupon by currency.

| *Currency* | *Bond Value* | *Coupon* |
|---|---|---|
| Russian roubles | Rbl 125 | 1.25 roubles |
| French francs | FF 500 | 5 francs |
| British pounds sterling | 19£, 15 sch, 6 p | 3 schillings, 11.5 pence |
| German marks | DM 404 | 4 marks, 4 pfennig |
| Dutch florins | *f*239 | 2 florins, 39 cents |
| U.S. gold dollars | $96.25 | 96.25 cents |

(The British pound sterling is the most complex for sub-components. At this time 12 pence ("P") equaled 1 schilling, and 20 schillings equaled 1 pound.)

2. **Create a chart which shows the fixed rate of exchange implied by the coupon for the six different currencies.**

The implied exchange rates are found by dividing the bond par values (or coupons) by currency pairs. For example, the Russian roubles per French franc exchange rate (Rbl/FF) is found by dividing Rbl 125 by FF 500, or Rbl 0.2500/FF.

| *Currency* | *Russian Roubles (per rouble)* | *French francs (per franc)* | *Pounds sterling (per pound)* | *German marks (per mark)* | *Dutch florins (per florin)* | *U.S. dollars (per dollar)* |
|---|---|---|---|---|---|---|
| Russian roubles | ----- | 0.2500 | 6.3211 | 0.3094 | 0.5230 | 1.2987 |
| French francs | 4.0000 | ----- | 25.2845 | 1.2376 | 2.0921 | 5.1948 |
| British pounds | 0.1582 | 0.0396 | ----- | 0.0489 | 0.0827 | 0.2055 |
| German marks | 3.2320 | 0.8080 | 20.4298 | ----- | 1.6904 | 4.1974 |
| Dutch florins | 1.9120 | 0.4780 | 12.0860 | 0.5916 | ---- | 2.4831 |
| U.S. gold dollars | 0.7700 | 0.1925 | 4.8673 | 0.2382 | 0.4027 | ----- |

3. **Create a second chart which compares these exchange rates with these same exchange rates today (use either the *Wall Street Journal* or *Financial Times* to find current exchange rates).**

Student assignment. The easiest approach would probably be to have the student reproduce the last column, the various currencies per U.S. dollar. Note that the French franc, German mark, and Dutch florin were all "retired" with the introduction of the euro, and their pegged rate to the euro will be needed to calculate an equivalent exchange rate (eg., florins/US$).

## Mini-Case: Tsar Alexander III's Russian Gold Loan

**What is the implied exchange rate between the currencies?**

| Currency | Par Value | Annual Coupon Rate | Annual Coupon (4% of Par) | Quarterly Coupon (coupon/4) | As described on the coupon |
|---|---|---|---|---|---|
| Russian gold roubles | 125.00 | 4.000% | 5.0000 | 1.2500 | In St. Petersburg 1.25 Roubles. |
| French francs | 500.00 | 4.000% | 20.0000 | 5.0000 | In Paris 5 Francs. |
| British pounds sterling | 19.775 | 4.000% | 0.7910 | 0.1978 | In London 3 Schill. 11 and 1/2 P. |
| German marks | 404.00 | 4.000% | 16.1600 | 4.0400 | In Berlin 4 Mark 4 Pf. |
| Dutch florins | 239.00 | 4.000% | 9.5600 | 2.3900 | In Amsterdam 2 Flor. 39 C. |
| US gold dollars | 96.25 | 4.000% | 3.8500 | 0.9625 | In New York 96 1/4 Cents. |

Of all the currencies, the British pound sterling is the most difficult for calculation. At this time 12 pence = 1 schilling, 20 schiling = 1 pound sterling.

The matrix of implied exchange rates is found by dividing the par values by currency.
For example, French francs/Russian roubles is found by dividing Rbl 125 by FF 500, giving an implied exchange rate of Rbl 0.2500/FF.

| Currency units | Russian roubles (per rouble) | French francs (per franc) | Pounds sterling (per pound) | German marks (per mark) | Dutch florins (per florin) | US gold dollars (per dollar) |
|---|---|---|---|---|---|---|
| Russian gold roubles | ---------- | 0.2500 | 6.3211 | 0.3094 | 0.5230 | 1.2987 |
| French francs | 4.0000 | ---------- | 25.2845 | 1.2376 | 2.0921 | 5.1948 |
| British pounds sterling | 0.1582 | 0.0396 | ---------- | 0.0489 | 0.0827 | 0.2055 |
| German marks | 3.2320 | 0.8080 | 20.4298 | ---------- | 1.6904 | 4.1974 |
| Dutch florins | 1.9120 | 0.4780 | 12.0860 | 0.5916 | ---------- | 2.4831 |
| US gold dollars | 0.7700 | 0.1925 | 4.8673 | 0.2382 | 0.4027 | ---------- |

These exchange rates can then be used to calculate the total issuance value in each of the respective currencies.

| Total issue value | Russian roubles (per rouble) | Total Bond Issuance By Currency |
|---|---|---|
| Russian gold roubles | ---------- | 113,600,000 |
| French francs | 4.0000 | 454,400,000 |
| British pounds sterling | 0.1582 | 17,971,520 |
| German marks | 3.2320 | 367,155,200 |
| Dutch florins | 1.9120 | 217,203,200 |
| US gold dollars | 0.7700 | 87,472,000 |

## CHAPTER 3: THE BALANCE OF PAYMENTS

*Questions*

### 3-1. Sources

The United States Department of Commerce (in its *Survey of Current Business*) and the International Monetary Fund (in its *Balance of Payments Statistics*).

### 3-2. Measuring activity

a. Current transactions having cash flows completed within one year, such as for the import or export of goods and services.
b. Capital and financial transactions, in which investors acquire ownership of a foreign asset, such as a company, or a portfolio investment, such as bonds or shares of common stock.

### 3-3. Purposes

a. Comparing the health and growth of one country with other countries.
b. Judging how the company's international operations will fit into and benefit or hurt a country's international financial position.
c. Judging the likelihood of a currency devaluation.

### 3-4. Balancing

The algebraic sum of all flows accounted for in the current account and the capital and financial accounts should, in theory, equal changes in a country's monetary reserves. Because data for the balance of payments is collected on a single entry basis and some data is missed, the equalization usually does not occur. The imbalance is plugged by an entry called "errors and omissions" which makes the accounts balance.

### 3-5. Accounting terms

A country's balance of payments is similar to a corporation's funds statement in that the balance of payments records events that cause the receipt (earnings) and disbursement (expenditures) of foreign exchange.

### 3-6. Current account

The main components and possible examples are:

*Trade in goods*:
Debit: U.S. firm purchases German machine tools.
Credit: Singapore Air Lines buys a Boeing jet.

*Trade in services*:
Debit: An American takes a cruise on a Dutch cruise line.
Credit: The Brazilian tourist agency places an ad in *The New York Times*.

*Income payments and receipts*:
Debit: The U.S. subsidiary of a Taiwan computer manufacturer pays dividends to its parent.
Credit: A British company pays the salary of its executive stationed in New York.

*Unilateral current transactions.*
Debit: The U.S.-based International Rescue Committee pays for an American working on the Afghan border.
Credit: A Spanish company pays tuition for an employee to study for an MBA in the United States.

### 3-7. Real vs. financial asserts

Real assets are goods (merchandise) and useful services. Financial assets are financial claims, such as shares of stock or bonds.

### 3-8. Direct vs. portfolio investments

A direct investment is made with the intent that the investor will have a degree of control over the asset acquired. Typical examples are the building of a factory in a foreign country by the subsidiary of a multinational enterprise or the acquisition of more than 10% of the voting shares of a foreign corporation. A portfolio investment is the purchase of less than 10% of the voting shares of a foreign corporation or the purchase of debt instruments. Multinational enterprises are more likely to engage in direct foreign investment than in portfolio investment.

### 3-9. Capital and financial accounts

The main components and possible examples are:

*Direct investment.*
Debit: Ford Motor Company builds a factory in Australia.
Credit: Ford Motor Company sells its factory in Britain to British investors.

*Portfolio investment.*
Debit: An American buys shares of stock of a European food chain on the Frankfurt Stock Exchange.
Credit: The government of Korea buys United States treasury bills to hold as part of its foreign exchange reserves.

*Other investment.*
Debit: A U.S. firm deposits $1 million in a bank balance in London.
Credit: A U.S. firm generates an account receivable for exports to Canada.

### 3-10. Classifying transactions

a. *A U.S. food chain imports wine from Chile.* Debit to U.S. goods part of current account, credit to Chilean goods part of current account.
b. *A U.S. resident purchases a euro-denominated bond from a German company.* Debit to U.S. portfolio part of financial account; credit to German portfolio of financial account.
c. *Singaporean parents pay for their daughter to study at a U.S. university. Credit to U.S. current transfers in current account; debit to Singapore current transfers in* current account.
d. *A U.S. university gives a tuition grant to a foreign student from Singapore.* If the student is already in the United States, no entry will appear in the balance of payments because payment is between U.S. residents. (A student already in the U.S. becomes a resident for balance of payments purposes.)

e. *A British Company imports Spanish oranges, paying with eurodollars on deposit in London.* A debit to the goods part of Britain's current account; a credit to the goods part of Spain's current account.

f. *The Spanish orchard deposits half the proceeds of its sale in a New York bank.* A debit to the income receipts/payments part of Spain's current account; a credit to the income receipts/payments part of the U.S. current account.

g. *The Spanish orchard deposits half the proceeds in a eurodollar account in London.* No recording in the U.S. balance of payments, as the transaction was between foreigners using dollars already deposited abroad. A debit to the income receipts/payments of the British current account; a credit to the income receipts/payments of the Spanish current account.

h. *A London-based insurance company buys U.S. corporate bonds for its investment portfolio.* A debit to the portfolio investment section of the British financial accounts; a credit to the portfolio investment section of the U.S. balance of payments.

i. *An American multinational enterprise buys insurance from a London insurance broker.* A debit to the services part of the U.S. current account; a credit to the services part of the British current account.

j. *A London insurance firm pays for losses incurred in the United States because of an international terrorist attack.* A debit to the services part of the British current account; a credit to the services part of the U.S. current account.

k. *Cathay Pacific Airlines buys jet fuel at Los Angeles International Airport so it can fly the return segment of a flight segment back to Hong Kong.* Hong Kong keeps its balance of payments separate from those of the People's Republic of China. Hence a debit to the goods part of Hong Kong's current account; a credit to the goods part of the U.S. current account.

l. *A California-based mutual fund buys shares of stock on the Tokyo and London stock exchanges.* A debit to the portfolio investment section of the U.S. financial account; a credit to the portfolio investment section of the Japanese and British financial accounts.

m. *The U.S. army buys food for its troops in South Asia from venders in Thailand.* A debit to the goods part of the U.S. current account; a credit to the goods part of the Thai current account.

n. *A Yale graduate gets a job with the International Committee of the Red Cross working in Bosnia and is paid in Swiss francs.* A debit to the income part of the Swiss current account; a credit to the income part of the Bosnia current account. This assumes the Yale graduate spends her earnings within Bosnia; should she deposit the sum in the United States then the credit would be to the income part of the U.S. current account.

o. *The Russian government hires a Dutch salvage firm to raise a sunken submarine.* A debit to the service part of Russia's current account; a credit to the service part of the Netherland's current account.

p. *A Colombian drug cartel smuggles cocaine into the United States, receives a suitcase of cash, and flies back to Colombia with that cash.* This would not get captured in the goods part of the U.S. or the Columbian current accounts. Assuming the cash was "laundered" appropriately, from the point of view of the smugglers, bank accounts in the U.S. or somewhere else (probably not Colombia, possibly Switzerland) would be credited. This imbalance would end up in the errors and omissions part of the U.S. balance of payments.

q. *The U.S. government pays the salary of a foreign service officer working in the U.S. embassy in Beirut.* Diplomats serving in a foreign country are regarded as residents of their home country, so this payment would not be recorded in any balance of payments accounts. If or when the diplomat spent the money in Beirut, at that time a debit should be incurred in the goods or services part of the U.S. current account and a contrary entry in the Lebanon balance of payments. It is doubtful that the goods or services transaction would get reported or recorded, although on a net basis changes in bank balances would reflect half of the transaction.

r. *A Norwegian shipping firm pays U.S. dollars to the Egyptian government for passage of a ship through the Suez canal.* If the Norwegian firm paid with dollar balances held in the U.S. and the Suez Canal Authority of Egypt redeposited the proceeds in the U.S. no entry would appear in the U.S. balance of payments. Norway would debit a purchase of services, and Egypt would credit a sale of services.

s. *A German automobile firm pays the salary of its business executive working for a subsidiary in Detroit.* Germany would record a debit in the income payments/receipts in its current account; the U.S. would record a credit in the income payments/receipts in its current account.

t. *An American tourist pays for a hotel in Paris with his American Express card.* A debit would be recorded in the services part of the U.S. current account; a credit would be recorded in the services part of the French current account.

u. *A French tourist from the provinces pays for a hotel in Paris with his American Express card.* A French resident most likely has a French-issued credit card, issued by the French subsidiary of American Express. In this instance, no entry would appear in either country's balance of payments. If, later, the French subsidiary of American express paid a dividend back to the U.S., that would be recorded in the income part of the current accounts.

v. *A U.S. professor goes abroad for a year and lives on a Fulbright grant.* The current transfers section of the U.S. current account would be debited for the salary paid to a foreign resident. (Even though an American, the professor is a foreign resident during the time he lives abroad.) The current transfers section of the host country's current account would be credited..

**3-11. The balance**

a. The *balance on goods* (also called the *balance of trade*) measures the balance on imports and exports of merchandise.

b. The *balance on current account* expands the balance on goods to include receipts and expenses for services, income flows, and unilateral transfers.

c. The *basic balance* measures all of the international transactions (current, capital, and financial) that come about because of market forces. I.e., the balance resulting from all decisions made for private motives. (This includes international operating expenses of the government.)

d. The *overall balance* (also called the *official settlements balance*) is the total change in a country's foreign exchange reserves caused by the basic balance plus any governmental action to influence foreign exchange reserves.

**3-12. Corporate objectives**

Two separate answers are possible for this question, and either is correct:

a. Control and profit, as mentioned in this chapter.

b. Risk and return, as mentioned in Chapter 1.

**3-13. Host country constraints**

a. The constraints may be based on several beliefs or assumptions. The belief that domestic land, business and industry should be owned and controlled by local residents.

b. In a slight restatement of the above, the concern that the home country is "selling out" its industries to foreigners.

c. The concern that foreigners might receive profits from an enterprise located in the host country.

d. In a slight restatement of the above, the concern that foreigners might receive profits from the labor of local workers.

e. Concerns over national sovereignty, often in the context of military self-sufficiency.
f. Concern over governmental (or oligarchy) ability to regulate and control companies operating within the country.
g. The assumption that business is a zero-sum game, so that if foreigners gain anything, it must have been at the expense of local citizens.
h. It is possible that other beliefs or assumptions also play a part. A complete list is probably impossible to compile.

**3-14. Nationalism**

Because both statements reflect a response to an inflow of foreign, presumably equity, capital, the difference is primarily one of political views. The first statement, "Foreign capital is showing its faith in our country," is essentially a political statement made in the context of welcoming foreign capital in recognition of the creation of more jobs, higher national income, and possibly expanded exports or diminished imports. The maker of the statement sees the benefits of greater capital investment and is not worried about the source.

The second statement, "Foreign capital is trying to take control and dominate our country," is a political statement by those who tend toward an isolationistic view of how a nation should act. The maker of the statement views the risk of loss of control and the possibility of foreign ideas and cultural intrusion as dangerous for the home country.

**3-15. Drugs and terrorists**

Quite obviously the merchandise involved in the import or export of marijuana, heroin, cocaine, or other drugs is not reported to customs officials and so does not appear in the goods section of the current account. For similar reasons, the cash payments used to finance terrorists are not reported in the current transfers section of the current account.

The opposite side to any of these transactions is changes in bank balances held by foreigners or foreign bank balances held by home country residents. These are usually reported, but only in the aggregate. That is, the total changes in holdings are reported by banks, but the parties to the millions and millions of individual transactions that lead to the total change are not reported. The imbalance shows up in the errors and omissions part of the balance of payments.

**3-16. Reserves and fixed rates**

The most likely effect of continued balance of payments deficits (either basic balance or official settlements balance) is an initial decrease in the country's foreign exchange reserves caused by increased flight from the local currency to stronger foreign currencies. If capital flight continues unabated, the next effect is likely to be a devaluation of the local currency.

**3-17. Reserves and floating rates**

Continued balance of payments deficits will cause private parties to judge the economy weak, and the currency will probably drop in value in the free foreign exchange markets. This drop might be self correcting because a cheaper local currency will encourage more exports and make imports more expensive. No specific reason exists to expect foreign exchange reserves to change.

However, the government might enter the foreign exchange market as one additional participant and use some of its foreign exchange to bolster or "stabilize" the value of its currency. Such trading activities by the government would probably use up some of the country's foreign exchange reserves. Stabilizing a foreign exchange rate implies a correct opinion about the proper foreign exchange rate, given all economic fundamentals. When undertaken by a government entity, it also implies that the government has a better view of the true value of the currency than the view implied in the impersonal and presumably efficient foreign exchange markets.

***Problems***

**3-1. Australia's current account**

| Problem 3.1 Australia's Current Account | | | |
|---|---|---|---|
| **Assumptions (millions of US dollars)** | **1998** | **1999** | **2000** |
| Goods: exports | 55,884 | 56,096 | 64,041 |
| Goods: imports | 61,215 | 65,826 | 68,752 |
| Balance on goods | -5,331 | -9,730 | -4,711 |
| Services: credit | 16,181 | 17,354 | 18,346 |
| Services: debit | 17,272 | 18,304 | 18,025 |
| Balance on services | -1,091 | -950 | 321 |
| Income: credit | 6,532 | 6,909 | 8,590 |
| Income: debit | 17,842 | 19,211 | 19,516 |
| Balance on income | -11,310 | -12,302 | -10,926 |
| Current transfers: credit | 2,651 | 3,003 | 2,629 |
| Current transfers: debit | 2,933 | 3,032 | 2,629 |
| Balance on current transfers | -282 | -29 | 0 |
| **Questions** | **1998** | **1999** | **2000** |
| a) What is Australia's balance on goods? | -5,331 | -9,730 | -4,711 |
| (goods exports - goods imports) | | | |
| b) What is Australia's balance on services? | -1,091 | -950 | 321 |
| (services credit - services debit) | | | |
| c) What is Australia's balance on goods and services? | -6,422 | -10,680 | -4,390 |
| (balance on goods + balance on services) | | | |
| d) What is Australia's current account balance? | -18,014 | -23,011 | -15,316 |
| (the sum of the four balances listed above, | | | |
| goods, services, income, and current transfers) | | | |

## 3-2. Uruguay's current account

| Problem 3.2 Uruguay's Current Account | | | |
|---|---|---|---|
| **Assumptions (millions of US dollars)** | **1998** | **1999** | **2000** |
| Goods: exports | 2,829 | 2,291 | 2,380 |
| Goods: imports | 3,601 | 3,187 | 3,316 |
| Balance on goods | -772 | -896 | -936 |
| Services: credit | 1,319 | 1,262 | 1,354 |
| Services: debit | 884 | 802 | 900 |
| Balance on services | 435 | 460 | 454 |
| Income: credit | 608 | 736 | 761 |
| Income: debit | 806 | 879 | 937 |
| Balance on income | -198 | -143 | -176 |
| Current transfers: credit | 75 | 78 | 71 |
| Current transfers: debit | 16 | 5 | 5 |
| Balance on current transfers | 59 | 73 | 66 |
| **Questions** | **1998** | **1999** | **2000** |
| a) What is Uruguay's balance on goods? | -772 | -896 | -936 |
| b) What is Uruguay's balance on services? | 435 | 460 | 454 |
| c) What is Uruguay's balance on goods and services? | -337 | -436 | -482 |
| d) What is Uruguay's balance on goods, services and income? | -535 | -579 | -658 |
| e) What is Uruguay's current account balance? | -476 | -506 | -592 |

**3-3. Myanmar's balance of payments**

| **Problem 3.3 Myanmar's Balance of Payments** | | | |
|---|---|---|---|
| **Assumptions (millions of US dollars)** | **1998** | **1999** | **2000** |
| A. Current account balance | -494.2 | -281.9 | -243.0 |
| B. Capital account balance | 0.0 | 0.0 | 0.0 |
| C. Financial account balance | 535.1 | 248.8 | 160.1 |
| D. Net errors and omissions | 18.8 | -12.3 | 59.6 |
| E. Reserves and related items | -59.7 | 45.4 | 23.3 |
| | | | |
| **Questions** | **1998** | **1999** | **2000** |
| a) Is Myanmar experiencing a net capital inflow or outflow? | 535.1 | 248.8 | 160.1 |
| | "inflow" | "inflow" | "inflow" |
| b) What is Myanmar's Total for Groups A and B? | -494.2 | -281.9 | -243.0 |
| c) What is Myanmar's Total for Groups A through C? | 40.9 | -33.1 | -82.9 |
| d) What is Myanmar's Total for Groups A through D? | 59.7 | -45.4 | -23.3 |

## 3-4. Argentina's balance of payments

| Problem 3.4 Argentina's Balance of Payments | | | |
|---|---|---|---|
| **Assumptions (millions of US dollars)** | **1998** | **1999** | **2000** |
| **A. Current Account** | | | |
| Goods: exports | 26,433 | 23,309 | 26,409 |
| Goods: imports | 29,532 | 24,103 | 23,851 |
| Balance on goods | -3,099 | -794 | 2,558 |
| | | | |
| Services: credit | 4,618 | 4,446 | 4,536 |
| Services: debit | 9,127 | 8,601 | 8,871 |
| Balance on services | -4,509 | -4,155 | -4,335 |
| | | | |
| Income: credit | 6,121 | 6,085 | 7,397 |
| Income: debit | 13,537 | 13,557 | 14,879 |
| Balance on income | -7,416 | -7,472 | -7,482 |
| | | | |
| Current transfers: credit | 711 | 688 | 641 |
| Current transfers: debit | 313 | 306 | 352 |
| Balance on current transfers | 398 | 382 | 289 |
| | | | |
| ***Current Account Balance (Group A)*** | -14,626 | -12,039 | -8,970 |
| | | | |
| **B. Capital Account (Group B)** | 73 | 88 | 87 |
| | | | |
| **C. Financial Account** | | | |
| Direct investment abroad | 2,326 | 1,354 | 1,113 |
| Direct investment in Argentina | 7,292 | 23,984 | 11,665 |
| Direct investment in Argentina, net | 4,966 | 22,630 | 10,552 |
| | | | |
| Portfolio investment assets, net | -1,905 | -2,129 | -1,060 |
| Portfolio investment liabilities, net | 10,693 | -4,782 | -1,332 |
| Balance on other investment assets and liabilities, net | 5,217 | -1,026 | -50 |
| | | | |
| **D. Net Errors and Omissions** | -328 | -729 | -403 |
| **E. Reserves and Related Items** | -4,090 | -2,013 | 1,176 |
| | | | |
| **Questions** | | | |
| | | | |
| a) What is Argentina's balance on goods and services? | -7,608 | -4,949 | -1,777 |
| b) What is Argentina's current account balance? | -14,626 | -12,039 | -8,970 |
| c) What seems to have been the primary driver in | | | |
| Argentina's current account balance? | income debit | income debit | income debit |
| d) What is Argentina's financial account balance? | 18,971 | 14,693 | 8,110 |
| e) What is Argentina's Total for Groups A through C? | 4,418 | 2,742 | -773 |
| f) What is Argentina's Total for Groups A through D? | 4,090 | 2,013 | -1,176 |

MINI-CASE: TURKEY'S KRIZ (A): DETERIORATING BALANCE OF PAYMENTS

1. **Where in the Current Account would the imported telecommunications equipment be listed? Would this correspond to the increase in magnitude and timing of the Financial Account?**

The telecom equipment would appear in the *Current Account* as an import of goods. *Net other investment* would include financing by the vendors that sold TelSim the equipment. This and other imports of capital equipment probably accounted for most of the increase in net other investment and thus the large negative balance in the *Financial Account* in the year 2000.

2. **Why do you think that net direct investment declined from $571 million in 1998 to $112 million in 2000?**

The decline was probably caused by a lack of confidence in Turkey's political stability and long-term growth prospects. Turkey's war on its own' inflation during the period 1999 to early 2000 must have included high interest rates and other macroeconomic policies to slow down the rate of growth. A slower rate of growth, if maintained in the long run, would reduce expected returns and direct investment inflows.

3. **Why do you think that TelSim defaulted on its payments for equipment imports from Nokia and Motorola?**

TelSim needed to invest heavily in capital equipment in order to create a modern high speed, high capacity network. Unfortunately, a considerable time gap typically exists between the time a network is created and it s capacity is utilized by revenue-paying customers. Thus long-term financing rather than short-term trade financing is needed. The timing gap experienced by TelSim was also experienced by many other telecommunications companies worldwide, including the highly-publicized case of Global Crossing, which also went bankrupt.

Expectations for the telecom industry and its ability to "monetize its customer base," the ability to generate significant revenues from installed networks, proved overly optimistic. A worldwide overcapacity of telecommunications networks led to cutthroat price competition, adding to the shortfall in revenues experience worldwide. The overcapacity continued for several years, however, as firms attempted to survive by covering variable costs but not fixed capital costs of providing services.

Finally, there has been a continuing debate over the intentions and ethics of the Uzan family itself – the controlling interest group of TelSim. The press has run a number of stories raising the question as to whether the Uzan family had ever truly intended to repay the massive infrastructure financing provided by Motorola and Nokia. At the time of this writing, however, there is no proof that this was the case.

## CHAPTER 4: FOREIGN EXCHANGE THEORY AND MARKETS

*Questions*

### 4-1. Purchasing power parity

The law of one prices states that producers' prices for goods or services of identical quality should be the same in different markets; i.e., different countries (assuming no restrictions on the sale and allowing for transportation costs). If a country has higher inflation than other countries, its currency should devalue or depreciate so that the real price remains the same as in all countries. Application of this law results in the theory of Purchasing Power Parity (PPP).

### 4-2. Undervalued and overvalued

In its semantic sense, *undervalued* means current value (current price) is lower than true intrinsic worth, and *overvalued* means current value (current price) is above true intrinsic worth. Application of these concepts to currencies implies that one has some basis, such as purchasing power parity, to determine true intrinsic worth.

a. An *undervalued currency* is a currency for which the current exchange rate (e.g., current value), stated as the foreign currency price for the base currency is lower than it should be. Assume the current exchange rate for the Slovak koruna is K50.0/$ at a time when the koruna's intrinsic worth is K40.0/$. Using reciprocals (1÷K50.0/$=$0.0200/K; 1÷K40/$=$0.0250/K), the koruna is currently priced in dollars at 2.0¢ per koruna at a time when its intrinsic worth is 2.5¢ per koruna. Hence at its present price it is *undervalued,* meaning the value placed on the koruna by the market (2.0¢) is below its true worth (2.5¢).

b. An *overvalued currency* is a currency for which the current exchange rate (e.g., current value), stated as the foreign currency price for the base currency is higher than it should be. Assume the current exchange rate for the Sri Lankan rupee is R100/$ at a time when the rupee's intrinsic worth is R125/$. Using reciprocals (1÷R100/$=$0.0100/R; 1÷R125/$=$0.0800/R), the rupee is currently priced in dollars at 1.0¢ per rupee at a time that its intrinsic worth is only 0.8¢ per koruna. Hence at its present price it is *overvalued,* meaning the value placed on the rupee by the market (1.0¢) is greater than its true worth (0.9¢).

Most exchange rates are stated as the number of foreign currency units needed to buy one U.S. dollar. For these currencies, then, an exchange rate where the stated rate is greater than the intrinsic worth of the currency is undervalued; and vice versa. One will note that in Exhibit 4.1 in the text, those currencies given a minus sign in column (5) are undervalued – see heading of column (5). I.e. their "actual exchange rate" (column 2, expressed as currency units per dollar) is greater than their inherent worth, the implied PPP vis à vise the dollar (column 4).

### 4-3. Hamburger standard

In Exhibit 4.1, currencies with a minus sign in column (5) are undervalued; see the heading to that column and the discussion in the solution to question 4-2 immediately above. Only two of the 30 listed countries have overvalued currencies.

Data in the current table suggest that hamburgers are cheaper in the rest of the world than they are in Britain, Denmark, Switzerland, and the United States. If the hamburger standard is a correct measure of overall purchasing power parity, goods in general are less expensive in all countries except Britain, Denmark,

Switzerland, and the United States.

| *Undervalued countries/currencies* | | | *Overvalued countries/currencies* |
|---|---|---|---|
| Argentina | Spain | Russia | Britain |
| Australia | Hong Kong | Singapore | Denmark |
| Brazil | Hungary | South Africa | Switzerland |
| Canada | Indonesia | South Korea | |
| Chile | Japan | Sweden | |
| China (PRC) | Malaysia | Taiwan | |
| Czech Rep | Mexico | Thailand | |
| France | New Zealand | | |
| Germany | Philippines | | |
| Italy | Poland | | |

Note that the exchange rate for the British pound is expressed as US$ per pound, rather than as pounds per U.S. dollar, the method used in all other currency rates in Exhibit 4.1.

**4-4. Relativity**

The *absolute* version of the theory of purchasing power parity states that exchange rates should reflect the difference in price indices for traded goods and services between two countries. The *relative* version of the theory uses changes in such price indices between two time periods to predict changes in the exchange rate (rather than the *absolute* exchange rate) relative to some past base period.

**4-5. PPP and BOP**

If a country's inflation rate exceeds that of its main trading partners and its exchange rate does not change, its exports of goods and services become evermore expensive while imports become evermore cheaper at home. These conditions lead to a deficit in the current account of the balance of payments.

**4-6. Validating PPP**

As a general matter research has shown (a) that PPP works well over the very long run but poorly over the short run, and (b) the theory holds better for countries with relatively high rates of inflation and underdeveloped capital markets.

**4-7. Exchange rate indices**

An exchange rate index is an index that measures the value of a given country's exchange rate against all other exchange rates in order to determine if that currency is overvalued or undervalued.

a. The *nominal* effective exchange rate index is based on a weighted average of actual exchange rates over a period of time. It is unrelated to PPP and simply measures changes in the exchange rate (i.e., currency value) relative to some arbitrary base period. It is used in calculating the real effective exchange rate index.

b. "The *real* effective exchange rate index adjusts the nominal effective exchange rate index to reflect differences in inflation. The adjustment is achieved by multiplying the nominal index by the ratio of domestic costs to foreign costs. The real index measures deviation from purchasing power parity, and consequently pressures on a country's current account and foreign exchange rate.

### 4-8. Interest rates

*Nominal* interest rates are simply the stated contractual rate of interest within a country. *Real* interest rates are the nominal interest rate less the rate of inflation. (If one earns 8% interest on a debt instrument, but inflation "eats away" 3 percentage points of those earnings, the real interest rate is only 5%. The purchasing power of debt holders rose only 5% during the year.)

### 4-9. International Fisher

Irving Fisher stated that the spot exchange rate should change in an equal amount but opposite in direction to the difference in nominal interest rates. Stated differently, the real return in different countries should be the same, so that if one country has a higher nominal interest rate, the gain from investing in that currency will be lost by a deterioration of its exchange rate.

### 4-10. Fisher effect

Irving Fisher stated that nominal interest rates in each country should equal the required rate of return plus compensation for inflation. Using i for the nominal rate, r for the real rate, and π for the rate of inflation, the Fisher effect may be stated two ways:

$$i = r + \pi, \text{ or } r = i - \pi$$

The Fisher effect also states that real interest rates in various countries should be the same.

***Problems***

### 4-1. Passing through

All prices are FOB Yokohama.

a. The dollar price of a Honda at the beginning of the year is the Japanese yen price converted to U.S. dollars at the beginning of the year spot exchange rate of ¥125.00/$:

$$\frac{¥4{,}000{,}000}{¥125.00/\$} = \$32{,}000.$$

b. The expected spot rate one year from now assuming purchasing power parity (PPP) is found by multiplying the current spot exchange rate by the ratio of expected inflation rates (Japanese yen over U.S. dollars):

$$\text{Expected spot rate} = ¥125.00/\$ \times \frac{(1 + .0100)}{(1 + .0300)} = ¥122.57/\$.$$

Note that the Japanese yen is expected to experience a lower rate of inflation than the U.S. dollar, and the yen correspondingly is seen to strengthen versus the dollar (it is expected to take fewer yen to get a dollar one year from now).

c. Assuming complete pass through, meaning that the full exchange rate change is to be reflected in the price of the automobile, the price of the Honda in U.S. dollars in one year is found as follows.

Price of the Honda will rise with Japanese inflation over the coming year:

$$¥4{,}000{,}000 \times 1.01 = ¥4{,}040{,}000$$

We then use the expected spot exchange rate one year from now calculated in part b) to estimate the dollar price at the end of one year:

$$\frac{¥4{,}040{,}000}{¥122.57/\$} = \$32{,}960.$$

If Honda were to pass through the entire exchange rate change, the price of the Honda automobile in U.S. dollar terms would rise from $32,000 to $32,960. This is complete – or 100% – pass through.

d. Assuming Honda prefers to only pass through 60% of the expected exchange rate change, the dollar price at the end of the coming year is found as follows.

Price of the Honda will rise with Japanese inflation over the coming year (as in the previous part c):

$$¥4{,}000{,}000 \times 1.01 = ¥4{,}040{,}000$$

PPP had predicted the exchange rate to change from ¥125.00/$ to ¥122.57/$, a change of 1.98%:

$$\frac{\text{Beginning rate} - \text{Ending rate}}{\text{Ending rate}} \times 100 = \frac{¥125.00/\$ - ¥122.57/\$}{¥122.57/\$} \times 100 = 1.98\%.$$

If Honda allows only 60% of this 1.98% change in the exchange rate to pass through into the price of the automobile, this is a change in the exchange rate of .6 x 1.98% or 1.188%. The effective exchange rate used to calculate the dollar price would be:

$$\frac{¥125.00/\$}{(1 + .01188)} = ¥123.532/\$.$$

The U.S. dollar price of the Honda automobile at the end of one year after passing through 60% of the expected exchange rate change of 1.98%, is $32,704.

$$\frac{¥4{,}040{,}000}{¥123.532/\$} = \$32{,}704.$$

## Problem 4.1 Passing Through

| Steps | | Value |
|---|---|---|
| Initial spot exchange rate (yen/$) | | 125.00 |
| Initial price of a Honda in, in yen | | 4,000,000 |
| Expected US dollar inflation rate for the coming year | | 3.000% |
| Expected Japanese yen inflation rate for the coming year | | 1.000% |
| Desired rate of pass through by Honda | | 60.000% |
| | | |
| **a. What was the dollar price for a Honda at the beginning of the year?** | | |
| Year-beginning price of a Honda (in yen) | | 4,000,000 |
| Spot exchange rate, Yen/US$ | | 125.00 |
| Year-beginning price of a Honda (in US$) | $ | 32,000.00 |
| | | |
| **b. What is the expected spot rate one year from now assuming PPP?** | | |
| Initial spot rate (yen/$) | | 125.00 |
| Expected US$ inflation | | 3.00% |
| Expected Japanese yen inflation | | 1.00% |
| Expected spot rate one year from now assuming PPP (yen/$) | | 122.57 |
| | | |
| **c. Assuming complete pass through, what will the price be in US$ in one year?** | | |
| Price of Honda at beginning of year, in yen | | 4,000,000 |
| Japanese yen inflation over the year | | 1.000% |
| Price of Honda at end of year, in yen | | 4,040,000 |
| Expected spot rate one year from now assuming PPP (yen/$) | | 122.57 |
| Price of Honda at end of year in US$ | $ | 32,960.00 |
| | | |
| **d. Assuming partial pass through, what will the price be in US$ in one year?** | | |
| Price of Honda at end of year, in yen | | 4,040,000 |
| Amount of expected exchange rate change, in percent | | 1.980% |
| Proportion of exchange rate change passed through by Honda | | 60.000% |
| Proportional percentage change | | 1.188% |
| Effective exchange rate used by Honda to price in US$ for end of year | | 123.532 |
| Price of Honda at end of year, in US$ | $ | 32,704 |

**4-2. Chilean pesos**

a. The "value" of one peso is its price in another currency. Thus:

$$\frac{1}{\text{Ps}\,500.00/\$} = \$0.0020/\text{Ps}.$$

If the peso lost 25% of this value, its subsequent value became \$0.0015/peso. The reciprocal, 1÷0.0015 gives the exchange rate quoted as pesos per dollar, which is Ps666.67/\$.

The percentage change can be checked by using the percentage change formula as follows:

$$\frac{\text{Beginning rate} - \text{Ending rate}}{\text{Ending rate}} \times 100 = \frac{\text{Ps}\,500.00/\$ - \text{Ps}\,666.67/\$}{\text{Ps}\,666.67/\$} \times 100 = -25.0\%.$$

b. Purchasing power parity dictates that an item should cost the same in two countries, and that exchange rates should adjust to this "rule." Using the formula for the relative version of purchasing power parity, the spot rate of exchange according to purchasing power parity is:

$$\text{Ps}\,500.00/\$ \times \frac{(1 + 0.22)}{(1 + 0.00)} = \text{Ps}\,610.00/\$.$$

or simply,

$$\text{Ps } 500.00/\$ \times 1.22 = \text{Ps } 610.00/\$.$$

To illustrate, assume a basket of goods in Chile cost Ps100,000 last year, Chilean inflation pushed the price up 22% to Ps122,000 this year. Last year, Ps100,000 was equal in value to \$200 [i.e., Ps100,000 ÷ Ps500/\$ = \$200]. At purchasing power parity, the basket should still cost \$200. Hence: Ps122,000 ÷ x = \$200, and x = Ps610/\$.

c. To estimate overvaluation or undervaluation, we must assume that purchasing power parity is the benchmark of what is the "correct value." The current spot rate of Ps 666.67/\$ compared to the purchasing power parity value of Ps 610.00/\$, indicates the market is currently undervaluing the peso by 8.50%.

$$\left(\left[\frac{\text{Ps}\,610.00/\$}{\text{Ps}\,666.67/\$}\right] - 1\right) \times 100 = -8.50\%.$$

Many students find undervaluation and overvaluation very confusing. One rule of thumb method of assuring logical results is to first say what the benchmark is, in this case, Ps 610.00/\$. Then compare that to the market's current valuation of the currency, Ps 666.67/$. The market is requiring more pesos per dollar than what PPP indicates is appropriate. Therefore, the market is undervaluing the peso compared to PPP.

| Problem 4.2 Chilean pesos | |
|---|---|
| **Assumptions** | **Value** |
| Spot exchange rate, one year ago, pesos per US$ | 500.00 |
| Change in value of peso over the year | -25.00% |
| US inflation over year | 0.00% |
| Chilean inflation over year | 22.00% |
| | |
| **a. What is the actual exchange rate today?** | |
| Beginning spot rate (pesos/US$) | 500.00 |
| Percentage change in the peso | -25.00% |
| Actual exchange rate today (pesos/US$) | 666.67 |
| | |
| Check: (Beginning-Ending)/(Ending) | -25.00% |
| | |
| **b. What should be the exchange rate today based on PPP?** | |
| Beginning spot rate (pesos/US$) | 500.00 |
| Chilean inflation | 22.00% |
| US inflation | 0.00% |
| PPP exchange rate | 610.00 |
| | |
| **c. By what percentage is the peso overvalued or undervalued?** | |
| Actual exchange rate today (pesos/US$) | 666.67 |
| PPP exchange rate (pesos/US$) | 610.00 |
| Percentage overvaluation (positive) or undervaluation (negative) | -8.500% |

### 4-3. International interest rates

Next year's spot foreign exchange rate must be such that a one-year investment in Great Britain yields the same as a one-year investment in the United States. Using a nominal amount of $10,000:

a. Invest in the United States: ($10,000)(1.06) = $10,600 one year hence.

b. Invest in Great Britain: $10,000 ÷ $1.4800/£ = £6,756.76 available to invest now.

c. £6,756.76 × 1.08 = £7,297.30 proceeds one year hence.

d. Next year's spot rate must be such that if you sell your £7,297.30 for dollars one year hence you will receive $10,600. ($10,600 ÷ £7,297.30 = $1.4526/£.)

e. If next year's spot rate is $1.4526/£, this result will be obtained: £7,297.30 × $1.4526/£ = $10,600.

Under the international Fisher effect one would expect next year's spot exchange rate to be $1.4526/£ because at this rate an investor is indifferent between investing at Britain's higher interest rate of 8% or the U.S. lower rate of 6%.

Alternatively, one can simply use the equation stated in the chapter for the International Fisher effect, which states that the future spot exchange rate is equal to the current spot rate multiplied by the ratio of interest rates:

$$\text{Expected spot rate in one year} = \$1.4800/£ \times \frac{(1 + 0.06)}{(1 + 0.08)} = \$1.4526/£.$$

**4-4. Trident borrows euros**

If Trident were to borrow €4,000,000 for one year at 5.000% per annum interest, Trident would need to repay a total of €4,200,000 (€4,000,000 x 1.05) principal and interest in one year.

The €4,000,000 at the current spot rate of $0.9000/€ is equal to $3,600,000.

The expected spot exchange rate at the end of the year is found by assuming purchasing power parity will hold. The PPP expectation is found by multiplying the current spot rate by the ratio of expected inflation rates:

$$\text{Expected rate in one year} = \$0.9000/€ \times \frac{(1 + 0.06)}{(1 + 0.02)} = \$0.9353/€.$$

The expected U.S. dollar cost of repaying the euro-denominated loan is found by calculating the amount of U.S. dollars required to repaying principal and interest assuming the PPP exchange rate is in effect at the end of the year:

$$€\,4{,}200{,}000 \times \$0.9353/€ = \$3{,}928{,}235.29.$$

Repaying $3,928,235.29 on a loan of an original amount in U.S. dollars of $3,600,000.00, is am implicit interest rate of:

$$\left[\frac{\$3,928,235.29}{\$3,600,000.00}\right] - 1 = .091176 \approx 9.1176\%.$$

Conclusion: Trident should have borrowed dollars in the United States at 8.00% per annum rather than euros in Europe at an all-in cost of 9.1176% per annum.

Note that 9.1176% is approximately the sum of the European interest rate (5%) and the inflation differential (6% – 2% = 4%). To be precise: (1.06 ÷ 1.02)(1.05)] – 1 × 100 = 9.1176%.

| Problem 4.4 Trident Borrowing euros | | |
|---|---|---|
| **Assumptions** | | **Value** |
| Trident is borrowing the following principal, in euros | | €4,000,000 |
| Trident's cost of borrowing euros | | 5.000% |
| Interest savings over borrowing rate in the US | | 3.000% |
| Current spot exchange rate (US$ per euro) | | 0.9000 |
| Expected US inflation rate for the coming year | | 6.000% |
| Expected euro inflation rate for the coming year | | 2.000% |
| | | |
| **Euro borrowing:** | | |
| Trident borrows the following euros | | €4,000,000 |
| At the following interest rate | | 5.000% |
| Repaying principal and interest of the following in one year | | €4,200,000 |
| | | |
| Proceeds of euro loan in US dollars | $ | 3,600,000 |
| | | |
| **Expected spot rate in one year:** | | |
| Current spot rate (US$/euro) | | 0.9000 |
| US inflation rate | | 6.000% |
| euro inflation rate | | 2.000% |
| Expected spot rate assuming PPP (US$/euro) | | 0.9353 |
| | | |
| **Repaying the euro loan in US dollars will cost:** | | |
| Required repayment in euros | | €4,200,000 |
| At the following expected spot rate | | 0.9353 |
| Will require this amount of US dollars | $ | 3,928,235.29 |
| | | |
| Cost of the loan in dollar terms is =(Repayment/Proceeds)-1 | | 9.1176% |
| This is the real cost of borrowing in euros as Trident would expect. | | |
| If the expected spot rate occurs, Trident should have borrowed dollars | | |
| in the beginning at the 5%+3% rate of 8%. | | |

## 4-5. Covering

*Arbitrage* involves investing so as to profit from a difference in available interest rates(or other prices) in different markets. If one can earn only 5% in one's home market, but a higher rate, say 7%, in a foreign market using that foreign currency, an interest arbitrage operation would involve removing funds from the 5% market, buying the foreign currency, investing in the 7% market, and changing the available currency at maturity (recovered principal and interest earned) back into the home currency. The interest gain is the 2 percentage point differential. The risk is that when the 7% investment matures, the exchange rate will have changed to the disadvantage of the investor, and that investor will lose 2 (or more) percentage points.

In an *uncovered* interest arbitrage investment, the investor assumes the risk that the exchange rate will turn against him or her by the time the investment matures. By taking this risk, the investor also opens up the possibility that the exchange rate will turn to his or her advantage, and more than 7% will be earned.

In a *covered* interest arbitrage investment, at the same time one invests in the higher 7% market, that investor sells the investment proceeds at maturity forward for the home currency. By covering (i.e., hedging) in this manner, the investor eliminates any possibility of loss, or gain, from a change in exchange rate. In most cases the forward cover itself costs something (in terms of spread from the spot rate), so that a portion (or all) of the additional 2 percentage points is given up.

## 4-6. Mary Smyth – CIA

If Ms. Smyth invests in the United States, her proceeds after 3 months will be:

$$\$1{,}000{,}000 \times 1.02 = \$1{,}020{,}000.$$

If Ms. Smyth invests in Switzerland and covers her foreign exchange risk with a forward contract, she would proceed as follows:

Day 1

1st: Exchange$1,000,000 for Swiss francs at the current spot rate:

$$\$1{,}000{,}00{,}000 \times SF1.6000/\$ = SF1{,}600{,}000.$$

2nd. Invest for 3 months in Swiss interest bearing instruments at 6.00% per annum.

$$(1.50\% \text{ per quarter}):\ SF1{,}600{,}000 \times 1.015 = SF1{,}624{,}000.$$

3rd. Sell SF1,624,000 forward 3 months at SF1.5800/$:

$$SF1{,}624{,}000 \div SF1.5800/\$ = \$1{,}027{,}848.$$

(Delivery will be made three months from now.)

Day 90

1st. Deliver the SF1,624,000 proceeds of the investment against the forward sale of dollars, and receive $1,027,848.

2nd. Subtracting the $1,000,000 principal from the $1,027,848 proceeds gives a gain of $27,848.

3rd. $1,027,848 proceeds via the Swiss franc investment, less $1,020,000 from investing in the United States yields a comparative gain from investing in Switzerland of $7,848.

4th. No additional risk is incurred in this covered arbitrage operation, so Ms. Smyth should invest in Switzerland and cover her exchange risk in the forward market.

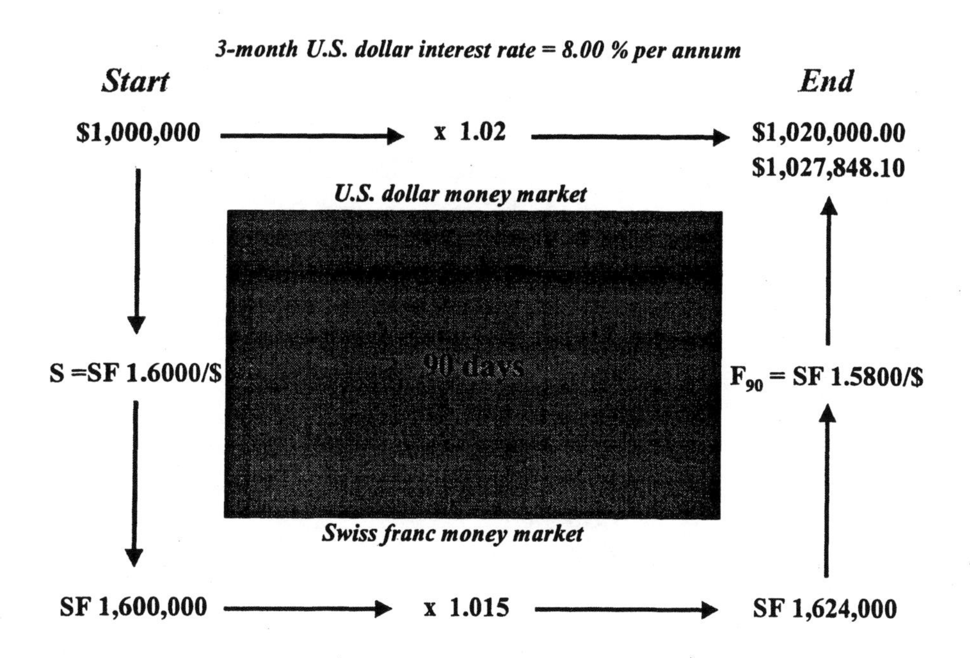

| Problem 4.6 Mary Smyth – CIA | | |
|---|---|---|
| **Assumptions** | | **Value** |
| Spot exchange rate (Swiss francs per US dollar) | | 1.6000 |
| 3-month forward ratae (Swiss francs per US dollar) | | 1.5800 |
| 3-month US dollar interest rate (per annum) | | 8.000% |
| 3-month Swiss franc interest rate (per annum) | | 6.000% |
| Principal to be invested | $ | 1,000,000.00 |
| | | |
| **Invest the Dollars in the US:** | | |
| Principal | $ | 1,000,000.00 |
| Interest for the 3-month period | | 2.000% |
| Gross return | $ | 1,020,000.00 |
| Net return in US dollars | $ | 20,000.00 |
| | | |
| | | |
| **Convert Dollars to Swiss francs and Cover:** | | |
| Principal | $ | 1,000,000.00 |
| Converted to Swiss francs at the current spot rate (SF/$) of | | 1.6000 |
| Yielding this principal of Swiss francs | | 1,600,000.00 |
| Invested at Swiss franc interest rate for the 3-month period | | 1.500% |
| Yielding this amount of Swiss francs at the end of one year | | 1,624,000.00 |
| Which are simultaneously sold forward at the forward rate of | | 1.5800 |
| Gross return in US dollars, fully covered, at the end of one year | $ | 1,027,848.10 |
| Net return in US dollars | $ | 27,848.10 |
| | | |
| **Mary Smyth is better off investing in the Swiss franc deposits.** | | |

**4-7. Mary Smyth – UIA**

This would be an uncovered interest arbitrage speculation. The steps would be as follows:

Day 1

1st. Exchange the $1,000,000 for Swiss francs at the current spot rate: $1,000,000 × SF1.60000/$ = SF1,600,000.

2nd. Invest for 3 months in Swiss interest bearing instruments at 6.00% per annum (1.50% per quarter):

SF1,600,000 × 1.015 = SF1,624,000.

Day 90

1st. Receive the SF1,624,000 proceeds of the investment.

2nd. Sell the SF1,624,000 proceeds for U.S. dollars at the then current spot rate, which could not have been known on Day 1. Many results are possible.

Among the possibilities:

a. If the spot rate were SF1.5800/$ (Day 1's forward rate), proceeds would be $1,027,848 the same as in the covered interest rate alternative – but riskier!

b. If the spot rate were SF1.6000/$ (Day 1's spot rate), proceeds would be $1,015,000, worse than the covered interest rate alternative.

c. If the spot rate were SF1.6200/$, proceeds would be $1,002,469, below both above alternatives.

Of course, the Swiss franc could be much weaker than SF1.6200/$ or much stronger than SF1.5800/$. The outcome of the uncovered interest rate arbitrage is uncertain and hence more risky than the covered alternative.

## Problem 4.7 Mary Smyth – UIA

| Assumptions | Value | | |
|---|---|---|---|
| Spot exchange rate (Swiss francs per US dollar) | 1.6000 | | |
| 3-month forward ratae (Swiss francs per US dollar) | 1.5800 | | |
| 3-month US dollar interest rate (per annum) | 8.000% | | |
| 3-month Swiss franc interest rate (per annum) | 6.000% | | |
| Principal to be invested | $ 1,000,000.00 | | |
| | | | |
| **Invest the Dollars in the US:** | | | |
| Principal | $ 1,000,000.00 | | |
| Interest for the 3-month period | 2.000% | | |
| Gross return | $ 1,020,000.00 | | |
| Net return in US dollars | $ 20,000.00 | | |
| | | | |
| **Convert Dollars to Swiss francs and Cover:** | | | |
| Principal | $ 1,000,000.00 | $ 1,000,000.00 | $ 1,000,000.00 |
| Converted to Swiss francs at the current spot rate (SF/$) of | 1.6000 | 1.6000 | 1.6000 |
| Yielding this principal of Swiss francs | 1,600,000.00 | 1,600,000.00 | 1,600,000.00 |
| Invested at Swiss franc interest rate for the 3-month period | 1.500% | 1.500% | 1.500% |
| Yielding this amount of Swiss francs at the end of one year | 1,624,000.00 | 1,624,000.00 | 1,624,000.00 |
| | | | |
| **The outcome of Uncovered Interest Arbitrage depends on the ending spot rate (SF/$):** | 1.6000 | 1.5800 | 1.5600 |
| Gross return in US dollars, fully covered, at the end of one year | $ 1,015,000.00 | $ 1,027,848.10 | $ 1,041,025.64 |
| Net return in US dollars | $ 15,000.00 | $ 27,848.10 | $ 41,025.64 |
| | | | |
| **Compared to investing in the US dollar markets,** | | | |
| **Mary Smyth, by investing uncovered in Swiss francs, earns:** | $ (5,000.00) | $ 7,848.10 | $ 21,025.64 |

**4-8. Mary Smyth – one month later.**

If Ms. Smyth attempts a covered interest arbitrage investment with these rates, she will face the results diagramed below:

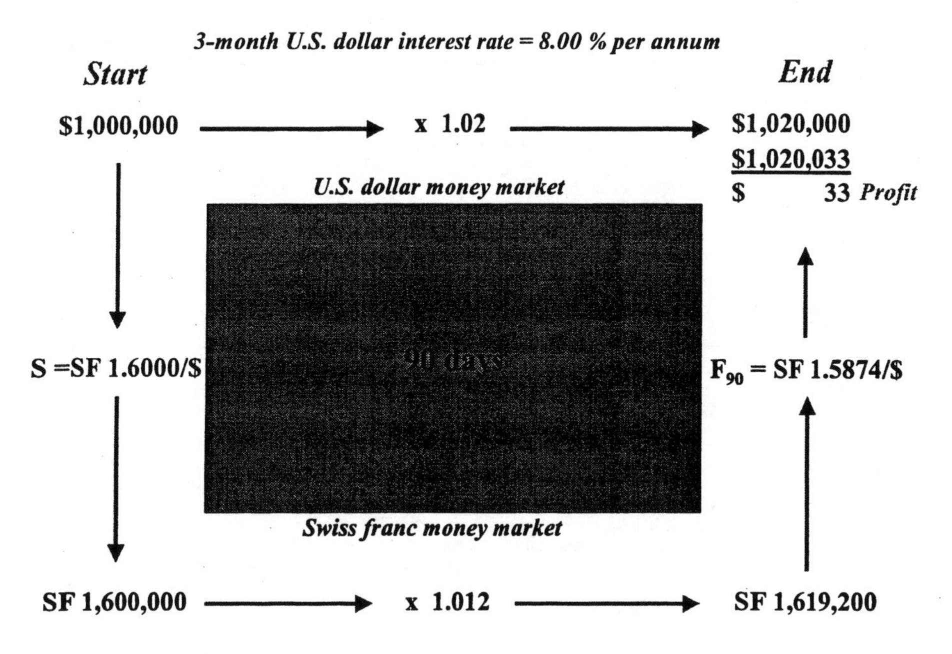


Although the markets are not precisely in equilibrium, they are very close. An investment principal of $1 million which earns only a CIA profit of $33 is for all intents and purposes not worth the effort (and surely does not cover the costs of Mary Smyth's employment).

## Problem 4.8 One Month Later

| Assumptions | | Value |
|---|---|---|
| Spot exchange rate (Swiss francs per US dollar) | | 1.6000 |
| 3-month forward ratae (Swiss francs per US dollar) | | 1.5874 |
| 3-month US dollar interest rate (per annum) | | 8.000% |
| 3-month Swiss franc interest rate (per annum) | | 4.800% |
| Principal to be invested | $ | 1,000,000.00 |
| | | |
| **Invest the Dollars in the US:** | | |
| Principal | $ | 1,000,000.00 |
| Interest for the 3-month period | | 2.000% |
| Gross return | $ | 1,020,000.00 |
| Net return in US dollars | $ | 20,000.00 |
| | | |
| **Convert Dollars to Swiss francs and Cover:** | | |
| Principal | $ | 1,000,000.00 |
| Converted to Swiss francs at the current spot rate (SF/$) of | | 1.6000 |
| Yielding this principal of Swiss francs | | 1,600,000.00 |
| Invested at Swiss franc interest rate for the 3-month period | | 1.200% |
| Yielding this amount of Swiss francs at the end of one year | | 1,619,200.00 |
| Which are simultaneously sold forward at the forward rate of | | 1.5874 |
| Gross return in US dollars, fully covered, at the end of one year | $ | 1,020,032.76 |
| Net return in US dollars | $ | 20,032.76 |
| | | |
| **Mary Smyth is better off investing in the US. dollar deposits.** | | |

**4-9. Langkawi Island Resort**

a. To estimate the dollars needed to pay for your 30-day vacation one year from now, we first estimate what the actual hotel charges would be at that time, and then the probable exchange rate in effect at that future date between the Malaysian ringgit (RM) and the U.S. dollar.

Hotel charges one year hence would be the current rate of RM760.00 increased for the expected rate of inflation in Malaysia in the coming year, 4%, multiplied by 30 days:

$$\text{RM } 760.00 \times 1.04 \times 30 = \text{RM } 23{,}712.$$

Next year's exchange, according to the theory of purchasing power parity, will be the current spot rate multiplied by the ratio of expected rates of inflation in Malaysian ringgit and U.S. dollar environments:

$$\text{Expected rate in one year} = \text{RM}3.8000/\$ \times \frac{(1 + 0.04)}{(1 + 0.01)} = \text{RM}3.9129/\$.$$

Therefore, the U.S. dollar price of this tropical 30-day vacation one year from now would be found by taking the expected price in ringgit and dividing that by the expected spot exchange rate one year from now:

$$\frac{\text{RM}23{,}712}{\text{RM}3.9129/\$} = \$6{,}060.$$

b. The percent increase in the dollar price of the 30-day vacation is:

$$(\$6{,}060 \div \$6{,}000) - 1 \times 100 = 1.0\%$$

The 1.0% increase in the dollar cost is equal to the U.S. dollar inflation rate. The additional inflation in Malaysia was offset by the change in the exchange rate. (Have a good trip.)

## Problem 4.9 Langkawi Island Resort

| Assumptions | | Value |
|---|---|---|
| Charge for suite plus meals (in ringgit) | | 760.00 |
| Spot exchange rate (ringgit per US$) | | 3.8000 |
| US$ cost today for a 30 day stay | $ | 6,000.00 |
| | | |
| Malaysian ringgit inflation rate expected to be | | 4.000% |
| U.S. dollar inflation rate expected to be | | 1.000% |
| | | |
| **a. How many dollars might you expecte to need one year hence for your 30-day vacation?** | | |
| | | |
| Spot exchange rate (ringgit per US$) | | 3.8000 |
| Malaysian ringgit inflation rate expected to be | | 4.000% |
| U.S. dollar inflation rate expected to be | | 1.000% |
| **Expected spot rate one year from now based on PPP (ringgit per US$)** | | 3.9129 |
| | | |
| **Hotel charges expected to be paid one year from now for a 30-day stay** | | 23,712.00 |
| | | |
| US dollars needed on the basis of these two expectations: | $ | 6,060.00 |
| | | |
| **b. By what percent has the dollar cost gone up? Why?** | | |
| | | |
| New dollar cost | $ | 6,060.00 |
| Original dollar cost | $ | 6,000.00 |
| **Percent change in US$ cost** | | 1.000% |
| | | |
| The dollar cost has risen by the US dollar inflation rate. This is a result of your | | |
| estimation of the future suite costs and exchange rate changing in relation to inflation. | | |

**4-10. Covered interest against the Norwegian krone**

a. If the trader invested the $500,000 in U.S. 3-month Treasury bills at 2.600% per annum (0.650% for 3 months), he would earn a gross amount of $503,250, or a net interest income of $3,250.

b. If he were to conduct a CIA investment in Norway, he would take the $500,000 and convert it to Norwegian krone at the current spot rate of NKr 8.8181/$, receiving NKr 4,409,050.

c. He would invest this NKr4,409,050 for 3 months at the Norwegian Treasury bill rate of 4.00% per annum (1.000% for 3 months), holding NKr4,453,140.50 at the end of 3 months.

d. At the same time he would sell the NKr4,453,140.50 forward 3 months at the 3 month forward rate of NKr8.9169/$, locking in U.S. dollar proceeds of $499,404.56.

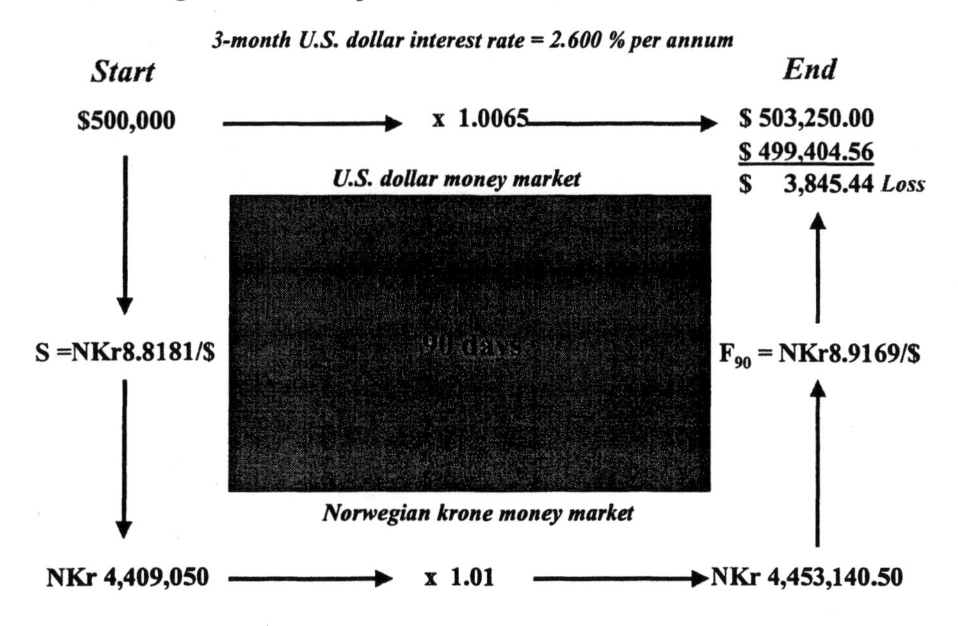


The trader would lose $3,845.44 through CIA (an opportunity loss of $3,250 he could have earned in the United States plus the 595.44 loss in principal investment). The trader has not only not failed to make a profit as large as he could have earned in the United States Treasury bill market, he has actually ended up with less than he started!

As is always the case with CIA, if going one way around the box loses money, the opposite direction would have gained. If the trader had begun with the equivalent of $500,000 in Norwegian kroner, Nkr4,409,050, exchanged the kroner for dollars spot, invested the $500,000 proceeds in the U.S. dollar money market for 90 days at a 2.60% per annum rate, and then sold the resulting $503,250 proceeds forward for Norwegian kroner at Nkr8.9169/$, the final proceeds from CIA would be Nkr4,487,429.93. This is a profit of NKr34,289.43 over simply investing the NKr4,409,050 for 90 days at the Norwegian treasury bill rate of 4.00% per annum (1% for 90 days), or Nkr4,453,140.50.

This is illustrated in the following diagram.

***3-month U.S. dollar interest rate = 2.600 % per annum***

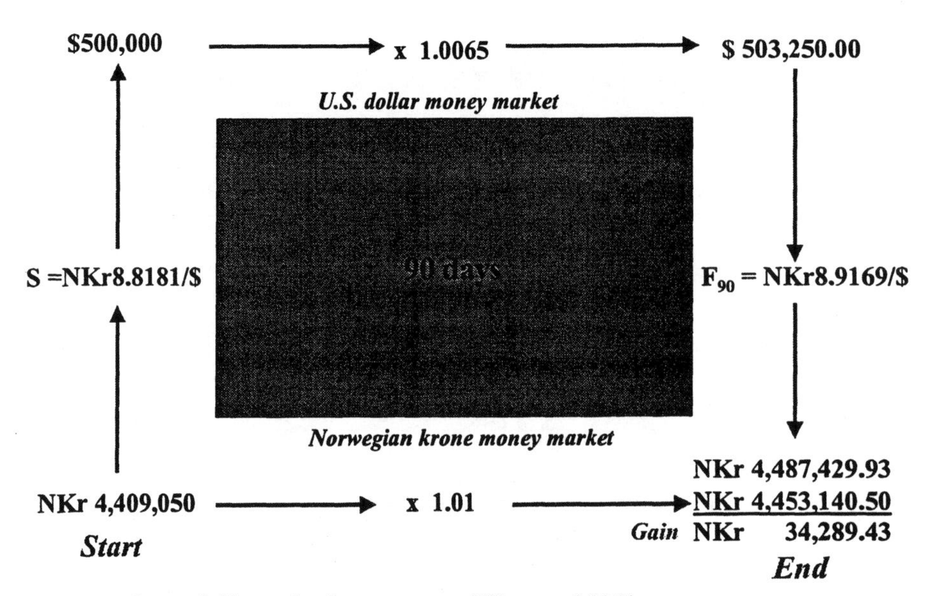


***3-month Norwegian krone treasury bill rate = 4.00 % per annum***

## Problem 4.10 Covered Interest Against the Krone

| Assumptions | | Value |
|---|---|---|
| Spot exchange rate (NKr/$) | | 8.8181 |
| 3-month forward rate (NKr/$) | | 8.9169 |
| US 3-month Treasury bill rate | | 2.600% |
| Norwegian 3-month Treasury bill rate | | 4.000% |
| Notional investment | $ | 500,000.00 |
| | | |
| **Invest the Dollars in the US:** | | |
| Principal | $ | 500,000.00 |
| Interest for the 3-month period | | 0.650% |
| Gross return | $ | 503,250.00 |
| Net return in US dollars | $ | 3,250.00 |
| | | |
| **Covered Interest Arbitrage in Norwegian Kroner:** | | |
| Principal | $ | 500,000.00 |
| Converted to Norwegian kroner at the spot rate (NKr/$) of | | 8.8181 |
| Yielding this principal in Norwegian kroner | | 4,409,050.00 |
| Invested at Norwegian Treasury bill rate for the 3-month period | | 1.000% |
| Yielding this amount of Norwegian kroner at the end of 3 months | | 4,453,140.50 |
| Which are simultaneously sold forward at the forward rate of | | 8.9169 |
| Gross return in US dollars, fully covered, at the end of one year | $ | 499,404.56 |
| Net return in US dollars | $ | (595.44) |
| | | |
| **Opportunity cost of investing in Norway over the US:** | $ | (3,845.44) |

**4-11. Frankfurt and New York**

a. According to the Fisher Effect, real interest rates should be the same in both Europe and the United States.

$$1+i_{eur} \div 1+i_{us} = 1 + r_{eur} \div 1+r_{us} ,$$

where i = interest rate and r = inflation rate.

$$1.065 \div 1.032 = 1 + r_{eur} \div 1.02$$

$$1 + r_{eur} = 1.0526$$

Hence the expected annual inflation rate for Europe is 5.26%.

b. The one-year forward exchange rate between the euro and the U.S. dollar is found by multiplying the current spot rate of \$0.9000/€ by the ratio of treasury bill rates:

$$\text{Forward rate}_{360\ \text{days}} = \$0.9000/€ \times \frac{(1 + 0.0320)}{(1 + 0.0650)} = \$0.8721/€.$$

Verification:
Invest \$1,000 in the U.S.: (\$1,000)(1.032) = \$1,032 one year hence.
Invest \$1,000 in Europe: \$1,000÷0.90 = € 1,111.11 available to invest.
€ 1,111.11 × 1.065 = € 1,183.33 at maturity.
€ 1,183.33 × \$0.8721/€ = \$1,032 one year hence.

Hence the two markets are in equilibrium. The forward discount on the euro exactly offsets the higher interest rate available on euros.

| Problem 4.11 Frankfurt and New York | | |
|---|---|---|
| **Assumptions** | **Frankfurt** | **New York** |
| Spot exchange rate (US$/euro) | 0.9000 | 0.9000 |
| One-year Treasury bill rate | 6.500% | 3.200% |
| Expected inflation rate | ? | 2.000% |
| | | |
| **a. What do the financial markets suggest for inflation in Europe next year?** | | |
| | | |
| According to the Fisher Effect, real interest rates should be the same in both Europe and the United States. | | |
| | | |
| Since the nominal rate = [ (1+real) x (1+expected inflation) ] - 1: | | |
| | | |
| 1 + real rate = (1 + nominal) / (1 + expected inflation) | | |
| 1 + nominal rate | 106.500% | 103.200% |
| 1 + expected inflation | ? | 102.000% |
| So 1 + real = | 101.176% <— | 101.176% |
| and therefore the real rate in the US is: | | 1.176% |
| | | |
| **The expected rate of inflation in Frankfurt is then:** | 5.262% | |
| | | |
| **b. Estimate today's one-year forward exchange rate between the dollar and the euro.** | | |
| | | |
| Spot exchange rate (US$/euro) | 0.9000 | |
| US dollar one-year Treasury bill rate | 3.200% | |
| European euro one-year Treasury bill rate | 6.500% | |
| **One year forward rate (US$/euro)** | 0.8721 | |

## 4-12. The Beer Standard

Overvaluation (+) or undervaluation (–) relative to South African rand (percentages are exact as calculated on the accompanying spreadsheets; occasional rounding in reported Implied rates are the source of rounding error here):

| | | |
|---|---|---|
| Botswana | $(0.96 \div 0.75) - 1 \times 100$ | = +27.9% overvalued |
| Ghana | $(521.74 \div 379.1) - 1 \times 100$ | = +37.6% overvalued |
| Kenya | $(17.93 \div 10.27) - 1 \times 100$ | = +74.6% overvalued |
| Malawi | $(8.04 \div 6.96) - 1 \times 100$ | = +15.6% overvalued |
| Mauritius | $(6.52 \div 4.03) - 1 \times 100$ | = +61.8% overvalued |

| | | |
|---|---|---|
| Namibia | (1.09 ÷ 1.00) – 1 × 100 | = + 8.7% overvalued |
| Zambia | (521.74 ÷ 340.68) – 1 × 100 | = +53.1% overvalued |
| Zimbabwe | (3.91 – 6.15) – 1 × 100 | = – 36.4% undervalued |

**Problem 4.12 The Beer Standard**

| | | Beer Prices | | | | | |
|---|---|---|---|---|---|---|---|
| | | Local | Local | In | Implied | Spot rate | Under or overvalued |
| Country | Beer | currency | currency | rand | PPP rate | 3/15/99 | to rand (%) |
| South Africa | Castle | Rand | 2.30 | — | — | — | — |
| Botswana | Castle | Pula | 2.20 | 2.94 | 0.96 | 0.75 | 27.9% |
| Ghana | Star | Cedi | 1,200.00 | 3.17 | 521.74 | 379.10 | 37.6% |
| Kenya | Tusker | Shilling | 41.25 | 4.02 | 17.93 | 10.27 | 74.6% |
| Malawi | Carlsberg | Kwacha | 18.50 | 2.66 | 8.04 | 6.96 | 15.6% |
| Mauritius | Phoenix | Rupee | 15.00 | 3.72 | 6.52 | 4.03 | 61.8% |
| Namibia | Windhoek | N$ | 2.50 | 2.50 | 1.09 | 1.00 | 8.7% |
| Zambia | Castle | Kwacha | 1,200.00 | 3.52 | 521.74 | 340.68 | 53.1% |
| Zimbabwe | Castle | Z$ | 9.00 | 1.46 | 3.91 | 6.15 | -36.4% |

Notes:

1. Beer price in South African rand = Price in local currency / spot rate on 3/15/99.
2. Implied PPP exchange rate = Price in local currency / 2.30.
3. Under or overvalued to rand = Implied PPP rate / spot rate on 3/15/99.

MINI-CASE: RUSSIAN PURCHASING POWER AND WESTERN AUTOMAKERS.

1. **How did the Russian rouble's collapse alter the structure of the Russian automobile market? How did this new structure affect the ability of importers to penetrate the Russian market?**

The rouble's collapse was devastating to the purchasing power of the average Russian consumer. Because purchasing power is measured in the ability of the domestic consumer and his currency to acquire foreign currency and subsequently foreign goods, the collapse of the rouble reduced the price of foreign goods which the average Russian could afford. (This was particularly acute in the Russian marketplace where more than 95% of all automobiles are purchased with cash. There is no national credit quality information base which would allow lenders to provide financing to Russian consumers.)

Strategies traditionally used by Western automakers would now have to be changed radically. This point is driven home by the case exhibit describing that 97% of the Russian auto market in 1999 was under $10,000. Western automakers would now have to produce in Russia with a Russian cost-base.

2. **Why do you think the kit-assembly approach was not more successful in Russia? It was a common automaker production/distribution strategy employed in much of the world's emerging markets, but was not working in Russia.**

In the past a foreign automaker would produce outside Russia and import the product into the Russian market, or manufacture automobile "kits" (typically termed *complete knockdown*, CKD, or *semi-knockdown*, SKD) into Russia where the final stages of assembly and finishing would be completed. Both of these strategies were now uncompetitive, as the cost-base for these autos would be too expensive. Although kit assembly has worked to a limited degree in other emerging markets, the Russian market was 'emerging' prior to the crisis; post-1998 Russian purchasing power was a step lower. That said, it does appear that Daewoo, even though now essentially owned by General Motors, is seeing some success in the Russian marketplace.

Interestingly in the Russian case, some Western automakers had attempted producing automobiles in a low-cost country such as Brazil in the past and then exporting the products to Russia. These had become infamous for their low quality – even in Russia. (In fact, the average Russian looks down on products produced in Latin America, specifically, Brazil.)

This extremely low purchasing power matched with a knowledge of and appreciation for higher quality and branded goods and services poses a very interesting problem for global business going forward. Simply because emerging markets do not at present have the purchasing power does not mean they do not know the difference or that they will be perennially stuck in that position.

3. **What do you think the prospective risks and returns were to the two joint venture partners, General Motors and AvtoVAZ? Was one firm gaining more than the other? Was one firm establishing a longer-term strategy at the risk of short-term costs?**

This should be a very fruitful question for class discussion. GM is gaining a partnership with the dominant automobile manufacturer in Russia. Jointly, they will be producing a high-quality highly visible product which is already quite successful in a more basic form. GM gains this beachhead without a major commitment of capital, and without risking any significant technology drain, as AvtoVAZ is to provide the majority of the engineering.

AvtoVAZ gains first and foremost the Chevrolet "badge" which has true brand value in the market. It gains increasing opportunities to learn higher quality manufacturing and operations techniques and management from one of the world leaders. And it furthers a relationship which could possibly continue to expand future domestic and international opportunities.

It can be argued that AvtoVAZ is risking more than GM. GM is putting up little real capital and little in terms of engineering and technology. (A side note to be offered as well is GM's recent investment in China amounted to more than $1 billion, 10 times that put at risk here.) If the venture fails, GM's losses are limited. AvtoVAZ, however, is investing one of its most successful models in the JV, and is providing a beachhead to GM's entry into the Russian marketplace. Without AvtoVAZ's aid, GM would likely remain a very small outside player in this market.

## CHAPTER 5: FOREIGN EXCHANGE RATE DETERMINATION

### *Questions*

### 5-1. Parity relationships

Under the international parity relationship approach, an assumption is made that international foreign exchange and short-term money markets are efficient. Hence funds will flow to the currency with the highest expected real rate of return. Exchange rates will then adjust so that neither investment gains nor losses can be made from covered interest arbitrage investments.

### 5-2. Asset market approach

Under the asset market approach, foreign exchange rates are determined by the willingness of foreign investors to hold monetary claims denominated in the local currency. This, in turn, is in part determined by expected real interest rates (as in the parity approach) and in part by expectations for the country's economic growth and profitability.

### 5-3. Fixed rates and the BOP approach

Under the balance of payments approach for a country with fixed exchange rates, imbalances in short-term money flows (current account) and longer-term money flows (investment and capital accounts) lead to a loss of foreign exchange reserves. As foreign exchange reserves are depleted, the government (or its central bank) is no longer able to give out foreign exchange for its own currency, and it must devalue so that smaller quantities of foreign exchange reserves are given out. Hopefully the devaluation will stop the outflow of local currency for foreign exchange.

### 5-4. Floating regimes and the BOP approach

Under a floating rate regime, the government (or its central bank) is not obligated to surrender its foreign exchange reserves to anyone who wants to exchange the local currency for a foreign currency. Increased deficits in the current account not matched by surpluses in the various investment accounts means that the free market demand and supply for the currency are not balanced. This imbalance is rectified in the free foreign exchange market: If buyers of the currency (at the present exchange rate) exceed sellers, the value of the currency rises until supply and demand are equalized. The opposite happens if buyers of the currency demand more than sellers want to sell.

### 5-5. Managed floats and the BOP approach

In a managed float regime, supply and demand for the currency determine its value, much as explained in question 5-4 above. However the government (or its central bank) intervene from time to time and probably anonymously on one side of the market so as to influence and/or force the direction of the exchange rate. However outsiders do not know if the government (or its central bank) are or are not intervening. Even if they do know, or suspect, government intervention, they have no way of knowing if that intervention will continue or will cease.

### 5-6. Technical analysis

In foreign exchange markets (as in the stock market) technical analysts look for patterns in recent past rate quotations and extrapolate those patterns into the future. The logic by which they work is that everything worth knowing about a price (foreign exchange or shares of stock) is built into recent past patterns, easily discerned by those accustomed to looking for recognizable patterns.

### 5-7. Infrastructure weakness

Infrastructure weakness refers to situations where public services (roads, railroads, electric power, impartial judicial system, minimum corruption by politicians, adequate police and fire services, reasonable health care systems, etc.) are dysfunctional. Lack of quality services increases the difficulty and risk of operating a business in that country, which in turn means domestic investment funds will tend to escape from the country and foreign investment funds will not enter. The flight of domestic currencies and the lack of foreign demand for the domestic currency force the exchange rate down (floating regime) or force the government to devalue (fixed exchange rate regime.)

### 5-8. Speculation

"Hot money" is a term used to describe funds held in one currency (country) that will move very quickly to another currency as soon as it is deemed weak. Such a quick flow will create severe short-term pressures on the exchange rate., forcing depreciation or a devaluation. This run on the currency may cause others to also try to exchange their local currency holdings for foreign money, aggravating the already apparent weakness.

If a currency is fundamentally weak, a speculator such as George Soros may lead a flight from that currency. He will succeed if he is correct in his assessment of the fundamentals, but if he is in error he will lose on the speculation. In the Malaysian situation, Soros correctly assessed the situation, and by moving first was probably instrumental in setting in motion underlying factors that would have influenced exchange rates in any case – possibly at a later date. In other words, Soros did not cause the currency crisis in a fundamental sense, but he may well have caused (and advanced) the timing of what would have occurred eventually in any case.

### 5-9. Cross-border investment flows

Cross-border investment flows are of two types: direct and portfolio. Investment flows into a country mean that foreigners are buying the local currency, which factor will drive up the value of that local currency. Such flows also give local entities, either private individuals and corporations or the central bank, foreign exchange balances that can be used to import goods and services or held as foreign exchange reserves. Together the investment inflows and their usage influence the country's exchange rate.

In the case of Thailand, investment flows went into the country before the 1997 crisis because Thai interest rates and expected returns on direct investments were high, because the outside world believed the Thai government would continue to support its currency, and because the outside world did not pay attention to the infrastructure weaknesses in Thailand. When Thailand devalued its baht, the outside world suddenly became aware of structural weaknesses and new investment inflows stopped at once. This precipitated the devaluation of the baht and the beginning of devaluation in neighboring countries.

### 5-10. Russian political risk

Political risk is a change in economic prospects caused by such political events as a radical change in government attitude toward foreigners and foreign investment, wars, revolutions, violent changes of government, and major terrorist attacks and attempts to end terrorism. Perceived political risk (i.e., future risk that is expected and discounted in advance) increases business risk and leads to capital outflows from the risky country and a drop off or cessation of capital inflows.

In 1998 the Russian government was borrowing large amounts of foreign currency, while at the same time having difficulty earning foreign exchange and collecting taxes because of inefficiency and corruption in its economic system. Russia was defaulting on its foreign debt, or surviving only because the International Monetary Fund was willing to keep on lending. The non-Russian world began to believe that Russia lacked the political will or ability to make its economy efficient and so would not be willing to pay its foreign exchange debts.

**5-11. Term forecasting**

a. Fixed exchange rate regimes: The major risk is of a sudden devaluation, not preceded by any apparent weakness of the currency in the foreign exchange market. Short-term investors focus on current changes in foreign exchange reserves in an attempt to discern both the timing of and amount of any devaluation. Near-term devaluation will cause losses to short-term investors who are holding funds in banks and/or purchasing short-term government securities. Long-term investors (such as companies making investments in productive factories) focus more on the long-run fundamentals because the safety of their principal and their investment returns depend on long-term growth.

b. Floating Rate Regimes Under a floating rate regime, the government has no responsibility for keeping the exchange rate constant and is not expected to intervene in the foreign exchange markets. In theory the exchange rate will adjust in the private market so that the current and investment accounts are in balance. Under these conditions forecasts focus more on fundamentals. Instead of a sudden drop in the foreign exchange value of the currency, as with a fixed rate regime, analysts try to predict a steady trend. Any loss experienced will be in the form of a gradual erosion of value, rather than a precipitous drop.

**5-12. Forecasting services**

Factors Ms. Gonzalez should consider are (1) the historic success of the forecasting service, and (2) whether the $20,000 cost of the service is too high relative to the level of Trident's foreign exchange transaction exposure that she is seeking to protect. More fundamentally, she should decide if Trident is going to take a position based on the recommendations of the service, such that she will gain if the service is correct and lose if the service is wrong; or if she is going to hedge her exposure anyway via any of the standard hedging techniques, in which case why pay for a foreign exchange forecast. Lastly she must ponder whether she will be criticized if she does not subscribe but makes poor forecasts herself.

**5-13. Cross rate consistency**

Management usually judges the performance of its subsidiaries and their managers by comparing actual performance against a budget established at the beginning of a budget period – usually one year. Assessment of performance for foreign subsidiaries is made difficult by the fact of exchange rate changes. If each foreign subsidiary is operating on a different exchange rate assumption, fair assessment is even more difficult. Hence it is important to have an internally-consistent company-wide forecast for all pairs of currencies of importance.

Companies usually make such a forecast within corporate headquarters. However subsidiaries very often trade directly with each other; e.g., the British and French subsidiaries of a U.S. parent trade between themselves. Hence local financial managers will have their own opinion of future exchange rates that do not necessarily involve the dollar, say pounds for euros. Such rates can be checked against the parent's forecast so that all combinations of foreign exchange rate forecasts are internally consistent.

**5-14. Southeast Asian crisis of 1997**

The basic cause was a period of large imports of goods (deficit on current account) financed by inflows of foreign capital (surplus on financial account), including local borrowing in cheaper overseas markets. Maintenance of exchange rates of the various southeast Asian currencies had been expected. The crisis was exacerbated by what came to be called "crony capitalism" where many dealings were driven by friendships and relationships to governing officials rather than by market factors.

Once the crisis was apparent, financial managers of MNEs should rationally stop expansion of local facilities and try to repatriate cash balances in local currencies, if possible. This would cause the financial component of the balance of payments to worsen for the countries involved. For companies manufacturing for local consumption, a drop in local demand, possibly caused by an increase in costs if imported components were needed, would lead to cut backs in production and resultant unemployment, making the crisis-caused depression even worse.

**5-15. Russian crisis of 1998**

This crisis was caused by a deterioration over the prior half decade or so of the Russian economy. During these years private and governmental Russian entities had borrowed large amounts of money abroad, most of which was denominated in U.S. dollars. To service this foreign currency debt Russia had to earn dollars from exports; however dollars earned, as well as dollars obtained by borrowing, flowed out almost at once in the form of capital flight. Furthermore, most dollar earnings came from the export of commodities, and commodity prices were falling worldwide, in part because of the Asian crisis.

Deteriorating conditions in Russia, combined with corruption and incompetence by governmental officials and continued capital flight meant that MNE financial managers should minimize the amount of cash held in any Russian subsidiary. In effect they should join the capital flight, although the form might be that of avoiding inflows of capital rather than flight of capital already in Russia. Plans for additional investments should be delayed until the Russian economy stabilized. Of course, such rational behavior on the part of managers of individual private entities worsens to some degree what is already happening.

**5-16. Trident and the Brazilian crisis of 1999**

Since the inception of the real, a new currency to replace the cruzeiro in 1994, the Brazilian government had kept the real's value artificially high in the hope that sustaining this higher peg would give confidence to holders of reals. The government was unable to keep the economy, and especially the current account, strong, and as it ran out of reserves it was forced to devalue.

Trident and other companies would rationally respond to factors leading up to the Brazilian crisis as they had to other crises: Inflows of capital for new or expanded manufacturing capacity would be curtailed, and if possible liquid capital (e.g., cash) would be repatriated. These steps would be driven by expectations of devaluation as well as deterioration in demand for local production intended for Brazilian consumption.

These steps, of course, do not help Brazil's economic position. After the devaluation, Trident and other MNEs would have to assess if the Brazilian economy would then recover. If this assessment were favorable, production for local consumption would again be expanded and capital inflows would resume. In addition to the above, insightful financial managers would look at the impact of the Brazilian devaluation on neighboring countries – in this case Argentina, and determined if their response should include a change in policy for that neighbor.

*Problems*

**5-1. Brazilian real**

The formula measuring the percentage amount of a devaluation when the exchange rate is stated on an indirect basis (foreign currency to the dollar, page 132) is:

$$\frac{\text{Beginning rate} - \text{Ending rate}}{\text{Ending rate}} \times 100 = \frac{1.21 - 1.43}{1.43} = -15.4\%.$$

**5-2. Turkish lire**

a. After a 20% devaluation the rate would be TL85,000/$, as follows :

$$\frac{\text{TL}68{,}000/\$}{0.80} = \text{TL}85{,}000/\$.$$

b. The percentage amount of devaluation is:

$$\frac{\text{Beginning rate} - \text{Ending rate}}{\text{Ending rate}} \times 100 = \frac{68{,}000 - 100{,}000}{100{,}000} \times 100 = -32.0\%.$$

**5-3. Mexican peso**

The percentage amount of devaluation is:

$$\frac{\text{Beginning rate} - \text{Ending rate}}{\text{Ending rate}} \times 100 = \frac{3.30 - 5.50}{5.50} = -40.0\%.$$

**5-4. Russian ruble**

The percentage amount of devaluation is:

$$\frac{\text{Beginning rate} - \text{Ending rate}}{\text{Ending rate}} \times 100 = \frac{6.25 - 20.00}{20.00} \times 100 = -68.75\%.$$

**5-5. Thai baht**

The percentage amount of devaluation is:

$$\frac{\text{Beginning rate} - \text{Ending rate}}{\text{Ending rate}} \times 100 = \frac{25.00 - 29.00}{29.00} \times 100 = -13.8\%.$$

**5-6. Ecuadorian sucre**

The percentage amount of devaluation is:

$$\frac{\text{Beginning rate} - \text{Ending rate}}{\text{Ending rate}} \times 100 = \frac{5{,}000 - 25{,}000}{25{,}000} \times 100 = -80.0\%.$$

## 5-7. Forecasting the Argentine peso

Using the chart, one could best forecast the future of the Argentine peso by extrapolating the trend from about January 23 to the end of the chart. However severe doubts might be expressed about this method, because the use of charts implies some sort of steady shift in economic fundamentals, whereas the future value of the peso is probably going to be more influenced by the presence or absence of political stability within the country.

| Problem 5.7 Forecating the Argentine peso | |
|---|---|
| What will be the peso's future value in the coming weeks? | |
| | "Eye-balled" |
| Date | Values |
| February 1st (Ps/$) | 2.00 |
| February 28th (Ps/$) | 2.20 |
| | |
| Percent change | -9.09% |
| | |
| If peso continued to fall at same rate for 1 month: | |
| | |
| March 1, 2002 (Ps/$) | 2.20 |
| Percent change | -9.09% |
| March 30, 2002 (Ps/$) | 2.42 |

## MINI-CASE: TURKEY'S KRIZ (B) UNCOVERED INTEREST ARBITRAGE

**1. Was the Turkish lira's collapse the result of a balance of payments crisis, an inflation crisis, a political crisis, or an economic crisis?**

Although we are tempted to say "all of the above," the more rigorous response is a political landscape which led to many of the common economic ills of a struggling emerging market. The inflationary pressures, continual volatility in current and financial balance of payment accounts, and struggling process of privatization – all reflect an economy in both political and structural transition. Although the struggles with BOP accounts and inflation had been recurring, the Turkish lira's fixed rate could probably have survived if it had not been for the dollar-debt obligations acquired by the Turkish banks. The activities of the banks served to not only undermine some of the economic reforms underway, they threatened the stability of the banking system itself – the pillar of any market economy's ability to grow and develop.

**2. Describe precisely how the Turkish banks were performing uncovered interest arbitrage. Do you feel this was an inappropriate investment policy?**

Turkish banks simply took advantage – at least for as long as it lasted – of a very easy arbitrage opportunity. As illustrated in the following diagram, the Turkish banks borrowed Eurodollars at relatively attractive rates, 8.000% per annum. They then exchanged the dollars for Turkish lira at the currently fixed or managed exchange rate, TL500,000/$. The Turkish lira proceeds were then invested in Turkish government bonds yielding the higher inflation-based rates of 20.00% per annum. At the end of the period, the Turkish lira were then converted back to U.S. dollars at the fixed exchange rate of TL500,000/$, yielding an uncovered interest rate arbitrage profit of $120,000.

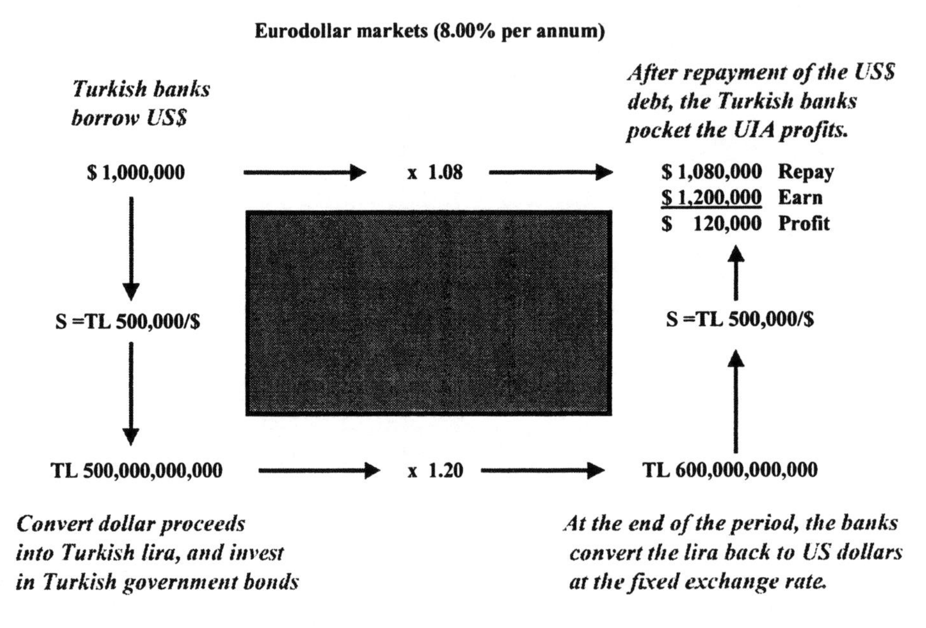

Note that the profits from the arbitrage activity as described here are in U.S. dollars. This was also a characteristic of the Turkish bank positions – ultimately positioning their profitability in the foreign hard currency, the U.S. dollar. The arbitrage activity could continue as long as the exchange rate at the end of the period did not change radically against the banks – a severe devaluation of the lira. This was what, in the end, occurred.

3. **How could the Turkish banks be contributing to financial crisis if they were purchasing Turkish government bonds and helping finance and support their own government?**

While it sounds helpful that the Turkish banks were promoting an active and growing market for Turkish government debt, and in the process allowing the government to finance its expenditures at a lower cost than without their activity, the source of their funds was the problem. By acquiring large quantities of dollar-denominated debt, for a country already running a current account deficit, this would inevitably lead to a currency crisis as the ability of the Turkish economy to generate sufficient hard-currency earnings (U.S. dollars in this case) in order to service this debt would fall short.

4. **Which do you think is more critical to a country such as Turkey, fighting inflation or fighting a large trade and current account deficit?**

The consensus among most international economists and various international organizations is that inflation is the first and foremost problem that must be controlled in order to establish a solid foundation for economic growth, industrial development, full employment, and managed trade. Current account deficits are not of themselves necessarily evil or destructive, but actually often a characteristic of a fully employed rapidly expanding economy.

5. **The quote from *Corporate Finance* magazine, although noting the outside possibility of a devaluation, was largely positive regarding Turkey's future in January 2001. What would you have thought?**

It seems that throughout history, after every currency crisis, there is the wailing voice crying out "why didn't you see this coming?" This quotation is rather useful in pointing out that in many (most?) currency crises there were at least murmurs in the marketplace prior to the crisis. The quotation points out that there have been some positive actions – the IMF capital injections – but that there are continuing problems with inflation. The latter was expected to drive the value of the lira down in the near future.

## CHAPTER 6: THE FOREIGN EXCHANGE MARKET

*Questions*

### 6-1. Foreign exchange

*Foreign exchange* means the money of a foreign country, with "money," in turn, meaning all of the means of making a payment: coins and banknotes, bank balances, checks drawn on bank balances, and drafts drawn on banks (bank drafts) or business firms (commercial drafts).

Examples would include euro banknotes (when held by Americans, but not when held by Europeans), U.S. dollar bank notes (when held by other than U.S. residents), international money orders, checks drawn on foreign banks (a U.S. resident writing a check on an account in Britain), foreign currency denominated checks being deposited in a U.S. bank (until deposited and exchanged for U.S. currency), and large foreign currency deposits held by banks in one country on banks in another country.

### 6-2. Spot transactions

A spot transaction is an agreement between two parties to exchange one currency for another, with the transaction being carried out at once for commercial customers and on the second following business day for most inter-bank (i.e., wholesale) trades.

### 6-3. Forward transactions

A forward transaction is an agreement made today to exchange one currency for another, with the date of the exchange being a specified time in the future – often one month, two months, or some other definitive calendar interval. The rate at which the two currencies will be exchanged is set today.

### 6-4. Foreign exchange transactions

A "foreign exchange transaction" is an agreement between two parties to exchange a given amount of one country's foreign exchange for the foreign exchange of another country. The parties are usually residents of two separate countries, unless the transaction is between residents of one country and a foreign exchange dealer (bank or non-bank dealer), in which case the foreign exchange dealer is operating directly or indirectly on behalf of holders of the foreign currency.

### 6-5. Time zones

a. Yes. New York City, USA (– 5 hours) is open from 11:00 am to 8:00 pm, GMT.
b. No. Los Angeles, California (– 8 hours) is open from 4:00 pm to 11:00 PM, GMT.
c. No. Sydney, Australia (+10 hours) is open from 4:00 pm to 1:00 am, GMT.
d. No. Tokyo, Japan (+9) is open from 3:00 pm to 12:00 midnight, GMT. Tokyo's 3:00 pm GMT opening is at the same moment London is closing, so Tokyo might decide to open earlier.
e. Yes. Singapore (+7) is open from 1:00 pm to 10:00 pm, GMT.
f. Yes. Assuming banks in Kabul, Afghanistan (+4 ½) are functioning during the stated business hours, they would be open from 10:30 am to 7:30 pm, GMT. Banks in central Asia, including India, Pakistan, and Sri Lanka, probably would move their operating hours ahead so as to overlap London.
g. Yes. Moscow, Russia (+3) is open from 9:00 am to 6:00 pm, GMT.
h. Yes. Rome, Italy (+1) is open from 7:00 am to 4:00 pm, GMT.

## 6-6. Functions of the foreign exchange market

a. To transfer purchasing power from one country and its currency to another. Typical parties would be importers and exporters, investors in foreign securities, and tourists.
b. To finance goods in transit. Typical parties would be importers and exporters.
c. To provide hedging facilities. Typical parties would be importers, exporters, and creditors and debtors with short-term monetary obligations.

## 6-7. Buying wholesale or retail?

The *wholesale* foreign exchange market is between banks and other financial institution, where trading is in blocks of even millions of dollars or the equivalent in other currencies. The *retail* foreign exchange market is between the banks and customers who need foreign exchange for their business or investment purposes. The size of transactions in the retail market is determined by the exact amount a customer wants to buy, and the spread between bid and ask is usually slightly greater than in the wholesale market.

## 6-8. Market participants

a. Foreign exchange dealers are banks and a few non-bank institutions that "make a market" in foreign exchange. They buy and sell foreign exchange in the wholesale market and resell or rebuy it from customers at a slight change from the wholesale price.
b. Foreign exchange brokers (not to be confused with dealers) act as intermediaries in bringing dealers together, either because the dealers do not want their identity revealed until after the transaction or because the dealers find that brokers and "shop the market," i.e., scan the bid and offer prices of many dealers very quickly.
c. Individuals and firms conducting international business consist primarily of three categories: importers and exporters, companies making direct foreign investments, and securities investors buying or selling debt or equity investments for their portfolios.
d. Speculators and arbitragers buy and sell foreign exchange for profit. Speculators and arbitragers buy or sell foreign exchange on the basis of which direction they believe a currency's value will change in the immediate or speculative horizon.
e. Central banks and treasuries buy and sell foreign exchange for several purposes, but most importantly, for intervention in the marketplace. Direct intervention, in which the central bank will buy (sell) its own currency in the market with its foreign exchange reserves to push its value up (down), is a very common activity by government treasuries and central banking authorities.

## 6-9. Big players

Data appears in Exhibit 6.3 in the text. The five largest foreign exchange markets by size in 2001 were:

1st: London
2nd: New York
3rd: Japan
4th: Singapore
5th: Germany.

In 1989, the foreign exchange markets of the U.S. and Japan were relatively equal is size, but by 2001 the U.S. market was perhaps 40% larger than the Japanese market. In 1989 the Japanese market was about twice the size of the Singapore market and the German market was almost non-existent. In 2001, twelve years later, Singapore was about 75% the size of the Japanese market and Germany was about 60% the size of the Japanese market.

### 6-10. Swap against forward

This is a transaction between two parties, usually banks, in which they engage in a spot transaction today and simultaneously agree to a forward transaction that will reverse the spot. To illustrate: Bank A buys €10,000,000 for dollars from Bank B today, at today's spot quote, and simultaneously sells €10,000,000 back to Bank B for dollars with delivery two months from now. Because both the spot and the forward exchange rates are set at the time of the transaction, neither party has any exchange risk. The transaction is, in effect, a 100% collateralized loan of one currency, with the difference in exchange for the spot and forward component representing the interest rate differential for the two currencies.

### 6-11. On whose terms?

| | | | |
|---|---|---|---|
| a. | Argentina: | Ps1.0017/$. | OK as is |
| b. | Brazil | $2.6080/*real* | *real*0.3834/$ |
| c. | Canada : | C$1.6000/US$ | OK as is |
| d. | Denmark: | DKr8.3156/$ | OK as is |
| e. | France: | FF7.3328/$ | OK as is |
| f. | Germany : | $0.4574/DM | DM2.1863/$ |
| g. | Indonesia : | $0.0000923/*rupiah* | *rupiah*10,834.2362/$ |
| h. | Hong Kong : | HK$7.8000/US$ | OK as is |
| i. | Japan | $0.008246/¥ | ¥121.2709/$ |
| j. | New Zealand : | US$0.4205/NZ$ | NZ$2.3781/US$ |
| k. | Russia: | $0.0336395/*ruble* | *ruble*29.7270/$ |
| l. | Turkey: | £1540000/$ | OK as is |

### 6-12. Direct or indirect?

a. In Norway, *NK*r8.8786/$ is direct.
b. In Kuwait $0.3056/*dinar* is indirect.
c. In New York $0.3056/*Kuwaiti dinars* is direct.
d. In China *Rmb*8.2767/$ is direct.
e. In Lebanon *L£*1,513.50/$ is direct.
f. In Miami, Florida, *Kuwaiti dinars 0.3056/$* is indirect.
g. In Ireland $0.8804/*punt* is indirect.
h. In South Korea, $0.0007752/$ is indirect.

### *Problems*

### 6-1. Ringgit up or down?

Before the Asian currency crisis, the cost of one dollar in Malaysia was RM2.7000. After the crisis the dollar cost more, RM3.7000/$. Because more ringgit were needed to buy one dollar, the ringgit dropped in value; i.e., *depreciated.* The formula for the percentage drop when the foreign currency price of the home currency is used is:

$$\frac{\text{Beginning rate} - \text{Ending rate}}{\text{Ending rate}} \times 100 = \frac{\text{RM2.70/\$} - \text{RM3.70/\$}}{\text{RM3.70/\$}} \times 100 = -27.03\%.$$

**6-2. Forward premiums and discounts**

The formula to be used depends upon whether the foreign exchange rates are stated as foreign currency units per U.S. dollar or U.S. dollars per foreign currency unit.

| Problem 6.2 Forward Premiums and Discounts | | | |
|---|---|---|---|
| **Calculate the percentage premium or discount.** | | | |
| | **Quoted** | **180-day** | |
| **Assumptions** | **Spot rate** | **Forward rate** | **Values** |
| Days forward | | 180 | |
| **European euro ($/euro)** | **0.8000** | **0.8160** | **4.0000%** |
| (F-S)/(F) x (360/180) | | | |
| **British pound ($/pound)** | **1.5620** | **1.5300** | **-4.0973%** |
| (F-S)/(F) x (360/180) | | | |
| **Japanese yen (yen/$)** | **120.00** | **118.00** | **3.3898%** |
| (S-F)/(F) x (360/180) | | | |
| **Swiss franc (SF/$)** | **1.6000** | **1.6200** | **-2.4691%** |
| (S-F)/(F) x (360/180) | | | |
| **Hong Kong dollar (HK$/$)** | **8.0000** | **7.8000** | **5.1282%** |
| (S-F)/(F) x (360/180) | | | |

**6-3. Trading in Switzerland**

a. Outright bid and ask, and the point spread, are:

| | *Bid* | *Ask* | *Spread* |
|---|---|---|---|
| Spot: | SF1.6075/$ | SF1.6085/$ | 10 points |
| 1-month | SF1.6085/$ | SF1.6100/$ | 15 points |
| 3-months | SF1.6089/$ | SF1.6107/$ | 18 points |
| 6-months | SF1.6095/$ | SF1.6115/$ | 20 points |

b. The point spread increases as the date of trade moves farther into the future. This is because the risk is greater for more distant maturities.

C. First calculate the spot and 6-month forward mid-rates:

Spot mid-rate: (SF1.6075/$+SF1.6085/$) ÷ 2 = SF1.6080/$.

6-month forward mid-rate: (SF1.6095/$+SF1.6115/$) ÷ 2 = SF1.6105/$.

Second use these mid-rates and the 5% cost of U.S. dollars per annum (2.5% interest for 6 months):

$$\frac{\text{SF}1.6080/\$ \times (1 + r)}{\text{SF}\,1.6105/\$} = 1.025.$$

Solving for r:

$$1+r = 1.026594$$

r = 2.6594 for 6 months, or 5.3188% per annum.

The probable yield on Swiss 6-month bills is 5.3188% per annum.

**6-4. Euro forward premiums**

The formula for forward premiums or discounts from a U.S. point of view, when the exchange rate is dollars per euro (i.e., direct), from the text is (Forward - Spot) / (Spot) x (360/days).

**Problem 6.4 Spot and Forward Quotes for the euro**

**Calculate the forward premiums for the euro in Exhibit 6.5.**

**Forward premium = (Forward - Spot) / (Spot) x (360/days)**

| | Euro ($/euro) | Implied | Calculated |
|---|---|---|---|
| **Assumptions** | **Mid Rates** | **Days Forward** | **Forward Premium** |
| Spot | 1.0899 | | |
| 1 week | 1.0903 | 7 | 1.8875% |
| 1 mo | 1.0917 | 30 | 1.9818% |
| 2 mo | 1.0934 | 60 | 1.9268% |
| 3 mo | 1.0953 | 90 | 1.9818% |
| 4 mo | 1.0973 | 120 | 2.0369% |
| 5 mo | 1.0992 | 150 | 2.0479% |
| 6 mo | 1.1012 | 180 | 2.0736% |
| 9 mo | 1.1075 | 270 | 2.1531% |
| 1 yr | 1.1143 | 360 | 2.2387% |
| | | | |
| 2 yr | 1.1401 | 720 | 2.3030% |
| 3 yr | 1.1679 | 1,080 | 2.3855% |
| 4 yr | 1.1899 | 1,440 | 2.2938% |
| 5 yr | 1.2102 | 1,800 | 2.2075% |

**6-5. Yen forward premiums**

The formula for forward premiums or discounts from a U.S. point of view, when the exchange rate is yen per dollars (i.e., indirect), from the text is (Spot - Forward) / (Forward) x (360/days).

**Problem 6.5 Spot and Forward Quotes for the yen**

**Calculate the forward premiums for the yen in Exhibit 6.5.**

**Forward premium = (Spot - Forward) / (Forward) x (360/days)**

| Assumptions | Yen (yen/$) Mid Rates | Implied Days Forward | Calculated Forward Premium |
|---|---|---|---|
| Spot | 118.32 | | |
| 1 week | 118.23 | 7 | 3.9149% |
| 1 mo | 117.82 | 30 | 5.0925% |
| 2 mo | 117.38 | 60 | 4.8049% |
| 3 mo | 116.91 | 90 | 4.8242% |
| 4 mo | 116.40 | 120 | 4.9485% |
| 5 mo | 115.94 | 150 | 4.9267% |
| 6 mo | 115.45 | 180 | 4.9718% |
| 9 mo | 114.00 | 270 | 5.0526% |
| 1 yr | 112.50 | 360 | 5.1733% |
| | | | |
| 2 yr | 106.93 | 720 | 5.3259% |
| 3 yr | 101.09 | 1,080 | 5.6814% |
| 4 yr | 96.82 | 1,440 | 5.5515% |
| 5 yr | 92.91 | 1,800 | 5.4698% |

The forward premium on the yen increases as maturity gets longer. The only exceptions to this smooth progression are for maturities of 1 month and for maturities of 4 and 5 years.

**6-6. Traveling: Copenhagen to St. Petersburg**

The cross rate is calculated:

$$\frac{\text{R}30.962/\$}{\text{Dkr}8.5515/\$} = \text{R}3.6207/\text{Dkr}$$

or inversely,

$$\frac{\text{Dkr}8.5515/\$}{\text{R}30.962/\$} = \text{Dkr}0.2762/\text{R}$$

Rubles received:

$$\text{Dkr}10{,}000 \times \text{R } 3.6207/\text{Dkr} = \text{R } 36.206.51,$$

or

$$\frac{\text{Dkr } 10{,}000}{\text{Dkr } 0.2762/\text{R}} = \text{R}36{,}206.51\,.$$

| Problem 6.6 Traveling: Copenhagen to St. Petersburg | |
|---|---|
| **What is the cross rate? What is left?** | |
| | |
| **Assumptions** | **Values** |
| Beginning your trip with Danish kroner | 10,000.00 |
| Spot rate (Dkr/$) | 8.5515 |
| Spot rate (Roubles/$) | 30.962 |
| | |
| **a) Calculate the cross rate** | |
| Cross rate (Dkr/rouble) = (Dkr/$) / (Roubles/$) | 0.2762 |
| | |
| **b) What would be the proceeds in Rubles?** | |
| Converting your Finnish markkas into Rubles | 36,206.51 |
| (Beginning Danish kroner / cross rate) | |

**6-7. Making a quick franc**

Yen/SF quote of Matterhorn Bank: ¥80.00/SF
Yen/SF cross rate: ¥120.00/\$÷SF1.6000/\$ = ¥75.00/SF

Because the cross rate is not equal to the direct quote, triangular arbitrage is possible.

1st. Exchange SF10,000,000 for yen at Matterhorn Bank:

SF10,000,000 × ¥80.00/SF = ¥800,000,000

2nd. Exchange ¥800,000,000 for dollars at Mt. Fuji Bank:

¥800,000,000 ÷ ¥120/\$ = \$6,666,666.67.

3rd. Exchange \$6,666,666.67 for Swiss francs at Mt. Rushmore Bank:

\$6,666,666.67 × SF1.6000/\$ = SF10,666.666.67.

Profit: SF10,666.666.67 – SF10,000,000 = SF666,666.67.

## Problem 6.7 Making a Quick franc

**Can you make a profit via triangular arbitrage?**

| **Assumptions** | **Values** |
| --- | --- |
| Beginning funds in Swiss francs (SF) | **10,000,000.00** |
| Mt. Fuji Bank (yen/$) | **120.00** |
| Mt. Rushmore Bank (SF/$) | **1.6000** |
| Matterhorn Bank (yen/SF) | **80.00** |
| | |
| **Try Number 1: Start with SF to $** | |
| Step 1: SF to $ | **6,250,000.00** |
| Step 2: $ to yen | **750,000,000.00** |
| Step 3: yen to SF | **9,375,000.00** |
| Profit? | **(625,000.00)** |
| | **A loss.** |
| | |
| **Try Number 2: Start with SF to yen** | |
| Step 1: SF to yen | **800,000,000.00** |
| Step 2: yen to $ | **6,666,666.67** |
| Step 3: $ to SF | **10,666,666.67** |
| Profit? | **666,666.67** |
| | **A profit.** |

## 6-8. Forward premiums on WSJ Quotes

**Problem 6.8 Forward Premiums on WSJ Quotes in Exhibit 6.6**

**Calculate the percentage premium or discount.**

| Assumptions | US$ equivalent Thu | US$ equivalent Wed | Currency/US$ Thu | Currency/US$ Wed |
|---|---|---|---|---|
| **Britain (Pound)** | 1.4443 | 1.4475 | 0.6924 | 0.6908 |
| 1-month forward | 1.4418 | 1.4452 | 0.6936 | 0.6919 |
| 3-months forward | 1.4371 | 1.4401 | 0.6958 | 0.6944 |
| 6-months forward | 1.4301 | 1.4336 | 0.6993 | 0.6975 |
| | | | | |
| **a) Forward premium (discount)** | | | | |
| 1-month forward | -2.0771% | -1.9067% | -2.0761% | -1.9078% |
| 3-months forward | -1.9940% | -2.0449% | -1.9546% | -2.0737% |
| 6-months forward | -1.9664% | -1.9206% | -1.9734% | -1.9211% |

**b) Why are the forward discounts not identical?**

**They would be if the "Currency/US$" quote is calculated as the reciprocal of "US$ equivalent" carrying the digits.**

| | | | | |
|---|---|---|---|---|
| **Britain (Pound)** | 1.4443 | 1.4475 | 0.6924 | 0.6908 |
| 1-month forward | 1.4418 | 1.4452 | 0.6936 | 0.6919 |
| 3-months forward | 1.4371 | 1.4401 | 0.6958 | 0.6944 |
| 6-months forward | 1.4301 | 1.4336 | 0.6993 | 0.6975 |
| | | | | |
| **Forward premium (discount)** | | | | |
| 1-month forward | -2.0771% | -1.9067% | -2.0771% | -1.9067% |
| 3-months forward | -1.9940% | -2.0449% | -1.9940% | -2.0449% |
| 6-months forward | -1.9664% | -1.9206% | -1.9664% | -1.9206% |

## 6-9. Geographic arbitrage

| Problem 6.9 Geographic Arbitrage | |
|---|---|
| **Can the arbitrageur make a profit with these quotes?** | |
| | |
| **Assumptions** | **Values** |
| Beginning funds | **$ 1,000,000.00** |
| Citibank NY quotes: | |
| Bid ($/euro) | **0.9650** |
| Ask ($/euro) | **0.9670** |
| Barclays London quotes: | |
| Bid ($/euro) | **0.9640** |
| Ask ($/euro) | **0.9660** |
| | |
| **Arbitrage Strategy #1** | |
| Initial investment | **$ 1,000,000.00** |
| Buy euros from Barclays London (at the Ask rate) | **1,035,196.69** |
| Sell euros to Citibank NY (at the Bid rate) | **$ 998,964.80** |
| Arbitrage profit (loss) | **$ (1,035.20)** |
| | |
| **Arbitrage Strategy #2** | |
| Initial investment | **$ 1,000,000.00** |
| Buy euros from Citibank NY (at the Ask rate) | **1,034,126.16** |
| Sell euros to Barclays London (at the Bid rate) | **$ 996,897.62** |
| Arbitrage profit (loss) | **$ (3,102.38)** |
| | |
| The arbitrager cannot make a profit from these quotes when starting in US$. | |

**6-10. Financial Times quotes**

The formula:

$$\frac{\text{Spot rate} - \text{Forward rate}}{\text{Forward rate}} \times \frac{360}{\text{days}} \times 100.$$

Spot means the closing mid-point rate.£

$$\text{One month: } \frac{\$1.4446/£ - \$1.4421/£}{\$1.4421/£} \times \frac{360}{30} \times 100 = 2.0803\% \approx 2.1\%..$$

A 2.1% annual premium on the dollar.

$$\text{Three months: } \frac{\$1.4446/£ - \$1.4374/£}{\$1.4374/£} \times \frac{360}{90} \times 100 = 2.0036\% \approx 2.0\%.$$

A 2.0% annual premium on the dollar.

$$\text{One year: } \frac{\$1.4446/£ - \$1.4183/£}{\$1.4183/£} \times \frac{360}{360} \times 100 = 1.8543\% \approx 1.85\%.$$

A 1.85% annual premium on the dollar.

**6-11. Venezuelan bolivar**

Reading from the chart, the exchange rate on February 1st was about Bs770/$. As given, the exchange rate on February 28th was Bs1025/$. The formula for percentage change from the text for indirect quotes is:

$$\frac{\text{Beginning rate} - \text{Ending rate}}{\text{Ending rate}} \times 100 = \frac{\text{Bs}770/\$ - \text{Bs}1025/\$}{\text{Bs}1025/\$} \times 100 = -24.88\%.$$

The bolivar lost 24.88% of its value during the month of February. (The minus sign indicates a loss in value versus the U.S. dollar.)

## Mini-Case: Willem Vandewater N.V. and the Euro

**1. Why might re-pricing lead to more inflation?**

When a local currency price is converted to a euro price the result will often be a whole number and fraction of a number such as 1.9 euros. Human nature might cause the price to be "rounded-up" to 2.0 euros. If the price turns out to be 1.1 euros, it is not as likely that the price will be rounded down.

**2. Why would the continued decline in value of the euro be a problem?**

If some of the suppliers price their goods in U.S. dollars but all sales are priced in euros, Willem Vandewater's gross margins will shrink unless it raises euro prices to match the extra currency costs. That action could reduce the volume of sales. If prices are not raised in euros, the smaller gross margin will lead to lower net income.

**3. What is meant by lower transaction and translation exposure?**

Since all sales and most costs will be priced in euros, there will be fewer "mismatches" of currencies such as existed prior to the introduction of the euro. The mismatch in currency can cause foreign exchange losses on "transactions," i.e. buying in one currency and selling an another currency after the exchange rate changes.

"Translation exposure" arises because Willem Vandewater needs to consolidate the financial statements of all its country sales subsidiaries into one company-wide statement. This was previously done by "translating" many European currencies into Dutch guilders. Any change in exchange rates would be reflected in translation gains or losses in the consolidated financial statements. The introduction of the euro will mean that "translation" will be unnecessary since all financial statements within the eurozone will already be stated in euro.

**4. Why would less cash in euros be needed than were previously required with multiple currencies?**

With multiple currencies Willem Vandewater needed to keep enough cash for change in each vending machine to cover expected sales in each currency, plus an extra amount for safety reasons in case transactions in a particular currency exceeded expectations.

With the euro Willem Vandewater still needs to keep enough cash for change in each vending machine. However, the safety margin would require less cash to cover one currency, the euro, than the previous multiple currencies.

**5. Has Willem Vandewater, Jr., forgotten to prepare for any other problems you can identify?**

This is an open-ended question for discussion. It is limited only by the discussants' imagination. Some possible topics include the following:

a. The potential for increased vandalism or terrorism as opposition to the euro by nationalistic forces increases. Many European citizens miss their old currencies and dislike the gradual concentration of power and authority in Brussels (European Union headquarters). Maybe they could express their anger and frustration by vandalizing the vending machines that now symbolically dispense euros.

b. Vending machines are a likely bet to "round-up" prices. This could lower sales and increase frustration by those opposed to the euro.

## CHAPTER 7: FOREIGN CURRENCY DERIVATIVES

### *Questions*

### 7-1. Options versus Futures

An option is a contract giving the buyer the right but not the obligation to buy or sell a given amount of foreign exchange at a fixed price for a specified time period. A *future* is an exchange-traded contract calling for future delivery of a standard amount of foreign currency at a fixed time, place, and price.

The essence of the difference is that an option leaves the buyer with the choice of exercising or not exercising. The *future* requires a mandatory delivery. The *future* is a standardized exchange-traded contract often used as an alternative to a forward foreign exchange agreement.

### 7-2. Trading location for futures

*The Wall Street Journal* reports on foreign exchange futures trading for the International Monetary Market in Chicago and for the Philadelphia Stock Exchange. These are the two major U.S. markets for foreign exchange futures.

### 7-3. Futures terminology

a. *Specific-sized contract:* Trading may be conducted only in pre-established multiples of currency units. This means that a firm wishing to hedge some aspect of its foreign exchange risk is not able to match the contract size with the size of the risk.

b. *Standard method of stating exchange rates*. Rates are stated in "American terms," meaning the U.S. dollar value of the foreign currency, rather than in the more generally accepted "European terms," meaning the foreign currency price of a U.S. dollar. This has no conceptual significance, although financial managers used to viewing exposure in European terms will find it necessary to convert to reciprocals.

c. *Standard maturity date*. All contracts mature at a pre-established date, being on the third Wednesday of eight specified months. This means that a firm wishing to use foreign exchange futures to cover exchange risk will not be able to match the contract maturity with the risk maturity.

d. *Collateral and maintenance margins*. An initial "margin," meaning a cash deposit made at the time a futures contract is purchased, is required. This is an inconvenience to most firms doing international business because it means some of their cash is tied up in a non-productive manner. Forward contracts made through banks for existing business clients do not normally require an initial margin. A *maintenance margin* is also required, meaning that if the value of the contract is marked to market every day and if the existing margin on deposit falls below a mandatory percentage of the contract, additional margin must be deposited. This constitutes a big nuisance to a business firm because it must be prepared for a daily outflow of cash than cannot be anticipated. (Of course, on some days the cash flow would be in to the firm.)

e. *Counterparty*. All futures contracts are with the clearing house of the exchange where they are traded. Consequently a firm or individual engaged in buying or selling futures contracts need not worry about the credit risk of the opposite party.

### 7-4. A futures trade

This data reports that 29,763 contracts, each contract being for € 125,000, were traded for settlement on the third Wednesday of the following December . The total euro value of all contracts traded on the day for which data is reported is the product of the two numbers: 29,763 × € 125,000 = € 3,720,375,000. The highest price during the day at which euro futures traded was $0.9147/€. The lowest price was $0.9098/€. The first trade of the day was at $0.9124/€ and the last trade, called "settlement," was at $0.9136/€. This closing price was 0.0027 above the previous day's close, from which one can determine that on the previous day euro contracts closed at $0.9136/€ – $0.0027/€ = $0.9109/€. The closing "settlement" price is the price used by futures exchanges to determine margin calls. Open interest is the sum of all long (buying futures) and short (selling futures) contracts outstanding.

### 7-5. Puts and calls

A *put* on pounds sterling is a contract giving the owner (buyer) the right but not the obligation to sell pounds sterling for dollars at the exchange rate stated in the put. A *call* on pounds sterling is a contract giving the owner (buyer) the right but not the obligation to buy pounds sterling for dollars at the exchange rate stated in the call.

### 7-6. Call contract elements

If you buy such an option, you may if you wish order the writer (opposite party) of the option to deliver pounds sterling to you and you will pay $1.460 for each pound. $1.460/£ is called the "strike price." You have this right (this "option") until next March, and for this right you will pay 3.67¢ per pound. The information provided to you does not tell you the size of each option contract, which you would have to know from general experience or from asking your broker. The contract size for pounds sterling on the IMM is £62,500 per contract, meaning that the option will cost you £62,500 × $0.0367 = $2,293.75.

### 7-7. The option cost

The amount you pay for the option is gone forever, whether or not you exercise the option. This is the amount paid to the writer of the option, who undertakes the open-ended obligation to deliver pounds to you should you so wish. If you do not exercise the option, this is the sunk cost of buying options. If you in fact do exercise the option, your direct profit on the option is reduced by this amount which has already been paid out.

### 7-8. Buying a European option

The only difference is that you may exercise the option *only* on the day that it matures. Of course, you may sell the option to another investor at any time, and that subsequent owner then must hold until maturity – or sell to yet another investors, and so forth.

### 7-9. Writing options

From the option writer's point of view, only two events can take place:

a. *The option is not exercised.* In this case the writer gains the option premium and still has the underlying stock.

b. *The option is exercised.* If the option writer owns the stock and the option is exercised, the option writer (a) gains the premium and (b) experiences only an *opportunity cost* loss. In other words, the loss is not a cash loss, but rather the opportunity cost loss of having foregone the potential of making even more profit had the underlying shares been sold at a more advantageous price. This is somewhat equivalent of having sold (call option writer) or bought (put option writer) at a price better than current market, only to have the market price move even further in a beneficial direction.

If the option writer does not own the underlying shares, the option is written "naked." Only in this instance can the cash loss to the option writer be a very large amount.

**7-10. Option valuation**

a. *Intrinsic value* for a call option is the amount of gain that would be made today if the option were exercised today and the underlying shares sold immediately. For a put, *intrinsic value* is the amount of gain that would be made if the underlying shares were purchased today and delivered immediately against the option. Intrinsic value can be zero, as when the option is not worth exercising today. However if a gain could be made by exercising the option today, the intrinsic value is positive because intrinsic value can never be less than what can be gained from an immediate exercise of the option. Note that gain is not the same as net profit because in all cases the option buyer has already paid the premium.

b. *Time value* of an option is related to what one will pay above intrinsic value because of the chance that between today and the maturity of the option intrinsic value will become positive (option with no intrinsic value) or greater than today (option having some positive intrinsic value today.) In effect, intrinsic value is the worth of the speculative component of the option.

## Problem 7.1 Peso Futures

**Amber McClain sells June futures**

| Assumptions | | a) Values | | b) Values | | c) Values |
|---|---|---|---|---|---|---|
| Number of pesos per futures contract | | 500,000 | | 500,000 | | 500,000 |
| Number of contracts | | 8.00 | | 8.00 | | 8.00 |
| Buy or sell the peso futures? | | Sell | | Sell | | Sell |
| | | | | | | |
| Ending spot rate ($/peso) | $ | 0.12000 | $ | 0.09800 | $ | 0.11000 |
| June futures contract, settle price ($/peso) | $ | 0.10773 | $ | 0.10773 | $ | 0.10773 |
| Spot - Futures | $ | 0.01227 | $ | (0.00973) | $ | 0.00227 |
| | | | | | | |
| Value of total position at maturity (US$) | $ | (49,080.00) | $ | 38,920.00 | $ | (9,080.00) |
| Value = - Notional x (Spot - Futures) x 8 | | | | | | |

**Interpretation**

Amber buys at the spot price and sells at the futures price.
If the futures price is greater than the ending spot price, she makes a profit.

## Problem 7.2 Pound Futures

**Michael Palin buying & selling pound futures**

| Assumptions | a) Values | b) Values | c) Values | d) Values |
|---|---|---|---|---|
| Number of pounds per futures contract | 62,500 | 62,500 | 62,500 | 62,500 |
| Maturity month | June | March | March | June |
| Number of contracts | 5 | 12 | 3 | 12 |
| Did he buy or sell the futures? | buys | sells | buys | sells |
| | | | | |
| Ending spot rate ($/peso) | $ 1.3980 | $ 1.4560 | $ 1.4560 | $ 1.3980 |
| Pound futures contract, settle price ($/pound) | $ 1.4162 | $ 1.4228 | $ 1.4228 | $ 1.4162 |
| Spot - Futures | $ (0.0182) | $ 0.0332 | $ 0.0332 | $ (0.0182) |
| | | | | |
| Value of position at maturity ($) | $ (5,687.50) | $ (24,900.00) | $ 6,225.00 | $ 13,650.00 |
| buys: Notional x (Spot - Futures) x contracts | | | | |
| sells: - Notional x (Spot - Futures) x contracts | | | | |

**Interpretation**

Buys a futures: Michael buys at the futures price and sells at the ending spot price.
He therefore profits when the futures price is less than the ending spot price.
Sells a future: Michael buys at the ending spot price and sells at the futures price.
He therefore profits when the futures price is greater than the ending spot price.

## Problem 7.3 Hans Schmidt, Speculator

**Hans Schmidt uses $10 million to speculate on the euro.**

| Assumptions | | a) Values | | b) Values |
|---|---|---|---|---|
| Initial investment (funds available) | $ | 10,000,000 | $ | 10,000,000 |
| Current spot rate (US$/euro) | $ | 0.8850 | $ | 0.8850 |
| 30-day forward rate (US$/euro) | $ | 0.9000 | $ | 0.9000 |
| Expected spot rate in 30 days (US$/euro) | $ | 0.8440 | $ | 0.9440 |
| **Strategy for Part a):** | | | | |
| 1. Sell euros 30-days forward (in euros) | | 11,111,111.11 | | |
| 2. At the end of 30 days, buy these euros spot | $ | (9,377,777.78) | | |
| 3. At the end of 30 days, sell euros at forward rate | $ | 10,000,000.00 | | |
| 4. Realize profit | $ | 622,222.22 | | |
| **Strategy for Part b):** | | | | |
| 1. Convert US$ to euros at the current spot rate (US$) | | | $ | (10,000,000.00) |
| (in euros) | | | | 11,299,435.03 |
| 2. At the end of 30 days, convert back to US$ at spot rate | | | $ | 10,666,666.67 |
| 3. Realize profit | | | $ | 666,666.67 |

## Problem 7.4 Hans Schmidt & the Swiss franc

**Hans Schmidt uses $100,000 to speculate on the Swiss franc.**

| Assumptions | | a) Values | | b) Values |
|---|---|---|---|---|
| Initial investment (funds available) | $ | 100,000 | $ | 100,000 |
| Current spot rate (US$/Swiss franc) | $ | 0.5820 | $ | 0.5820 |
| Six-month forward rate (US$/Swiss franc) | $ | 0.5640 | $ | 0.5640 |
| Expected spot rate in six months (US$/Swiss franc) | $ | 0.6250 | $ | 0.6250 |

| Strategy for Part a): | | |
|---|---|---|
| 1. Use the $100,000 today to buy SF at spot rate | | SFr. 171,821.31 |
| 2. Hold the SF indefinitely. | | |
| 3. At the end of six months, convert SF at expected rate | $ | 0.6250 |
| 4. Yielding expected dollar revenues of | $ | 107,388.32 |
| 5. Realize profit (revenues less $100,000 initial invest) | $ | 7,388.32 |

| Strategy for Part b): | | |
|---|---|---|
| 1. Buy SF forward six months (no cash outlay required) | | |
| 2. Fulfill the six months forward in six months | | 177,304.96 |
| cost in US$ | $ | (100,000.00) |
| 3. Convert the SF into US$ at expected spot rate | $ | 110,815.60 |
| 4. Realize profit | $ | 10,815.60 |

## Problem 7.5 Katya and the yen

**Katya Berezovsky wishes to speculate on the fall of the yen against the dollar**

| **Assumptions** | | **Values** |
|---|---|---|
| Current spot rate (Japanese yen/US$) | | **120.00** |
| in US$/yen | **$** | **0.00833** |
| Maturity of option (days) | | **90** |
| Expected ending spot rate in 90 days (yen/$) | | **140.00** |
| in US$/yen | **$** | **0.00714** |

| | | **Call on yen** | | **Put on yen** |
|---|---|---|---|---|
| Strike price (yen/US$) | | **125.00** | | **125.00** |
| in US$/yen | **$** | **0.00800** | **$** | **0.00800** |
| Premium (US$/yen) | **$** | **0.00046** | **$** | **0.00003** |

**a) Should she buy a call on yen or a put on yen?**

Katya should buy a put on yen to profit from the rise of the dollar (the fall of the yen).

**b) What is Katy'as break even price on her option of choice in part a)?**

Katya buys a put on yen. Pays premium today.
In 90 days, exercises the put, receiving US$.

| | | | **in yen/$** |
|---|---|---|---|
| Strike price | **$** | **0.00800** | 125.00 |
| Less premium | **$** | **(0.00003)** | |
| Breakeven | **$** | **0.00797** | **125.47** |

**c) What is Katya's gross profit and net profit if the end spot rate is 140 yen/$?**

| | | **Gross profit (US$/yen)** | | **Net profit (US$/yen)** |
|---|---|---|---|---|
| Strike price | **$** | **0.00800** | **$** | **0.00800** |
| Less spot rate | | **(0.00714)** | | **(0.00714)** |
| Less premium | | | | **(0.00003)** |
| Profit | **$** | **0.00086** | **$** | **0.00083** |

## Problem 7.6 Samuel and the Singapore dollar

**Samuel Samosir wishes to speculate on the rise of the Singapore dollar versus the US dollar.**

| **Assumptions** | | **Values** | | |
|---|---|---|---|---|
| Current spot rate (US$/Singapore dollar) | $ | **0.6000** | | |
| Days to maturity | | **90** | | |
| Expected spot rate in 90 days (US$/Singapore dollar) | $ | **0.7000** | | |
| Option choices on the Singapore dollar: | | **Call option** | | **Put option** |
| Strike price (US$/Singapore dollar) | $ | **0.6500** | $ | **0.6500** |
| Premium (US$/Singapore dollar) | $ | **0.0002** | $ | **0.0449** |

**a) Which option should Samuel buy?**

Since Samuel expects the Singapore dollar to appreciate versus the US dollar, he should buy a call on Singapore dollars.

**b) What is Samuel's breakeven price on the option purchased in part a)?**

| | | |
|---|---|---|
| Strike price | $ | **0.65000** |
| Plus premium | $ | **0.00020** |
| Breakeven | $ | **0.65020** |

**c) What is Samuel's gross profit and net profit (including premium) if the ending spot rate is $0.70/S$?**

| | | **Gross profit (US$/S$)** | | **Net profit (US$/S$)** |
|---|---|---|---|---|
| Spot rate | $ | **0.70000** | $ | **0.70000** |
| Less strike price | | **(0.65000)** | | **(0.65000)** |
| Less premium | | | | **(0.00020)** |
| Profit | $ | **0.05000** | $ | **0.04980** |

**d) What is Samuel's gross profit and net profit (including premium) if the ending spot rate is $0.80/S$?**

| | | **Gross profit (US$/S$)** | | **Net profit (US$/S$)** |
|---|---|---|---|---|
| Spot rate | $ | **0.80000** | $ | **0.80000** |
| Less strike price | | **(0.65000)** | | **(0.65000)** |
| Less premium | | | | **(0.00020)** |
| Profit | $ | **0.15000** | $ | **0.14980** |

## Problem 7.7 How Much Profit -- Calls?

**A call option is written on euros.**

| Assumptions | a) Values | b) Values | c) Values | d) Values | e) Values | f) Values | g) Values |
|---|---|---|---|---|---|---|---|
| Notional principal (euros) | € 100,000.00 | € 100,000.00 | € 100,000.00 | € 100,000.00 | € 100,000.00 | € 100,000.00 | € 100,000.00 |
| Maturity (days) | 90 | 90 | 90 | 90 | 90 | 90 | 90 |
| Strike price (US$/euro) | $ 0.9400 | $ 0.9400 | $ 0.9400 | $ 0.9400 | $ 0.9400 | $ 0.9400 | $ 0.9400 |
| Premium (US$/euro) | $ 0.0090 | $ 0.0090 | $ 0.0090 | $ 0.0090 | $ 0.0090 | $ 0.0090 | $ 0.0090 |
| Ending spot rate (US$/euro) | $ 0.9000 | $ 0.9200 | $ 0.9400 | $ 0.9600 | $ 0.9800 | $ 1.0000 | $ 1.0200 |
| | | | | | | | |
| Gross profit on option | $ - | $ - | $ - | $ 0.0200 | $ 0.0400 | $ 0.0600 | $ 0.0800 |
| Less premium | (0.0090) | (0.0090) | (0.0090) | (0.0090) | (0.0090) | (0.0090) | (0.0090) |
| Net profit (US$/euro) | $ (0.0090) | $ (0.0090) | $ (0.0090) | $ 0.0110 | $ 0.0310 | $ 0.0510 | $ 0.0710 |
| | | | | | | | |
| Net profit, total | $ (900.00) | $ (900.00) | $ (900.00) | $ 1,100.00 | $ 3,100.00 | $ 5,100.00 | $ 7,100.00 |

## Problem 7.8 How Much Profit -- Puts?

**A put option on yen is written.**

| | a) | b) | c) | d) | e) | f) | g) |
|---|---|---|---|---|---|---|---|
| **Assumptions** | **Values** | **Values** | **Values** | **Values** | **Values** | **Values** | **Values** |
| Notional principal (yen) | 12,500,000 | 12,500,000 | 12,500,000 | 12,500,000 | 12,500,000 | 12,500,000 | 12,500,000 |
| Maturity (days) | 180 | 180 | 180 | 180 | 180 | 180 | 180 |
| Strike price (US$/yen) | $ 0.008000 | $ 0.008000 | $ 0.008000 | $ 0.008000 | $ 0.008000 | $ 0.008000 | $ 0.008000 |
| Premium (US$/yen) | $ 0.000080 | $ 0.000080 | $ 0.000080 | $ 0.000080 | $ 0.000080 | $ 0.000080 | $ 0.000080 |
| | | | | | | | |
| Ending spot rate (yen/US$) | 110.00 | 115.00 | 120.00 | 125.00 | 130.00 | 135.00 | 140.00 |
| in US$/yen | $ 0.009091 | $ 0.008696 | $ 0.008333 | $ 0.008000 | $ 0.007692 | $ 0.007407 | $ 0.007143 |
| | | | | | | | |
| Gross profit on option | $ - | $ - | $ - | $ - | $ 0.0003 | $ 0.0006 | $ 0.0009 |
| Less premium | (0.000080) | (0.000080) | (0.000080) | (0.000080) | (0.000080) | (0.000080) | (0.000080) |
| Net profit (US$/yen) | $ (0.000080) | $ (0.000080) | $ (0.000080) | $ (0.000080) | $ 0.000228 | $ 0.000513 | $ 0.000777 |
| | | | | | | | |
| Net profit, total | $ (1,000.00) | $ (1,000.00) | $ (1,000.00) | $ (1,000.00) | $ 2,846.15 | $ 6,407.41 | $ 9,714.29 |

## Problem 7.9 Giri and the Canadian dollar

**Giri Patel wishes to speculate on the rise of the Canadian dollar versus the US dollar.**

| **Assumptions** | | **Values** |
|---|---|---|
| Current spot rate (US$/Canadian dollar) | $ | 0.6750 |
| Days to maturity | | 90 |

| Option choices on the Canadian dollar: | | **Call option** | | **Put option** |
|---|---|---|---|---|
| Strike price (US$/Canadian dollar) | $ | 0.7000 | $ | 0.7000 |
| Premium (US$/Canadian dollar) | $ | 0.0249 | $ | 0.0003 |

**a) Which option should Giri buy?**

Since Giri expects the Canadian dollar to appreciate versus the US dollar, he should buy a call on Canadian dollars.

**b) What is Giri's breakeven price on the option purchased in part a)?**

| | | |
|---|---|---|
| Strike price | $ | 0.7000 |
| Plus premium | | 0.0249 |
| Breakeven | $ | 0.7249 |

**c) What is Giri's gross profit and net profit (including premium) if the ending spot rate is $0.7600/C$?**

| | | **Gross profit (US$/C$)** | | **Net profit (US$/C$)** |
|---|---|---|---|---|
| Spot rate | $ | 0.7600 | $ | 0.7600 |
| Less strike price | $ | (0.7000) | $ | (0.7000) |
| Less premium | | | $ | (0.0249) |
| Profit | $ | 0.0600 | $ | 0.0351 |

**d) What is Giri's gross profit and net profit (including premium) if the ending spot rate is $0.8250/C$?**

| | | **Gross profit (US$/C$)** | | **Net profit (US$/C$)** |
|---|---|---|---|---|
| Spot rate | $ | 0.8250 | $ | 0.8250 |
| Less strike price | $ | (0.7000) | $ | (0.7000) |
| Less premium | | | $ | (0.0249) |
| Profit | $ | 0.1250 | $ | 0.1001 |

## Problem 7.10 Braveheart

**Andy Furstow of Braveheart wishes to speculate on the fall of the British pound.**

| **Assumptions** | | **Values** |
|---|---|---|
| Current spot rate (US$/pound) | $ | **1.4260** |
| Expected endings spot rate in 30 to 60 days (US$/pnd) | $ | **1.3200** |
| Potential investment principal per person (pounds) | | **£250,000.00** |

| **Put options on pounds** | | **Put #1** | | **Put #2** | | **Put #3** |
|---|---|---|---|---|---|---|
| Strike price (US$/pound) | $ | **1.36** | $ | **1.34** | $ | **1.32** |
| Maturity (days) | | **30** | | **30** | | **30** |
| Premium (US$/pound) | $ | **0.00081** | $ | **0.00021** | $ | **0.00004** |

| **Put options on pounds** | | **Put #4** | | **Put #5** | | **Put #6** |
|---|---|---|---|---|---|---|
| Strike price (US$/pound) | $ | **1.36** | $ | **1.34** | $ | **1.32** |
| Maturity (days) | | **60** | | **60** | | **60** |
| Premium (US$/pound) | $ | **0.00333** | $ | **0.00150** | $ | **0.00060** |

**Issues for Andy Furstow to consider:**

1. Because his expectation is for "30 to 60 days" he should confine his choices to the 60 day options to be sure and capture the timing of the exchange rate change. (We have no explicit idea of why he believes this specific timing.)

2. The choice of which strike price is an interesting debate.
   * The lower the strike price (1.34 or 1.32), the cheaper the option price.
   * The reason they are cheaper is that, statistically speaking, they are increasingly less likely to end up in the money.
   * The choice, given that all the options are relatively "cheap," is to pick the strike price which will yield the required return.
   * The $1.32 strike price is too far 'down,' given that Andy Furstow only expects the pound to fall to about $1.32.

| | | **Put #4**<br>**Net profit** | | **Put #5**<br>**Net profit** | | **Put #6**<br>**Net profit** |
|---|---|---|---|---|---|---|
| Strike price | $ | **1.36000** | $ | **1.34000** | $ | **1.32000** |
| Less expected spot rate | | **(1.32000)** | | **(1.32000)** | | **(1.32000)** |
| Less premium | | **(0.00333)** | | **(0.00150)** | | **(0.00060)** |
| Profit | $ | **0.03667** | $ | **0.01850** | $ | **(0.00060)** |
| If Andy invested an individual's principal purely in this specific option, they would purchase an option of the following notional principal (pounds): | | **£75,075,075.08** | | **£166,666,666.67** | | **£416,666,666.67** |
| Expected profit, in total (profit rate x notional): | $ | **2,753,003.00** | $ | **3,083,333.33** | $ | **(250,000.00)** |
| Initial investment at current spot rate | $ | **356,500.00** | $ | **356,500.00** | $ | **356,500.00** |
| **Return on Investment (ROI)** | | **772%** | | **865%** | | **-70%** |
| **Risk: They could lose it all (full premium)** | | | | | | |

## MINI-CASE: ROGUE TRADER, NICHOLAS LEESON

**This mini-case is based on "Baring Brothers & Company," by Professor Mark Griffiths, Thunderbird Case #E06-99-0021. Used with the permission of the Thunderbird Case Series.**

1. **What was Nick Leeson's strategy to earn trading profits on derivatives?**

   Nick Leeson was trading futures and options on the Nikkei 225, an index of Japanese securities. He was long Nikkei 225 futures, short Japanese government bond futures, and short both put and call options on the Nikkei Index. He was betting that the Nikkei index would rise, but instead, it fell, causing him to lose $1.39 billion.

2. **What went wrong that caused his strategy to fail?**

   Nick Leeson's strategy failed because the Nikkei 225 index kept falling while he continued to bet that it would rise.

3. **Why did Nick Leeson establish a bogus error account (88888) when a legitimate account (99002) already existed?**

   Nick Leeson established a bogus error account (88888) when a legitimate account (99002) already existed in order to conceal his unauthorized trading activities. While the legitimate error account was known to Barings Securities in London, the bogus account was not. However, the bogus account was known to SIMEX as a customer account, not as an error account. In this way Leeson could hide his balances and losses from London – but not Singapore. One the other hand, SIMEX thought the bogus error account, 88888, was a legitimate customer account rather than a proprietary Barings account.

4. **Why did Barings and its auditors not discover that the error account was used by Leeson for unauthorized trading?**

   Internal Reasons. Leeson engaged in unauthorized trading, as well as fraud. However, it is clear that he was hidden in the organized chaos that characterized Barings. "There were no clearly laid down reporting lines with regard to Leeson, through the management chain to Ron Baker [Head of Financial Products Group for Barings]" (Bank of England, p. 235). In fact, it seems there were several people responsible for monitoring Leeson's performance, each of whom assumed the other was watching more closely than he.

   In August 1994, James Baker completed an internal audit of the Singapore office. He made several recommendations that should have alerted Barings executives to the potential for unauthorized trading: 1) segregation of front and back office activities—a fundamental principle in the industry, 2) a comprehensive review of Leeson's funding requirements, and 3) position limits on Leeson's activities. None of these had been acted upon by the time of the bank's collapse.

   With regard to the first concern, Simon Jones, Director of BFS and Finance Director of BSS, in Singapore, offered assurances that he would address the segregation issue. However, he never took action to segregate Leeson's front and back office activities. Tony Hawes, Barings Treasurer in London agreed to complete a review of the funding requirements within the coming year. Ian Hopkins, Director and Head of Treasury and Risk in London, placed the issue of position limits on the risk committee's agenda, but it had not been decided when the collapse occurred.

According to the Bank of England report, senior management in London considered Jones a poor communicator and were concerned that he was not as involved as he should have been in the affairs of BFS. In fact, Peter Norris, the chief executive officer for Baring Securities Limited wanted to replace Jones. Jones, however, was protected by James Bax, Managing Director of Baring Securities Singapore, who was well liked in London.

The Bank of England also found fault with the process of funding Leeson's activities from London. First, there was no clear understanding of whether the funds were needed for clients or for Baring's own accounts, making reconciliation impossible. Second, given the large amounts, credit checks should have been completed as well. The report places the responsibility for the lack of due diligence with Tony Hawes, Ian Hopkins, and the Chairman of the Barings Credit Committee.

The issue of proper reconciliation arose as early as April 1992 when Gordon Bowser, the risk manager in London, recommended that a reconciliation process be developed. Unfortunately, Bowser left Simon Jones and Tony Dickel, who had sent Leeson to Singapore, to agree on a procedure. With internal conflict over who was responsible for Leeson's activities, no agreement was reached between those two, and Leeson was left to establish reconciliation procedures for himself.

There are numerous similar examples of internal conflict benefitting Leeson's covert trading throughout the three years. But one of the late failures occurred in January 1995 when SIMEX raised concern over Barings' ability to meet its large margins. In a letter dated January 11, 1995, and addressed to Simon Jones, SIMEX officials noted that there should have been an additional $100 million in the margin account for 88888. Jones passed the letter to Leeson to draft a response.

External Reasons. In January 1995, SIMEX was getting close to Leeson's activities, but had not yet managed to determine what was happening. In response to a second letter dated January 27, 1995 and sent to James Bax in Singapore, SIMEX expressed concerns regarding Barings' ability to fund its margin calls. Bax referred the letter to London, and SIMEX received reassurance that opposite positions were held in Japan. Unfortunately, SIMEX officials did not follow up with the Osaka Stock Exchange to verify the existence of those positions.

**5. Why did none of the regulatory authorities in Singapore, Japan, and the United Kingdom not discover the true use of the error account?**

SIMEX assumed that Barings was hedging and not speculating when it granted an exemption on the number of contracts that Barings could hold. Due to Barings' reputation for being a conservative firm, the exchange and clearing houses were operating under a false sense of security. In addition, the speculative position of Barings was hidden due to use of an omnibus account to clear trades. With an omnibus account, the identity of the broker's customers is hidden from the exchange and the clearinghouse.

Several incidents in London also made Leeson's activities easier to manage and hide. The Bank of England had a Large Exposure rule where a bank could not lend more than 25% of its capital to any one entity. However, Barings had requested that an exception be made, arguing that an exchange should not be treated as one entity. Christopher Thompson, the supervisor in charge of Barings activities, acknowledged receipt of the request and said he would review it. In the meantime, he offered an informal concession for Japan, which Barings took the liberty of also applying to Singapore and Hong Kong. Thompson did not respond for a year, and when he did on February 1, 1995, the answer was that an exception could not be made for exchanges and that the positions taken under the informal concession should be unwound.

The second incident was the solo-consolidation of Baring Securities Ltd and Baring Brothers & Co. This allowed them to be treated as one entity for capital adequacy and large exposure purposes. This meant Leeson had access to a larger amount of capital. The Bank of England found the process of solo-consolidation to have been too informal and the results to have facilitated Leeson's fraudulent activities.

**6. Why was Barings Bank willing to transfer large cash sums to Barings Futures Singapore?**

Barings Bank believed that the large cash sums transferred to Barings Futures Singapore was for loans to customers as portrayed on the Barings Futures Singapore balance sheet.

**7. Why did the attempt by the Bank of England to organize a bailout for Barings fail?**

The attempt by the Bank of England to organize a bailout for Barings failed because no one would assume the contingent risk of additional, but as yet undiscovered losses.

**8. Suggest regulatory and management reforms that might prevent a future debacle of the type that bankrupted Barings.**

Due to incidents of staggering losses to corporate and banking entities as early as 1993, calls for financial reforms, particularly in relation to derivatives, had been ongoing for quite some time. However, it took the Baring Brothers bankruptcy to finally bring about action. The Bank of England, SIMEX and the Group of Thirty all created reports on how regulators, administrators, legislators, international firms and associations could address the issues of regulating financial activities.

The Bank of England wrote a report describing how the losses occurred, why they went unnoticed within and outside Barings, and lessons learned. How the losses occurred and why they went unnoticed has already been explained. The Bank produced five lessons from the bankruptcy. They are (Bank of England Report):

1. Management teams have a duty to understand fully the businesses they manage
2. Responsibility for each business activity has to be clearly established and communicated;
3. Clear segregation of duties is fundamental to any effective control system;
4. Relevant internal controls, including independent risk management, have to be established for all business activities;
5. Top management and the Audit Committee have to ensure that significant weaknesses, identified to them by internal audit or otherwise, are resolved quickly.

Despite these simplistic recommendations, at least one and usually several, of the points was the reason why firms lost large sums of money within the derivatives market.

SIMEX, like the other exchanges in the world, implemented changes to decrease default and counterparty risk as well as systemic risks. These changes were made as a direct result of the Barings collapse. SIMEX joined with other exchanges to share information about similar positions participants held on different exchanges. To reduce the risk of non-payment of contracts, SIMEX and other exchanges placed the resources of their entire membership behind the settlements.

The Group of Thirty based out of Washington, DC, has become particularly concerned with the risks derivatives pose. Since 1995, it has issued several publications to address these problems. The first of these was published in August 1996, and is titled "International Insolvencies in the Financial Sector, Discussion Draft." This document advances fourteen ideas to reduce the risk in the financial sector particularly with regard to derivatives (see Exhibit 2 for the complete list). The second publication printed in April of 1997 is titled "International Insolvencies in the Financial Sector, Summary of Comments from Respondent Countries on Discussion Draft." This publication gives the responses and opinions of those member countries to the proposed reforms. The support for these reforms was generally very strong among all the countries that responded. Germany and other countries did mention several drawbacks to some of the reforms, but they, too, were generally supportive. Ironically, Singapore expressed reservations or outright opposition to five of the reforms (#1, 2, 4, 6 and 9).[1]

A third publication dealing with the aftermath of Barings, is titled "Global Institutions, National Supervision and Systemic Risk" (1997). This discusses reforms that have already been put in place. These reforms include "expanded use of netting and collateral; improvements in measuring risk; greater disclosure of off-balance-sheet risk; substantial increases in equity capital of major financial institutions; financial sector consolidation; and the growth of securitization."[2]

---

[1] Group of Thirty, "International Insolvencies in the Financial Sector," *Summary of Comments from Respondent Countries on Discussion Draft*, April 1997, pp. I-iii.

[2] Group of Thirty, *Global Institutions, National Supervision and Systemic Risk*, 1997, p.v.

## Postscript

ING, a Dutch insurance company, was looking to enter the banking business, especially in Asia. It paid one pound sterling for Baring Brothers and added an additional $1 billion to pay off the debts Baring Brothers had accumulated and restore the bank's capital position. In addition, ING also had to pay $677 million to the holders of subordinated debt that was issued by Barings plc, the holding company, just before the bankruptcy.[3] Legally, ING was not liable for the bonds, but since the bondholders were Barings best customers, ING had to make good on the notes in order to save the customer relationships.[4]

On February 23, 1995, Nick Leeson fled in his Mercedes across the bridge from Singapore to Malaysia. He hid out in Thailand for the next week with his wife and was caught flying into Germany one week later. He was extradited back to Singapore, stood trial and was subsequently sentenced to 6.5 years in a Singapore prison for fraud. In August 1998, Leeson underwent surgery for colon cancer and began receiving chemotherapy. Despite his condition, authorities in Singapore did not release Leeson until June 1999.

Christopher Thompson was the Bank of England supervisor in charge of Baring Brothers at the time of the bankruptcy. He was responsible for allowing Baring Brothers to invest over the legal limit of 25% of its capital in the SIMEX and OSE. The day before the Bank of England report was to be published about the Baring Brothers collapse, Thompson resigned.[5]

---

[3] Hans R. Stoll, "Lost Barings: A Tale in Three Parts Concluding with a Lesson," *The Journal of Derivatives,* Fall 1995, Vol. 3, No.1.

[4] Mayer, *The Bankers.*

[5] Fay, *Collapse.*

CHAPTER 8: TRANSACTION EXPOSURE

*Questions*

**8-1. Foreign exchange exposure**

In its most general sense, foreign exchange exposure is the possibility of either beneficial or harmful effects on a company caused by a change in foreign exchange rates. The effect on the company may be on its profits, its cash flows, or its market value.

**8-2. Exposure types**

a. *Transaction exposure* is the potential for a gain or loss in contracted-for near term cash flows caused by a foreign exchange rate-induced change in the value of amounts due to the MNE or amounts that the MNE owes to other parties. As such, it is a change in the home currency value of cash flows that are already contracted for.

b. *Operating exposure* is the potential for a change in the value of a MNE, usually viewed as the present value of all future cash inflows, caused by unexpected exchange rate changes. As such, it is a change in expected long-term cash flows; i.e., future cash flows expected in the course of normal business but not yet contracted for.

c. *Translation exposure* is the possibility of a change in the equity section (common stock, retained earnings, and equity reserves) of a MNE's consolidated balance sheet, caused by a change (expected or not expected) in foreign exchange rates. As such it is not a cash flow change, but is rather the result of consolidating into one parent company's financial statement the individual financial statements of related subsidiaries and affiliates.

**8-3. Translation versus transaction exposure**

*Translation exposure* measures accounting (book) gains and losses from a change in exchange rates. *Transaction exposure* measures cash (realized) gains and losses from a change in exchange rates.

**8-4. Tax exposure**

*Tax exposure* is separate from the triumvirate of transaction, operating, and accounting exposure because it basically the tax consequences of a gain or loss caused by this triumvirate. *Transaction exposure* is a cash loss and so results in a tax savings – in the sense that a lowering of profits because of a transaction loss lowers income taxes, other things being equal. Any loss from operating exposure is difficult to measure; a resultant drop in market value of a MNE's shares has no tax consequences for the company – although it may have tax consequences for investors holding the shares. To the extent that operating exposure causes a lowering of corporate profits in future years, taxes in those years are reduced. *Translation exposure* is a measurement loss, rather than a cash loss, and so has no tax consequences.

**8-5. Hedging**

A "hedge" is the acquisition of a contract or a physical asset that will offset a change in value of some other contract or physical asset. Hedges are entered into to reduce or eliminate risk.

**8-6. Cash flow variability**

a. The areas toward the center of the distributions where the "hedged" line is higher than the "unhedged" line, implies that a greater proportion of expected values will be near the expected mean value when the cash flows are hedged. Variability of expected results is reduced.

b. The areas toward the outlying edges of the distributions, where the "unhedged" line is higher than the "hedged" line, imply that a greater likelihood exists for significantly higher cash flows as well as significantly lower cash flows than exist when the cash flows are hedged.

c. Hedging is not cost free; something is paid to obtain the hedge. Hence the expected value for hedged cash flows should be that of the unhedged cash flow less the cost of the hedge. Thus one might argue that the mean expected value of the hedged cash flow should be to the left of that for the unhedged cash flow. (No reason exists for the mean cash flow of the hedged flows to be to the right of that for the unhedged cash flows.)

**8-7. Investor expectations**

Proponents of the efficient market hypothesis believe that the current market price of a MNE's shares of stock fully and appropriately discounts all the risks of the firm, including foreign exchange risk, and that the firm should not pay the cash cost of hedging because investors can individually hedge or not as they see fit, and that the present share price already reflects this risk. These proponents also argue that the propensity to carry risk is different for management than for shareholders, and that risk hedging is often undertaken by management to protect its own interests, which differ from the interests of shareholders. Lastly they argue that management is more likely to hedge accounting risks, which are more precisely measured, than operating risks, which are conceptual and deal with future expectations.

The argument that management might appropriately hedge its foreign currency risks is based on the logic that management has firsthand knowledge of foreign currency risks, that the nature and magnitude of these risks change from day to day (or at least month to month), and that the specifics of such risks cannot be known (and so discounted) by the impersonal forces of an "efficient" market. Other arguments in favor of hedging include improved cash flow management for the firm and the need to preserve liquidity for debt service and/or unexpected variations in near-term cash flows.

**8-8. Creating transaction exposure**

Assume a hypothetical U.S. company named Smith Company.

a. *Purchasing or selling on open account.* Smith Company sells goods to a buyer in Great Britain with the sale denominated in British pounds sterling and payment due in 60 days. When Smith Company receives the pounds sterling 60 days after the sale, the U.S. dollar value of those pounds may be less, or more, than was expected at the time of sale.

b. *Borrowing and lending.* Smith Company finds that it can borrow Swiss francs at 4% per annum interest, and exchange them for the needed U.S. dollars, whereas borrowing dollars in the U.S. will cost 7% per annum. Hence it borrows Swiss francs for one year in order to "save" on the interest cost. One year hence the Swiss franc has strengthened against the dollar by more than the 3% interest differential, and the Swiss franc borrowing ends up costing more than 7% in U.S. dollar terms.

c. *Owning an unperformed foreign exchange forward contract.* Believing that the Japanese yen will weaken within three months, Smith Company decides to speculate by selling yen forward. It hopes to profit by buying the yen to deliver against this forward sale at a cheaper exchange rate in three months. In fact the yen strengthens and Smith Company must buy yen to cover its forward yen obligation at a price higher than will be received via the forward sale.

d. *Acquiring assets or incurring liabilities denominated in foreign currencies*. Having excess cash and faced with euro interest rates of 8% and U.S. rates of 5%, Smith Company invests the cash in euro money market obligations. At maturity the euro has weakened by more than three percentage points and Smith Company ends up earning in dollars less than the 5% it could have earned by investing in a U.S. dollar asset.

**8-9. Cash balances**

Transaction exposure arises from the payment of one currency to a party wanting, in the end, a different currency. Thus a movement of currency value from one currency to another is required. Foreign currency cash balances held for operating purposes by a foreign subsidiary are not inherently intended for exchange for another currency, nor is such an exchange required. Hence they do not create transaction exposure. (They do, however, create translation exposure.)

**8-10. Natural vs. contractual hedges**

A *natural hedge* is one that results from matching foreign currency cash flows that come about from the normal operations of a MNE. An example would be for a MNE that had euro operating inflows from sales to borrow an equivalent amount of euros to finance working capital. Should the dollar/euro exchange rate change, any gain or loss from the euro operating inflows would be offset by a loss or gain on the euro borrowing. In effect, the euro operating inflows would be used to pay the euro debt. Any foreign exchange transaction is avoided.

A *contractual hedge* is a contract specifically entered into as a financial rather than operating hedge. Examples are forward and future foreign exchange agreements, money market hedges, and the purchase of options.

**8-11. Risk tolerance**

*Risk tolerance* is the psychological or philosophical willingness of a firm, or of its managers, to bear risk. As such, it cannot be measured or quantified, although observations and comparisons of management decisions over time can provide a rough inkling of such managements' risk tolerance. Variations in risk tolerance reflect the fact that different individuals have different opinions about whether or not a risk is worth bearing, or conversely, whether or not a risk should be left open ended or hedged.

*Problems*

**8-1. Vamo Road Industries**

Vamo's goal is to minimizing the dollar payment required in the face of a possible devaluation of the Guatemalan quetzel (Q). The exposure is a debt of Q8,400,000, payable in quetzals in six months.

a. *Alternatives:* Vamo can (1) remain uncovered -- do nothing -- and buy quetzels spot six months from now, (2) buy quetzels six months forward, or (3) buy quetzels now and invest them in Guatemala for six months.

*Remain uncovered.* If the present spot rate of Q7.0000/$ does not change, the required payment in six months would be:

$$\frac{Q8{,}400{,}000}{Q7.0000/\$} = \$1{,}200{,}000.$$

Using Vamo's three separate spot rate forecasts, the range of expected payments in six months is:

| | |
|---|---|
| Highest expected cost: | Q8,400,000 ÷ Q6.4000/$ = $1,312,500.00. |
| Most likely cost: | Q8,400,000 ÷ Q7.3000/$ = $1,150,684.93. |
| Lowest expected cost: | Q8,400,000 ÷ Q8.0000/$ = $1,050,000.00. |

The Guatemalan quetzel interest rate is higher than the U.S. dollar interest rate. If the International Fisher Effect is to be believed, the quetzel is expected to depreciate versus the U.S. dollar by an amount equal to the interest rate differential. However the forecasts of Vamo's treasury manager differ from a simple International Fisher effect solution. One question for the manager is whether or not to rely on his or her own exchange rate forecast, accept the forward market quotation as the best indicator of future spot rate, or assume it is not possible to forecast future spot exchange rates.

*Forward cover.* If Vamo buys Q8,400,000 forward at the forward rate of Q7.1000/$ it would pay in six months exactly:

$$\frac{Q8{,}400{,}000}{Q7.1000/\$} = \$1{,}183{,}098.59.$$

*Money market hedge.* Exchange dollars for quetzels now and invest in Guatemalan securities for the 6 month period. Since Q8,400,000 is needed in 6 months to make the payment, we will work backwards to determine the exact number of quetzels needed today. Vamo can earn 14.000% per annum on quetzel deposits, or 7.000% for the 6 month period.

Q8,400,000 ÷ 1.07 = Q7,850,467.29 needed today.

This means that Q7,850,467.29 invested today in Guatemala at 14.000% per annum will grow to

Q8,400,000 in 6 months. We now find the dollar amount needed to acquire these quetzels in the present – using the present spot rate of Q7.0000/$:

$$\frac{Q7{,}850{,}467}{Q7.0000/\$} = \$1{,}121{,}495.33.$$

It would require Vamo to come up with $1,121,495.33 today, to obtain the needed Guatemalan quetzels.

In order to compare the cost of this alternative versus the previous alternatives, this dollar cost needs to be carried forward in time 6 months. Vamo would carry forward all dollar amounts at its weighted average cost of capital, 20.000% per annum, 10.000% for 6 months.

The future value in six months of this to Vamo at its 20% WACC is:

$$\$1{,}121{,}495.33 \times 1.10 = \$1{,}233{,}644.86.$$

(The comparison can be made with present values instead of future values. The necessary step is to bring all payments to the same date.)

b. Which is the best choice?

(1) If Vamo remains uncovered:

If the exchange rate remains unchanged, a future payment of $1,200,000 will be required. This amount is uncertain.
If the ending exchange rate is Q6.4000/$, a future payment of $1,312,500 will be required. This higher amount is uncertain.
If the ending exchange rate is Q7.3000/$, a future payment of $1,150,685 will be required. Although "most likely," the actual amount is uncertain.
If the ending exchange rate is Q8.0000/$, a future payment of $1,050,000 will be required. Although the lowest payment, the actual amount is uncertain.

(2) If Vamo uses a forward hedge a future payment of $1,183,098.59 will be required. This amount is certain.

(3) If Vamo uses a money market hedge a present payment with a future value of $1,233,645 will be required. His amount is certain.

Of the two certain cost alternatives, the forward hedge cost of $1,183,098.59 is less than the money market hedge cost of $1,233,644.86. The forward hedge is thus preferable on a cost basis.

To remain unhedged is to take a chance on a lower payment in six months (possibly as low as $1,050,000 if the quetzel drops significantly in value.) against the chance of a much higher payment (possibly $1,312,500 – although the payment could be even higher as there is no upper limit). Remaining unhedged seems very risky.

c. The choice among the alternatives depends in part on whether Vamo's 20% weighted average cost of capital (WACC) is the appropriate discount rate to use to price the money market hedge. Finance theory advocates using a firm's WACC on the assumption that a firm will always be undertaking in all projects having an internal rate of return above the WACC, plus the added the assumption that a firm in fact has a supply of potential projects. In this case one must note that the money market hedge is more expensive than the forward hedge because of the use of a 20% WACC. If Vamo lacked any proposals for additional projects, or was unable to undertake them because of non-financial constraints such as insufficient managerial or technical staff, then the best alternate use of funds would be to invest them at, perhaps, the 6.000% U.S. dollar interest rate.

If the money market hedge is recalculated using only an available 6.000% rate of return on the money for the six months, the cost becomes:

$$\$1,121,495.33 \times 1.03 = \$1,155,140.19.$$

This is <u>less</u> that the $1,183,098.59 cost of the forward rate hedge, and shifts the advantage to the money market hedge. The point of this calculation is that the preference for one alternative over the other is in part based on theoretical concepts and assumptions that may not apply in a given "real-world" situation.

## Problem 8.1 Vamo Road Industries

**Hedging foreign exchange risk: a payable**

| Assumptions | Values |
|---|---|
| Construction payment due in six-months (A/P, quetzals) | **8,400,000** |
| Present spot rate (quetzals/$) | **7.0000** |
| Six-month forward rate (quetzals/$) | **7.1000** |
| Guatemalan six-month interest rate (per annum) | **14.000%** |
| U.S. dollar six-month interest rate (per annum) | **6.000%** |
| Vamo's weighted average cost of capital (WACC) | **20.000%** |
| Expected spot rate in six-months (quetzals/$): | |
| Highest expected rate | **8.0000** |
| Expected rate | **7.3000** |
| Lowest expected rate | **6.4000** |

| a) What realistic alternatives are available to Vamo? | Cost | Certainty? |
|---|---|---|
| **1. Wait six months and make payment at spot rate** | | |
| Highest expected rate | **$ 1,050,000.00** | **Risky** |
| Expected rate | **$ 1,150,684.93** | **Risky** |
| Lowest expected rate | **$ 1,312,500.00** | **Risky** |
| **2. Purchase quetzals forward six-months** | **$ 1,183,098.59** | **Certain** |
| (A/P divided by the forward rate) | | |
| **3. Transfer dollars to quetzals today, invest for six-months** | | |
| quetzals needed today (A/P discounted 180 days) | **7,850,467.29** | |
| Cost in dollars today (quetzals to $ at spot rate) | **$ 1,121,495.33** | |
| factor to carry dollars forward 180 days (1 + (WACC/2)) | **1.10** | |
| Cost in dollars in six-months ($ carried forward 180 days ) | **$ 1,233,644.86** | **Certain** |

The second choice, the forward contract, results in the lowest cost alternative among certain alternatives.

**8-2. Wilmington Chemical Company**

Wilmington might hedge its exposure in the forward market, in the money market, or via an options hedge; or it might decide not to hedge at all.

a. *Remain unhedged.* Wilmington could remain uncovered and hope spot exchange rates would be favorable six months hence. If the spot rate in six months were the same as today's spot rate, a guess based on the logic that the exchange rate is either fixed or relatively stable over time, Wilmington could end up paying the following in 6 months:

$$\frac{\text{dirhams } 6{,}000{,}000}{\text{dirhams } 10.00/\$} = \$600{,}000.00.$$

This is uncertain and risky. The final dollar payment could actually be anything – higher or lower.

b. *Forward market hedge.* Wilmington can buy dirhams forward at the six month forward rate:

$$\frac{\text{dirhams } 6{,}000{,}000}{\text{dirhams } 10.40/\$} = \$576{,}823.$$

This is certain and risk free.

c. *Money market hedge.* Wilmington could use U.S. dollars now to buy dirhams in the spot market and invest those dirhams for six months at 7.000% per annum in Morocco.

6,000,000 dirhams ÷ 1.035 = 5,797,101.45 dirhams needed today.
5,797,101.45 dirhams ÷ 10.00 dirhams per dollar = $579,710.14 needed today.

This dollar amount is then carried forward six months at Wilmington's WACC of 14.000% per annum, a 1.070 factor for six months:

$579,710.14 x 1.070 = $620,289.86 future value of payment.

Note that the forward market and the money market are in equilibrium so that the proceeds received are almost identical before the funds from the money market hedge are time-adjusted. The higher cost of capital for Wilmington makes the future value of the payment via the money market hedge larger.

d. *Options hedge.* Because Wilmington needs Moroccan dirhams for a future payment, it must buy a call on those dirhams. With the call option strike price of 10.00 dirhams per dollar, Wilmington would exercise the call if the spot exchange rate in six months were below 10.00 dirhams per dollar, i.e., the dirham had appreciated versus the dollar. The call option assures Wilmington of always getting at least 10 dirhams for each dollar.

In the worst case scenario, if the call option were exercised it would yield $600,000 in six months:

$$\frac{\text{dirhams } 6{,}000{,}000}{\text{dirhams } 10.00/\$} = \$600{,}000.00.$$

The cost of the call option would be equal to 2.00% of the face amount of the 600,000 dirhams valued at the current spot exchange rate of 10.00 dirhams per dollar, 2.00% of $600,000:

$600,000 x 0.02 = $12,000, paid today.

The total future cost of the payment if hedged via an option, where the option premium has been carried six months forward at the WACC, would be:

$600,000 + ($12,000 x 1.07) = $612,840.00.

If the spot rate at the end of the six-month period were higher than 10.00 dirhams per dollar (i.e., lower value of the dirham), Wilmington would discard the option and purchase the necessary dollars in the spot market at the lower cost.

Summary:

| | | |
|---|---|---|
| Remain uncovered | $600,000.00 | Maybe. Unknown and risky. |
| Forward market hedge | $576,923.08 | Certain. |
| Money market hedge | $620,289.86 | Certain |
| Option hedge | $612,840.00 | Maximum, could be lower. |

Among the certain alternatives, the forward market hedge dominates the money market hedge. This is because adjusting the time of payment six months with Wilmington's cost of capital made the later payment (via the forward hedge) more desirable. The call option hedge assures Wilmington of a maximum payment, but its final value is not known until the end of the six month period. If the dirham were to depreciate against the dollar during that six month period, the option hedge could result in a lower cost than the forward hedge (option would expire out of the money and the dirhams would be purchased by Wilmington on the open market).

## Problem 8.2 Wilimington Chemical Company

**Hedging foreign exchange risk: a payable**

| **Assumptions** | **Values** | |
|---|---|---|
| Shipment of phosphates from Morocco, Moroccan dirhams | 6,000,000 | |
| Wilmington's cost of capital (WACC) | 14.000% | |
| Spot exchange rate, dirhams/$ | 10.00 | |
| Six-month forward rate, dirhams/$ | 10.40 | |
| | | |
| Options on Moroccan dirhams: | **Call Option** | **Put Option** |
| Strike price, dirhams/$ | 10.00 | 10.00 |
| Option premium (percent) | 2.000% | 3.000% |
| | | |
| | **United States** | **Morocco** |
| Six-month interest rate for borrowing (per annum) | 6.000% | 8.000% |
| Six-month interest rate for investing (per annum) | 5.000% | 7.000% |

| **Risk Management Alternatives** | | **Values** | **Certainty** |
|---|---|---|---|
| **1. Remain uncovered, making the dirham payment in six months at the spot rate in effect at that date** | | | |
| Account payable (dirhams) | | 6,000,000 | |
| Possible spot rate in six months (dirhams/$) | | 10.00 | |
| Cost of settlement in six months (US$) | $ | 600,000.00 | Uncertain. |
| **2. Forward market hedge. Buy dirhams forward six months.** | | | |
| Account payable (dirhams) | | 6,000,000 | |
| Six month forward rate, dirhams/$ | | 10.40 | |
| Cost of settlement in six months (US$) | $ | 576,923.08 | Certain. |
| **3. Money market hedge. Exchange dollars for dirhams now, invest for six months.** | | | |
| Account payable (dirhams) | | 6,000,000.00 | |
| Discount factor at the dirham investing rate for 6 months | | 1.035 | |
| Dirhams needed now for investing (payable/discount factor) | | 5,797,101.45 | |
| Current spot rate (dirhams/$) | | 10.00 | |
| US dollars needed now | $ | 579,710.14 | |
| Carry forward rate for six months (WACC) | | 1.070 | |
| US dollar cost, in six months, of settlement | $ | 620,289.86 | Certain. |
| **4. Call option hedge. (Need to buy dirhams = call on dirhams)** | | | |
| Option principal | | 6,000,000.00 | |
| Current spot rate, dirhams/$ | | 10.00 | |
| Premium cost of option | | 2.000% | |
| Option premium (principal/spot rate x % pm) | $ | 12,000.00 | |
| | | | |
| If option exercised, dollar cost at strike price of 10.00 dirhams/$ | $ | 600,000.00 | |
| Plus premium carried forward six months (pm x 1.07, WACC) | | 12,840.000 | |
| Total net cost of call option hedge if exercised | $ | 612,840.00 | Maximum. |

The lowest cost certain alternative is the forward. If Wilmington were to expect the dirham to depreciate significantly over the next six months, it may choose the call option.

**8-3. Plasti-Grip, Inc.**

a. The primary alternatives for managing this foreign exchange exposure are:

*Remain Uncovered.* Plasti-Grip could wait six months and then purchase Won6,030 million at the spot rate, whatever it might be at that time. If the spot rate were the same as the current spot rate, Plasti-Grip would pay in six months:

$$\frac{\text{Won}\,6{,}030{,}000{,}000}{\text{Won}\,1{,}200/\$} = \$5{,}025{,}000.00.$$

This amount is uncertain.

*Forward Cover.* Plasti-Grip could cover the entire payment of Won6,030,000,000 at the forward rate of Won1260/$, paying in six months:

$$\frac{\text{Won}\,6{,}030{,}000{,}000}{\text{Won}\,1{,}260/\$} = \$4{,}785{,}714.29.$$

This amount is certain.

*Money Market Hedge.* The money market hedge alternative is to use U.S. dollars today to purchase Korean won at the current spot rate and invest the won received for six months in Korea. The final payment would be made with the proceeds of this investment. The necessary value of the cost today is found by discounting the Won6,030 million principal for six months at the Korean interest rate for investment of 16.00% p.a., and then finding today's dollar value of purchasing that amount of won:

$$\frac{\text{Won}\,6{,}030{,}000{,}000}{\left[1 + \left(0.16 \times \frac{180}{360}\right)\right]} \times \frac{1}{\text{Won}\,1{,}200/\$} = \$4{,}652{,}777.78.$$

To compare this alternative at the same point in time as other alternatives, the dollar value must be carried forward six months. The future dollar value for six months at Plasti-Grip's WACC of 25% per annum is:

$$\$4{,}652{,}777.78 \times \left[1 + \left(0.25 \times \frac{180}{360}\right)\right] = \$5{,}234{,}375.00.$$

*Call Option Hedge.* Because Plasti-Grip must obtain Korean won to make a future payment, it needs a call (not a put) option on won. The dollar cost today of purchasing a call option on Won 6,030,000 at a premium of 3.0% is:

$$\frac{\text{Won}\,6{,}030{,}000{,}000}{\text{Won}\,1{,}200/\$} \times .03 = \$150{,}750.00.$$

This cost, carried forward at Plasti-Grip's WACC of 25% (or a factor of 1.125 for six months) gives a future value of:

$$\$150{,}750.00 \times 1.125 = \$169{,}593.75.$$

If the option were to be exercised (the worst case outcome for a call option hedge) the final cost in six months would be:

$$\frac{\text{Won}\,6{,}030{,}000{,}000}{\text{Won}\,1{,}200/\$} + \$169{,}593.75 = \$5{,}194{,}593.75.$$

*Recommendations*: The four primary alternatives (one of which has two different compounding assumptions) and the certainty regarding each are:

| | | |
|---|---|---|
| Remain uncovered | Pay $5,025,000.00 | very uncertain |
| Forward contract hedge | Pay $4,785,714.29 | certain |
| Money market hedge (at WACC) | Pay $5,234,375.00 | certain |
| Call option hedge (worst case) | Pay $5,194,593.75 | maximum; only if exercised |

The forward contract hedge is the cheapest certain choice. If the Korean won were expected to depreciate in the coming six months against the U.S. dollar, and Plasti-Grip was willing to accept the call option hedge's worst case outcome (in the event the won did not fall in value), the call option could be the preferred choice over the forward.

## Problem 8.3 Plasti-Grip, Inc.

**Hedging foreign exchange risk: a payable**

| **Assumptions** | **Values** | |
|---|---|---|
| Purchase price of Korean manufacturer, in Korean won | 7,030,000,000 | |
| Less initial payment, in Korean won | (1,000,000,000) | |
| Net settlement needed, in Korean won, in six months | 6,030,000,000 | |
| Current spot rate (Won/$) | 1,200 | |
| Six month forward rate (Won/$) | 1,260 | |
| Plasti-Grip's cost of capital (WACC) | 25.00% | |
| | | |
| Options on Korean won: | **Call Option** | **Put Option** |
| Strike price, won | 1,200.00 | 1,200.00 |
| Option premium (percent) | 3.000% | 2.400% |
| | | |
| | **United States** | **Korea** |
| Six-month investmentinterest rate (per annum) | 4.000% | 16.000% |
| Six-month borrowing rate (investment rate + 2%) | 6.000% | 18.000% |

| **Risk Management Alternatives** | | **Values** | **Certainty** |
|---|---|---|---|
| **1. Remain uncovered, making the won payment in 6 months at the spot rate in effect at that date** | | | |
| Account payable (won) | | 6,030,000,000 | |
| Possible spot rate in six months (won/$) | | 1,200 | |
| Cost of settlement in six months (US$) | $ | 5,025,000.00 | Uncertain. |
| **2. Forward market hedge. Buy won forward six months** | | | |
| Account payable (won) | | 6,030,000,000 | |
| Forward rate (won/$) | | 1,260.00 | |
| Cost of settlement in six months (US$) | $ | 4,785,714.29 | Certain. |
| **3. Money market hedge. Exchange dollars for won now, invest for six months.** | | | |
| Account payable (won) | | 6,030,000,000.00 | |
| Discount factor at the won interest rate for 6 months | | 1.080 | |
| Won needed now (payable/discount factor) | | 5,583,333,333.33 | |
| Current spot rate (won/$) | | 1,200.00 | |
| US dollars needed now | $ | 4,652,777.78 | |
| Carry forward rate for six months (WACC) | | 1.125 | |
| US dollar cost, in six months, of settlement | $ | 5,234,375.00 | Certain. |
| **4. Call option hedge. (Need to buy won = call on won)** | | | |
| Option principal | | 6,030,000,000.00 | |
| Current spot rate (won/$) | | 1,200.00 | |
| Premium cost of option (%) | | 3.000% | |
| Option premium (principal/spot rate x % pm) | $ | 150,750.00 | |
| | | | |
| If option exercised, dollar cost of won | $ | 5,025,000.00 | |
| Premium carried forward six months (pm x 1.125, WACC) | | 169,593.750 | |
| Total net cost of call option hedge if exercised | $ | 5,194,593.75 | Maximum. |

**8-4. Swing-a-Long Equipment Company**

This problem highlights the management of a transaction exposure when the goal of the firm to "protect the value" of the proceeds of a foreign currency-denominated sale.

a. *Alternative hedges*. When Swing-a-Long shipped the playground equipment to Japan, it recorded both an account receivable in its balance sheet and a sale on its income statement. These were recorded at the spot rate of exchange in effect on the date of sale. Thus the "value" of the sale was:

$$\frac{¥200{,}000{,}000}{¥118.255/\$} = \$1{,}691{,}260.41.$$

Swing-a-Long's treasury staff is charged with maximizing the dollar amount to be received when the yen receivable is collected. Alternatives for the management of this exposure are the following.

*Remain uncovered.* This is inconsistent with Swing-a-Long's goal of protecting value. The spot rate in 90 days when payment is made to Swing-a-Long could be higher or lower. If the spot rate remains the same, receipts would be exactly the same as that which was booked as the sale – $1,691,260, received three months hence. But this is highly uncertain..

*Forward hedge.* If Swing-a-Long sold the entire proceeds of the transaction forward 3 months at ¥116.830/$, Swing-a-Long would receive:

$$\frac{¥200{,}000{,}000}{¥116.830/\$} = \$1{,}711{,}889.07.$$

This is received 3 months hence.

This is $20,628.66 ($1,711,889.07 - $1,691,260.41) more than the sales value booked by the firm. This increase in proceeds represents added time value of money in the U.S. dollar markets (higher interest rates) for the 90 days period.

*Money market hedge.* Swing-a-Long could borrow against the receivable in Japan at (2.000% + 0.09375%) = 2.09375% p.a. (i.e., 0.5234% for 90 days), and exchange the yen received at the current spot rate into U.S. dollars, eliminating the currency exposure.

$$\frac{¥200{,}000{,}000}{\left[1 + \left(0.209375 \times \frac{90}{360}\right)\right]} \times \frac{1}{¥118.255/\$} = \$1{,}682{,}453.82.$$

This is received today.

The first half of the equation determines that the amount to be borrowed is ¥198,958,650. Exchanged today at the spot rate of ¥118.255/$ yields $1,682,453.82 to Swing-a-Long today. The loan would be repaid with the ¥200,000,000 received from Nagasaki in 90 days.

This dollar value must be carried forward in time in order to compare it with the other hedging alternatives. If it is carried forward at Swing-a-Long's cost of capital of 16% per annum (4% for 3 months) it is:

$$\$1,682,453.82 \times 1.04 = \$1,749,751.97.$$

Value 3 months hence.

*Put option hedge.* Because Swing-a-Long will be receiving yen and wishes to be assured a rate for selling those yen for U.S. dollars, Swing-a-Long could buy a put option on yen. The put would be purchased for 3.0% of the current market value of the principal, at the ¥118.255/$ spot rate. The cost of the option is:

$$\frac{¥200,000,000}{¥118.255/\$} \times .03 = \$50,737.81.$$

This premium expense must be carried forward 90 days at Swing-a-Long's cost of capital of 16% per annum (4% for 90 days), for a total premium cost in 90 days of:

$$\$50,737.81 \times 1.04 = \$52,767.325.$$

If the spot rate in 90 days were greater (e.g., the yen weaker) than the strike price of ¥118.000/$, the option would be exercised yielding a net total dollar revenue of:

$$\frac{¥200,000,000}{¥118.000/\$} - \$52,767.81 = \$1,642,147.93.$$

Value 3 months hence. If the dollar proceeds from such a put option would be the worst case outcome, the put option would obviously not completely assure or protect Swing-a-Long's desired sales proceeds of $1,691,260.41. However, the option also has an upside potential if the yen should appreciate more than expected.

*Summary:* Booked receivable from sale: $ 1,691,260.41
Amount received under various alternatives:

| | |
|---|---|
| Uncovered: | Unknown amount. |
| Forward hedge: | $1,711,889.07 received, certain. |
| Money market hedge @WACC: | $1,749,751.97 received, certain. |
| Options hedge: | $1,642,147.93 minimum, worst case, only if exercised. |

The money market hedge is preferable unless the yen appreciates more than expected.

b. *Break-even reinvestment rate*. Only the forward contract hedge and money market hedge assure Swing-a-Long of a specific dollar receipt at the end of 90 days. The forward's valuation is simply the stated \$1,711,889. The money market hedge's valuation depends on "what the funds are worth" to Swing-a-Long.

One way to isolate a critical value for valuing these cash flows internally to Swing-a-Long is to calculate the break-even interest rate which equates the forward contract proceeds with money market proceeds before adjusting for the time differential:

$$\$1,711,889.07 = \$1,682,453.82 \quad \text{x} \quad (1+\text{breakeven})$$

Reducing the equation,

$$(1 + \text{breakeven}) = 1.017495$$

This is 1.017495% per quarter or 6.998% per annum. If Swing-a-Long values funds in-hand at a rate equal to or greater than about 7.000% per annum (which it most likely does, because it regards its cost of capital as being 16%), the money market hedge provides a better solution to Swing-a-Long's problem.

This is theory. However a "real world" constraint exists. Japan's published interest rates are extremely low, which is why the money market hedge appears favorable. However, Swing-a-Long might not be able to borrow in Japan – the statement in the problem to the contrary. Japanese banks have traditionally loaned at published rates only to Japanese firms associated with the same *keiretsu* or business alliance.

Additionally, in the late 1990s and early 2000s Japanese banks incurred extremely large losses on loans and so were inhibited by inadequate capital from making more loans, even as the Ministry of Finance kept interest rates low to encourage economic recovery. This situation is cited here as an example where 'published rates" may not reveal the totality of being able to finance in a particular way in a foreign country.

## Problem 8.4 Swing-a-Long Equipment Company

**Hedging foreign exchange risk: a receivable**

| Assumptions | Values |
|---|---|
| Amount of receivable, Japanese yen | 200,000,000 |
| Spot exchange rate at time of sale (yen/$) | 118.255 |
| Booked value of sale | $ 1,691,260.41 |
| Days receivable due | 90 |
| Swing-a-Long Equipment's WACC | 16.0% |
| Competitor borrowing premium, yen | 2.0% |

| Forward rates and premiums | Forward Rate | Premium |
|---|---|---|
| One-month forward rate (yen/$) | 117.760 | 5.04% |
| Three-month forward rate (yen/$) | 116.830 | 4.88% |
| One-year forward rate (yen/$) | 112.450 | 5.16% |

| Money Rates (Investment rates) | United States | Japan | Differential |
|---|---|---|---|
| 1 month | 4.8750% | 0.09375% | 4.78125% |
| 3 months | 4.9375% | 0.09375% | 4.84375% |
| 12 months | 5.1875% | 0.31250% | 4.87500% |

| 3 Month Options on yen | Strike (yen/$) | Call Option | Put Option |
|---|---|---|---|
| Premium on strike price | 118.000 | 1.0% | 3.0% |

| a. Alternative Hedges | Values | Certainty |
|---|---|---|
| **1. Remain uncovered.** | | |
| Account receivable (yen) | 200,000,000 | |
| Possible spot rate in 90 days (yen/$) | 118.255 | |
| Cash settlement in 90 days (US$) | $ 1,691,260.41 | Uncertain. |
| **2. Forward market hedge.** | | |
| Account receivable (yen) | 200,000,000 | |
| Forward rate (won/$) | 116.830 | |
| Cash settlement in 90 days (US$) | $ 1,711,889.07 | Certain. |
| **3. Money market hedge.** | | |
| Account receivable (yen) | 200,000,000 | |
| Discount factor for 90 days | 1.00523 | |
| Yen proceeds up front | 198,958,576 | |
| Current spot rate (won/$) | 118.255 | |
| US dollars needed now | $ 1,682,453.82 | |
| Carry forward (WACC) | 1.040 | |
| Proceeds in 90 days | $ 1,749,751.97 | Certain. |
| **4. Put option hedge. (Need to sell yen = put on yen)** | | |
| Option principal | 200,000,000 | |
| Current spot rate (won/$) | 118.255 | |
| Premium cost of option (%) | 3.000% | |
| Option pm (principal/spot rate x % pm) | $ 50,737.81 | |
| If option exercised, dollar proceeds | $ 1,694,915.25 | |
| Less Pm carried forward 90 days | (52,767.325) | |
| Net proceeds in 90 days | $ 1,642,147.93 | Minimum. |

The put option does not GUARANTEE the company of settling for the booked amount.
The money market and forward hedges do; the money market yielding the higher proceeds.

## 8-5. Arva Watch Company

a. Covering or hedging an amount greater than the exposure amounts to taking two separate positions: 1) hedging 100% of the exposure itself, and 2) taking an additional forward position that is an outright forward speculation on the expected change in exchange rates. This latter position is not "hedging" as it *protects* nothing. It seeks to gain by betting on an exchange rate change with some of the company's money.

b. The most conservative approach would be the full forward hedge (100%) of all exposures. The use of selective approaches such as 70% simply hedges a portion of the total exposure; it does not eliminate the risk completely. Options cannot be considered a truly conservative hedge because they require the user to formulate a *directional view* of where the exchange rate is headed and those views may prove wrong.

The following numerical example highlights this common fallacy in hedging. Assume Arva Watch Company possesses a €1,000,000 90-day account receivable. It may choose to hedge the minimum (70% of the total exposure) or the maximum (120% of the total exposure).

At a forward rate of $0.9460/€, the minimum hedge yields $662,200, the maximum hedged proportion locks in gross proceeds of $1,135,200. But in each case, there is an uncovered component – either the 30% left uncovered of the total exposure (in the case of minimum hedge) – or the additional 20% forward contract sale which is now a short position (in the case of the maximum hedge).

Case #1: Ending spot rate is $0.9000/€.
The minimum hedge position has total net proceeds of $662,200 (forward cover, 70%) + $270,000 (30% left uncovered and redeemed at the spot rate), or $932,200. Arva would have been better off fully-hedged (100%) at $946,000.

The maximum hedge position has total net proceeds of $1,135,200 (forward cover, 120%) + a loss of $180,000 (cost of covering the 20% over-sold forward), or $955,2000. Arva only marginally improved over fully-hedged (100%) position at $946,000.

Case #2: Ending spot rate is $1.0000/€.
The minimum hedge position has total net proceeds of $662,200 (forward cover, 70%) + $300,000 (30% left uncovered and redeemed at the spot rate), or $962,200. Arva is better off than fully-hedged (100%) at $946,000.

The maximum hedge position has total net proceeds of $1,135,200 (forward cover, 120%) + a loss of $200,000 (cost of covering the 20% over-sold forward), or $935,200. Arva marginally worse than fully-hedged (100%) position at $946,000.

## Problem 8.5 Arva Watch Company

**Hedging policy**

| **Assumptions** | | **Values** |
|---|---|---|
| Account recievable in 90 days (euros) | | 1,000,000 |
| Initial spot exchange rate ($/euro) | $ | 0.9650 |
| Forward rate, 90 days ($/euro) | $ | 0.9460 |

| **If Arva Watch Company ......** | | **Hedged the Minimum** | | **Hedged the Maximum** |
|---|---|---|---|---|
| **Proportion of exposure to be hedged** | | 70% | | 120% |
| Total exposure (euros) | | 1,000,000 | | 1,000,000 |
| hedged proportion | | 70% | | 120% |
| Minimum hedge in euros (exposure x min prop) | | 700,000 | | 1,200,000 |
| at the forward rate ($/euro) | $ | 0.9460 | $ | 0.9460 |
| locking in ($) | $ | 662,200.00 | $ | 1,135,200.00 |
| **Case #1: Ending spot rate is $0.9000/euro** | | | | |
| Proportion uncovered (short) | | 300,000 | | (200,000) |
| If ending spot rate is ($/euro) | $ | 0.9000 | $ | 0.9000 |
| value of uncovered proportion ($) | $ | 270,000 | $ | (180,000) |
| Total net proceeds | $ | 932,200 | $ | 955,200 |
| **Case #2: Ending spot rate is $1.0000/euro** | | | | |
| Proportion uncovered (short) | | 300,000 | | (200,000) |
| If ending spot rate is ($/euro) | $ | 1.0000 | $ | 1.0000 |
| value of uncovered proportion ($) | $ | 300,000 | $ | (200,000) |
| Total net proceeds | $ | 962,200 | $ | 935,200 |
| **Benchmark: Full (100%) forward cover** | $ | 946,000 | $ | 946,000 |

This is not a conservative hedging policy. Any time a firm may choose to leave any proportion uncovered, or purchase cover for more than the exposure (creating a short position) the firm could experience nearly unlimited losses or gains.

## 8-6. Redwall Pump Company

Redwall's goal is to maximize the expected U.S. dollar future value of the euros to be received from the sale to Volendam. (A present value approach is equally valid.) Four possibilities are a forward hedge, money market hedge, options hedge, or doing nothing. Redwall could also calculate a break-even foreign exchange rate, and it could consider how it might hedge the exposure between the time it made the quote and the time it received the order. These aspects are considered at the end of this solution.

A separate issue is whether, on March 1st when the firm order is received, Redwall should hedge the $4,320,000 of the original sale or the $4,400,000 current value of the receivable. A strong case can be made for hedging (if hedging is desirable) the $4,400,000 of current value. However because most students will follow the "traditional" approach of hedging just $4,320,000, the remainder of this solution is based on that approach.

Background calculations

| | |
|---|---|
| T-bill rate of 3.6% p.a.: | 3-mo. factor = 1.009, 6-mo. factor = 1.018. |
| euro borrowing rate of 8.00% p.a.: | 3-mo. factor = 1.020, 6-mo. factor = 1.040 |
| Cost of equity of 12.0% p.a.: | 3-mo. factor = 1.030, 6-mo. factor = 1.060 |

The cost of equity, in the presence of no long-term or permanent debt component in Redwall's capital structure, is also the WACC, in this case 12%. We will use 12% in the remainder of this solution.

The basic exposure problem is illustrated in the following time line:

**Spot rate:** $1.08/€ $1.10/€

| **Date:** | Feb 1 | Mar 1 | Apr 1 | May 1 | Jun 1 | Jul 1 | Aug 1 | Sept 1 |
|---|---|---|---|---|---|---|---|---|
| **Event:** | Quote | Sale | | | €2,000,000 | | | €2,000,000 |

*Forward Market Hedge.* Redwall can sell forward the June and September euro proceeds for dollars at $1.1060/€ and $1.1130/$, respectively:

June: €2,000,000 x $1.1060/€ = $2,212,000 received June 1st
Sept: €2,000,000 x $1.1130/€ = $2,226,000 received September 1st.

To compare alternatives, all cash flows must be measured at the same point in time. The June 1st payment carried forward 3 months at the 12% per annum rate (3% per quarter) plus the September payment add to a total forward future value of:

($2,212,000 x 1.03) + $2,226,000 = $4,504,360. Dollar value on September 1st.

*Money Market Hedge.* Redwall can borrow euros in London at 8.00% per annum, and exchange those euros for dollars at today's spot rate of $1.1000/€. Sales proceeds would repay the euro loan. For meaningful comparison, the dollar proceeds must be carried forward six months to the same point in time as all other alternatives.

The amount to borrow today so that the June 1st receipt can repay the loan, and exchanged for U.S. dollars at today's spot exchange rate, is:

$$\frac{€2{,}000{,}000}{1.02} \times \$1.1000/€ = \$2{,}156{,}863.$$

This dollar amount is received March 1st.

The amount to borrow today so the September 1st receipt can repay the loan and exchanged for U.S. dollars at today's spot rate is:

$$\frac{€2{,}000{,}000}{1.04} \times \$1.1000/€ = \$2{,}115{,}385.$$

This is received March 1st.

Total dollars received today (March 1st) are \$2,156,863 + \$2,115,385 = \$4,272,248. Carried forward six months at the 12% per annum Redwall cost of equity (6% for six months) results in a money market total of:

$4,272,248 × (1.06) = $4,528,582.88. Value on September 1st.

*Option hedge*. Redwall can buy euro put options for June with a strike price of \$1.1000/€ for a premium of 2.0%. The premium cost in dollars would be:

€2,000,000 × 0.02 x $1.1000/€ = $44,000. Paid March 1st.

The $44,000 carried forward 6 months at the 12% per annum cost of equity for September valuation:

$44,000 × 1.06 = $46,640. Value on September 1st.

Euro put options for September with a strike price of $1.1000/€ have a premium of 1.2%. They would cost:

€2,000,000 × 0.012 x $1.1000/€ = $26,400.

This is paid March 1st.

This $26,400 carried forward 6 months at the 12% per annum cost of equity for September valuation:

$26,400 × 1.06 = $27,984.

This is the dollar value on September 1st.

If exercised, the option hedge provides the following, which is a floor or "worst case" scenario.

| | |
|---|---|
| Cost of June put, carried forward 6 months | ($46,640) |
| Cost of September put, carried forward 6 months | ( 27,984) |
| June put proceeds, exercised, carried forward 3 months | |
| € 2,000,000 × $1.1000/€ × 1.03 = | 2,266,000 |
| September put proceeds, exercised: | |
| € 2,000,000 × $1.1000/€ = | 2,200,000 |
| Total net proceeds in six months | $4,391,376 |

If in June and September the euro were stronger than $1.1000/€, Redwall would sell its euros received at that higher spot rate and allow the options to expire out-of-the-money (OTM). Although the "worst case" provides less dollar revenue than either the forward or money market hedges, this alternative allows Redwall to gain from any possible strengthening of the mark.

*Do nothing*. Redwall can decide to just wait, bearing itself the full risk of any drop in the value of the euro and gaining from any appreciation. Although "expected" proceeds might be deemed to be the same as those received under the forward market option, on the logic that the forward is an unbiased predictor of future spot rates, this outcome is not certain and hence the alternative is riskier. (See the discussion of break-even analysis, below, for additional analysis of the risk of remaining unhedged.)

*Summary of Four Basic Hedge Alternatives*. The four methods are summarized as follows:

| | |
|---|---|
| Forward Hedge | $4,504,360 certain |
| Money Market Hedge | $4,528,583 certain |
| Option Hedge (if exercised) | $4,391,376 worst case |
| Do Nothing | Unknown & risky |

*Break-even Analysis*. Redwall might calculate the lowest value of the euro at which it could still break even, and use that break-even exchange rate as the basis for a hedging decision. Because two payments are involved in this instance, any number of combined 3-month and 6-month rates would provide an overall break-even result. To simplify, assume that spot rates in 3 months and 6 months are identical.

a. Break-even on hoped-for sales revenue:

| | |
|---|---|
| Implied dollar price of sale: | $4,320,000 |
| Actual sales price in euros: | €4,000,000 |
| Break-even exchange rate: | $4,320,000 ÷ €4,000,0000 = $1.0800/€ |

At a future spot exchange rate of $1.0800/€ (which was the exchange rate at the time Redwall quoted the sale in euros), Redwall would break even. I.e., it would receive in dollars the amount it hoped for (dare one say "expected?"). The likelihood of the euro being weaker than $1.0800/€ in June and September is the analysis that Redwall must make.

b. Break-even on total costs. In a variation of break-even analysis, assume that the hoped-for dollar sales price included a profit margin of 12%. Hence the cost of filling the export order is only 0.88 x $4,320,000 = $3,801,600. Redwall might be willing to remain unhedged (so as to benefit from any strengthening of the euro) as long as its net proceeds did not fall below $3,801,600 because up to that point any exchange loss reduces profit on the sale but the cost of the goods sold are still recovered. I.e.,

Redwall might risk its profit on the sale but not risk a failure to recover costs.

Dollars needed to break even on cost: $3,801,600
Actual sales price in euros: € 4,000,000
Break-even exchange rate: $3,801,600 , €4,000,000 = $0.9504/€

As long as the euro does not drop in value below $0.09504/€, Redwall will at least recover all of its costs. If Redwall judges such a drop in the value of the euro within six months to be extremely unlikely, it might decide not to hedge.

*Open Period Exposure*: Between February 1st, when Redwall offered to sell at a fixed price, and March 1st, when the sale was agreed upon, Redwall was at risk for *quotation exposure*: the risk that the exchange rate changes between the time an offer or bid on a project is made and the order is received. In the above instance, Redwall gained during this open period because the euro strengthened. However, Redwall could equally have lost. This exposure can not readily be hedged in the forward or money market because, in this instance, Redwall does not know if it will receive the order. If the order were not received, Redwall would not have future euro cash inflows (in June and September) to deliver against the forward sale or to repay the euro bank debt. Hence, if the order is not received, a forward or money market hedge creates a risk exposure exactly opposite to the risk if the order is received.

From a financial instruments point of view, the best hedge during this open period is an options hedge: Redwall could buy a put option on February 1st that matures on the last day that the fixed price offer remains valid, say March 1st. If the order is received and the euro has weakened, the loss *during this open period* is offset by profit on the option. If the order is not received, Redwall can either resell the option, if it is in the money, or discard it if it expires out of the money. Under the worst of conditions, Redwall is out only the cost of the option.

*Quotation exposure* can also be addressed by *non-hedging approaches*. In all instances, open bids or offers should have a specific time limit. Additionally, a fixed price bid or offer in a foreign currency might have an escalator clause for changes in the spot rate. In the above example, Redwall's offer price of €4,000,000 was based on an exchange rate of $1.0800/€. The offer could carry a provision that if the euro fell below, say, $1.0600/€ the euro price would be adjusted upward or the offer no longer stood.

## Problem 8.6 Redwall Pump Company

**Hedging foreign exchange risk: a receivable**

| Assumptions | | Values |
|---|---|---|
| 90-day Forward rate, $/euro | $ | 1.1060 |
| 180-day Forward rate, $/euro | $ | 1.1130 |
| US Treasury bill rate | | 3.600% |
| Redwall's borrowing rate, euros, per annum | | 8.000% |
| Redwall's cost of equity | | 12.000% |

| Today is March 1 | | |
|---|---|---|
| Date | | Exchange Rate ($/euro) |
| February 1 | $ | 1.0800 |
| March 1 | $ | 1.1000 |

| Options on euros | | Strike ($/euro) | Call Option | Put Option |
|---|---|---|---|---|
| June maturity options | $ | 1.1000 | 3.0% | 2.0% |
| September maturity options | $ | 1.1000 | 2.6% | 1.2% |

| Valuation of Alternative Hedges | | June Receivable | | Sept Receivable |
|---|---|---|---|---|
| Amount of receivable, in euros | | € 2,000,000 | | € 2,000,000 |
| **a. Hedge in the forward market** | | | | |
| Amount of receivable, in euros | | € 2,000,000 | | € 2,000,000 |
| Respective forward rates ($/euro) | $ | 1.1060 | $ | 1.1130 |
| US dollar proceeds as hedged ($) | $ | 2,212,000 | $ | 2,226,000 |
| Carry forward to Sept 1st at WACC | | 1.03 | | ---- |
| Total US$ proceeds on Sept 1st | $ | 2,278,360 | $ | 2,226,000 |
| | $ | | | 4,504,360 |
| **b. Hedge in the money market** | | | | |
| Amount of receivable, in euros | | € 2,000,000 | | € 2,000,000 |
| Discount factor for euro funds, period | | 1.02 | | 1.04 |
| Current proceeds from discounting, euros | | € 1,960,784 | | € 1,923,077 |
| Current spot rate ($/euro) | $ | 1.1000 | $ | 1.1000 |
| Current US dollar proceeds | $ | 2,156,863 | $ | 2,115,385 |
| Carry forward rate for the period | | 1.06 | | 1.06 |
| US dollar proceeds on future date | $ | 2,286,275 | $ | 2,242,308 |
| | $ | | | 4,528,582 |
| **c. Hedge with options** | | | | |
| Amount of receivable, in euros | | € 2,000,000 | | € 2,000,000 |
| Buy put options for maturities (% x spot value) | $ | (44,000) | $ | (26,400) |
| Carry forward for the period | | 1.06 | | 1.06 |
| Premium cost carried forward to Sept 1 | $ | (46,640) | $ | (27,984) |
| Gross put option value if exercised | $ | 2,200,000 | $ | 2,200,000 |
| Carried forward 3 months to Sept 1 | | 1.03 | | ---- |
| Gross proceeds, Sept 1 | $ | 2,266,000 | $ | 2,200,000 |
| Total net proceeds, after premium deduction, Sept 1 | $ | | | 4,391,376 |
| **d. Do nothing (remain uncovered)** | | | | |
| Amount of receivable, in euros | | € 2,000,000 | | € 2,000,000 |
| Ending spot exchange rate ($/euro) | | ??? | | ??? |

The money market hedge provides the highest certain outcome.
If Redwall believes the euro will strengthen versus the dollar over the coming months, and it is willing to take the currency risk, the put option hedges could be considered.

## MINI-CASE: LUFTHANSA'S PURCHASE OF BOEING 737S

1. **Do you think Heinz Ruhnau's hedging strategy made sense?**

   Although Ruhnau was correct in his assessment that the dollar was too high ("overvalued"), the position he constructed to manage the position was not really effective. By hedging half the DM 7.6 million exposure, he basically divided the exposure in half, hedging half and leaving half uncovered. The resulting positions will move opposite in their valuation as the exchange rate moves (in either direction).

2. **To what degree did he limit the upside and downside exposure of the transaction by hedging one-half of it? Do you agree with his critics that he was *speculating*?**

   Ruhnau did not effectively manage his exchange rate risk. A completely uncovered position would have no upper or lower limit to its exposure. A position which is one-half covered would still have no limit to it upside or downside, only half the slope or rate of movement as the totally uncovered position. A call option on dollars (or put option on marks) would have placed an absolute upper limit on how much Ruhnau and Lufthansa would have to pay to settle the Boeing purchase.

   It is difficult to truly agree with the argument that he was speculating. Ruhnau was indeed trying to manage or hedge the exposure, but his strategy was definitely flawed. To accuse him of speculating on the component which was covered with the forward contract is to not understand the concept of transaction exposure and how a short position in a foreign currency could potentially cause severe monetary losses or excessive expenses in the event the foreign currency appreciated significantly before cash settlement.

3. **Is it fair to judge transaction exposure management effectiveness with 20-20 hindsight?**

   Although most would agree it is not "fair" to judge exposure management effectiveness with perfect hindsight, it is a common practice in industry. Managerial behavior and results must always be interpreted on the basis of both decision-making at specific points in time – recognizing the risks and uncertainties of decisions made about the future – and the eventual results and outcomes of those decisions. Outcomes cannot be ignored, but management decision-making to protect the firm, its shareholders and creditors against adverse impacts of exchange rate movements, is a necessary part of risk management.

   A more effective and fair measure of performance is probably to measure outcomes as hedged against corporate benchmarks which are agreed upon prior to the hedging. Common benchmarks are a full forward cover outcome, or an average of the full forward and completely uncovered position (which is indeed what Ruhnau did!).

## CHAPTER 9. OPERATING EXPOSURE

### *Questions*

### 9-1. By any other name

*Economic exposure* emphasizes that the exposure is created by the economic consequences of an unexpected exchange rate change. Economic consequences, in turn, suggests that the impact is due to the response of external forces in the economy, rather than, say, something directly under the control of management. *Competitive exposure* suggests that the consequences of an unexpected exchange rate change are due to a shift in the competitive position of a firm, vis-á-vis its competitors. *Strategic exposure* suggests that matters of long-range cost changes and price setting, needed to anticipate or adjust to an unexpected change in exchange rates, are matters of corporate strategy; i.e., how the company positions itself in anticipation of risks caused by exchange rate changes.

### 9-2. Exposure type comparison

Both exposures deal with changes in expected cash flows. *Transaction exposure* deals with changes in near-term cash flows that have already been contracted for (such as foreign currency accounts receivable, accounts payable, and other debts). *Operating exposure* deals with changes in long-term cash flows that have not been contracted for but would be expected in the normal course of future business. One might view operating exposure as "anticipated future transactions exposure," although the concept is broader because the impact of the exposure might be through sales volume or operating cost changes.

Given a known exchange rate change, the cash flow impact of transaction exposure can be measured precisely whereas the cash flow impact of operating exposure remains a conjecture about the future.

### 9-3. Intra-company cash flows

*Operating cash flows*. These flows arise from normal business (production, marketing, selling) between parent and subsidiary.

a. *Payment for goods and services*: Parents and subsidiaries frequently buy and sell components and/or services from each other as a matter of seeking the most cost efficient way of doing business.

b. *Rent and lease payments* Parents and subsidiaries often use each other's physical facilities. Examples of rented or leased physical assets range from factory buildings to corporate aircraft. Decisions on ownership vs. renting from a related company may be based on the search for efficiency, on tax laws, or on the historical evolution of the multinational firm.

c. *Royalties and license fees*. Subsidiaries often use or produce goods that are patented by the parent, and they also sell under brand names controlled by the parent. For these "benefits" to the subsidiary the subsidiary usually pays a royalty (often a percent of sales) or a license fee (often a flat fee).

d. *Management fees and distributed overhead.* Certain expense of the parent are incurred on behalf of the subsidiary. Examples include the salaries of parent staff temporarily working for the subsidiary and subsidiary share of overhead (headquarters costs) that are incurred for the benefit of the world-wide enterprise. Subsidiaries pay their share by remitting management fees and overhead contribution to the parent.

*Financial cash flows.* These flows arise because of managerial decisions to transfer funds from subsidiary to parent or vice versa. They are optional in the sense that they are not made for a compelling operating purpose but rather from a decision over which management exercises greater discretion.

a. *Dividends paid to parent.* Whether or not the subsidiary pays dividends to its parent is at the discretion of the board of directions.

b. *Parent invested equity capital.* The parent may or may not choose to advance additional ownership capital into its subsidiary. Additional equity investment is only one of several ways by which the parent can add cash to its investment in the subsidiary. (See next item.)

c. *Parent lending to subsidiary.* Instead of investing additional equity capital, a parent may decide to make a long-term loan to its subsidiary. The same amount of cash can be invested, but under a legal form that allows repayment of the principal (as well as interest), whereas "repayment" of an equity investment amounts to a liquidating dividend.

d. *Interest on intrafirm lending.* If the parent loans funds to its subsidiary, interest on that loan represents a financial cash flow back to the parent.

e. *Intrafirm principal repayment.* If the parent loans funds to its subsidiary, repayment of the principal represents a cash flow back to the parent.

**9-4. Expected exchange rate changes**

Expected changes in foreign exchange rates should be incorporated in all financial plans of a MNE, including both operating and financial budgets. Hence the arrival of an expected exchange rate change should not be a surprise requiring alteration of existing plans and procedures.

Unexpected exchange rate changes are those that could not have been anticipated or built into existing plans. Hence a reevaluation of existing plans and procedures must be considered.

One must note that because budgets are built around expected exchange rate changes, the unexpected exchange rate is the deviation from the expected exchange rate, rather than the deviation from the actual exchange rate at the time a budget was prepared.

**9-5. Macroeconomic uncertainty**

Macroeconomic uncertainty is the sensitivity of the firm's future cash flows to macroeconomic variables in addition to foreign exchange, such as changes in interest rates and inflation rates.

**9-6. Who owns whom?**

As suggested, any answer is pure conjecture. The purpose of the question is to point out how in fact operating exposure can be quite complicated to anticipate.

One possible response is that a devaluation of the Indian rupee would make products manufactured by the French firm in India cheaper and thus allow for greater sales volume and possibly greater cash flows in India. If the French parent imported components from India, costs in France might fall, sales increase, and

French cash flow might increase. If the Indian sub-subsidiary in France were only a marketing and distribution subsidiary, its franc cash flow should increase. However if the Indian sub-subsidiary in France provided components to India, Indian costs would rise, and sales and cash flow might fall in India.

All in all, it would be a complicated task for French management to figure out exactly what its operating exposure is – which is the point of this somewhat convoluted example.

## 9-7. Strategic responses

The key to effective preparations for an unexpected devaluation is *anticipation*. Major changes to protect a firm after an unexpected devaluation are minimally effective. Possibilities include:

*Diversifying operations*. World-wide diversification in effect pre-positions a firm to make a quick response to any loss from operating exposure.

- The firm's own internal cost control system and the alertness of its foreign staff should give the firm an edge in anticipating countries where the currency is weak. Recognizing a weak currency is different from being able to predict the time or amount of a devaluation, but it does allow some defensive planning.

- If the firm is already diversified, it should be able to shift sourcing, production or sales effort from one country/currency to another in order to benefit from the change in the post-devaluation economic situation. Such shifts could be marginal or major.

*Diversifying financing*. Unexpected devaluations change the cost of the several components of capital – in particular, the cost of debt in one market relative to another.

- If a firm has already diversified its sources of financing, that is, established itself as a known and reputable factor in several capital markets, it can quickly move to take advantage of any temporary deviations from the international Fisher effect by changing the country or currency where borrowings are made.

## 9-8. Proactive policies to offset foreign exchange exposure

The four most common proactive policies and a brief explanation are:

a. *Matching currency cash flows*. The essence of this approach is to create operating or financial foreign currency cash outflows to match equivalent foreign currency inflows. Often debt is incurred in the same foreign currency in which operating cash flows are received.

b. *Risk-sharing agreements*. Contracts, including sales and purchasing contracts, between parties operating in different currency areas can be written such that any gain or loss caused by a change in the exchange rate will be shared by the two parties.

c. *Back-to-back loans*. Two firms in different countries lend their home currency to each other and agree to repay each other the same amount at a latter date. This can be viewed as a loan between two companies (independent entities or subsidiaries in the same corporate family) with each participant both making a loan and receiving 100% collateral in the other's currency. A back-to-back loan appears as both a debt (liability side of the balance sheet) and an amount to be received (asset side of the balance sheet) on the financial statements of each firm.

d. *Currency swap*. In terms of financial flows, the currency swap is almost identical to the back-to-back loan. However in a currency swap, each participant gives some of its currency to the other participant and receives in return an equivalent amount of the other participant's currency. No debt or receivable shows on the financial statements as this is in essence a foreign exchange transaction. The swap allows the participants to use foreign currency operating inflows to unwind the swap at a later date.

**9-9. Paradox?**

An exchange rate change causes a shift in both the cash flow needed to settle existing financial obligations (transaction exposure) and the future cash flows from operating the foreign affiliate (operating exposure.) It is possible that these will work in opposite directions, as in the chapter example for Trident Corporation. Each change individually is the consequence of both the price and the volume (i.e., the elasticity) for that account.

*Overview:* In its essence, a devaluation might cause a transaction loss because more local currency is needed to settle outstanding foreign-currency debts, and less is received from outstanding foreign-currency receivables. However if the devaluation results in a surge in volume because the local subsidiary is more competitive in its home market or in export markets, overall future cash flows (and future profits) may rise. Assuming for discussion a devaluation of the currency of the subsidiary, individual accounts may be influenced as follows:

*Sales*: Local sales prices may increase or remain the same in local currency terms, depending on local competition. This depends in part on whether competing goods in the local market are sourced domestically or from foreign countries. Export sales prices could increase in local currency terms if the firm chooses to maintain the foreign currency price fixed. If the foreign currency price is reduced (fixed local currency price) export volume might increase depending on the price elasticity of demand.

*Direct costs*: Whether or not direct costs in local currency terms rise depends, in the first instance, on whether they represent imported or local content. The replacement cost of imported content rises as soon as new imports are purchased; production may be costed at "old" imported prices for a while (increasing reported profit margins), but eventually the "new" and higher import prices must be charged to cost of goods sold. Local material and goods do not inherently increase with a depreciation of the local currency; however, depreciation may lead to inflationary conditions that cause local suppliers and local labor to demand more. Often a lag exists between increased cost of local goods and labor, but generalizations are difficult.

*Fixed costs*: In theory fixed costs should remain "fixed," but in practice they may creep up, possibly with a time lag, for the same reasons mentioned above for local direct costs.

*Volume*: Sales volume, and consequent changes in the profit contribution of marginal sales, may change in any direction. In theory a rise in local prices should cause demand to fall, but if the rise leads to an expectation of more future price increases, buyers may "rush" to buy more before additional price increases. Short-run and long-run consequences are likely to be different in this regard.

## 9-10. Subsidiary borrowing from parent

The greater the amount of local currency debt a subsidiary can acquire, the greater the proportion of its free cash flows (cash remaining after cash operating expenses) that is naturally hedged. This is because a portion of the subsidiary's free cash flow (roughly net income plus depreciation) can be used to service the local currency debt, rather than be exchanged for the parent's currency, remitted to the parent, and used by the parent to service parent-currency debt.

*Problems*

**9-1. Subscribing to *the Economist* in 2002**

a. Calculated implied euro subscription rates are in the spreadsheet table on the following page (right-hand column).

b. *The Economist* was most expensive in France at an implied euro cost of €167.08 per year. It was least expensive in Portugal at an implied euro cost of €139.74 per year. The French price was 19.6% above the Portuguese price. (Note: The December 2001 subscription price for Greece was stated in U.K. pounds sterling, rather than Greek drachmas.)

c. Subscribers and potential subscribers might be unhappy to see price discrimination based on national location. If subscription prices vary significantly by country in the months after January 1, 2002, one might expect some sort of "next door subscription" system developing such that subscribers near the borders of low-cost countries arrange to receive their copies "just across the border."

d. In fact, most euro-zone subscriptions were set at €164 per year, but five countries have different rates. These rates are posted at www.economist.com. The subscription information states specifically that it is for the "country that your printed copies will be delivered to." May 2002 subscription prices, the conversion prices from the table above, and the gain or loss are shown below. As noted, most subscriptions prices were set at €164 per year. For five countries, shown in italics, the subscription price was set at a different level. (As of May, 2002, a subscription in Greece was still quoted in pounds at £92.)

Within those countries where the price was set at €164 per year, prices increased in Belgium, Germany, and Luxembourg and fell in Austria and the Netherlands. In Finland the new subscription price was set at €155, a 1.8% increase from the effective pre-euro price. In Ireland and Italy the new subscription price was set at €145, an increase for Ireland of 0.2% - hardly significant, and a decrease for Italy of a miniscule 0.05%. It is worth noting, however, that if the price in Italy were the same as in the general heartland of Europe, i.e., €164, the price increase would have been 13.0%. In Portugal and Spain the new subscription price was set at €142, a small price increase in both countries.

e. With all euro-zone prices quoted in euros, *The Economist* has eliminated transaction exposure for those countries. A potential for operating exposure remains, however, for subscriptions could fall off in the five countries where the price has gone up. Insofar as subscribers to *The Economist* are among the more sophisticated and thus possibly more affluent members of the population, and given that the greatest increase (France) was only €2.7893 per year, *The Economists's* managers may have decided that subscription demand was relatively inelastic to price changes.

## Problem 9.1 Subscribing to the Economist in 2002

| Country | Cost of a one-year subscription to the Economist (local currency) | Official exchange rate with the euro (per euro) | a) Implied euro cost | b) by extreme |
|---|---|---|---|---|
| Austria | 2,258.00 | 13.7603 | € 164.10 | |
| Belgium | 6,537.00 | 40.3399 | € 162.05 | |
| Finland | 905.00 | 5.94573 | € 152.21 | |
| France | 1,096.00 | 6.55957 | € 167.08 | Most expensive |
| Germany | 316.00 | 1.95583 | € 161.57 | |
| Ireland | 114.00 | 0.787564 | € 144.75 | |
| Italy | 280,908.00 | 1,936.27 | € 145.08 | |
| Luxembourg | 6,537.00 | 40.3399 | € 162.05 | |
| Netherlands | 365.00 | 2.20371 | € 165.63 | |
| Portugal | 28,016.00 | 200.482 | € 139.74 | Least expensive |
| Spain | 23,317.00 | 166.386 | € 140.14 | |

c) According to European Union law, differences in prices across countries should reflect only differences associated with the provision of goods or services, not on any basis related to currency.

## Problem 9.2 Trident Europe - Case 4

### Balance Sheet Information, End of Fiscal 2002

| Assets | | Liabilities and net worth | |
|---|---|---|---|
| Cash | € 1,600,000 | Accounts payable | € 800,000 |
| Accounts receivable | 3,200,000 | Short-term bank loan | 1,600,000 |
| Inventory | 2,400,000 | Long-term debt | 1,600,000 |
| Net plant and equipment | 4,800,000 | Common stock | 1,800,000 |
| | | Retained earnings | 6,200,000 |
| Sum | € 12,000,000 | Sum | € 12,000,000 |

### Important Ratios to be Maintained and Other Data

| | |
|---|---|
| Accounts receivable, as percent of sales | 25.00% |
| Inventory, as percent of annual direct costs | 25.00% |
| Cost of capital (annual discount rate) | 20.00% |
| Income tax rate | 34.00% |

| | Base Case | Case 1 | Case 2 | Case 3 | Case 4 |
|---|---|---|---|---|---|
| **Assumptions** | | | | | |
| Exchange rate, $/€ | 1.2000 | 1.0000 | 1.0000 | 1.0000 | 1.0000 |
| Sales volume (units) | 1,000,000 | 1,000,000 | 2,000,000 | 1,000,000 | 500,000 |
| Export sales volume (case 4) | | | | | **500,000** |
| Sales price per unit | € 12.80 | € 12.80 | € 12.80 | € 15.36 | € 12.80 |
| Export sales price per unit (case 4) | | | | | **€ 15.36** |
| Direct cost per unit | € 9.60 | € 9.60 | € 9.60 | € 9.60 | € 9.60 |
| **Annual Cash Flows before Adjustments** | | | | | |
| Sales revenue | € 12,800,000 | € 12,800,000 | € 25,600,000 | € 15,360,000 | € 14,080,000 |
| Direct cost of goods sold | 9,600,000 | 9,600,000 | 19,200,000 | 9,600,000 | 9,600,000 |
| Cash operating expenses (fixed) | 890,000 | 890,000 | 890,000 | 890,000 | 890,000 |
| Depreciation | 600,000 | 600,000 | 600,000 | 600,000 | 600,000 |
| Pretax profit | € 1,710,000 | € 1,710,000 | € 4,910,000 | € 4,270,000 | € 2,990,000 |
| Income tax expense | 581,400 | 581,400 | 1,669,400 | 1,451,800 | 1,016,600 |
| Profit after tax | € 1,128,600 | € 1,128,600 | € 3,240,600 | € 2,818,200 | € 1,973,400 |
| Add back depreciation | 600,000 | 600,000 | 600,000 | 600,000 | 600,000 |
| Cash flow from operations, in euros | € 1,728,600 | € 1,728,600 | € 3,840,600 | € 3,418,200 | **€ 2,573,400** |
| Cash flow from operations, in dollars | $ 2,074,320 | $ 1,728,600 | $ 3,840,600 | $ 3,418,200 | **$ 2,573,400** |
| **Adjustments to Working Capital for 2003 and 2007 Caused by Changes in Conditions** | | | | | |
| Accounts receivable | € 3,200,000 | € 3,200,000 | € 6,400,000 | € 3,840,000 | € 3,520,000 |
| Inventory | 2,400,000 | 2,400,000 | 4,800,000 | 2,400,000 | 2,400,000 |
| Sum | € 5,600,000 | € 5,600,000 | € 11,200,000 | € 6,240,000 | € 5,920,000 |
| Change from base conditions in 2003 | € - | € - | € 5,600,000 | € 640,000 | **€ 320,000** |
| **Year** | **Year-End Cash Flows** | | | | |
| 1 (2003) | $ 2,074,320 | $ 1,728,600 | $ (1,759,400) | $ 2,778,200 | $ 2,253,400 |
| 2 (2004) | $ 2,074,320 | $ 1,728,600 | $ 3,840,600 | $ 3,418,200 | $ 2,573,400 |
| 3 (2005) | $ 2,074,320 | $ 1,728,600 | $ 3,840,600 | $ 3,418,200 | $ 2,573,400 |
| 4 (2006) | $ 2,074,320 | $ 1,728,600 | $ 3,840,600 | $ 3,418,200 | $ 2,573,400 |
| 5 (2007) | $ 2,074,320 | $ 1,728,600 | $ 9,440,600 | $ 4,058,200 | $ 2,893,400 |
| **Year** | **Change in Year-End Cash Flows from Base Conditions** | | | | |
| 1 (2003) | na | $ (345,720) | $ (3,833,720) | $ 703,880 | $ 179,080 |
| 2 (2004) | na | $ (345,720) | $ 1,766,280 | $ 1,343,880 | $ 499,080 |
| 3 (2005) | na | $ (345,720) | $ 1,766,280 | $ 1,343,880 | $ 499,080 |
| 4 (2006) | na | $ (345,720) | $ 1,766,280 | $ 1,343,880 | $ 499,080 |
| 5 (2007) | na | $ (345,720) | $ 7,366,280 | $ 1,983,880 | $ 819,080 |
| **Present Value of Incremental Year-End Cash Flows** | | | | | |
| | na | **$ (1,033,914)** | **$ 2,866,106** | **$ 3,742,892** | **$ 1,354,489** |

## Problem 9.3 Trident Europe - Case 5

**Balance Sheet Information, End of Fiscal 2002**

| Assets | | Liabilities and net worth | |
|---|---|---|---|
| Cash | € 1,600,000 | Accounts payable | € 800,000 |
| Accounts receivable | 3,200,000 | Short-term bank loan | 1,600,000 |
| Inventory | 2,400,000 | Long-term debt | 1,600,000 |
| Net plant and equipment | 4,800,000 | Common stock | 1,800,000 |
| | | Retained earnings | 6,200,000 |
| Sum | € 12,000,000 | Sum | € 12,000,000 |

| Important Ratios to be Maintained and Other Data | |
|---|---|
| Accounts receivable, as percent of sales | 25.00% |
| Inventory, as percent of annual direct costs | 25.00% |
| Cost of capital (annual discount rate) | 20.00% |
| Income tax rate | 34.00% |

| | Base Case | Case 1 | Case 2 | Case 3 | Case 5 |
|---|---|---|---|---|---|
| **Assumptions** | | | | | |
| Exchange rate, $/€ | 1.2000 | 1.0000 | 1.0000 | 1.0000 | 1.0000 |
| Sales volume (units) | 1,000,000 | 1,000,000 | 2,000,000 | 1,000,000 | 500,000 |
| Export sales volume (case 4) | | | | | **500,000** |
| Sales price per unit | € 12.80 | € 12.80 | € 12.80 | € 15.36 | **€ 15.36** |
| Export sales price per unit (case 4) | | | | | **€ 15.36** |
| Direct cost per unit | € 9.60 | € 9.60 | € 9.60 | € 9.60 | **€ 11.52** |
| **Annual Cash Flows before Adjustments** | | | | | |
| Sales revenue | € 12,800,000 | € 12,800,000 | € 25,600,000 | € 15,360,000 | € 15,360,000 |
| Direct cost of goods sold | 9,600,000 | 9,600,000 | 19,200,000 | 9,600,000 | 11,520,000 |
| Cash operating expenses (fixed) | 890,000 | 890,000 | 890,000 | 890,000 | 1,068,000 |
| Depreciation | 600,000 | 600,000 | 600,000 | 600,000 | 600,000 |
| Pretax profit | € 1,710,000 | € 1,710,000 | € 4,910,000 | € 4,270,000 | € 2,172,000 |
| Income tax expense | 581,400 | 581,400 | 1,669,400 | 1,451,800 | 738,480 |
| Profit after tax | € 1,128,600 | € 1,128,600 | € 3,240,600 | € 2,818,200 | € 1,433,520 |
| Add back depreciation | 600,000 | 600,000 | 600,000 | 600,000 | 600,000 |
| Cash flow from operations, in euros | € 1,728,600 | € 1,728,600 | € 3,840,600 | € 3,418,200 | **€ 2,033,520** |
| Cash flow from operations, in dollars | $ 2,074,320 | $ 1,728,600 | $ 3,840,600 | $ 3,418,200 | **$ 2,033,520** |
| **Adjustments to Working Capital for 2003 and 2007 Caused by Changes in Conditions** | | | | | |
| Accounts receivable | € 3,200,000 | € 3,200,000 | € 6,400,000 | € 3,840,000 | € 3,840,000 |
| Inventory | 2,400,000 | 2,400,000 | 4,800,000 | 2,400,000 | 2,880,000 |
| Sum | € 5,600,000 | € 5,600,000 | € 11,200,000 | € 6,240,000 | € 6,720,000 |
| Change from base conditions in 2003 | € - | € - | € 5,600,000 | € 640,000 | **€ 1,120,000** |
| **Year** | **Year-End Cash Flows** | | | | |
| 1 (2003) | $ 2,074,320 | $ 1,728,600 | $ (1,759,400) | $ 2,778,200 | $ 913,520 |
| 2 (2004) | $ 2,074,320 | $ 1,728,600 | $ 3,840,600 | $ 3,418,200 | $ 2,033,520 |
| 3 (2005) | $ 2,074,320 | $ 1,728,600 | $ 3,840,600 | $ 3,418,200 | $ 2,033,520 |
| 4 (2006) | $ 2,074,320 | $ 1,728,600 | $ 3,840,600 | $ 3,418,200 | $ 2,033,520 |
| 5 (2007) | $ 2,074,320 | $ 1,728,600 | $ 9,440,600 | $ 4,058,200 | $ 3,153,520 |
| **Year** | **Change in Year-End Cash Flows from Base Conditions** | | | | |
| 1 (2003) | na | $ (345,720) | $ (3,833,720) | $ 703,880 | $ (1,160,800) |
| 2 (2004) | na | $ (345,720) | $ 1,766,280 | $ 1,343,880 | $ (40,800) |
| 3 (2005) | na | $ (345,720) | $ 1,766,280 | $ 1,343,880 | $ (40,800) |
| 4 (2006) | na | $ (345,720) | $ 1,766,280 | $ 1,343,880 | $ (40,800) |
| 5 (2007) | na | $ (345,720) | $ 7,366,280 | $ 1,983,880 | $ 1,079,200 |
| **Present Value of Incremental Year-End Cash Flows** | | | | | |
| | na | **$ (1,033,914)** | **$ 2,866,106** | **$ 3,742,892** | **$ (605,247)** |

## Problem 9.4 Cleveland Pneumatic Company (A)

| Assumptions | | Values |
|---|---|---|
| Sales volume per year | | 1,000,000 |
| US dollar price per unit | $ | 24.00 |
| Direct costs as % of US$ sales price | | 75% |
| Direct costs per unit | $ | 18.00 |
| Spot exchange rate, Rmb/$ | | 8.0000 |
| Expected spot rate, Rmb/$ | | 10.0000 |
| Unit volume decrease if price increased | | -10% |

| Sales to China | | Case 1<br>Same Rmb Price | | Case 2<br>Same US$ Price |
|---|---|---|---|---|
| US dollar price per unit | $ | 19.20 | $ | 24.00 |
| Unit volume | | 1,000,000 | | 900,000 |
| | | | | |
| Sales revenue, Rmb | $ | 19,200,000 | $ | 21,600,000 |
| Less direct costs | | (18,000,000) | | (16,200,000) |
| Gross profits, Rmb | $ | 1,200,000 | $ | 5,400,000 |
| | | | | Better. |

## Problem 9.5 Cleveland Pneumatic Company (B)

| Assumptions | Values |
|---|---|
| Sales volume per year | 1,000,000 |
| US dollar price per unit | $ 24.00 |
| Direct costs as % of US$ price | 75% |
| Direct costs per unit | $ 18.00 |
| Spot exchange rate, Rmb/$ | 8.0000 |
| Expected spot rate, Rmb/$ | 10.0000 |

| Assumptions | Values |
|---|---|
| Volume change (if price increased) | 1% |
| Volume growth (same Rmb price) | 12% |
| WACC | 10% |

**Alternative 1: Keep Same Chinese Sales Price**

| Year | Volume | Revenue | Direct Costs | Gross Margin | Present Value Factor | Present Value of Margin |
|---|---|---|---|---|---|---|
| 1 | 1,000,000 | $ 19,200,000 | $ 18,000,000 | $ 1,200,000 | 0.9091 | $ 1,090,909 |
| 2 | 1,120,000 | $ 21,504,000 | $ 20,160,000 | $ 1,344,000 | 0.8264 | $ 1,110,744 |
| 3 | 1,254,400 | $ 24,084,480 | $ 22,579,200 | $ 1,505,280 | 0.7513 | $ 1,130,939 |
| 4 | 1,404,928 | $ 26,974,618 | $ 25,288,704 | $ 1,685,914 | 0.6830 | $ 1,151,502 |
| 5 | 1,573,519 | $ 30,211,572 | $ 28,323,348 | $ 1,888,223 | 0.6209 | $ 1,172,438 |
| 6 | 1,762,342 | $ 33,836,960 | $ 31,722,150 | $ 2,114,810 | 0.5645 | $ 1,193,755 |
| 7 | 1,973,823 | $ 37,897,396 | $ 35,528,808 | $ 2,368,587 | 0.5132 | $ 1,215,460 |
| 8 | 2,210,681 | $ 42,445,083 | $ 39,792,265 | $ 2,652,818 | 0.4665 | $ 1,237,559 |
| **Cum PV of Gross Margin** | | | | | | **$ 9,303,306** |

**Alternative 2: Raise Chinese Sales Price**

| Year | Volume | Revenue | Direct Costs | Gross Margin | Present Value Factor | Present Value of Margin |
|---|---|---|---|---|---|---|
| 1 | 900,000 | $ 21,600,000 | $ 16,200,000 | $ 5,400,000 | 0.9091 | $ 4,909,091 |
| 2 | 909,000 | $ 21,816,000 | $ 16,362,000 | $ 5,454,000 | 0.8264 | $ 4,507,438 |
| 3 | 918,090 | $ 22,034,160 | $ 16,525,620 | $ 5,508,540 | 0.7513 | $ 4,138,648 |
| 4 | 927,271 | $ 22,254,502 | $ 16,690,876 | $ 5,563,625 | 0.6830 | $ 3,800,031 |
| 5 | 936,544 | $ 22,477,047 | $ 16,857,785 | $ 5,619,262 | 0.6209 | $ 3,489,119 |
| 6 | 945,909 | $ 22,701,817 | $ 17,026,363 | $ 5,675,454 | 0.5645 | $ 3,203,646 |
| 7 | 955,368 | $ 22,928,835 | $ 17,196,626 | $ 5,732,209 | 0.5132 | $ 2,941,529 |
| 8 | 964,922 | $ 23,158,124 | $ 17,368,593 | $ 5,789,531 | 0.4665 | $ 2,700,859 |
| **Cum PV of Gross Margin** | | | | | | **$ 29,690,361** |

Cleveland Pneumatic is much better off raising the Chinese sales price to maintain the US dollar price, and suffering the lower volumes. The volume decrease does not offset the stronger US dollar price per unit receieved.

## Problem 9.6 Autocars, Ltd.

| Assumptions | Values | |
|---|---|---|
| Invoice price of car | **£12,000** | |
| Spot exchange rate, NZ$/pound | **1.6400** | |
| Risk-sharing band, percentage | **5.00%** | |
| **Sales to New Zealand Distributors** | **Lower Band** | **Upper Band** |
| **a. What are the outside ranges?** | **1.7220** | **1.5580** |
| (initial spot rate + or - 5%) | | |
| **b. New current spot rate is** | **1.7000** | |
| Is this within the band? | **Yes** | |
| **The effective exchange rate is:** | | |
| The base spot rate | **1.6400** | |
| Plus .5 of the deviation from base | **0.0300** | |
| Effective exchange rate | **1.6700** | |
| **c. Cost to the distributor for 10 cars, NZ$** | **200,400** | |
| Receipts to Autocar in British pounds (NZ$ invoice amount at current spot rate) | **£117,882** | |

This is less than 12,000 pounds per car.

**d. How does this shift the currency risk?**
Autocars bears more of the currency risk within the band, allowing the New Zealand distributor to pay a "dampened" movement.

**e. Who benefits from this risk-sharing agreement?**
Both parties in practice. The manufacturer in this case carries roughly all the currency risk within the range, allowing the distributor to have more stable pricing to pass on to the customer. This also benefits the manufacturer as it now probably enjoys a more stable and sustainable distributor sales outlet.

## MINI-CASE: TOYOTA'S EUROPEAN OPERATING EXPOSURE

1. **Why do you think Toyota had waited so long to move much of its manufacturing for European sales to Europe?**

Automobile manufacturing is a very complex and capital intensive industry. Toyota, like most manufacturers, wished to continue to enjoy the benefits of scale and scope economies in manufacturing as long as possible, and had resisted the movement of more and more of its manufacturing into the local and regional markets. Time, however, was now running out.

2. **If the British pound were to join the European Monetary Union would the problem be resolved? How likely do you think this is?**

The British joining the EMU would eliminate the currency risk between the UK and Europe, but not between Japan and Europe. The UK joining the EMU would eliminate the deviations in currency value between the British pound and the euro only.

Although there has been continuing and heated debate over the possibility of Britain joining the EMU, there is at present no specific plan to do so. In many ways the UK believes itself to be somewhat the beneficiary of being the single large "European" country which is not euro-based.

3. **If you were Mr. Shuhei, how would you categorize your problems and solutions? What was a short-term and what was a long-term problem?**

The problems, at least on the basis of the data presented, appear to be primarily exchange rate-induced pricing problems. The fall in the value of the euro against the yen throughout 1999 and early 2000 was significant (for example calculate the percentage change in the value of the euro between January 1999 and July 2000). For some unknown reason most of Toyota's North American operations had moved to manufacturing bases in North America, while Toyota had continued to try and service European sales via exports from Japan. The recent decision to manufacture a new European-targeted product, the Yaris, from production in Japan was in the continuing strategy. It did not appear to be a good strategy given the recent direction of exchange rate movements.

The primary short-term solution was to continue to absorb yen-based cost increases in lower margins on European sales – assuming that the market would not bear passing-through the exchange rate changes. In the medium-to-long-term, Toyota must inevitably move more of the automobile's content into manufacturing operations within the EMU (and not the United Kingdom).

4. **What measures would you recommend Toyota Europe take to resolve the continuing operating losses?**

If Toyota was willing to continue incurring the operating losses in Europe, and put market share goals above profit goals, then continuing the current operating and pricing policy would be in order. The euro had regained some of its weakness against the yen in the recent year.

The fact that significant Toyota operations existed in the United Kingdom would be a continuing dilemma as long as the UK stayed out of the EMU. The strength of the pound against the euro – and the new-found stability in that rate seen in 2000 and 2001 – did not bode well for UK-based operations for European sales. In the longer-term, Toyota, like many other multinationals, would have to consider moving more of its manufacturing and cost structure to within the EMU, not in Japan and not in the UK.

## CHAPTER 10. TRANSLATION EXPOSURE

### *Questions*

### 10-1. By any other name

Translation refers to the process by which the financial statements of separately incorporated subsidiaries are added to the financial statements of a parent in order to prepare a *consolidated financial statement* that will reflect the economic reality of the entire enterprise, rather than just the financial status of one separately-incorporated segment. Consolidation of domestic subsidiaries (same country as parent) is simple because only one currency is involved. The financial statements of subsidiaries of a multinational enterprise are kept in other currencies, so consolidation involves adjusting each year for changes in the value of those separate currencies. The process of restating the foreign currency financial statements of a foreign subsidiary is called *translation.*

Because translation occurs as a result of the accounting process, the restatement is most often called "accounting." Because exchange rates change from one time period to another, imbalances occur. These imbalances may cause an accounting-derived gain or loss, which is taken into the equity section of the parent's consolidated statement. The possibility of gain or loss gives rise to the word "exposure."

### 10-2. Converting financial assets

They are *not* synonyms. To *translate* is to express the value of a financial account (assets, liability, revenue, or expense) originally measured in one currency in another currency. Translation is pure measurement; no transaction is involved.

To *convert* is to engage in a transaction in which an asset or liability originally measured in one currency is physically exchanged for as asset or liability measured in another currency. Exchanging pounds sterling for dollars in the foreign exchange market is converting sterling into dollars. Swapping yen-denominated debt for dollar-denominated debt is converting the debt from once currency to another.

### 10-3. The central problem

The central problem arises from the fact that exchange rates change from one time period to another, combined with the accounting tradition that accounts are supposed to be kept on a historic cost basis. The value in the parent's home currency of assets and liabilities measured on a historic cost basis in a foreign currency is not clear if the exchange rate has changed. Different countries have different rules on how to treat the discrepancy that arises when exchange rates change.

### 10-4. Self-sustaining subsidiaries

A *self-sustaining* foreign subsidiary is an entity that operates in the local economy more or less independently of its parent. To a large degree its operations, including purchasing, production, and sales, are tied into the local economy; and the entity could probably operate on its own without foreign parent ownership. An example would be the operations of Shell Petroleum in the United States; although owned by a Dutch-British parent, the U.S. operations of Shell in refining and transporting stand pretty much on their own. (Most of Shell's petroleum stations in the United States are owned by local operators.)

An *integrated* foreign subsidiary is one that operates as an extension of the parent's operations, with cash flows and general business lines highly integrated into those of the parent. An example would be a Ford

Motor Company plant that manufactures automobile transmissions in France, with the transmissions shipped only to Ford assembly lines around the world.

### 10-5. Functional currency

A *functional currency* is the currency of the primary economic environment in which a subsidiary operates and in which it generates cash flows. As a general matter the functional currency of self-sustaining foreign entities is their local currency, whereas the functional currency of an integrated foreign entity is usually the currency of the parent.

Insofar as the authors know, there is no such thing as a *non-functional* currency. However one might consider the currencies of countries with extremely high rates of inflation as being "non-functional," in that they fail to act as a dependable medium of exchange, measure of value, or store of value.

### 10-6. Translating assets

Under the current rate method, all assets are translated at the exchange rate in effect on the date the accounts are translated. Under the temporal method, monetary assets (cash, marketable securities, and accounts receivable) are translated (accountants prefer the technical term *remeasured)* at the current exchange rate, but inventory and fixed assets are translated at the exchange rate that was in effect at the time the asset was acquired. (Exceptions exist where the local inflation rate exceeds 100% over a three year period.)

### 10-7. Translating liabilities

Under both the current rate method and the temporal method all liabilities (but not equity accounts) are translated at the current exchange rate. The two methods do not differ in the manner in which they translate liabilities.

### 10-8. Hyperinflation

*Hyperinflation* is, by definition, a "very high and rapid monetary inflation, or the period during which this occurs." (*Encarta World English Dictionary*). The prefix, *hyper*, means "over, beyond, over much, above measure." (*The Shorter Oxford English Dictionary on Historical Principles.*) In the context of practical international accounting for multinational companies, *hyperinflation* is deemed to exist when accumulated inflation is 100% or more over a three-year period.

### 10-9. Foreign exchange losses by any other name

Losses from *transaction exposure* are cash losses incurred in the near term because of a change in the amount of cash to be received or paid on account of already-existing receivables or payables. The focus is on a loss from an already-existing balance sheet account. These are "realized" losses and therefore can be deducted from income for tax purposes.

Losses from *operating exposure* are potential cash losses that will probably be incurred at some time in the future because of changes in future expenses, revenues, or sales volume that result from an unexpected exchange rate change. The focus is on a loss from future income statement accounts.

Losses from *translation exposure* are changes in the size of the equity section of a parent company issuing consolidated financial statements that result from a change in how foreign subsidiary financial statements are measured for translation purposes. As such, losses from translation exposure are not cash losses. The focus is on translation ("remeasurement, if you prefer) of both balance sheet and income statement accounts.

**10-10. Reacting to potential losses**

Financial managers should first address the question of protecting the firm from losses due to operating exposure because these are probable future cash losses and thus affect the value of the firm. After operating exposure is dealt with, financial managers should then consider whether or not they wish to deal with translation exposure, and if so, what to do.

The logic of this sequence is that future cash flows are more important to the value of the firm than are non-cash accounting losses. Additionally, protecting against operating exposure may increase or decrease future translation exposure, and vice versa. Notwithstanding the above logic, many financial managers address translation exposure losses first in the belief that investors are guided more by reported earnings than by the more nebulous expected future cash flows.

**10-11. Trident and a strong dollar**

An appreciation of the dollar is the same as a weakening of the euro. Trident's German subsidiary with its euro-denominated earnings would find those earnings translated into fewer dollars. Consequently Trident's consolidated earnings would decrease from this effect.

Nevertheless if the weakened euro led to an offsetting increase in volume in Trident's German subsidiary, unmatched by increasing costs, the German subsidiary might earn and report more. This would be an instance where Trident's gain from operating exposure more than offset its loss from translation exposure.

**10-12. Trident and a weak dollar**

A weakening of the dollar is the same as an appreciation of the euro. Trident's German subsidiary with its euro-denominated earnings would find those earnings translated into more dollars. Consequently Trident's consolidated earnings would increase from this effect.

Nevertheless if the strengthened euro led to an offsetting decrease in volume in Trident's German subsidiary, unmatched by decreased costs, the German subsidiary might earn and report less. This would be an instance where Trident's loss from operating exposure more than offset its gain from translation exposure.

## Problem 10.1 Montevideo Products, S.A.

**Balance Sheet (thousands of pesos Uruguayo)**

| Assets | January 1st | Exchange Rate ($U/US$) | | US$ |
|---|---|---|---|---|
| Cash | 60,000 | 20.00 | $ | 3,000 |
| Accounts receivable | 120,000 | 20.00 | | 6,000 |
| Inventory | 120,000 | 20.00 | | 6,000 |
| Net plant & equipment | 240,000 | 20.00 | | 12,000 |
| | 540,000 | | | 27,000 |

| Liabilities & Net Worth | | | | |
|---|---|---|---|---|
| Current liabilities | 30,000 | 20.00 | $ | 1,500 |
| Long-term debt | 90,000 | 20.00 | | 4,500 |
| Capital stock | 300,000 | 15.00 | | 20,000 |
| Retained earnings | 120,000 | 15.00 | | 8,000 |
| | 540,000 | | | 34,000 |

| | | | January 1st $U/US$ | | December 31st $U/US$ |
|---|---|---|---|---|---|
| **a. Calculation of Accounting Exposures:** | **$U (000s)** | | **15.00** | | **20.00** |
| Exposed assets (all assets) | 540,000 | $ | 36,000 | $ | 27,000 |
| Less exposed liabilities (curr liabs + lt debt) | (120,000) | | (8,000) | | (6,000) |
| Net exposure | 420,000 | $ | 28,000 | $ | 21,000 |

| | | |
|---|---|---|
| **b. Change in translation exposure: Gain (Loss)** | $ | (7,000) |

**Alternatively, the translation loss arising from the fall in the value of the peso Uruaguayo can be found as follows:**

| | | |
|---|---|---|
| Net exposed assets (US$) | $ | 28,000 |
| Percentage change in the value of the $U | | -25.0% |
| Translation gain (loss) | $ | (7,000) |

## Problem 10.2 Siam Toys, Ltd.

### TRANSLATION BY THE CURRENT RATE METHOD

| Balance Sheet (thousands) | | Before Devaluation | | | After Devaluation | | |
|---|---|---|---|---|---|---|---|
| Assets | Thai baht Statement | Exchange Rate (Baht/US$) | | Translated Accounts US dollars | Exchange Rate (Baht/US$) | | Translated Accounts US dollars |
| Cash | ฿24,000 | 30 | $ | 800 | 40 | $ | 600 |
| Accounts receivable | 36,000 | 30 | | 1,200 | 40 | | 900 |
| Inventory | 48,000 | 30 | | 1,600 | 40 | | 1,200 |
| Net plant & equipment | 60,000 | 30 | | 2,000 | 40 | | 1,500 |
| Total | ฿168,000 | | $ | 5,600 | | $ | 4,200 |
| | | | | | | | |
| **Liabilities & Net Worth** | | | | | | | |
| Accounts payable | ฿18,000 | 30 | $ | 600 | 40 | $ | 450 |
| Bank loans | 60,000 | 30 | | 2,000 | 40 | | 1,500 |
| Common stock | 18,000 | 20 | | 900 | 20 | | 900 |
| Retained earnings | 72,000 | 34 | | 2,100 | 34 | | 2,100 |
| CTA account (loss) | 0 | | | - | | $ | (750) |
| Total | ฿168,000 | | $ | 5,600 | | $ | 4,200 |

Note: Dollar retained earnings before devaluation are the cumulative sum of additions to retained earnings of all prior years, translated at exchange rates in effect in each of those years.

This cumulative translation account (CTA) loss of $750,000 would be entered into the company's consolidated balance sheet under equity.

### TRANSLATION BY THE TEMPORAL METHOD

| Balance Sheet (thousands) | | Before Devaluation | | | After Devaluation | | |
|---|---|---|---|---|---|---|---|
| Assets | Thai baht Statement | Exchange Rate (Baht/US$) | | Translated Accounts US dollars | Exchange Rate (Baht/US$) | | Translated Accounts US dollars |
| Cash | ฿24,000 | 30 | $ | 800 | 40 | $ | 600 |
| Accounts receivable | 36,000 | 30 | | 1,200 | 40 | | 900 |
| Inventory | 48,000 | 30 | | 1,600 | 30 | | 1,600 |
| Net plant & equipment | 60,000 | 20 | | 3,000 | 20 | | 3,000 |
| Total | ฿168,000 | | $ | 6,600 | | $ | 6,100 |
| | | | | | | | |
| **Liabilities & Net Worth** | | | | | | | |
| Accounts payable | ฿18,000 | 30 | $ | 600 | 40 | $ | 450 |
| Bank loans | 60,000 | 30 | | 2,000 | 40 | | 1,500 |
| Common stock | 18,000 | 20 | | 900 | 20 | | 900 |
| Retained earnings | 72,000 | 23 | | 3,100 | 23 | | 3,100 |
| CTA account (loss) | 0 | | | - | | $ | 150 |
| Total | ฿168,000 | | $ | 6,600 | | $ | 6,100 |

Note a: Dollar retained earnings before devaluation are the cumulative sum of additions to retained earnings of all prior years, translated at exchange rates in effect in each of those years.

Note b: Retained earnings after devaluation are translated at the same effective rate (see Note a) as before devaluation.

**The translation gain of $150,000 would be passed-through to the consolidated income statement.**

### EXPLANATION OF DIFFERENT OUTCOME BY TRANSLATION METHODOLOGY

The Temporal Method results in a translation gain, as opposed to the CTA loss found under the Current Rate Method, because of the different exchange rates used against Net plant & equipment and the inventory line items. This gain would be impossible under the Current Rate Method because ALL assets are exposed under that method, whereas the Temporal Method carries Net plant & equipment and inventory at relevant historical exchange rates.

## Problem 10.3 Egyptian Ingot, Ltd.

**Translation Using the Current Rate Method**

| Balance Sheet of Egyptian Ingot, Ltd. | | Before Exchange Rate Change | | | After Exchange Rate Change | | |
|---|---|---|---|---|---|---|---|
| | Egyptian pounds | Exchange Rate | | Translated Accounts | Exchange Rate | | Translated Accounts |
| **Assets** | Statement | (Egyptian L/UKL) | | US dollars | (Egyptian L/UKL) | | US dollars |
| Cash | 16,500,000 | 5.50 | $ | 3,000,000 | 6.00 | $ | 2,750,000 |
| Accounts receivable | 33,000,000 | 5.50 | | 6,000,000 | 6.00 | | 5,500,000 |
| Inventory | 49,500,000 | 5.50 | | 9,000,000 | 6.00 | | 8,250,000 |
| Net plant & equipment | 66,000,000 | 5.50 | | 12,000,000 | 6.00 | | 11,000,000 |
| Total | 165,000,000 | | $ | 30,000,000 | | $ | 27,500,000 |
| **Liabilities & Net Worth** | | | | | | | |
| Accounts payable | 24,750,000 | 5.50 | $ | 4,500,000 | 6.00 | $ | 4,125,000 |
| Long-term debt | 49,500,000 | 5.50 | | 9,000,000 | 6.00 | | 8,250,000 |
| Invested capital | 90,750,000 | 5.50 | | 16,500,000 | 5.50 | | 16,500,000 |
| CTA account (loss) | - | | | - | | $ | (1,375,000) |
| Total | 165,000,000 | | $ | 30,000,000 | | $ | 27,500,000 |

| a. Calculation of Actg Exposures: | Egyptian pounds | | December 31st 5.50 | | End of Quarter 6.00 |
|---|---|---|---|---|---|
| Exposed assets (all assets) | 165,000,000 | $ | 30,000,000 | $ | 27,500,000 |
| Less exposed liabilities (c.liabs + lt debt | (74,250,000) | | (13,500,000) | | (12,375,000) |
| Net exposure | 90,750,000 | $ | 16,500,000 | $ | 15,125,000 |

**b. Change in translation exposure: Gain (Loss)** $ (1,375,000)

Alternatively, the translation loss arising from the fall in the value of the peso Uruaguayo can be found as follows:

| | | |
|---|---|---|
| Net exposed assets (US$) | $ | 16,500,000 |
| Percentage change in the value of the $U | | -8.3% |
| Translation gain (loss) | $ | (1,375,000) |

## Problem 10.4 Trident Europe (A)

**Translation Using the Current Rate Method: euro depreciates from $1.2000/euro to $0.9000/euro.**

| Balance Sheet of Egyptian Ingot, Ltd. | | Just before devaluation | | | Just after devaluation | | |
|---|---|---|---|---|---|---|---|
| | Euros | Exchange Rate | | Translated Accounts | Exchange Rate | | Translated Accounts |
| **Assets** | **Statement** | **(US$/euro)** | | **US dollars** | **(US$/euro)** | | **US dollars** |
| Cash | 1,600,000 | 1.2000 | $ | 1,920,000 | 0.9000 | $ | 1,440,000 |
| Accounts receivable | 3,200,000 | 1.2000 | | 3,840,000 | 0.9000 | | 2,880,000 |
| Inventory | 2,400,000 | 1.2000 | | 2,880,000 | 0.9000 | | 2,160,000 |
| Net plant & equipment | 4,800,000 | 1.2000 | | 5,760,000 | 0.9000 | | 4,320,000 |
| Total | 12,000,000 | | $ | 14,400,000 | | $ | 10,800,000 |
| **Liabilities & Net Worth** | | | | | | | |
| Accounts payable | 800,000 | 1.2000 | $ | 960,000 | 0.9000 | $ | 720,000 |
| Short-term bank debt | 1,600,000 | 1.2000 | | 1,920,000 | 0.9000 | | 1,440,000 |
| Long-term debt | 1,600,000 | 1.2000 | | 1,920,000 | 0.9000 | | 1,440,000 |
| Common stock | 1,800,000 | 1.2760 | | 2,296,800 | 1.2760 | | 2,296,800 |
| Retained earnings | 6,200,000 | 1.2000 | | 7,440,000 | 1.2000 | | 7,440,000 |
| CTA account (loss) | - | | $ | (136,800) | | $ | (2,536,800) |
| Total | 12,000,000 | | $ | 14,400,000 | | $ | 10,800,000 |

| **a. The translation gain (loss) is:** | | |
|---|---|---|
| | $ | (2,536,800) |
| | | 136,800 |
| | $ | (2,400,000) |

b. The translation gain (loss) for the year is added to the balance in the Cumulative Translation adjustment account, which is carried as a separate balance sheet account within the equity section of the consolidated balance sheet. The loss does not pass through the income statement under the current rate method in which the currency of the foreign subsidiary is a local currency functional.

## Problem 10.5 Trident Europe (B)

**Translation Using the Temporal Method: euro depreciates from $1.2000/euro to $0.9000/euro.**

| Balance Sheet of Egyptian Ingot, Ltd. | | Just before devaluation | | | Just after devaluation | | |
|---|---|---|---|---|---|---|---|
| | | | | Translated | | | Translated |
| | Euros | Exchange Rate | | Accounts | Exchange Rate | | Accounts |
| **Assets** | **Statement** | **(US$/euro)** | | **(US dollars)** | **(US$/euro)** | | **(US dollars)** |
| Cash | 1,600,000 | 1.2000 | $ | 1,920,000 | 0.9000 | $ | 1,440,000 |
| Accounts receivable | 3,200,000 | 1.2000 | | 3,840,000 | 0.9000 | | 2,880,000 |
| Inventory | 2,400,000 | 1.2180 | | 2,923,200 | 1.2180 | | 2,923,200 |
| Net plant & equipment | 4,800,000 | 1.2760 | | 6,124,800 | 1.2760 | | 6,124,800 |
| Total | 12,000,000 | | $ | 14,808,000 | | $ | 13,368,000 |
| | | | | | | | |
| **Liabilities & Net Worth** | | | | | | | |
| Accounts payable | 800,000 | 1.2000 | $ | 960,000 | 0.9000 | $ | 720,000 |
| Short-term bank debt | 1,600,000 | 1.2000 | | 1,920,000 | 0.9000 | | 1,440,000 |
| Long-term debt | 1,600,000 | 1.2000 | | 1,920,000 | 0.9000 | | 1,440,000 |
| Common stock | 1,800,000 | 1.2760 | | 2,296,800 | 1.2760 | | 2,296,800 |
| Retained earnings | 6,200,000 | 1.2437 | | 7,711,200 | 1.2437 | | 7,711,200 |
| CTA account (loss) | - | | $ | (0) | | $ | (240,000) |
| Total | 12,000,000 | | $ | 14,808,000 | | $ | 13,368,000 |

**a. The translation gain (loss) is:**

| | | |
|---|---|---|
| | $ | (240,000) |
| | | 0 |
| | $ | (240,000) |

b. Under the Temporal Method, the translation loss of $240,000 would be closed into retained earnings through the income statement, rather than as a separate line item. It is shown as a separate line item above for pedagogical purposes only. Actual year-end retained earnings would be $7,711,200 - $240,000 = $7,471,200.

c. The translation gain (loss) differs from the Current Rate Method because "exposed assets" under the Current Rate Method are larger than under the temporal method by the amount of inventory and net plant & equipment.

## Problem 10.6 Trident Europe (C)

**Translation Using the Current Rate Method: euro appreciates from $1.2000/euro to $1.5000/euro.**

| **Balance Sheet of Egyptian Ingot, Ltd.** | | **Just before revaluation** | | | **Just after revaluation** | | |
|---|---|---|---|---|---|---|---|
| | **Euros** | **Exchange Rate** | | **Translated Accounts** | **Exchange Rate** | | **Translated Accounts** |
| **Assets** | **Statement** | **(US$/euro)** | | **US dollars** | **(US$/euro)** | | **US dollars** |
| Cash | 1,600,000 | 1.2000 | $ | 1,920,000 | 1.5000 | $ | 2,400,000 |
| Accounts receivable | 3,200,000 | 1.2000 | | 3,840,000 | 1.5000 | | 4,800,000 |
| Inventory | 2,400,000 | 1.2000 | | 2,880,000 | 1.5000 | | 3,600,000 |
| Net plant & equipment | 4,800,000 | 1.2000 | | 5,760,000 | 1.5000 | | 7,200,000 |
| Total | 12,000,000 | | $ | 14,400,000 | | $ | 18,000,000 |
| | | | | | | | |
| **Liabilities & Net Worth** | | | | | | | |
| Accounts payable | 800,000 | 1.2000 | $ | 960,000 | 1.5000 | $ | 1,200,000 |
| Short-term bank debt | 1,600,000 | 1.2000 | | 1,920,000 | 1.5000 | | 2,400,000 |
| Long-term debt | 1,600,000 | 1.2000 | | 1,920,000 | 1.5000 | | 2,400,000 |
| Common stock | 1,800,000 | 1.2760 | | 2,296,800 | 1.2760 | | 2,296,800 |
| Retained earnings | 6,200,000 | 1.2000 | | 7,440,000 | 1.2000 | | 7,440,000 |
| CTA account (loss) | - | | $ | (136,800) | | $ | 2,263,200 |
| Total | 12,000,000 | | $ | 14,400,000 | | $ | 18,000,000 |

**a. The translation gain (loss) is:**

| | | |
|---|---|---|
| | $ | 2,263,200 |
| | | 136,800 |
| | $ | 2,400,000 |

b. The translation gain for the year is added to the balance in the Cumulative Translation adjustment account, which is carried as a separate balance sheet account within the equity section of the consolidated balance sheet. The gain does not pass through the income statement under the current rate method in which the currency of the foreign subsidiary is a local currency functional.

## Problem 10.7 Trident Europe (D)

**Translation Using the Temporal Method: euro appreciates from $1.2000/euro to $1.5000/euro.**

| Balance Sheet of Egyptian Ingot, Ltd. | | Just before revaluation | | | Just after revaluation | | |
|---|---|---|---|---|---|---|---|
| Assets | Euros Statement | Exchange Rate (US$/euro) | | Translated Accounts (US dollars) | Exchange Rate (US$/euro) | | Translated Accounts (US dollars) |
| Cash | 1,600,000 | 1.2000 | $ | 1,920,000 | 1.5000 | $ | 2,400,000 |
| Accounts receivable | 3,200,000 | 1.2000 | | 3,840,000 | 1.5000 | | 4,800,000 |
| Inventory | 2,400,000 | 1.2180 | | 2,923,200 | 1.2180 | | 2,923,200 |
| Net plant & equipment | 4,800,000 | 1.2760 | | 6,124,800 | 1.2760 | | 6,124,800 |
| Total | 12,000,000 | | $ | 14,808,000 | | $ | 16,248,000 |
| | | | | | | | |
| **Liabilities & Net Worth** | | | | | | | |
| Accounts payable | 800,000 | 1.2000 | $ | 960,000 | 1.5000 | $ | 1,200,000 |
| Short-term bank debt | 1,600,000 | 1.2000 | | 1,920,000 | 1.5000 | | 2,400,000 |
| Long-term debt | 1,600,000 | 1.2000 | | 1,920,000 | 1.5000 | | 2,400,000 |
| Common stock | 1,800,000 | 1.2760 | | 2,296,800 | 1.2760 | | 2,296,800 |
| Retained earnings | 6,200,000 | 1.2437 | | 7,711,200 | 1.2437 | | 7,711,200 |
| CTA account (loss) | - | | $ | (0) | | $ | 240,000 |
| Total | 12,000,000 | | $ | 14,808,000 | | $ | 16,248,000 |

**a. The translation gain (loss) is:**

| | | |
|---|---|---|
| | $ | 240,000 |
| | | 0 |
| | $ | 240,000 |

b. Under the Temporal Method, the translation loss of $240,000 would be closed into retained earnings through the income statement, rather than as a separate line item. It is shown as a separate line item above for pedagogical purposes only. Actual year-end retained earnings would be $7,711,200 - $240,000 = $7,471,200.

c. The translation gain (loss) differs from the Current Rate Method because "exposed assets" under the Current Rate Method are larger than under the temporal method by the amount of inventory and net plant & equipment.

## MINI-CASE: HEDGING THE EURO AWAY

1. **Do you believe multinational firms should hedge their reported earnings?**

   There is the "academic" answer and the "business-in-practice" answer. Academia has always taken a firm stand that issues which do not affect cash flows of any kind directly, including tax obligations, should not be the subject of resource-using managerial action. But business-in-practice has always emphasized that the markets respond quite regularly to earnings levels, regardless of the cause of the change in earnings. If the analysts and investor public in general understood when a multinational company reported changes in consolidated earnings as a result of translation, and they concluded these were not real changes in earnings or cash flows, then "no" a multinational firm should not hedge reported earnings. The question is whether that is the world we live in.

2. **What exactly would the firm have to do in order to actually hedge the reported earnings of its European subsidiary for the coming quarter?**

   A U.S.-based firm wishing to hedge its reported European earnings for the coming quarter would need to first forecast its expected earnings in euros. This can be done by most companies with some degree of accuracy several months in advance. Those euro earnings could then be hedged with either a forward contract (sell euros forward) an option (put option on euros), or a balance sheet hedge (specific currency-denominated debt).

3. **Do you believe an investor should evaluate earnings differently depending on whether the reported earnings were before or after hedging?**

   An investor would ideally like to know and differentiate the types or categories of earnings which make up reported earnings. For example, changes in the pure euro earnings of European operations would tell the investor about the company's relative competitive performance in the European marketplace. The fact that those earnings may be "hedged" and therefore protected against exchange rate losses through translation would tell more about the company's centralized corporate management system and its aggressiveness (in hedging reported earnings), than it would about the company's core competencies in business.

4. **Does hedging reported earnings reduce their transparency, an increasing concern since the Enron debacle?**

   There is a distinction between actions taken and disclosure. Most of modern corporate financial and market theory focuses on giving investors in the marketplace adequate and appropriate information so that they may make their own decisions as to whether the firm's performance is appropriate and adequate. There is arguably nothing wrong with hedging reported earnings as long as the firm openly discloses that is what they have and will be doing going forward, allowing the investor to differentiate what was earned – for example in euros – and what was reported in consolidation results are earnings after hedging.

## CHAPTER 11. GLOBAL COST AND AVAILABILITY OF CAPITAL

*Questions*

### 11-1. Benefits

Two benefits may be considered major: Lower cost and greater access to new capital.

### 11-2. Illiquid markets

An illiquid market is one in which it is difficult to buy or sell shares, and especially an abnormally large number of shares, without a major change in price. From a company perspective, an illiquid market is one in which it is difficult to raise new capital because there are insufficient buyers for a reasonably sized offering. From an investors perspective, an illiquid market means that the investor will have difficulty selling any shares owned without a major drop in price.

### 11-3. Segmented markets

If all capital markets are fully integrated, securities of comparable expected return and risk should have the same required rate of return in each national market after adjusting for foreign exchange risk and political risk. In a *segmented market* capital market segmentation is a financial market imperfection caused mainly by government constraints, institutional practices, and investor perceptions. In a segmented market shares of stock are priced at levels that ignore valuation in major world markets, with the consequence that prices in the segmented market, relative to the value of the underlying shares, may be greatly at odds with prices and values in world markets in general.

### 11-4. WACC

The weighted average cost of capital is normally viewed as the weighted average of the cost of equity and the cost of debt. They are combined, in words and symbols as follows:

| Overall cost of of capital | = | Cost of equity | Weight of equity | + | Cost of debt | After-tax consequence | Weight of debt. |
|---|---|---|---|---|---|---|---|
| $K_{WACC}$ | = | $k_e$ | E/V | + | $k_d$ | (1-t) | D/V |

$k_{WACC}$ represents the overall cost of capital.

$k_e$ represents the cost of equity.

E/V represents the weight of equity within the total capital section of the balance sheet. E is the amount of equity, and V is the sum of equity and debt capital.

$k_d$ represents the cost of debt.

(1-t) means 1 minus the tax rate, such that if the tax rate is 40%, (1-t) will equal 60%. In other words, (1-t) is a factor which changes a pre-tax cost into the cost after adjustment for income taxes.

D/V represents the weight of debt within the total capital section of the balance sheet. D is the amount of debt, and V is the sum of equity and debt. Note that E/V plus D/V should add to the number 1, that is, to 100%.

### 11-5. Capital structure goal

No, the firm should strive to find the lowest weighted average cost of capital (WACC), which is a blend of the product and sum of three variables: One, certainly, is to seek the lowest cost of equity capital. However the other two are to seek the lowest cost of debt and to find a near-optimal mix of debt and equity so that the weighted average of the two costs is lowest. The overall goal of the firm is to maximize the sum of capital gains and dividend even if that requires using a higher cost of capital then its minimum cost.

### 11-6. Beta

*Beta* is a measure of the systematic risk of a firm, where "systematic risk" means that risk that cannot be diversified away. *Beta* measures the amount of fluctuation expected in a firm's share price, *relative to* the stock market as a whole. Thus a *beta* of 0.8 would indicate an expectation that the share price of a given company would rise or fall at 80% of the rise or fall in the stock market in general. The stock is expected to be less volatile than the market as a whole. A *beta* of 1.6 would indicate an expectation that the share price of a given company would rise or fall at 60% more that the rise or fall in the market. If the market rose, say, 20% during a year, a stock with a *beta* of 1.6 would be expected to rise (0.20)(1.6) = 0.32, or 32%.

### 11-7. Systematic and unsystematic risk

*Systematic risk* is the risk of share price changes that can not be avoided by diversification. In other words, it is the risk that the stock market as a whole will rise or fall and the price of shares of an individual company will rise and fall with the market. Systematic risk is sometimes called *market risk.*

*Unsystematic risk* is risk that can be avoided by diversification. It arises because some of the characteristics of a given company are peculiar to that company, causing it to perform in a way that differs from the performance of the market as a whole. Unsystematic risk is also called unique risk, residual risk, specific risk, or diversifiable risk.

### 11-8. Sourcing abroad

The goal is to minimize the weighted average cost of capital (WACC), which can be accomplished in part by lowering either the cost of equity or the cost of debt – or both.

The cost of equity might be lowered by positioning trading in a multinational's share of stock so that they appeal to foreigners as well as local investors. Investors presumably select shares of stock that will lower the risk in their portfolios. Buying foreign shares whose price movement is not correlated with domestic price movements lowers systematic risk in the portfolio, and consequently foreign investors may be willing to pay more for foreign shares than domestic investors.

The cost of debt may be lower in an international offering because world interest rate levels may be below those of a segmented capital market after controlling for foreign exchange risk, because competition is greater.

### 11-9. WACC for a MNE

What questions might one ask if trying to find out if a MNE has a lower cost of capital than a domestic-only enterprise:

a. Can the MNE achieve an optimal capital structure with some of the international components having a lower cost than comparable domestic components?

b. Does being multinational change the systematic risk of the company?

c. Is additional capital available from foreign sources in amounts not easily available within the home country at the time additional capital is needed?

d. What is the level of the optimal capital budget? The so-called "riddle" showed that at high capital budget levels MNEs have lower costs of capital. At low capital budget levels domestic firms may have lower cost of capital than MNEs.

**11-10. Novo and Acer**

This is a student project question. It is intentionally constructed to push the student to do web-based research on the subject firm (Acer Group, Taiwan), and to seriously consider the technical aspects of globalizing the cost and availability of capital.

The Acer Group was chosen for a number of reasons:

1. It is a major non-U.S. multinational firm, with production facilities in a number of countries. It must compete with other world computer manufacturers, such as Dell, Compaq, and IBM.
2. After trading only on the Taiwan Stock Exchange in its early years, shares were listed in both Singapore and London (as Global Depository Receipts.) starting in 1995.
3. Acer publishes a very detailed annual report, which is available from its web site.

**11-11. Differing premia**

The difference in equity premia reflect differences in perceived risk and growth rates for countries as well as firms located in those countries. A high equity risk premium for a country suggests that firms located there would have a higher cost of equity and WACC. But all costs of capital, including equity risk premia, are also currency specific (remember, interest rates reflect the currency environments in which they reside), making a direct comparison difficult at best.

## 11-12. Equity outlook

Even though individual investors may have individual investment horizons of about 20 years, picking a 20-year period to use as a base for expectations is risky because individual 20-yearperiods during the 19th century showed great variations. (1930-1950 was substantially different from 1980-2000!) Hence selecting a 20-year interval would most likely not be useful, contrary to the suggestion in the question.

Nevertheless, the arithmetic mean is probably more useful than the geometric mean because the latter considers only the first and last year of the interval, and the shorter the time period the greater the chance that either the first or the last year was highly atypical.. Atypical first or last years greatly distorts the geometric mean.

## 11-13. Equity premiums and competitive advantage

If the lower premia over the cost of risk-free debt results in a lower total cost of equity capital, a MNE could take advantage of the differential equity risk premia by raising more equity capital in those countries where the premia are lowest.

## 11-14. Explaining differences in equity premia

The mean risk premium for the entire 20th century is probably lower in Denmark because Danish domestic investors regard local publicly traded companies as being of low risk – meaning only slightly riskier than debt. This in turn would result from governmental policies that tend to protect local industries, One would have to consider this in the context of the entire 20th century, where the earliest two-thirds or so were years in which private common stock ownership was not as common as in the latter third, and where such common stock ownership as did exist was held and traded only by Danish investors, not by foreigners.

The mean risk premium for the 20th century for Japan would be influenced by the lack of public ownership of shares of stock in the Meiji, Taisho, and early Showa years (well into the post World War II era). After World War II artificially low interest rates were used as a device to finance reconstruction and Japanese rapid economic growth through 1990, as well as its attempt to recover from the long-lived depression that started in 1990. If the cost of equity was "normal," abnormally low interest rtes would result in the premium, the difference between cost of equity and the risk-free interest rate, being large.

*Problems*

**11-1. Schmidt Company**

The cost of equity capital for Schmidt is:

$$k_e = k_{rf} + B(k_m - k_{rf}) = 0.04 + 1.3(0.14 - 0.04) = 0.1700,$$

or 17.00%. Schmidt's weighted average cost of capital is:

$$k_{WACC} = k_e(E/V) + k_d(1 - t)(D/V)$$

$$k_{WACC} = (0.1700)(0.70) + (0.06)(0.70)(0.30) = 0.1316 \text{ or } 13.16\%$$

| Problem 11.1 Schmidt Company | |
|---|---|
| **What is Schmidt's weighted average cost of capital?** | |
| | |
| **Assumptions** | **Values** |
| Schmidt's beta | **1.30** |
| Cost of debt, before tax | **6.000%** |
| Risk-free rate of interest | **4.000%** |
| Corporate income tax rate | **30.000%** |
| General return on market portfolio | **14.000%** |
| Optimal capital structure: | |
| Proportion of debt | **30%** |
| Proportion of equity | **70%** |
| | |
| **Calculation of the WACC** | |
| Cost of debt, after-tax | **4.200%** |
| Cost of equity, after-tax | **17.000%** |
| | |
| **WACC** | **13.160%** |

## Problem 11.2 Sunshine Pipelines Inc.

| Assumptions | Values |
|---|---|
| Combined federal and state tax rate | 40% |
| Desired capital structure: | |
| Proportion debt | 50% |
| Proportion equity | 50% |
| Capital to be raised | $ 120,000,000 |

| Costs of Raising Capital in the Market | Cost of Domestic Equity | Cost of Domestic Debt | Cost of European Equity | Cost of European Debt |
|---|---|---|---|---|
| Up to $40 million of new capital | 12% | 8% | 14% | 6% |
| $41 million to $80 million of new capital | 18% | 12% | 16% | 10% |
| Above $80 million | 22% | 16% | 24% | 18% |

| a. To raise $120,000,000 | Debt Market | Debt Cost | Equity Market | Equity Cost | Incremental WACC |
|---|---|---|---|---|---|
| First $40,000,000 | European | 6.00% | Domestic | 12.00% | 7.80% |
| Second $40,000,000 | European | 10.00% | European | 16.00% | 11.00% |
| Third $40,000,000 | Domestic | 16.00% | Domestic | 22.00% | 15.80% |
| Weighted average cost | | 10.67% (equal weights) | | 16.67% (equal weights) | 11.53% |

| b. To raise $60,000,000 | Debt Market | Debt Cost | Equity Market | Equity Cost | Incremental WACC |
|---|---|---|---|---|---|
| First $40,000,000 | European | 6.00% | Domestic | 12.00% | 7.80% |
| Additional $20,000,000 | European | 10.00% | European | 16.00% | 11.00% |
| Weighted average cost | | 7.33% (2/3 & 1/3 weights) | | 13.33% (2/3 & 1/3 weights) | 8.87% |

## Problem 11.3 Trident's Cost of Equity

**What is Trident's cost of equity?**

| **Original assumptions in Chapter** | **Values** |
|---|---|
| Trident's beta | **1.20** |
| Cost of debt, before tax | **8.000%** |
| Risk-free rate of interest | **5.000%** |
| Corporate income tax rate | **35.000%** |
| General return on market portfolio | **15.000%** |
| Optimal capital structure: | |
| Proportion of debt | **40%** |
| Proportion of equity | **60%** |
| | |
| **Trident's original cost of equity** | **17.000%** |
| | |
| **a. US Treasury bond rate rises to** | **5.500%** |
| Trident's cost of equity is now | **16.900%** |
| | |
| **b. Trident's beta rises to** | **1.50** |
| Trident's cost of equity is now | **20.000%** |
| | |
| **c. Market risk premium reduced from 10% to** | **6.000%** |
| Trident's cost of equity is now | **12.200%** |
| | |
| **d. Combined impact on cost of equity if:** | |
| Treasury bond rate is | **5.500%** |
| Trident's beta is | **1.50** |
| Market risk premium reduced from 10% to | **6.000%** |
| Trident's cost of equity is now | **14.500%** |

## Problem 11.4 Trident's Cost of Debt

**What is Trident's cost of debt?**

| **Original assumptions in Chapter** | **Values** |
|---|---|
| Trident's beta | **1.20** |
| Cost of debt, before tax | **8.000%** |
| Risk-free rate of interest | **5.000%** |
| Corporate income tax rate | **35.000%** |
| General return on market portfolio | **15.000%** |
| Optimal capital structure: | |
| Proportion of debt | **40%** |
| Proportion of equity | **60%** |
| | |
| **Trident's original cost of debt, after-tax** | **5.200%** |
| | |
| **a. Trident's debt is an average of:** | |
| One-half at | **6.000%** |
| One-half at | **10.000%** |
| Average cost of debt | **8.000%** |
| Average cost of debt, after-tax | **5.200%** |
| | |
| **b. Trident's long-term debt component cost changes** | |
| One-half at | **6.000%** |
| One-half at | **9.000%** |
| Average cost of debt | **7.500%** |
| Average cost of debt, after-tax | **7.110%** |
| | |
| **c. US corporate tax rate changes to** | **30.000%** |
| Average cost of debt, after-tax | **5.600%** |

## Problem 11.5 Trident's Weighted Average Cost of Capital

**What is Trident's weighted average cost of capital?**

| **Original assumptions in Chapter** | **Values** |
|---|---|
| Trident's beta | **1.20** |
| Cost of debt, before tax | **8.000%** |
| Risk-free rate of interest | **5.000%** |
| Corporate income tax rate | **35.000%** |
| General return on market portfolio | **15.000%** |
| Optimal capital structure: | |
| Proportion of debt | **40%** |
| Proportion of equity | **60%** |
| | |
| **Trident's original cost of capital** | |
| Cost of equity | **17.000%** |
| Cost of debt | **5.200%** |
| WACC | **12.280%** |
| | |
| **a. Desired debt proportion rises from 40% to** | **50%** |
| Trident's WACC is now | **11.100%** |
| | |
| **b. Desired debt proportion falls from 40% to** | **30%** |
| Trident's cost of equity is now | **13.460%** |
| | |
| **c. Combined impact on cost of capital of:** | |
| Desired debt rises from 40% to | **50%** |
| Average cost of debt rises to | **8.500%** |
| Trident's beta rises to | **1.40** |
| | |
| Cost of equity | **19.000%** |
| Cost of debt, after-tax | **5.525%** |
| **WACC** | **12.263%** |

## MINI-CASE: BANG & OLUFSEN & PHILIPS N.V.

1. **Why might an industrial purchaser, such as Philips, be willing to pay a higher price for B&O's stock than a typical international portfolio investor?**

   Philip's expected to receive operating synergies from B&O that would improve Philips' own operating performance and not just B&O's operating performance. If B&O's operating performance also improved as a result of the purchase, that would create additional benefits of significant value to Philips.

   An international portfolio investor would price B&O's stock based on the normal risk versus return tradeoff. Such an investor could not anticipate synergies for B&O from a strategic alliance in the future. Clearly, the international investor would not see the 'value' in B&O which Philips would see.

2. **What are the likely synergies that both Philip's and B&O expected to achieve through their strategic alliance?**

   The operating synergies for Philips were:

   - gaining a better position in the upscale consumer electronics market than it had been unable to attain on its own
   - guaranteeing that B&O would continue to be a major purchaser of components from Philips
   - maintaining a political ally in the EU's effort to defend the few remaining European-based consumer electronics firms from Japanese competitors. (B&O itself was a potential acquisition target of Japanese competitors.)

   The operating synergies for B&O were:

   - gaining more rapid access to Philips' new technology discoveries
   - receiving assistance from Philips in converting its technology into B&O product applications
   - guarantee of timely delivery of components at large volume discounts from Philips itself
   - access to Philips large network of suppliers under terms enjoyed by Philips
   - gaining an equity infusion from Philips to strengthen its own shaky financial position

***Postscript:*** B&O and Philips eventually realized their expected synergies. In fact, it went so well for B&O that the firm eventually bought back the 25% ownership held by Philips while renewing the strategic alliance.

3. **What are the advantages and disadvantages to B&O of using a strategic alliance equity infusion from Philips compared to attracting international portfolio investors, assuming that both alternatives would lead to a lower cost and greater availability of capital?**

   - The equity infusion from Philips has minimal up-front costs, mainly the negotiating time
   - The 35% premium in B&O's stock price from its strategic alliance was probably much higher than it could have achieved with international portfolio investors.
   - In order to attract international portfolio investors, and retain them as investors, B&O would have a very high initial cost. This would include the cost of preparing a prospectus, using international accounting principles and level of disclosure, and the cost of investor relations.
   - International portfolio investors would not bring any operating synergies to B&O like those offered by Philips.

## Chapter 12. Sourcing Equity Globally

*Questions*

### 12-1. Trident's capital strategy

A variety of responses to this question are both possible and reasonable. (See Exhibit 12.1.)

1. *Locate a credible international investment banker.* Generally speaking, firms such as Trident that initially excel in making and selling a product domestically, and that initially finance their operations domestically, do not have in-house expertise in dealing with foreign capital markets. Investment bankers can help the firm navigate the institutional barriers and requirements needed and avoid major pitfalls.

2. *List bonds in less liquid markets.* This is the equivalent of a first step to "get your toes wet." Additionally it is a first step in creating an awareness of the firm in foreign markets.

3. *Sell a bond issue in a target foreign capital market and/or in the eurobond market.* Bonds are more easily sold than new shares of stock, so this step is one additional operation to make the firm better acquainted to foreign investors.

4. *List existing equity shares in a less liquid foreign market.* This is the next logical step in making foreign investors aware of the firm and its investment characteristics. Except in the rare instance of a firm of world-wide prominence and recognition, an initial listing in New York or London is probably not possible at this point. This step also gives the firm perspective and experience on such matters as complying with exchange-determined requirements on public disclosure of corporate information.

5. *Sell new equity shares in the less liquid market.* This is simply a follow-on to the previous step which (1) provides the firm with additional capital, (2) creates a greater awareness of the firm in foreign markets, and (3) "tests the water" to see if foreign investors are in fact interested in the firm. It also expands the number of foreign investors, thus creating a pool of investors such that trading on a more liquid market is nearer to possibility.

6. *List equity shares on a liquid major world exchange – the "target" exchange.* This is the ultimate objective in creating a body of global investors aware of the firm and its characteristics. This step, in effect, creates the global cost of equity capital.

7. *Sell equity shares in the global market.* Step (6) above globalizes the firm's cost of equity capital; however, the firm has net yet taken advantage of this globalization. Selling new shares in the global market is the step that the firm uses its presumably lower cost of equity capital to raise additional capital at a lower cost.

### 12-2. Depositary receipts

A *depositary receipt* is a negotiable certificate issued by a bank to represent the deposit of underlying shares of stock held in trust at a foreign custodian bank. As such, it is an equity security with a claim on the underlying shares, which security may be traded in a foreign stock market.

Depositary receipts exist so that investors in one market may buy, hold, or sell foreign shares without the complexities of transferring or holding securities in a foreign country. Investors need not deal with foreign language reports and other information, receive foreign currency dividends, or have to probate part of an estate in a foreign court, among other advantages.

## 12-3. ADRs

An ADR is an *American Depositary Receipt*, which is the form of depositary receipts listed and traded in various U.S. markets. ADRs are issued by commercial banks operating in the United States, and are based on deposits of the underlying securities held in trust by banks in the country in which foreign company is headquartered

## 12-4. Arbitrage

*Arbitrage* is the simultaneous buying and selling of a security (or a commodity) in different markets in order to make an immediate risk-free profit from price differences between the two markets. If share prices at home and abroad get out of line with each other, depositary receipt holders may sell their shares in that market where the price is higher. They may also buy the underlying shares if the foreign market price is below the equivalent depositary receipt price at home. The possibility of arbitrage tends to keep foreign and domestic prices close to being identical, which in turn means that the possibility of arbitrage tends to provide the best price in both markets.

## 12-5. Sponsorship

*Sponsored* ADRs are created at the request of a foreign firm wishing its shares to be traded in the United States. The firm applies to the Securities and Exchange Commission (SEC) and a U.S. bank for registration and issuance of ADRs. The foreign firm pays all costs of creating such sponsored ADRs.

*Unsponsored* ADRs are issued at the request of U.S. investors or U.S. securities firm because of their interest in an ability to trade in the foreign shares on a depositary receipt basis. Unsponsored ADRs must be approved by the foreign firm whose shares are involved.

## 12-6. ADR levels

The three levels differ in the degree of compliance with U.S. accounting standards and S.E.C. registration requirements. Thus they also differ in terms of the cost to the foreign firm of complying with these requirements and the expected degree of liquidity.

*Level I* compliance allows ADR trading on the U.S. over-the-counter market without being registered with the SEC As such, it is least costly and also least likely to have any impact on the liquidity of the shares.

*Level II* compliance allows ADR trading on organized exchanges, such as the New York Stock Exchange and American Stock Exchange, as well as trading on that portion of the equity markets quoted on the NASDAQ (National Association of Securities Dealers Automated Quotation) quotation system. Such ADRs are fully registered with the SEC Trading liquidity is increased.

*Level III* compliance allows the sale of new issues of shares to the U.S. investing public, and in turn means that the foreign financial statements must be issued in a form that fully complies with U.S. generally accepted accounting practices. Trading liquidity is increased and the firm's share price and availability are more fully freed from the influence of a segmented market at home.

## 12-7. Listing objectives

By cross listing in a foreign stock market a firm tries to accomplish one or more of the following:

1. Improve the liquidity of its existing shares and support a liquid secondary market for new equity issues in foreign markets.

2. Increase its share price by overcoming mispricing in a segmented and illiquid home capital market.

3. Increase the firm's visibility and political acceptance to its customers, suppliers, creditors, and host governments.

4. Establish a secondary market for shares used to acquire other firms in the host market.

5. Create a secondary market for shares than can be used to compensate local management and employees of foreign subsidiaries.

## 12-8. Degrees of liquidity

In an *illiquid* market, any significant number of shares may not be purchased or sold without such purchase or sale influencing the share price. At the other extreme, in a *fully liquid* market, large numbers of shares may be sold without the size of the order having more than a minimal impact on share prices. In other words, these are the two extreme poles where an order may be executed with or without having significant effect on market quotations.

A *semi-liquid* market, quite obviously, is a point between these extremes – the purchase or sale of a reasonable numbers of shares of stock can be accomplished with some impact on share price.

## 12-9. Private placement

A private placement under SEC Rule 144a is the sale of a new issue of securities to a small set of qualified institutional buyers (QIBs), such as insurance companies and investment companies. Under SEC Rule 144a, qualified institutional buyers may trade privately placed securities without the previously required holding period and without SEC registration. Foreign firms, especially new or rapidly growing foreign firms, are likely to use the Rule 144a route to raise capital in the United States because they do not need to spend the time and money that would be required for a fully-registered U.S. offering.

## 12-10. Private equity

Private equity funds are usually limited partnerships of institutional and wealthy individual investors that have raised their capital in the most liquid capital markets, such as the United States. They are then able to invest their private equity funds in mature, family-owned foreign firms in emerging markets. Thus they provide funds for smaller, often family owned, firms that are more or less invisible to foreign investors, lack managerial depth, and are unable to fund the up-front costs of globalizing their cost of capital. The funds are useful for firms in emerging markets because they may invest directly without the costs of an SEC registration such as would be needed if the firms in emerging markets sought a public issue in one of the larger world capital markets.

## 12-11. Alternative approaches

A *directed public share issue* is an initial issue of shares of stock of a company sold to the investing public in a single foreign country. The issue is underwritten in whole or part by investment bankers in the country where the shares are to be sold. The issue may or may not be priced in the currency of the target market and the shares may or may not be cross-listed on a stock exchange in the target market.

A *euro equity issue* is an issue of shares sold anywhere in the world. Usually a *tranche,* that is, a segment of the total issue, is given to underwriters who are expected to resell the shares in their predetermined territories. Underwriters in the firm's home market also sell shares in that market.

Directed public share issues will be used when the issuer has the visibility and attractiveness to appeal to investors in the target market, while euro-equity issues are used when the issuer seeks to internationalize its cost of equity capital through a large share issue that is too big for any single national market.

## 12-12. Strategic alliances

A strategic alliance is a set of contractual agreements between two (or more) firms to operate some portion of their businesses in conjunction with each other. An example of a firm strategic alliance is Bang & Olufsen A/S, a strategic alliance created by Denmark's Bang & Olufsen and the Netherlands' Philips N.V. An example of a contractual agreement strategic alliance is the *One World* alliance between Aer Lingus, American Airlines, British Airways, Cathay Pacific, Finnair, Iberia Airlines, LanChile, Quantas, Quantas New Zealand, Dragon Air, Japan Airlines, Japan Asia Airways, and Swissair. In an informal sense, one might think of a strategic alliance as a cooperative agreement of some but not all of the functions of the partners.

A number of business reasons may compel firms to join in strategic alliances. From a financial point of view, some members of the alliance may have a lower cost of equity capital than others. These low-equity cost firms may thus be the vehicle through which funds needed for the alliance are raised.

## MINI-CASE: DEUTSCHE BANK'S GLOBAL REGISTERED SHARES

**1. Do you believe the differences between ADRs and GRSs are real or cosmetic? Why?**

The differences are real and not cosmetic for the following reasons:

a. GRSs are actual shares in Deutsche Bank (DB), identical to all other shares in DB. ADRs are only receipts that evidence the underlying actual shares in DB held in a depositary bank.

b. GRSs entitle the shareholder to have equal voting rights and access to rights offerings that are not always available to ADR holders.

c. GRSs can be traded, denominated, and quoted in local currency in any market. ADRs are limited to being denominated in U.S. dollars and are traded in the U.S. market.

d. GRSs have a flat $5 fee per trade regardless of the quantity of shares traded. This is an advantage if trades are being made in large blocks. The ADRs' trading costs are between 3 and 5 cents per share.

e. GRSs have no conversion fees, ADRs do have conversion fees.

f. Based on the past experience of DaimlerChrysler and seven other European companies that listed on the NYSE using ADRs, it appears that the initial cost of establishing the ADRs was lower than for the GRSs and their liquidity in the U.S. marketplace greater.

**2. Why do you think Deutsche Bank would proceed with a GRS listing when so many others have not?**

DB probably wanted to be perceived as a leader in establishing the GRS system as an alternative to ADRs that were already well known and established. By being the leader DB could build up the service business of its subsidiary, Registrar Services. Celanese was already using this service.

DB also probably wanted its share to trade globally rather than be concentrated mainly in Germany and the United States, which GRSs would be appropriate for.

**3. What do you think Deutsche Bank concluded from DaimlerChrysler's experience with GRSs?**

They probably concluded that GRSs needed to fight an uphill battle to overtake the liquidity available in the ADR market. The DaimlerChrysler experience was that the large majority of trading in GRSs gravitated to Germany. This was not a promising way to globalize DB's stock unless they could market their GRSs better in other markets.

## CHAPTER 13: OPTIMAL FINANCIAL STRUCTURE

*Questions*

### 13-1. Objective

The objective sought in pursuit of an optimal capital structure is a mix of debt and equity that minimizes a firm's weighted average cost of capital for a given level of business risk.

### 13-2. Varying debt proportions

*a.* *Cost of debt:* The cost of debt tends to remain low and constant for lower proportions of debt, up to about 30% debt and 70% equity. (The proportions will vary from industry to industry and company to company.) As a firm's debt moved from zero to about 30% markets tend to regard the additional debt as adding nothing to the financial risk of the firm and the firm's cost of debt remains constant. As debt increases above about 30%, financial market tend to view the debt of the firm as creating an increasing degree of financial risk, for which the market typically demands a higher rate of interest. This higher rate of interest is required on *all* debt, not just the marginal debt.

b. Cost of equity: If a firm has no debt, the cost of equity will be the return demanded (but not always achieved) by common shareholders who invest in the shares of stock. As the proportion of equity in the company decreases (and thus the proportion of debt increases), stockholders initially view the change in capital structure favorably, in that the benefits from modest to reasonable degrees of leverage outweigh the perceived slight increase in financial risk.

c. At the point where equity decreases to about 70% (meaning debt has increased to 30% or more), shareholder perceptions of financial risk tend to offset the expected gain from financial leverage, and the cost of equity starts to increase. As the proportion of equity continues to decrease (and the proportion of debt to increase), shareholders tend to view the amount of financial risk as increasing evermore, and the cost of equity rises sharply.

d. Weighted average cost of capital (WACC): WACC is the proportional weighting of the cost of equity and cost of debt lines. With no debt, the WACC is only the cost of equity. Were the firm to reach a point of 99.9% debt and 0.1% equity (from a practical point an impossibility), the WACC line would have to converge with the cost of debt line. At a 50% debt and 50% equity point, the WACC line would have to lie exactly between the cost of debt line and the cost of equity line. The objective in determining an optimal capital structure is to find the low point of the WACC line.

### 13-3. Availability of capital

The theory of optimal capital structure assumes that new debt and new equity funds can be raised in rough proportion to the point on the WACC lines that is lowest. If a multinational firm can raise funds in a separate, presumably foreign capital market at a lower cost for either component than is obtainable in its domestic capital market, that will lower the weighted average cost of capital.

### 13-4. Diversified cash flows

The dominant argument would be that an internationally diversified set of cash inflows would reduce cash flow risk because flows from several countries, or in several currencies, would have less than perfect correlation. I.e., at a time when cash inflows from Country A were falling, cash inflows from Country B might increase or, at the extreme, decrease at a lesser rate. Hence overall cash flows available to service debt are likely to be more constant, the risk to investors holding that debt diminished, and the interest cost of that debt lowered.

A contrary argument might be built around the idea that for a given industry or product line the world is so economically integrated that cash flows in different countries would be highly correlated. A counter argument also might be built around the fact that cash flows in a currency other than the currency needed for debt service are subject to a foreign exchange risk.

**13-5. Ex-post cost of borrowing**

The change from nominal cost at time of borrowing to market yield at a later date is caused by foreign exchange transaction exposure. This change has an impact on investors holding the bonds, but does not change in any way the ex-post cost of borrowing for the two entities. Deutsche Bank pays 9.59% per annum in deutschemarks for the life of this debt, and the Kingdom of Thailand pays 8.70% per annum in Thai baht for the life of its debt.

After the debt is sold, the borrower is locked in at the contractual rate. Investors are the ones that gain or lose. When the market yield on the Deutsche Bank debt fell from 9.59% to 7.24%, the bonds rose to a premium, price-wise, in the market. Investors in those bonds gained. When the market yield on the Thai bonds rose from 8.70% to 11.87%, the bonds fell in price and investors lost.

The implications for management are complex. Had Deutsche Bank delayed borrowing until market rates fell to 7.24% it would, of course, have benefited from the lower rate. However Deutsche Bank presumably needed the funds for operations at the time it did borrow, so this alternative is most likely impractical. The Kingdom of Thailand, of course, did benefit from borrowing when rates were lower.

From a practical point of view, Deutsche Bank should have had a call provision incorporated into the indenture of its bond issue. Thus as its rate of interest fell and the bonds tended to rise in price, Deutsche Bank could have "called" the bonds – that is, redeemed them early at a stated price that is typically 102% or 103% of par. Deutsche Bank could refinance at the lower current rate. I.e., Deutsche Bank would preserve the option to borrow at 7.24% and use the funds to retire the higher-costing 9.59% debt at a modest premium over par.

The Kingdom of Thailand has little it can do that is the opposite of the call provision available to Deutsche Bank. In fact, because it is paying the nominal 8.70% contracted for, it is better off than had it waited and then borrowed at 11.87%.

The overall conclusion is to include call provisions in debt expected to appreciate because of a fall in interest rates, and to borrow in a soft currency if possible.

**13-6. Local norms**

The main advantages of ascribing to local capital structure norms are:

a. Reduction of local criticism for having too high debt by local standards.
b. Easier to evaluate return on equity relative to local competitors.

c. Reminder to management that local operations should cover local costs of capital if resources are to be allocated properly.

The main disadvantages of ascribing to local capital structure norms are:

a. Loss of comparative advantage over local firm where local capital markets are imperfect.
b. Creation of illogical capital structure on parent's consolidated financial statement if all subsidiaries follow local standards.
c. Local capital structure may be cosmetic only because investors will look to parent and worldwide company for funds to service local debt.

**13-7. Argentina**

Had the pending bankruptcy of the Argentine subsidiary been the result of a business-caused failure, the argument for parent rescue would be strong. When, as in this case, the failure is caused by maladroit economic policies of the government, the moral case for paying off the subsidiary's debt is lacking.

If the parent did not intend to stay in or return to business in Argentina, it should probably let the local subsidiary go bankrupt and not pay the subsidiary's debt. This is the logical consequence of having separately incorporated subsidiaries, which creditors should fully understand. However if the parent intended to remain in or return to Argentina at some future date, it should probably pay the subsidiary's debt so as to benefit from a greater credit standing within Argentina in the future.

**13-8. Internal financing**

*Internal financing* refers to funds acquired from other entities within the multinational enterprise. Some of these are:

1. Funds derived from the parent, such as additional equity, cash loans, or leading or lagging payments to and from the parent.
2. Funds from sister subsidiaries, such as cash loans or leading or lagging intra-subsidiary payments.
3. Borrowing from capital markets with formal parent or sister subsidiary guarantees.
4. Funds generated internally from the operations of the subsidiary, such as retained earnings plus non-cash charges.

External financing refers to funds acquired directly from capital markets, without parent or sister subsidiary involvement. Some of these are:

1. Borrowing from sources in the host country.
2. Borrowing directly from sources in the parent's country or in other countries, without parent or sister subsidiary involvement. (Name recognition of the parent might help this, even though no parent guarantee is involved.)
3. Selling share of stock directly to local interests.
4. Entering into a joint venture so that funding from the joint venture partner comes into the enterprise.

### 13-9. Eurodollars

a. Yes. This is a U.S. dollar deposit held in a bank outside of the United States.
b. Yes. The fact that the London banking office is U.S. owned is irrelevant. The deposit is held in a banking facility in London.
c. Yes. The "Euro" in Eurodollars is historical in nature because the first offshore deposits were in Europe. However the term encompasses deposits in any bank outside of the United States, so a dollar deposit in Tokyo is a eurodollar deposit.
d. No. Because the deposit is held in a bank within the United States it is not a eurodollar. The European ownership of the deposit is irrelevant.
e. No. The deposit is held by a banking office in the United States, and the fact that the banking office is a branch of a European bank is irrelevant.
f. Yes. The U.S. dollar deposit is held in a bank outside the United States. See answer to number c. above.
g. No. The fact that the bank is not a U.S. bank is irrelevant. The deposit is held by a U.S. located banking office.
h. No. The name "euros" for Europe's new currency does not make euro deposits into eurodollar deposits.
i. No. This is not a eurodollar deposit because the currency is the euro, not the dollar. However it would be considered a *eurocurrency* deposit because it is a currency deposited outside of the country (or area, in the case of euros) of issue.
j. The answer to this is confusing. The deposit is in fact a *eurocurrency* deposit, as it is in a bank outside of the country of issue, and furthermore the deposit is of dollars – albeit of Australian rather than U.S. dollars. Because the term "eurodollars" universally refers to U.S. dollars on deposit outside of the United States, calling the offshore deposit of Australian dollars "eurodollars" would lead to confusion everywhere. The deposit would more appropriately be called "euro Australian dollars" or an "offshore deposit of Australian dollars."

### 13-10. Eurodollar deposits

Several reasons exist:

1. Interest earned on such deposits is greater than interest earned on deposits of the same risk and maturity within the United States.
2. The interest cost of borrowing eurodollars is less than the cost of borrowing dollars within the United States. Both this and the answer to 1. above are possible because the spread between bid and ask is smaller, this in turn being possible because the eurodollar (and eurocurrency) market is a wholesale market between banks and large institutions in which multiples of $1 million are normally traded.
3. Political risk for entities not friendly to the United States is reduced. Cuba under Fidel Castro, Iraq under Sadam Hussein, the Taliban and Al Qaeda all need or have needed dollars to conduct international business. Obviously none of these parties, nor parties similarly estranged from the United States, can deposit their dollars in the United States without a well-grounded fear that such accounts will be frozen. Hence financially astute enemies of the United States tend to keep their U.S. dollars in eurodollar form. Of course this is not without some risk, as the United States has prevailed upon many countries to freeze accounts deemed held by Al Qaeda cells.
4. A time zone advantage exists for certain industries in Europe, such as insurance companies, that need to transfer U.S. dollars during European, rather than U.S., business hours.

### 13-11. Euro-euros

*Euro-euro* (hyphen supplied by authors) is the obviously confusing generic name for a deposit of euros, Europe's new common currency, in a bank outside of the Euro zone. As of the current writing no better name has been devised and generally accepted for such an overseas deposit.

### 13-12. International debt instruments

Each of these compared to bank loans:

a. *Syndicated loans*. Syndication of loans allows a group of banks to spread the risk of a very large loan between themselves. Thus loans that would be too large for the risk taking capability of a single bank can be made.
b. *Euronotes*. Euronotes represent the conversion to security form (i.e., securitization) of loans. This technique allows non-bank financial institutions to join banks in providing funds to borrowing corporations and governments while, at the same time, providing liquidity in case the lender (the investor holding the notes) needs to liquidate its holdings. Because euronotes are typically medium term in maturity, such ability to liquidate a holding is important.
c. *Commercial Paper*. These are similar in most attributes to Euro-notes, except that maturities are typically very short – less than six months. The main advantage relative to bank notes is their liquidity.
d. *Euro-Medium Term Notes*. The distinguishing characteristic of these notes is that they are issued under a facility that allows continuous issuance, and they are usually sold directly rather than underwritten by a syndicate of investment bankers. Consequently they are much more flexible than either bank loans or euronotes.
e. *International bonds*. These are long-term bonds, which provide funds for much longer terms than are typically available from commercial banks.

### 13-13. Euro- versus foreign bonds

A *eurobond* is sold in countries other than the country in whose currency it is denominated and is not available to residents of that country. Consequently the bonds do not need to be registered in the country whose currency is being used.

A *foreign bond* is sold within the country in whose currency it is denominated, primarily to local investors – although some buyers may be from other countries. Hence it is registered and must comply with all disclosure requirements of that country.

### 13-14. Separation

In project financing, the project is a separate entity from its owners because of the (usually) large scale and high risk of the project. Consequently the owning corporations want to be free of the credit risk of the project, and creditors are forced to evaluate the project's cash flows by themselves without relying on the additional cash flows of the corporate owners.

### 13-15. Singular Project

One of the reasons for the use of project financing is that, projects financed in this manner tend to be long-lived, capital intensive, and singular. *Singular* means the project stands alone in terms of construction, operation, and size (capacity). *Stands alone,* in turn, means that the project operates as an entity separate from the operations of its parent corporations, with the latter often being suppliers or customers of the project.

### 13-16. Predictability

Another aspect of project financing is that it is used to finance projects with cash flow predictability. Third parties are usually committed to buying the output at fixed prices. This predictability of cash flows allows the proportion of debt to be relatively high, relative to equity.

### 13-17. Infinite lives

Investors engaged in project financing realize that they will receive only current cash flow from the project, but not appreciation. Under project financing, no cash flow is reinvested to seek growth. Given that investors may rely only on current cash flow, they want to know of a specific and finite terminal date at which the project will be wound up.

### 13-18. Maximizing present value

Like all investors, investors in project financing do seek to maximize the present value of their investment. However with no capital appreciation and no increase in cash flow other than what might have been predicted at the start of the project, "maximizing present value" means no more than taking the present value of the predictable cash flows and discounting them at the desired rate of return. If the net present value that results after the cash outflow is subtracted from the present value of the inflows is negative, investors simply do not invest. Thus investors' desire to maximize net present value is more a matter of jumping over a fixed hurdle than it is of considering probabilities of an uncertain future stream of cash inflows.

## Problem 13.1 Global Manufacturing, Inc.

**What is Global's weighted average cost of capital?**

| Assumption | | Value |
|---|---|---|
| **Tax rate** | | **30.00%** |
| **10-year euro bonds (euros)** | | **6,000,000** |
| **20-year yen bonds (yen)** | | **750,000,000** |
| **Spot rate ($/euro)** | $ | **0.9000** |
| **Spot rate ($/pound)** | $ | **1.5000** |
| **Spot rate (yen/$)** | | **125.00** |

| Component | | US Dollar Amount | Proportion | Pre-tax Cost (%) | Post-tax Cost (%) | Weighted Component Cost (%) |
|---|---|---|---|---|---|---|
| 25 year US dollar bonds | $ | 10,000,000 | 13.26% | **6.000%** | 4.200% | 0.5570% |
| 5 year US dollar euronotes | | 4,000,000 | 5.31% | **4.000%** | 2.800% | 0.1485% |
| 10 year euro bonds | | **5,400,000** | 7.16% | **5.000%** | 3.500% | 0.2507% |
| 20 year yen bonds | | **6,000,000** | 7.96% | **2.000%** | 1.400% | 0.1114% |
| Shareholders' equity | | 50,000,000 | 66.31% | **20.000%** | 20.000% | 13.2626% |
| Total | $ | **75,400,000** | 100.00% | | **WACC =** | **14.3302%** |

The component coupon costs (for example the 6% coupon on the 25-year US dollar bonds) are the same as the current yields to maturity that would be needed to sell similar bonds in the marketplace today. Current yields to maturity is the proper rate to use.

The interest costs used for the euro and yen bonds reflect actual expected interest costs after any exchange rate changes. This calculation assumes there is no expected change in the exchange rate over the life of the debt issue (which is indeed highly unlikely).

## Problem 13.2 Mississippi Company

**What is the dollar cost of this debt?**

| **Assumptions** | | **Value** |
|---|---|---|
| Principal borrowed (British pounds) | | **£3,000,000** |
| Pound interest rate, one year (percent per annum) | | **9.000%** |
| Beginning of year spot rate, $/pound | **$** | **1.6000** |
| End of year spot rate, $/pound | **$** | **1.5000** |

| **Calculation of the dollar cost of pound debt** | | |
|---|---|---|
| Pound-denominated debt, in pounds sterling: | | |
| Principal | | **£3,000,000.00** |
| Interest | | **270,000.00** |
| Principapl & interest due at end of year | | **£3,270,000.00** |
| | | |
| Repayment cost of pounds, in US dollars (ending spot rate) | **$** | **4,905,000.00** |
| Divided by the US dollar value of initial pound debt proceeds (at beginning of period spot rate) | **$** | **4,800,000.00** |
| Equals | | **1.02188** |
| Minus 1 | | **1.00000** |
| Equal the implied US dollar cost of pound-denominated debt | | **0.02188** |
| **US dollar cost of pound debt** | | **2.188%** |

## Problem 13.3 Virginia Company

**What is the effective US dollar cost of this debt?**

| **Assumptions** | | **Value** |
|---|---|---|
| Principal borrowed for three years, in euros | | **€ 80,000,000** |
| Interest rate on loan, percent per annum | | **6.000%** |
| Beginning spot rate, $/euro | $ | **0.9000** |
| Expected % change in the euro versus the dollar | | **-3.000%** |

| **Calculation of the dollar cost of euro debt** | | **Year 0** | | **Year 1** | | **Year 2** | | **Year 3** |
|---|---|---|---|---|---|---|---|---|
| Proceeds from borrowing euros | | **€ 80,000,000** | | | | | | |
| Interest payment due, in euros | | | | **-€ 4,800,000** | | **-€ 4,800,000** | | **-€ 4,800,000** |
| Repayment of principal in year 3 | | | | | | | | **-€ 80,000,000** |
| Total cash flows of euro-denominated debt | | **€ 80,000,000** | | **-€ 4,800,000** | | **-€ 4,800,000** | | **-€ 84,800,000** |
| (check calculation: IRR of cash flow stream) | | **6.000%** | | | | | | |
| Expected exchange rate, $/euro (spot rate x (1 - .03)) | **$** | **0.9000** | **$** | **0.8730** | **$** | **0.8468** | **$** | **0.8214** |
| US dollar equivalent of euro-denominated cash flows | **$** | **72,000,000** | **$** | **(4,190,400)** | **$** | **(4,064,688)** | **$** | **(69,655,203)** |
| IRR of cash flow stream (the implied US dollar cost) | | **2.820%** | | | | | | |

The internal rate of return, IRR, of any stream of cash flows will determine the rate of discount (interest) which results in a NPV of the cash flow stream of exactly zero.

## Problem 13.4 Quatrefoil Construction Company

**What are the debt and equity proportions in the consolidated balance sheet?**

| **Assumptions** | | **Value** |
|---|---|---|
| Q-Malaysia (in ringgits): | | |
| Long-term debt | | **11,400,000** |
| Shareholders' equity | | **15,200,000** |
| Q-Mexico (in pesos): | | |
| Long-term debt | | **20,000,000** |
| Shareholders' equity | | **60,000,000** |
| **Quatrefoil Construction Company (non-consolidated)** | | |
| Investment in subsidiaries (US dollars): | | |
| in Q-Malaysia | **$** | **4,000,000** |
| in Q-Mexico | **$** | **6,000,000** |
| Parent long-term debt | **$** | **12,000,000** |
| Common stock | **$** | **5,000,000** |
| Retained earnings | **$** | **20,000,000** |
| Current exchange rates: | | |
| Malaysian ringgit per dollar (RM/$) | | **3.80** |
| Mexican pesos per dollar (Ps/$) | | **10.00** |

| **Consolidated Balance Sheet (US$)** | | **Value** | **Percent** |
|---|---|---|---|
| Debt: | | | |
| Malaysian ringgit debt (RM converted to US$) | $ | 3,000,000 | |
| Mexican peso debt (Ps converted to US$) | | 2,000,000 | |
| Parent company debt | | 12,000,000 | |
| Consolidated long-term debt | **$** | **17,000,000** | **40.48%** |
| Shareholders' equity (common + retained) | **$** | **25,000,000** | **59.52%** |
| Total capital | **$** | **42,000,000** | **100.00%** |

Note that the equity accounts of the subsidiaries are matched by "investment in subsidiaries" asset account held in the non-consolidated books of the parent company. In consolidation these two accounts cancel each other out.

## Problem 13.5 Gung Ho Enterprises

**Which course of action do you recommend and why?**

| Alternatives | Japanese yen bonds | euro bonds | US dollar bonds |
|---|---|---|---|
| Coupon rate | 3.000% | 7.000% | 5.000% |
| Current spot rate, yen/$ | 125.00 | $ 0.9200 | |
| Expected change in the value of the foreign currency | 2.000% | -2.000% | 0.000% |
| Principal needed by Gung Ho | $ 100,000,000 | | |

| Calculation of the dollar cost debt alternatives | Year 0 | Year 1 | Year 2 | Year 3 | Year 4 |
|---|---|---|---|---|---|
| **Japanese yen bonds:** | | | | | |
| Proceeds and principal and interest payments | 12,500,000,000 | (375,000,000) | (375,000,000) | (375,000,000) | (12,875,000,000) |
| Expected exchange rate (yen/$) | 125.00 | 122.55 | 120.15 | 117.79 | 115.48 |
| US dollar equivalent in expected cash flows | $ 100,000,000 | $ (3,060,000) | $ (3,121,200) | $ (3,183,624) | $ (111,490,512) |
| IRR of US$ cash flow stream (cost of funds) | 5.060% | | | | |
| **euro-denominated bonds:** | | | | | |
| Proceeds and principal and interest payments | € 108,695,652 | -€ 7,608,696 | -€ 7,608,696 | -€ 7,608,696 | -€ 116,304,348 |
| Expected exchange rate (yen/$) | 0.9200 | 0.9016 | 0.8836 | 0.8659 | 0.8486 |
| US dollar equivalent in expected cash flows | $ 100,000,000 | $ (6,860,000) | $ (6,722,800) | $ (6,588,344) | $ (98,693,393) |
| IRR of US$ cash flow stream (cost of funds) | 4.860% | | | | |
| **US dollar bonds:** | | | | | |
| Proceeds and principal and interest payments | $ 100,000,000 | $ (5,000,000) | $ (5,000,000) | $ (5,000,000) | $ (105,000,000) |
| IRR of US$ cash flow stream (cost of funds) | 5.000% | | | | |

Given the expected exchange rate changes, the euro-denominated bonds have the lowest all-in-cost of funds for the US-based company, Gung Ho Entrprises. (Note that it is the expected changes in exchange rates which determine this outcome. In the event that all currencies were expected to remain fixed, an expected change of 0%, then the Japanese yen bonds are clearly the cheapest source of capital.)

## Problem 13.6 Matterhorn Airlines

| Assumptions | | Value |
|---|---|---|
| Funds retained in New York | $ | 12,000,000 |
| Mid-Manhattan Bank deposit rate, on dollars | | 5.00% |
| Docklands Bank, London, deposit rate on eurodollars | | 5.50% |

| Journal Entries | | Debit | | Credit |
|---|---|---|---|---|
| ***On the books of Matterhorn Airlines:*** | | | | |
| Cash deposit with Docklands Bank | $ | 12,000,000 | | |
| Cash deposit with Mid-Manhattan Bank | | | $ | 12,000,000 |
| ***On the books of Mid-Manhattan Bank:*** | | | | |
| Deposit of Materhorn Airlines | $ | 12,000,000 | | |
| Deposit of Docklands Bank | | | $ | 12,000,000 |
| ***On the books of Docklands Bank:*** | | | | |
| Deposit in Mid-Manhattan Bank | $ | 12,000,000 | | |
| Deposit of Matterhorn Airlines | | | $ | 12,000,000 |

a. Bank deposits of US banks have not changed because the deposit of Matterhorn Airlines in a US bank has been replaced by the deposit of Docklands Bank in a US bank.

b. Docklands Bank would transfer its deposit in Mid-Manhattan Bank to the US Treasury and receive in return US government bonds. Mid-Manhattan Bank would lose (debit) its deposit liability to Docklands Bank and simultaneously lose (credit) its reserve account at the New York Federal Reserve Bank, which is the fiscal agent of the US Treasury.

Note: This assumes that Docklands Bank purchased the US government bonds from the US Treasury in a new issue of bonds. If the US government bonds were purchased in the secondary market, say from a bond dealer such as Goldman Sachs, Goldman Sachs would receive the deposit at Mid-Manhattan Bank. Goldman Sachs might leave that deposit with Mid-Manhattan Bank, or it might transfer the funds to another bank.

## Problem 13.7 Gas du Ardennes

**What is the effective interst cost for the first year?**

| **Initial Issuance** | | **Value** |
|---|---|---|
| Principal borrowed for six years, in US$ | **$** | **800,000,000** |
| Issuance fees | | **1.20%** |

| **Interest Costs** | **First 6-months** | **2nd 6-months** |
|---|---|---|
| LIBOR | **8.000%** | **7.000%** |
| Spread over LIBOR | **0.800%** | **0.800%** |
| Total interest cost | **8.800%** | **7.800%** |

| **Calculation of the effective cost of funds** | | **Issuance** | | **First 6-months** | | **2nd 6-months** |
|---|---|---|---|---|---|---|
| Face value of syndicated loan | $ | 800,000,000 | | | | |
| less fees for issuance | | (9,600,000) | | | | |
| **Net proceeds of syndicated loan** | $ | 790,400,000 | | | | |
| Interest payment due at end of 6-month period | | | $ | (35,200,000) | $ | (31,200,000) |
| (annual rate divided by 2 for 6-month period) | | | | | | |
| **Total interest payments in first year of loan** | $ | (66,400,000) | | | | |
| **Effective interest cost (interest payment/proceeds)** | | **8.401%** | | | | |

## Problem 13.8 River Thames Insurance Company

**What will be the immediate proceeds of the CP issuance?**

| **Assumptions** | | **Value** |
|---|---|---|
| Principal of Euro Commercial Paper issuance | **$** | **1,000,000** |
| Maturity (days) | | **60** |
| Yield to maturity at issuance | | **6.000%** |

| **Proceeds of issuance** | | **Value** |
|---|---|---|
| Face value | **$** | **1,000,000.00** |
| Discount rate (1 + ((days/360) x (ytm))) | | **1.01000** |
| Proceeds equal (Face value / Discount rate) | **$** | **990,099.01** |

## Problem 13.9 Mediterranean Alliance, S.A.

**How much in US$ will Mediterranean receive for each $1,000 note sold?**

| Assumptions | Value |
|---|---|
| Face value of each note sold | $ 1,000.00 |
| Annual coupon | 8.00% |
| Semi-annual coupon | 4.00% |
| (paid June 30th and December 31st) | |
| Date of issuance | February 28, 2003 |
| Maturity | August 31, 2005 |

| Cash payment (payment date) | Days Since Previous Date | Cumultive Days From Start | Cash Flows (par x coupon x days/180) | Discount Factor Calculation: Compound Factor (cum days/180) | Discount Factor 04) compounded | Discounted Cash Flows (US dollars) |
|---|---|---|---|---|---|---|
| First coupon (30 June 2003) | 122 | 122 | $ 27.11 | 0.6778 | 1.0269 | $ 26.40 |
| Second coupon (31 December 2003) | 180 | 302 | $ 40.00 | 1.6778 | 1.0680 | $ 37.45 |
| Third coupon (30 June 2004) | 180 | 482 | $ 40.00 | 2.6778 | 1.1107 | $ 36.01 |
| Fourth coupon (31 December 2004) | 180 | 662 | $ 40.00 | 3.6778 | 1.1552 | $ 34.63 |
| Fifth coupon (30 June 2005) | 180 | 842 | $ 40.00 | 4.6778 | 1.2014 | $ 33.30 |
| Sixth and final coupon (31 August 2005) | 62 | 904 | $ 13.78 | 5.0222 | 1.2177 | $ 11.31 |
| Principal repayment | | 904 | $ 1,000.00 | 5.0222 | 1.2177 | $ 821.21 |
| | | | | | | $ 1,000.31 |

Note: That the reason these Euro Medium Term Notes each have a market value which exceeds their face value is because the first coupon is paid sooner than the six month period separating coupon payments. For example, if all coupons payments were made in 180 days increments ("days since previous date"), the market value of notes would be at the par value of $1,000.

## Problem 13.10 Yunnan Airlines

**At what exchange rate would Yunnan be indifferent between debt sources?**

| **Assumptions** | | **Value** |
|---|---|---|
| Working capital debt needed for one year | $ | 5,000,000 |
| Borrowing US dollars in London: | | |
| Interest rate, percent per annum | | 9.000% |
| Principal borrowed | $ | 5,000,000 |
| Borrow Hong Kong dollars in Hong Kong | | |
| Interest rate, percent per annum | | 7.000% |
| Initial spot rate, HK$/US$ | | 7.8000 |
| Principal borrowed | | 39,000,000 |

| **Calculation of the breakeven exchange rate** | | |
|---|---|---|
| Cost of repaying the Hong Kong dollar loan in HK$ | | 41,730,000 |
| Cost of repaying the US dollar loan in US$ | $ | 5,450,000 |
| **Breakeven exchange rate (HK$ cost/US$ cost)** | | 7.6569 |

MINI-CASE: THE FINANCING OF PETROZUATA

1. **Why was getting an investment grade rating so critical to the financing of the Petrozuata project?**

   Project financing utilizes a significantly higher level of debt than traditional methods of financing business activities. The cost of that debt, therefore, becomes critically important to the economics of the project. In the case of Petrozuata, the sponsors of the project had based their financial expectations on debt which was funded on the investment grade level – BBB or higher. A credit rating below this level would be equivalent to falling off a cliff; it would not be a minor step, but a very large one. The costs of debt would rise significantly threatening the viability of the project.

2. **Is a project finance venture like Petrozuata of lower or higher risk than if the project had simply been funded by the two joint venture partners as in most investments?**

   This is actually not a simple question. From the perspective of the individual investors, the project undertaken with a project finance structure reduces the risk to the individual investors significantly. First, they share the costs, returns, and risks. Projects of this magnitude – both scale, technical resources, and financial resources, would represent an overly large singular risk to an individual enterprise.

   Secondly, the liability to losses associated with the investment is limited to the project itself – once the project is in operation (they have substantially higher obligations prior to startup). The project itself, however, if undertaken with a normal joint venture structure or through a sole investment, would typically be considered too risky for the individual investor to undertake.

3. **Did the Petrozuata finance team "over-sell" the project? Were the economic and political events that followed the financing predictable?**

   This is a very controversial subject. First, the Petrozuata "team" included not only the corporate sponsors of the project, Conoco and PDVSA, but also members of the lead managing banks who would underwrite and syndicate parts of the financing. The lead managers under this set of conditions also have some conflicts of interest, depending on how much of the debt they end up syndicating (selling to other banks and institutions, thereby earning a fee) versus how much they kept of the original debt financing (thereby suffering the credit risk changes of the project).

   Were the negative events predictable? The financing participants were obviously aware of the potential for negative events to occur, but evidently were pacified by the various structures and agreements that the Petrozuata financing deal provided to pacify their concerns. In retrospect, they most certainly underestimated the political risks associated with the Venezuelan government's role as owner and operator of one of the sponsors, PDVSA, and the willingness of a new political regime to tamper with what many considered the sacred cow of the Venezuelan economy, the oil export sector.

4. **Did the investors – the debt providers in particular – not assess the risk of the project appropriately?**

   The decision by the various investors and lending institutions to break the sovereign ceiling for Venezuela was in retrospect a mistake. The Petrozuata financing team and structure had sought to form a venture which would be largely "immune" from the political risks of the host country, Venezuela. However, as the subsequent events proved, the project and its expected returns were still impacted by those events. To be fair, however, the project's expectations on the future crude oil price were generally conservative, and the depths to which oil prices were driven in the following year(s) are still considered by all analysts as largely beyond what even a prudent investor may have foreseen.

## Chapter 14. Interest Rate and Currency Swaps

### *Questions*

### 14-1. Triumvirate of risks

a. *Interest rate risk*: The risk that a change in the level of interest rates will have (1) an adverse impact on the liquidity and cash flows of the firm, and (2) an adverse impact on the firm's holding of interest-sensitive securities.

b. *Foreign exchange rate risk*: The risk that a change in exchange rates will lead to losses from transaction exposure, operating exposure, and/or translation exposure.

c. *Commodity price risk*: The risk that changes in commodity prices will have an impact on the profit and loss situation of a firm.

### 14-2. Reference rates

A *reference rate* is an average interest rate taken from a sample of banking firms at a specified time each day. In London, where LIBOR (London Interbank Offered Rate) is the main reference rate for Eurocurrency loans, the reference rate is that rate charged by banks in their lending to each other in the specified currency. As such, it is the lowest commercial rage available for the best credit sources for a very short maturity.

### 14-3. Risk and return

a. Performance of a *service*, or *cost center,* is measured by how operating costs compare with budgeted operating costs. The center is not expected to "make a profit." The advantage of having a corporate treasury department be a service center is that the department is not tempted to make a profit by taking risky positions in anticipation of changes in interest or foreign exchange rates. The disadvantages are that the employees of the department may become excessively conservative, there being no advantage job-wise for taking any risks; and that the firm lacks any way to determine if the treasury department is operating efficiently – other than by complying with its budget, which is not a very good measure of efficiency.

b. As a *profit center*, a certain amount of revenue is attributed to the center in addition to its expenses. The difference measures the within-the-firm profit contributed by the treasury department. The advantage is that the treasury department is encouraged to think of itself in terms of how much it adds to overall corporate profit, while the disadvantage is that the department may take excessive risks that do not work out and cause big losses for the firm.

### 14-4. Forecast types

A *specific* forecast provides a specific anticipated number, say an interest rate or a foreign exchange rate, that the forecaster anticipates will be in effect at a specific future date. A *directional* forecast only suggests that the anticipated number will be above or below the present number; it does not provide a specific target number, however. As a general matter, directional forecasts are easier to make and are often sufficient to suggest what type of risk control a firm might wish to engage in.

### 14-5. Policy statements

A *goal statement* prescribes desired objective (such as a certain level of profits) but does not prescribe how management might seek to reach that goal. A *policy statement* is more precise; it states what specific things management should do, or what specific things management may not do.

Policy statements are established to protect the firm's stockholders and creditors from management, and in many ways, to protect management from itself. By establishing specific rules and restrictions – such as "the firm will not write uncovered options" – the firm eliminates discretionary behavior which management on occasion may be tempted to undertake, but the firm as a whole has stated is not worth the commensurate risks.

### 14-6. Credit and repricing risk

a. Credit risk for the borrower is the chance that a borrower's credit worthiness will deteriorate and at the time that a credit is rolled over, the lower credit ranking will lead to higher interest rates. A firm minimizes its credit risk by attending to the adequacy of its internal cash flows relative to budgeted cash expenses and financial expenses. A simple measure sometimes mentioned is attention to a "times interest earned" ratio, in which for good quality credit ratings cash flow available to pay interest should be five to seven times the amount of interest.

b. Repricing risk for the borrower is the chance that interest rates in the economy will rise, so that when a credit is rolled over a higher interest rate will be charged. The causes of the repricing are factors in the economy and its financial markets. A firm can do little directly to avoid repricing risk because the cause is not within the firm. However a firm can plan for contingency financing so that if the cost of a given credit rises funds can be raised from an alternate source of financing.

### 14-7. Forward rate agreement

Under a forward rate agreement, a borrower would contract with a party willing to carry interest rate risk to pay to the risk taker the difference between the initial floating interest rate and any lower reset of that rate, and to received from the risk taker the difference between the initial floating interest rate and any higher reset of that rate.

### 14-8. Eurodollar futures

Annual yield is (100.00 – 93.55) = 6.45%.

### 14-9. Defaulting on an interest rate swap

Jones Company would resume paying the fixed interest for which it is obligated to its creditors because from the creditors' point of view only Jones is obligated. The creditors would probably not know about the interest rate swap. Jones Company would also stop making floating payments to Smith Company. Consequentially the loss to Jones Company is only the interest differential. It is not the full amount of any series of payments.

## 14-10. Currency swaps

Presumably the company borrowed pounds sterling, perhaps because the company was well regarded and had a credit history that made borrowing pounds feasible at a time when borrowing in U.S. dollars was not possible. The interest rate paid on pounds might also have been lower than the U.S. dollar rate, if it could borrow in the United States, because the firm was better known in Britain.

However the company earns its revenue in U.S. dollars, meaning that the cash flow to service the loan is in dollars. Rather than risk an adverse change in exchange rates between the dollars (cash source) and pounds (cash payments) at each interest payment date, the company swaps the entire amount of sterling interest payments for dollar interest payments. This eliminates the need to go through a foreign exchange transaction at each interest date.

## 14-11. Counterparty risk

In exchange-traded swaps and other derivatives, the exchange rather than the actual other party to the swap is the counterparty. Hence if one participant in the swap defaults, the exchange will carry on with the agreement

*Problems*

**14-1. Andina, S.A.**

Annual interest on $8,000,000 at 4.00% per annum would be $320,000.

a. New York will charge interest for 56 days based on a 360-day year.
Interest costs will be (56/360)($320,000) = $49,777.78.

b. Great Britain will charge interest for 56 days based on a 365 day year.
Interest costs will be (56/365)($320,000) = $49,095,89.

c. Switzerland will charge interest for 60 days (2 months) based on a 360 day year.
Interest costs will be (60/360)($320,000) = $53,333.33.

Andina, S.A. should borrow the funds in Great Britain because the real interest cost is lower.

| Problem 14.1 Andina, S.A. | | |
|---|---|---|
| **From which source should Andina borrow?** | | |
| | | |
| **Assumptions** | | **Values** |
| Principal borrowing need | $ | 8,000,000 |
| Maturity needed, in weeks | | 8 |
| Rate of interest charged by ALL potential lenders | | 4.000% |
| | | |
| **New York interest rate practices** | | |
| Interest calculation uses: | | |
| Exact number of days in period | | 56 |
| Number of days in financial year | | 360 |
| So the interest charge on this principal is | $ | 49,777.78 |
| | | |
| **Great Britain interest rate practices** | | |
| Interest calculation uses: | | |
| Exact number of days in period | | 56 |
| Number of days in financial year | | 365 |
| So the interest charge on this principal is | $ | 49,095.89 |
| | | |
| **Swiss interest rate practices** | | |
| Interest calculation uses: | | |
| Assumed 30 days per month for two months | | 60 |
| Number of days in financial year | | 360 |
| So the interest charge on this principal is | $ | 53,333.33 |
| | | |
| Andina should borrow in Great Britain because it has the lowest interest cost. | | |

**14-2. Adelaide Corporation**

Adelaide's management could group the risks and costs of the three alternatives as follows:

*Choice 1*: Alternative 1, the fixed 5% loan, is free of risk and has a known cost. By comparison, alternatives 2 and 3 both possess a risk of a higher cost the second year, as well as having the potential for a lower cost the second year.

- A risk adverse management might well decide that this risk, which is a financial risk, should not be undertaken because the firm already has business (product, manufacturing, and sales) risks. Thus it would chose alternative 1.

- A management willing to add financial risk to its already existing business risk would move on to select between alternatives 2 and 3.

*Choice 2*: As between the second and third alternatives, alternative 2 provides the same rate as alternative 1 for the first six months, and is open ended after that. Alternative 3 provides a lower rate than alternative 1 for the first whole year and alternative 2 for the first six months, and is open ended after that. Six-month LIBOR rates and second year refinancing rates would probably move in the same direction, so no need exists to chose one over the other from a directional point of view.

- A firm might have specific forecasts for future exchange rates, in which case the cost of the two remaining alternatives could be calculated. However most research indicates that accurate forecasting of near-term interest rate changes is not very successful.

- Alternative three has one additional risk that alternative 2 lacks, which is the risk of not being able to obtain new financing one year hence. Alternative 2 provides for a full two years of financing, and so might be considered less risky than alternative 3 which includes the possibility of financing drying up.

## Problem 14.2 Adelaide Corporation

**Compare the alternatives and make a recommendation.**

| **Assumptions** | | **Values** |
|---|---|---|
| Principal borrowing need | $ | 30,000,000 |
| Maturity needed, in years | | 2.00 |
| Fixed rate, 2 years | | 5.000% |
| Floating rate, six-month LIBOR + spread | | |
| Current six-month LIBOR | | 3.500% |
| Spread | | 1.500% |
| Fixed rate, 1 year, then re-fund | | 4.500% |

| | First 6-months | Second 6-months | Third 6-months | Fourth 6-months |
|---|---|---|---|---|
| **#1: Fixed rate, 2 years** | | | | |
| Interest cost per year | | $ 1,500,000 | | $ 1,500,000 |
| Certainty over access to capital | Certain | Certain | Certain | Certain |
| Certainty over cost of capital | Certain | Certain | Certain | Certain |
| **Floating rate, six-month LIBOR + #2: spread** | | | | |
| Interest cost per year | $ 750,000.00 | $ 750,000.00 | $ 750,000.00 | $ 750,000.00 |
| Certainty over access to capital | Certain | Certain | Certain | Certain |
| Certainty over cost of capital | Certain | Uncertain | Uncertain | Uncertain |
| **#3: Fixed rate, 1 year, then re-fund** | | | | |
| Interest cost per year | | $ 1,350,000.00 | ??? | ??? |
| Certainty over access to capital | Certain | Certain | Uncertain | Uncertain |
| Certainty over cost of capital | Certain | Certain | Uncertain | Uncertain |

Only alternative #1 has a certain access and cost of capital for the full 2 year period.
Alternative #2 has certain access to capital for both years, but the interest costs in the final 3 of 4 periods is uncertain.
Alternatvie #3, possessing a lower interest cost in year 1, has no guaranteed access to capital in the second year.
Depending on the company's business needs and tolerance for interest rate risk, it should choose between #1 and #2.

## Problem 14.3 The Wineries

**Given interest rate expectations, who has the best deal?**

| **Assumptions** | **Values** | **Expected Chg in LIBOR** |
|---|---|---|
| Principal borrowing need | $ 20,000,000 | |
| Maturity needed, in years | 4.00 | |
| Current LIBOR | 4.000% | |
| Cabernet's bank spread & expectation | 2.000% | 0.500% |
| Cabernet's bank initiation fee | 1.800% | |
| Sauvignon's bank spread & expectation | 2.500% | -0.500% |
| Sauvignon's bank inititiation fee | 0.000% | |

| **Cabernet's Expected Cost of Funds** | **Year 0** | **Year 1** | **Year 2** | **Year 3** | **Year 4** |
|---|---|---|---|---|---|
| Expected interest rates & payments: | | | | | |
| Expected LIBOR | 4.000% | 4.500% | 5.000% | 5.500% | 6.000% |
| Bank spread | 2.000% | 2.000% | 2.000% | 2.000% | 2.000% |
| Interest rate | 6.000% | 6.500% | 7.000% | 7.500% | 8.000% |
| | | | | | |
| Funds raised, net of fees | $ 19,640,000 | | | | |
| Expected interest costs | | $ (1,300,000) | $ (1,400,000) | $ (1,500,000) | $ (1,600,000) |
| Repayment of principal | | | | | (20,000,000) |
| Total cash flows | $ 19,640,000 | $ (1,300,000) | $ (1,400,000) | $ (1,500,000) | $ (21,600,000) |
| All-in-cost of funds (IRR) | 7.744% | | | | |

| **Sauvignon's Expected Cost of Funds** | **Year 0** | **Year 1** | **Year 2** | **Year 3** | **Year 4** |
|---|---|---|---|---|---|
| Expected interest rates & payments: | | | | | |
| Expected LIBOR | 4.000% | 3.500% | 3.000% | 2.500% | 2.000% |
| Bank spread | 2.500% | 2.500% | 2.500% | 2.500% | 2.500% |
| Interest rate | 6.500% | 6.000% | 5.500% | 5.000% | 4.500% |
| | | | | | |
| Funds raised, net of fees | $ 20,000,000 | | | | |
| Expected interest costs | | $ (1,200,000) | $ (1,100,000) | $ (1,000,000) | $ (900,000) |
| Repayment of principal | | | | | (20,000,000) |
| Total cash flows | $ 20,000,000 | $ (1,200,000) | $ (1,100,000) | $ (1,000,000) | $ (20,900,000) |
| All-in-cost of funds (IRR) | 5.282% | | | | |

If LIBOR does indeed RISE 50 basis points per year (Cabernet's expectation), then Cabernet will pay 7.744%, Sauvignon will end up paying 7.704%.

If LIBOR FALLS 50 basis points per year (Sauvignon's expectation), then Cabernet will pay 5.293%, Sauvignon will end up paying 5.282%.

## Problem 14.4 Sauvignon's Interest Rate Risk

| Assumptions | Values |
|---|---|
| Principal borrowing need | $ 20,000,000 |
| Maturity needed, in years | 4.00 |
| Current LIBOR | 4.000% |
| Sauvignon's bank spread | 2.500% |
| Cost of FRA | $ 100,000 |

| If LIBOR Falls 50 Basis Pts Per Year | Year 0 | Year 1 | Year 2 | Year 3 | Year 4 |
|---|---|---|---|---|---|
| Expected annual change in LIBOR | | -0.500% | | | |
| LIBOR | 4.000% | 3.500% | 3.000% | 2.500% | 2.000% |
| Bank spread | 2.500% | 2.500% | 2.500% | 2.500% | 2.500% |
| Interest rate | 6.500% | 6.000% | 5.500% | 5.000% | 4.500% |
| Funds raised, net of fees | $ 20,000,000 | | | | |
| Expected interest (interest rate x principal) | | $ (1,200,000) | $ (1,100,000) | $ (1,000,000) | $ (900,000) |
| **Forward Rate Agreement** | $ (100,000) | $ (100,000) | $ (200,000) | $ (300,000) | $ (400,000) |
| Repayment of principal | | | | | (20,000,000) |
| Total cash flows | $ 19,900,000 | $ (1,300,000) | $ (1,300,000) | $ (1,300,000) | $ (21,300,000) |
| All-in-cost of funds (IRR) | 6.646% | | | | |

| If LIBOR Rises 50 Basis Pts Per Year | Year 0 | Year 1 | Year 2 | Year 3 | Year 4 |
|---|---|---|---|---|---|
| Expected annual change in LIBOR | | 0.500% | | | |
| LIBOR | 4.000% | 4.500% | 5.000% | 5.500% | 6.000% |
| Bank spread | 2.500% | 2.500% | 2.500% | 2.500% | 2.500% |
| Interest rate | 6.500% | 7.000% | 7.500% | 8.000% | 8.500% |
| Funds raised, net of fees | $ 20,000,000 | | | | |
| Expected interest (interest rate x principal) | | $ (1,400,000) | $ (1,500,000) | $ (1,600,000) | $ (1,700,000) |
| **Forward Rate Agreement** | $ (100,000) | $ 70,000 | $ 140,000 | $ 210,000 | $ 280,000 |
| Repayment of principal | | | | | (20,000,000) |
| Total cash flows | $ 19,900,000 | $ (1,330,000) | $ (1,360,000) | $ (1,390,000) | $ (21,420,000) |
| All-in-cost of funds (IRR) | 7.010% | | | | |

This rather unusual forward rate agreement is somewhat one-sided in the favor of the insurance company. When Sauvignon is correct, Sauvignon pays the full difference in rates to the insurance company, but when Sauvignon is incorrect, the insurance company pays Sauvignon only 70% of the difference in rates. And all of that is after Sauvignon paid $100,000 up front for the agreement regardless of outcome.

A final note of significance is that since Sauvignon only receives 70% of the difference in rates, its total cost of funds is not effectively "capped" -- they could in fact rise with no limit over the period as interest rates rose.

## Problem 14.5 John Jones

**How will John Jones do using interest rate futures?**

| **Assumptions** | **Values** |
|---|---|
| Interest rate futures, closing price | **93.07** |
| Effective yield on interest rate futures | **6.930%** |

| | **Three Months From Now** | |
|---|---|---|
| | **Floating Rate is** | **Floating Rate is** |
| **John Jones' interest rate payments with futures** | **6.000%** | **8.000%** |
| Interest payment due in three months | **6.000%** | **8.000%** |
| Sell a future (take a short position) | **-6.930%** | **-6.930%** |
| Gain or loss on position | **-0.930%** | **1.070%** |
| | **Loss** | **Gain** |

## Problem 14.6 Canon Candy Company

**Calculate gains or losses from swap position.**

| **Assumptions** | **Values** |
|---|---|
| Notional principal | $ 5,000,000 |
| LIBOR, per annum | 4.000% |
| Spread paid over LIBOR, per annum | 2.000% |
| Swap rate, to pay fixed, per annum | 7.000% |

| **Interest & Swap Payments** | | **First 6-months** | | **Second 6-months** | | **Third 6-months** | | **Fourth 6-months** |
|---|---|---|---|---|---|---|---|---|
| **a. LIBOR increases 50 basis pts/6 months** | | 0.500% | | | | | | |
| Expected LIBOR | | 4.500% | | 5.000% | | 5.500% | | 6.000% |
| **Current loan agreement:** | | | | | | | | |
| Expected LIBOR (for 6 months) | | -2.250% | | -2.500% | | -2.750% | | -3.000% |
| Spread (for 6 months) | | -1.000% | | -1.000% | | -1.000% | | -1.000% |
| Expected interest payment | | -3.250% | | -3.500% | | -3.750% | | -4.000% |
| **Swap Agreement:** | | | | | | | | |
| Pay fixed (for 6-months) | | -3.500% | | -3.500% | | -3.500% | | -3.500% |
| Receive floating (LIBOR for 6 months) | | 2.250% | | 2.500% | | 2.750% | | 3.000% |
| **Net interest (loan + swap)** | | -4.500% | | -4.500% | | -4.500% | | -4.500% |
| **Swap savings?** | | | | | | | | |
| Net interest after swap | $ | (225,000) | $ | (225,000) | $ | (225,000) | $ | (225,000) |
| Loan agreement interest | | (162,500) | | (175,000) | | (187,500) | | (200,000) |
| **Swap savings (swap cost)** | $ | (62,500) | $ | (50,000) | $ | (37,500) | $ | (25,000) |
| **b. LIBOR decreases 25 basis pts/6 months** | | -0.250% | | | | | | |
| Expected LIBOR | | 3.750% | | 3.500% | | 3.250% | | 3.000% |
| **Current loan agreement:** | | | | | | | | |
| Expected LIBOR (for 6 months) | | -1.875% | | -1.750% | | -1.625% | | -1.500% |
| Spread (for 6 months) | | -1.000% | | -1.000% | | -1.000% | | -1.000% |
| Expected interest payment | | -2.875% | | -2.750% | | -2.625% | | -2.500% |
| **Swap Agreement:** | | | | | | | | |
| Pay fixed (for 6-months) | | -3.500% | | -3.500% | | -3.500% | | -3.500% |
| Receive floating (LIBOR for 6 months) | | 1.875% | | 1.750% | | 1.625% | | 1.500% |
| **Net interest (loan + swap)** | | -4.500% | | -4.500% | | -4.500% | | -4.500% |
| **Swap savings?** | | | | | | | | |
| Net interest after swap | $ | (225,000) | $ | (225,000) | $ | (225,000) | $ | (225,000) |
| Loan agreement interest | | (143,750) | | (137,500) | | (131,250) | | (125,000) |
| **Swap savings (swap cost)** | $ | (81,250) | $ | (87,500) | $ | (93,750) | $ | (100,000) |

**In both cases Canon Candy Company is suffering higher total interest costs as a result of the swap.**

## Problem 14.7 Xavier and Zulu

**Make a recommendation on potential swaps.**

| **Assumptions** | **Xavier** | **Zulu** |
|---|---|---|
| Credit rating | **AAA** | **BBB** |
| Prefers to borrow | **Floating** | **Fixed** |
| Fixed-rate cost of borrowing | **8.000%** | **12.000%** |
| Floating-rate cost of borrowing: | | |
| LIBOR (value is unimportant) | **5.000%** | **5.000%** |
| Spread | **1.000%** | **2.000%** |
| Total floating-rate | **6.000%** | **7.000%** |

| **Comparative Advantage in Borrowing** | **Values** |
|---|---|
| Xavier's absolute advantage: | |
| in fixed rate borrowering | **4.000%** |
| in floating-rate borrowing | **1.000%** |
| Comparative advantage in fixed rate | **3.000%** |

| **One Possibility** | **Xavier** | **Zulu** |
|---|---|---|
| Xavier borrows fixed | **-8.000%** | **---** |
| Zulu borrows floating | **---** | **-7.000%** |
| Xavier pays Zulu floating (LIBOR) | **-5.000%** | **5.000%** |
| Zulu pays Xavier fixed | **8.500%** | **-8.500%** |
| Net interest after swap | **-4.500%** | **-10.500%** |

| **Savings (own borrowing versus net swap):** | | |
|---|---|---|
| If Xavier borrowed floating | **6.000%** | |
| If Xavier borrows fixed & swaps with Zulu | **4.500%** | |
| | **1.500%** | |
| If Zulu borrowes fixed | | **12.000%** |
| If Zulu borrows floating & swaps with Xavier | | **10.500%** |
| | | **1.500%** |

The 3.0% comparative advantage enjoyed by Xavier represents the opportunity set for improvement for both parties. This could be 1.5% savings for each (as in the example shown), or any other combination which distributes the 3.0% between the two parties.

## MINI-CASE: MCDONALD'S CORPORATION'S BRITISH POUND EXPOSURE

This problem is particularly useful at focusing students on the currency exposures that are created within the structure of a MNE, as well as the use of swaps as a currency hedging tool. It also highlights something most finance academics do not – the concern and emphasis placed on accounting-based measures of corporate performance by financial management. The public equity markets are demanding in their assessment of corporate earnings and ability to meet earnings expectations. Management in practice has to be diligent in their attention to reported earnings and EPS, whether academics will admit it or not!

**1. How does the cross currency swap effectively hedge the three primary exposures McDonald's has relative to its British subsidiary?**

The U.S. parent company possesses three pound-denominated exposures arising from the British subsidiary:

1. the equity capital the parent company has in the subsidiary (originally US$ but now pound-denominated)
2. intra-company debt in the form of a 4-year fixed rate (5.30%) £125 million loan
3. an inflow stream of royalties arising from payment by the British subsidiary of a percentage of sales (£) to the parent company in the U.S.

In addition to these exposures, a detail of U.S. accounting practices is noted about the "permanence" of the intra-company loan.

- If the loan is designated by McDonald's as *permanently invested* in the British subsidiary, it is in essence equity capital in character and any foreign exchange gains and losses arising from debt service flow only to the CTA account on the consolidated books.

- If the loan is designated by McDonald's as not permanently invested in the British subsidiary, the foreign exchange gains and losses arising from debt service will flow to the profit and loss statement of the parent company itself, possibly altering consolidated earnings (and EPS) of the company.

Whether a particular company will find this attractive or not depends on at least three factors:

1) corporate philosophy towards foreign exchange gains/losses in general,
2) whether the investment in the foreign subsidiary is for the very long-run, and
3) whether the currency – in this case the British pound – will trend up or down versus the dollar over an extended period.

**2. How does the cross-currency swap hedge the long-term equity exposure in the foreign subsidiary?**

Cross-Currency Swap as Hedge. The use of the cross-currency swap as hedge to the parent is best explained visually, with a simple balance sheet of the U.S. parent company by the nature of the exposures.

| Assets of US Parent Company | | Liabilities of US Parent Company |
|---|---|---|
| | | Swap dollar $ payments for £ payments: |
| £ inflow over time -----> | A/R of royalties | interest payment on swap ------> £ outflow |
| £ inflow over time -----> | interest on loan | |
| £ exposure, long term --> | equity in subsidiary | outstanding notional principal on swap –> £ exposure |

All in all, this is by most measures a very effective use of cross currency swaps for hedging currency exposures on an on-going or operating basis.

## 3. Should Anka – and McDonald's – worry about OCI?

The newly proposed accounting standard at the time, FAS 133, would require that McDonald's mark-to-market the value of the outstanding swap on a regular (quarterly) basis, and include the resulting gains/losses on the swap in Other Comprehensive Income (OCI). With a little prompting, this should spark some interesting debate among students. The problem can be broken down into a few sub-components for detailed debate:

1. Marking-to-market a cross currency swap will likely result in very large swings in the value of the position from period to period. This is a result of what was demonstrated in the chapter about unwinding a cross currency swap. As both interest rates and exchange rates change, long term swaps with large notional principals outstanding in the distant future will change significantly in value.

2. Other Comprehensive Income (OCI) is another measure of consolidated income which firms conforming to U.S. accounting practices (US-GAAP) must report. What is it? It is in essence the normal consolidated profits of the firm plus change in the retained earnings account of the firm – which is often largely the value of the CTA account for a MNE. Obviously, combining the CTA account change in value with current consolidated income could potentially result in volatile movements in the combined OCI measure. (Some of the older professors out there might remember this as the basic problem of translation and consolidation under FAS #8 prior to the adoption of FAS #52 in 1981.)

3. The cross-currency swap is hedging actual cash flows which are moving between the subsidiary and the parent, whereas the concern over FAS #133 is primarily an accounting-based measurement issue. Which is more important, actual cash flow or accounting-based measurements? Cash flow.

4. Should management worry about volatility in the OCI? This is not the measure of earnings which is popularly reported and focused on by Wall Street, and most of the true analysts who follow firms will understand the distinctions.

But all things considered, if two different firms had the same basic performance on an EPS basis, but one firm had a significant deterioration in its reported OCI as a result of marking-to-market its cross-currency swap (hedge) position as in the case of McDonald's, would the firm be punished by the market? To date, McDonald's has continued to follow the FAS #133 debate closely and continually reviews its currency hedging strategies and accounting policies and practices.

# CHAPTER 15. FOREIGN DIRECT INVESTMENT THEORY AND STRATEGY

## *Questions*

### 15-1. Evolving into multinationalism

a. If a firm lacks sufficient competitive advantage to compete effectively in its home market, it is unlikely to have sufficient advantages of any type to be successful in a foreign market. This is because the competitive advantages of the home market must be enduring, transferable, and sufficiently powerful to enable the firm to overcome the assorted difficulties of operating in a foreign environment.

b. Foreign operations must be located where market imperfections are such that the firm can take advantage of its competitive advantages to the degree necessary to earn a risk-adjusted rate of return above the firm's cost of capital.

c. The firm must decided upon the degree of control it will need over the foreign operation, recognizing that greater control usually involves both greater risk and a greater investment. Viewing a spectrum of degrees of control, licensing and management contracts provide a low level of control (along with a low level of financial investment); joint ventures necessitate a somewhat higher level of control; and Greenfield direct investments and/or acquisition of an existing foreign firm require the highest degree of control (along with a higher level of financial investment).

d. The spectrum of investment approaches (licensing, management contracts, joint ventures, and direct investment) require in that order ever increasing investment of more monetary capital. The firm must decide if the benefits of greater investment (presumably greater profits, plus possibly acquiring market share or forestalling competitors from gaining a greater market share) are worth the differing amounts of monetary capital needed.

### 15-2. Theory of comparative advantage

The essence of the theory of comparative advantage is that a country should specialize in producing those goods and services for which it has a ***relative*** cost advantage compared to other countries, export a portion of those goods and services, and use the proceeds from those exports to import goods and services for which it has a ***relative*** cost disadvantage.

The theory focuses on the concept of "relative advantage" for each country. Relative advantage means a comparison of the ratio of costs between items within one country to the ratio of costs within another country. A country might have an absolute advantage in everything, but it will still gain by specializing where its relative advantage is greatest.

### 15-3. The theory of competitive advantage

Recognizing that the basic concept of the theory of competitive advantage is the same as the theory of comparative advantage, the theory of competitive advantage speaks to advantages obtained through (a) variations in a country's endowment of land, labor, capital and technology, (b) variations in demand conditions, (c) availability of related and supporting industries, and (d) differences in firm strategy, structure, and rivalry.

## 15-4. Comparative vs. competitive advantages

The terms are essentially synonyms, common usage for each having arisen from the different time periods in which the term was first used. "Comparative advantage" came into economic vogue in the middle of the 19th century through the writings of John Stuart Mill, who was writing about nations. "Competitive advantage" was first used by Michael Porter in *The Competitive Advantage of Nations,* in1990. The context of Porter's work is more often of multinational firms operating in a competitive global economy.

## 15-5. Owner-specific advantages

Disney's owner-specific advantages are based around Mickey Mouse and his friends, who for decades have been important in creating fun and joy for children. Intel's owner-specific advantages are a reputation for being first in the design of ever-faster computer chips, and for being able to sell them at comparatively low prices. Volvo's owner-specific advantages are a reputation for building high-quality, very durable and safe automobiles.

## 15-6. Location-specific advantages

Semiconductor technology firms have a location-specific advantage in places with large numbers of young scientists and engineers, located near firms that make products that use semiconductors. Silicon Valley in the San Francisco Bay Area is a prime example. Semiconductor manufacturing firms need low cost power, water, and a clean environment such as in the Pacific Northwest of the United States and the Penang Peninsula in Malaysia.

Oil exploration firms obtain their location-specific advantage by being near integrated oil producers, who are the main customers who hire such exploration firms. In the United States such firms have tended to congregate in the state of Texas, which possesses this location-specific advantage because it was the site of major petroleum discoveries in the early part of the 20th century. It was at that time and in that place that the petroleum industry first blossomed. Oil exploration firms also locate close to existing or expected oil fields such as the Middle East. Petrochemical refining firms have a location-specific advantage in being either (1) near other firms in the petroleum industry, and (2) being near ports where oil tankers can deliver petroleum to refineries, or being in locations that enjoy low political risk.

## 15-7. Internalization

Internalization in the OLI Paradigm means that a MNE is better off to enter foreign locations through direct investment (100% owned) rather than alternative modes. The reason is that 100% control allows the MNE to receive all of the benefits on its own research and development while minimizing agency costs.

## 15-8. Exporting

Production abroad allows a firm to exploit its research and development skills, to preempt foreign markets from competitors that might find costs of producing abroad lower than at home, and to use the foreign production base as a lower-cost location for supplying the host country market and thus enabling the firm to lower its sales prices and capture more volume.

## 15-9. Unbundling

In a wholly-owned operation (foreign or domestic), a firm's profits result from the sum of return on invested capital, return on proprietary knowledge and skills, return on managerial expertise, and possibly others. It is not necessary to break apart the various sources of profit. Owners receive their return in the form of dividends ("bundled").

Some foreign governments question the justification of a rate of return earned by foreigners within their country. "Unbundling" allows the firm to price each contribution separately, as well as to desegregate components of a total investment. Thus licensing allows the parent to be paid for use of its proprietary knowledge and skills, and a management contract allows a firm to be paid for its managerial expertise. The unbundled payments are "transparent," in that payment for each contribution is priced separately and that payment is known to governing authorities.

## 15-10. Joint ventures

Possible advantages of a joint venture include:

a. Quicker access to the European market through already-established marketing and distribution networks.
b. Ability to use physical facilities (popping ovens) already in place.
c. Possible use of a European brand name, if desirable.
d. Availability of experience European managers to guide the project, without having to find and hire new managers acquainted with Europe.
e. Physical closeness between the popping facility and the consumer market.

Possible disadvantages of a joint venture include:

a. Loss of the company secret that makes its popcorn so unique and different from other brands.
b. A risk of loss of sales if other products branded by the European joint venture partner are found to be unsafe. (Hypothetical example: The joint venture partner also bakes bread, which is found to have microbes that make people sick. Consumers avoid all products from the joint venture partner, including your popcorn.)
c. Disagreements over the price of popcorn, especially in the context of lowering prices to achieve greater growth and market penetration, versus raising prices to make more profit on existing volume.
d. Disagreement on distribution of profits as dividends versus retention of earnings for growth.
e. Differing attitudes by your firm and your joint venture partner on putting new equity capital into the joint venture firm. Differing ability to inject more equity capital is also a possible disadvantage.
f. Disagreement over the right to export European or U.S. manufactured popcorn to Asia and Africa, where a potentially big market is assumed to exist.
g. Inability to sell your equity in the joint venture, if you want to liquidate your European holding, because potential European buyers do not want the risk of sharing control with your existing joint venture partner.

## 15-11. Comparative advantage and Twenty-First Century Reality

One can argue either way on this proposition, in part because the diverse factors that now give rise to comparative advantages at the start of the 21st century are complex. The basic argument in favor would be that if comparable products can be manufactured less expensively and thus sold for lower prices, both exporting and importing country will benefit from such specializing.

With regards to the individual original factors of production, capital is ever more mobile as the techniques of international fund flows and of risk-adjustment become increasingly sophisticated. Labor mobility now includes the movement of individuals of highly valuable expertise (e.g., managers, engineers and designers) who may serve as expatriates in other countries for fixed periods of several years but who return to their homeland after such overseas duty. Cultural, ethnographic, linguistic and religions barriers preclude some labor mobility. However jet-age transportation facilitates "limited time migration;" as persons can live in a foreign country for a while with the expectation of returning to their homeland in due course. In "olden days" most labor mobility was of physical laborers who for the most part sought jobs in low-paying factories, and most of those moves were permanent – for the remainder of the immigrant's life. Political turmoil in the world has also increased the "labor mobility" of higher trained persons, who are often the first to flee such countries as Cuba, Iraq, Iran, and Afghanistan.

Perhaps more important in the 21st century is the mobility of ideas and technologies. Ideas are spread via the ever-greater number of foreign students and by such communication innovations as the internet. Technology is spread by the practice of large companies becoming multinational and thus utilizing their technology in countries other than the homeland.

**15-12. International automotive mergers**

Any answer to this question must be based on current research at the time information is are sought. Students should be encouraged to consider other, more contemporary mergers including those in industries other than automotive, and to ponder if other criteria not mentioned in the text are relevant.

**15-13. Advantages**

a. Producing at home for foreign sales gives the firm complete and secure control over technology and quality while avoiding almost all political risk and the need to monitor and control distant subsidiaries. Managers and their families need not be sent abroad for extended periods of time. *Producing abroad* places the manufacturing process closer to customers and facilitates managers becoming acquainted with market conditions and cultural aspects of the foreign market. An on-the-scene presence makes the firm less vulnerable to competitors attempting to enter the same market.

b. With a *wholly owned subsidiary* the parent firm has complete control over the foreign operation, with the possibility of greater earnings. Of course, any greater earnings are the result of a greater exposure of capital and greater time devoted by management. *Joint ventures* allow the firm to maintain a smaller presence in the foreign country and to be able to work with managers who already understand the culture and languages and have the political contacts and know how needed for success. A joint venture is less likely to be perceived as a foreign company and so is probably less exposed to political risk.

c. Licensing allows the firm a limited profit from its expertise and technology, such as patents, trademarks, and brand names, without risking loss of capital. Licensing is a way to "unbundle" the valuable attributes owned by a firm and capture a return on one (say patents and trademarks) without risking others (say, invested capital or time and energy diverted from home-country activities.) Licensing has little risk of direct financial loss, although at times an opportunity cost may be incurred because a commitment must be made for the contractual time, and a change in strategy (say, deciding to export to that market or manufacture there directly) is precluded until the license contract expires. *Full control of assets*, meaning foreign direct investment, has the advantage that the firm need not worry about actions taken by a licensee, such as a lowering of quality or exporting to a third country, that the parent firm does not like. Additionally, full control of assets means the firm is free to change its strategy or possibly substitute new technology very quickly, as market conditions dictate, without having to renegotiate a contract. Full control of assets is also likely to produce greater profits, albeit at the risk of incurring greater losses.

d. Acquisition of an existing firm provides an immediate presence already staffed by persons acquainted with the local country. The foreign operation is "up and running' right at the start. The risk is that after acquiring an existing firm, the parent discovers that assets are obsolete or that managers are incompetent. If new managers are to be installed, the associated firing of old managers may create significant local ill will. *A greenfield* investment takes a much longer time interval for planning, construction, ramping up production, and creating a new staff. However it does allow the investing parent to design the investment exactly in the way that it wishes, and in the long run allows the parent firm to gain permanent knowledge about the foreign country.

**15-15. DFI motivations**

| | | |
|---|---|---|
| Market seekers | ----> | McDonalds (USA) |
| Raw material seekers | ----> | Shell Oil (Netherlands/UK) |
| Production efficiency seekers | ----> | Acer Electronics (Taiwan) |
| Knowledge seekers | ----> | Compaq Computers (USA) |
| Political safety seekers | ----> | Jardine Matheson (Hong Kong) |

## MINI-CASE: THE THEORY OF COMPARATIVE ADVANTAGE

1. **Using data from the case, explain the difference between absolute advantage and comparative advantage.**

Thailand has an *absolute advantage* over Brazil in the production of both sports shoes and stereo equipment. Using 1,000 production units Thailand produces 12 containers of sports shoes compared to only 10 in Brazil, an absolute advantage of 12 to 10. Thailand also has an *absolute advantage* in producing stereo equipment of 6 to 2.

As long as these ratios are different, *comparative advantage* exists. *Comparative advantage* exists because Thailand has a larger relative advantage over Brazil in producing stereo equipment (6 to 2) than shoes (12 to 10). Therefore the world's consumption is better off if Thailand specializes in producing stereo equipment and trades Brazil stereo equipment for shoes. Brazil should specialize in shoes and trade Thailand for stereo equipment.

2. **This mini-case assumes that free bargaining leads to a price of 4 to 1, meaning that for each container of stereo equipment exported to Brazil, Thailand imports 4 containers of shores from Brazil. Recalculate what happens to production and trade between Brazil and Thailand if the price were 3 to 1 (3 containers of shoes equals 1 container of stereo equipment).**

Trade at a price of 3 containers of shoes to one container of stereo equipment. (See Exhibit A.4).

| | *Shoe Production Plus/minus trade* | *Stereo Production Plus/minus trade* |
|---|---|---|
| Thailand produces 6,000 containers of stereo equipment and exports 1,600 containers | 0 + 4,800 = 4,800 | 6,000 - 1,600 = 4,400 |
| Brazil produces 10,000 containers of shoes and exports 4,800 containers | 10,000 - 4,800 = 5,200 | 0 + 1,600 = 1,600 |
| World production and consumption | 10,000 ctrs | 6,000 ctrs |

3. **What bargaining factors will determine the actual price terms of exchange between the two countries? How might exchange rates enter into this price determination?**

Bargaining factors must include the political consequences of complete specialization. Shoe workers in Thailand and stereo equipment workers in Brazil will lose their jobs. Another factor would be the influence of other countries on supply and demand worldwide. Given the current globalization of markets, it is unlikely that bargaining only between Brazil and Thailand will determine the final trade price. It will be a global price.

Exchange rate changes could make the competitiveness of both shoes and stereo equipment increase or decrease. For example, if Brazil's exchange rate weakened it would reduce its market demand for imported stereo equipment that might force a reduction in the price of stereos such as a 2 to 1 ratio of shoes for stereos.

## MINI-CASE: BENECOL'S GLOBAL LICENSING AGREEMENT

**1. How does the global licensing agreement split *risk* and *return*, in a financial sense, between Raisio and McNeil?**

The success of a global license such as this one depends primarily on how diligently and effectively the licensor (McNeil) pursues its distribution rights. For the most part, the investments in product production, distribution, and promotion would be funded by McNeil. Thus McNeil carries significat financial risks associated with adequate returns on its own investments and expenditures. For Raisio, although it is not investing capital in any significant way to support the global distribution of its licensed property, it is subject to the risk that the distributor does not do a very good job with its exclusive rights. Raisio would therefore suffer the opportunity losses associated with a lost potential market, but not out-of-pocket expenses or investments as would McNeil.

**2. How will the returns to Raisio accrue over the short-to-medium-to-long term under the agreement, assuming the product is met with relative success?**

Under the agreement Raisio receives returns three ways.

- In the short-term, the milestone payments represent a known and assured series of cash inflows to Raisio for its intellectual property. Raisio incurs no direct expenses related to these payments; they are simply returns on the intellectual property held by Raisio, and in which it has invested years of capital and intellectual resources to create.

- On a continuing basis, as Benecol gains wider and wider acceptance and distribution, Raisio would continue to provide all of the stanol estor – Benecol's key chemical ingredient manufactured by Raisio alone – assuring a continuing sale at an acceptable transfer price. Note that this is more consistent with Raisio's traditional core competencies, the manufacturing of industrial chemicals. (By the way, students may be surprised to find that margarine is generally regarded as a chemical product.)

- Over the life of the agreement Raisio would receive a royalty payment calculated as a percentage of the final retail product price of any product containing Benecol. This is a very attractive element of the agreement to a company like Raisio, as it in no way requires Raisio to be involved or concerned with the variety of different products or ways in which it may finally be distributed. As such, it simply reaps an income stream on the basis of sales, not profitability.

**3. What are some of the possible motivations to Raisio and McNeil behind a *milestone agreement*? Assume the milestone payments are agreed upon payments from McNeil to Raisio if:**

**a. Raisio successfully completes the expansion of its manufacturing capabilities for stanol ester**

McNeil may be worried that it will invest and expend in developing and marketing Benecol-based products only to find that Raisio is not prepared to provide sufficient stanol estor for rapidly expanding sales.

**b. McNeil successfully introduces Benecol products in major industrial markets, overcoming regulatory hurdles and reaching specific sales goals.**

Given the risks associated with these new products, termed *nutriceuticals*, McNeil may have wished for Raisio to share the risks of overcoming initial barriers to market penetration. If Raisio were to only receive the payments with successful market introduction (however that is measured in practice in this case), McNeil has reduced its total financial risks associated with the Benecol product line.

*Note:* Raisio has never fully described the conditions which had to be met in order for the "milestone payments" to be made. They are generally thought to be a required up-front payment to Raisio, representing a minimum return to the global license and providing an incentive for McNeil to diligently pursue distribution in order to generate some return on this early payment to Raisio.

## CHAPTER 16: MULTINATIONAL CAPITAL BUDGETING

*Questions*

### 16-1. Initial decision

Factors usually involved are a mix of strategic, behavioral, and economic aspects of the firm's total worldwide operations.

### 16-2. Follow-up analysis

Factors are the type of plant needed, the mix of labor and capital appropriate for that particular economy; the kinds of equipment needed; the method of financing; and the impact of the proposed foreign project on consolidated net earnings, on cash flows from other subsidiaries, and on the market value of the parent's share of stock.

### 16-3. NPV or IRR

Yes, they are useful, but they must be modified in certain ways to reflect the differing attributes of cash flow generation and recovery in a foreign country. Some of these differing attributes are listed in the solution to question 4 which follows.

### 16-4. Foreign complexities

Complications include:
1. Distinguishing between project cash flows and parent cash flows
2. Recognizing that parent cash flows depend on the form of financing
3. Looking at the impact of cash flows from the new investment on cash flows of other already-existing subsidiaries
4. Tax and political constraints on the flow of funds back to the parent
5. The various mechanics by which cash may be returned to the parent
6. Differing rates of local inflation
7. The possibility of an unanticipated change in foreign exchange rates
8. The impact of segmented capital markets on the cost of capital
9. The possibility of using host-government subsidized loans
10. Political risk
11. How to treat terminal value.

### 16-5. Which cash flow?

Domestic operating cash flows are automatically and instantaneously available to the parent, so the manner by which an investment is financed can be kept separate from the operating cash flows.. Internationally, cash flows available to the parent must pass through a second step, which in most cases involves converting them to a financial flow. This arises because the foreign subsidiary is a separate corporate entity and probably receives its cash flows in a different currency than the currency of the parent.

In other words, operating cash flows of a subsidiary must pass through some type of "conduit" to become available to the parent, and one task of evaluating a potential foreign investment is to assess several types of conduits that might be used to repatriate funds to the parent.

## 16-6. Risk-adjusted return

Both of the above. Expected return for a proposed foreign project should be compared to alternative home country proposals, with two caveats. One, the returns should be compared on a risk-adjusted basis. And two, the proposed foreign project contributes to a portfolio effect for the consolidated parent company because fluctuations in returns in foreign countries are not necessarily correlated with returns in the home country. Hence total worldwide consolidated return may be more stable than returns in the home country alone.

A multinational firm should also earn a risk-adjusted return greater than local-based competitors can earn on the same project. Otherwise the multinational firm should simply buy shares in local firms.

## 16-7. Blocked cash flows

Where the blockage of cash flows is temporary and/or reinvestment opportunities in the host country have a risk-adjusted rate of return equal to the firm's required rate of return, such blocked cash flows do not lose significant value. If the blocked funds lose value because of low host country rates of return and a progressive weakening of the host country's currency, value is lost.

Blocked cash flows may be included within the traditional net-present-value approache by first compounding them *forward* to the date when the blockage is expected to end, using a compounding rate equal to what can be earned by reinvesting in the host country, reduced by the expected annual depreciation rate of the local currency; and then discounting this hypothetical terminal value back to the present by the firm's required rate of return.

## 16-8. Host country inflation

The multinational firm can multiply each year's expected spot rate by the fraction (1+ host country inflation rate) ÷ (1+home country inflation rate), recognizing that this calculation must be cumulative. This approach is, in effect, discounting future exchange rates by a purchasing power parity factor.

## 16-9. Cost of equity

A foreign subsidiary does not have an independent cost of equity. However, in order to estimate the discount rate for a comparable host country firm, one could try to calculate a hypothetical cost of equity.

$k_{rf}$ is the risk free rate in the host country. This should be the nearest equivalent to the risk free rate in the host country, which will most likely not be the same as the risk free rate in the home country.

$k_m$ is the market rate of return on shares of stock in the host country. Where this is not available in a credible form, because host country markets either do not exist or are dominantly speculative forums, a guess as to the rate local entrepreneurs expect for family-owned enterprises of the average risk class for "normal" or "average" businesses should be used.

$\beta$ is *beta*, the ratio of returns earned in the particular risk class to "normal" or "average" returns earned on equity investments in the host country. In countries without an efficient stock market, this variable is usually a very subjective guess.

## 16-10. Viewpoints

The answer to this question is embodied in Exhibit 16.5 and Exhibit 16.6. Project cash flows are EBITDA (earnings before interest, income taxes, depreciation, and amortization), less recalculated income taxes calculated on this amount as if it were all available to equity investors (the so-called "all equity" approach), less any required additions to net working capital. The impact of interest payments is taken into account in the discount rate used, rather than in the cash flow calculation.

Parent cash flows are the sum of dividends remitted (less any withholding taxes), license and royalty fees remitted, any cash flows recovered by other means (such as altering transfer prices), interest on parent-supplied debt, and repayment of the principal on parent-supplied debt.

## 16-11. Real option analysis

*Real option analysis* inserts a possible preliminary expenditure into the evaluation process. NPV valuation is uncertain in that the expected cash flows might well be either greater or smaller than their mean – but the NPV approach involves using the most likely (e.g., mean) expected cash flows. The question is whether an expenditure of an additional certain amount before making the investment will lower the range of uncertainty. After this preliminary expenditure, the investing firm will hopefully have a more precise set of future cash flows to invest. I.e, the range of uncertainty is narrowed.

This approach is called "real option analysis" because the additional preliminary expenditures can be viewed as the cost of an option to make the investment after the range of uncertainly is reduced.

If it is possible to make such a preliminary analysis, and expenditure, to narrow the range of expected cash flows, real option analysis is a worthy way to supplement traditional capital budgeting analysis. Real option analysis is better regarded as a way to supplement traditional analysis, rather than as a possibly better (or not better) method,

## Problem 16.1 Sarasota Corporation

| Assumptions | | | Values |
|---|---|---|---|
| Cash dividends to be received (euros) | | | € 720,000 |
| Expected dividend growth rate per year | | | 10.0% |
| Current spot exchange rate ($/euro) | | $ | 0.9180 |
| Sarasota's weighted average cost of capital | | | 12.0% |

| **a) PV of dividend stream if euro appreciates 4%** | | 0 | 1 | 2 | 3 |
|---|---|---|---|---|---|
| Dividend stream expected from investment, in euros | | | € 720,000 | € 792,000 | € 871,200 |
| Current and expected spot rate ($/euro) : spot x ( 1 + .04) | **4.0%** | **$ 0.9180** | **$ 0.9547** | **$ 0.9929** | **$ 1.0326** |
| Dividends, in US dollars | | | $ 687,398 | $ 786,384 | $ 899,623 |
| Present value factor | | 1.0000 | 0.8929 | 0.7972 | 0.7118 |
| Present value of dividends, in US dollars | | | $ 613,749 | $ 626,900 | $ 640,334 |
| Cumulative NPV | | **$ 1,880,983** | | | |

| **b) PV of dividend stream if euro depreciates 3%** | | 0 | 1 | 2 | 3 |
|---|---|---|---|---|---|
| Dividend stream expected from investment, in euros | | | € 720,000 | € 792,000 | € 871,200 |
| Current and expected spot rate ($/euro) : spot x ( 1 - .03) | **-3.0%** | **$ 0.9180** | **$ 0.8905** | **$ 0.8637** | **$ 0.8378** |
| Dividends, in US dollars | | | $ 641,131 | $ 684,087 | $ 729,921 |
| Present value factor | | 1.0000 | 0.8929 | 0.7972 | 0.7118 |
| Present value of dividends in US dollars | | | $ 572,439 | $ 545,350 | $ 519,543 |
| Cumulative NPV | | **$ 1,637,332** | | | |

## Problem 16.2 Trefica de Honduras

| Assumptions | Values |
|---|---|
| Expected free cash flow in 2003 | **13,000,000** |
| Expected growth rate in free cash flow | **8.00%** |
| Assumed sale multiple of FCF in year 3 | **10** |
| Spot exchange rate, Lempiras/$ (2002) | **14.80** |
| US dollar inflation rate | **2.0%** |
| Honduran lempira inflation rate | **16.0%** |
| Texas Pacific required return (annual rate) | **20.0%** |

| | 0 | 1 | 2 | 3 |
|---|---|---|---|---|
| **a) Trefica's value if exchange rate fixed** | **2002** | **2003** | **2004** | **2005** |
| Trefica's expected free cash flow (Lp) | | 13,000,000 | 14,040,000 | 15,163,200 |
| Expected sale value in year 3 | | | | 151,632,000 |
| Total expected free cash flow (Lp) | | 13,000,000 | 14,040,000 | 166,795,200 |
| Expected exchange rate (Lp/$) | **14.8000** | **14.8000** | **14.8000** | **14.8000** |
| Trefica's expected FCF in US$ | | $ 878,378 | $ 948,649 | $ 11,269,946 |
| Present value factor | 1.0000 | 0.8333 | 0.6944 | 0.5787 |
| Present value of expected FCF in US$ | | $ 731,982 | $ 658,784 | $ 6,521,959 |
| Cumulative present value in US$ | **$ 7,912,725** | | | |

| | 0 | 1 | 2 | 3 |
|---|---|---|---|---|
| **b) Trefica's value assuming PPP** | **2002** | **2003** | **2004** | **2005** |
| Trefica's expected free cash flow (Lp) | | 13,000,000 | 14,040,000 | 15,163,200 |
| Expected sale value in year 3 | | | | 151,632,000 |
| Total expected free cash flow (Lp) | | 13,000,000 | 14,040,000 | 166,795,200 |
| Expected exchange rate (Lp/$)<br>(PPP: spot * (1+inf in Lp) / (1 + inf in $) | **14.8000** | **16.8314** | **19.1416** | **21.7688** |
| Trefica's expected FCF in US$ | | $ 772,367 | $ 733,483 | $ 7,662,110 |
| Present value factor | 1.0000 | 0.8333 | 0.6944 | 0.5787 |
| Present value of expected FCF in US$ | | $ 643,639 | $ 509,363 | $ 4,434,091 |
| Cumulative present value in US$ | **$ 5,587,094** | | | |

## Problem 16.3 Baltimore Tile Company

| Assumptions | Values | Assumptions | Values |
|---|---|---|---|
| Initial investment in India (Rs) | **50,000,000** | Dividend distribution per year | **75.00%** |
| Indian corporate tax rate | **50.00%** | US corporate tax rate | **40.00%** |
| Sale price in year 5 (Rs) | **100,000,000** | India risk premium to WACC | **6.00%** |
| Baltimore Tile's WACC | **14.00%** | | |

| **Pro forma income and cash flow** | | **0** | **1** | **2** | **3** | **4** | **5** |
|---|---|---|---|---|---|---|---|
| **(December 31st)** | | **2002** | **2003** | **2004** | **2005** | **2006** | **2007** |
| Sales revenue | | | 30,000,000 | 30,000,000 | 30,000,000 | 30,000,000 | 30,000,000 |
| Less cash operating expenses | | | (17,000,000) | (17,000,000) | (17,000,000) | (17,000,000) | (17,000,000) |
| Gross income | | | 13,000,000 | 13,000,000 | 13,000,000 | 13,000,000 | 13,000,000 |
| Less depreciation expenses | | | (1,000,000) | (1,000,000) | (1,000,000) | (1,000,000) | (1,000,000) |
| Earnings before interest and taxes | | | 12,000,000 | 12,000,000 | 12,000,000 | 12,000,000 | 12,000,000 |
| Less Indian taxes at 50% | | | (6,000,000) | (6,000,000) | (6,000,000) | (6,000,000) | (6,000,000) |
| Net income | | | 6,000,000 | 6,000,000 | 6,000,000 | 6,000,000 | 6,000,000 |
| | | | | | | | |
| Add back depreciation | | | 1,000,000 | 1,000,000 | 1,000,000 | 1,000,000 | 1,000,000 |
| Annual cash flow | | | 7,000,000 | 7,000,000 | 7,000,000 | 7,000,000 | 7,000,000 |
| Initial investment | | (50,000,000) | | | | | |
| Terminal value, sales | | | | | | | 100,000,000 |
| Cash flows for discounting | | (50,000,000) | 7,000,000 | 7,000,000 | 7,000,000 | 7,000,000 | 107,000,000 |
| Present value factor | **20%** | 1.0000 | 0.8333 | 0.6944 | 0.5787 | 0.4823 | 0.4019 |
| Present value of cash flow | | (50,000,000) | 5,833,333 | 4,861,111 | 4,050,926 | 3,375,772 | 43,000,900 |
| | | | | | | | |
| NPV of India investment (project view) | | **11,122,042** | | | | | |
| IRR of Indian investment (project view) | | **25.96%** | | | | | |
| | | | | | | | |
| **Cash inflows & outflows to US** | | | | | | | |
| Initial investment (Rs) | | (50,000,000) | | | | | |
| Dividends received in the US (Rs) | | | 4,500,000 | 4,500,000 | 4,500,000 | 4,500,000 | 4,500,000 |
| Sales value (Rs) | | | | | | | 100,000,000 |
| Net cash flows to parent after-tax (Rs) | | (50,000,000) | 4,500,000 | 4,500,000 | 4,500,000 | 4,500,000 | 104,500,000 |
| | | | | | | | |
| Expected exchange rate (Rs/$) | | **50.00** | **54.00** | **58.00** | **62.00** | **66.00** | **70.00** |
| | | | | | | | |
| Net cash flows to parent after-tax (US$) | | $ (1,000,000) | $ 83,333 | $ 77,586 | $ 72,581 | $ 68,182 | $ 1,492,857 |
| Present value factor | **20%** | 1.0000 | 0.8333 | 0.6944 | 0.5787 | 0.4823 | 0.4019 |
| Present value of cash flow | | (1,000,000) | 69,444 | 53,879 | 42,003 | 32,881 | 599,946 |
| | | | | | | | |
| NPV of cash flows (parent viewpoint) | | **(201,847)** | | | | | |
| IRR of cash flows (parent viewpoint) | | **13.94%** | | | | | |

## Problem 16.4 Berkeley Devices

| Assumptions | Values |
|---|---|
| Current spot rate (ringgit/$) | **3.80** |
| Current spot rate (pesos/$) | **50.00** |
| Malaysian ringgit expectation (% change) | **2.000%** |
| Phillippine peso expectation (% change) | **-5.000%** |
| WACC for Berkeley Devices | **14.000%** |

| **Berkeley in Penang (after-tax)** | | **0**<br>**2002** | **1**<br>**2003** | **2**<br>**2004** | **3**<br>**2005** | **4**<br>**2006** | **5**<br>**2007** |
|---|---|---|---|---|---|---|---|
| Net ringgit cash flows | | (26,000) | 8,000 | 6,800 | 7,400 | 9,200 | 10,000 |
| Expected exchange rate (ringgit/$)<br>(spot / (1+.02)) | | **3.8000** | **3.7255** | **3.6524** | **3.5808** | **3.5106** | **3.4418** |
| Ringgit cash flows in dollars | | $ (6,842) | $ 2,147 | $ 1,862 | $ 2,067 | $ 2,621 | $ 2,905 |
| Dollar cash outflows | | - | (100) | (120) | (150) | (150) | - |
| Net total cash flows (US$) | | $ (6,842) | $ 2,047 | $ 1,742 | $ 1,917 | $ 2,471 | $ 2,905 |
| Present value factor | **14%** | 1.0000 | 0.8772 | 0.7695 | 0.6750 | 0.5921 | 0.5194 |
| Present value of cash flow | | $ (6,842) | $ 1,796 | $ 1,340 | $ 1,294 | $ 1,463 | $ 1,509 |
| **Net present value (NPV)** | | **$ 560** | | | | | |

| **Berkeley in Manila (after-tax)** | | **0**<br>**2002** | **1**<br>**2003** | **2**<br>**2004** | **3**<br>**2005** | **4**<br>**2006** | **5**<br>**2007** |
|---|---|---|---|---|---|---|---|
| Net peso cashflows | | (560,000) | 190,000 | 180,000 | 200,000 | 210,000 | 200,000 |
| Expected exchange rate (pesos/$)<br>(spot / ( 1 - .05)) | | **50.00** | **52.63** | **55.40** | **58.32** | **61.39** | **64.62** |
| Net peso cashflows in dollars | | $ (11,200) | $ 3,610 | $ 3,249 | $ 3,430 | $ 3,421 | $ 3,095 |
| Dollar cash outflows | | | (100) | (200) | (300) | (400) | - |
| Net dollar cashflows, total | | $ (11,200) | $ 3,510 | $ 3,049 | $ 3,130 | $ 3,021 | $ 3,095 |
| Present value factor | **14%** | 1.0000 | 0.8772 | 0.7695 | 0.6750 | 0.5921 | 0.5194 |
| Present value of cash flow | | $ (11,200) | $ 3,079 | $ 2,346 | $ 2,112 | $ 1,789 | $ 1,608 |
| **Net present value (NPV)** | | **$ (266)** | | | | | |

**Neither project looks very promising. Berkeley Penang does, however, possess a positive NPV.**

## Problem 16.5 Superior Machine Oil Company

| **Assumptions** | | **0** | **1** | **2** | **3** |
|---|---|---|---|---|---|
| Original investment (Czech korunas, K) | | **250,000,000** | | | |
| Spot exchange rate (K/$) | | **50.00** | **50.00** | **40.00** | **30.00** |
| Unit demand | | | **700,000** | **900,000** | **1,000,000** |
| Unit sales price | | | **$ 10.00** | **$ 10.30** | **$ 10.60** |
| Fixed cash operating expenses | | | **$ 1,000,000** | **$ 1,030,000** | **$ 1,060,000** |
| Depreciation | | | **$ 500,000** | **$ 500,000** | **$ 500,000** |
| Investment in working capital (K) | | **100,000,000** | | | |
| **Project Viewpoint (in US$)** | | **0** | **1** | **2** | **3** |
| Initial investment | | $ (5,000,000) | | | |
| Revenues | | | $ 7,000,000 | $ 9,270,000 | $ 10,600,000 |
| Less costs of manufacturing | **50%** | | (3,500,000) | (4,635,000) | (5,300,000) |
| Gross profit | | | $ 3,500,000 | $ 4,635,000 | $ 5,300,000 |
| Less fixed cash operating expenses | | | (1,000,000) | (1,030,000) | (1,060,000) |
| Less depreciation | **10.0** | | (500,000) | (500,000) | (500,000) |
| Earnings before taxes | | | $ 2,000,000 | $ 3,105,000 | $ 3,740,000 |
| Less Czech corporate income taxes | **25%** | | (500,000) | (776,250) | (935,000) |
| Net income | | | $ 1,500,000 | $ 2,328,750 | $ 2,805,000 |
| Add back depreciation | | | 500,000 | 500,000 | 500,000 |
| Less additional working capital investment | | $ (2,000,000) | | | |
| Sale value | | | | | 5,500,000 |
| Free cash flow for discounting | | $ (7,000,000) | $ 2,000,000 | $ 2,828,750 | $ 8,805,000 |
| Present value factor | **18%** | 1.0000 | 0.8475 | 0.7182 | 0.6086 |
| Present value of cash flows | | $ (7,000,000) | $ 1,694,915 | $ 2,031,564 | $ 5,358,995 |
| Cumulative NPV | | **$ 2,085,474** | | | |
| **Parent Viewpoint (US$)** | | **0** | **1** | **2** | **3** |
| Dividends remitted to US parent | | | $ 1,500,000 | $ 2,328,750 | $ 2,805,000 |
| Add back Czech taxes deemed paid | | | 500,000 | 776,250 | 935,000 |
| Grossed up dividend | | | $ 2,000,000 | $ 3,105,000 | $ 3,740,000 |
| Tentative US tax liability | **40%** | | $ 800,000 | $ 1,242,000 | $ 1,496,000 |
| Less credit for Czech taxes paid | | | (500,000) | (776,250) | (935,000) |
| Additional US taxes due on foreign income | | | $ 300,000 | $ 465,750 | $ 561,000 |
| Cash dividend less added US taxes | | | $ 1,200,000 | $ 1,863,000 | $ 2,244,000 |
| Initial investment & working capital | | $ (7,000,000) | | | |
| Plus sale value at end of 3 years | | | | | 5,500,000 |
| Parent cash flows (US$) | | $ (7,000,000) | $ 1,200,000 | $ 1,863,000 | $ 7,744,000 |
| Present value factor | **18%** | 1.0000 | 0.8475 | 0.7182 | 0.6086 |
| Present value of cash flow | | $ (7,000,000) | $ 1,016,949 | $ 1,337,978 | $ 4,713,237 |
| Cumulative NPV | | **$ 68,164** | | | |

## Problem 16.6 Tostada de Baja, S.A.

| Assumptions | | Value |
|---|---|---|
| Sales price per unit, 2003 (US$) | $ | 5.00 |
| Sales price increase, per year | | 3.00% |
| Initial sales volume, 2003, units | | 1,000,000 |
| Sales volume increase, per year | | 10.00% |
| Production costs per unit, 2003 | $ | 4.00 |
| Production cost per unit increase, per year | | 4.00% |
| General and administrative expenses per year | $ | 100,000 |
| Depreciation expenses per year | $ | 80,000 |
| Tostada de Baja's WACC (pesos) | | 16.00% |
| Terminal value discount rate | | 20.00% |

| Capital Budgeting Analysis | | 2002 | | 2003 | | 2004 | | 2005 |
|---|---|---|---|---|---|---|---|---|
| Sales price, US$ | | | $ | 5.00 | $ | 5.15 | $ | 5.30 |
| Sales volume | | | | 1,000,000 | | 1,100,000 | | 1,210,000 |
| Revenue | | | $ | 5,000,000 | $ | 5,665,000 | $ | 6,418,445 |
| | | | | | | | | |
| Costs per package | | | $ | (4.00) | $ | (4.16) | $ | (4.33) |
| Total costs | | | | (4,000,000) | | (4,576,000) | | (5,234,944) |
| Gross profit | | | $ | 1,000,000 | $ | 1,089,000 | $ | 1,183,501 |
| | | | | | | | | |
| Less general & administration expenses | | | | (100,000) | | (100,000) | | (100,000) |
| Less depreciation expenses | | | | (80,000) | | (80,000) | | (80,000) |
| Operating profit before tax | | | $ | 820,000 | $ | 909,000 | $ | 1,003,501 |
| | | | | | | | | |
| Less U.S. corporate income taxes | 30% | | | (246,000) | | (272,700) | | (301,050) |
| Net income | | | $ | 574,000 | $ | 636,300 | $ | 702,451 |
| | | | | | | | | |
| Dividends distributed ($) (80% of net income) | 80% | | $ | 459,200 | $ | 509,040 | $ | 561,961 |
| Exchange rate (Ps/$) | | 8.00 | | 9.00 | | 10.00 | | 11.00 |
| | | | | | | | | |
| Dividends remitted to parent (pesos) | | | | 4,132,800 | | 5,090,400 | | 6,181,566 |
| Additional taxes due in Mexico | | | | 0 | | 0 | | 0 |
| Dividend received, after-tax (pesos) | | | | 4,132,800 | | 5,090,400 | | 6,181,566 |
| | | | | | | | | |
| Terminal value, US$ (discounted @ 20%) (dividend in 2005/.20) | | | | | | | $ | 2,809,803 |
| Terminal value, pesos | | | | | | | | 30,907,831 |
| | | | | | | | | |
| Total cash flows for discounting (pesos) | | | | 4,132,800 | | 5,090,400 | | 37,089,397 |
| Present value factor (@ 16%) | | 1.0000 | | 0.8333 | | 0.6944 | | 0.5787 |
| Present value of total cash flows (pesos) | | | | 3,444,000 | | 3,535,000 | | 21,463,771 |
| | | | | | | | | |
| Cumulative present value (pesos) | | 28,442,771 | | | | | | |
| in US dollars | | $ 3,555,346 | | | | | | |

## 16-7. Semen Indonesia & Cemex

This is a problem with a multitude of potential solutions. Use the separate spreadsheet analysis for the chapter problem – ***Semen Indonesia.xls*** – and conduct a myriad of sensitivity and scenario analyses using the valuation model.

A few illustrations of objectives or scenarios could be used from the following:

- **Parent versus Project Viewpoint.** Are there specific variables or components of the valuation which benefit one at the direct expense of the other? Are there any specific variables which move both prospective returns in the same directions?

- **Operating versus Financing Cash Flows.** One particularly instructive technique is to have student groups separate those components of the parent's viewpoint capital budget into the two different cash flow streams of operating and financing cash flows. It is also of note to students that traditional capital budgeting analysis performed domestically is based on operating cash flow returns alone, with financing cash flows or components captured by the discount rate (with the exception of APV analysis).

MINI-CASE: TRIDENT'S CHINESE MARKET ENTRY – AN APPLICATION OF REAL OPTION ANALYSIS

1. **How does real option analysis differ from traditional expected value analysis?**

   Stated simply, expected value analysis assumes all events will occur according to their stated or assumed probabilities. Real option analysis assumes that many decisions are *conditional* – that is, they will only proceed in the event of specific outcomes. This means that the negative outcomes are not eventualities according to the stated probability.

2. **How does real option analysis use information gathering differently from discounted cash flow analysis?**

   Discounted cash flow analysis (DCF) analyzes all future cash inflows and outflows as expected outcomes. They are not assumed to change sequentially in time in any response to what occurs before them. Real option analysis assumes that the decisions about subsequent events – cash inflows and outflows – is conditional upon the information and learning which occurs along the path of development.

3. **Recalculate both the expected return analysis and the real option analysis for the Chinese market entry assuming that the revenue probabilities were 25% high and 75% low. Is the project acceptable under either of the decision-making methodologies?**

   _Expected value analysis:_
   Expected value of revenues would now be = (.25 x $130) + (.75 x $50) = $70.
   Expected value of costs remains = $80.
   Expected value of net revenues = ($10).
   Expected value of project = ($15) + ($10) = ($25).

   An unacceptable project.

   _Real option analysis:_
   Expected value of revenues would now be = (.25 x $130) + (.75 x $50) = $70.
   After expending the $15 up-front for R&D, the firm would know which cost path is to occur.

- If it is the High cost path, the project has an expected net revenue of $70 - $120 = ($50). The project is terminated, and no additional expenditure is made.

- If it is the Medium cost path, the project has an expected net revenue of $70 - $80 = ($10). The project would be terminated, and no additional expenditure is made.

- If it is the Low cost path, the project has an expected net revenue of $70 - $40 = $30. The project would be pursued.

Expected value of project = ($15) + [ (0.333 x $0) + (0.333 x $0) + (0.333 x $30)] = $10.

## CHAPTER 17. POLITICAL, ECONOMIC, AND FINANCIAL RISK

*Questions*

### 17-1. Defining risk

Possibilities include:

a. *Fundamentals of Multinational Finance*: p. 374: The possibility of suffering harm or loss, or a course involving uncertain danger or hazard.

b. *Encarta Dictionary*: Chance of something going wrong. The danger that injury, damage, or loss will occur.

c. *American Heritage Dictionary*: To expose to a chance of loss or damage.

d. *The Shorter Oxford English Dictionary on Historical Principles:* Hazard, danger; exposure to mischance or peril.

e. Brealey & Myers, *Principles of Corporate Finance, 6th ed*: Risk, in investment, means that future returns are unpredictable. (p. 179.) Risk is usually measured by the variance of returns or the standard deviation, which is simply the square root of the variance.

f. *Encyclopædia Britannica* (1771 edition - 231 years ago!): In gaming, chance. Chance, in turn, is defined as "In a general sense, a term applied to events not necessarily produced as the natural effects of any proper foreknown cause."

### 17-2. Nature of risk

A *qualitative* risk is inherently subjective, meaning that it proceeds from or takes place within an individual's mind based upon whatever perceptions that individual may have. It can not be measured in numerical terms. A *quantitative* risk is one for which numerical measurements are possible.

### 17-3. Types of risk

*One-sided* risks are those that emphasize only the potential for loss; that is, the possibility that events will turn out worse than some expected norm. An example is a corporate bond, in which a fixed interest payment plus repayment of principal at maturity is promised. No up-side "risk," i.e., possibility, exists because the holder can never receive more than the promised payments. However a down-side risk exists because the company could default on its interest payments or on repaying the principal.

A *two-sided* risk emphasizes the potential for either loss or gain; that is, the possibility events may turn out either better or worse than the expected norm. An example is a share of corporate stock. The value (market price) of the shares could rise or fall, so the holder might gain or might lose.

### 17-4. Sovereign risk

This is a project. Returns may be found, among other places, in *The Wall Street Journal* and *The Financial Times*.

## 17-5. Foreign investment risk

This is a project for which different responses will be found depending on the year that it is undertaken. As of early 2002, an example of a *firm-specific risks* would be the risks taken by Ford Motor Company in buying control of Volvo Motors (Sweden) or Jaguar Motors (England).

*Country-specific risks* in early 2002 would certainly include the risk of starting a new venture in Afghanistan or Iraq. The risk of investing in India or Pakistan when they might be considered on the brink of war would also be a country-specific risk.

A *global-specific risk* would be the demonstrations against an expanding global economy held outside annual meetings of the World Bank, International Monetary Fund and World Economic Forum. These demonstrations could lead to political or economic actions that hurt MNEs.

## 17-6. Business risk

The main attributes of *business risk* are that business results, such as sales, costs, and profits will differ (for better or worse – a *two-sided* risk) from those that had been anticipated.

*Sensitivity analysis* uses an array of "what if?" projections, in which future results are predicted for a set of circumstances having a range of possibilities. Sensitivity analysis is more easily done by computer simulation than by "hand and pencil" techniques – where the effort would drive most evaluators crazy!

*Diversification* reduces business risk by having a set of business operations kept separate so that under-performance by one or more operations can be offset by the chance of over-performance in others.

If a multinational firm can identify particular segments of its business that are *overly-risky*, spinning off or otherwise disposing of those segments (i.e., those assets) may reduce the risk of the whole. However accurately identifying which assets are mostly as risk is difficult, and the logic of diversification is to admit that asset-specific or location-specific assets are extremely difficult to identify in advance.

*Insurance* can be purchased against specifically identified risks, but a firm must consider the cost of the insurance relative to any possible loss.

Losses in the airline and other travel industries after the September 11, 2001, terrorist attacks on the World Trade Center and Pentagon might be considered business risk, in the sense that the damages to the buildings themselves were terrorist risks, but the economic fallout was a business risk.

## 17-7. Ford Motor Company

Sensitivity analysis can treat the additional risk of selling Mazda automobiles under the Ford name plate while retaining the Volvo and Jaguar name plates by either (1) increasing the discount rate for these foreign operations to account for any perceived greater risk, or (2) adjusting the cash flows. Note that such approaches differentiate between these three types of cars and Ford's long-established sales of "normal" Ford cars and trucks under its own nameplate.

Alternatively, one could argue that Ford parent's relationship to these three foreign models of cars and companies increases Ford's worldwide diversification and so reduced risk.

### 17-8. Preferences

One might argue the answer to this question either way, although the authors prefer adjusting the cash flows through a variety of sensitivities, scenarios, and other common budgeting methods.

Argentina, at this writing, has recently devalued its peso and is under great domestic political pressure, such as rioting in the streets and expecting a new president (the third president within two months, at latest count) to do something to reverse the country's economic downturn. One might argue that the risks of Argentina are entire-country derived and so are better treated by increasing the discount rate. This is because the risks arise from factors much broader than just the performance of a single company (subsidiary) within a predictable economic environment. The entire Argentine economy will be affected by political events there, and company success will simply be carried away by these non-company events.

Given the political instability of Argentina, a reasonable prediction of future cash flow, with or without an adjustment for political risk, seems impossible.

### 17-9. Discount rate

The appropriate discount rate should be taken from the rate demanded by local investors. However in countries where capital markets are underdeveloped; and where most ventures are owned by individuals or families, where results (financial statement) are not reported and the shares not traded, no market reference points exist from which to estimate what a local discount rate would be. The decision (the rough guess) of the appropriate discount rate should be made by a mix of local and headquarter financial officers, after sleuthing around to get what fragments of information can be gleaned from local investors.

(One of the authors once reviewed for publication a manuscript in which it was argued that membership in local country clubs, jockey clubs, and so forth, in Chile was a normal cost of acquiring business and economic information Lacking informed business publications due to corporate secrecy, such clubs were the normal means by which business information was passed from one business person to another.)

### 17-10. Success!

Despite the fact that foreign investments provide benefits to both country and multinational company, the two may differ about the magnitude of benefits received relative to the cost. Host governments often prefer more control over firms operating within their country, while multinational investors need to have control over their foreign operations to achieve business success. A large MNC investment may have an impact on a country's balance of payments or foreign exchange rate that the government considers undesirable. Employment of local staff and management versus headquarters assigned personnel for critical jobs may be a cause of disagreement. In addition to these and similar substantive differences, governments may be concerned about the image of a foreign-controlled entity having a significant impact on local economic affairs.

### 17-11. Investment agreements

a. Remittance of fund flows: Primarily MNE. (But host government has a concern over the impact on balance of payments and exchange rate.)

b. Setting transfer prices: Primarily government. (MNE would prefer they not be set in advance.)

c. Third-country exports: About equal – but with opposite motives. Firm wants to control and probably limit so other subsidiaries not hurt, whereas government wants more exports to create more employment.

d. Funding social overhead projects: Primarily government. (Although the firm gains in the long run from more educated, healthier employee base.)

e. Taxation methods: Primarily government.

f. Access to local capital markets: Primarily MNE.

g. Some local ownership required: Primarily government.

h. Price controls: Primarily government.

i. Local sourcing requirement: Primarily government.

j. Use of expatriate managers and technical staff: Primarily MNE.

k. Arbitration provision: Both equally.

l. Planned divestment: Both equally

*Comment:* In classifying the above a general observation is possible. The MNE will tend to prefer flexibility, so that it can adjust more quickly to changed economic circumstances. Other things being equal, governments would always prefer to retain the power to regulate or to change regulations at some future date, so they do not give up their sovereign responsibilities.

**17-12. OPIC**

Student project

**17-13. Post-FDI management**

Student project.

**17-14. Country-specific risk**

Student project.

### 17-15. Corruption

Student project. The authors got the following mean rankings by continent:

| | | |
|---|---|---|
| 2 South Pacific countries | Mean of 9.0 | Australia and New Zealand. |
| 2 North America countries | Mean of 8.3 | Mexico was not in the list. |
| 24 European countries | Mean of 7.0 | Range from 10.0 to 3.9 (Belarus) |
| 6 Asian countries | Mean of 6.2 | |
| 2 Mid-east countries | Mean of 5.9 | Israel and Jordan |
| 8 African countries | Mean of 4.8 | |
| 6 Latin American countries | Mean of 4.8 | |

### 17-16. U.S. anti-bribery law

From an ethical point of view, as well as a long-run collective economic point of view, the ethics laws are correct in that they support American principles of honesty in business dealings. Additionally the general knowledge that American firms and/or officers can not be bribed will (one hopes) lead to fewer attempts to bribe.

On the other hand, because business practice in much of the world involves bribery (*guanxi* in China, *la mordida* or "the bite" in Mexico), American business undoubtedly loses substantial current business, and the United States as a country has a greater deficit in its currency account because of the law. One important question is whether European countries and Japan will eventually follow the U.S. lead, or will attempt to take advantage of the restrictions placed on U.S. companies by its government.

The major non-government organization devoted to exposing and ending bribery and other forms of corruption is Germany-based Transparency International (TI). Their annual report provides a lengthy list and discussion of bribery around the world and actions taken to end it. (Transparency International, Heylstrasse 33, D-10825 Berlin, Germany. Email: ti@kabissa.com. Website: http://www.transparency.de)

*Problems*

### 17-1. Cool Cola Company

Goal conflict may arise from the interaction of Cool Cola Company with the basic economic policies of India and from certain non-economic policy areas. Because Cool Cola Company will be moving capital into and out of India at various times, its actions will have an influence on Indian monetary and fiscal policy, balance of payments, exchange rate policies, and development policies. Cool Cola Company' activities may also have an influence on India's perceptions of the degree to which it should protect local beverage producers from "more efficient" foreign firms. For example, what would India do if Cool Cola become so popular that domestic soft drink bottlers are driven out of business?

Goal conflict is also possible in such areas as perceptions of "cultural pollution." If Cool Cola becomes truly popular and is consumed by most of the young students in India, would elderly Indians believe that their culture was being subverted by an American import? Would they tolerate this?

Goal conflict may also arise from private groups within Europe and North America where Cool Cola Company sells most of its production. If India were to initiate an attack on Pakistan, would consumer boycotts take place? Would consumer boycotts take place if Cool Cola Company's factory work force included otherwise unemployed children who are in any case not able to attend schools because of general poverty?

### 17-2. Political risk forecast – India

This project must be completed with the use of current periodicals describing the current situation in India, including India's desire for economic development versus preserving its traditional way of life, India's conflict with Pakistan over Kashmir, and India's decision to text nuclear bombs after Pakistan did so.

### 17-3. Operating strategies – India

*Marketing strategies* should include agreement on domestic market competition, such as whether or not competing soft drink companies (Coca Cola and Pepsi Cola) will be allowed to set up bottling plants in India, either at all or only after a designated period during which Cool Cola has a protected monopoly. Requirements and/or limitations on the export of Cool Cola drinks to other countries must be considered; India would undoubtedly like Cool Cola to export to the maximum, but Cool Cola bottlers in other countries would object. Trademark protection in India should be assured.

*Production strategies* should include agreements on local sourcing of bottles and water – one resumes the secret syrup will be imported from the parent. Any desires (by Cool Cola) or constraints (by India) on the location of both the present and any future bottling plants should be considered.

*Finance strategies* should include agreements on capital structure proportions, such as using foreign currency debt, access to foreign exchange markets, restrictions on repatriation of funds (interest, dividends, and debt principal), and present or future local ownership vs. Cool Cola Company's initial 100% ownership. Cool Cola Company's right to use such techniques as hedging, swaps, linked financing, and export credit insurance must be negotiated (especially if domestic Indian firms are not granted free access to all aspects of international money and capital markets), as must be Cool Cola Company' right to borrow from either foreign or local banks.

*Organizational strategies* should include discussions on the degree of joint ownership of a joint venture, even if the present venture is 100% owned by Cool Cola, because future Indian government might change the rules for wholly owned subsidiaries of foreign companies. Fees, licensing royalties, and management agreements with the parent must be approved by India. Availability of visas for foreign employees must be agreed upon, as well as import duties that might be levied on the personal possessions of foreign employees transferred to India. The tax status of foreign employees must be made clear, both for salaries and for such benefits as housing, school allowances and use of corporate-owned cars.

**17-4. Crisis plan – India**

The crisis plan should include provisions for evacuating all non-Indian personnel and protecting key corporate records if the Indian political environment becomes so chaotic as to be dangerous for foreign firms and people within the country.

**17-5. Divestment – China**

This is a project, the results of which depend on when it is undertaken. In essence, the plan will evolve around three questions:

a. Can a buyer willing to pay U.S. dollars be found, or must the bottling plants be sold for Chinese renminbi? The convertibility of the renminbi at the time the bottling plants are sold, as well as future expectations for China's economy, are critical variables.

b. If the bottling plants can only be sold for non-convertible renminbi, can Cool Cola find some way of using those renminbi -- such as buying Chinese goods to export to the U.S. for sale through some outlet. Does a cola company have any ability and expertise in non-beverage items?

c. Can Cool Cola design its original investment plan so that it can divest at a minimum loss or maximum gain relative to its original investment?

**17-6. McGregor's Coffee Canteens**

One method of evaluating Tom Broderick's issues is to construct an expected value tree of compounded probabilities.

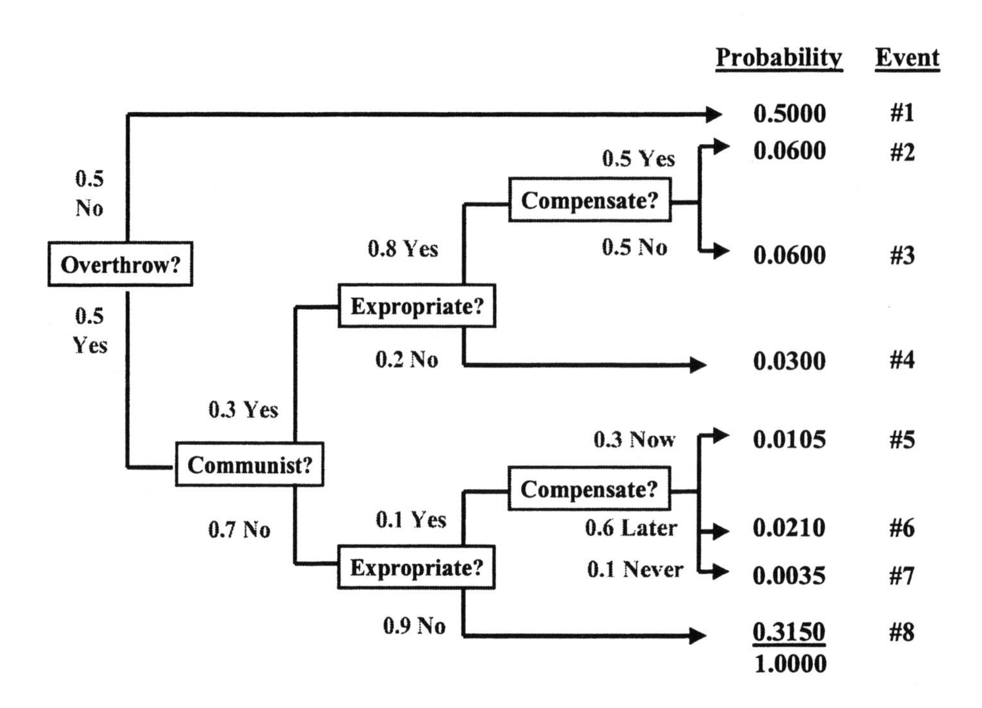


<u>Present value calculations of compensation amounts:</u>

| | | |
|---|---|---|
| Full value of compensation now | $2,500,000 | |
| Full compensation 1 year from now | $2,155,172 | ($2,500,000 ÷ 1.16) |
| 30% compensation now | $750,000 | |
| 30% compensation 2 years from now | $557,372 | ($750,000 ÷ $(1.16)^2$ ) |

<u>Value calculations (thousands of dollars):</u>

| Event # | Probability | Value if no insurance | Prob x value | Value with insurance | Prob x value |
|---|---|---|---|---|---|
| 1 (full, now) | 0.5000 | 2,500 | $1,250 | $2,480 | $1,240 |
| 2 (30%in 2 yrs) | 0.0600 | 557 | 33 | 2,480 | 149 |
| 3 (none) | 0.0600 | 0 | 0 | 2,480 | 149 |
| 4 (full now) | 0.0300 | 2,500 | 75 | 2,480 | 74 |
| 5 (full now) | 0.0105 | 2,500 | 26 | 2,480 | 26 |
| 6 (full in 1 yr) | 0.0210 | 2,155 | 45 | 2,480 | 52 |
| 7 (none) | 0.0035 | 0 | 0 | 2,480 | 9 |
| 8 (full now) | 0.3150 | 2,500 | 788 | 2,480 | 781 |
| Sum | 1,0000 | | $2,217 | | $2,480 |

| | | |
|---|---|---|
| Cost of insurance: | $20,000 | ($2,500,000 x $0.80/$100) |
| Expected value without insurance | $2,217,000 | |
| Expected value with insurance | $2,480,000 | |

Because the estimated expected value with insurance is greater, Tom Roderick should purchase OPIC insurance for McGregor's Coffee Canteens.

## MINI-CASE: MOTOROLA & TELSIM OF TURKEY

**a. Why does a company like Motorola, a telecommunications company, get into the business of lending and financing?**

Telecommunications is a capital intensive industry. In order to provide even startup services in an emerging market, the provider must build the entire infrastructure for most of the system – before there is any possibility of cash inflows. Motorola knew that whichever telecom manufacturer like itself provided financing, making it easier and cheaper to buy the equipment, would get the sale. Sales were increasingly hard to find in the year 2000, and the potential of the Turkish market great.

**b. Should Motorola have extended so much credit to a privately-held telecom company in an emerging market like Turkey?**

Difficult to say. Of course in retrospect, it appears a very unsound decision. But in the context of the telecommunications market in 1999 and 2000, as the market which had previously been growing at such an astronomical pace slowed, companies like Nokia and Motorola were faced with declining sales and more intense competition. The Turkish market was promising, the partner a well-established political family of considerable wealth and influence.

It is also important to note that Motorola had attempted to protect itself against possible default by the Uzan family by holding the equity shares in TelSim against the vendor financing obligations. Motorola had obviously not anticipated that, under Turkish corporate governance laws, that TelSim could issue more shares at will – without its approval – effectively undermining Motorola's equity holdings and implicit insurance.

**c. What did Motorola hope to gain by providing both technology and financing to TelSim?**

The real strategic motivation for Motorola was establishing its equipment as the foundation for the system. This would give it the upper hand in future purchases, and establish its technology as the basis for the Turkish market.

## CROSS-BORDER MERGERS, ACQUISITIONS & VALUATION

### 18-1. Cross-border trends

Recent trends in cross-border mergers and acquisitions have been dominated by capital movements among the developed countries, not the developing. Total cross-border M&A activity in the developing or emerging countries totaled only $86 billion in the year 2000, a mere 8% of global M&A activity.

### 18-2. Shareholder value

The question is really what the "true value" of the target firm is. Acquisition targets are typically expected to yield major synergistic benefits to the acquiring company. These synergies are typically not known to the seller (hopefully), allowing many sellers to sell at a price which they consider attractive and true, while the buyer is able to acquire a business at a price which will allow it to create more than adequate value as a result of its actions after acquiring the company.

### 18-3. Management and shareholder value

This is a question which will be an increasing lightning rod for debate in the post-Enron/WorldCom business environment. Internal growth, what is often termed *organic growth*, requires a firm to steadily continue the pursuit of its traditional business lines and expansion through primarily expanding existing businesses in existing markets. Acquisition of an existing business, *inorganic growth*, allows a company to leap-frog the early stages of building a business, and acquire existing businesses which already possess customers, suppliers, markets, and operating cash flows.

The growing debate is on what the actual goal is that management is pursuing in its organic and inorganic growth strategies. The Enron/WorldCom debacles illustrated the singular pursuit of accounting-based earnings – in the belief that the creation of shareholder value was purely about earnings growth. However, the markets, after taking a closer look at the earnings quality of these and other companies, have altered their opinions of their value considerably. Senior management in many firms has long been accused of being more interested in expansion of power than creation of shareholder value. Acquisitions have long offered a major opportunity for the exertion and expansion of that power.

### 18-4. Cross-border drivers

The six primary drivers for cross-border mergers and acquisitions are:

1. To gain access to strategic proprietary assets
2. To gain market power and dominance
3. To achieve synergies in local/global operations and across different industries
4. To become larger, and then to reap the benefits of size in competition and negotiation
5. To diversify and spread their risks wider
6. To exploit financial opportunities which they may possess and others desire.

### 18-5. Stages of acquisition

*Stage II: Completion of the ownership change transaction (the tender).* As seen in a number of recent contested cross-border acquisitions, the strategy and process of affecting the tender – acquiring control over a target firm – is equally important in a financial sense. For example, the requirement by many countries that a tender be made to all remaining shareholders after hitting some government-established threshold can have an enormous impact on the capital cost of an acquisition. Although effective control may be increasingly gained through a so-called creeping acquisition, in which shares accumulated gradually from the open market without a public tender, the requirement that further share purchases be made only if acquired as a whole at a premium establishes a financial barrier to rapid and free-form acquisition strategies.

*Stage III: Management of the post-acquisition transition; integration of business and cultures.* It depends on how the acquired company is to be operated. If it is to be operated independently as a stand-alone business with its own operations, financial structure, and corporate culture, or integrated into the family of businesses of the acquiring company, every aspect of financial management is not only present but intensified. Differences in performance evaluation systems, risk-taking behavior, capital structure, the use of credit terms and net working capital structures, etc., all influence the relative success or failure of the third and last stage of the acquisition process.

### 18-6. Shareholder rights

All markets need rules and regulatory processes to operate fairly – at least in the eyes of that country or culture. Few business arenas demonstrate the power and value of information like that in the market for corporate control. Issues such as insider trading, public tender offers, and one-share-one-vote debates highlight the fact that those investors or agents holding information about probable future events before that of the general market have a distinct advantage in making a great return or profit on their trading activities. Most countries have established a series of securities trading laws which attempt to level the playing field for big versus small investors.

### 18-7. Settlement

The decision over whether settlement of an acquisition is to be in cash or shares of stock is very important, and has been known to make the critical difference over who wins an acquisition bidding battle. Depending on who the seller is, payment in cash in many countries results in immediate tax liabilities which may or may not be desirable. Secondly, depending on whether the acquiring company's shares are considered overvalued or undervalued at the time, accepting shares may be considered a risky replacement for cash. Typical of the field of finance, it is not always how much you pay, but when and how you pay which may eventually make the difference.

### 18-8. Corporate cascades

Countries have very different belief systems over how market economies and share trading and ownership should work. A system like that seen in the Telecom Italia case would not be acceptable in a country like the United States in which transparency of control and influence is considered necessary for all publicly traded companies in order that investors have sufficient and timely information for making rational investment decisions. The corporate cascades demonstrated by the Telecom Italia case are considered by many in different countries as an abuse of majority ownership control in which only the voice of the plural or major owner is heard, and the rights and opinions of minority shareholders become in effect null and void.

### 18-9. Free Cash Flow versus Profit

> *Academia always focuses on the present value of free cash flow as the definition of value, yet companies seem to focus on "earnings" or "profits."*

This is useful either as the basis for class discussion or simply a self-help question for the individual reader. The following notes may be helpful in initiating a dialogue.

a) "Academia" or outsiders valuing companies focus on the ability of a firm to create value as we know it, which is cash flow. "Companies," meaning management, have a tendency to focus on those issues which they have the largest degree of direct managerial control of – and responsibility for – which is more immediately profitability. The market looks to earnings and EPS growth as indicators of general performance, but will look much further and deeper – to cash flow eventually – for valuation.

b) *Profit* is an accounting measure of residual earnings available to equity holders. *Cash flow* is the actual liquid cash balances and flows available to management within a period of time. A classic distinction is that of the concept of *depreciation*. *Depreciation* expenses are charged against income, and deductible towards tax liabilities. They are, however, what is termed a *non-cash expense*, since the payment is actually to the company itself, not to any external party. The cash flow represented by the depreciation charge never leaves the firm.

c) As noted in the text, the equation for Free Cash Flow (FCF) is derived from the financial statements of the firm (including the measure of profitability – Earnings Before Interest, Taxes, Depreciation and Amortization -- EBITDA):

$$FCF = EBITDA - Taxes - Chg\ NWC - Capex$$

Note that the first two terms are pulled from the Income Statement of the firm, representing the basic earnings of the business before financial and accounting changes, and payments to government. The second two terms represent ongoing investment which may or may not be required to sustain the business.

**18-10. Discounted Cash Flow Valuation**

a) The discount rate and the cash flows should be on an after-tax basis. Students often forget that most calculations of the weighted average cost of capital for a firm include the deductibility of interest towards taxes (the (1-t) term). The tax basis of the discount rate and the cash flows being measured should be on the same basis.

b) The proper discount rate is the risk-adjusted cost of capital. This includes the cost of acquiring the capital in the proportions of debt and equity which the project is to be funded. In addition, the opportunity cost of this capital is for investments of similar expected risk and return; therefore, if the investment is potentially riskier, the discount rate should include a risk premium which reflects the expected returns investors receive for undertaking similar projects of similar risk.

c) The most direct approach to refuting the statement is the simple fact that $1 invested in an interest-bearing account will compound in its value over time. Cash flows occurring at future dates must therefore be valued on the basis of their opportunity costs, which are calculated as the compounded value of the next best alternative use of the funds.

### 18-11. Comparables and market multiples

The traditional method of discounted cash flow focuses on the firm itself and captures little of the market-based value concepts of the competitive landscape in which the firm operates. Market multiples and earnings multiples of comparable firms in that industry provide a bit more detailed insight into the investment choices made inside the target firm and outside by investors as they view the target firm amongst its competitors. Discounted cash flow may not always capture value residing in assets or knowledge held by the firm (real option analysis may, however), while a number of different multiples may capture portions of it in their varied mix.

### 18-12. Market-to-book

The M/B ratio provides some measure of the market's assessment of the employed capital per share versus what the capital cost. The *book value* of a firm is the value of common stock as recorded on the firm's balance sheet plus the retained earnings (cumulative capital reinvested from earnings). If the M/B ratio exceeds 1, it implies that the firm's equity is currently valued in excess of what stockholders invested in the firm. Like the PE ratio, the magnitude of the M/B ratio, as compared to its major competitors, reflects the market's perception of the quality of the firm's earnings, management, and general strategic opportunities.

***Problems***

### 18-1. PE valuation of Global.com

Mechanically, we first calculate the P/E multiples of 35 and 40 for the current EPS and the expected EPS.

| *Time* | *EPS* | *P/E of 35* | *P/E of 40* |
|---|---|---|---|
| Last year | ($1.20) | | |
| This year | $0.75 | $26.25 | $30.00 |
| Next year | $1.85 | $64.75 | $74.00 |

Since equity markets are forward-looking, they are focused on the expected earnings of $1.85 per share, and would be driving the value of the share towards the $64 to $75 range (assuming the multiple approach works).

### 18-2. Bidding on Sao Paulo cellular rights

This problem is a classic example of the distinction between a project level valuation viewpoint and the viewpoint of a foreign investor or parent company.

*Brazilian real Viewpoint (Project Viewpoint)*

A discounted cash flow analysis on the local level, in Brazilian real, utilizes the real discount rate of 32.0%. This discount rate reflects the risk-adjusted weighted average cost of capital for this specific investment, and reflects (invisibly) the actual financing structure in terms of debt and equity utilized.

| *Cash flow estimate* | *NPV (R$)* | R$1.70/$ *NPV ($)* |
|---|---|---|
| Best case | 1,867 | 1,098 |
| Moderate case | 1,376 | 810 |
| Worst case | 293 | 172 |

*U.S. dollar Viewpoint (Foreign Investor Viewpoint)*
A discounted cash flow analysis in U.S. dollar terms would utilize the expected exchange rate scenarios as part of the discounting process. Each of the expected Brazilian real cash flows is first converted to U.S. dollars and then discounted by the U.S. dollar discount rate of 18.0%. Because there are 9 different potential cash flow streams (3 cases x 3 exchange rate expectations), the following three combinations would provide a combined Best Case, Moderate Case, and Worst Case range.

| *Cash Flow Estimate* | *Year 0* | *Year 1* | *Year 2* | *Year 3* | US$ *NPV* |
|---|---|---|---|---|---|
| Best CF with Best Exchange Rate | (794) | 324 | 1,176 | 2,235 | $1,685 |
| Moderate CF with Moderate Exchange Rate | (794) | 306 | 842 | 1,600 | $1,043 |
| Worst CF with Worst Exchange Rate | (794) | 275 | 455 | 600 | $ 131 |

The bids from the Brazilian perspective could range as high as R$1,867 (US$1,098), and from a U.S. dollar-based perspective as high as $1,685. The bid needed to assure competitiveness is one which falls between these two values. The bid is not likely to be much higher than the $1,098 value given that from a U.S. perspective, the Moderate/Moderate case itself is $1,043.

Final Note: It may be also helpful to point out to students that in a perfect world in which all exchange rates and interest rates reflected all pure international equilibrium conditions – particularly purchasing power parity – that it would not matter from which perspective the cash flows and discounting was performed. Alas, we do not live in that world. The markets for capital (debt and equity, credit quality, liquidity, corporate governance structure, etc.) and currencies (relative inflation, balance of payments, economic growth expectations, political stability, etc.) are not so aligned.

**18-3. Tsingtao Brewery Company (A)**

The spreadsheet, Tsingtao.xls, which accompanies this book's teaching supplements, is useful in either checking or aiding in the construction of student spreadsheets. Using the spreadsheet, a variety of sensitivities on the drivers of free cash flow are easily run.

**18-4. Tsingtao Brewery Company (B)**

Student project.

## MINI-CASE: CEMEX OF MEXICO BIDS FOR SEMEN GRESIK OF INDONESIA

1. **What was the bias of the bidding process as structured? Did it benefit the seller over the buyer?**

   The bidding process was structured to benefit the seller. By having two rounds, where the winner of the first round had the right to match the highest bidder in the second round, it provided additional incentive for bidders to bid higher in the first round. Because one of the primary motivations of privatization is to raise capital for the owner, government, this biased bidding structure was accepted by all.

2. **Why did Cemex want Semen Gresik? Why did the Indonesian government want to sell Semen Gresik?**

   Cemex was now a global player in the cement industry. If Cemex was to consolidate its strategic future, it needed to expand its presence in Asia, and the Semen Gresik property provided an excellent opportunity to buy new assets and state of the art facilities at a fraction of the cost of building from ground up. The Indonesian government's motivations for selling government-owned industries was the same as all major privatization efforts — a movement toward free markets and private ownership of assets and industries, a desire to upgrade the technical aspects and international competitiveness of domestic industry, and ultimately, to raise capital.

3. **Do you think Cemex should have anticipated the political opposition to the privatization of Semen Gresik? Should that have affected its bidding?**

   Indonesia was in the midst of historical political change. The resignation of President Suharto in May of 1998 had set the stage for a tumultuous period of transition from a totalitarian leader to more democratic governance. The sale of national industries and assets would be clearly controversial. But the leader of the privatization effort had continued to reassure the principal bidders such as Cemex that the privatization program would be pushed through. What Cemex had not anticipated was how fragmented Indonesia quickly became in the months following Suharto's resignation.

4. **Should Cemex bid the second time around, or walk-away? If it did win the second round bidding and gain the 14% ownership share, how would it actually implement its strategy in Asia using Semen Gresik?**

   This question always leads to substantial class debate.

   Many students believe that Cemex should not bid a second time because Cemex would now be unable to gain majority ownership (at maximum, they would now gain the 14% sold plus, if buying all free float shares, another 35%, totaling 49%). Without majority ownership, the question would the be to what degree of control could Cemex exercise over Semen Gresik's operations and sales. Cemex could possibly end up spending hundreds of millions of dollars in acquiring the privatized shares to gain nothing but passive ownership in a marginally profitable business. With renewed threats of privatization on the horizon.

   The opposing viewpoint is, however, a bit more sophisticated. First, given the fact that Cemex is an outsider and Indonesia highly protective of foreign intervention, it is questionable whether Cemex could ever have exerted dominant unilateral control regardless of ownership percentage. (This point frustrates many students who are used to the Anglo-American concept that majority equity ownership gives an entity dictatorial powers. That is simply not the case in corporate wealth maximizing countries, and generally, in most of the world's emerging markets.) If Cemex were to bid again, it could still possibly "win" the bid, if nothing else, keeping any of its major competitors from gaining influence over a prime cement producing firm in the South Asia regional marketplace. Possibly, with extended negotiations and relationship-building, Cemex may at least be able to spearhead export market development sales efforts, a non-threatening value-added activity to current management and stakeholders. Operating control, however, where Cemex could also add value from its experience as a world-class operator, would still be largely out of their direct influence. Time would tell.

**Postscript: What Happened.**

Cemex did indeed bid a second time, basically bidding the same price of $1.39 per share, plus a put option to the government (call option to Cemex) of acquiring the remaining government held shares over the coming five years. Cemex viewed this still as a strategic opportunity of gaining a foothold in the region, preventing major competitors from acquiring these attractive assets (operating margins were so large they were unheard of in the global industry – a testimony to the impacts of real operating exchange rate exposure), and slowly and steadily expanding global operations. Cemex believed that over time it would eventually gain not only operating influence, but ultimately, majority ownership.

As of July 2002 the Indonesian government continued to struggle with the political debate over the sale of the remaining shares of Semen Gresik to Cemex according to the put option component of the winning bid.

## CHAPTER 19: INTERNATIONAL PORTFOLIO THEORY & INVESTMENT

### 19-1. Diversification benefits

The diversification of a portfolio results primarily in the reduction of risk. For a domestic portfolio, the diversification of the portfolio results in a weighted average expected return, but a reduction in risk as the returns of individual securities will be less than perfectly correlated.

This principle also applies to international diversification, but the definition of the "market" is expanded with many new securities with their respective risks, returns, and correlations being added. The other added component of international diversification is the introduction of currency risk.

### 19-2. Risk reduction

A diversified portfolio has *systematic risk* and *unsystematic risk. Systematic risk* is the risk of the market itself. *Unsystematic risk* is the risk of individual securities within the market and the portfolio. Increasing the number of securities in the portfolio reduces and ultimately eliminates the unsystematic risk -- the risk of the individual securities -- leaving only the risk of the market, the systematic risk.

### 19-3. Measurement of risk

If we assume a portfolio consists of two assets, asset 1 and asset 2, The weights of investment in the two assets are $w_1$ and $w_2$ respectively, and $w_1 + w_2 = 1$. The risk of the portfolio ($\sigma_p$), usually expressed in terms of the standard deviation of the portfolio's expected return, is given by the following equation:

$$\sigma_p = \sqrt{w_1^2\sigma_1^2 + w_2^2\sigma_2^2 + 2w_1w_2\rho_{12}\sigma_1\sigma_2}$$

where $\sigma_1^2$ and $\sigma_2^2$ are the variances of the expected returns of risky assets 1 and 2, respectively. $\sigma_1$ and $\sigma_2$ are their respective standard deviations. $\rho_{12}$ is the correlation coefficient between the two assets' returns.

### 19-4. Market risk

All market risk is not the same because all markets, like individual assets, are not perfectly correlated in their returns. The addition of additional markets to the potential portfolio of the investor reduces the overall market risk below that of any individual market.

### 19-5. Currency risk

Currency risk for a portfolio, like currency risk for a firm or a currency speculator, can be positive or negative. If an individual investors buys a security denominated in a currency, which then appreciates against the home currency of the investor, it increases the expected returns of the investor in home currency terms. Different international portfolios and portfolio managers deal with this concern very differently. Some international portfolios wish to hedge the currency risk as much as possible, focusing on the expected returns and risks of the individual assets for their portfolio goals. Other managers, however, use the currency of denomination of the asset as part of the expected returns and risks from which the manager is trying to profit.

### 19-6. Optimal domestic portfolio

An investor may choose any portfolio of assets which lie within the *domestic portfolio opportunity set*. In order to maximize expected return while minimizing expected risk, the investor will find a combination of the risk-free asset available in the market with some portfolio of risky assets as found in the domestic portfolio opportunity set. The optimal domestic portfolio is then found as that portfolio which provides the highest expected return when combined with the riskless asset and the lowest possible expected portfolio risk.

### 19-7. Minimum risk portfolios

The portfolio with the lowest expected risk is not the same thing as the optimal portfolio. The portfolio with minimum risk is measured only on that basis – risk – and does not consider the relative amount of expected return per unit of expected risk. Modern portfolio theory assumes that investors are risk averse, but are in search of the highest expected return per unit of risk which they can achieve.

### 19-8. International risk

This means that, at least from their perspective, they do not expect that international diversification will result in any net reduction in the potential portfolio opportunity set's risk. This is equivalent to saying that internationally diversifying the portfolio does not cause an inward shift of the portfolio opportunity set as illustrated in Exhibits 19.4 and 19.5.

### 19-9. Correlation coefficients

Many experts have expected the correlations between markets to slowly but steadily increase over time as the world "globalizes." There are, however, many political and institutional frictions and barriers which may cause this to be a very, very long process.

One important development over the past decade complicates this process. While more and more countries have opened their markets to foreign investors and firms, more and more of the world's publicly traded firms are listing and trading in the world's primary equity markets of London and New York in addition to their individual domestic equity markets. This reduces market segmentation, increases correlation, and increases liquidity.

### 19-10. Relative risk and return

The Sharpe measure (SHP) defines risk as the standard deviation of the returns of the portfolio. The Treynor measure (TRN) uses a measure of risk which measures the systematic risk of the portfolio versus the world market portfolio. If a portfolio is poorly diversified, it is possible for it to show a high ranking on the basis of the Treynor measure, but a lower ranking on the basis of the Sharpe measure. The two measures provide different information, but are useful in their own ways when evaluating portfolios which are not always adequately diversified.

### 19-11. International equities and currencies

What sounds so simple at first glance is not. First, exchange rate values change as a result of many factors (as described in earlier chapters of this book), not just business cycles. Expected changes in inflation, real interest rates, political and country risk, current account balances, to name a few, all influence the movement of exchange rates. Secondly, even if business cycles were a primary driver of currency values, business cycles are not perfectly correlated globally. In fact, one way to appreciate this phenomenon is to consider that in 2001-2002 most of the major industrial economies were either in recession or near-recession, but currencies still fluctuated widely. For example, the Japanese yen first depreciated against the dollar in the early part of 2002, but still appreciated significantly by mid-year.

### 19-12. Are MNEs global investments?

Actually, many investors do consider ownership in the securities of a MNE listed on their local exchange as a substitute for international diversification. Although generating its earnings partially in different countries and currencies, its results are reported in the home currency of the parent company. The MNE bears the currency risk of 'international diversification' internally, rather than the investor bearing the explicit risk of international diversification.

### 19-13. ADRs versus direct holdings

The ownership of ADRs on Cementos de Mexico (Cemex) rather than buying shares directly on the Mexico City Bolsa provides a number of attractive advantages to the individual U.S.-based investor.

a. The currency risk is not explicitly observed by the investor, but still exists in practice. The shares which are traded in pesos in Mexico City are translated into U.S. dollars as listed on the NYSE. The shares still possess the currency risk, but the individual investor is not confronted with explicitly translating the currency value of the share prices.

b. The primary advantage of ADRs is the ease by which a domestic investor can acquire equity stakes in companies traded on equity markets around the world. The investor does not have to explicitly worry about translating local currency results into the investor's home currency for performance and management purposes. The costs of conducting transactions is significantly less as ADRs are bought and sold through domestic trading houses and brokers, rather than through a foreign broker relationship, which would be more costly and difficult for a domestic investor to employ.

   The primary disadvantage of ADRs for an individual investor is that he or she is seeing a share price which has already had the exchange rate change embedded in its value. This makes it more difficult to separate the equity change from the exchange rate change in the interpretation of performance. Secondly, the values of some ADRs are often dictated by the foreign market – like that of the NYSE – rather than the fundamental drivers of equity values reflected on the home local stock exchange. This is often due to the magnitude of trading volume as seen on the NYSE in comparison to the home stock exchange

c. The asset manager of a predominantly domestic corporation would probably be well-served in investing in ADRs as a method of internationally diversifying its portfolio, rather than buying shares internationally direct. The relative transaction costs and difficulties would probably dominate.

## Problem 19.1 Investing on the DAX

**The best way to work this problem is to assume a notional principal, say, $100,000.**

| Element | | Jan 1st Purchase | | Dec 31st Sale | Distributions |
|---|---|---|---|---|---|
| Share price, euros | | € 135.00 | | € 157.60 | € 15.00 |
| Exchange rate, US$/euro | $ | 1.0660 | $ | 1.1250 | |

| | Currency | Percentage |
|---|---|---|
| **a. Return on the security in local currency terms** | | |
| Capital appreciation | 22.60 | 16.74% |
| Dividend distribution | 15.00 | 11.11% |
| Total return | 37.60 | 27.85% |

**b. Return on the security in US$ terms**

| | | | |
|---|---|---|---|
| Initial investment in US$ | $ | 100,000.00 | <--------- Assumed notional principal |
| Converted to euros | | € 93,808.63 | |
| Purchases shares at initial price | | € 135.00 | |
| Holding this number of shares | | 694.88 | |
| | | | |
| Which earn this dividend per share | | € 15.00 | |
| Total dividend income | | € 10,423.18 | |
| | | | |
| Ending share price | | € 157.60 | |
| Total euro proceeds, Dec 31 | | € 119,936.07 | |
| | | | |
| End of period exchange rate, US$/euro | $ | 1.1250 | |
| End of period proceeds, US$ | $ | 134,928.08 | |
| | | | |
| Rate of return in US$ terms (ending/beginning)-1 | | 34.93% | |

c. Although both returns appear to be very good for a one year period, the relative return on an individual security should always be compared to that of the market as a whole (or some index of the market).

## Problem 19.2 Portfolio Risk and Return: Boeing and Unilever

| Assumptions | Expected Return | Expected Risk | Correlation |
|---|---|---|---|
| Boeing (US) | 18.60% | 22.80% | 0.60 |
| Unilever (UK) | 16.00% | 24.00% | |

**PORTFOLIO ANALYSIS**

| Weight of Boeing in Portfolio | Weight of Unilever in Portfolio | Expected Risk (percent) | Expected Return (percent) |
|---|---|---|---|
| 1.00 | 0.00 | 22.80% | 18.60% |
| 0.95 | 0.05 | 22.40% | 18.47% |
| 0.90 | 0.10 | 22.04% | 18.34% |
| 0.85 | 0.15 | 21.73% | 18.21% |
| 0.80 | 0.20 | 21.47% | 18.08% |
| 0.75 | 0.25 | 21.25% | 17.95% |
| 0.70 | 0.30 | 21.08% | 17.82% |
| 0.65 | 0.35 | 20.97% | 17.69% |
| 0.60 | 0.40 | 20.90% | 17.56% |
| 0.55 | 0.45 | 20.89% | 17.43% |
| 0.50 | 0.50 | 20.93% | 17.30% |
| 0.45 | 0.55 | 21.02% | 17.17% |
| 0.40 | 0.60 | 21.17% | 17.04% |
| 0.35 | 0.65 | 21.36% | 16.91% |
| 0.30 | 0.70 | 21.61% | 16.78% |
| 0.20 | 0.80 | 22.24% | 16.52% |
| 0.25 | 0.75 | 21.90% | 16.65% |
| 0.20 | 0.80 | 22.24% | 16.52% |
| 0.15 | 0.85 | 22.62% | 16.39% |
| 0.10 | 0.90 | 23.04% | 16.26% |
| 0.05 | 0.95 | 23.50% | 16.13% |
| 0.00 | 1.00 | 24.00% | 16.00% |

| | Expected Return | Expected Risk | Correlation |
|---|---|---|---|
| a. Equally weighted portfolio has | 17.30% | 20.93% | +.6 |
| b. 70% Boeing & 30% Unilever | 17.82% | 21.08% | +.6 |
| c. Optimal portfolio 55% Boeing, 45% Unilever (assume 'optimal' is minimum risk) | 17.43% | 20.89% | +.6 |

## Problem 19.3 Monthly Returns for Major Markets

**Exhibit 19.7 presents monthly returns for 18 major stock markets for the 1977-1996 period. All of the returns have been converted into U.S. dollars and include all dividends paid.**

**These returns as stated would obviously be most directly applicable to investors based in the United States.**

**However, they would also be increasingly relevant to global investors who focus their investment portfolios, and portfolio performance, on the US and London markets. In many cases, the common reference currency for global portfolio performance is the US dollar.**

**Problem 19.4 Sharpe & Treynor Performance Measures**

| Market | Mean Return | Risk-Free Rate | Standard Deviation | Beta | Sharpe | Treynor |
|---|---|---|---|---|---|---|
| Hong Kong | | 5.10% | | | | |
| Monthly | 1.50% | 0.42% | 9.61% | 1.09 | 0.113 | 0.010 |
| Estonia | 1.12% | 0.42% | 16.00% | 1.65 | 0.044 | 0.004 |
| Latvia | 0.75% | 0.42% | 22.80% | 1.53 | 0.015 | 0.002 |
| Lithuania | 1.60% | 0.42% | 13.50% | 1.20 | 0.088 | 0.010 |

## Mini-Case: Private Equity in Latin America -- The Soto Group

**A priori analysis. Revenue enhancement and financing expense reduction not included (set to zero).**

| **Assumptions** | | **Year 1** | **Year 2** | **Year 3** |
|---|---|---|---|---|
| Revenue growth | | **12%** | **15%** | **20%** |
| Revenue enhancement | | **0%** | **0%** | **0%** |
| Direct cost reduction | | **15%** | **20%** | **25%** |
| Financing expense reduction | | **0%** | **0%** | **0%** |

| **(Millions of Argentine pesos)** | **Year 0** | **Year 1** | **Year 2** | **Year 3** |
|---|---|---|---|---|
| Gross revenues | **210** | **235** | **270** | **325** |
| Less direct costs | **(132)** | **(144)** | **(162)** | **(190)** |
| Gross profit | **78** | **91** | **108** | **135** |
| *Gross margin* | ***37%*** | ***39%*** | ***40%*** | ***41%*** |
| Less G&A | **(16)** | **(17)** | **(18)** | **(19)** |
| EBITDA | **62** | **74** | **90** | **116** |
| Less depreciation | **(24)** | **(24)** | **(24)** | **(24)** |
| EBIT | **38** | **50** | **66** | **92** |
| Less interest | **(28)** | **(30)** | **(30)** | **(28)** |
| EBT | **10** | **20** | **36** | **64** |
| Less taxes @ 30% | **(3)** | **(6)** | **(11)** | **(19)** |
| Net profit | **7** | **14** | **26** | **45** |
| *Return on sales* | ***3%*** | ***6%*** | ***9%*** | ***14%*** |

**Ex post analysis. Revenue enhancement and financing expense reductions active.**

| **Assumptions** | **Year 0** | **Year 1** | **Year 2** | **Year 3** |
|---|---|---|---|---|
| Revenue growth | | **12%** | **15%** | **20%** |
| Revenue enhancement | | **5%** | **5%** | **5%** |
| Direct cost reduction | | **15%** | **20%** | **25%** |
| Financing expense reduction | | **25%** | **25%** | **35%** |

| **(Millions of Argentine pesos)** | **Year 0** | **Year 1** | **Year 2** | **Year 3** |
|---|---|---|---|---|
| Gross revenues | **210** | **247** | **298** | **376** |
| Less direct costs | **(132)** | **(144)** | **(162)** | **(190)** |
| Gross profit | **78** | **103** | **136** | **186** |
| *Gross margin* | ***37%*** | ***42%*** | ***46%*** | ***49%*** |
| Less G&A | **(16)** | **(17)** | **(18)** | **(19)** |
| EBITDA | **62** | **86** | **118** | **167** |
| Less depreciation | **(24)** | **(24)** | **(24)** | **(24)** |
| EBIT | **38** | **62** | **94** | **143** |
| Less interest | **(28)** | **(23)** | **(23)** | **(18)** |
| EBT | **10** | **39** | **72** | **125** |
| Less taxes @ 30% | **(3)** | **(12)** | **(22)** | **(37)** |
| Net profit | **7** | **28** | **50** | **87** |
| *Return on sales* | ***3%*** | ***11%*** | ***17%*** | ***23%*** |

## Mini-Case: Private Equity in Latin America -- The Soto Group (continued)

**1. What is the difference between a priori and ex post earnings and cash flows?**

| Difference in earnings (NI): | Year 0 | Year 1 | Year 2 | Year 3 |
|---|---|---|---|---|
| *ex post* | 7 | 28 | 50 | 87 |
| *a priori* | 7 | 14 | 26 | 45 |
| Improvement in earnings | - | 13 | 25 | 43 |

Gross cash flow is assumed here to be: Gross CF = EBITDA - taxes

| Difference in cash flows: | Year 0 | Year 1 | Year 2 | Year 3 |
|---|---|---|---|---|
| *ex post* | 59 | 74 | 97 | 129 |
| *a priori* | 59 | 68 | 80 | 97 |
| Improvement in cash flow | - | 6 | 17 | 33 |

**2. What is the difference between a priori and ex post sale value at the end of year 3?**

| | | Sale Value at Multiple of: | |
|---|---|---|---|
| Difference in valuation: | FCF in Year 3 | 18 | 20 |
| *ex post* | 129 | 2,329 | 2,588 |
| *a priori* | 97 | 1,737 | 1,930 |
| Difference in sale values | | 592 | 657 |

**3. What is Guga Avionics worth?**

Guga is worth different things to different people. To the Soto Group, who is willing to put capital and management expertise into the business, the company is worth between 2,329 and 2,588 Argentine pesos three years into the future (less in present value terms).

This higher value assigned the property by the Soto Group over the existing management group is a result of the buyout, rebuild, resell sequence of the private equity group's expertise.

To the current owners and management of Guga, however, who may not either know the values placed on the business by the Soto Group, or have access to the expertise and capital needed to create the value, it is worth considerably less. This leaves the Soto Group with a wide range of potential bids which may enable it to capture substantial profits from the deal if their expectations prove correct.

**4. What would you recommend -- in addition to the current Soto plan -- to enhance the profit and cash flow outlook for Guga if acquired?**

Anything which would increase cash flow by year 3 would potentially create additional value. For example, although additional capital expenditure would be somewhat costly up-front, given the additional depreciation expenses which they would generate, and potential additional operation cost reductions over the three year period, they may generate added cash flows which more than pay for the additional up-front investment (remember the concept of multiple valuation here).

## Chapter 20: Multinational Tax Management

*Questions*

### 20-1. Foreign tax credits

Governments give tax credits for taxes paid on income generated in other countries in order to prevent double taxation of the same income. At the extreme, imagine two countries that both levy a 55% income tax on the same income. For each $1,000 of income, a total of $550 (to first country) and $550 (to second country) would be levied, making total taxes $1,100 on income of $1,000 – a combined tax rate of 110%. If tax credits were not given, the total tax take would be so high that companies would not find it worthwhile to have foreign operations. And then, of course, the home country would collect no taxes at all.

### 20-2. Tax neutrality

Tax neutrality has several objectives beyond collecting revenue from the tax. They are:

a. Neutralizing tax incentives that might favor or disfavor private investment in other countries.
b. Providing an incentive for home country private investment in other countries.
c. Improving the home country balance of payments by removing any advantages of artificial tax havens and encouraging the repatriation of funds.

### 20-3. Tax environments

Under the *worldwide* approach, taxes are levied on income regardless of where the income was earned – at home or abroad. The home country levies taxes on all income, domestic or foreign, earned by domestic companies. Under the *territorial* approach, taxes are levied on firms within the legal jurisdiction of the home country. That is, income earned within the home country is taxed regardless of whether earned by a domestic or foreign firm, but income earned outside of the country is not taxed, even if earned by a domestic company.

### 20-4. Tax treaties

Tax treaties typically are established to reduce double taxation. They cover taxation in one country of income earned in another country; taxation of dividends, interest, and royalty payments; use or non-use of withholding taxes.

### 20-5. Tax averaging

Tax averaging allows corporate tax payers to apply excess foreign tax credits on income from one country against income taxes levied on income from another country, if all of the income is derived from the same type of business. What this means is that income earned and income taxes paid from a high-tax country can be averaged with income from a low-tax country for purposes of using the foreign tax credit.

### 20-6. Passive income

Passive income consists of dividends, interest, and royalties. Thus passive income is differentiated from *active* income which is earned through operations. Because foreign recipients of passive income are unlikely to file income tax returns in the foreign country (say the U.S.) from which they receive passive income, passive income is most often taxed by a withholding tax.

## 20-7. Value-added taxes

The value added tax is in effect a sales tax on the value added at every step of the production and distribution process, adjusted so that the tax is not cumulative; i.e., a later stage of production does not pay tax on taxes already levied at earlier stages. The advantages of the value-added tax include (1) it is probably more neutral in its effect on economic decisions, (2) the populace is generally more aware that they are paying the tax, and (3) it can be rebated in the case of exports. The latter "advantage" puts countries using the value-added tax at an advantage over those that rely on income taxes on the profit from exports because income taxes can not be rebated.

## 20-8. Branch income

A foreign *branch* is an integral part of the parent company. It is not a separate company. Losses of a foreign branch, therefore, can be deducted from other taxable income of the parent before the parent's income is taxed by the home country. If the foreign subsidiary is organized as a corporation, its losses can not be deducted from taxable income of the parent.

## 20-9. FSCs

A Foreign Sales Corporation (FSC) is a separate corporation that derives all of its income from gross receipts of exports, lease or rental of export property, incidental services provided with the sale or lease of export property, and fees for various services. Such income (subject to some limits) pays reduced U.S. income taxes. Other countries argue that FSCs are illegal under the World trade Organization (WTO) because it is a subsidy to U.S.-exporters.

## 20-10. Tax havens

If all foreign operating subsidiaries were owned by a holding company subsidiary in a tax haven country, income from the operating subsidiaries could be paid as dividends to the holding company and so defer any parent country (U.S.) taxes into the far future – assuming that at some date in the far future a dividend was paid to the parent company itself.) The holding company could reinvest the funds in other foreign countries, free of the burden of U.S. taxes.

## 20-11. Russia

A general discussion question. A definitive answer is not possible because morality (ours presumably being better than that of Russian businesses) might suggest not evading taxes, while competitive necessity might suggest following local practices.

## 20-12. Success?

By words, one might acknowledge the nature of the balance of payments problem being created. By action, the company should do something to rectify the impact it is having. This is necessary both (1) to be a responsible business within the country and not have a longer-run negative impact on that country, and (2) as a matter of showing a willingness to be publicly responsible. Concrete actions might include shifting to local suppliers instead of foreign suppliers – and even helping local suppliers get started or develop the quality of production necessary. Additionally, the firm might see if it could increase its exports from this country.

## 20-13. No home

In general you would prefer to incorporate your headquarters in a country that applies taxes on a territorial approach. Income earned from operations within that country would be taxed, but because you are forming a holding company you would not be taxed again on income earned and already taxed in foreign countries. The worldwide approach would be disadvantageous because you would pay additional taxes, albeit calculated on a "grossed up" basis, on income earned in foreign countries.

## 20-14. Active income

a. Royalties received from a wholly-owned foreign subsidiary - PASSIVE.
b. Royalties received from a non-affiliated foreign company - PASSIVE
c. Royalties received from a foreign branch operation –ACTIVE, in the special sense that all earnings of a non-incorporated foreign branch are automatically taxed as part of the income of the parent company. In this instance, all income of the foreign branch would be taxed, and the royalties as such are not part of the home country tax calculation. Stated differently, income before royalties would be fully taxed; and the payment of royalties is irrelevant for taxation.
d. Profit earned from domestic sales of items manufactured at home – ACTIVE.
e. Profit earned from domestic sales of items imported by the parent from a subsidiary - ACTIVE
f. Profit earned from exports of items manufactured at home to a foreign subsidiary - ACTIVE
g. Profit earned by the parent from sale of a building no longer needed - ACTIVE
h. Interest received from domestic treasury bills held by the parent for liquidity purposes - ACTIVE
i. Interest received from a parent loan to a wholly-owned subsidiary – PASSIVE, unless challenged on the basis that the parent loan was in fact a form of equity investment.
j. Interest received from foreign bank deposits held by the parent as part of its international cash depository system – PASSIVE.

## 20-15. Tax types

a. Corporate income tax paid by a Japanese subsidiary on its operating income – DIRECT TAX.
b. Royalties paid to Saudi Arabia for oil extracted and shipped to world markets – TECHNICALLY NOT A TAX, BUT IN FACT SIMILAR TO A DIRECT TAX.
c. Interest received by a U.S. parent on bank deposits held in a London Bank. Any tax on such interest would be a DIRECT TAX.
d. Interest received by a U.S. parent on a loan to a subsidiary in Mexico – DIRECT TAX.
e. Principal repayment received by U.S. parent from Belgium on a loan to a wholly-owned subsidiary in Belgium – NOT A TAX
f. Excise tax paid on cigarettes manufactured and sold within the United States – INDIRECT TAX..
g. Property taxes paid on the corporate headquarters building in Seattle – INDIRECT TAX.
h. A direct contribution to the International Committee of the Red Cross for refugee relief – NOT A TAX
i. Deferred income tax, shown as a deduction on the U.S. parent's consolidated income state – DIRECT TAX.
j. Withholding taxes withheld by Germany on dividends paid to a United Kingdom parent corporation – DIRECT TAX.

## 20-16. Jurisdictional characteristics

The selection of "natural groups" is subjective, but a rigid grouping by continents seems to collect too many dissimilar regimes. The authors' calculation, with which others might disagree, is as follows. Where multiple rates exist, either the mean or the rate applicable to foreign-owned businesses was used.

| | Mean | Range | | Number in 30s |
|---|---|---|---|---|
| Africa – 21 countries. | 36.0 | 10% | (Botswana) to 50% (Zaire) | 16 |
| Asia – 16 countries | 31.2 | 16½% | (HKG) to 48% (Papua New Guinea) | 9 |
| Caribbean – 11 countries | 23.6 | 0% | (3 countries) to 40% (Barbados) | 4 |
| Europe – 30 Countries | 31.8 | 20% | (4 countries) to 40% (Bulgaria) | 17 |
| Former USSR – 6 cos. | 28.3 | 25% | (2 countries) to 35% (Russia) | 1 |
| Latin America - 20 cos. | 29.8 | 15% | (Brazil) to 45% (Guyana) | 13 |
| Mid-East – 5 countries | 37.0 | 0% | (Bahrain) to 55% (Kuwait) | none |
| North America – 2 cos. | 36.5 | 35% | (U.S.A.) to 38% (Canada) | 2 |
| South Pacific – 4 cos. | 33.5 | 30% | (New Caledonia) to 326% (Australia) | 4 |

Perhaps the most striking thing about the list in Exhibit 20.2 is that 66 of the 115 countries, or 57%, have a corporate tax rate between 30% and 39%. As a general matter, no particular grouping seems to deviate from the general trend of rates in the 30%s, except for the three Caribbean countries (Bahamas, Bermuda, and Cayman islands) that have a zero tax rate.

## 20-17. Value-added taxation

The value added tax is in effect a sales tax at every step of the production and distribution process, adjusted so that the tax is not cumulative; i.e., a later stage of production does not pay tax on taxes already levied at earlier stages. A sales tax could end up being a compound tax if it is assessed at every stage of production and distribution.

## 20-18. Tax credits

Using a hypothetical before-tax foreign income of $100,000:

| | Without foreign *tax credits* | With foreign *tax credits* |
|---|---|---|
| Before-tax foreign income | $ 100,000 | $ 100,000 |
| less foreign tax at 25% | –25,000 | –25,000 |
| Available to parent & paid as dividend | $ 75,000 | $ 75,000 |
| Less additional parent-country tax at 40% | –30,000 | |
| Less incremental tax paid, after credits | | –15,000 |
| Profit after all taxes | $ 45,000 | $ 60,000 |
| | | |
| Total taxes, both jurisdictions | $55,000 | $ 40,000 |
| Effective overall tax rate | 55% | 40% |

Note that with tax credits the effective tax rate is that of the highest jurisdiction through which the income passes, but no higher. Without tax credits, the effect tax rate can be higher than the highest rate of one of the jurisdictions. The tax of $15,000 actually paid in the second jurisdiction is calculated as follows:

| | |
|---|---|
| Available to parent & paid as dividend | $ 75,000 |
| Add back income taxes paid 1st jurisdiction (25%) | + 25,000 |
| Grossed-up dividend | $100,000 |
| Taxes calculated by 2nd jurisdiction (40%) | $40,000 |
| Less credit for taxes already paid | –25,000 |
| Incremental tax paid, after credits, 2nd jurisdiction | $ 15,000 |

**20-19. Indifference**

Income taxes collected by the foreign government are a direct tax. Value-added taxes collected by the foreign government are an indirect tax. Indirect taxes can be rebated, meaning that the European corporation would have one less significant tax to add to its cost base for the sale. Hence the European corporation could sell in the U.S. and compete with U.S. firms at lower prices because it does not have to cover a European tax collection. U.S. firms can not get rebates for the income tax component of their costs.

**20-20. Profitable – eventually**

The branch form of organization would be preferred for the initial years, but after five years the foreign branch should be incorporated in the foreign country. The reason is that income or loss of a foreign branch is automatically income or loss of the parent; hence the losses of the first five years can be deducted in full from home country domestic taxes. When or if the foreign branch is incorporated in the host country, home country taxes are paid only on dividends received from that subsidiary. Incorporating after the first five years would protect the foreign income from home-country taxation until it was remitted as a dividend.

A second consideration is liability. Liabilities (on loans or performance contracts, or caused by losing legal suits) entered into by a branch are the liability of the parent. Liabilities of a separately incorporated subsidiary are not the legal liability of the parent.

## Problem 20.1 U.S. Taxation of Foreign-Source Income

| | Baseline Values | Case 1 | Case 2 |
|---|---|---|---|
| a | Foreign corporate income tax rate | **28%** | **45%** |
| b | U.S. corporate income tax rate | **35%** | **35%** |
| c | Foreign dividend witholding tax rate | **15%** | **0%** |
| d | U.S. ownership in foreign firm | **100%** | **100%** |
| e | Dividend payout rate of foreign firm | **100%** | **100%** |

| | Foreign Subsidiary Tax Computation | | Case 1 | | Case 2 |
|---|---|---|---|---|---|
| 1 | Taxable income of foreign subsidiary | $ | 3,400,000 | $ | 3,400,000 |
| 2 | Foreign corporate income tax | | (952,000) | | (1,530,000) |
| 3 | Net income available for distribution | $ | 2,448,000 | $ | 1,870,000 |
| 4 | Retained earnings | | - | | - |
| 5 | Distributed earnings | | 2,448,000 | | 1,870,000 |
| 6 | Distribution to U.S. parent company | | 2,448,000 | | 1,870,000 |
| 7 | Withholding taxes on dividends | | 367,200 | | - |
| 8 | Net remittance to U.S. parent | $ | 2,080,800 | $ | 1,870,000 |

| | U.S. Corporate Tax Computation on Foreign-Source Income | | Case 1 | | Case 2 |
|---|---|---|---|---|---|
| 9 | Dividend received (before withholding) | $ | 2,448,000 | $ | 1,870,000 |
| 10 | Add-back foreign deemed-paid tax | | 952,000 | | 1,530,000 |
| 11 | Grossed-up foreign dividend | $ | 3,400,000 | $ | 3,400,000 |
| 12 | Tentative U.S. tax liability | | 1,190,000 | | 1,190,000 |
| 13 | Less credit for foreign taxes | | | | |
| | a. foreign income taxes paid | | (952,000) | | (1,530,000) |
| | b. foreign withholding taxes paid | | (367,200) | | - |
| | c. total | $ | (1,319,200) | $ | (1,530,000) |
| 14 | Additional U.S. taxes due | | - | | - |
| 15 | Excess foreign tax credits | | 129,200 | | 340,000 |
| 16 | After-tax income from foreign subsidiary | $ | 2,080,800 | $ | 1,870,000 |

| | Tax Burden Measurement | | Case 1 | | Case 2 |
|---|---|---|---|---|---|
| 17 | Total taxes paid on remitted income | $ | 1,319,200 | $ | 1,530,000 |
| 18 | Effective tax rate on foreign income | | **38.8%** | | **45.0%** |

## Problem 20.2 Discovery Bay Airlines/Hong Kong

| Country | Hong Kong | United States |
|---|---|---|
| Corporate income tax rate | **16.5%** | **35.0%** |
| Dividend payout rate | **75.0%** | |
| Withholding tax on dividends | **15.0%** | |

| Dbay-Hong Kong Income Items (millions US$) | 2002 | 2003 | 2004 | 2005 |
|---|---|---|---|---|
| Earnings before interest and taxes (EBIT) | 8,000 | 10,000 | 12,000 | 14,000 |
| Less interest expenses | (800) | (1,000) | (1,200) | (1,400) |
| Earnings before taxes (EBT) | 7,200 | 9,000 | 10,800 | 12,600 |
| Less Hong Kong corporate income taxes | (1,188) | (1,485) | (1,782) | (2,079) |
| **a. Net income** | **6,012** | **7,515** | **9,018** | **10,521** |
| Retained earnings | 1,503 | 1,879 | 2,255 | 2,630 |
| Dividend remitted to U.S. parent | 4,509 | 5,636 | 6,764 | 7,891 |

| United States Taxation: Grossup | 2002 | 2003 | 2004 | 2005 |
|---|---|---|---|---|
| Gross dividend remitted | $ 4,509 | $ 5,636 | $ 6,764 | $ 7,891 |
| Less withholding taxes | (676) | (845) | (1,015) | (1,184) |
| **b. Net dividend remitted** | **$ 3,833** | **$ 4,791** | **$ 5,749** | **$ 6,707** |
| Add back proportion of corp income tax | $ 891 | $ 1,114 | $ 1,337 | $ 1,559 |
| Add back withholding taxes paid | (676) | (845) | (1,015) | (1,184) |
| Grossed-up dividend for US tax purposes | $ 4,047 | $ 5,059 | $ 6,071 | $ 7,083 |
| Theoretical US tax liability | (1,417) | (1,771) | (2,125) | (2,479) |
| Foreign tax credits (FTCs) | (215) | (268) | (322) | (376) |
| Additional US taxes due? | (1,202) | (1,502) | (1,803) | (2,103) |
| Excess foreign tax credits? | - | - | - | - |
| **c. Net dividend, after-tax** | **$ 2,631** | **$ 3,288** | **$ 3,946** | **$ 4,604** |
| Total taxes paid on this income | 1,417 | 1,771 | 2,125 | 2,479 |
| Income before tax | 4,047 | 5,059 | 6,071 | 7,083 |
| **d. Effective tax rate (taxes paid/income before tax)** | **35.0%** | **35.0%** | **35.0%** | **35.0%** |

## Problem 20.3 Stutz of Germany

| | Part a) | Part b) | Part b) |
|---|---|---|---|
| Dividend payout rate | **50.0%** | **40.0%** | **60.0%** |
| Corporate income tax rate, retained | **45.0%** | **45.0%** | **45.0%** |
| Corporate income tax rate, distributed | **30.0%** | **30.0%** | **30.0%** |
| Added tax for retained over distributed | **15.0%** | **15.0%** | **15.0%** |
| **Stutz' Income Items (euros)** | | | |
| Earnings before taxes (EBT) | € 580,000,000 | € 580,000,000 | € 580,000,000 |
| Less corporate income taxes @ 30% | (174,000,000) | (174,000,000) | (174,000,000) |
| Net income (preliminary) | € 406,000,000 | € 406,000,000 | € 406,000,000 |
| Distributed income | € 203,000,000 | € 162,400,000 | € 243,600,000 |
| Less any added corporate tax | - | - | - |
| Distributed income after-tax | € 203,000,000.0 | € 162,400,000.0 | € 243,600,000.0 |
| Retained income | € 203,000,000 | € 243,600,000 | € 162,400,000 |
| Less added tax | (30,450,000) | (36,540,000) | (24,360,000) |
| Retained income after-tax | € 172,550,000 | € 207,060,000 | € 138,040,000 |
| Total net income, after-tax | **€ 375,550,000** | **€ 369,460,000** | **€ 381,640,000** |
| Total taxes paid | **€ 204,450,000** | **€ 210,540,000** | **€ 198,360,000** |

## Problem 20.4 Odessa Petroleum

| Country | Zaire | United States | |
|---|---|---|---|
| Corporate income tax rate | 50.0% | 35.0% | |
| Withholding tax on dividends paid | 20.0% | | |
| Dividend payout rate | 50.0% | | |
| Current spot exchange rate (ZRN/US$) | 100,000 | | |
| Inflation rate | 20.0% | 3.0% | |

| Odessa's Zaire Income Items (ZRN) | 2002 | 2003 | 2004 |
|---|---|---|---|
| Expected price per barrel of oil (US$) | $ 18.50 | $ 19.50 | $ 19.00 |
| Estimated all-in-cost of production per barrel (US$) | $ 7.50 | $ 6.25 | $ 4.50 |
| Barrels of oil produced (expected) | 1,000,000 | 10,000,000 | 15,000,000 |
| Expected oil revenues (US$) | $ 18,500,000 | $ 195,000,000 | $ 285,000,000 |
| **Expected Exchange Rate (ZRN/US$): PPP** | 100,000 | 116,505 | 135,734 |
| Earnings from oil (ZRN) | 1,850,000,000,000 | 22,718,446,601,942 | 38,684,136,110,849 |
| All in cost of production | (750,000,000,000) | (7,281,553,398,058) | (9,162,032,236,780) |
| Earnings before taxes (EBT) | 1,100,000,000,000 | 15,436,893,203,884 | 29,522,103,874,069 |
| Less Zaire corporate income taxes | (550,000,000,000) | (7,718,446,601,942) | (14,761,051,937,035) |
| **a. Net income** | **550,000,000,000** | **7,718,446,601,942** | **14,761,051,937,035** |
| Retained earnings | 275,000,000,000 | 3,859,223,300,971 | 7,380,525,968,517 |
| Dividend remitted to U.S. parent | 275,000,000,000 | 3,859,223,300,971 | 7,380,525,968,517 |
| **Expected Exchange Rate (ZRN/US$)** | 100,000 | 116,505 | 135,734 |

| United States Taxation: Grossup | 2002 | 2003 | 2004 |
|---|---|---|---|
| Gross dividend remitted | $ 2,750,000 | $ 33,125,000 | $ 54,375,000 |
| Less withholding taxes | (550,000) | (6,625,000) | (10,875,000) |
| **b. Net dividend remitted** | **$ 2,200,000** | **$ 26,500,000** | **$ 43,500,000** |
| Add back proportion of corp income tax | $ 2,750,000 | $ 33,125,000 | $ 54,375,000 |
| Add back withholding taxes paid | 550,000 | 6,625,000 | 10,875,000 |
| Grossed-up dividend for US tax purposes | $ 5,500,000 | $ 66,250,000 | $ 108,750,000 |
| Theoretical US tax liability | (1,925,000) | (23,187,500) | (38,062,500) |
| Foreign tax credits (FTCs) | (3,300,000) | (39,750,000) | (65,250,000) |
| Additional US taxes due? | - | - | - |
| Excess foreign tax credits? | (1,375,000) | (16,562,500) | (27,187,500) |
| **c. Net dividend, after-tax** | **$ 2,200,000** | **$ 26,500,000** | **$ 43,500,000** |
| Total taxes paid on this income | 3,300,000 | 39,750,000 | 65,250,000 |
| Income before tax | 5,500,000 | 66,250,000 | 108,750,000 |
| **d. Effective tax rate** | **60.0%** | **60.0%** | **60.0%** |

## Problem 20.5 Hildalgo's Tax Averaging

| Subsidiary Income Statement | | | BELIZE | | | COSTA RICA | | Total Income |
|---|---|---|---|---|---|---|---|---|
| Earnings before taxes | | $ | 1,000,000 | | $ | 1,500,000 | | |
| Less corporate income tax | 40% | | (400,000) | 30% | | (450,000) | | |
| Net income | | $ | 600,000 | | $ | 1,050,000 | | |
| Retained earnings | | | 300,000 | | | 525,000 | | |
| Distributed earnings | 50% | | 300,000 | 50% | | 525,000 | | |
| Less withholding taxes on dividends | 10% | | (30,000) | 0% | | - | | |
| Net dividend remitted to U.S. parent | | | 270,000 | | | 525,000 | | |
| **US Tax Calculation (individually)** | | | | | | | | |
| Net dividend remitted | | $ | 270,000 | | $ | 525,000 | $ | 795,000 |
| Gross-up: | | | | | | | | |
| Withholding taxes paid | | | 30,000 | | | - | | |
| Foreign corporate income tax paid | | | 200,000 | | | 225,000 | | |
| Grossed-up dividend | | $ | 500,000 | | $ | 750,000 | $ | 1,250,000 |
| Theoretical U.S. tax liability | 35% | | 175,000 | 35% | | 262,500 | $ | 437,500 |
| Foreign tax credits | | | 230,000 | | | 225,000 | $ | 455,000 |
| Additional US taxes due? | | $ | - | | $ | 37,500 | $ | **37,500** |
| Excess foreign tax credits? | | $ | 55,000 | | $ | - | $ | 55,000 |
| **TAX AVERAGING (combined)** | | | | | | | | |
| Total additional US taxes due after averaging | | | | | | | $ | - |
| Excess FTCs to carry forward/back? | | | | | | | $ | 17,500 |
| Effective tax rate on foreign source income | | | | | | | | **36.4%** |

## Mini-Case: Romanian Communications and Cyprus Offshore

1. **How does the creation of the Cyprus Offshore business unit, a type of middle-man, change the credit quality of the buyer?**

   Multinational telecom equipment manufacturers were interested in making sales and financing those sales to Romanian companies, but the current state of business law and creditor rights in Romania made it impossible. By booking the purchases by Romanian Communications through the Cyprus subsidiary, Cypriot business law applied to the purchase and financing contracts, meeting the needs of both buyer and seller.

2. **What benefits and costs accrue to both Romanian and Cypriot government tax authorities as a result of this structure?**

   The Cypriot government gains substantial tax revenues as a result of attracting corporate financing subsidiaries. Although the tax rate itself is quite low, these financial subsidiaries impose little if any cost on Cyprus, and attract some infrastructure and business development while generating tax haven tax returns.

   The Romanian government tax authorities most likely suffer significant tax losses as a result of the use of these offshore facilities. Not only is the Cypriot subsidiary booking the purchases and fronting for the business law and financing structures, it is re-selling product and financing to the parent company, Romanian Communications (RC), at a relatively higher transfer price, thereby reducing the taxable profits of RC in Romania itself.

3. **Although this particular arrangement would be illegal under existing rules and practices among most Western industrial countries, including the United States, do you believe the Cyprus International Business Companies as designed serve a useful purpose other than as a method of reducing tax liabilities?**

   Yes. They provide both parties a type of credit "shield" which allows each to enter into a business agreement in which both parties are satisfied with the result, but both parties also remain consistent with their own prerequisites and requirements for business counterparties.

## CHAPTER 21. REPOSITIONING FUNDS

### *Questions*

### 21-1. Constraints on positioning funds

a. Government mandated restrictions on moving funds out of the country.
   1. Governments may want to preserve or enhance their foreign exchange reserves, so as to maintain or influence their exchange rate.
   2. MNEs might argue that such constraints inhibit capital investment and so in the long run lead to less production, less employment, and less taxes paid by successful business operations.

b. *Withholding taxes on dividend distributions to foreign owners.*
   1. Governments want and often need more tax revenue to finance governmental projects. Additionally, if local investors pay personal income taxes on dividends received, the government may argue quite reasonably that a withholding tax on dividends to foreign investors is simply a way of treating all dividend recipients equally because foreign investors do not file local income tax returns. Governments might also argue that a tax on dividends paid encourages the retention and reinvestment of earnings. Lastly, they might note in some circumstances that the withholding tax on dividends is a tax credit in the home country, and so simply transfers tax collection from home government to host government without any net increase in overall taxation. (This depends on the home government having a higher overall tax rate than the host government.)
   2. MNEs might argue that tax withholding simply adds to the cost of doing the business, which in turn results in higher prices for consumers. They might also argue that ability to move cash from one location to another via the dividend route is a necessary part of being an efficient multinational firm, and that only by being efficient can the firm survive in a competitive world economy. If the firm does not survive, there will be no local jobs.

c. *Dual currency regimes, with one rate for imports and another rate for exports.*
   *1.* Governments may argue that different rates produce more governmental income. An artificially low exchange rate for imports (mean more local currency units are need to import a given import) is in effect a hidden import duty on imports. A higher rate for exports (meaning more local currency units are received for a given export) subsidizes exporters by producing greater export revenue.
   2. MNEs might argue that a subsidy to exports and a penalty on imports misallocates resources and causes the local standard of living to be lower than it might otherwise be because imports are more expensive. They might also argue that a frequent accompanying requirement that foreign currency export receipts must be turned over to the central bank leads to corruption because local firms will use double invoices for exports – an official invoice at a lower price for which the proceeds must be surrendered to the central bank, and a separate unofficial invoice for the real (and higher) price, with the difference deposited in a foreign bank and not reported to the home government.

d. *Refusal to allow foreign firms in the country to net cash inflows and outflows into a single payment.*
   1. Governments might argue this is necessary to keep reasonable statistics on all foreign payments.
   2. MNEs might argue that such a rule is primarily a subsidy to local banks that raises costs for firms doing international business. Anything that impedes firm efficiency has the ending effect of lessening local employment and discouraging (at the margin) foreign investment in the country.

## 21-2. Unbundling

A foreign parent provides a multitude of services for its foreign subsidiary: capital invested, technology made available, engineering expertise, management guidance, and marketing skills, to name the more obvious. Traditionally the foreign parent would be compensated for this mix of inputs with dividends from the subsidiary. However a local government may consider dividends as being too high – in part because they may relate the dividend amount only to monetary capital invested. If the return to owners for the basket of services provided is broken into its component parts, the reasonableness of each component may be more apparent.

Within a single country funds may be moved from subsidiary to parent, or vice versa, without restriction because only one currency and tax jurisdiction is involved. Hence unbundling has little domestic value

## 21-3. Conduits

a. *Imports of components from the parent.* When the subsidiary pays for the imports, funds are moved from host country to home country. The cost of imports is a business expense in the host country and so is deductible in calculating taxable income. In the home country, the export creates taxable income.

b. *Payment to cover overhead expenses of parent managers temporarily assigned to the subsidiary.* Visiting managers might normally receive their compensation from the home office. If their expenses are paid by the subsidiary, the subsidiary ends up with less cash and the parent with more cash – even though no "transfer" has occurred. The tax deductibility is transferred from home to host country.

c. *Payment of royalties for the use of proprietary technology.* This is unbundling, with the subsidiary paying a price (which can usually be judged by the host government as reasonably appropriate or clearly inappropriate) that leads to a fund movement from subsidiary to parent. Royalties are deductible in the host country and create taxable income in the home country.

d. *Subsidiary borrowing of funds of an intermediate- or long-term maturity from the parent.* A parent may use this as an alternative to investing permanent equity capital into the subsidiary. The advantage is that repayment of both interest and principle over future years provides a conduit to move funds from subsidiary to parent. Local retained earnings, over a period of time, can be used to "replenish" the capital originally supplied via the intra-firm loan. Interest payments are deductible in the host country (whereas dividend payments are not). Principal repayment is not taxable in the home country.

e. *Payment of dividends to the parent.* Dividends are the "normal" way of compensating owners for their investment contribution. Dividends are not tax deductible in the host country and create taxable income in the home country. Dividend withholding taxes paid to the host country reduce the cash transferred to the parent firm.

## 21-4. Transfer pricing motivation

A *transfer price* is the amount paid by one unit of a company (domestic or international) for goods or services purchased from another unit of the same firm. As such, a transfer price is needed for every intra-firm transaction. Where buyer and seller are in different tax jurisdictions (i.e., countries), governments are concerned with the possibility that transfer prices are raised or lowered from a "normal" or "appropriate" level in order to avoid taxes.

In most countries tax authorities have the right to declare a given international transfer price as a tax avoidance device. Such countries have the right to reset taxable income to a higher level. The motives for the parent MNE are to minimize taxes and the difficulty is that the burden of proof is on the MNE, not the tax collector, to show proof as to why a given transfer price is reasonable.

## 21-5. Sister subsidiaries

Each subsidiary can produce the currently traded items at approximately the same price as is being paid for the import-export transactions. Hence the only gain must come from either the avoidance of foreign exchange costs (as intended by the present firm) or from the tax effect. The foreign exchange spread is probably minimal. The tax effect suggests that the worldwide firm would be better off if income were transferred from Country Able to Country Baker.

Income could be transferred from Country Able to Country Baker by having Beta, Inc., continue to manufacture and ship to Alpha, Inc. The profit on this transaction would be taxed at only 20%, whereas if Alpha, Inc., makes the goods and includes the same implied market up in its international costing, Alpha, Inc. will pay more income taxes.

## 21-6. Correct pricing

A "correct price," according to the IRS, is one that best reflects an arm's length transaction; i.e., what price one would charge if selling to a completely unrelated buyer. Within this definition are three possibilities, ranked in order of desirability:

a. *Comparable uncontrolled price* – being the same price as for a *bona fide* sale of the same item to an unrelated buyer.

b. *Resale price method* – in which the final selling price of similar items to unrelated independent purchasers becomes a base from which an appropriate markup for costs and profit is calculated. The resulting net markup is then used as the appropriate transfer price for similar but not necessarily identical items.

c. *Cost-plus method* – in which an appropriate markup over the seller's full cost is allowed. Full cost is the accounting definition of direct costs plus allocation of overhead.

## 21-7. Over- and under-pricing

| *Countries with over-priced imports* | | *Countries with under-priced exports* | |
|---|---|---|---|
| *Country* | *Tax Rate* | *Country* | *Tax Rate* |
| France | 33.3% | Mexico | 34% |
| United Kingdom | 33.0 | Romania | 38.0 |
| Germany | 30.0 (34.0) | Netherlands | 35.0 |
| India | 40.0 | El Salvador | 25.0 |
| Canada | 38.0 | Bolivia | 25.0 |
| Japan | 37.5 | Hong Kong | 16.5 |
| Slovenia | not given | St.Lucia | 33.3 |
| Colombia | 35.0 | Malta | 35.0 |
| Switzerland | 22.0 (46.0) | United Kingdom | 33.0 |

| | | | |
|---|---|---|---|
| Mean for 8 countries | 33.6% (lower rates) | Mean for 9 countries | 30.5% |
| Mean for 8 countries | 37.1% (higher rate) | | |

Although this is a crude test, it does tend to support the hypothesis. Two means are possible for the over-priced import countries because Germany and Switzerland have split tax rates. The mean of 37.1%, using the higher rate for Germany and Switzerland, is above the U.S. rate of 35.0%, while the mean using the lower rate of 33.6% is below. Both means are above the mean for the countries with under-priced exports. (If Switzerland's low 22.0% is excluded from the mean of eight lower rates, the mean for the seven remaining countries is 39.3%. If Switzerland's high 46.0% is excluded from the mean of the eight higher rates, the mean for the seven remaining countries is 35.8%. The impact of Switzerland as an outlier must be considered.

In the countries with under-priced exports, the mean of 30.5% is clearly below the U.S. rate of 35.0%, and is also below the lower of the two possible means for countries with over-priced imports. If the outlying mean of 16.5% for Hong Kong is excluded from the group, the mean for the remaining 8 countries is 32.3% - still below the U.S. rate. One might argue with testing a hypothesis with this comparatively crude method, but the results do at least suggest that transfer pricing is probably influenced by the tax rates of the two countries involved in the trade.

**21-8. Allocated fees – 1**

License fees and royalty charges are similar in that they are charges by a parent company for use of its expertise (in many areas) by a subsidiary. They differ primarily in the manner in which they are calculated, with a license fee normally being charged as part of the cost of each unit of expertise used, whereas a royalty charge is normally a percent of the final sales price. In other words, for the subsidiary a license fee is an additional cost whereas a royalty fee is a sharing of sales receipts.

Because license fees and royalty charges can also be charged for providing expertise (in many areas) to non-related companies, an "arms' length" base for comparison exists. If transfer prices are to be regulated at all, a strong case can be made that license and royalty fees should also be covered by the tax rules.

**21-9. Allocated fees – 2**

A management fee is a charge for supplying general management expertise. A technical assistance fee is a charge for providing more specific technical help, such as engineering or marketing advice. A license fee for patent usage is a payment to a parent to cover portions of the research and development costs already incurred to discover, invent, or design the product.

No reason has been presented why these three types of allocated fees should be treated differently than any other cost. In all instances the base for the allocated fee should be specified clearly in organizational contracts before the services are provided so that the reasonableness of the amount charged can be documented.

**21-10. Distributed overhead**

The method of charging (allocating) overhead costs to various products or to various units of a company should be the same for both domestic units and foreign units. Such an allocation, which cost accountants have traditionally allocated as a percent of direct labor costs, will seem fair if allocated the same way both domestically and internationally.

If a different method is used to allocate to foreign subsidiaries, the documentation and logic must be very clearly spelled out. (The appropriateness of overhead allocation as a percent of direct labor is questioned by many cost accountants as being out-of-step in a technological world dominated by the indirect costs of technology, where direct labor is only a small part of total costs.)

### 21-11. Fee treatment

Fees are charged for specific benefits received by a subsidiary, and the reasonableness can be judged against the benefit received. Governments seeking foreign investment but sensitive to populist political charges of allowing a foreign company to make "excess" profits may find it politically easier to allow the parent MNE to recover funds by charging fees than by earning a profit margin which also includes compensation for services. For the subsidiary, fees are deductible in calculating local income taxes. For the parent, fees are taxable in the year charged. Profits would be taxable only in the year in which they were returned to the parent as a cash dividend.

### 21-12. Downstream tax rates

The lower tax rate in Brazil, relative to the other three countries, would have attracted investment to Brazil rather than to the other three. For trade between the countries, transfer prices might be set so as to record more profit in Brazil than in Argentina, in particular, or Paraguay or Uruguay (much smaller markets). The combination of the 28% drop in the value of Brazil's real in early 2001 and Brazil's lower tax rates probably hurt the economy of Argentina is a way that contributed to the resignation of two presidents and the drop in the external value of the peso in early 2002.

### 21-13. Leading foreign payments

The main motive would be to preserve the worldwide real purchasing power of cash balances by getting them out of a country with a weak currency, where devaluation and subsequent loss of external purchasing power of cash balances is expected. Preserving purchasing power (or enhancing it, if the cash balances are to be returned to the country after devaluation) is probably a more urgent motive than tax minimization.

### 21-14. Lagging foreign payments

The motives would be the same as for leading foreign receipts, but used when the currency of the importing country is weak. The firm will want to minimize any cash balances subject to loss of world purchasing power, and/or to increase the purchasing power locally by transferring funds back after a devaluation. (See answer to previous question.)

### 21-15. Reinvoicing centers

a. All *foreign exchange risk* is centered in the Reinvoicing Center. Neither the exporting entity nor the importing entity has any foreign exchange risk. It is possible, however, that the actual sales price somehow discounts the foreign exchange risk.

b. The *goods are shipped* directly to the buyer in South Africa. The Reinvoicing Center does not take physical possession of the goods at any time.

c. *Income tax avoidance* is probably impossible because U.S. tax laws levy income taxes on all income earned by non-manufacturing subsidiaries. Hence the Reinvoicing Center would pay full U.S. taxation. If the reinvoicing Center is within the United States, its tax return may be consolidated with that of the parent.

The Reinvoicing Center can be used to reposition cash because the center can buy or sell foreign exchange in its possession as it deems best for the worldwide corporate operation. By netting it probably accomplishes this at a lower cost than if each transaction were paid for with foreign exchange purchased from the banking system. There is no apparent tax advantage in the U.S. for having the Reinvoicing Center reposition cash.

(Many non-U.S. countries do not tax profits of foreign holding or finance companies (such as reinvoicing centers) unless their profits are remitted to the home country. Such non-taxation of foreign financial subsidiaries is believed to give their MNEs a comparative advantage over U.S. MNEs.)

## Problem 21.1 Kowloon Blade Company

**Transfer pricing and tax differences**

| Assumptions | Hong Kong | Great Britain |
|---|---|---|
| Corporate income tax rate | 16.0% | 30.0% |
| Desired markup on transfers | 2,000 | 3,000 |

| (Hong Kong dollars, HK$) | Kowloon Blade | Cranfield Eversharp | Consolidated |
|---|---|---|---|
| Direct costs | 10,000 | 16,000 | |
| Overhead | 4,000 | 1,000 | |
| Total costs | 14,000 | 17,000 | |
| Desired markup | 2,000 | 3,000 | |
| Transfer/sales price | 16,000 | 20,000 | |
| | | | |
| Sales price | 16,000 | 20,000 | |
| Less total costs | 14,000 | 17,000 | |
| Taxable income | 2,000 | 3,000 | |
| Less taxes | 320 | 900 | |
| Post-tax profit | 1,680 | 2,100 | 3,780 |

**a. What happens to profits if Kowloon Blade raises its transfer price to $18.000?**

This is accomplished by raising Kowloon's desired markup to HK$4,000.

| (Hong Kong dollars, HK$) | Kowloon Blade | Cranfield Eversharp | Consolidated |
|---|---|---|---|
| Direct costs | 10,000 | 18,000 | |
| Overhead | 4,000 | 1,000 | |
| Total costs | 14,000 | 19,000 | |
| Desired markup | 4,000 | 3,000 | |
| Transfer/sales price | 18,000 | 22,000 | |
| | | | |
| Sales price | 18,000 | 22,000 | |
| Less total costs | 14,000 | 19,000 | |
| Taxable income | 4,000 | 3,000 | |
| Less taxes | 640 | 900 | |
| Post-tax profit | 3,360 | 2,100 | 5,460 |

| Profits | Kowloon Blade | Cranfield Eversharp | Consolidated |
|---|---|---|---|
| After transfer price change | 3,360 | 2,100 | 5,460 |
| Before transfer price change | 1,680 | 2,100 | 3,780 |
| Differential | 1,680 | - | 1,680 |

Kowloon's Hong Kong operations are substantially more profitable, Great Britain unchanged, and consolidated profits increased by HK$1,680.

**b. What happens if the transfer price is raised to HK$18,000, but British tax authorities do not recognize the change for tax purposes?**

It yields the identical results to part a), because Great Britain's profits are unaffected by the transfer price change.

## Problem 21.2 Balanced Tire Company

**Is Balanced Tire's pricing strategy for US-Canadian operations correct?**

| **US Profit Calculation, C$** | **US Sales** | | **to Canada** |
|---|---|---|---|
| US sales price per tire, in C$ | **80.00** | | |
| less direct labor in US | **20.00** | | |
| less direct material in US | **20.00** | | |
| less US manufacturing overhead | **12.00** | | |
| Total manufacturing costs | **52.00** | -----------> | **52.00** |
| US factory margin | **28.00** | | **4.00** |
| less selling & admin costs | **10.00** | **Price** | **56.00** |
| Pre-tax profit per tire | **18.00** | | |
| less US corporate income taxes | **7.20** | | |
| After-tax profit per tire in the US | **10.80** | | |
| Current unit volume sold in US | **300,000** | | |
| Total profit on US sales | **3,240,000** | | |

| **Canadian dollars, C$** | | | | | |
|---|---|---|---|---|---|
| Unit sales price | **85.00** | **80.00** | **75.00** | **70.00** | **65.00** |
| less import (transfer price) | **56.00** | **56.00** | **56.00** | **56.00** | **56.00** |
| less shipping | **2.00** | **2.00** | **2.00** | **2.00** | **2.00** |
| Unit profit before tax | **27.00** | **22.00** | **17.00** | **12.00** | **7.00** |
| less Canadian income taxes | **-10.80** | **-8.80** | **-6.80** | **-4.80** | **-2.80** |
| Unit profit after-tax | **16.20** | **13.20** | **10.20** | **7.20** | **4.20** |
| expected unit volume | **110,000** | **150,000** | **180,000** | **250,000** | **400,000** |
| Total profit on Canadian sales | **1,782,000** | **1,980,000** | **1,836,000** | **1,800,000** | **1,680,000** |

The company has excess capacity (its producing 450,000 and is capable of producing 700,000). There are no differences in tax rates. All tires are manufactured in the US; the only additional Canadian costs are shipping. In this case, Balanced Tire needs to determine what final sales price in Canada will increase the sales volume allowing the firm to expand sales. As long as Canadian prices cover costs plus minimum profits, it will pay the firm to cut its Canadian sales price.

| **Finding Optimal Combination** | | | | | |
|---|---|---|---|---|---|
| Unit sales price | **85.00** | **80.00** | **75.00** | **70.00** | **65.00** |
| less direct labor | **20.00** | **20.00** | **20.00** | **20.00** | **20.00** |
| less direct material | **20.00** | **20.00** | **20.00** | **20.00** | **20.00** |
| less shipping | **2.00** | **2.00** | **2.00** | **2.00** | **2.00** |
| Total direct cost | **42.00** | **42.00** | **42.00** | **42.00** | **42.00** |
| Pre-tax contribution | **43.00** | **38.00** | **33.00** | **28.00** | **23.00** |
| less 40% corporate tax | **-17.20** | **-15.20** | **-13.20** | **-11.20** | **-9.20** |
| After-tax contribution | **25.80** | **22.80** | **19.80** | **16.80** | **13.80** |
| expected unit volume | **110,000** | **150,000** | **180,000** | **250,000** | **400,000** |
| Total profit | **2,838,000** | **3,420,000** | **3,564,000** | **4,200,000** | **5,520,000** |
| | | | | | **Maximum** |

Balanced Tire should cut its Canadian sales price to C$65, and increase volume to capacity.
The transfer price at which it is sold to the Canadian plant is immaterial.

## Problem 21.3 FinFones, Ltd.

**Note: This solution employs corrected assumptions from errors in the first printing of the text. Assume that FinFones (Finland) sells equal units to the two foreign subsidiaries.**

| **Assumptions** | | **United States** | **Finland** | **Japan** |
|---|---|---|---|---|
| Corporate income tax rate | | **40.0%** | **30.0%** | **25.0%** |
| Spot rate, US$/euro | **$** | **0.9000** | ---------- | ---------- |
| Spot rate, yen/euro | | ---------- | ---------- | **108.00** |
| Additional local costs | **$** | **3.00** | ---------- | **250.00** |
| Adjustment to transfer price (+/- 20%) | | | **0.00%** | |

| **Income items (euros)** | **U.S. Subsidiary** | **Finnish Parent** | **Japanese Subsidiary** |
|---|---|---|---|
| Sales price per unit | **€ 40.00** | **€ 30.00** | **€ 40.00** |
| Less direct labor | | **(12.50)** | |
| Less direct material | | **(6.25)** | |
| Less cost of importing (transfer) | **(30.00)** | | **(30.00)** |
| Less parent overhead | | **(5.00)** | |
| Less additional local costs | **(3.33)** | | **(2.31)** |
| Pre-tax profit per unit | **€ 6.67** | **€ 6.25** | **€ 7.69** |
| Less corporate income taxes | **(2.67)** | **(1.88)** | **(1.92)** |
| Post-tax profit | **€ 4.00** | **€ 4.38** | **€ 5.76** |
| | | | |
| Consolidated profits (euros) | | **€ 14.14** | |

a. Current consolidated profit of FinFones is 14.14 euros.

b. If the transfer price were increased by 20% (adjustment cell above increases both transfer prices), the consolidated profit of FinFones falls to 10.24 euros.

If the transfer price were decreased by 20% (adjustemnt cell above decreases both transfer prices), the consolidated profit of FinFones rises to 18.04 euros.

c. Using the baseline assumptions (which create consolidated profits of 14.14 euros), if the dollar were to fall to say, $1.00 per euro, consolidated profits would actually increase to 14.34 euros.

## Problem 21.4 Adams Corporation

| Assumptions | | Values | | Values |
|---|---|---|---|---|
| Brazilian income tax rate | | 15.0% | | 15.0% |
| US income tax rate | | 30.0% | | 30.0% |
| Spot exchange rate, R$/$ | | 2.60 | | 2.60 |
| Royalty paid, in US$ | $ | - | $ | 5,000,000 |
| Dividend paid, in US$ | $ | 10,000,000 | $ | 5,000,000 |

| Income Items (Brazilian real) | Brazilian Subsidiary Dividend Only (reais) | Brazilian Subsidiary Dividend + Royalty (reais) |
|---|---|---|
| Profits before royalties | R$61,176,471 | R$61,176,471 |
| Less royalties | - | (13,000,000) |
| Earnings before taxes | R$61,176,471 | R$48,176,471 |
| Less corporate income taxes | (9,176,471) | (7,226,471) |
| Net profits | R$52,000,000 | R$40,950,000 |
| | | |
| Dividend paid to US parent | R$26,000,000 | R$13,000,000 |
| Retained earnings | R$26,000,000 | R$27,950,000 |

| Remittance to US Parent | | | | |
|---|---|---|---|---|
| Dividend remitted to US, R$ | | R$26,000,000 | | R$13,000,000 |
| Spot exchange rate, R$/$ | | 2.60 | | 2.60 |
| Dividend remitted to US, $ | $ | 10,000,000 | $ | 5,000,000 |
| | | | | |
| **Dividend tax gross-up calculation:** | | | | |
| Dividend remitted to US, $ | $ | 10,000,000 | $ | 5,000,000 |
| Add back corp taxes deemed paid, $ | | 1,764,706 | | 882,353 |
| Grossed-up dividiend income, $ | $ | 11,764,706 | $ | 5,882,353 |
| | | | | |
| Tentative US tax at 30% | $ | 3,529,412 | $ | 1,764,706 |
| Tax credit for taxes paid in Brazil | | 1,764,706 | | 882,353 |
| Additional US taxes due on dividend | $ | 1,764,706 | $ | 882,353 |
| | | | | |
| **Royalty tax gross-up calculation:** | | | | |
| Royalty remitted to US, $ | $ | - | $ | 5,000,000 |
| Add back corp taxes deemed paid, $ | | - | | - |
| Grossed-up royalty income, $ | $ | - | $ | 5,000,000 |
| | | | | |
| Tentative US tax at 30% | $ | - | $ | 1,500,000 |
| Tax credit for taxes paid in Brazil | | - | | - |
| Additional US taxes due on royalty | $ | - | $ | 1,500,000 |
| | | | | |
| **Total returns and taxes to US parent** | | | | |
| Dividend received, before-tax | $ | 10,000,000 | $ | 5,000,000 |
| Less additional taxes due on dividend | | (1,764,706) | | (882,353) |
| Royalty received, before-tax | | - | | 5,000,000 |
| Less additional taxes due on royalty | | - | | (1,500,000) |
| Total returns, after-tax | $ | 8,235,294 | $ | 7,617,647 |

Although $10 million was paid out of the Brazilian subsidiary in both cases, the net proceeds of those payments in the US were different. The pure dividend distribution results in a greater dollar proceed, after-tax, because of the tax rate differences. In this case, because Brazil has a lower tax rate, Adams is better off positioning its tax liabilities in Brazil than in the US.

## Problem 21.5 Surgical Tools, Inc.

| Assumptions | | Values | | Values |
|---|---|---|---|---|
| Korean income tax rate | | 28.0% | | 28.0% |
| US income tax rate | | 34.0% | | 34.0% |
| Spot exchange rate, won/$ | | 1,342 | | 1,342 |
| License fee, won | | - | | 362,340,000 |
| Dividend distribution, won | | 362,340,000 | | - |
| | | | | |
| Income Items (Korean won) | | Korean Subsidiary Dividend Only (Korean won) | | Korean Subsidiary License fee only (Korean won) |
| Sales | | 2,684,000,000 | | 2,684,000,000 |
| Cash manufacturing expenses | | (1,342,000,000) | | (1,342,000,000) |
| Depreciation expenses | | (335,500,000) | | (335,500,000) |
| Less license fee | | - | | (362,340,000) |
| Pretax profit | | 1,006,500,000 | | 644,160,000 |
| Korean taxes | | (281,820,000) | | (180,364,800) |
| Profit after taxes | | 724,680,000 | | 463,795,200 |
| | | | | |
| Dividend paid to US parent | | 362,340,000 | | - |
| Retained earnings | | 362,340,000 | | 463,795,200 |
| | | | | |
| **Remittance to US Parent** | | | | |
| Dividend remitted to US, won | | 362,340,000 | | - |
| Spot exchange rate, won/$ | | 1,342 | | 1,342 |
| Dividend remitted to US, $ | $ | 270,000 | $ | - |
| | | | | |
| **Dividend tax gross-up calculation:** | | | | |
| Dividend remitted to US, $ | $ | 270,000 | $ | - |
| Add back corp taxes deemed paid, $ | | 105,000 | | - |
| Grossed-up dividend income, $ | $ | 375,000 | $ | - |
| | | | | |
| Tentative US tax at 34% | $ | 127,500 | $ | - |
| Tax credit for taxes paid in Korea | | 105,000 | | - |
| Additional US taxes due on dividend | $ | 22,500 | $ | - |
| | | | | |
| **License fee tax gross-up calculation:** | | | | |
| License fee remitted to US, $ | $ | - | $ | 270,000 |
| Add back corp taxes deemed paid, $ | | - | | - |
| Grossed-up license fee income, $ | $ | - | $ | 270,000 |
| | | | | |
| Tentative US tax at 34% | $ | - | $ | 91,800 |
| Tax credit for taxes paid in Korea | | - | | - |
| Additional US taxes due on license fee | $ | - | $ | 91,800 |
| | | | | |
| **Total returns and taxes to US parent** | | | | |
| Dividend received, before-tax | $ | 270,000 | $ | - |
| Less additional taxes due on dividend | | (22,500) | | - |
| License fee received, before-tax | | - | | 270,000 |
| Less additional taxes due on license fee | | - | | (91,800) |
| Total returns, after-tax | $ | 247,500 | $ | 178,200 |

a. A dividend of 362,340,000 won results in a net remittance after-tax in the US of $247,500.

b. A license fee of 362,340,000 won results in a net remittance after-tax in the US of $178,200. The license fee results in a smaller net proceed as it results in the entire remittance being taxed in the US at the higher US corporate tax rate, whereas the dividend "split" the tax liabilities between the two countries.

## MINICASE: FORD RANGER ASIA PACIFIC

1. **What possible advantages would Ford gain by positioning all profits and losses within the FTC business unit?**

The FTC business unit was designed to be the repository of gains or losses, and to assure the businesses on either end – the manufacturers and the distributors – a stable price and margin. This allowed Ford to sustain a reliable and profitable value-chain on the way to market for its business. If the FTC unit itself made substantial profits, it could be managed appropriately to reduce its tax burden.

2. **What types of incentives or disincentives does the transfer pricing structure described create with manufacturers like AAT and local distributors?**

One of the primary drivers of this arrangement was to set a price and relatively fixed margin for all distributors and maintain it. This allowed those businesses closest to the consumer to have stable pricing and margins, assuring them of adequate return for their efforts. Or at least that was Ford's intention, but when sales slowed markedly and these same distributors began discounting the truck prices, problems arose because the same fixed-dollar margin was allotted the discounted Ford Ranger unit prices. The lower revenue per truck was then absorbed by FTC; FTC did not pass along the lower realized revenues to its manufacturing units. Product continued to be purchased from them at the same price in effect prior to the slowdown in sales and initiation of discounts. FTC moved into the red.

Under this structure, the distributors suffered no pressure to preserve price. In fact, they were incentivized to simply sell a truck for whatever they could get, since they would earn the same margin regardless of their sales price. They simply began dumping inventory at close to cost, but they still earned their same profit per unit.

The manufacturers, meanwhile, could continue to produce trucks at the same price and margin, even though the retail markets were no longer able to sustain the previous price/cost basis. They were increasingly insulated from market pressures, and did not suffer any profitability from the drop in market demand and pricing.

3. **What would you suggest Ford do to improve the workings of its transfer pricing structure within the Ford Ranger value chain?**

FTC itself was designed to be the locus of profits or losses, and that was exactly what it continued to do. Ford's senior management had seemingly forgotten that was its designed purpose, as is commonly the case in global business, many senior executives believe they can motivate business units to perform more effectively with increasing pressure for better results. That may or may not be correct in this case.

The actual transfer pricing mechanism in place here with FTC is doing what it was designed to do. Unfortunately, price discipline and pressures are missing on the retail distribution side. Distributors need additional incentives to preserve prices. If they do not, they should at least suffer declining margins per unit as a result. The concept that they will always realize a profit regardless of their own pricing and inventory-volume sales strategy is a flawed business proposition from Ford's perspective.

## CHAPTER 22. WORKING CAPITAL MANAGEMENT

### *Questions*

#### 22-1. The cycle

1. *Quotation period.* No cash flow is associated with the period, which starts with a stated willingness by the seller to deliver goods or services at a specified price (an offer to sell) and ends with either an order received or the offer not being accepted by the targeted buyer. A promise involving future cash is associated with the offer because if the targeted buyer accepts at the quoted price future revenues (from the sale) and future expenses (to produce the good or service) are locked into place.

2. *Input sourcing period.* Over the course of this period cash will flow out for direct labor and possibly for direct material. Normally these are cash outflows that precede in time any cash inflow from the sale of the goods or services. However in some lines of business a down payment or partial payment may bring cash into the firm during the input sourcing period. The supplier of the goods or services enters into promises involving future cash payments for direct labor at the end of a payroll period (perhaps every two weeks) and for paying for direct material purchased on credit (perhaps payable 30 days after purchase). The buyer of the goods or services enters into a promise to pay cash to the seller at some future date. At the end of the period, some cash is probably still due to venders.

3. *Inventory period.* During this period the seller has a cash outflow for direct material purchased on credit during the previous input sourcing period, plus cash payments for direct labor. At the end of the period some (probably small) cash outflow is necessary to pay for shipping the goods or services to the buyer. The buyer has no cash outflow. At the end of the period the seller records an account receivable for the sale and the buyer records an account payable for the same amount. At this time the existing promise to pay for the goods or services (created by the purchase-sale agreement) is formalized and the date of the future payment is determined precisely. (The date may or may not have been specified precisely at the time the order was placed.)

4. *Accounts receivable period.* During the course of this period neither cash flows nor new obligations to make a future payment are involved. On the last day of the period cash will flow from the buyer to the seller. (If the buyer fails to pay on the last day, the accounts receivable period is extended by definition, since it can only end with payment – or by bankruptcy of the buyer!.)

#### 22-2. Accounts payable period

Note from Exhibit 22.1 that the Inventory Period includes any time needed for production. Strictly speaking, an inventory period consists of a raw material holding period, a work-in-process period, and a finished goods holding period. In some industries, such as selling fresh fruit or vegetables, the "raw material" period will be only a few hours or possibly days. In merchandising operations (reselling of purchased inventory with no manufacturing involved) no work-in-process period is involved.

An answer to the question, the Accounts Payable Period may well be shorter than the Inventory Period. This will occur when material purchased must be paid for before it can be processed and shipped to the buyer. An extreme example would be a vintner who buys grapes from independent grape growers, pays for them, processes them into wine, and ages the wine for five years before selling. The grape growers are neither willing nor financially able to wait five years for payment! The construction industry (everything from buildings to hydroelectric power projects) is another industry where the accounts payable period is normally shorter than the inventory period – primarily because the work-in-process period is extremely long.

The cash implication of the Accounts Payable Period being shorter than the Inventory Period is that the producer must pay cash out during the Inventory Period before cash is received from the sale.

### 22-3. Payables and receivables

The financial manager's ideal situation would be for the Accounts Payable Period to extend all the way to the end of the Accounts Receivable Period. Should this be the case, the supplier of the material inputs need not be paid until the final customer pays the manufacturer. The manufacturing firm itself need not advance any cash for inputs prior to being reimbursed by the final customer. Such an idea is almost always impossible, so realistically a financial manager would prefer that the Accounts Payable Period last as long as possible.

### 22-4. Transaction exposure

*Time $t_0$ :* Although not a part of the question itself, it is worthwhile noting that if the offer to sell (denominated in a foreign currency) is made at $t_0$, the seller incurs an "offer-period" or "conditional" transaction exposure because the price of the potential sale is established in a foreign currency but the exchange rate at $t_5$, when payment will be received and exchanged for the home currency, is not known. This is a special type of transaction exposure because an offer to sell in a foreign currency has been extended but not yet accepted. The exposure will not materialize if the offer is rejected; hence the exposure is considered "conditional" or "tentative" rather than already booked. If the offer to sell is made in the home currency, no tentative transaction exposure is created.

*Time $t_1$:* When the order is placed (time $t_1$), the seller incurs transaction exposure; this might be viewed as a continuation of the offer-period exposure referred to above. (If the offer had been made and accepted in the seller's home currency, the buyer rather than the seller incurs transaction exposure.) During the Input Sourcing Period that begins at $t_1$, the seller incurs additional transaction exposure if raw material or component parts are purchased in a foreign currency with payment to follow at the end of the Accounts Payable Period. (Note that if raw material or components parts are purchased in the same foreign currency as the final goods or services are sold, a natural hedge is created for a portion of the exposure.)

*Time $t_5$:* All exposure ends at $t_5$ when the final payment is made. On this date, any remaining transaction exposure is realized as a loss or gain. If the separate transaction exposure were created when the seller purchased raw material or components from a foreign supplier, that exposure would have ended when those raw material or components were paid for.

### 22-5. Operating exposure

*Operating exposure*, as defined in Chapter 9, is the potential for a change in expected future cash flows, and thus in value, of a foreign subsidiary as a result of an unexpected change in exchange rates. This exposure is entirely different from the transaction exposure (Chapter 8) that may result from the "operating cycle" shown in Exhibit 23.1.

The word "operating" is used in two separate contexts that are unrelated to each other. The operating cycle (Exhibit 22.1) reflects current exposure and so is separate from operating exposure which looks to the long-term future (not yet booked) changes in expected cash flows.

### 22-6. Translation exposure

If the operating cycle shown in Exhibit 22.1 begins in one accounting period (say $t_1$ is in 2002) but ends in another accounting period (say $t_5$ in 2003), then a translation exposure is created because the receivables or payables might be translated at a different exchange rate. The "exposure" exists even if the exchange rate did not change, as long as the accounts receivable or payable are outstanding. If the entire operating cycle is within one accounting period, translation exposure does not exist. (Although accounting periods are normally thought of in terms of years, if quarterly financial statements are published then the translation exposure comes into being over the turn of the quarter.)

### 22-7. Reducing NWC

*Operating techniques:*

1. Operate with a lower level of inventory – albeit with some risk of being out of stock at the time a customer orders.
2. Shorten the time allowed customers to pay for your sales; i.e., reduce the cycle time for accounts receivable – albeit with some risk of losing sales to competitors willing to grant longer payment terms.
3. Stretch out the time for payment of the firm's own accounts payables – albeit it at the risk of being denied purchases because venders have alternate customers who are willing to pay on time.
4. Shift purchasing of inventory to the same country in which the final product is sold, thus creating some degree of balance between receivables and payables in a single currency.

### 22-8. Trade terms

*1.* *Cost of trade credit.* The Swedish supplier is offering a 3% discount if payment is made within the first 15 days. 3% of SKr1,000,000 is SKr30,000. The net purchase is for SKr970,000 if paid in the first 15 days, but an additional SKr30,000 is charged for waiting an additional 30 days. SKr30,000 ÷ SKr970,000 = 3.0928% for 30 days. This rate compounded into a full year is $[(1.030928)^{12} - 1] =$ 0.4412, or 44.12% per annum.

*2.* *Taking the discount.* If the British company can finance its investment in inventory for the additional 30 days at less than 44.12% per annum (which should be possible for a British firm having any credit rating at all) it should take the discount by paying in 15 days and then finance inventory by some other method.

*3.* *Exchange rates change.* Not withstanding the above, if the British firm expected the Swedish krona to drop in value by more than 3% within the next 45 days, it might wait and buy krona at the end of 45 days. This course of action puts the payment in sterling terms at risk because the spot krona in 45 days might not have dropped in value more than 3%.

### 22-9. Inventory turnover

Day's inventory turnover is an average of 19 days for the United States, and ranges from 20 days (a Netherlands company) to 59 days (a French-Italian company) for the European companies shown, with great variation depending on the country. "Just-in-time" for a Japanese company means that the raw material holding time is only a few hours rather than a matter of days. Of course, work-in-process time in Japan as elsewhere is tied to the engineering technology of the production process, and finished goods inventory time is based on other variables such as how much inventory is needed to assure a supply for customers whose arrival may be unpredictable.

(One of the authors visited the Toyota Corolla assembly plant near Nagoya, Japan. He estimates that on that day one car rolled off the end of the production line about every 3 to 5 minutes. At the beginning of the line, large trucks carrying six assembled engines were arriving every 20 minutes or so, and about 20 engines were "in line" waiting. Inventory of 20 engines waiting on the floor was thus somewhere between 60 and 100 minutes worth of production time.)

The low level of inventory held with a "just-in-time" system reduces the cost of investing in inventory that is "sitting around" waiting to be used. It also saves on storage space. On the other hand, if a steady supply is not very assured, the risk and cost of running out of inventory and stopping a whole production process because of the non-availability of a single item can be very high. Increased truck traffic on Japanese roads increases the risk that inventory arriving from some distance may not arrive on time. Additionally, just-in-time delivery by truck increases road congestion during the day, whereas a less frequent delivery schedule might mean deliveries could take place at night.

Another example of the risk of just-in-time delivery arose shortly after the September 11, 2001, terrorist attacks on the World Trade Center and the Pentagon. Inspection delays at the bridge bringing automobile parts from Windsor, Ontario, to Detroit, Michigan, had a significant impact on ready availability of some automobile parts in Detroit-area automobile assembly lines.

Japanese firms in Thailand and Malaysia may try to emulate the within-Japan just-in-time system, but the quality of roads and the willingness to depend upon suppliers to be able to deliver on time are probably less in those two countries.

### 22-10. Receivables turnover

When funds flow between related subsidiaries of a multinational firm, the basic issue is only "in which [corporate] pocket" money is to be kept. A decision on when to pay can be based on minimizing foreign exchange risk and/or optimizing cash location for the multinational firm as a while. For transactions between non-related companies, the paying company always has an incentive to pay as late as possible (not counting possible loss of discounts) and the receiving company will always want to collect as soon as possible (which is why it offers discounts). Unlike multinational subsidiaries, the underlying interests of non-related companies are always at odds with each other.

### 22-11. Devaluation risk

A wait of 20 days after the initial ten days costs the firm $(2 \div 98) = 2.0408\%$ for twenty days. Because there are eighteen 20-day periods per year, the annual cost of not taking the discount is $(1.0211^{20} - 1) = 0.4979$ or 49.79% per annum. However this calculation of annual cost is not particularly relevant in the present situation.

Merlin will gain 36% if the Indonesian rupiah falls in value during this 30-day period, and the cost of not taking the discount is only 2%. So the issue is whether or not Merlin should give up 2% in return for the possibility of saving 36%. Risk-return tradeoffs are personal and so a universal conclusion is not possible; however, a possible 36% gain for a 2% cost does not seem unreasonable.

**22-12. Free-trade zones**

A free trade zone allows a firm to import components or finished goods duty free into an earmarked zone near where additional production and/or sales will take place, while also allowing the firm to delay payment of import duties until the goods are needed. Investment in inventory is thus lessened. In some instances goods in a free trade zone are processed further there, and then exported, without the need to pay any import duty. The total cost of such goods is less than it would be if the components parts also carried the cost of the import duty because the duty need not be added to the import purchase price.

**22-13. Motives**

The *transaction motive* for holding cash is to hold cash against anticipated day-to-day variations in disbursement for operations, as well as against the risk that day-to-day cash receipts will vary within some small margin based on prior experience.

The *precautionary motive* for holding cash is to hold cash against major unanticipated variations from budgeted cash flows. These potential variations can be substantially greater in magnitude than the small daily variations experienced as a matter of normal business procedures.

**22-14. Cash cycle**

A firm can shorted its cash cycle as follows:

1. Cash due from customers should be collected as soon as possible. Where different currencies are involved, the firm may borrow the expected foreign currency from a bank, exchange that currency at once for the more desirable home currency, and repay the bank with the foreign funds eventually collected from customers.

2. Cash held for anticipated transactions should probably be exchanged for the currency of the eventual payments as soon as possible. This reduces risk. Exceptions might be made when the currency of eventual payment is expected to depreciate, but that involves taking added risks that the firm may be unable to evaluate.

3. If cash has been exchanged for the currency of eventual payment, that cash should be invested in local money-market instruments with a maturity equal to the date of eventual payment.

**22-15. Electro-Beam Company**

Because the centralized system for Quad Corporation, U.K. in the text is all in the euro one-currency area, foreign exchange problems do not arise. From a foreign exchange point of view, Quad Corporation is in effect a domestic company.

Where several currencies are involved, as in the case of Singapore, Malaysia, Thailand, and Vietnam, a base operating currency must first be decided upon. This might be the Singapore dollar, the strongest of the four currencies, or it might even be an external currency such as the U.S. dollar. Until 1990 Electro-Beam might even have selected the Japanese yen, but Japanese economic deterioration over the last dozen years would now make the yen seem an ill advised choice.

Given selection of a base currency, say the Singapore dollar, each subsidiary would transfer to a Singapore financial office (which might be different from the finance office of the Singaporean operating subsidiary) at the end of each day all funds not needed for normal transaction disbursements on the following day or two – the exact number of days would be set by corporate policy depending on historical variations in fund flows and the cost of foreign exchange transactions. This is another way of saying that transaction funds needed in the near term will be held at the local level, but all precautionary funds will be centralized in Singapore.

The Singapore office will invest the precautionary funds in such money market instruments as it deems appropriate, bearing in mind that if funds are needed by any of the three non-Singaporean operating units, such emergency funds will be wired back almost instantaneously. Singapore would also (1) send back funds, (2) instruct operating units to retain extra funds, or (3) instruct one subsidiary to send funds directly to another, bypassing Singapore, at any time that near-term cash budgets indicated a probable net disbursement of funds in the next day or so.

### 22-16. France

The French government undoubtedly imposed such a rule in order to subsidize, indirectly, French banks. The efficiency of French multinationals and foreign firms operating in France, and the enhancement of their economic strength in a world of global competition, was either not considered or not deemed important. Because a multinational firm can control the timing of funds sent into France, MNEs should delay remitting funds to their French subsidiary and should remit such funds in, for example, one monthly block rather than on a transaction by transaction basis.

### 22-17. Foreign bank office

The *branch* of a foreign bank is an integral part, both legally and operational, of the home bank, and its profits or losses are those of the home office. Its employees work for the home office. Nevertheless it does maintain a separate set of books for its branch operation, and it will be taxed in the host jurisdiction.

A *subsidiary* office of a foreign bank is a separate corporation, with its own corporate charter in the host country and its own board of directors. As such, its lending limits and other operational characteristics must comply with the laws of the host country that govern all banks in that country.

### 22-18. Representative office

The *advantage* of a foreign representative office for a bank is that it provides a location where traveling and expatriate business persons can come to seek information, business contacts, and referrals to local banks – presumably correspondent banks of the home office of the representive office.. It also allows the bank to have a foreign presence to learn about the country before making a decision to establish a full service bank branch or subsidiary.

The *disadvantage* is that the representative office cannot carry on a normal banking business. It cannot accept deposits or make loans. If the client firm is thinking of establishing a permanent business presence in that foreign country, the client firm almost inevitably will have already taken its regular banking business to a fully functioning local bank. If the bank later decides to replace the representative office with a full service bank, potential clients will already have established themselves with other local banks.

## Problem 22.1 Quinlan Company

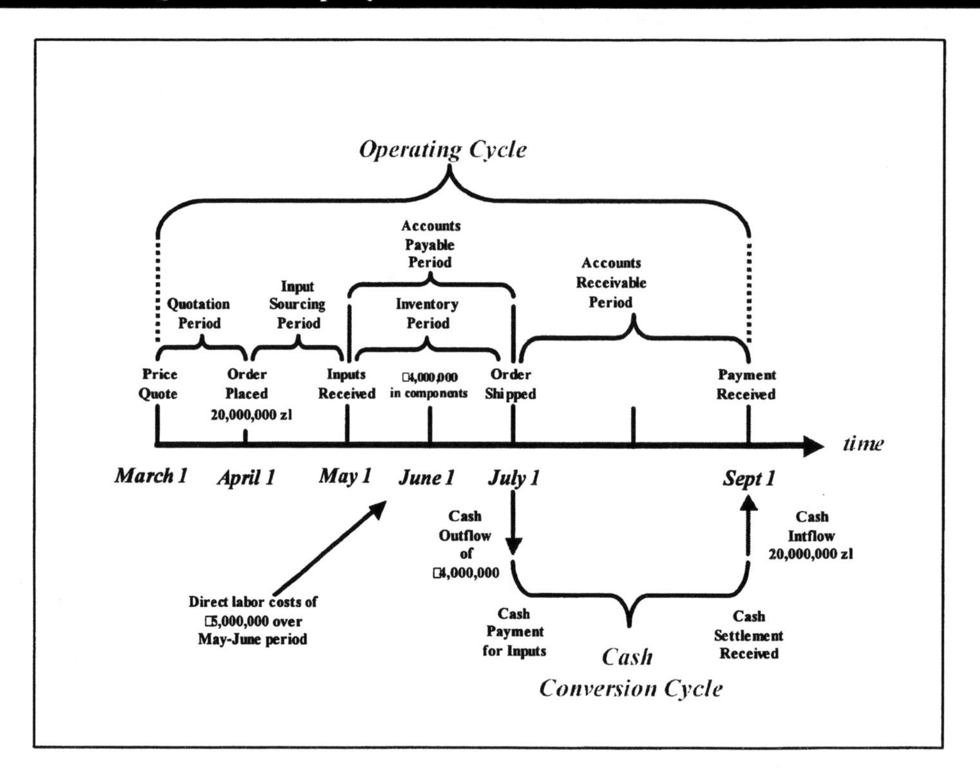


Working capital techniques. Quinlan accepted foreign exchange risk by quoting its sales price in the foreign currency (Polish zloty) equivalent of its €10,000,000 sales price. The following techniques might have been used by Quinlan in managing its currency exposure:

1. Quinlan might have denominated its offer in euros rather than zloty. Of course, this increases the possibility it might not receive the order.
2. If the offer had to be denominated in zloty for competitive reasons, Quinlan might have purchased a put option to deliver zloty against euros on April 1st. If the order were received, the put would provide some protection against deterioration of the zloty during the month of March, and if the order were not received the put could be sold in the market.
3. The March 1st offer might also have had a deadline by which it has to be accepted, perhaps two weeks, although competition would influence this.
4. Regardless of whether or not Quinlan decides to hedge its risk during the period between making the offer and receiving the order, on April 1st Quinlan should probably hedge the anticipated receipt of zloty in September. Note that this hedge would extend for a period two months longer than the period during which Quinlan had a formal accounts receivable on its books. This hedge might be in the forward market or via a money market hedge, or possibly by some other technique.
5. Quinlan could have purchased some inputs from venders in the customer's country, paying them in zloty to be received from the sale. This approach ignores established vender lines and their assurances of quality, as well as the possible time and money costs of locating a new supplier.

## Problem 22.2 Shimoda, K.K.

**Should Shimoda be taking the discount?**

| **Assumptions** | **Values** |
|---|---|
| Shimoda KK's accounts receivable in yen | **100,000,000** |
| Receivable credit terms: | |
| Discount given if paid in first 30 days | **2.000%** |
| Days in which full invoice is due | **60** |
| Shimoda KK's accounts payable in yen | **60,000,000** |
| Payable credit terms: | |
| Discount given if paid in first 10 days | **3.000%** |
| Days in which full invoice is due | **60** |
| Shimoda's average cash balance | **30,000,000** |

| **Shimoda could be paying its A/P early:** | |
|---|---|
| Discount given for 60 day paybles | **3.000%** |
| This discount could be compounded for 6 periods of 60 days per year (360/60) | **6.00** |
| For an effective cost of funds of (1.03) to the sixth power, -1 | **19.41%** |

Since Shimoda does not normally carry enough cash to completely make its A/P payments, and it cannot necessarily rely on A/R arriving exactly as hoped, it would have to draw upon corporate credit lines with its banks.

If Shimoda can borrow at less than 19.41%, Shimoda should be paying early (taking the discount).

| **How much cash would Shimoda save?** | |
|---|---|
| Current A/P, due in 60 days on average (yen) | **60,000,000** |
| Annual discount or savings, percentage | **3.000%** |
| Annual cash savings (discount x A/P) (yen) | **1,800,000** |

## Problem 22.3 Alpine Ski Company

**Combining precautionary cash balances**

| a.<br>**Country of subsidiary** | **Expected cash need** | **One standard deviation** |
|---|---|---|
| Switzerland | **€ 5,000,000** | **€ 1,000,000** |
| Italy | **3,000,000** | **400,000** |
| France | **2,000,000** | **300,000** |
| Germany | **800,000** | **40,000** |
| Total | **€ 10,800,000** | **€ 1,740,000** |

| **Current total cash balance:** | | |
|---|---|---|
| Sum of total cash expected need | **€ 10,800,000** | |
| Plus 2 times one standard deviation | **3,480,000** | |
| Current total cash balance | **€ 14,280,000** | |
| | | |
| **Using a single combined account:** | | |
| Sum of total cash expected need | **€ 10,800,000** | |
| Calculation of centralized precautionary balance: | | |
| a) Sum of squared individual std dev's | | **€ 1,251,600,000,000** |
| b) square root of a) | | **€ 1,118,749** |
| c) 2 x b | | **€ 2,237,499** |
| | | |
| Centralized precautionary balance | **€ 2,237,499** | |
| Combined account total cash balance | **€ 13,037,499** | |
| | | |
| **Savings using combined account:**<br>(current cash balance - combined cash balance) | **€ 1,242,501** | |

b. Transaction costs should be lower for the single cash account than for four separate accounts. Any foreign exchange transactions can be implemented more efficiently by being centralized.

## Problem 22.4 Futebal do Brasil, S.A.

| Anticipated cash flows (000s) | | *Companhia Futebal do Brasil* | | *Compania Futbal de Argentina* | | *Compania Futbal de Chile* |
|---|---|---|---|---|---|---|
| Day end cash balance | $ | 6,000 | $ | 5,000 | $ | 5,000 |
| Minimum operating balance required | $ | 5,000 | $ | 1,000 | $ | 1,000 |
| Excess cash balance | $ | 1,000 | $ | 4,000 | $ | 4,000 |
| Expected receipts (+) or disbursements (-): | | | | | | |
| + 1 day | $ | 3,000 | $ | (2,000) | $ | 5,000 |
| + 2 days | $ | - | $ | 1,000 | $ | (3,000) |
| + 3 days | $ | (5,000) | $ | (3,000) | $ | 2,000 |

**Today (Day 0)**

Argentina would normally be required to remit its excess cash balance of $4,000 to Brasil, but because $2,000 would have to be returned the next day (Day +1), Argentina should be instructed to retain $3,000 in cash and remit $2,000 to Brazil.

Chile remits its excess cash balance of $4,000 to Brasil today. It will be having a net receipt the next day.

Brasil receives $6,000 in total from its two subsidiaries, leaving it with a day-end cash balance of $12,000. Because Brasil needs only $5,000 in daily operating balances, and because some $3,000 is expected the next day, Brasil should invest $7,000 in the money market.

**Tomorrow (Day +1)**

Argentina uses $2,000 of its $3,000 balance to cover the day's cash shortfall. No funds are received or remitted to Brasil.

Chile recieves another $5,000, all of which would normally be remitted to Brasil. However, Chile expects a short fall on Day + 2 of $3,000. Hence it retains $3,000 of Day + 1's cash receipts and remits only $2,000 to Brasil.

Brasil receives $2,000 from Chile plus receives $3,000 from its own operations. Hence it invests $5,000 in the money market.

**Day after tomorrow (Day + 2)**

Argentina receives $1,000, which it retains overnight against Day +3's expected short fall of $3,000.

Chile uses the $3,000 held overnight from Day + 1 to cover its cash shortage.

Brazil receives no cash from either subsidiary or on its own.

**Day + 3**

*Note: Transfers on Day +3 would in fact be based on forecasts for Day +4, which we do not have.*
Ignoring Day +4, transfers for Day +3 might be as follows.

Argentina needs $3,000 and kept an extra $1,000 overnight. Hence Argentina needs an extra $2,000 for the day from its Brazilian parent or from another subsidiary.

Chile recieves an extra $2,000. Rather than remit this to Brasil, and have Brasil also send $2,000 to Argentina, Chile should be instructed to remit its excess of $2,000 directly to Argentina.

Brasil has resolved its Argentine deficit with funds from Chile. Hence Brasil need only liquidate $5,000 of money market instruments to cover its own shortfall.

## Problem 22.5 Earth Technology, Inc.

**Intra-company multilateral netting**

**Foreign exchange transaction spreads** **0.400%**

| | Amount | Transaction costs |
|---|---|---|
| **Earth Technology China:** | | |
| Owes to Spanish subsidiary | $ 8,000,000 | $ 32,000 |
| Owes to Iowa parent | $ 9,000,000 | $ 36,000 |
| **Earth Technology Spain:** | | |
| Owes to Chinese subsidiary | $ 5,000,000 | $ 20,000 |
| Owes to Iowa parent | $ 6,000,000 | $ 24,000 |
| **Earth Technology Iowa:** | | |
| Owes to Chinese subsidiary | $ 4,000,000 | $ 16,000 |
| Owes to Spanish subsidiary | $ 10,000,000 | $ 40,000 |
| | | $ 168,000 |

**NETTING MATRIX**

Earth Technology would first construct a netting matrix to determine the net receipts (payments) by unit.

| | Receiving Unit | | | |
|---|---|---|---|---|
| **Paying Unit** | **China** | **Spain** | **Iowa** | **Total** |
| **China** | 0 | $ 8,000,000 | $ 9,000,000 | $ 17,000,000 |
| **Spain** | $ 5,000,000 | 0 | $ 6,000,000 | 11,000,000 |
| **Iowa** | $ 4,000,000 | $ 10,000,000 | 0 | 14,000,000 |
| **Total Paid** | $ 9,000,000 | $ 18,000,000 | $ 15,000,000 | $ 42,000,000 |

| **Net Settlements** | **Payments** | **Receipts** | **Net Payment (-) or receipt (+)** |
|---|---|---|---|
| **China** | $ 17,000,000 | $ 9,000,000 | -8,000,000 |
| **Spain** | $ 11,000,000 | $ 18,000,000 | 7,000,000 |
| **Iowa** | $ 14,000,000 | $ 15,000,000 | 1,000,000 |
| **Total Paid** | $ 42,000,000 | $ 42,000,000 | $ - |

The interpretation of the net settlements calculation is for China to make a net payment of $8 million, $7 million to Spain and $1 million to Iowa (parent).

| **Savings on transaction costs** | | |
|---|---|---|
| Transaction costs prior to netting | $ 168,000 | |
| Transaction costs on netted payments | 32,000 | (.04 x total payments of $7 million + $1 million) |
| Savings on transaction spreads | $ 136,000 | |

## Problem 22.5 Earth Technology, Inc. (Part b)

**Foreign exchange transaction spreads** **0.400%**

NETTING MATRIX

Earth Technology would first construct a netting matrix to determine the net receipts (payments) by unit.

| | Receiving Unit | | | | |
|---|---|---|---|---|---|
| **Paying Unit** | **China** | **Spain** | **Iowa** | **Phillipines** | **Total** |
| **China** | $ - | $ 8,000,000 | $ 9,000,000 | $ - | $ 17,000,000 |
| **Spain** | $ 5,000,000 | $ - | $ 6,000,000 | $ - | $ 11,000,000 |
| **Iowa** | $ 4,000,000 | $ 10,000,000 | $ - | $ 6,000,000 | $ 20,000,000 |
| **Phillipines** | $ - | $ - | $ - | $ - | $ - |
| **Total Paid** | **$ 9,000,000** | **$ 18,000,000** | **$ 15,000,000** | **$ 6,000,000** | **$ 48,000,000** |

| **Net Settlements** | **Payments** | **Receipts** | **Net Payment (-) or receipt (+)** |
|---|---|---|---|
| **China** | $ 17,000,000 | $ 9,000,000 | **-8,000,000** |
| **Spain** | $ 11,000,000 | $ 18,000,000 | **7,000,000** |
| **Iowa** | $ 20,000,000 | $ 15,000,000 | **-5,000,000** |
| **Phillipines** | $ - | $ 6,000,000 | **6,000,000** |
| **Total Paid** | **$ 48,000,000** | **$ 48,000,000** | **$ -** |

There are several settlement possibilities.

**Settlement Possibility #1:** China, owing $8 million, pays $7 million to Spain and $1 million to the Phillipines. Iowa pays $5 million to the Phillipines.

| **Savings on transaction costs** | | |
|---|---|---|
| Transaction costs prior to netting | **$ 192,000** | (.04 * $48 million in payments) |
| Transaction costs on netted payments | **52,000** | (.04 x total payments of $7 million + $1 million + $5 million) |
| Savings on transaction spreads | **$ 140,000** | |

**Settlement Possibility #2:** China, owing $8 million, pays $2 million to Spain and $6 million to the Phillipines. Iowa pays $5 million to Spain

| **Savings on transaction costs** | | |
|---|---|---|
| Transaction costs prior to netting | **$ 192,000** | (.04 * $48 million in payments) |
| Transaction costs on netted payments | **52,000** | (.04 x total payments of $7 million + $1 million + $5 million) |
| Savings on transaction spreads | **$ 140,000** | |

Important final note is that regardless of the settlement pattern (#1 or #2 for example), the total cost of settlement is minimized.

## Problem 22.6 Crystal Publishing Company

**Creating an in-house bank**

| **Assumptions** | **Per annum** | **Monthly** |
|---|---|---|
| Interest paid on deposits | **4.800%** | **0.400%** |
| Interest charged on advances | **5.400%** | **0.450%** |
| Spot exchange rate, euros/pound | **1.6000** | |

**a. What would be the net interest earnings for Crystal's in-house bank in April?**

| **Deposits on April 1:** | **In euros** | **In pounds** |
|---|---|---|
| From Crystal Germany | **€ 20,000,000** | |
| From Crystal Spain | **€ 5,000,000** | |
| From Crystal Britain (in pounds) | | **£12,000,000** |
| in euros (1.6 euros per pound) | **€ 19,200,000** | |
| Total deposits (funds available), in euros | **€ 44,200,000** | |
| times monthly deposit rate | **-0.400%** | |
| **Total interest paid on deposits** | **-€ 176,800** | |

| **Advances on April 1:** | **In euros** |
|---|---|
| To Crystal France | **€ 12,000,000** |
| To Crystal Italy | **€ 8,000,000** |
| To Crystal Greece | **€ 6,000,000** |
| Total advances, in euros | **€ 26,000,000** |
| times monthly rate on advances | **0.450%** |
| **Total interest earned on advances** | **€ 117,000** |
| | |
| **Net interest earnings for the month of April:** | **-€ 59,800** |

This "loss" is a paper or opportunity cost loss, as all cash flows remain within Crystal.

**b. If the parent subsidized the in-house bank for all operating expenses, how much more could the in-house bank loan at the beginning of April?**

| | |
|---|---|
| Total funds available from depositors | **€ 44,200,000** |
| Less advances by in-house bank | **-€ 26,000,000** |
| Plus net interest "loss" by in-house bank | **€ 59,800** |
| Funds available | **€ 18,259,800** |

## MINI-CASE: HONEY WELL AND PAKISTAN INTERNATIONAL AIRWAYS

This case analysis is one of the authors' favorites. It combines exchange rate risk, the timing associated with cash flows (and commensurate currency risk), emerging market financial management practices, corporate performance goals for working capital management, pricing and invoicing decisions, and the most difficult of all – *managerial judgement*.

**1. Estimate what cash flows in which currencies the proposal would probably yield What is the expected U.S. dollar value that would, in the end, be received?**

The spreadsheet analysis on the following page is helpful in understanding the complexity of the proposed transaction.

*Original Agreement.* The original proposal which Honeywell had thought it had negotiated was for all payments to be made in U.S. dollars. The original contract price of $23,700,000, would be paid in two installments, 20% on contract signing ($4,740,000), and the remaining balance would be invoiced at the end of one year upon completion of the cockpit retrofits ($18,960,000). (It is a bit unclear as to whether the original contract under negotiation had included any type of up-front payment; it was evidently smaller than the 20% now on the negotiating table.) The second payment invoice would be due in 180 days. All payments would be in U.S. dollars, and Honeywell's Pakistani agent, Makran, would broker the transaction for the standard 5% fee.

*Pakistani Rupee Invoicing.* The Pakistan Airways counterproposal, for all invoicing and payments to be made in Pakistani rupee, constituted serious issues and risks for Honeywell.

- First, it was against corporate policy to receive payment in any other currency than U.S. dollars (not unusual in the global airline industry). This specific transaction was already considered a troubled one internally within Honeywell, as it did not meet corporate goals on return on sales and had been continually postponed. Unfortunately, the division within Honeywell had already included it in their prospective sales goals for the period, so the pressures were numerous.

- Secondly, the rupee appeared to be a currency subject to near-term devaluation. It had experienced a relatively recent devaluation of 7.86% which by traditional exchange rate standards was a small – and possibly incomplete – devaluation. Most devaluations were 15% to 25% in recent history, and the rumors of further devaluation were strong. The black market rate of Rp50.00/$ represented a devaluation from the current rate of Rp40.4795/$ of about 23.5%.

If Honeywell were to accept payment in rupee, it would be incurring substantial currency risk. If the payments were to occur on schedule, 20% advance payment upon contract signing and the 80% balance settled 180 days following invoice for completed work in 360 days (180 + 360 = 540 days from the present, contract signing), and no currency devaluation were to take place, the present value of the sale was estimated at $18,662,397. If, however, the rupee suffered a 20% devaluation after the advance payment but before balance settlement, the sale has a present value of only $16,262,997. This will sure not meet corporate margin on sales goals!

If Honeywell were to use Makran to both facilitate the transaction (mandatory) and provide currency conversion services, the exchange rate risk would be eliminated for a 5% fee, and the 80% balance would be settled in 360 + 30 days (390 days total), rather than 540 days.

## Mini-Case: Honeywell and Pakistan International Airways

| Components of the Transaction | *Original Negotiated Agreement* Event Timing | | Original Agreement | *Makran Solution to Currency Invoicing* Event Timing | | Makran Covers Currency Risks |
|---|---|---|---|---|---|---|
| Contract price | t | | $ 23,700,000 | t | | $ 23,700,000 |
| Up-front advance payment | t | 20% | $ 4,740,000 | t | 20% | $ 4,740,000 |
| Less agent (Makran) commission | t | 10% | (474,000) | t | 10% | (474,000) |
| Less currency charges (Makran) | t | 0% | - | t | 5% | (237,000) |
| Net up-front payment after fees | t | | $ 4,266,000 | t | | $ 4,029,000 |
| Remaining balance invoiced at t+360 | t+360+180 | | $ 18,960,000 | t+540 | | $ 18,960,000 |
| (price less up-front payment) | (540 days) | | | (540 days) | | |
| Less agent (Makran) commission | t+360+180 | 10% | (1,896,000) | t+360+30 | 10% | (1,896,000) |
| Less currency charges (Makran) | t+360+180 | 0% | - | 390 | 5% | (948,000) |
| Net balance after fees | t+360+180 | | $ 17,064,000 | 390 | | $ 16,116,000 |
| Discount factor for present value | **540** | 12% | 0.8437 | **390** | 12% | 0.8845 |
| Present value of net balance | t | | $ 14,396,397 | t | | $ 14,254,032 |
| Present value of all payments | t | | **$ 18,662,397** | t | | **$ 18,283,032** |

*Honeywell Bears Currency Risk*

| Components of the Transaction | Event Timing | Invoice Amounts (in Rupee, Rp) | Expected Rate (Rp/$) | | Effective Amount (in US$) |
|---|---|---|---|---|---|
| Contract price | t | 959,364,150 | 40.4795 | | $ 23,700,000 |
| Up-front advance payment | t | 191,872,830 | 40.4795 | 20% | $ 4,740,000 |
| Less agent (Makran) commission | t | | | 10% | $ (474,000) |
| Less currency charges (Makran) | t | | | 0% | $ - |
| Net up-front payment after fees | t | | | | 4,266,000 |
| | | Assumed devaluation of | 20% | | |
| Remaining balance invoiced at t+360 | t+360+180 | 767,491,320 | 48.5754 | | $ 15,800,000 |
| (price less up-front payment) | (540 days) | | | | |
| Less agent (Makran) commission | t+360+180 | | | 10% | (1,580,000) |
| Less currency charges (Makran) | t+360+180 | | | 0% | - |
| Net balance after fees | t+360+180 | | | | $ 14,220,000 |
| Discount factor for present value | **540** | | | 12% | 0.8437 |
| Present value of net balance | t | | | | $ 11,996,997 |
| Present value of all payments | t | | | | **$ 16,262,997** |

2. **Do you think the services that Makran is offering are worth the costs?**

Yes. If Honeywell were to use Makran for currency services, it would eliminate the currency exposure and accelerate the remaining payment. This would provide a present value of $18,283,032, only $379,365 less than originally envisioned. This is far superior to incurring the currency risk, and waiting possibly 540 days or longer to receive rupees which would be worth who knows what in U.S. dollars at that time. And the Makran solution also aids in reducing the days sales outstanding of the division, another divisional goal.

This does not assume, however, that the sale is a good one from Honeywell's perspective. It would still be up to Honeywell to decide whether the sale is sufficiently profitable and important from a corporate perspective.

3. **What would you do if you were heading the Honeywell SAC group negotiating the deal?**

The spreadsheet analysis is helpful in understanding a variety of the negotiating alternatives. If the 20% advance payment is indeed a pivotal point, this could be reduced against either price or timing alternatives. A number of options could be explored here, including reducing the 20% to 10% in exchange for accelerated payment of the balance (guaranteed?).

If Honeywell wishes to pursue the Makran currency management alternative, it may wish to tradeoff when Makran itself receives payment against the currency charge. (A reduction of the currency charge on both payments from 5% to 4% results in a present value of total payments of $18,498,127.)

*Postscript.* Honeywell never completed the agreement as PIA continued to throw obstacles in the way of the contract signing, evidently not wishing to pursue the cockpit retrofit in the end.

## CHAPTER 23. INTERNATIONAL TRADE FINANCE

### *Questions*

### 23-1. Unaffiliated buyers

A new non-affiliated buyer presents a credit risk for the exporter because the exporter may be unable to assess the credit worthiness of that importer due to geographic distance, language, culture or lack of a record of payments to other suppliers. A letter of credit, accompanied by other documents, allows the exporter to rely on the credit standing of a bank, which is presumed to be of greater credit worthiness than just an unknown manufacturing firm.

After successful trade goes on for some time the importer becomes a known entity, in which case the exporter will have more faith in the importer's willingness and ability to pay. Because the letter of credit and other documents have both a financial cost and a cost for the time and energy involved in handling the documents, direct billing for exports is easier, faster, and lowers the final end-cost to the ultimate customer.

### 23-2. Affiliated buyers

An export to a parent or sister subsidiary has no credit risk because both exporter and importer are part of the same corporate unit. Non-payment to an exporter in this situation is just a matter of keeping the firm's cash in another corporate account. In fact, very late payment for an export to an affiliated importer might be desirable because the firm wants to keep cash in one location and not in another. (This is referred to as "leads and lags," a topic explained in Chapter 21.) Nevertheless an export to an affiliated buyer might pass through the standard documentation as a way to obtain financing that is easy to obtain, is possibly cheaper than alternative sources of short-term financing, or provides some protection against political or country-based interruption to payment for the transaction.

### 23-3. Related party trade

The globalization of world business means that multinational firms manufacture as well as sell in many international markets simultaneously. Firms that move part of their manufacturing operation abroad to lower costs and thus enable them to compete more effectively in the home and other markets find themselves specializing in certain products or components in one location and then exporting those items to sister subsidiaries in other countries. The globalization of enterprise means that an ever-greater portion of a firms' products are produced in one country and sold in another. (This is no different than large domestic U.S. firms manufacturing in one state and selling in another.)

### 23-4. Documents – LC/draft

A Letter of Credit (L/C) is a document issued by a bank promising to pay if certain documents are delivered to that bank  A draft is an order sent to that bank written by a business firm ordering the bank to make payment. (A personal check is a simple form of a bank draft.) L/Cs and drafts are linked because the L/C states the conditions under which the bank promises to honor a draft drawn on (e.g., directed to) that bank.

### 23-5. Documents – B/L

A *straight* bill of lading is a document in which a common carrier promises to deliver merchandise to a designated addressee. The addressee does not need any particular document to obtain possession of the shipment.

An *order* bill of lading is a document in which a common carrier promises to deliver merchandise only to a party holding a copy of the order bill of lading. Although the merchandise is shipped to the addressee's address, that addressee can not obtain possession unless that addressee has a copy of the order bill of lading. Hence an order bill of lading is a document of ownership of the merchandise, meaning usually that the addressee must pay for the goods to obtain the order bill of lading and consequently possession of the merchandise.

**23-6. Consular invoices and certificates or origin**

A bank honors (e.g., pays) a draft drawn in accordance with its L/C only if other required documents are attached. Neither the bank nor the importer can know for certain that the containers do in fact contain the merchandise claimed. Hence banks and importers often require verification of the contents by an independent third party. The consular invoice provides statistical information for customs purposes, and thus facilitates entry of the goods into the importing country. A certificate of origin verifies where the goods originated.

**23-7. Certificates of analysis**

As mentioned in the solution to the previous question, a bank honors (e.g., pays) a draft drawn in accordance with its L/C only if other required documents are attached. Neither the bank nor the importer can know for certain that the containers do in fact contain the merchandise claimed. If the importer wants to know with certainty that the shipment is what it purports to be (say, a particular quantity or quality of oil or grain) it will ask an independent certifying company to issue a warranty, guarantee, or certificate attesting to the validity of the contents.

**23-8. Risks**

*Currency risk* is the risk that the currency designated for payment of the import changes in value relative to the other currency. A U.S. firm exporting to France wants dollars, while the French importer wants to pay euros. If the sale contract specifies payment in dollars, the French importer has a currency risk – more euros than expected might be needed when payment is due. If the sales contract specifies payment in euros, the U.S. exporter has a currency risk – fewer dollars than expected might be received when the euros are exchanged for dollars.

*Risk of non-completion* is the risk that one of the parties fails to fulfill its obligations. The importer may refuse to pay for the goods, or the exporter may fail to ship the goods. Events not under the control of the parties to the trade, such as major storms, disease epidemics, terrorist acts, or war, may make completion of the trade impossible. The several documents involved in international trade are intended to reduce financial loss from non completion.

**23-9. Letter of credit**

A *bank* issues a letter of credit, promising to pay for an international trade transaction if certain documents are presented to the bank. The *applicant* for the letter of credit (usually the importer) applies to the bank for the letter of credit. The *beneficiary* of the letter of credit (usually the exporter) is to receive payment under a set of conditions specified in the letter of credit.

## 23-10. Revocable letter of credit

A *revocable letter of credit* is used as a document to facilitate payment when the nature or quantity of the goods is not determined beforehand. A revocable letter of credit functions primarily as a means to arrange payment. For example, a department store buyer might be traveling in south Asia looking for merchandise to buy for the home company, yet that buyer does not know exactly what he or she will buy or what it will cost. Because the merchandise is not known, a normal L/C can not be used. But if the buyer finds merchandise appropriate for the home company, he or she can purchase it and arrange payment through a revocable letter of credit. In this case, the seller might have to wait a few days for assurance that the funds are available. The buyer need not carry many thousands of dollars in cash or travelers' checks, with the risk of loss or theft.

## 23-11. Confirming a letter of credit

Most letters of credit are unconfirmed, meaning the exporter relies on the credit quality of the issuing bank, rather than the importer. However the exporter may be uncertain of the quality of the issuing bank, especially if that bank is in a remote country about which the importer knows little. The confirmation of the letter of credit is by a better-known bank in a major country. For example, a U.S. exporter with an order from Morocco accompanied by a L/C from a Casablanca bank may not know if the bank in Casablanca is dependable. The exporter may then ask a Paris bank to guarantee (i.e., "confirm") the L/C of the Casablanca bank. The confirming bank may be acquainted with the Casablanca bank because it has had long-standing correspondent banking relationships going back to earlier French control of parts of Morocco, and so be willing – for a fee – to guarantee the L/C of the Casablanca bank.

## 23-12. Documenting an export of hard drives

1. The San Jose importer applies for a letter of credit (L/C) from its California bank.
2. California bank issues an L/C in favor of the San Jose importer and sends the L/C to exporter's Malaysian bank.
3. Malaysian bank advises the Penang exporter of the opening of the L/C.
4. Penang exporter ships the hard drives to the San Jose importer, shipping on an order bill of lading made deliverable to itself; i.e., deliverable to the exporter itself so that the exporter retains legal title to the merchandise at this stage of the transaction.
5. The Penang exporter draws a sight draft against the California bank in accordance with the terms of the L/C and presents the draft, along with any other required documents, to its own Malaysian bank.
6. Malaysian bank forwards the draft, accompanied by the order bill of lading and any other required documents, to the California bank.
7. California bank pays the Malaysian bank for the sight draft, receiving the order bill of lading, now endorsed by the Malaysian bank. At this point the California bank has legal title to the merchandise.
8. Malaysian bank, having received the proceeds from the sale (via the sight draft paid by the California bank), pays the Penang exporter (less any fees).
9. California bank collects the proceeds of the sale from the San Jose importer and endorses the order bill of lading over to the importer so the importer, in turn, can collect the merchandise from the shipper. (The California bank could endorse the order bill of lading over to the San Jose importer without collecting at that time. In such an instance, the California bank is making an unsecured loan to the importer, a lending transaction entirely separate from the import/export transaction.)

## 23-13. Documenting an export of lumber from Portland, Oregon, to Yokohama

1. Yokohama importer applies for a letter of credit (L/C) from its Japanese bank.
2. Japanese bank issues an L/C in favor of the Yokohama importer and sends the L/C to exporter's Oregon bank, asking the Oregon back to confirm (i.e., guarantee) the letter of credit.
3. Oregon bank confirms the L/A and advises Portland exporter of the opening of the L/C.
4. Portland exporter ships the lumber to the Yokohama importer, shipping on an order bill of lading made deliverable to itself; i.e., deliverable to the exporter itself so that the exporter retains legal title to the merchandise at this stage of the transaction.
5. The Portland exporter draws a 120-day time draft against the Yokohama bank in accordance with the terms of the L/C and presents the draft, along with any required documents, to its own Oregon bank.
6. The Oregon bank endorses (i.e., applies its own guarantee) to the 120-day draft and forwards it, accompanied by the order bill of lading and any other required documents, to the Japanese bank.
7. The Japanese bank accepts the time draft, which at this point becomes a *banker's acceptance*, and returns the accepted time draft to the exporter. The exporter may (1) hold the acceptance to maturity, or (2) discount it in the acceptance market. At this point the Japanese bank has legal title to the lumber.
8. The Japanese bank retains the order bill of lading and other documents for the moment. The Japanese bank collects the funds from the Yokohama importer, and then gives the order bill of lading to the importer so the importer may obtain both legal title and physical possession of the shipment of lumber. Several other possibilities exist, depending on the security arrangements between the Japanese bank and the Yokohama importer.
9. At maturity (120 days after the Japanese bank accepted the time draft) the holder of the acceptance presents it to the Japanese bank. The holder might be the exporter or it might be an investor in banker's acceptances. If the acceptance is still held by the Portland exporter, that exporter presents it to its Oregon bank, which in turn forwards it to the Japanese bank for collection. When the Oregon bank receives funds it credits the account of the Portland exporter.

## Problem 23.1 Inca Breweries of Peru

**Hold the acceptance or discount it at once?**

| Assumptions | | Values |
|---|---|---|
| Value of shipment | $ | 720,000 |
| Credit terms, days | | 90 |
| Discount rate on 3-month bankers acceptance, per annum | | 8.000% |
| Commission for sale of bankers acceptances | | 1.200% |
| Inca's weighted average cost of capital | | 20.000% |

| Alternative #1: Inca Breweries Holds the Draft | | |
|---|---|---|
| Inca waits 90 days to receive payment in full | $ | 720,000.00 |
| Present value factor for payment received in 90 days | | 0.9524 |
| Present value of payment (amount x pv factor) | $ | 685,714.29 |

| Alternative #2: Inca Breweries Sells the Acceptance | | |
|---|---|---|
| Face amount of bankers acceptance | $ | 720,000.00 |
| Less commission for sale of acceptance | | (8,640.00) |
| Net amount of acceptance, after commission | $ | 711,360.00 |
| Discount charged against acceptances, 90 days | | (14,400.00) |
| Amount received up-front, net of all fees | $ | 696,960.00 |

## Problem 23.2 Swishing Shoe Company

**Hold the draft or discount it?**

| **Assumptions** | **Values** |
|---|---|
| Value of shipment | **£400,000.00** |
| Credit terms, days | **120** |
| Discount rate on 3-month bankers acceptance, per annum | **12.000%** |
| Commission for sale of bankers acceptances | **2.000%** |
| Swishing's weighted average cost of capital | **18.000%** |

| **Alternative #1: Swishing Holds the Draft** | |
|---|---|
| Swishing waits 120 days to receive payment in full | **£400,000.00** |
| Present value factor for payment received in 120 days | **0.9434** |
| Present value of payment (amount x pv factor) | **£377,358.49** |

| **Alternative #2: Swishing Sells the Acceptance** | |
|---|---|
| Face amount of bankers acceptance | **£400,000.00** |
| Less commission for sale of acceptance | **-£8,000.00** |
| Discount charged against acceptances, 120 days | **-£16,000.00** |
| Amount received up-front, net of all fees | **£376,000.00** |

b. Swishing's gain should be calculated in present value terms. Swishing will receive 376,000 pounds today by discounting the banker's acceptance. The present value of the 400,000 to be received in 120 days, discounted at Swishing's WACC of 18% is 377,358.49 pounds. The difference is 1,358.49. Swishing would gain - in present value terms - by waiting.

c. Swishing has assumed the foreign exchange transaction risk. That is, the risk that the pounds to be received from the export will be worth fewer dollars when received. If Swishing discounts the banker's acceptance at the time of sale, it receives dollars at once at the current spot exchange rate.

## Problem 23.3 Going Abroad

If Swishing shifts manufacturing to Ireland from North Carolina, it avoids the 10% import duty and the discount on such bankers' acceptances as it now might be incurring. Alternatively, Swishing would avoid waiting 120 days for its cash and undertaking the associate transaction risk. Note that the solution to Problem 2 previous, is unique to that moment in time. A week or a month later discount rates may change and the alternative might then be preferable.

If Swishing decides to open a plant and manufacture in Ireland, the following factors must be considered:

1. Corporate income tax rates in Ireland and the United States
2. Present and possible future changes in shipping costs.
3. Expected production volume in Ireland, relative to the designed manufacturing capacity of a new factory there. The cost of manufacturing shoes in Ireland will depend on both the volume for which that plant is designed and the percent of capacity expected to be used in the near future.
4. The cost of labor and material in Ireland versus North Carolina; and the availability and level of education and skill of potential workers.
5. The existence or non-existence of excess capacity in the North Carolina factory, both at present and in the near future.
6. The political risk of investing in Ireland for the British market.
7. The possibility that valuable technology or other intellectual property of Swishing's could be lost.

This is only a partial and preliminary list, but it does provide an overview of the complexity of such sourcing and investing decisions.

## Problem 23.4 Governmentally Supplied Credit

The cost to local taxpayers is a contingent loss, to be covered by the government's tax revenues in case the foreign importer fails to pay the exporter. Failure could be deliberate by the importer, but it could also be imposed because of wars, natural disasters, or other international events.

The benefits to the exporting country are the current jobs created by the manufacturing process and any future jobs that might follow from recurring exports by the same firm. The government has determined that these benefits outweigh the possibility of loss. Furthermore, government insurance and guarantee programs charge a fee to the exporter for coverage. The fees are determined by actuarial experience just like any insurance.

MINI-CASE: CROSSWELL INTERNATIONAL'S PRECIOUS ULTRA-THIN DIAPERS

1. **How are pricing, currency of denomination, and financing interrelated in the value-chain for Crosswell's penetration of the Brazilian market? Can you summarize them using Exhibit 2?**

   A variety of sensitivities can be analyzed using the cost analysis of Exhibit 2; the spreadsheet on the following page reproduces the analysis.

   For successful market penetration, Crosswell needs to hit the consumer market at a price of about R$0.65 to R$0.68; the preliminary cost analysis indicates a price of R$0.70 – t0o high. Obviously, currency risk will always be present for Crosswell/Sosa because the product is being imported from the United States with a dollar-cost basis, and the primary competitors are all manufactured locally. According to the preliminary analysis, a case of small diapers which costs R$97.95 in the Santos harbor (port city closest to Sao Paulo), ends up costing R$245.48 per case to consumers.

   Financing is a significant cost concern in the competitive analysis. The cost of financing the diaper inventory needed for distribution in Brazil, according to Sosa, is 7.000% for a one month inventory period, exceedingly high by either U.S. or international standards. Crosswell should explore this cost with Sosa, and evaluate to what degree this rate truly reflects Brazilian costs of funds, whether they can be reduced, and what types of alternative (cheaper) financing may be available.

2. **How important is Sosa to the value-chain of Crosswell? What worries might Crosswell have regarding Sosa's ability to fulfill its obligations?**

   The role that the distributor, in this case Sosa, plays in the success of a product for a consumer product is critical. Crosswell's entire success in the Brazilian marketplace will depend on not only the price-quality offering of Crosswell's products, but also the ability of Sosa to search out and penetrate retail distribution outlets to reach the consumer.

   If Sosa is not a credible or reliable distributor, it could very possibly result in a failed market entry and Crosswell's name and future being tainted for time to come. If Sosa is not adequately financed or staffed to handle the scope of the distribution, costs and reliability may hender market entry, again resulting in either poor service, higher prices than competitors, or both.

   *Note:* Because it is always difficult for a company like Crosswell, with no presence or knowledge of the Brazilian market, to find good business partners in a country like Brazil, the role of institutions like the American Chamber of Commerce (AmCham) in Sao Paulo, Brazil, is critical. AmCham seeks to provide information and introductions for U.S. firms wishing to enter the Brazilian marketplace on a reliable and successful basis.

3. **If Crosswell is to penetrate the market, some way of reducing its prices will be required. What do you suggest?**

   As discussed in question 1, financing expenses may be one area where savings could still be found. Sosa's margin on distribution, 20% in Exhibit 2, also is relatively high given that the retailer's themselves will add on another30%. Retailers themselves carry differing levels of negotiating strength, depending on whether they are major chains such as Carrefour, or smaller corner mom and pop shops called *tienditas* across Latin America. Taxes and government charges are clearly not negotiable, and represent the costs and complexities of attempting to compete through importation.

## Mini-Case: Crosswell International's Precious Ultra-Thin Diapers

| | | Price / case | Rate | Calculation |
|---|---|---|---|---|
| Cases per container | | | 968 | |
| | | | | |
| **Export to Brazil Costs & Pricing** | | | | |
| FOB price per case (US$) | $ | 34.00 | | |
| Freight, loading, & documentation | | 4.32 | 4180 | $4180 per container |
| CFR price | $ | 38.32 | | |
| | | | | |
| Export insurance | | 0.86 | 2.250% | % of CFR |
| CIF/case to distributor (US$) | $ | 39.18 | | |
| | | | | |
| Exchange rate (R$/US$) | | 2.50 | 2.50 | |
| CIF price/case to distributor (R$) | | R$97.95 | | |
| | | | | |
| **Brazilian Importation Costs** | | | | |
| Import duties (ID) | | 1.96 | 2.000% | % of CIF |
| Merchant marine renovation fee (MMRF) | | 2.70 | 25.00% | % of freight |
| Port storage | | 1.27 | 1.300% | % of CIF |
| Port handling fees | | 0.01 | 14.00 | R$12 per container |
| Additional handling tax | | 0.26 | 20.000% | % of storage & handling |
| Customs brokerage fees | | 1.96 | 2.000% | % of CIF |
| Import license | | 0.05 | 50.00 | R$50 per container |
| Local transportation | | 1.47 | 1.500% | % of CIF |
| Total cost to distributor (R$) | | R$107.63 | | |
| | | | | |
| **Distributor's Costs & Pricing** | | | | |
| Storage cost | | 1.47 | 1.500% | % of CIF * months |
| Cost of financing diaper inventory | | 6.86 | 7.000% | % of CIF * months |
| Distributor's margin | | 23.19 | 20.000% | % of Price + storage + cc |
| Price to retailer (R$) | | 139.15 | | |
| | | | | |
| **Brazilian Retailer Costs & Pricing** | | | | |
| Industrial product tax (IPT-2) | | 20.87 | 15.000% | % of price to retailer |
| Tax on merc circulation services (ICMS-2) | | 28.80 | 18.000% | % of price + IPT2 |
| Retailer costs and markup | | 56.65 | 30.000% | % of price + IPT2 + ICMS2 |
| Price per case to consumer (R$) | | 245.48 | | |

| DIAPER PRICES | Bags of 8 per case | Diapers per case | Price to Consumer (R$/diaper) |
|---|---|---|---|
| **Small** | 44 | 352 | R$0.70 |
| **Medium** | 32 | 256 | R$0.96 |
| **Large** | 24 | 192 | R$1.28 |
| **Extra Large** | 22 | 176 | R$1.39 |

# Test Bank

## Preface

The multiple-choice questions for *Fundamentals of Multinational Finance* by Michael Moffett, Arthur Stonehill, and David Eiteman carry two kinds of labels—one that identifies the topic and one that identifies the style or category of question. In terms of categorization, the questions cluster under three types: recognition, conceptual, and analytical. The recognition questions typically refer to a definition or a list of characteristics about a particular topic. The conceptual questions attempt to test the student's understanding of a topic. The analytical questions generally require a calculation to determine the correct answer.

Because this is an introductory text I have tried very hard to restrict the questions to only those concepts presented in the text, and I have not assumed that students have a significant background in finance.

Though I have attempted to provide good questions with accurate answers, errors will occur and they are my responsibility. I would appreciate any corrections or suggestions for improvement that you might have.

Curtis J. Bacon
Southern Oregon University

# Table of Contents

# Chapter 1
# The Globalization Process

**Topic: The Globalization Process Fundamentals**
**Skill: Recognition**
1. The phase of the globalization process characterized by imports from foreign suppliers and exports to foreign buyers is called the

a. domestic phase.
b. multinational phase.
c. international trade phase.
d. import-export banking phase.

**Topic: The Globalization Process Fundamentals**
**Skill: Recognition**
2. The authors describe the multinational phase of globalization for a firm as one characterized by the

a. ownership of assets and enterprises in foreign countries.
b. potential for international competitors or suppliers even though all accounts are with domestic firms and are denominated in dollars.
c. imports from foreign suppliers and exports to foreign buyers.
d. requirement that all employees be multilingual.

**Topic: The Globalization Process, Financial Management**
**Skill: Recognition**
3. Of the following, which was NOT mentioned by the authors as an increase in the demands of financial management services due to increased globalization by the firm?

a. Evaluation of the credit quality of foreign buyers and sellers.
b. Foreign consumer method of payment preferences.
c. Credit risk management.
d. Evaluation of foreign exchange risk.

**Topic: Foreign Direct Investment**
**Skill: Recognition**
4. Which of the following forms of *foreign direct investment* requires greater foreign investment?

a. Joint venture.
b. Domestic production and exporting.
c. Licensing management contracts.
d. Greenfield investment.

**Topic: Foreign Direct Investment**
**Skill: Recognition**

5. A *Greenfield Investment* could be defined as
   a. shared investment in new plant and equipment in a foreign country.
   b. the purchase and subsequent operation of an already existing facility in a foreign country.
   c. building a new operational facility in a foreign country.
   d. all of the above.

**Topic: Foreign Direct Investment**
**Skill: Recognition**

6. A *Joint Venture* could be defined as

   a. the purchase and subsequent operation of an already existing facility in a foreign country.
   b. shared investment in new plant and equipment in a foreign country.
   c. building a new operational facility in a foreign country.
   d. all of the above.

**Topic: Foreign Direct Investment**
**Skill: Recognition**

7. Which of the following is an example of a *Cross-border acquisition*?

   a. Tektronics purchases a chip-manufacturing plant in Thailand.
   b. Ford Motor Company purchases automotive parts from a supplier in Mexico.
   c. Braun builds a new small appliance factory in Tennessee.
   d. A dental supply company in San Francisco purchases a warehouse in Arizona.

**Topic: Fundamentals of Finance**
**Skill: Recognition**

8. Anglo-American is defined to mean

   a. North, Central, and South America.
   b. the United States, Canada, and Western Europe.
   c. the United States, United Kingdom, Canada, Australia and New Zealand.
   d. the United States, France, Britain, and Germany.

**Topic: Fundamentals of Finance**
**Skill: Recognition**

9. In finance, an efficient market is one in which

   a. prices are assumed to be correct.
   b. prices adjust quickly and accurately to new information.
   c. prices are the best allocators of capital in the macro economy
   d. all of the above.

**Topic: Fundamentals of Finance**
**Skill: Recognition**

10. In the Anglo-American model of corporate governance, the primary goal of management is to

   a. maximize the wealth of all stakeholders.
   b. maximize shareholder wealth.
   c. minimize costs
   d. minimize risk.

**Topic: Fundamentals of Finance**
**Skill: Recognition**

11. Systematic risk can be defined as

   a. the total risk to the firm.
   b. the risk of the individual security.
   c. the added risk that a firm's shares bring to a diversified portfolio.
   d. the risk that can be systematically diversified away.

**Topic: Fundamentals of Finance**
**Skill: Recognition**

12. Unsystematic risk can be defined as

   a. the total risk to the firm.
   b. the risk of the individual security.
   c. the added risk that a firm's shares bring to a diversified portfolio.
   d. the risk that can be systematically diversified away.

**Topic: Alternative Management Objectives**
**Skill: Recognition**

13. "Maximize corporate wealth"

   a. is the primary objective of the European/Japanese model of management.
   b. as a management objective treats shareholders on a par with other corporate stakeholders such as creditors, labor, and local community.
   c. has a broader definition than just financial wealth.
   d. all of the above.

**Topic: Alternative Management Objectives**
**Skill: Recognition**
14. Corporate wealth maximization, also known as the stakeholder capitalism model, holds that total risk (operational and financial) is more important than just systematic risk.

a. True
b. False

**Topic: Alternative Management Objectives**
**Skill: Recognition**
15. The Corporate Wealth Maximization Model

a. clearly places shareholders as the primary stakeholder.
b. combines the interests and inputs of shareholders, creditors, management, employees, and society.
c. has financial profit as its goal and is often termed impatient capital.
d. is the Anglo–American model of corporate governance.

**Topic: Alternative Management Objectives**
**Skill: Recognition**
16. The Shareholder Wealth Maximization Model

a. combines the interests and inputs of shareholders, creditors, management, employees, and society.
b. is being usurped by the Corporate Wealth Maximization Model as those types of MNEs dominate their global industry segments.
c. clearly places shareholders as the primary stakeholder.
d. is the dominant form of corporate management in the European-Japanese governance system.

**Topic: Alternative Management Objectives**
**Skill: Recognition**
17. In recent years the trend has been for markets to increasing focus on the shareholder wealth form of wealth maximization.

a. True
b. False

**Topic: Corporate Governance**
**Skill: Conceptual**

18. Under the Shareholder Wealth Maximization Goal of Corporate Governance, poor firm performance is likely to be faced with all but which of the following?

a. Sale of shares by disgruntled current shareholders.
b. Shareholder activism to attempt a change is current management.
c. As a maximum threat, initiation of a corporate takeover.
d. Prison time for executive management.

**Topic: Corporate Governance**
**Skill: Conceptual**

19. Non-Anglo-American markets are dominated by the "one-vote-one-share" rule.

a. True
b. False

**Topic: Corporate Governance**
**Skill: Conceptual**

20. Which of the following is a reason why managers act to maximize shareholder wealth in Anglo-American markets?

a. The use of stock options to align the goals of shareholders and managers.
b. The market for corporate control that allows for outside takeover of the firm.
c. Performance based compensation for executive management.
d. All of the above.

**Topic: Firm Value**
**Skill: Recognition**

21. Which of the following was NOT identified by the authors as a knowledge asset?

a. Customer care.
b. Foreign macroeconomic issues.
c. Brand value.
d. Management skill.

**Topic: Operational Goals**
**Skill: Conceptual**

22. Which of the following is generally NOT considered to be a viable operational goal for a firm?

a. Maintaining a strong local currency.
b. Maximization of after-tax income.
c. Minimization of the firm's effective global tax burden.
d. Correct positioning of the firm's income, cash flows and available funds as to country and currency.

**Topic: Operational Goals**
**Skill: Conceptual**
23. The primary operational goal for the firm is to

a. maximize after-tax profits in each country where the firm is operating.
b. minimize the total financial risk to the firm.
c. maximize the consolidated after-tax profits of the firm.
d. maximize the total risk to the firm.

**Topic: Operational Goals**
**Skill: Conceptual**
24. Which of the following is an *operational* process that can destroy firm value?

a. Interest rate fluctuations.
b. Competitive pressures.
c. Natural disasters
d. Accounting irregularities.

**Topic: Operational Goals**
**Skill: Conceptual**
25. Privatization is a term used to describe

a. firms that are purchased by the government.
b. government operations that are purchased by corporations and other investors.
c. firms that do not use publicly available debt.
d. non-public meetings held by members of interlocking directorates.

**Topic: Operational Goals**
**Skill: Conceptual**
26. The goal of all international corporations is to maximize shareholder wealth.

a. True
b. False

**Topic: The Globalization Process Fundamentals**
**Skill: Conceptual**
27. Typically, a firm in its domestic stage of globalization has all financial transactions in its domestic currency.

a. True
b. False

**Topic: The Globalization Process Fundamentals**
**Skill: Conceptual**

28. A firm in the International Trade Phase of Globalization

a. makes all foreign payments in foreign currency units and all foreign receipts in domestic currency units.
b. receives all foreign receipts in foreign currency units and makes all foreign payments in domestic currency units.
c. bears direct foreign exchange risk.
d. none of the above.

**Topic: The Globalization Process Fundamentals**
**Skill: Conceptual**

29. The exposure to foreign exchange risk known as Translation Exposure may be defined as

a. changes in reported owners' equity in consolidated financial statements caused by a change in exchange rates.
b. the impact of settling outstanding obligations entered into before change in exchange rates but to be settled after change in exchange rates.
c. the change in expected future cash flows arising from an unexpected change in exchange rates.
d. all of the above.

**Topic: Operational Goals**
**Skill: Conceptual**

30. The exposure to foreign exchange risk known as Operating Exposure may be defined as

a. changes in reported owners' equity in consolidated financial statements caused by a change in exchange rates.
b. the impact of settling outstanding obligations entered into before change in exchange rates but to be settled after change in exchange rates.
c. the change in expected future cash flows arising from an unexpected change in exchange rates.
d. all of the above.

**Topic: Operational Goals**
**Skill: Conceptual**

31. The exposure to foreign exchange risk known as Transaction Exposure may be defined as

a. the change in expected future cash flows arising from an unexpected change in exchange rates.
b. changes in reported owners' equity in consolidated financial statements caused by a change in exchange rates.
c. the impact of settling outstanding obligations entered into before change in exchange rates but to be settled after change in exchange rates.
d. all of the above.

**Topic: Operational Goals**
**Skill: Conceptual**

32. Unlike domestic firms, MNEs should use a capital budgeting framework to evaluate projects.

a. True
b. False

**Topic: Risk**
**Skill: Conceptual**

33. Of the following types of risk, which is NOT identified by the authors as a type associated with foreign direct investment?

a. Seasonal
b. Political
c. Economic
d. Financial

**Topic: Operational Goals**
**Skill: Recognition**

34. The prices charged on sales of goods and services between units of a firm globally are known as

a. royalties.
b. licensing fees.
c. blocked funds.
d. transfer pricing.

**Topic: Risk**
**Skill: Conceptual**
35. Systematic risk can be eliminated through portfolio diversification.

a. True
b. False

**Topic: Corporate Governance**
**Skill: Recognition**
36. According to the authors, dual classes of voting stock are the norm in non-Anglo-American markets.

a. True
b. False

**Topic: The Globalization Process Fundamentals**
**Skill: Recognition**
37. Which of the following is not a form of direct foreign investment?

a. Joint ventures
b. Acquisitions of existing operations in a foreign country
c. Franchising
d. International trade

**Topic: The Globalization Process Fundamentals**
**Skill: Recognition**
38. Typically, Licensing is considered to be a greater foreign investment than a Greenfield investment

a. True
b. False

**Topic: Corporate Governance**
**Skill: Recognition**
39. The deliberation of the of the process demonstrated in the European-Japanese system of corporate governance has sometimes been termed
a. socialism.
b. impatient capital.
c. patient capital.
d. communism.

**Topic: Corporate Governance**
**Skill: Recognition**
40. With shareholder wealth maximization as the manager's goal, capital may be termed
a. impatient.
b. patient.
c. borrowed.
d. bought.

## Short Answer Questions:

1. Why is it more appropriate to use the term multinational enterprise rather than international corporation to describe the firms engaged in the globalization process?

**Answer**
Multinational is a more accurate descriptive term for firms operating in several countries. Enterprise is more appropriate because many of the techniques for going global do not require incorporation. Many businesses "go global" by entering into franchise or licensing agreements, strategic alliances, or simple operating agreements with private firms and governments that are not incorporated.

2. Describe the management objectives of a firm governed by the shareholder wealth maximization model and one governed by the stakeholder wealth maximization model. Give an example of how these two models may lead to different decision-making by executive management.

**Answer**
Shareholder wealth maximization attempts to do just that, typically through the maximization of share price. Stakeholder wealth maximization is much more difficult because of the necessity to satisfy many stakeholders all having approximately equal claim on the objectives of management. These stakeholders may include shareholders, creditors, customers, employees, and community. Differing decisions may occur in a situation that involves significant social costs. For example, in the U.S. the decision to shift production from a local factory to a foreign one may be in large based on the change in NPV as the result of the move with only minor consideration of the impact that a change in location would have on the community at large or the local employees. A manager of a stakeholder driven firm may place equal or greater emphasis on the local employees and community and choose to maintain the current facility rather than move even if the foreign operation provided a much greater NPV. Ultimately, the latter may cause an inefficient allocation of scarce resources and lead to an overall lower standard of living.

## Chapter 1: The Globalization Process
## Multiple Choice and True/False Answer Key

| | | | | | | | |
|---|---|---|---|---|---|---|---|
| 1 | C | 11 | C | 21 | B | 31 | C |
| 2 | A | 12 | A | 22 | A | 32 | B |
| 3 | B | 13 | D | 23 | C | 33 | A |
| 4 | D | 14 | A | 24 | D | 34 | D |
| 5 | C | 15 | B | 25 | B | 35 | B |
| 6 | B | 16 | C | 26 | B | 36 | A |
| 7 | A | 17 | A | 27 | A | 37 | D |
| 8 | C | 18 | D | 28 | C | 38 | B |
| 9 | D | 19 | B | 29 | A | 39 | C |
| 10 | B | 20 | D | 30 | C | 40 | A |

# 12

# Chapter 2
# History of Foreign Exchange Rates

**Topic: Currency Terminology**
**Skill: Recognition**
1. The price of one country's currency in units of another currency or commodity is the

a. foreign interest rate.
b. foreign currency exchange rate.
c. par value.
d. international rate.

**Topic: Currency Terminology**
**Skill: Recognition**
2. A country that regulates the rate at which its currency is exchanged for all other currencies is considered to have a ____________ exchange rate system.

a. fixed or managed
b. floating or flexible
c. forward
d. spot

**Topic: Currency Terminology**
**Skill: Conceptual**
3. You check the CNNfn web site and find that the Japanese yen is trading at a rate of 130 yen per dollar. This rate of exchange is typically referred to as the ___________.

a. forward rate
b. par rate
c. spot rate
d. 130 rate

**Topic: Currency Terminology**
**Skill: Conceptual**
4. The drop in value of a currency pegged to gold or another currency is known as __________________.

a. revaluation
b. depreciation
c. deterioration
d. devaluation

**Topic: Currency Terminology**
**Skill: Conceptual**
5. A _____________ currency is expected to devalue or depreciate relative to major currencies.

a. soft or weak
b. hard or strong
c. deteriorated
d. devalued

**Topic: Currency Terminology**
**Skill: Conceptual**
6. The increase in value of a currency pegged to gold or another currency is known as _______________.

a. appreciation
b. revaluation
c. strengthened
d. hardened

**Topic: Currency Terminology**
**Skill: Conceptual**
7. A currency that has increased in foreign exchange value relative to a floating rate currency has _____________.

a. revalued
b. violated international trade agreements
c. appreciated
d. deteriorated

**Topic: Currency Terminology**
**Skill: Conceptual**
8. A currency that has decreased in foreign exchange value relative to a floating rate currency has _____________.

a. devalued
b. appreciated
c. devalued
d. depreciated

**Topic: Currency Terminology**
**Skill: Recognition**

9. The _____________, the most recent currency regime, is the common currency for 12 of the 15 countries that are members of the European Union.

a. SDR (Special Drawing Rights)
b. ECU (European Currency Unit)
c. Euro
d. Yugo

**Topic: Currency Terminology**
**Skill: Recognition**

10. A United States firm had chosen to deposit money in a British bank and have it denominated in U.S. dollars. This is an example of a (an) _____________ deposit.

a. imPounded
b. Euroyen
c. Europound
d. Eurodollar

**Topic: Gold Standard**
**Skill: Analytical**

11. Under the gold standard of currency exchange that existed from 1879 to 1914, an ounce of gold cost $20.67 in U.S. dollars and £4.2474 in British pounds. Therefore, the exchange rate of pounds per dollar under this fixed exchange regime was

a. £4.8665/$.
b. £0.2055/$.
c. always changing because the price of gold was always changing.
d. unknown because there is not enough information to answer this question.

**Topic: Gold Standard**
**Skill: Conceptual**

12. World War I caused the suspension of the gold standard for fixed international exchange rates because the war

a. cost too much money.
b. interrupted the free movement of gold.
c. lasted too long.
d. used gold as the main ingredient armament plating.

**Topic: Currency Speculation**
**Skill: Conceptual**

13. A speculative technique whereby the speculator sells as asset that he/she doesn't own, such as a currency, to another party for delivery at a future date is called _______.

a. selling ahead
b. selling behind
c. selling short
d. selling long

**Topic: Currency Speculation**
**Skill: Conceptual**

14. Which of the following investment strategies will allow me to make a profit if I anticipate that the value of the Euro, a currency that I do not own, is going to fall over the next 90 days and I am correct in my prediction?

a. Sell Euros short.
b. Buy Euros short.
c. Sell dollars short.
d. Buy Euros long.

**Topic: Bretton Woods Agreement**
**Skill: Recognition**

15. The post WWII international monetary agreement that was developed in 1944 is known as the ____________________.

a. United Nations
b. League of Nations
c. Yalta Agreement
d. Bretton Woods Agreement

**Topic: Bretton Woods Agreement**
**Skill: Recognition**

16. Another name for the International Bank for Reconstruction and Development is

a. the Recon Bank.
b. the European Monetary System.
c. the Marshall Plan.
d. the World Bank.

**Topic: Bretton Woods Agreement**
**Skill: Recognition**
17. The International Monetary Fund (IMF)

a. in recent years has provided large loans to Russia, South Korea, and Brazil.
b. was created as a result of the Bretton Woods Agreement.
c. aids countries with balance of payment and exchange rate problems.
d. is all of the above.

**Topic: Bretton Woods Agreement**
**Skill: Recognition**
18. Under the terms of Bretton Woods countries tried to maintain the value of their currencies to within 1% of a hybrid security made up of the U.S. dollar, British pound, and Japanese yen.

a. True
b. False

**Topic: Bretton Woods Agreement**
**Skill: Recognition**
19. Members of the International Monetary Fund may settle transactions among themselves by transferring Special Drawing Rights (SDRs).

a. True
b. False

**Topic: Bretton Woods Agreement**
**Skill: Analytical**
20. Today, the United States has been ejected from the International Monetary Fund for refusal to pay annual dues.

a. True
b. False

**Topic: Exchange Rate Regimes**
**Skill: Conceptual**
21. Which of the following led to the eventual demise of the fixed currency exchange rate regime worked out at Bretton woods?

a. Widely divergent national monetary and fiscal policies among member nations.
b. Differential rates of inflation across member nations.
c. Several unexpected economic shocks to member nations.
d. All of the above.

**Topic: Exchange Rate Regimes**
**Skill: Recognition**

22. The IMFs exchange rate regime classification identifies _________ as the most rigidly fixed, and ______________ as the least fixed.

a. exchange arrangements with no separate legal tender; independent floating
b. crawling pegs; managed float
c. currency board arrangements; independent floating
d. pegged exchange rates within horizontal bands; exchange rates within crawling pegs

**Topic: Exchange Rate Regimes**
**Skill: Conceptual**

23. Which of the following correctly identifies exchange rate regimes from less fixed to more fixed?

a. Independent floating, currency board arrangement, crawling pegs.
b. Independent floating, currency board arrangement, managed float.
c. Independent floating, crawling pegs, exchange arrangements with no separate legal tender.
d. exchange arrangements with no separate legal tender, currency board arrangement, crawling pegs.

**Topic: Exchange Rate Regimes**
**Skill: Recognition**

24. As of January 2002, the Independent Floating regime of exchange rate classifications was used by over 75% of the 186 countries identified by the IMF.

a. True
b. False

**Topic: Exchange Rate Regimes**
**Skill: Conceptual**

25. A small economy country whose GDP is heavily dependent on trade with the United States could use a (an) ______________ exchange rate regime to minimize the risk to their economy that could arise due to unfavorable changes in the exchange rate.

a. pegged exchange rate with the United States
b. pegged exchange rate with the Euro
c. independent floating
d. managed float

**Topic: Exchange Rate Regimes**
**Skill: Recognition**
26. The United States currently uses a ____________ exchange rate regime.

a. crawling peg
b. pegged
c. floating
d. fixed

**Topic: Exchange Rate Regimes**
**Skill: Conceptual**
27. Based on the premise that, other things equal, countries would prefer a fixed exchange rate: Variable rates provide stability in international prices for the conduct of trade.

a. True
b. False

**Topic: Exchange Rate Regimes**
**Skill: Recognition**
28. Based on the premise that, other things equal, countries would prefer a fixed exchange rate, which of the following statements is NOT true.

a. Fixed rates provide stability in international prices for the conduct of trade.
b. Fixed exchange rate regimes necessitate that central banks maintain large quantities of international reserves for use in the occasional defense of the fixed rate.
c. Fixed rates are inherently inflationary in that they require the country to follow loose monetary and fiscal policies.
d. Stable prices aid in the growth of international trade and lessen exchange rate risks for businesses.

**Topic: Exchange Rate Regimes**
**Skill: Conceptual**
29. Which of the following is not an attribute of the "ideal" currency?

a. Monetary independence.
b. Full financial integration.
c. Exchange rate stability.
d. All are attributes of an ideal currency.

**Topic: Exchange Rate Regimes**
**Skill: Conceptual**
30. If exchange rates were fixed, investors and traders would be relatively certain about the current and near future exchange value of each currency.

a. True
b. False

**Topic: Currency Regimes**
**Skill: Conceptual**
31. The authors discuss the concept of the "Impossible Trinity" or the inability to achieve simultaneously the goals of exchange rate stability, full financial integration, and monetary independence. If a country chooses to have a pure float exchange rate regime, which two of the three goals is a country most able to achieve?

a. Monetary independence and exchange rate stability.
b. Exchange rate stability and full financial integration.
c. Full financial integration and monetary independence.
d. A cannot attain any of the exchange rate goals with a pure float exchange rate regime.

**Topic: Currency Regimes**
**Skill: Recognition**
32. The attempt by many countries to stimulate their domestic economies and to gain access to global financial markets, is causing more and more countries to choose a ____________ or ____________ exchange rate regime.

a. floating; monetary union
b. monetary union; full capital controls
c. full capital controls; floating
d. pegged; fixed

**Topic: Currency Regimes**
**Skill: Recognition**
33. Beginning in 1991 Argentina conducted its monetary policy through a currency board. In January 2002, Argentina abandoned the currency board and allowed it currency to float against other currencies. The country took this step because

a. the Argentine Peso had grown too strong against major trading powers thus the currency board policies were hurting the domestic economy.
b. the United States required the action as a prerequisite to finalizing a free trade zone with all of North, South, and Central America.
c. the Argentine government lost the ability to maintain the pegged relationship as in fact investors and traders perceived a lack of equality between the Argentine Peso and the U.S. dollar.
d. of all of the above.

**Topic: Currency Regimes**
**Skill: Analytical**
34. In January 2002, the Argentine Peso changed in value from Peso1.00/$ to Peso1.40/$, thus, the Argentine Peso ___________ against the U. S. dollar.

a. strengthened
b. weakened
c. remained neutral
d. all of the above

**Topic: Currency Regimes**
**Skill: Conceptual**
35. On September 9, 2000 Ecuador officially replaced its national currency, the Ecuadorian sucre, with the U.S. dollar. This practice is known as ___________.

a. bi-currencyism
b. sucrerization
c. a Yankee bailout
d. dollarization

**Topic: Currency Regimes**
**Skill: Conceptual**
36. You have been hired as a consultant to the central bank for a country that has for many years suffered from repeated currency crises and depends heavily on the U.S. financial and product markets. Which of the following policies would have the greatest effectiveness for reducing currency volatility of the client country with the United States?

a. Dollarization.
b. An exchange rate pegged to the U. S. dollar.
c. An exchange rate with a fixed price per ounce of gold.
d. An internationally floating exchange rate.

**Topic: Bank Holiday**
**Skill: Recognition**
37. A bank holiday

a. occurs every day after 3:00 p.m.
b. is a term used when a country's central government freezes (temporarily) all deposits in commercial banks.
c. is observed in Europe every fourth Friday.
d. occurs the last three working days of the year to prepare financial statements for tax purposes.

**Topic: Currency Regimes**
**Skill: Conceptual**

38. Which of the following is NOT an argument against Dollarization?

a. The dollarized country's central bank can no longer act as a lender of last resort.
b. The dollarized country can no longer profit from seignorage (the ability to profit from the creation of money within its economy).
c. The dollarized country losses sovereignty over its own monetary policy.
d. All of the above are arguments against dollarization from the viewpoint of the affected country.

**Topic: The Euro**
**Skill: Recognition**

39. The Euro currency is fixed against other currencies on the international currency exchange markets, but allows member country currencies to float against each other.

a. True
b. False

**Topic: The Euro**
**Skill: Recognition**

40. Even though the Euro currency has been designed and printed, it is still not available for general use by the public in the European Union.

a. True
b. False

**Topic: The Euro**
**Skill: Recognition**

41. Which of the following is NOT a required convergence criteria to become a full member of the European Economic and Monetary Union (EMU)?

a. National birthrates must be at 2.0 or lower per person.
b. The fiscal deficit should be no more than 3% of GDP.
c. Nominal inflation should be no more than 1.5% above the average inflation rate for the three members with the lowest inflation rates in the previous year.
d. Government debt should be no more than 60% of GDP.

**Topic: The Euro**
**Skill: Recognition**
42. Since its introduction in January 1999 at $1.19/Euro, the Euro has realized a more or less steady ____________ value relative to the U.S. dollar.

a. constant
b. increase in
c. decrease in
d. The Euro is not yet available for trade versus the U.S. dollar.

**Topic: The Euro**
**Skill: Recognition**
43. Which of the following groups of countries have replaced their individual currencies with the Euro?

a. France, Germany, and the United Kingdom.
b. Sweden, Denmark, and Greece.
c. The United Kingdom, The Netherlands, and Austria.
d. Germany, The Netherlands, and Italy.

**Topic: Emerging markets**
**Skill: Conceptual**
44. The tremendous international mobility of financial capital is forcing emerging market nations to adopt one of two polarized choices, free float or currency board, for their foreign currency exchange regimes. Which of the following would NOT be a reason for an emerging nation to choose to have their currency freely float?

a. The country desires to lose political influence on the valuation of their currency.
b. The emerging nation desires an independent monetary policy
c. The emerging nation is willing to tradeoff exchange rate stability to gain free movement of capital.
d. All of the above.

**Topic: The Euro**
**Skill: Conceptual**
45. According to the authors, what is the single most important mandate of the European Central Bank?

a. Promote international trade for countries within the European Union.
b. Price, in Euros, all products for sale in the European Union.
c. Promote price stability within the European Union.
d. Establish an EMU trade surplus with the United States.

**Topic: The Euro**
**Skill: Analytical**

46. Ignoring transaction costs and based solely on the change in currency exchange rates, a speculator who sold short a three year contract for the Euro (receiving dollars) in January 1999 would have realized a profit upon the exercise of the contract in January 2002.

a. True
b. False

**Topic: The Euro**
**Skill: Conceptual**

47. Which of the following is a way in which the Euro affects markets?

a. Countries within the Euro zone enjoy cheaper transaction costs.
b. Currency risks and costs related to exchange rate uncertainty are reduced.
c. Consumers and business enjoy price transparency and increased price-based competition.
d. All of the above.

**Topic: International Monetary Fund**
**Skill: Recognition**

48. A special Drawing Right is a unit of account established by

a. the Federal Reserve Bank.
b. the World Bank.
c. the International Monetary Fund.
d. the European Central Bank.

**Topic: Currency Terminology**
**Skill: Recognition**

49. A currency is considered *hard* if

a. it is expected to be revalued or appreciate.
b. it is expected to be devalued or depreciate.
c. it is backed in part by a precious metal such as gold.
d. it is difficult to trade on the international currency exchange markets.

**Topic: Currency Regimes**
**Skill: Recognition**
50. Under a fixed exchange rate regime, the government of the country is officially responsible for:

a. intervention in the foreign exchange markets using gold and reserves.
b. setting the fixed/parity exchange rate.
c. maintaining the fixed/parity exchange rate.
d. all of the above.

## Short Answer Essay Questions:

1. The mobility of international capital flows is causing emerging market nations to choose between a free-floating currency exchange regime and a currency board (or taken to the limit, dollarization). Describe how each of the regimes would work and identify at least two likely economic results for each regime.

**Answer**
With free float the exchange rate is market determined and beyond the control of the country's central bank or government. The economic results are likely to be an independent monetary policy, free movement of capital, but less stability in the exchange rate. Such instability may be more than an emerging market country's small financial market can bear. A currency board on the other hand is an implied legislative commitment to fix the foreign exchange rate with a specific currency, generally the country's major trading partner. Dollarization is taking this policy to the extreme whereby the emerging market nation forgoes its currency for that of its major trading partner. An example of Dollarization is Panama using U.S. dollars as the official Panamanian currency. With such a regime, independent monetary policy is lost and political influence on monetary policy is eliminated. However, the benefits accruing to countries as a result of the ability to print its own money, seignorage, is lost.

2. On January 4, 1999 the member nations of the EMU introduced a new unified currency, the Euro, to replace the individual national currencies of many member nations. Identify and explain several of the arguments made both for and against the Euro. Do you think the Euro has proven to be a "good" idea? Why/Why not?

**Answer**
Arguments for the Euro include a stable currency for trading among the several member nations and eliminating the need to exchange currencies to make cross-border transactions among member nations thus increasing transactional efficiency and eliminating exchange rate risk. Other advantages include unification of the several European markets, transparency of prices in the member countries, and a larger market to compete against the United States.

Arguments against the Euro include a loss of national heritage and pride in losing a long-held domestic currency. Governments lose exclusive control over seignorage, lack of

national autonomy in fiscal and monetary policy, and inequality among member states in their production and financial market strengths and weaknesses. Member nations are forced to go along with the group even if a particular action does not maximize value to the individual countries.
As for whether the Euro has been good or bad, this is an opinion piece for each student.

3. Most Western nations were on the gold standard for currency exchange rates from 1876 until 1914. Today we have several different exchange rate regimes in use, but most larger economy nations have freely floating exchange rates today and are not obligated to convert their currency into a predetermined amount of gold on demand. Today several parties till call for the "good old days" and a return to the gold standard. Develop an argument as to why this is a good idea.

**Answer**
The gold standard forces a nation to maintain sufficient reserves of gold to back its currency's value. This helps control inflation, as a country cannot print additional money without sufficient gold to back it up. The gold standard eases international transactions as there is little uncertainly about exchanges rates for trade with foreign countries.

## Chapter 2: History of Foreign Exchange Rates
## Multiple Choice and True/False Answer Key

| | | | | | | | | | |
|---|---|---|---|---|---|---|---|---|---|
| 1 | B | 11 | B | 21 | D | 31 | C | 41 | A |
| 2 | A | 12 | B | 22 | A | 32 | A | 42 | C |
| 3 | C | 13 | C | 23 | C | 33 | C | 43 | D |
| 4 | D | 14 | A | 24 | B | 34 | B | 44 | A |
| 5 | A | 15 | D | 25 | A | 35 | D | 45 | C |
| 6 | B | 16 | D | 26 | C | 36 | A | 46 | A |
| 7 | C | 17 | D | 27 | B | 37 | B | 47 | D |
| 8 | D | 18 | B | 28 | C | 38 | D | 48 | C |
| 9 | C | 19 | A | 29 | D | 39 | B | 49 | A |
| 10 | D | 20 | B | 30 | A | 40 | B | 50 | D |

# Chapter 3
# The Balance of Payments

**Topic: BOP Introduction**
**Skill: Conceptual**
1. The *balance of payments* as applied to a course in international finance may be defined as:

a. The amount still owed by an exporting firm after making an initial down payment.
b. The amount still owed by governments to the International Monetary Fund.
c. The measurement of all international economic transactions between the residents of a country and foreign residents.
d. The amount of a country's merchandise trade deficit of surplus.

**Topic: BOP Introduction**
**Skill: Conceptual**
2. Balance of payment (BOP) data may be important for any of the following reasons:

a. BOP data helps to forecast a country's market potential, especially in the short run.
b. The BOP is an important indicator of a country's foreign exchange rate.
c. Changes in a country's BOP may signal a change in controls over payment of dividends and interest.
d. All of the above.

**Topic: BOP Understanding**
**Skill: Analytical**
3. A country experiencing a serious BOP _________ is more likely to __________ imports than otherwise.

a. surplus; contract
b. deficit; contract
c. deficit; expand
d. None of the above.

**Topic: BOP Understanding**
**Skill: Conceptual**
4. Which of the following would NOT be considered a typical BOP transaction?

a. Toyota U.S.A is a U.S. distributor of automobiles manufactured in Japan by its parent company.
b. The U.S. subsidiary of European financial giant, Credit Suisse, pays dividends to its parent in Zurich.
c. A U.S. tourist purchases gifts at a museum in London.
d. All are example of BOP transactions.

**Topic: BOP Introduction**
**Skill: Recognition**
5. The authors identify a tip for understanding BOP accounting. They recommend that you "follow the cash flow."

a. True
b. False

**Topic: Current Account**
**Skill: Recognition**
6. The BOP must be in balance but the current account need not be.

a. True
b. False

**Topic: Current Account**
**Skill: Recognition**
7. Which of the following is NOT a part of the *Current Account* of BOP?

a. Net export/import of goods.
b. Balance of Trade.
c. Net portfolio investment.
d. Net exports/imports of services.

**Topic: Financial Account**
**Skill: Recognition**
8. Which of the following is NOT part of the *Financial Account* of the BOP?

a. Net foreign direct investment.
b. Net imports/exports of services.
c. Net portfolio investment.
d. Other Financial items.

**Topic: BOP Understanding**
**Skill: Recognition**
9. Expenditures by U.S. tourists in foreign countries for foreign goods or services are NOT factored into BOP payment calculations.

a. True
b. False

**Topic: BOP Understanding**
**Skill: Conceptual**
10. Which of the following is NOT an item to be considered in BOP calculations?

a. Purchase of a U.S. Treasury Bill by a foreign resident.
b. A U.S.-based firm manages the development of an oil field in Kazakhstan.
c. A consumer buys a VCR made in Korea from a Wal-Mart store.
d. A U.S. citizen living in Minnesota travels to Winnipeg, Canada and buys a case of LaBatt's Canadian beer.

**Topic: Balance of payments**
**Skill: Recognition**
11. The *balance of payments* is most like a(an) ____________.

a. cash flow statement
b. balance sheet
c. income statement
d. proxy statement

**Topic: Balance of payments**
**Skill: Recognition**
12. The *balance of payments*

a. determines the eligibility of countries for IMF aid.
b. adds up the value of all assets and liabilities of a country on a specific date.
c. records all international transactions for a country over a period of time.
d. all of the above.

**Topic: Balance of Payments**
**Skill: Conceptual**
13. According to the authors, the following types of transactions dominate the *balance of payments:*

a. The exchange of guns for butter.
b. The exchange of stocks and bonds.
c. The exchange of goods and services.
d. The exchange of real and financial assets.

**Topic: Current Account**
**Skill: Conceptual**
14. Which of the following is NOT an example of an exchange of financial assets?

a. The exchange of travel services.
b. The exchange of stocks.
c. The exchange of bonds.
d. Loans.

**Topic: Balance of Payments**
**Skill: Recognition**
15. Because current and financial/capital account balances use double-entry booking, it is unusual to find mistakes serious discrepancies in the debits and credits.

a. True
b. False

**Topic: Balance of payments**
**Skill: Recognition**
16. Which of the following is NOT part of the *balance of payments* account?

a. The current account.
b. The financial/capital account.
c. The official reserves account.
d. All of the above are BOP accounts.

**Topic: Current account**
**Skill: Recognition**
17. The __________ includes all international economic transactions with income or payment flows occurring within the year.

a. capital account
b. current account
c. financial account
d. IMF account

**Topic: Current account**
**Skill: Conceptual**
18. If your company were to import and export textiles, the transactions would be recorded in the current account subcategory of ________________.

a. services trade
b. income trade
c. goods trade
d. current transfers

**Topic: Current account**
**Skill: Conceptual**
19. The travel services provided to international travelers by United Airlines would be recorded in the current account subcategory of ______________.

a. services trade
b. income trade
c. goods trade
d. current transfers

**Topic: Current account**
**Skill: Conceptual**
20. Anaconda Copper Inc. created a subsidiary in Chile last year to mine copper ore. The proportion of net income paid back to the parent company as a dividend would be recorded in the current account subcategory of ______________.

a. services trade
b. income trade
c. goods trade
d. current transfers

**Topic: Current account**
**Skill: Recognition**
21. The subcategory that typically dominates the current account is ___________.

a. goods (merchandise) trade
b. services trade
c. income trade
d. transfer accounts

**Topic: Current account**
**Skill: Conceptual**
22. Over the last several years, the United States has run a ________ in the goods trade balance and a __________ in the services trade balance.

a. surplus; deficit
b. surplus; surplus
c. deficit; deficit
d. deficit; surplus

**Topic: Current account**
**Skill: Recognition**
23. In general, the United States goods trade balance has grown increasing positive over the last 3 years.

a. True
b. False

**Topic: Current account**
**Skill: Recognition**
24. In 1999 the United States posted a current account deficit of -$331 billion. The bulk of the negative value came from

a. a net transfer deficit.
b. an income balance deficit.
c. a goods trade deficit.
d. an income trade deficit.

**Topic: Economic Theory**
**Skill: Conceptual**
25. In general, as a country's income increases, so does the demand for imports.

a. True
b. False

**Topic: Economic Theory**
**Skill: Conceptual**
26. In general, a country's exports increase as foreign income decreases.

a. True
b. False

**Topic: Balance of Trade**
**Skill: Recognition**
27. Over the last two decades the surplus on U.S. services trade has typically been __________ the deficit on U.S. goods trade.

a. greater than
b. equal to
c. less than
d. The relationship is constantly shifting from greater than to less than.

**Topic: Capital/Financial Account**
**Skill: Recognition**
28. The ________________ of the balance of payments measures all international economic transactions of financial assets.

a. current account
b. merchandise trade account
c. services account
d. capital/financial account

**Topic: Capital/Financial Account**
**Skill: Recognition**
29. The financial account consists COMPLETELY of which three components?

a. Stock investment, bond investment, and mutual fund investment.
b. Direct investment, stock investment, and bond investment.
c. Direct investment, portfolio investment, and other asset investment.
d. Mutual fund investment, portfolio investment, and stock investment.

**Topic: Capital/Financial Account**
**Skill: Recognition**
30. When categorizing investments for the financial account component of the balance of payments the ________________ is an investment where the investor has no control whereas the ________________ is an investment where the investor has control over the asset.

a. direct investment; portfolio investment
b. direct investment; indirect investment
c. portfolio investment; indirect investment
d. portfolio investment; direct investment

**Topic: Capital/Financial Account**
**Skill: Conceptual**
31. Which of the following would NOT be considered a direct investment either into or from the United States?

a. The purchase of U.S. Treasury (debt) securities.
b. Ford Motor Company building an assembly plant in Mexico.
c. Honda of Japan building a manufacturing plant in Alabama.
d. Intel purchasing a chip manufacturing plant in Thailand.

**Topic: Capital/Financial Account**
**Skill: Recognition**

32. International debt security purchases and sales are defined as portfolio investments for financial account purposes because by definition debt securities do not provide the buyer with ownership or control.

a. True
b. False

**Topic: International Investment**
**Skill: Conceptual**

33. In general there is consensus that ________________ should be free but there is no such consensus that ________________ should be free.

a. international investment; international goods trade
b. international investment; international trade
c. international trade; international goods trade
d. international trade; international investment

**Topic: International Investment**
**Skill: Conceptual**

34. The two major concerns about foreign direct investment are

a. national defense and taxes.
b. who controls the assets and who receives the profits.
c. who receives the profits and taxes.
d. who pays the taxes and who receives the taxes.

**Topic: Capital/Financial Account**
**Skill: Recognition**

35. Portfolio investment is capital invested in activities that are ____________ rather than made for ______________.

a. short term; the long term
b. long term; profit
c. profit motivated; control
d. control motivated; profit

**Topic: Capital/Financial Account**
**Skill: Recognition**
36. Most U.S. debt purchased by foreigners is denominated in __________ and most foreign debt issued by countries such as Russia, Mexico, and Brazil is issued in ________________.

a. U.S. dollars; the purchasing investor's domestic currency
b. the purchasing investor's domestic currency; the issuing country's domestic currency
c. U.S. dollars; the issuing country's domestic currency
d. U.S. dollars; U.S. dollars

**Topic: Capital/Financial Account**
**Skill: Conceptual**
37. Significant amounts of United States Treasury issues are purchased by foreign investors, therefore the U.S. must earn foreign currency to repay this debt.

a. True
b. False

**Topic: Capital/Financial Account**
**Skill: Conceptual**
38. The role of official reserves is ____________ under a __________exchange rate regime.

a. enhanced; floating
b. diminished; fixed
c. enhanced; fixed
d. None of the above apply.

**Topic: Capital/Financial Account**
**Skill: Conceptual**
39. If most major economies are operating under a regime of fixed exchange rates, then a ___________ in a country's balance of payments suggests that the country should ____________ its currency.

a. surplus; revalue
b. surplus; devalue
c. deficit; revalue
d. All of the above.

**Topic: Capital/Financial Account**
**Skill: Conceptual**

40. Under an international regime of fixed exchange rates, countries with a BOP ________ should consider ____________ their currency while countries with a BOP ____________ should consider ___________ their currency.

a. deficit, revaluing; surplus, revaluing
b. deficit, devaluing; surplus, devaluing
c. surplus, devaluing; deficit, revaluing
d. surplus, revaluing; deficit, devaluing

**Topic: Capital Mobility**
**Skill: Recognition**

41. The era between 1880 and 1914, when the gold standard was in use, was characterized by increasing capital mobility.

a. True
b. False

**Topic: Capital Mobility**
**Skill: Recognition**

42. The time from 1971 to today has predominately used a regime of variable exchange rates. It has also seen a decrease in capital mobility.

a. True
b. False

**Topic: Capital Mobility**
**Skill: Recognition**

43. Which of the following is the best definition of money laundering?

a. Legal transfer of funds through the usual international payments mechanisms.
b. The transfer of cash into collectibles that are then transferred across borders.
c. The cross-border purchase of assets that are then managed in a way that hide the movement of money and its ownership.
d. False invoicing of international trade transactions.

**Topic: Balance of Trade**
**Skill: Recognition**

44. The _____________ is the difference between merchandise imports and exports and a measure of a country's international trade in goods and services.

a. balance of payments
b. current account
c. capital account
d. balance of trade

**Topic: Balance of Trade**
**Skill: Recognition**
45. The United States experienced a balance of trade __________ during the 1980s and a balance of trade ___________ during the 1990s.

a. surplus; surplus
b. surplus; deficit
c. deficit; deficit
d. deficit; surplus

**Topic: Current Account**
**Skill: Recognition**
46. The largest single component of the United States current account is ________.

a. current transfers
b. income payments and receipts
c. goods (merchandise) imports and exports
d. services imports and exports

**Topic: Balance of Trade**
**Skill: Conceptual**
47. An excess of merchandise imports over merchandise exports results in a balance of trade deficit.

a. True
b. False

**Topic: Capital/Financial Account**
**Skill: Recognition**
48. Portfolio investments are transactions that involve long-term financial assets and affect the transfer of control.

a. True
b. False

**Topic: Capital Mobility**
**Skill: Recognition**
49. Which of the following does NOT represent a possible mechanism by which capital can be moved from country to country?

a. Transfers via the usual international payments mechanism such as regular bank transfers.
b. Transfers via a physical bearer such as smuggling.
c. The transfer of cash into collectibles.
d. All of the above are mechanisms for moving capital from country to country.

**Topic: Balance of Payments**
**Skill: Recognition**

50. Which of the following statements about the balance of payments is not true?

a. The BOP is the summary statement of all international transactions between one country and all other countries.
b. The BOP is a flow statement, summarizing all international transactions that occur across the geographic borders over a period of time, typically a year.
c. Although the BOP must always balance in theory, in practice there are substantial imbalances as a result of statistical errors and misreporting of current account and financial account flows.
d. All of the above are true.

## Essay Questions:

1. What is a country's balance of (merchandises) trade and why is it so widely reported in the financial and popular press?

**Answer**
The balance of trade (BOT) is the largest and most important subset of a country's current account. It measures the difference in a country's imports and exports over a specified time period. It is often reported because it is intuitively easy to understand (i.e., we either sell more or buy more from foreign countries) and it is a reasonable representation of the total current account balance. (For example, for the U. S. the BOT was -$343B in 1999 while the current account balance was -$331B.

2. What is the Official Reserves Account (ORA) and why is it more important for countries under a fixed exchange rate regime than for ones under a floating exchange rate regime?

**Answer**
The ORA is the total reserves held by official monetary authorities within the country. Under a fixed exchange regime a country's currency is convertible into a fixed amount of another country's currency. To keep the relationship between currencies at equilibrium, it may become necessary for the government to buy or sell official reserves until the equilibrium is restored. Under a variable rate regime this is not necessary as exchange rates are allowed to change and official reserves no longer serve the same purpose as under the fixed rate regime.

## Chapter 3: The Balance of Payments
## Multiple Choice and True/False Answer Key

| | | | | | | | | | |
|---|---|---|---|---|---|---|---|---|---|
| 1 | C | 11 | A | 21 | A | 31 | A | 41 | A |
| 2 | D | 12 | C | 22 | D | 32 | A | 42 | B |
| 3 | B | 13 | D | 23 | B | 33 | D | 43 | C |
| 4 | D | 14 | A | 24 | C | 34 | B | 44 | D |
| 5 | A | 15 | B | 25 | A | 35 | C | 45 | C |
| 6 | A | 16 | D | 26 | B | 36 | D | 46 | C |
| 7 | C | 17 | B | 27 | C | 37 | B | 47 | A |
| 8 | B | 18 | C | 28 | D | 38 | C | 48 | B |
| 9 | B | 19 | A | 29 | C | 39 | A | 49 | D |
| 10 | C | 20 | B | 30 | D | 40 | D | 50 | D |

# Chapter 4
# International Parity Conditions

**Topic: The Law of One Price**
**Skill: Recognition**

1. If an identical product can be sold in two different markets, and no restrictions exist on the sale or transportation costs, the product's price should be the same in both markets. This is know as

   a. relative purchasing power parity.
   b. interest rate parity.
   c. the law of one price.
   d. equilibrium.

**Topic: PPP**
**Skill: Recognition**

2. ____________ states that the spot exchange rate is determined by the relative prices of similar baskets of goods.

   a. Absolute purchasing power parity
   b. Relative purchasing power parity
   c. Interest rate parity
   d. The Fisher Effect

**Topic: PPP**
**Skill: Analytical**

3. *The Economist* publishes annually the "hamburger standard" by which they compare the prices of the McDonalds Corporation Big Mac hamburger around the world. The index estimates the exchange rates for currencies based on the assumption that the burgers in question are the same across the world and therefore, the price should be the same. If a Big Mac costs $2.54 in the United States and 294 yen in Japan, what is the estimated exchange rate of yen per dollar as hypothesized by the Hamburger index?

   a. $.0086/¥
   b. 124¥/$
   c. $.0081/¥
   d. 115.75¥/$

**Topic: PPP**
**Skill: Analytical**
4. If the current exchange rate is 124 Japanese yen per U.S. dollar, the price of a Big Mac hamburger in the United States is $2.54, and the price of a Big Mac hamburger in Japan is 294 yen, then other things equal, the Big Mac hamburger in Japan is ________.

a. correctly priced
b. under priced
c. over priced
d. not enough information to determine if the price is appropriate or not.

**Topic: Law of One Price**
**Skill: Analytical**
5. If according to the law of one price the current exchange rate of dollars per British pound is $1.43/£, then at an exchange rate of $1.28/£, the dollar is ________.

a. overvalued
b. undervalued
c. correctly valued
d. unknown relative valuation

**Topic: PPP**
**Skill: Recognition**
6. Generally speaking, the theory of absolute purchasing power parity works better for single goods than for a market basket of goods.

a. True
b. False

**Topic: Law of One Price**
**Skill: Analytical**
7. Other things equal, and assuming efficient markets, if a Honda Accord costs $18, 365 in the U.S. then at an exchange rate of $1.43/£, the Honda Accord should cost __________ in Great Britain.

a. 26,262£
b. 18,365£
c. 12,843£
d. 9,183£

**Topic: PPP**
**Skill: Conceptual**
8. The assumptions for relative PPP are more rigid than the assumptions for absolute PPP.

a. True
b. False

**Topic: PPP**
**Skill: Recognition**
9. ________________ states that differential rates of inflation between two countries tend to be offset over time by an equal but opposite change in the spot exchange rate.

a. The Fisher Effect
b. The International Fisher Effect
c. Absolute Purchasing Power Parity
d. Relative Purchasing Power Parity

**Topic: PPP**
**Skill: Analytical**
10. One year ago the spot rate of U.S. dollars for Canadian dollars was $1/C$1. Since that time the rate of inflation in the U.S. has been 4% greater than that in Canada. Based on the theory of Relative PPP, the current spot exchange rate of U.S. dollars for Canadian dollars should be approximately ____________.

a. $.96/C$
b. $1/C$1
c. $1.04/C$1
d. relative PPP provides no guide for this type of question.

**Topic: PPP**
**Skill: Recognition**
11. Empirical tests prove that PPP is an accurate predictor of future exchange rates.

a. True
b. False

**Topic: PPP**
**Skill: Recognition**

12. Two general conclusions can be made from the empirical tests of purchasing power parity (PPP):

a. PPP holds up well over the short run but poorly for the long run and the theory holds better for countries with relatively low rates of inflation.
b. PPP holds up well over the short run but poorly for the long run and the theory holds better for countries with relatively high rates of inflation.
c. PPP holds up well over the long run but poorly for the short run and the theory holds better for countries with relatively low rates of inflation.
d. PPP holds up well over the long run but poorly for the short run and the theory holds better for countries with relatively high rates of inflation.

**Topic: Currency Valuation**
**Skill: Conceptual**

13. A country's currency that strengthened relative to another country's currency by more than that justified by the differential in inflation is said to be _________ in terms of PPP.

a. overvalued
b. over compensating
c. undervalued
d. under compensating

**Topic: Real Effective Exchange Rate**
**Skill: Conceptual**

14. If a country's *real effective exchange rate index* were to be less than 100, this would suggest an _____________ currency.

a. overvalued
b. over compensating
c. undervalued
d. under compensating

**Topic: Real Effective Exchange Rate**
**Skill: Analytical**

15. If we set the *real effective exchange rate index* between Canada and the United States equal to 100 in 1998, and find that the U.S. dollar has risen to a value of 112.6, then from a competitive perspective the U.S. dollar is

a. overvalued.
b. undervalued.
c. very competitive.
d. There is not enough information to answer this question.

**Topic: Real Effective Exchange Rate**
**Skill: Conceptual**
16. The government just released international exchange rate statistics and reported that the *real effective exchange rate index* for the U.S. dollar vs the Japanese yen decreased from 105 last year to 95 currently and is expected to fall still further in the coming year. Other things equal U.S. ___________ to/from Japan think this is good news and U.S. _________ to/from Japan think this is bad news.

a. importers; exporters
b. importers; importers
c. exporters; exporters
d. exporters; importers

**Topic: Exchange Rate Pass-through**
**Skill: Recognition**
17. *Exchange rate pass-through* may be defined as

a. the bid/ask spread on currency exchange rate transactions.
b. the degree to which the prices of imported and exported goods change as a result of exchange rate changes.
c. the PPP of lesser-developed countries.
d. the practice by Great Britain of maintaining the relative strength of the currencies of the Commonwealth countries under the current floating exchange rate regime.

**Topic: Exchange Rate Pass-through**
**Skill: Analytical**
18. Sony of Japan produces DVD players and exports them to the United States. Last year the exchange rate was 130¥/$ and Sony charged $150 per DVD player. Currently the spot exchange rate is 110¥/$ and Sony is charging $170 per DVD player. What is the degree of pass through by Sony of Japan on their DVD players?

a. 95.9%
b. 86.7%
c. 73.2%
d. 4.1%

**Topic: Price Elasticity**
**Skill: Conceptual**
19. Consider the price elasticity of demand. If a product has price elasticity less than one it is considered to have relatively *elastic* demand.

a. True
b. False

**Topic: Price Elasticity**
**Skill: Analytical**

20. The price elasticity of demand for DVD players manufactured by Sony of Japan is greater than one. If the Japanese yen appreciates against the U.S. dollar by 10% and the price of the Sony DVD players in the U.S also rises by 10%, then other things equal, the total dollar sales revenues of Sony DVDs would ____________.

a. decline
b. increase
c. stay the same
d. insufficient information

**Topic: Fisher Effect**
**Skill: Recognition**

21. ______________ states that nominal interest rates in each country are equal to the required real rate of return plus compensation for expected inflation.

a. Absolute PPP
b. Relative PPP
c. The Law of One Price
d. The Fisher Effect

**Topic: Fisher Effect**
**Skill: Recognition**

22. In its approximate form the Fisher effect may be written as ____________.
Where: $i$ = the nominal rate of interest, $r$ = the real rate of return and $\pi$ = the expected rate of inflation.

a. $i = (r)(\pi)$
b. $i = r + \pi + (r)(\pi)$
c. $i = r + \pi$
d. $i = r + 2\pi$

**Topic: Fisher Effect**
**Skill: Recognition**

23. The final component of the equation for the Fisher Effect, $(r)(\pi)$, where $r$ = the real rate of return and $\pi$ = the expected rate of inflation, is often dropped from the equation because the number is simply too large for most Western economies.

a. True
b. False

**Topic: Fisher Effect**
**Skill: Analytical**
24. Assume a nominal interest rate on one-year U.S. Treasury Bills of 4.60% and a real rate of interest of 2.50%. Using the Fisher Effect Equation, what is the approximate expected rate of inflation in the U.S. over the next year?

a. 2.10%
b. 2.05%
c. 2.00%
d. 1.90%

**Topic: Fisher Effect**
**Skill: Analytical**
25. Assume a nominal interest rate on one-year U.S. Treasury Bills of 3.80% and a real rate of interest of 2.00%. Using the Fisher Effect Equation, what is the exact expected rate of inflation in the U.S. over the next year?

a. 1.84%
b. 1.80%
c. 1.76%
d. 1.72%

**Topic: Fisher Effect**
**Skill: Conceptual**
26. Empirical studies show that the Fisher Effect works best for short-term securities.

a. True
b. False

**Topic: International Fisher Effect**
**Skill: Recognition**
27. The relationship between the percentage change in the spot exchange rate over time and the differential between comparable interest rates in different national capital markets is known as ____________________.

a. absolute PPP
b. the law of one price
c. relative PPP
d. the international Fisher Effect

**Topic: International Fisher Effect**
**Skill: Conceptual**

28. From the viewpoint of a U.S. investor or trader, the indirect quote for a currency exchange rate would be quoted in ____________.

a. terms of dollars per unit of foreign currency (e.g., $/£)
b. cents
c. 1/8ths
d. terms of foreign currency units per dollar (e.g., £/$)

**Topic: International Fisher Effect**
**Skill: Analytical**

29. According to the international Fisher Effect, if an investor purchases a five-year U.S. bond that has an annual interest rate of 5% rather than a comparable British bond that has an annual interest rate of 6%, then the investor must be expecting the _________ to ___________ at a rate of at least 1% per year over the next 5 years.

a. British pound; appreciate
b. British pound; revalue
c. U.S. dollar; appreciate
d. U.S. dollar; depreciate

**Topic: International Fisher Effect**
**Skill: Recognition**

30. ___________ states that the spot exchange rate should change in an equal amount but in the opposite direction to the difference in interest rates between two countries.

a. Fisher-open
b. Fisher-closed
c. The Fisher Effect
d. None of the above

**Topic: Forward Rate**
**Skill: Recognition**

31. A _____________ is an exchange rate quoted today for settlement at some time in the future.

a. spot rate
b. forward rate
c. currency rate
d. yield curve

**Topic: Forward Rate**
**Skill: Analytical**
32. Assume the current U.S. dollar-British spot rate is 0.6993£/$. If the current nominal one-year interest rate in the U.S. is 5% and the comparable rate in Britain is 6%, what is the approximate forward exchange rate for 360 days?

a. 1.42£/$
b. 1.43£/$
c. 0.6993£/$
d. 0.7060£/$

**Topic: Forward Rate**
**Skill: Analytical**
33. Assume the current U.S. dollar-yen spot rate is 125¥/$. Further, the current nominal 180-day rate of return in Japan is 3% and 4% in the United States. What is the approximate forward exchange rate for 180 days?

a. 123.80¥/$
b. 124.00¥/$
c. 124.39¥/$
d. 124.67¥/$

**Topic: Forward Rate Premium/Discount**
**Skill: Conceptual**
34. The current U.S. dollar-yen spot rate is 125¥/$. If the 90-day forward exchange rate is 127 ¥/$ then the yen is at a forward premium.

a. True
b. False

**Topic: Forward Rate Premium/Discount**
**Skill: Analytical**
35. The current U.S. dollar-yen spot rate is 125¥/$. If the 90-day forward exchange rate is 127 ¥/$ then the yen is selling at a per annum _________ of ___________.

a. premium; 1.57%
b. premium; 6.30%
c. discount; 1.57%
d. discount; 6.30%

**Topic: Forward Rate Premium/Discount**
**Skill: Conceptual**
36. The premium or discount on forward currency exchange rates between any two countries is visually obvious when you plot the interest rates of each country on the same yield curve. The currency of the country with the higher yield curve should be selling at a forward discount.

a. True
b. False

**Topic: Interest Rate Parity**
**Skill: Recognition**
37. The theory of __________ states that the difference in the national interest rates for securities of similar risk and maturity should be equal to but opposite in sign to the forward rate discount or premium for the foreign currency, except for transaction costs.

a. international Fisher Effect
b. absolute PPP
c. interest rate parity
d. the law of one price

**Topic: Interest Rate Parity**
**Skill: Analytical**
38. Use interest rate parity to answer this question. A U.S. investor has a choice between a risk-free one-year U.S. security with an annual return of 4%, and a comparable British security with a return of 5%. If the spot rate is $1.43/£, the forward rate is $1.44/£, and there are no transaction costs, the investor should invest in the U.S. security.

a. True
b. False

**Topic: Covered Interest Arbitrage**
**Skill: Recognition**
39. With *covered interest arbitrage*,

a. the market must be out of equilibrium.
b. a "riskless" arbitrage opportunity exists.
c. the arbitrageur trades in both the spot and future currency exchange markets.
d. all of the above.

**Topic: Covered Interest Arbitrage**
**Skill: Conceptual**
40. Covered interest arbitrage moves the market _________ equilibrium because

a. toward; purchasing a currency on the spot market and selling in the forward market narrows the differential between the two.
b. toward; investors are now more willing to invest in risky securities.
c. away from; purchasing a currency on the spot market and selling in the forward market increases the differential between the two.
d. away from; demand for the stronger currency forces up interest rates on the weaker security.

**Topic: Interest Rate Arbitrage**
**Skill: Conceptual**
41. Both covered and uncovered interest arbitrage are risky operations in the sense that even without default in the securities, the returns are unknown until all transactions are complete.

a. True
b. False

**Topic: Forward Rate**
**Skill: Recognition**
42. If the forward rate is an unbiased predictor of the expected spot rate, which of the following is NOT true?

a. The expected value of the future spot rate at time 2 equals the present forward rate for time 2 delivery, available now.
b. The distribution of possible actual spot rates in the future is centered on the forward rate.
c. The future spot rate will actually be equal to shat the forward rate predicts.
d. All of the above are true.

**Topic: Market Efficiency**
**Skill: Recognition**
43. Which of the following is NOT an assumption of market efficiency?

a. Instruments denominated in other currencies are perfect substitutes for one another.
b. Transaction costs are low or nonexistent.
c. All relevant information is quickly reflected in both spot and forward exchange markets.
d. All of the above are true.

**Topic: Market Efficiency**
**Skill: Recognition**

44. Empirical evidence has yielded __________ evidence about market efficiency with a general consensus developing that foreign markets are ___________.

a. conflicting; not efficient
b. conflicting; efficient
c. consistent; inefficient
d. consistent; inefficient

**Topic: Market Efficiency**
**Skill: Conceptual**

45. If exchange markets were not efficient, it would pay for a firm to spend resources on forecasting exchange rates.

a. True
b. False

**Topic: Forward Rates**
**Skill: Conceptual**

46. If the forward exchange rate is an unbiased predictor of future spot rates, then future spot rates will always be equal to current forward rates.

A. True
B. False

**Topic: PPP**
**Skill: Recognition**

47. The _______ version of the theory of PPP says that the spot exchange rate is determined by the relative prices of a similar market basket of goods. The _______version of PPP says that changes in differential rates of inflation over the years tend to be offset by an equal and opposite change in the spot exchange rate.

a. absolute; absolute
b. relative; absolute
c. absolute; relative
d. relative; relative

**Topic: The Law of One Price**
**Skill: Recognition**
48. If the identical product can be sold in two different markets, and there are no restrictions on its sale or transportation costs of moving the product between markets, the product's price should be the same in both markets. This is called _______________.

a. arbitrage
b. interest rate parity
c. the Fisher Effect
d. the law of one price

**Topic: Interest Rate Parity**
**Skill: Recognition**
49. According to the theory of interest rate parity, the difference in national interest rates for securities of similar risk and maturity should be __________ and ___________ sign to the forward rate discount or premium for the foreign currency, except for transaction costs.

a. equal to; of the same
b. less than; of the same
c. greater than; opposite in
d. equal to; opposite in

**Topic: Covered Interest Arbitrage**
**Skill: Recognition**
50. When the spot and forward exchange markets are not in equilibrium as described by interest rate parity, the potential for "riskless" arbitrage profit exists. This is called

_______________________.

a. covered interest arbitrage (CIA)
b. interest rate parity
c. the Fisher Effect
d. dancing on the head of a pin

**Essay Questions:**
1. The authors describe an application of uncovered interest arbitrage (UIA) known as "yen carry trade". Define UIA and describe the example of yen carry trade. Why would an investor engage in the practice of yen carry trade and is there any risk of loss or lesser profit from this investment strategy?

**Answer**
UIA is the practice of investors borrowing money in countries where interest rates are relatively low, converting the loan proceeds into a currency where rates are relatively high, investing at the higher rate, subsequently converting the proceeds back into the original currency to repay the proceeds from the loan and hopefully realizing a greater return from this practice than if the borrowing and investing had all taken place in the original currency. The arbitrage is uncovered because at the time of the investment the investor does not lock in a forward exchange rate and therefore bears the risk that currency exchange rates will change in an unfavorable manner. The yen carry trade exists because rates in Japan are so very low that investors borrow yen, convert to another currency, say U.S. dollars, invest at much higher interest rates, often in default-risk free Treasury securities, then convert back to yen, repay the original loan and walk away with a significantly greater return than otherwise available. The risk in this process is neither from the investment nor from the loan. The risk is that exchange rates may change unfavorably and the investor takes a loss rather than a profit.

2. The authors state that empirical tests of purchasing power parity "have, for the most part, not proved PPP to be accurate in predicting future exchange rates." The authors then state that PPP does hold up reasonable well in two situations. What are some reasons why PPP does not accurately predict future exchange rates, and under what conditions might we reasonable expect PPP to hold?

**Answer**
PPP does not hold because goods and services do not move without cost between countries and markets. Often, goods and services are nor perfect substitutes in every market for reasons of availability, taste, quality, and production techniques. Having said that, PPP does appear to work reasonably well over the long run and especially in countries with higher rates of inflation and underdeveloped capital markets.

3. The Fisher Effect is a familiar economic theory in the domestic market. In words, define the Fisher Effect and explain why you think it is also appropriately applied to international markets.

**Answer**
Irving Fisher was an early 20th century economist who hypothesized that all market determined nominal interest rates had at least two basic components. First, a real return is required to compensate investors for postponing current consumption. This real rate is constant and unaffected by expectations about inflation. Second, an expected inflation component is required so that investors would not expect to lose purchasing power by the act of forgoing current consumption. Intuitively, if capital can move freely among international markets these same requirements must exist in each of the capital markets and the Fisher Effect would apply internationally as well as domestically.

## Chapter 4: International Parity Conditions
## Multiple Choice and True/False Answer Key

Multiple Choice Answer Key:

| | | | | | | | | | |
|---|---|---|---|---|---|---|---|---|---|
| 1 | C | 11 | B | 21 | D | 31 | B | 41 | B |
| 2 | A | 12 | D | 22 | C | 32 | D | 42 | C |
| 3 | D | 13 | A | 23 | B | 33 | C | 43 | D |
| 4 | B | 14 | C | 24 | A | 34 | B | 44 | A |
| 5 | A | 15 | A | 25 | C | 35 | D | 45 | A |
| 6 | B | 16 | D | 26 | A | 36 | A | 46 | B |
| 7 | C | 17 | B | 27 | D | 37 | C | 47 | C |
| 8 | B | 18 | C | 28 | D | 38 | B | 48 | D |
| 9 | D | 19 | B | 29 | C | 39 | D | 49 | D |
| 10 | C | 20 | A | 30 | A | 40 | A | 50 | A |

# Chapter 5
# Foreign Exchange Rate Determination

**Topic: Complementary Theories**
**Skill: Recognition**

1. The important thing to remember about foreign exchange rate determination is that parity conditions, asset approach, and balance of payments approaches are _______________ theories rather than _______________ theories.

a. competing; complementary
b. competing; contemporary
c. complementary; contiguous
d. complementary; competing

**Topic: Market Collapse**
**Skill: Recognition**

2. Which of the following did NOT contribute to the exchange rate collapse in emerging markets in the 1990s?

a. Infrastructure weaknesses.
b. Speculation on the part of market participants.
c. The sharp reduction of cross-border foreign direct investment.
d. All of the above contributed to the emerging markets exchange rate collapse of the 1990s.

**Topic: Determinants of Spot Exchange Rates**
**Skill: Conceptual**

3. It is safe to say that most determinants of the spot exchange rate are also affected by changes in the spot rate. I.e., they are linked AND mutually determined.

a. True
b. False

**Topic: International Speculation**
**Skill: Recognition**

4. A popular speculation in the 1990s was

a. U.S. investors investing in Japanese securities to take advantage of Japan's higher nominal and real interest rates.
b. Japanese investors investing in the United States securities to take advantage of the higher U.S. nominal and real interest rates.
c. selling short the U.S. dollar against the Russian Ruble.
d. None of the above was a popular speculation technique in the 1990s.

**Topic: Balance of Payments**
**Skill: Recognition**
5. The ___________ provides a means to account for international cash flows in a standardized and systematic manner.

a. parity conditions
b. asset approach
c. balance of payments
d. international Fisher effect

**Topic: Current Account**
**Skill: Conceptual**
6. Which of the following is NOT a current account activity?

a. Net import/export of goods (Balance of Trade)
b. Net import/export of services
c. Net portfolio investment
d. All of the above are activities of the current account.

**Topic: Fixed Exchange Rate Regimes**
**Skill: Recognition**
7. Under a ____________ the government bears the responsibility to ensure a ___________ near zero.

a. fixed exchange regime; BOP
b. fixed exchange regime; balance of trade
c. variable exchange regime; BOP
d. variable exchange regime; balance of trade

**Topic: Fixed Exchange Rate Regimes**
**Skill: Conceptual**
8. Under a fixed exchange regime, if the sum of the sum of the current and capital accounts is greater than zero a ____________ demand for the currency exists. To maintain the fixed exchange rate the government must intervene and _________ the domestic currency or gold.

a. deficit; sell
b. surplus; sell
c. deficit; buy
d. surplus; buy

**Topic: Fixed Exchange Rate Regimes**
**Skill: Conceptual**
9. Under a fixed exchange regime, if the sum of the current and capital accounts is less than zero a ___________ demand for the currency exists. To maintain the fixed exchange rate the government must intervene and ___________ the domestic currency or gold.

a. deficit; sell
b. surplus; sell
c. deficit; buy
d. surplus; buy

**Topic: Change in the Value of Currency**
**Skill: Recognition**
10. A positive change in the value of a currency is called a ___________ under a fixed rate regime and a ___________ under a variable rate regime.

a. revaluation; appreciation
b. appreciation; revaluation
c. appreciation; depreciation
d. revaluation; devaluation

**Topic: Floating Exchange Rate Regimes**
**Skill: Conceptual**
11. Under a floating exchange rate regime, a country has no responsibility to peg its foreign exchange rate.

a. True
b. False

**Topic: Floating Exchange Rate Regimes**
**Skill: Recognition**
12. In theory, a country with a ___________ exchange rate regime, a large current account deficit, and a near zero balance on its capital and financial accounts will have a currency that _____________ in value.

a. fixed; falls
b. variable; increases
c. fixed; falls
d. variable; increases

**Topic: Managed Float**
**Skill: Recognition**

13. Countries with a ____________ exchange rate regime allow market conditions to determine day-to-day foreign exchange rates, but will intercede to maintain their desired exchange rates.

   a. fixed
   b. variable
   c. managed float
   d. none of the above

**Topic: Asset Market**
**Skill: Recognition**

14. The ___________ approach to the determination of spot exchange rates hypothesizes that the most important factors are the relative real interest rate and a country's outlook for economic growth and profitability.

   a. balance of payments
   b. parity conditions
   c. managed float
   d. asset market

**Topic: Key Factors for Equilibrium in Foreign Exchange Markets**
**Skill: Conceptual**

15. The authors compromise as to the key factors for exchange rate determination. They conclude that ____________ is important in the short run, but that _________ determines long run exchange rates.

   a. Fisher effect; PPP
   b. asset markets, interest rates, and expectations; PPP
   c. PPP, Fisher effect
   d. Fisher effect; asset prices, interest rates, and expectations

**Topic: Technical Analysis**
**Skill: Recognition**

16. _______________, Traditionally referred to as chartists, focus on price and volume data to determine past trends that are expected to continue into the future.

   a. Mappists
   b. Trappist Monks
   c. Filibusters
   d. Technical Analysts

**Topic: Technical Analysis**
**Skill: Conceptual**
17. The longer the time horizon of the technical analyst the more accurate the prediction of foreign exchange rates is likely to be.

a. True
b. False

**Topic: Key Factors for Equilibrium in Foreign Exchange Markets**
**Skill: Recognition**
18. Short-term foreign exchange forecasts are often motivated by such activities as ____________ whereas long-term forecasts are more likely motivated by __________.

a. long-term investment; long-term capital appreciation
b. long-term capital appreciation; desire to hedge a receivable
c. the desire to hedge a payable; the desire for long-term investment
d. the desire for long-term investment; the desire to hedge a payable

**Topic: Market Efficiency**
**Skill: Conceptual**
19. The more efficient the foreign exchange market is the more likely it is that exchange rate movements are random walks.

A. True
B. False

**Topic: Currency Cross Rates**
**Skill: Analytical**
20. A major U.S. multinational firm has forecast the Euro/dollar rate to be 1.10/$ one year hence, and an exchange rate of $1.40 for the British pound (£) in the same time period. What does this imply the companies expected rate for the Euro per pound to be in one year?

a. 1.40Euro/£
b. 1.40£/Euro
c. 1.54£/Euro
d. 1.54Euro/£

**Topic: Key Factors for Equilibrium in Foreign Exchange Markets**
**Skill: Recognition**
21. The authors claim that theoretical and empirical studies appear to show that fundamentals do apply to the long-term for foreign exchange.

a. True
b. False

**Topic: Key Factors for Equilibrium in Foreign Exchange Markets**
**Skill: Recognition**

22. The authors claim that random events, institutional frictions, and technical factors may cause currency values to deviate significantly from their long-term fundamental path.

a. True
b. False

**Topic: Key Factors for Equilibrium in Foreign Exchange Markets**
**Skill: Recognition**

23. The authors claim that the theories of international currency values hold better for less liquid and poorly capitalized markets.

a. True
b. False

**Topic: International Currency Crises**
**Skill: Recognition**

24. Which of the following was not an international currency crisis in the 1990s?

a. The Asian Crisis
b. The Russian Crisis
c. The Brazilian Crisis
d. All of the above were currency crises in the 1990s.

**Topic: International Currency Crises**
**Skill: Recognition**

25. The Asian Currency crisis appeared to begin in which country?

a. South Korea
b. Taiwan
c. Thailand
d. Japan

**Topic: International Currency Crises**
**Skill: Recognition**

26. Prior to July 2, 1997, the Thai government

a. allowed the Thai Bhat to float against major currencies.
b. fixed the Bhat's value against the Korean won only.
c. fixed the Bhat's value against major currencies especially the U.S. dollar.
d. None of the above.

**Topic: International Currency Crises**
**Skill: Recognition**
27. The "tequila effect" is a slang term used to describe a form of financial panic called _____________.

a. run on the market
b. speculation
c. contrary investing
d. contagion

**Topic: International Currency Crises**
**Skill: Conceptual**
28. The authors did not identify which of the following as a root of the Asian currency crisis?

a. the collapse of some Asian currencies
b. the rate of inflation in the United States
c. corporate socialism
d. banking stability and management

**Topic: International Currency Crises**
**Skill: Recognition**
29. Corporate socialism in the Asian markets could be contributed in part

a. to the relatively short and stable post-WWII history of capitalism in their markets.
b. a belief by the owners of Asian companies that their governments would not allow them to fail.
c. the practice of lifetime employment at many corporations.
d. all of the above.

**Topic: International Currency Crises**
**Skill: Recognition**
30. The authors refer practice of many Asian firms being largely controlled by families of groups related to the governing body of the country as _____________.

a. illegal
b. insider trading
c. cronyism
d. not in my backyard

**Topic: Asian Crisis**
**Skill: Recognition**

31. The principle focus of the IMF bailout of the efforts during the Asian financial crisis was ___________________.

a. banking liquidity
b. shareholder's wealth
c. reestablishing fixed currency exchange rates in Asia
d. dollarization of Asian currencies

**Topic: 1990s International Economic Crises**
**Skill: Recognition**

32. The chronological order of the major currency crises of the 1990s from fist to last is:

a. Russia, Brazil, Asia
b. Asia, Russia, Brazil
c. Russia, Asia, Brazil
d. Brazil, Russia, Asia

**Topic: Asian Crisis**
**Skill: Recognition**

33. In the years immediately preceding 1998 the Russian Ruble operated under what type of exchange rate regime?

a. Fixed
b. Free floating (market determined)
c. Managed floating
d. Pegged (to the U.S. dollar)

**Topic: Asian Crisis**
**Skill: Recognition**

34. Which of the following is the official Chinese currency?

a. Baht
b. Won
c. Ringgit
d. Renminbi

**Topic: Russian Crisis**
**Skill: Recognition**

35. The stability of the Russian Ruble in the 1990s (until the Russian debt crisis) was considered an observable success of the Yeltsin administration.

a. True
b. False

**Topic: Russian Crisis**
**Skill: Conceptual**

36. When the Russian Ruble reached the limits of the bands about its managed float targets (Ru5.70/$ to Ru6.35/$) in 1997, the Russian government would intervene in the markets to stabilize the Ruble. If the exchange rate approached Ru5.70/$ the government would _________ Rubles using foreign exchange and gold, or if the exchange rate approached Ru6.35/$ they would _________ Rubles.

a. buy; sell
b. sell; buy
c. buy; buy
d. sell; sell

**Topic: Russian Crisis**
**Skill: Recognition**

37. After the Russian government (in August 1998) allowed the Ruble to move outside its official trading range of between Ru5.70/$ - Ru6.35/$, the value of he Ruble eventually ____________ to around ____________ by May 1999.

a. increased; Ru13/$
b. increased; Ru4.50/$
c. decreased; Ru13/$
d. decreased; Ru25/$

**Topic: Russian Crisis**
**Skill: Recognition**

38. It is safe to say that the Russian transition from a communist economy to a capitalist economy has been smooth for the Russian people

a. True
b. False

**Topic: Brazilian Crisis**
**Skill: Recognition**

39. The ____________ is the Brazilian currency unit.

a. peso
b. dollar
c. real
d. peseta

**Topic: Brazilian Crisis**
**Skill: Conceptual**

40. Fundamentally, a country with a relatively high inflation rate should see its currency ____________ in value relative to countries with lower rates of inflation and this ______ the case for the Brazilian currency from 1994 - 1998.

a. fall; was not
b. fall; was
c. rise; was not
d. rise; was

**Topic: Exchange Rate Equilibrium**
**Skill: Conceptual**

41. Under a fixed exchange rate regime, the government of the country is officially responsible for:

a. intervention in the foreign exchange markets using reserves and gold.
b. setting the fixed/parity exchange rate.
c. maintaining the fixed/parity exchange rate.
d. all of the above.

**Topic: Exchange Rate Equilibrium**
**Skill: Recognition**

42. Which of the following is NOT a factor in determining exchange rate equilibrium?

a. Relative inflation rates
b. Relative interest rates
c. Market expectations
d. All of the above are factors in determining equilibrium exchange rates.

**Topic: Fixed Exchange Rate Regime**
**Skill: Conceptual**

43. Under a fixed exchange rate regime, if the BOP deviates significantly from the zero, the government is expected to intervene.

a. True
b. False

**Topic: Floating Exchange Rate Regime**
**Skill: Conceptual**

44. Under a floating exchange rate regime, if the BOP deviates significantly from the zero, the government is expected to intervene.

a. True
b. False

**Topic: Asian Crisis**
**Skill: Recognition**
45. The Asian currency crisis was primarily a

a. parity conditions problem.
b. an asset markets problem.
c. balance of payments problem.
d. PPP problem.

**Topic: Russian Crisis**
**Skill: Recognition**
46. The Russian Ruble crisis of 1998 was a complex combination of speculative pressures best explained by ________________ to exchange rate determination.

a. parity conditions approach
b. asset approach
c. balance of payments approach
d. PPP approach

**Topic: Brazilian Crisis**
**Skill: Recognition**
47. The Brazilian real crisis of 1999 was most likely a combination of a disequilibrium in international parity conditions (differential rtes of inflation) and balance of payments disequilibrium (current account deficits combined with financial account outflows).

a. True
b. False

**Topic: Fixed Exchange Rate Regimes**
**Skill: Conceptual**
48. Under a fixed exchange rate regime which of the following would NOT likely be a government action taken to correct a BOP imbalance?

a. Selling domestic currency to correct a BOP surplus.
b. Buying domestic currency to correct a BOP deficit.
c. Allowing exchange rates to float freely.
d. All of the above.

**Topic: Variable Exchange Rate Regimes**
**Skill: Conceptual**
49. Under a variable exchange rate regime which of the following would NOT likely be a government action taken to correct a BOP imbalance?

a. Selling domestic currency to correct a BOP surplus.
b. Allowing the currency to appreciate if BOP surplus exits.
c. Allowing the currency to depreciate if a BOP deficit exits.
d. All of the above.

**Topic: Exchange Rate Regimes**
**Skill: Recognition**
50. It is easier to predict forward rates under a fixed exchange regime than under a floating rate regime.

a. True
b. False

## Essay Questions:

1. Foreign exchange forecasting can be either long-term, or short-term in duration. Compare and contrast the motivation for and the techniques a forecaster might use for each of the time periods.

**Answer**
Short-run forecasts are usually more tactical in nature as a firm may desire to reduce exchange rate risk associated with foreign receivable or payables. Technical factors and short-term market expectations are often more important for short-run forecasters than long-run parity or fundamental economic conditions.

Long-run forecasts are more strategic in nature as firms make key decisions about entering new foreign markets. Longer time horizons tend to be less accurate but also require less accuracy. What forecasters typically desire is a general long-run understanding of the relationships between markets. Fundamental analysis and parity conditions tend to be more important than technical factors in this type of forecasting.

2. Describe the asset market approach to exchange rate determination. How is this consistent with economic theory of (say, security) prices in general?

**Answer**
The asset market approach to exchange rate determination looks at relative interest rates and prospects for economic growth and profitability. This is consistent with the pricing of equity securities in that the price of a share of stock should reflect expectations about the timing, magnitude, and risk of future cash flows. In other words, expectations about what is to come is more important to the price of an asset, including currency prices, than what has occurred in the past.

3. Assume your country has a balance of payments surplus. How would the government and markets react to "correct" this imbalance under a fixed exchange rate regime? Under a floating exchange rate regime?

**Answer**
A BOP surplus means there is a surplus demand for the country's currency most likely due to a surplus of exports of goods and services. Under a fixed exchange regime, the government is obligated to attempt to keep the BOP at or near zero. This surplus demand for currency means the government must supply it to the international markets by using currency to buy gold or foreign currencies in the international market place.

Under a floating exchange rate regime, the excess demand for the home currency would result in an appreciating currency on the foreign exchange markets. Demand for the currency would in theory push the value up, thus reducing exports, increasing imports, and moving the balance of payments toward equilibrium.

## Chapter 5: Foreign Exchange Rate Determination
## Multiple Choice Answer Key:

| | | | | | | | | | |
|---|---|---|---|---|---|---|---|---|---|
| 1 | D | 11 | A | 21 | A | 31 | A | 41 | D |
| 2 | D | 12 | B | 22 | A | 32 | B | 42 | D |
| 3 | A | 13 | C | 23 | B | 33 | C | 43 | A |
| 4 | B | 14 | D | 24 | D | 34 | D | 44 | B |
| 5 | C | 15 | B | 25 | C | 35 | A | 45 | C |
| 6 | C | 16 | D | 26 | C | 36 | B | 46 | B |
| 7 | A | 17 | B | 27 | D | 37 | D | 47 | A |
| 8 | B | 18 | C | 28 | B | 38 | B | 48 | C |
| 9 | C | 19 | A | 29 | D | 39 | C | 49 | A |
| 10 | A | 20 | D | 30 | C | 40 | A | 50 | A |

# Chapter 6
# Foreign Exchange Markets

**Topic: Introduction to the Foreign Exchange Market**
**Skill: Recognition**

1. Which of the following is NOT true regarding the market for foreign exchange?

   a. The market provides the physical and institutional structure through which the money of one country is exchanged for another.
   b. The rate of exchange is determined in the market.
   c. Foreign exchange transactions are physically completed in he foreign exchange market.
   d. All of the above are true.

**Topic: Introduction to the Foreign Exchange Market**
**Skill: Recognition**

2. A/An __________________ is an agreement between a buyer and seller that a fixed amount of one currency will be delivered at a specified rate for some other currency.

   a. Eurodollar transaction
   b. import/Export exchange
   c. foreign exchange transaction
   d. interbank market transaction

**Topic: Introduction to the Foreign Exchange Market**
**Skill: Recognition**

3. While trading in foreign exchange takes place worldwide, the major currency trading centers are located in

   a. London, New York, and Tokyo
   b. New York, Zurich, and Bahrain
   c. Paris, Frankfurt, and London
   d. Los Angeles, New York, and London

**Topic: Introduction to the Foreign Exchange Market**
**Skill: Recognition**

4. Because the market for foreign exchange is worldwide, the volume of foreign exchange currency transactions is level throughout the 24-hour day.

   a. True
   b. False

**Topic: Foreign Exchange Market Functions**
**Skill: Recognition**
5. Which of the following is NOT a motivation identified by the authors as a function of the foreign exchange market?

a. The transfer of purchasing power between countries.
b. Obtaining or providing credit for international trade transactions.
c. Minimizing the risks of exchange rate changes.
d. All of the above were identified as functions of the foreign exchange market.

**Topic: Foreign Exchange Market Tiers**
**Skill: Recognition**
6. The authors identify two tiers of foreign exchange markets;

a. bank and nonbank foreign exchange.
b. commercial and investment transactions.
c. interbank and client markets.
d. client and retail market.

**Topic: Foreign Exchange Market Efficiency**
**Skill: Conceptual**
7. The foreign exchange market is NOT efficient because

a. markets participants do not compete with one another due to the fact that exchange takes place around the world and not in a single centralized location.
b. dealers have ask prices that are higher than bid prices.
c. central governments dominate the foreign exchange market and everybody knows that by definition, central governments are inefficient.
d. none of the reasons listed above cause the foreign exchange market to be inefficient.

**Topic: Foreign Exchange Market Dealers and Brokers**
**Skill: Recognition**
8. Dealers in foreign exchange departments at large international banks act as market makers and maintain inventories of the securities in which they specialize.

a. True
b. False

**Topic: Foreign Exchange Market Profitability**
**Skill: Recognition**
9. Currency trading lacks profitability for large commercial and investment banks but is maintained as a service for corporate and institutional customers.

a. True
b. False

**Topic: Foreign Exchange Market Dealers**
**Skill: Recognition**

10. It is characteristic of foreign exchange dealers to

a. bring buyers and sellers of currencies together but never to buy and hold an inventory of currency for resale.
b. act as market makers, willing to buy and sell the currencies in which they specialize.
c. trade only with clients in the retail market and never operate in the wholesale market for foreign exchange.
d. All of the above are characteristics of foreign exchange dealers.

**Topic: Foreign Exchange (FX) Market Participants**
**Skill: Recognition**

11. Which of the following may be participants in the foreign exchange markets?

a. Bank and nonbank foreign exchange dealers
b. Central banks and treasuries
c. Speculators and arbitragers
d. All of the above

**Topic: Foreign Exchange (FX) Market Participants**
**Skill: Recognition**

12. The following seek to profit from trading in the market itself rather than having the foreign exchange transaction being incidental to the execution of a commercial or investment transaction.

a. Speculators and arbitragers
b. Foreign exchange brokers
c. Central banks
d. Treasuries

**Topic: Foreign Exchange (FX) Market Participants**
**Skill: Recognition**

13. In the foreign exchange market, ____________ seek all of their profit from exchange rate changes while _____________ seek to profit from simultaneous exchange rate differences in different markets.

a. wholesalers; retailers
b. central banks; treasuries
c. speculators; arbitragers
d. dealers; brokers

**Topic: Foreign Exchange (FX) Market Participants**
**Skill: Recognition**
14. Foreign exchange _______________ earn a profit by a bid-ask spread on currencies they purchase and sell. Foreign exchange _________________, on the other hand earn a profit by bringing together buyers and sellers of foreign currencies and earning a commission on each sale and purchase.

a. central banks; treasuries
b. dealers; brokers
c. brokers; dealers
d. speculators; arbitragers

**Topic: Foreign Exchange (FX) Market Participants**
**Skill: Recognition**
15. The primary motive of foreign exchange activities by most central banks is profit.

a. True
b. False

**Topic: Foreign Exchange (FX) Market Participants**
**Skill: Recognition**
16. Dealers sometimes use brokers in the foreign exchange market because the dealers desire

a. speed.
b. accuracy.
c. to remain anonymous.
d. all of the above.

**Topic: FX Trading Volume**
**Skill: Recognition**
17. Daily trading volume in the foreign exchange market was about __________ per _______ in 2001.

a. $1,200 billion; month
b. $500 billion; month
c. $1,200 billion; day
d. $500 billion; day

**Topic: FX Trading Volume**
**Skill: Recognition**
18. Daily trading volume of foreign exchange had actually decreased in 2001 from the levels reported in 1998.

a. True
b. False

**Topic: FX Trading Volume**
**Skill: Recognition**
19. Which of the following is NOT one of the three categories reported for foreign exchange?

a. Spot transactions
b. Swap transactions
c. Strip transactions
d. Futures transactions

**Topic: FX Trading Volume**
**Skill: Recognition**
20. Foreign exchange swaps were larger in 1998 than in 2001. The Bank for International Settlements attributes this to

a. the introduction of the Euro.
b. growing electronic brokering in the spot interbank market.
c. consolidation in general.
d. all of the above.

**Topic: Foreign Exchange Market Locations**
**Skill: Recognition**
21. The greatest amount of foreign exchange trading takes place in the following three cities:

a. New York, London, and Tokyo
b. New York, Singapore, and Zurich
c. London, Frankfurt, and Paris
d. London, Tokyo, and Zurich

**Topic: Foreign Exchange Market Currencies**
**Skill: Recognition**
22. The "big three" currencies that dominate foreign exchange trading are:

a. U.K pound, U.S. dollar, and Japanese yen
b. U.S. dollar, euro, and U.K. pound
c. U.S. dollar, Japanese yen, euro
d. U.S. dollar, U.K. pound, euro

**Topic: Foreign Exchange Market Transactions**
**Skill: Recognition**
23. A __________ transaction in the foreign exchange market requires an almost immediate delivery of foreign exchange.

a. spot
b. forward
c. futures
d. none of the above

**Topic: Foreign Exchange Market Transactions**
**Skill: Recognition**
24. A ________ transaction in the foreign exchange market requires delivery of foreign exchange at some future date.

a. spot
b. forward
c. swap
d. currency

**Topic: Foreign Exchange Market Spot Transactions**
**Skill: Recognition**
25. A spot transaction in the interbank market for foreign exchange would typically involve a two-day delay in the actual delivery of the currencies, while such a transaction between a bank and its commercial customer would not necessarily involve a two-day wait.

a. True
b. False

**Topic: Foreign Exchange Market Forward Transactions**
**Skill: Recognition**
26. A forward contract to deliver British pounds for U.S. dollars could be described either as
__________________ or _______________.

a. buying dollars forward; buying pounds forward
b. selling pounds forward; selling dollars forward
c. selling pounds forward; buying dollars forward
d. selling dollars forward; buying pounds forward

**Topic: Foreign Exchange Market Swaps**
**Skill: Recognition**

27. A common type of swap transaction in the foreign exchange market is the ____________ where the dealer buys the currency in the spot market and sells the same amount back to the same bank in the forward market.

a. "forward against spot"
b. "forspot"
c. repurchase agreement
d. "spot against forward"

**Topic: Foreign Exchange Market Swaps**
**Skill: Recognition**

28. Swap and forward transactions account for an insignificant portion of the foreign exchange market.

a. True
b. False

**Topic: Foreign Exchange Market Derivatives**
**Skill: Recognition**

29. The ______________ is a new derivative forward contract that was created in the 1990s. It has the same characteristics and documentation requirements as traditional forward contracts except that they are only settled in U.S. dollars and the foreign currency involved in the transaction is not delivered.

a. nondeliverable forward
b. dollar only forward
c. virtual forward
d. internet forward

**Topic: Foreign Exchange Market NDFs**
**Skill: Conceptual**

30. Which of the following is NOT true regarding nondeliverable forward (NDF)contracts?

a. NDFs are used primarily for emerging market currencies.
b. Pricing of NDFs reflects basic interest rate differentials plus an additional premium charged for dollar settlement.
c. NDFs can only be traded by central banks.
d. All of the above are true.

**Topic: Foreign Exchange Market Rates and Quotes**
**Skill: Recognition**
31. A foreign exchange _________ is the price of one currency expressed in terms of another currency. A foreign exchange ______________ is a willingness to buy or sell at the announced rate.

a. quote; rate
b. quote; quote
c. rate; quote
d. rate; rate

**Topic: Foreign Exchange Market Terms**
**Skill: Recognition**
32. Most foreign exchange transactions are through the U.S. dollar. If the transaction is expressed as the foreign currency per dollar this known as ______________ whereas ____________ are expressed as dollars per foreign unit.

a. European terms; indirect
b. American terms; direct
c. American terms; European terms
d. European terms; American terms

**Topic: Foreign Exchange Market Terms**
**Skill: Recognition**
33. The following is an example of an American term foreign exchange quote:

a. \$20/£.
b. 0.85€/\$.
c. 100¥/€.
d. None of the above.

**Topic: Foreign Exchange Market Terms**
**Skill: Recognition**
34. The European and American terms for foreign currency exchange are square roots of one another.

a. True
b. False

**Topic: Foreign Exchange Market Terms**
**Skill: Recognition**
35. With several exceptions, most interbank quotes are stated in European terms (meaning foreign currency unit per U.S. dollar).

a. True
b. False

**Topic: Billion**
**Skill: Recognition**
36. American and British meanings differ for the word billion. Therefore, when traders refer to an American billion, they call it a/an ________________.

a. Kiwi
b. Loony
c. Uncle Sam
d. Yard

**Topic: Foreign Exchange Terms**
**Skill: Recognition**
37. Major exceptions to using European terms in foreign exchange include:

a. Trading yen and euros
b. pounds and euros
c. Mexican Pesos and euros
d. All of the above.

**Topic: Direct Quote**
**Skill: Recognition**
38. From the viewpoint of a British investor, which of the following would be a direct quote in the foreign exchange market?

a. SF2.40/£
b. $1.50/£
c. £0.55/€v
d. $0.90/€

**Topic: Direct and Indirect Quotes**
**Skill: Recognition**
39. A/an _________ quote in the United States would be foreign units per dollar, while a/an _____________ quote would be in dollars per foreign currency unit.

a. direct; direct
b. direct; indirect
c. indirect; indirect
d. indirect; direct

**Topic: Direct Quote**
**Skill: Analytical**

40. If the direct quote for a U.S. investor for British pounds is $1.43/£, then the indirect quote for the U.S. investor would be ________ and the direct quote for the British investor would be ___________.

a. £0.699/$; £0.699/$
b. $0.699/£; £0.699/$
c. £1.43/£; £0.699/$
d. £0.699/$; $1.43/£

**Topic: Dealers**
**Skill: Recognition**

41. ___________ make money on currency exchanges by the difference between the ________ price, or the price they offer to pay, and the ____________ price, or the price at which they offer to sell the currency.

a. Dealers; ask; bid
b. Dealers; bid; ask
c. Brokers; ask; bid
d. Brokers; bid; ask

Use the table to answer questions 42 - 46

| | Yen: Spot and Forward (¥/$) | | | | Pound: Spot and Forward ($/£) | | |
|---|---|---|---|---|---|---|---|
| | Mid Rates | Bid | Ask | | Mid Rates | Bid | Ask |
| Spot | 129.87 | 129.82 | 129.92 | | 1.4484 | 1.4481 | 1.4487 |
| Forward Rates | | | | | | | |
| 1 month | 129.68 | -20 | -18 | | 1.4459 | -26 | -24 |
| 6 months | 128.53 | -136 | -132 | | 1.4327 | -160 | -154 |
| Swaps | | | | | | | |
| 2 year | 117.65 | 1232 | 1212 | | 1.4250 | -238 | -230 |
| 3 year | 115.50 | 1452 | 1422 | | 1.4225 | -265 | -253 |

**Topic: Spot Rate Calculation**
**Skill: Analytical**

42. The current spot rate of dollars per pound as quoted in a newspaper is ________ or __________.

a. £1.4484/$; $0.6904/£
b. $1.4481/£; £0.6906/$
c. $1.4484/£; £0.6904/$
d. £1.4487/$; $0.6903/£

**Topic: Forward Rates**
**Skill: Analytical**

43. The one-month forward bid price for dollars as denominated in Japanese yen is______ .

a. -¥20
b. -¥18
c. ¥129.74/$
d. ¥129.62/$

**Topic: Swap Rates**
**Skill: Analytical**

44. The ask price for the two-year swap for a British pound is _______ .

a. $1.4250/£
b. $1.4257/£
c. -$230
d. -$238

**Topic: Forward Premium Calculation**
**Skill: Analytical**

45. According to the information provided in the table, the 6-month yen is selling at a forward ___________ of approximately ___________ per annum. (Use the mid rates to make your calculations.)

a. discount; 2.09%
b. discount; 2.06%
c. premium; 2.09%
d. premium; 2.06%

**Topic: Cross Rates**
**Skill: Recognition**

46. Cross rates

a. are often reported in the form of a matrix in the financial newspapers.
b. can be used to check on opportunities for intermarket arbitrage.
c. for the spot market in the table are ¥188.10/£ (using the mid rates).
d. are all of the above.

**Topic: Currency Arbitrage**
**Skill: Analytical**
47. Given the following exchange rates, which of the multiple-choice choices represents a potentially profitable intermarket arbitrage opportunity?

¥129.87/$
€1.1226/$
€0.00864/¥

a. ¥115.69/€
b. ¥114.96/€
c. $0.8908/€
d. $0.0077/¥

**Topic: Currency Arbitrage**
**Skill: Conceptual**
48. For arbitrage opportunities to be practical,

a. participants must have instant access to quotes.
b. participants must have instant access to executions.
c. bank traders must be able to execute the arbitrage trades without an initial sum of money relying on their bank's credit standing.
d. all of the above must be true.

**Topic: Foreign Exchange**
**Skill: Analytical**
49. The U.S. dollar suddenly changes in value against the euro moving from an exchange rate of $0.8909/€ to $.08709/€. Thus, the dollar has ____________ by ________.

a. appreciated; 2.30%
b. depreciated; 2.30%
c. appreciated; 2.24%
d. depreciated; 2.24%

**Topic: Triangular Arbitrage**
**Skill: Recognition**
50. When the cross rate for currencies offered by two banks differs from the exchange rate offered by a third bank, a triangular arbitrage opportunity exists.

a. True
b. False

## Essay Questions:

1. What are some of the reasons central banks and treasuries enter the foreign exchange markets, and in what important ways are they different from other foreign exchange participants?

**Answer**

Central banks and treasuries enter the foreign exchange market to acquire/spend their own foreign exchange reserves and to influence the price at which their own currency is traded. Unlike other market participants, they are not profit oriented. Instead, they may willingly take a loss if they think it is in their best national interest.

2. Define spot, forward, and swap transactions in the foreign exchange market and give an example of how each could be used.

**Answer**

Spot transactions are exchanging one currency for another right now. Spot transactions are typically entered into because the parties need to exchange foreign currencies that they have received into their domestic currency, or because they have an obligation that requires them to obtain foreign currency.

Forward foreign exchange transactions are agreements entered into today to exchange currencies at a particular price at some point in the future. Forwards may be speculative or a hedge against unexpected changes in the price of the other currency.

Swaps are the simultaneous purchase and sale of a given amount of a foreign exchange for two different dates. Both transactions are conducted with the same counterparty. A swap may be considered a technique for borrowing another currency on a fully collateralized basis.

## Chapter 6: Foreign Exchange Markets
## Multiple Choice Answer Key:

| | | | | | | | | | |
|---|---|---|---|---|---|---|---|---|---|
| 1 | D | 11 | D | 21 | A | 31 | C | 41 | B |
| 2 | C | 12 | A | 22 | C | 32 | D | 42 | C |
| 3 | A | 13 | C | 23 | A | 33 | A | 43 | D |
| 4 | B | 14 | B | 24 | B | 34 | B | 44 | B |
| 5 | D | 15 | B | 25 | A | 35 | A | 45 | C |
| 6 | C | 16 | D | 26 | C | 36 | D | 46 | D |
| 7 | D | 17 | C | 27 | D | 37 | B | 47 | B |
| 8 | A | 18 | A | 28 | B | 38 | C | 48 | D |
| 9 | B | 19 | C | 29 | A | 39 | D | 49 | A |
| 10 | B | 20 | D | 30 | C | 40 | A | 50 | A |

# Chapter 7
# Foreign Currency Derivatives

**Topic: Financial Derivatives**
**Skill: Recognition**
1. Financial derivatives are powerful tools that can be used by management for purposes of

a. speculation.
b. hedging.
c. human resource management.
d. all of the above.

**Topic: Futures Contract**
**Skill: Recognition**
2. A foreign currency __________ contract calls for the future delivery of a standard amount of foreign exchange at a fixed time, place, and price.

a. futures
b. forward
c. option
d. swap

**Topic: Futures Contract**
**Skill: Recognition**
3. Currency futures contracts are still unusual enough that they trade in only a few of the world money centers.

a. True
b. False

**Topic: Futures Contract**
**Skill: Recognition**
4. The major difference between currency futures and forward contracts is that futures contracts are standardized for ease of trading on an exchange market whereas forward contracts are specialized and tailored to meet the needs of they clients.

a. True
b. False

**Topic: Futures Contract**
**Skill: Recognition**
5. Which of the following is NOT a contract specification for currency futures trading on an organized exchange?

a. Size of the contract
b. Maturity date
c. Last trading day
d. All of the above are specified

**Topic: Futures Contract**
**Skill: Analytical**
6. About ______ of all futures contracts are settled by physical delivery of foreign exchange between buyer and seller.

a. 0%
b. 5%
c. 50%
d. 95%

**Topic: Futures Contract Provisions**
**Skill: Recognition**
7. Futures contracts require that the purchaser deposit an initial sum as collateral. This deposit is called a

a. collateralized deposit.
b. marked market sum.
c. margin.
d. settlement.

**Topic: Currency Speculation**
**Skill: Conceptual**
8. A speculator in the futures market wishing to lock in a price at which they could _______ a foreign currency will ________ a futures contract.

a. buy; sell
b. sell; buy
c. buy; buy
d. none of the above

**Topic: Currency Speculation**
**Skill: Recognition**
9. A speculator that has ______ a futures contract has taken a ________ position.

a. sold; long
b. purchased; short
c. sold; short
d. purchased; sold

**Topic: Currency Speculation**
**Skill: Conceptual**
10. Peter Simpson thinks that the U.K. pound will cost $1.43/£ in six months. A 6-month currency futures contract is available today at a rate of $1.44/£. If John was to speculate in the currency futures market, and his expectations are correct, which of the following strategies would earn him a profit?

a. Sell a pound currency futures contract.
b. Buy a pound currency futures contract.
c. Sell pounds today.
d. Sell pounds in six months.

**Topic: Currency Futures**
**Skill: Analytical**
11. Jack Hemmings bought a 3-month British pound futures contract for $1.4400/£ only to see the dollar appreciate to a value of $1.4250 at which time he sold the pound futures. If each pound futures contract is for an amount of £62,500, how much money did Jack gain or lose from his speculation with pound futures?

a. $937.50 loss
b. $937.50 gain
c. £937.50 loss
d. £937.50 gain

**Topic: Currency Futures/Forwards**
**Skill: Conceptual**
12. Which of the following is NOT a difference between a currency futures contract and a forward contract?

a. A futures contract is a standardized amount per currency whereas the forward contact is for any size desired.
b. A futures contract is for a fixed maturity whereas the forward contract is for any maturity you like up to one year.
c. Futures contracts trade on organized exchanges whereas forwards take place between individuals and banks with other banks via telecom linkages.
d. All of the above are true.

**Topic: Currency Futures/Forwards**
**Skill: Conceptual**
13. Which of the following is NOT a difference between a currency futures contract and a forward contract?

a. The futures contract is marked to market daily whereas the forward contract is only due to be settled at maturity.
b. The counterparty to the futures participant is unknown with the clearinghouse stepping into each transaction whereas the forward contract participants are in direct contact setting the forward specifications.
c. A single sales commission covers both the purchase and sale of a futures contract whereas there is no specific sales commission with a forward contract because banks earn a profit through the bid-ask spread.
d. All of the above are true.

**Topic: Currency Options**
**Skill: Recognition**
14. A foreign currency ___________ gives the purchaser the right, not the obligation, to buy a given amount of foreign exchange at a fixed price per unit for a specified period.

a. future
b. forward
c. option
d. swap

**Topic: Currency Options**
**Skill: Recognition**
15. A foreign currency _______ option gives the holder the right to _______ a foreign currency whereas a foreign currency _______ option gives the holder the right to _________ an option.

a. call, buy, put, sell
b. call, sell, put, buy
c. put, hold, call release
d. none of the above

**Topic: Currency Options**
**Skill: Recognition**
16. The writer of the option is referred to as the buyer, and the seller of the option is referred to as the holder.

a. True
b. False

**Topic: Currency Options**
**Skill: Recognition**
17. The price at which an option can be purchased is called the __________.

a. premium
b. spot rate
c. strike price
d. commission

**Topic: Currency Options**
**Skill: Recognition**
18. An _________ option can be exercised only on its expiration date, whereas an ________ option can be exercised anytime between the date of writing up to and including the exercise date.

a. American; European
b. American; British
c. Asian; American
d. European; American

**Topic: Currency Options**
**Skill: Recognition**
19. An option whose exercise price exceeds the spot rate is said to be ___________.

a. in-the-money
b. at-the-money
c. out-of-the-money
d. around-the-money

**Topic: Currency Options**
**Skill: Recognition**
20. An option whose exercise price is less than the spot rate is said to be ___________.

a. in-the-money
b. at-the-money
c. out-of-the-money
d. around-the-money

**Topic: Currency Options**
**Skill: Recognition**
21. An option whose exercise price is equal to the spot rate is said to be ____________.

a. in-the-money
b. at-the-money
c. out-of-the-money
d. around-the-money

**Topic: Currency Options**
**Skill: Recognition**
22. Foreign currency options are available both over-the-counter and on organized exchanges.

a. True
b. False

**Topic: Currency Options**
**Skill: Recognition**
23. The main advantage(s) of over-the-counter foreign currency options over exchange traded options is(are)

a. expiration dates tailored to the needs of the client.
b. amounts that are tailor made.
c. client desired expiration dates.
d. all of the above.

**Topic: Currency Options**
**Skill: Recognition**
24. As a general statement, it is safe to say that businesses generally use the _________ for foreign currency option contracts, and individuals and financial institutions typically use the _________.

a. exchange markets; over-the-counter
b. over-the-counter; exchange markets
c. private; government sponsored
d. government sponsored; private

**Topic: Currency Options**
**Skill: Recognition**
25. All exchange-traded options are settled through a clearing house but over-the-counter options are not and are thus subject to greater ________ risk.

a. exchange rate
b. country
c. counterparty
d. none of the above

**Topic: Currency Futures**
**Skill: Recognition**
26. When reading the futures quotation in the financial section of the newspaper, the column heading indicating the number of contracts outstanding is called ______________.

a. contracts outstanding
b. settle
c. open interest
d. short positions

**Topic: Currency Options**
**Skill: Recognition**
27. The amount that an investor pays to obtain an option may be described as the _________.

a. premium
b. price
c. cost
d. all of the above

Use the following table to answer questions 28 – 30

April 19, 2002, British Pound Option Prices (cents per pound, 62,500 pound contracts).

| Option & | Strike | Calls - Last | | | Puts - Last | | |
|---|---|---|---|---|---|---|---|
| Underlying | Price | May | June | July | May | June | July |
| 1448 | 1440 | 0.88 | 1.42 | 1.42 | 0.52 | 1.06 | ----- |
| 1448 | 1450 | 0.42 | 1.02 | ----- | ----- | ----- | ----- |
| 1448 | 1460 | 0.20 | 0.68 | 0.72 | ----- | 2.32 | ----- |

**Topic: Currency Options**
**Skill: Analytical**
28. What was the closing price of the British pound on April 18, 2002?

a. \$1.448/£
b. £1.448/\$
c. \$14.48/£
d. None of the above

**Topic: Currency Options**
**Skill: Analytical**
29. The exercise price of __________ giving the purchaser the right to sell pounds in June has a cost per pound of ______ for a total price of ___________.

a. 1460, 0.68 cents, \$425.00
b. 1440, 1.06 cents, \$662.50
c. 1450, 1.02 cents, \$637.50
d. 1440, 1.42 cents, \$887.50

**Topic: Currency Options**
**Skill: Analytical**
30. The May call option on pounds of 1440 means ___________.

a. \$88/£ per contract
b. \$0.88/£
c. \$.0088/£
d. none of the above

**Topic: Foreign Currency Exchange Speculation**
**Skill: Conceptual**
31. Andrea Cujoli is a currency speculator who enjoys "betting" on changes in the foreign currency exchange market. Currently the spot price for the Japanese yen is ¥129.87/\$ and the 6-month forward rate is ¥128.53/\$. Andrea thinks the yen will move to ¥128.00/\$ in the next six months. Andrea should _______ at _________ to profit from changing currency values.

a. buy yen,
b. buy dollars,
c. sell yen,
d. not enough information to answer this question

**Topic: Foreign Currency Exchange Speculation**
**Skill: Analytical**

32. Andrea Cujoli is a currency speculator who enjoys "betting" on changes in the foreign currency exchange market. Currently the spot price for the Japanese yen is ¥129.87/$ and the 6-month forward rate is ¥128.53/$. Andrea thinks the yen will move to ¥128.00/$ in the next six months. If Andrea buys $100,000 worth of yen at today's spot price and sells within the next six months at ¥128/$ she will earn a profit of _____________.

a. $146.09
b. $101,460.94
c. $1460.94
d. Nothing, she will lose money.

**Topic: Foreign Currency Exchange Speculation**
**Skill: Analytical**

33. Andrea Cujoli is a currency speculator who enjoys "betting" on changes in the foreign currency exchange market. Currently the spot price for the Japanese yen is ¥129.87/$ and the 6-month forward rate is ¥128.53/$. Andrea thinks the yen will move to ¥128.00/$ in the next six months. Andrea's potential gain is _______ and her potential loss is ________.

a. $100,000, unlimited
b. unlimited, unlimited
c. $100,000, $100,000
d. unlimited, $100,000

**Topic: Foreign Currency Exchange Speculation**
**Skill: Analytical**

34. Andrea Cujoli is a currency speculator who enjoys "betting" on changes in the foreign currency exchange market. Currently the spot price for the Japanese yen is ¥129.87/$ and the 6-month forward rate is ¥128.53/$. Andrea thinks the yen will move to ¥128.00/$ in the next six months. If Andrea's expectations are correct, then she could profit in the forward market by _________ and then _______.

a. buying yen for ¥128.00/$, selling yen at ¥128.53/$
b. buying yen for ¥128.53/$, selling yen at ¥128.00/$
c. there is not enough information to answer this question
d. she could not profit in the forward market.

**Topic: Currency Options**
**Skill: Conceptual**
35. The maximum gain for the purchaser of a call option contract is _________ while the maximum loss is _________.

a. unlimited, the premium paid
b. the premium paid, unlimited
c. unlimited, unlimited
d. unlimited, the value of the underlying asset

**Topic: Currency Options**
**Skill: Conceptual**
36. Most option profits and losses are realized through offsetting contracts rather than taking actual delivery of the currency.

a. True
b. False

**Topic: Currency Options**
**Skill: Conceptual**
37. The buyer of a long call option

a. has a maximum loss equal to the premium paid.
b. has a gain equal to but opposite in sign to the writer of the option.
c. has an unlimited maximum gain potential.
d. all of the above.

**Topic: Currency Options**
**Skill: Conceptual**
38. Which of the following is NOT true for the writer of a call option?

a. The maximum loss is unlimited.
b. The maximum gain is unlimited.
c. The gain or loss is equal to but of the opposite sign of the buyer of a call option.
d. All of the above are true.

**Topic: Currency Options**
**Skill: Conceptual**
39. Which of the following is NOT true for the writer of a put option?

a. The maximum loss is limited to the strike price of the underlying asset less the premium.
b. The gain or loss is equal to but of the opposite sign of the buyer of a put option.
c. The maximum gain is the amount of the premium.
d. All of the above are true.

**Topic: Currency Options**
**Skill: Conceptual**

40. The buyer of a long put option

a. has a maximum loss equal to the premium paid.
b. has a gain equal to but opposite in sign to the writer of the option.
c. has maximum gain potential limited to the difference between the strike price and the premium paid.
d. all of the above

**Topic: Currency Options**
**Skill: Recognition**

41. The value of a European style call option is the sum of two components, the

a. present value plus the intrinsic value.
b. time value plus the present value.
c. intrinsic value plus the time value.
d. the intrinsic value plus the standard deviation.

**Topic: Currency Options Pricing**
**Skill: Recognition**

42. Which of the following is NOT a factor in determining the premium price of a currency option?

a. The present spot rate.
b. The time to maturity.
c. The standard deviation of the daily spot price movement.
d. All of the above are factors in determining the premium price.

**Topic: Currency Options**
**Skill: Conceptual**

43. Other things equal, the __________the exercise price of the currency call option, the _______ the call option premium price.

a. greater, greater
b. greater, lesser
c. lesser, greater
d. There is no general rule for the relationship between the premium and exercise price of a currency call option.

**Topic: Currency Options Intrinsic Value**
**Skill: Recognition**
44. The __________ of an option is the value if the option were to be exercised immediately. It is the options ___________ value.

a. intrinsic value, maximum
b. intrinsic value, minimum
c. time value, maximum
d. time value, minimum

**Topic: Currency Options Intrinsic Value**
**Skill: Analytical**
45. Assume that a call option has an exercise price of $1.50/£. At a spot price of $1.45/£, the call option has

a. a time value of $0.04
b. a time value of $0.00
c. an intrinsic value of $0.00
d. an intrinsic value of -$0.04

**Topic: Currency Options Time Value**
**Skill: Conceptual**
46. The time value is symmetric in value as you move away from the strike price. (I.e., the time value at two cents above the strike price is the same as the time value two cents below the strike price.)

a. True
b. False

**Topic: Currency Options Volatility**
**Skill: Conceptual**
47. Other things equal, the price of an option is directly related to the volatility of the underlying exchange rates.

a. True
b. False

**Topic: Currency Options Volatility**
**Skill: Recognition**
48. Volatility cannot be directly observed for calculation purposes of the option pricing model. Therefore, it may be determined from

a. historic volatility.
b. forward-looking volatility.
c. implied volatility.
d. any of the above.

**Topic: Currency Options Volatility**
**Skill: Conceptual**
49. Volatilities are the only judgmental aspect of currency option pricing and are therefore, the least important component therein.

a. True
b. False

**Topic: Currency Options Volatility**
**Skill: Recognition**
50. ____________ volatility are calculated by being backed out of the market option premium values traded.

a. Historic
b. Forward-looking
c. Implied
d. None of the above

## Essay Questions

1. Why are foreign currency futures contracts more popular with individuals and banks while foreign currency forwards are more popular with businesses?

**Answer**
Foreign currency futures are standardized contracts that lend themselves well to speculation purposes but less so for hedging purposes. The standardized nature of the futures contract makes it easy to trade futures and to make bets about general changes in the value of currencies. Forward contracts are better for hedging in that they are tailored to meet the specific needs of the client, typically a business, and can be quite useful in reducing exchange rate risk. Banks are involved in the foreign currency futures market in part to offset positions that they may have taken in the forward markets as dealers.

2. Compare and contrast foreign currency future options and futures. Identify situations when you may prefer one vs. the other when speculating on foreign exchange.

**Answer**
Foreign currency futures are derivative securities that allow the holder to lock in a price today for another currency at some point in the future. The foreign currency future contract is an obligation on the part of the parties to fulfill the terms of the contract. Even if prices change in an unanticipated way, the parties are obligated to fulfill the terms of the contract. The foreign currency option contract on the other hand is a right not an obligation to purchase/sell a currency at some point in the future at a price agreed upon today. If prices change in an unexpected manner, the buyer of the contract is under no obligation to exercise the contract. Option contracts are better suited to situations where price changes are anticipated, but the direction of the change is highly uncertain.

## Chapter 7: Foreign Currency Derivatives
## Multiple-Choice Questions Answer Key:

| | | | | | | | | | |
|---|---|---|---|---|---|---|---|---|---|
| 1 | D | 11 | B | 21 | B | 31 | A | 41 | C |
| 2 | A | 12 | D | 22 | A | 32 | C | 42 | D |
| 3 | B | 13 | D | 23 | D | 33 | D | 43 | A |
| 4 | A | 14 | C | 24 | B | 34 | B | 44 | B |
| 5 | D | 15 | A | 25 | C | 35 | A | 45 | C |
| 6 | B | 16 | B | 26 | C | 36 | A | 46 | B |
| 7 | C | 17 | C | 27 | D | 37 | D | 47 | A |
| 8 | C | 18 | D | 28 | A | 38 | B | 48 | D |
| 9 | C | 19 | C | 29 | B | 39 | C | 49 | B |
| 10 | A | 20 | A | 30 | C | 40 | D | 50 | C |

# Chapter 8
# Transaction Exposure

**Topic: Transaction Exposure**
**Skill: Recognition**
1. ____________exposure deals with cash flows that result from existing contractual obligations.

a. Operating
b. Transaction
c. Translation
d. Economic

**Topic: Operating Exposure**
**Skill: Recognition**
2. __________ exposure measures the change in the present value of the firm resulting from unexpected changes in exchange rates.

a. Operating
b. Transaction
c. Translation
d. Accounting

**Topic: Accounting Exposure**
**Skill: Recognition**
3. Each of the following is another name for operating exposure EXCEPT

a. economic exposure
b. strategic exposure
c. accounting exposure
d. competitive exposure

**Topic: Transaction and Operating Exposure**
**Skill: Recognition**
4. Transaction exposure and operating exposure exist because of unexpected changes in future cash flows. The difference between the two is that __________ exposure deals with cash flows already contracted for, while __________ exposure deals with future cash flows that might change because of changes in exchange rates.

a. transaction; operating
b. operating; transaction
c. operating; accounting
d. none of the above

**Topic: Accounting Exposure**
**Skill: Recognition**

5. ___________ exposure is the potential for accounting-derived changes in owner's equity to occur because of the need to translate foreign currency financial statements into a single reporting currency.

a. Transaction
b. Operating
c. Economic
d. Accounting

**Topic: Transaction and Accounting Exposure**
**Skill: Recognition**

6. Losses from __________ exposure generally reduce taxable income in the year they are realized. ___________ exposure losses may reduce taxes over a series of years.

a. accounting; operating
b. operating; transaction
c. transaction; operating
d. transaction; accounting

**Topic: Transaction and Accounting Exposure**
**Skill: Recognition**

7. Losses from ___________ exposure generally reduce taxable income in the year they are realized. ________ exposure losses are not cash losses and therefore, are not tax deductible.

a. transaction; operating
b. accounting; operating
c. accounting; transaction
d. transaction; accounting

**Topic: MNE Cash Flow Risk**
**Skill: Recognition**

8. MNE cash flows may be sensitive to changes in which of the following?

a. Exchange rates
b. Interest rates
c. Commodity prices
d. All of the above

**Topic: MNE Cash Flow Risk**
**Skill: Recognition**
9. Which of the following is a technique used by MNEs to deal with currency exposure?

a. Do nothing
b. Speculation
c. Hedging
d. All are techniques MNEs could use

**Topic: MNE Cash Flow Risk**
**Skill: Conceptual**
10. Hedging, or reducing risk, is the same as adding value or return to the firm.

a. True
b. False

**Topic: Hedging**
**Skill: Conceptual**
11. Assuming no transaction costs (i.e., hedging is "free"), hedging currency exposures should __________ the variability of expected cash flows to a firm and at the same time, the expected value of the cash flows should _________.

a. increase; not change
b. decrease; not change
c. not change; increase
d. not change; not change

**Topic: Hedging**
**Skill: Recognition**
12. Which of the following is NOT cited as a good reason for hedging currency exposures?

a. Reduced risk of future cash flows is a good planning tool.
b. Reduced risk of future cash flows reduces the probability that the firm may not meet required cash flows.
c. Currency risk management increases the expected cash flows to the firm.
d. Management is in a better position to assess firm currency risk than individual investors.

**Topic: Hedging**
**Skill: Recognition**
13. There is little question among investors and managers that hedging is a good and necessary tool.

a. True
b. False

**Topic: Hedging**
**Skill: Recognition**
14. Which of the following is cited as a good reason for NOT hedging currency exposures?

a. Shareholders are more capable of diversifying risk than management.
b. Currency risk management through hedging does not increase expected cash flows.
c. Hedging activities are often of greater benefit to management than to shareholders.
d. All of the above are cited as reasons NOT to hedge.

**Topic: Hedging**
**Skill: Conceptual**
15. The key arguments in opposition to currency hedging such as market efficiency, agency theory, and diversification have financial theory at their core.

a. True
b. False

**Topic: Hedging**
**Skill: Conceptual**
16. ___________ exposure may result from a firm having a payable in a foreign currency.

a. Transaction
b. Accounting
c. Operating
d. None of the above

**Topic: Transaction Exposure**
**Skill: Recognition**

17. The stages in the life of a transaction exposure can be broken into three distinct time periods. The first time period is the time between quoting a price and reaching an actual sale agreement or contract. The next time period is the time lag between taking an order and actually filling or delivering it. Finally, the time it takes to get paid after delivering the product. In order, these stages of transaction exposure may be identified as,

a. backlog, quotation, and billing exposure.
b. billing backlog, and quotation exposure.
c. quotation, backlog, and billing exposure.
d. quotation, billing, and backlog exposure.

**Topic: Transaction Exposure**
**Skill: Analytical**

18. A U.S. firm sells merchandise to a British company for £100,000. If the current exchange rate is $1.43/£, the U.S. firm is at risk of a loss if

a. the exchange rate changes to $1.42/£.
b. the exchange rate changes to $1.44/£.
c. the exchange rate doesn't change.
d. all of the above.

**Topic: Transaction Exposure**
**Skill: Analytical**

19. A U.S. firm sells merchandise to a British company for £100,000 at a current exchange rate of $1.43/£. If the exchange rate changes to $1.45/£ the U.S. firm will realize a ________ of ________.

a. loss; $2000
b. gain; $2000
c. loss; £2000
d. gain; £2000

**Topic: Contractual Hedges**
**Skill: Recognition**

20. Which of the following is NOT a popular contractual hedge against foreign exchange transaction exposure?

a. Forward market hedge
b. Money market hedge
c. Options market hedge
d. All of the above are contractual hedges

**Topic: Natural Hedge**
**Skill: Recognition**
21. A _________ hedge refers to an offsetting operating cash flow such as a payable arising from the conduct of business.

a. financial
b. natural
c. contractual
d. futures

**Use the following information for problems 22 – 26 and 29 - 35**

Plains States Manufacturing has just signed a contract to sell agricultural equipment to Boschin, a German firm, for €1,250,000. The sale was made in June with payment due six months later in December. Because this is a sizable contract for the firm and because the contract is in Euros rather than dollars, Plains States is considering several hedging alternatives to reduce the exchange rate risk arising from the sale. To help the firm make a hedging decision you have gathered the following information.

- The spot exchange rate is $.8924/€
- The six month forward rate is $.8750/€
- Plains States' cost of capital is 11%
- The Euro zone 6-month borrowing rate is 9% (or 4.5% for 6 months)
- The Euro zone 6-month lending rate is 7% (or 3.5% for 6 months)
- The U.S. 6-month borrowing rate is 8% (or 4% for 6 months)
- The U.S. 6-month lending rate is 6% (or 3% for 6 months)
- December put options for €625,000; strike price $.90, premium price is 1.5%
- Plains States' forecast for 6-month spot rates is $.91/€
- The budget rate, or the lowest acceptable sales price for this project, is $1,075,000 or $.86/€

**Topic: Forward Hedge Computation**
**Skill: Analytical**
22. If Plains States chooses not to hedge their euro receivable, the amount they receive in six months will be ____________.

a. $1,125,000
b. $1,137,500
c. $1,115,500
d. undeterminable today

**Topic: Forward Hedge Computation**
**Skill: Analytical**
23. If Plains States chooses to hedge its transaction exposure in the forward market, it will __________ €1,250,000 forward at a rate of __________.

a. sell; $.8750/€
b. sell; $.8924/€
c. buy; $.8750/€
d. buy; $.8924/€

**Topic: Forward Hedge Computation**
**Skill: Analytical**
24. Plains States chooses to hedge its transaction exposure in the forward market at the available forward rate. The payoff in 6 months will be __________.

a. $1,137,500
b. $1,125,000
c. $1,093,750
d. $1,075,000

**Topic: Forward Hedge Computation**
**Skill: Analytical**
25. If Plains States locks in the forward hedge at $.8750/€, and the spot rate when the transaction was recorded on the books was $.8924/€, this will result in a "foreign exchange loss" accounting transaction of ____________.

a. $0
b. $21,750
c. This was not a loss, it was a gain of $21,750.
d. There is not enough information to answer this question.

**Topic: Forward Hedge Computation**
**Skill: Analytical**
26. Plains States would be ___________ by an amount equal to ___________ with a forward hedge than if they had not hedged and their predicted exchange rate for 6 months had been correct.

a. better off; $43,750
b. better off; $62,500
c. worse off; $43,750
d. worse off; $62,500

**Topic: Money Market Hedge**
**Skill: Conceptual**
27. The structure of a money market hedge is similar to a forward hedge. The difference is the cost of the money market hedge is determined by the differential interest rates, while the forward hedge is a function of the forward rates quotation.

a. True
b. False

**Topic: Money Market Hedge**
**Skill: Conceptual**
28. In efficient markets, interest rate parity should assure that the costs of a forward hedge and money market hedge should be approximately the same.

a. True
b. False

**Topic: Money Market Hedge**
**Skill: Analytical**
29. Plains States could hedge the Euro receivables in the money market. Using the information provided, how much would the money market hedge return in six months assuming Plains States reinvests the proceeds at the U.S. investment rate?

a. $1,250,000
b. $1,232,057
c. $1,215,596
d. $1,207,371

**Topic: Money Market Hedge**
**Skill: Conceptual**
30. Money market hedges almost always return more than forward hedges because of the greater risk involved.

a. True
b. False

**Topic: Money Market Hedge**
**Skill: Analytical**
31. If Plains States chooses to implement a money market hedge for the Euro receivables, how much money will the firm borrow today?

a. €1,201,923
b. $1,201,923
c. €1,196,172
d. $1,196,172

**Topic: Put Option Hedge**
**Skill: Conceptual**

32. A ________ hedge allows Plains States to enjoy the benefits of a favorable change in exchange rates for their Euro receivables contract while protecting the firm from unfavorable exchange rate changes.

a. forward
b. call option
c. put option
d. money market

**Topic: Put Option Hedge**
**Skill: Analytical**

33. What is the cost of a put option hedge for Plains States' Euro receivable contract? (Note: Calculate the cost in future value dollars and assume the firm's cost of capital as the appropriate interest rate for calculating future values.)

a. $17,653
b. $16,733
c. €17,653
d. €16,733

**Topic: Put Option Hedge**
**Skill: Analytical**

34. The cost of a call option to Plains States would be ___________.

a. $17,653
b. $16,733
c. $18,471
d. there is not enough information to answer this question

**Topic: Put Option Hedge**
**Skill: Analytical**

35. If Plains States purchased the put option, and the option expires in six months on the same day that Plains States receives the €1,250,000, the firm will exercise the put at that time if the spot rate is $.91/€.

a. True
b. False

**Topic: Multiple Hedges**
**Skill: Conceptual**
36. A ________ hedge and a _______ hedge guarantee fixed payoffs but a ________ hedge or ________ hedge offer uncertain outcomes.

a. money market, currency option, forward, no hedge at all
b. no hedge at all, currency option, forward, money market
c. money market, forward, currency option, no hedge at all
d. forward, no hedge at all, money market, currency option

**Topic: Transaction Exposure**
**Skill: Conceptual**
37. Choosing which transaction exposure hedging strategy is best for a particular transaction depends on all of the following:

a. the firm's risk tolerance.
b. the firm's expectations about changes in currency exchange rates.
c. the costs associated with each alternative.
d. all of the above.

**Topic: Options**
**Skill: Conceptual**
38. Hedging accounts payable foreign currency exchange risk would likely consider the purchase of a _______ option whereas hedging accounts receivable currency exchange risk would be likely be to purchase a __________ option.

a. put, call
b. put, put
c. call, put
d. call, call

**Use the following information for problems 39 - 43**

Oregon Transportation Inc. (OTI) has just signed a contract to purchase light rail cars from a manufacturer in Germany €2,500,000. The purchase was made in June with payment due six months later in December. Because this is a sizable contract for the firm and because the contract is in Euros rather than dollars, OTI is considering several hedging alternatives to reduce the exchange rate risk arising from the sale. To help the firm make a hedging decision you have gathered the following information.

- The spot exchange rate is $.8924/€
- The six month forward rate is $.8750/€
- OTI's cost of capital is 11%
- The Euro zone 6-month borrowing rate is 9% (or 4.5% for 6 months)
- The Euro zone 6-month lending rate is 7% (or 3.5% for 6 months)
- The U.S. 6-month borrowing rate is 8% (or 4% for 6 months)

- The U.S. 6-month lending rate is 6% (or 3% for 6 months)
- December call options for €625,000; strike price $.90, premium price is 1.5%
- OTI's forecast for 6-month spot rates is $.91/€
- The budget rate, or the highest acceptable purchase price for this project, is $2,300,000 or $.92/€

**Topic: Transaction Exposure**
**Skill: Analytical**

39. If OTI chooses not to hedge their euro payable, the amount they pay in six months will be ____________.

a. $2,231,000
b. $2,187,500
c. €2,231,000
d. unknown today.

**Topic: Forward Hedge**
**Skill: Analytical**

40. If OTI chooses to hedge its transaction exposure in the forward market, it will _________ €2,500,000 forward at a rate of __________.

a. buy, $.8750
b. buy, $.8924
c. sell, $.8750
d. sell, €.8924

**Topic: Forward Hedge**
**Skill: Analytical**

41. OTI chooses to hedge its transaction exposure in the forward market at the available forward rate. The required amount in dollars to pay off the accounts payable in 6 months will be _________.

a. $2,500,000
b. $2,187,500
c. $2,300,000
d. $2,231,000

**Topic: Forward Hedge**
**Skill: Analytical**
42. If OTI locks in the forward hedge at $.8750/€, and the spot rate when the transaction was recorded on the books was $.8924/€, this will result in a "foreign exchange _______" accounting transaction of ____________.

a. loss, $43,500
b. loss, €43,500
c. gain, $43,500
d. gain, €43,500

**Topic: Forward Hedge**
**Skill: Analytical**
43. OTI would be ___________ by an amount equal to ___________ with a forward hedge than if they had not hedged and their predicted exchange rate for 6 months had been correct.

a. better off, $87,500
b. better off, €87,500
c. worse off. $87,500
d. worse off, €87,500

**Topic: Call Option**
**Skill: Analytical**
44. What is the cost of a call option hedge for OTI's Euro receivable contract? (Note: Calculate the cost in future value dollars and assume the firm's cost of capital as the appropriate interest rate for calculating future values.)

a. $33,750
b. $35,606
c. $34,500
d. $36,398

**Topic: Put Option**
**Skill: Analytical**
45. The cost of a put option to OTI would be ____________.

a. $33,750
b. $35,606
c. $34,500
d. there is not enough information to answer this question

**Topic: Profit Centers**
**Skill: Recognition**
46. The treasury function of most firms, the group typically responsible for transaction exposure management, is usually considered a profit center.

a. True
b. False

**Topic: Anticipated Exposure**
**Skill: Recognition**
47. _______________ are transactions for which there are, at present, no contracts or agreements between parties.

a. Backlog exposure
b. Quotation exposure
c. Anticipated exposure
d. None of the above

**Topic: Proportional Hedging**
**Skill: Recognition**
48. According to the authors, firms that employ proportional hedges decrease the percentage of forward-cover as the maturity of the exposure lengthens.

a. True
b. False

**Topic: Transaction Exposure**
**Skill: Recognition**
49. According to a survey by Bank of America, which type of foreign exchange risk do firms most often hedge?

a. Translation exposure
b. Transaction exposure
c. Contingent exposure
d. Economic exposure

**Topic: Forward Hedges**
**Skill: Recognition**
50. According to a survey by Bank of America, when firms do hedge, the most common type of hedging instruments are _____________.

a. forwards
b. options
c. money markets
d. call and puts

## Essay Questions:

1. Does foreign currency exchange hedging both reduce risk and increase expected value? Explain, and list several arguments in favor of currency risk management and several against.

**Answer**
Foreign exchange currency hedging can reduce the variability of foreign currency receivables or payables by locking in a specific exchange rate in the future via a forward contract, converting currency at the current spot rate using a money market hedge, or minimizing unfavorable exchange rate movement with a currency option. None of these hedging techniques, however, increases the expected value of the foreign currency exchange. In fact, expected value should fall by an amount equal to the cost of the hedge.

Generally, those in favor of currency risk management find value in the reduction of variability of uncertain cash flows. Those opposed to currency risk management argue the NPV of such activities are $0 or less and that shareholders can reduce risk themselves more efficiently. For a more complete answer to this question, see page 4 where the author outlines several arguments for and against currency risk management.

2. Currency risk management techniques include forward hedges, money market hedges, and option hedges. Draw a diagram showing the possible outcomes of these hedging alternatives for a foreign currency receivable contract. In your diagram, be sure to label the X and Y-axis, the put option strike price, and show the possible results for a money market hedge, a forward hedge, a put option hedge, and an uncovered position. (Note: Assume the forward currency receivable is British pounds and the put option strike price is $1.50/£, the price of the option is $.04 the forward rate is $1.52/£ and the current spot rate is $1.48/£.

**Answer**
The student should draw and label a diagram that looks similar to the one found on page 14.

### Chapter 8: Transaction Exposure
### Multiple Choice Answer Key:

| | | | | | | | | | |
|---|---|---|---|---|---|---|---|---|---|
| 1 | B | 11 | B | 21 | B | 31 | C | 41 | B |
| 2 | A | 12 | C | 22 | D | 32 | C | 42 | C |
| 3 | C | 13 | B | 23 | A | 33 | A | 43 | A |
| 4 | A | 14 | D | 24 | C | 34 | D | 44 | B |
| 5 | D | 15 | A | 25 | B | 35 | B | 45 | D |
| 6 | C | 16 | A | 26 | C | 36 | C | 46 | B |
| 7 | D | 17 | C | 27 | A | 37 | D | 47 | C |
| 8 | D | 18 | D | 28 | A | 38 | C | 48 | A |
| 9 | D | 19 | A | 29 | B | 39 | D | 49 | B |
| 10 | B | 20 | D | 30 | B | 40 | A | 50 | A |

# Chapter 9
# Operating Exposure

**Topic: Operating Exposure**
**Skill: Recognition**
1. Another name for operating exposure is __________ exposure.

a. economic
b. competitive
c. strategic
d. all of the above

**Topic: Operating Exposure**
**Skill: Recognition**
2. What type of international risk exposure is measures the change in present value of a firm resulting from changes in future operating cash flows caused by any unexpected change in exchange rates?

a. transaction exposure
b. accounting exposure
c. operating exposure
d. translation exposure

**Topic: Operating Exposure**
**Skill: Conceptual**
3. The goal of operating exposure analysis is to identify strategic operating techniques the firm might adopt to enhance value in the face of unanticipated exchange rate changes.

a. True
b. False

**Topic: Operating and Financial Cash Flows**
**Skill: Recognition**
4. ________ cash flows arise from intracompany and intercompany receivables and payments while __________ cash flows are payments for the use of loans and equity.

a. Financing; operating
b. Operating; financing
c. Operating; accounting
d. Accounting; financing

**Topic: Operating and Financial Cash Flows**
**Skill: Recognition**
5. Operating cash flows may occur in different currencies and at different times, but financing cash flows may occur only in a single currency.
  a. True
  b. False

**Topic: Financial Cash Flows**
**Skill: Recognition**
6. Which of the following is NOT an example of a financial cash flow?

  a. Dividend paid to parent company
  b. Interest on intrafirm lending
  c. Rent and lease payments
  d. Intrafirm principle payments

**Topic: Operating Cash Flows**
**Skill: Recognition**
7. Which of the following is NOT an example of an operating cash flow?

  a. Management fees and distributed overhead
  b. Royalties and license fees
  c. Payment for goods and services
  d. Parent invested equity capital

**Topic: Operating, Transaction, and Translation Exposure**
**Skill: Conceptual**
8. ____________ exposure is far more important for the long-run health of a business than changes caused by ___________ or ____________ exposure.

  a. Operating; translation, transaction
  b. Transaction; operating, translation
  c. Accounting; translation, transaction
  d. Translation; operating, transaction

**Topic: Expectations**
**Skill: Conceptual**
9. Expected changes in foreign exchange rates should already be factored into anticipated operating results by management and investors.

  a. True
  b. False

**Topic: Forward Rate**
**Skill: Conceptual**
10. Under conditions of equilibrium, management would use _________ exchange rate as an unbiased predictor of future spot rates when preparing operating budgets.

a. the current spot
b. the forward rate
c. black market
d. none of the above

**Topic: Exchange Rate Equilibrium**
**Skill: Conceptual**
11. In equilibrium, expected cash flow to amortize international debt obligations should reflect the __________.

a. current spot rate
b. the spot rate when the loan was contracted
c. the international Fisher effect
d. none of the above

**Topic: Exchange Rate Equilibrium**
**Skill: Conceptual**
12. From an investor's perspective, if the foreign exchange market is efficient, information about expected changes in exchange rates should be widely known and thus reflected in a firm's market value. Only ___________ in exchange rates or an __________ foreign exchange market, should cause market value to change.

a. expected changes; efficient
b. unexpected changes; efficient
c. expected changes, inefficient
d. unexpected changes; inefficient

**Topic: Foreign Exchange Diversification**
**Skill: Recognition**
13. Which of the following is NOT an example of diversifying operations?

a. Diversifying sales.
b. Diversifying location of operations.
c. Raising funds in more than one country.
d. Sourcing raw materials in more than one country.

**Topic: Foreign Exchange Diversification**
**Skill: Recognition**
14. Which of the following is NOT an example of diversifying financing?

a. Raising funds in more than one market.
b. Raising funds in more than one country.
c. Financing with stocks, bonds, and bank loans.
d. All of the above qualify.

**Topic: Foreign Exchange Diversification**
**Skill: Conceptual**
15. Management must be able to predict disequilibria in international markets to take advantage of diversification strategies.

a. True
b. False

**Topic: Foreign Exchange Diversification**
**Skill: Conceptual**
16. When disequilibria in international markets occur, management can take advantage by

a. doing nothing if they are already diversified and able to realize beneficial portfolio effects.
b. recognizing disequilibria faster than purely domestic competitors.
c. shifting operational of financing activities to take advantage of the disequilibria.
d. All of the above.

**Topic: Foreign Exchange Diversification**
**Skill: Conceptual**
17. Purely domestic firms will be at a disadvantage to MNEs in the event of market disequilibria because

a. domestic firms lack comparative data from its own sources.
b. international firms are already so large.
c. all of the domestic firm's raw materials are imported.
d. None of the above. Domestic firms are not at a disadvantage.

**Topic: Foreign Exchange Diversification**
**Skill: Recognition**
18. Which of the following is probably NOT an advantage of foreign exchange risk management?

a. The reduction of the variability of cash flows due to domestic business cycles.
b. Increased availability of capital.
c. Reduced cost of capital.
d. All of the above are potential advantages of foreign exchange risk management.

**Topic: Political Risk**
**Skill: Recognition**
19. Which of the following is NOT an example of a form of *political* risk that might be avoided or reduced by foreign exchange risk management?

a. Expropriation of assets.
b. Destruction of raw materials through natural disaster.
c. War.
d. Unfavorable legal changes.

**Topic: Management of Foreign Exchange Risk**
**Skill: Recognition**
20. Which of the following is NOT identified by your authors as a proactive management technique to reduce exposure to foreign exchange risk?

a. Matching currency cash flows.
b. Currency swaps.
c. Remaining a purely domestic firm.
d. Parallel loans.

**Topic: Management of Foreign Exchange Risk**
**Skill: Conceptual**
21. Which one of the following management techniques is likely to best offset the risk of long-run exposure to receivables denominated in a particular foreign currency?

a. Borrow money in the foreign currency in question.
b. Lend money in the foreign currency in question.
c. Increase sales to that country.
d. Increase sales in this county.

**Topic: Management of Foreign Exchange Risk**
**Skill: Conceptual**
22. Which one of the following management techniques is likely to best offset the risk of long-run exposure to payables denominated in a particular foreign currency?

a. Borrow money in the foreign currency in question.
b. Lend money in the foreign currency in question.
c. Rely on the Federal Reserve Board to enact monetary policy favorable to your exposure risk.
d. None of the above.

**Topic: Management of Foreign Exchange Risk**
**Skill: Recognition**
23. The particular strategy of trying to offset stable inflows of cash from one country with outflows of cash in the same currency is known as _______________.

a. hedging
b. diversification
c. matching
d. balancing

**Topic: Management of Foreign Exchange Risk**
**Skill: Recognition**
24. Which of the following is NOT an acceptable hedging technique to reduce risk caused by a relatively predictable long-term foreign currency inflow of Japanese yen?

a. Import raw materials from Japan denominated in yen to substitute for domestic suppliers.
b. Pay suppliers from other countries in yen.
c. Import raw materials from Japan denominated in dollars.
d. Acquire debt denominated in yen.

**Topic: Natural Hedge**
**Skill: Recognition**
25. An MNE has a contract for a relatively predictable long-term inflow of Japanese yen that the firm chooses to hedge by seeking out potential suppliers in Japan. This hedging strategy is referred to as _______________.

a. a natural hedge
b. currency-switching
c. matching
d. diversification

**Topic: Currency-Switching**
**Skill: Recognition**
26. An MNE has a contract for a relatively predictable long-term inflow of Japanese yen that the firm chooses to hedge by paying for imports from Canada in Japanese yen. This hedging strategy is known as _____________.

a. a natural hedge
b. currency-switching
c. matching
d. diversification

**Topic: Risk-Sharing**
**Skill: Conceptual**
27. A U.S. timber products firm has a long-term contract to import unprocessed logs from Canada. To avoid occasional and unpredictable changes in the exchange rate between the U.S. dollar and the Canadian dollar, the firms agree to split between the two firms the impact of any exchange rate movement. This type of agreement is referred to as _____________.

a. risk-sharing
b. currency-switching
c. matching
d. a natural hedge

**Topic: Back-to-Back Loan**
**Skill: Recognition**
28. A _____________ occurs when two business firms in separate countries arrange to borrow each other's currency for a specified period of time.

a. natural hedge loan
b. forward loan
c. currency switch loan
d. back-to-back loan

**Topic: Back-to-Back Loan**
**Skill: Conceptual**
29. A Canadian firm with a U.S. subsidiary and a U.S. firm with a Canadian subsidiary agree to a parallel loan agreement. In such an agreement, the Canadian firm is making a/an _________ loan to the ___________ subsidiary while effectively financing the ____________ subsidiary.

a. indirect; U.S, Canadian
b. indirect; Canadian; U.S.
c. direct; U.S.; Canadian
d. direct; Canadian; U.S.

**Topic: Back-to-Back Loan**
**Skill: Conceptual**
30. Which of the following is NOT an important impediment to widespread use of parallel loans?

a. Difficulty in finding an appropriate counterparty.
b. The risk that one of the parties will fail to return the borrowed funds when agreed.
c. The process does not avoid exchange rate risk
d. All of the above are significant impediments.

**Topic: Currency Swap**
**Skill: Conceptual**
31. A ____________ resembles a back-to-back loan except that it does not appear on a firm's balance sheet.

a. forward loan
b. currency hedge
c. counterparty
d. currency swap

**Topic: Currency Swap**
**Skill: Recognition**
32. A _______ is the term used to describe a foreign currency agreement between two parties to exchange a given amount of one currency for another, and after a period of time, to give back the original amounts.

a. matched flow
b. currency swap
c. back-to-back loan
d. none of the above

**Topic: Currency Swap**
**Skill: Recognition**
33. Currency swaps are exclusively for periods of time under one year.

a. True
b. False

**Topic: Currency Swap**
**Skill: Conceptual**

34. A British firm and a U.S. Corporation each wish to enter into a currency swap hedging agreement. The British firm is receiving U.S. dollars from sales in the U.S. but wants pounds. The U.S. firm is receiving pounds from sales in Britain but wants dollars. Which of the following choices would best satisfy the desires of the firms?

a. The British firm pays dollars to a swap dealer and receive pounds from the dealer. The U.S. firm pays pounds to the swap dealer and receives dollars.
b. The U.S. firm pays dollars to a swap dealer and receive pounds from the dealer. The British firm pays pounds to the swap dealer and receives dollars.
c. The British firm pays pounds to a swap dealer and receive pounds from the dealer. The U.S. firm pays dollars to the swap dealer and receives dollars.
d. The British firm pays dollars to a swap dealer and receive dollars from the dealer. The U.S. firm pays pounds to the swap dealer and receives pounds.

**Topic: Currency Swap**
**Skill: Recognition**

35. Most swap dealers arrange swaps so that each firm that is a party to the transaction does not know who the counterparty is.

a. True
b. False

**Topic: Currency Swap**
**Skill: Recognition**

36. Swap agreements are treated as off-balance sheet transactions via U.S. accounting methods.

a. True
b. False

**Topic: Currency Swap**
**Skill: Recognition**

37. After being introduced in the 1980's, currency swaps have remained a relatively insignificant financial derivative instrument.

a. True
b. False

**Topic: Diversification**
**Skill: Recognition**

38. The primary method by which a firm may protect itself against operating exposure impacts is:

a. money market hedges
b. diversification
c. forward contract hedges
d. balance sheet hedging

**Topic: Operating Exposure**
**Skill: Recognition**

39. Operating exposure

a. creates foreign exchange accounting gains and losses.
b. causes exchange rates to fluctuate.
c. is the possibility that future cash flows will change due to an unexpected change in foreign exchange rates.
d. measures a country's propensity to import and export.

**Topic: Transaction Exposure**
**Skill: Recognition**

40. When an enterprise has a receivable or payable denominated in a foreign currency and settlement of the obligation has not yet taken place, that firm is said to have _________ exposure.

a. accounting
b. operating
c. tax
d. transaction

**Topic: Diversification**
**Skill: Recognition**

41. An Advantage of international diversification is the

a. reduction in the variability of future cash flows due to domestic business cycles.
b. increase in the availability of capital.
c. diversification of political risk.
d. all of the above.

**Topic: Exchange Rates**
**Skill: Conceptual**
42. An unexpected change in exchange rates impacts firms cash flows at what level(s)?

a. Short run
b. Medium run, (equilibrium case)
c. Long run
d. All of the above

**Topic: Hedging**
**Skill: Recognition**
43. Which of the following is NOT one of the commonly employed financial policies used to manage operating and transaction exposure?

a. Use of natural hedges by matching currency cash flows.
b. Back-to-back or parallel loans.
c. Currency swaps
d. All of the above are commonly used financial policies for managing operating exposure.

**Topic: Operating Cash Flows**
**Skill: Recognition**
44. Which of the following is not an operating cash flow?

a. Intra-firm payable
b. Account receivable from an unrelated party.
c. Interest payment by a subsidiary to a parent company.
d. Account payable to a foreign subsidiary

**Topic: Types of Foreign Exchange Risk**
**Skill: Recognition**
45. The three main types of foreign exchange risk are:

a. operating, transaction, and translation
b. translation, accounting, and operating
c. transaction, accounting, and translation
d. operating, currency, and market

**Topic: Operating Exposure**
**Skill: Recognition**
46. ________________ risk measures the change in value of the firm that results from changes in future operating cash flows caused by unexpected changes in exchange rates.

a. Transaction
b. Accounting
c. Operating
d. Translation

**Topic: Contractual Hedging**
**Skill: Conceptual**
47. Contractual approaches (i.e., options and forwards) have occasionally been used to hedge operating exposure, but are costly and possible ineffectual.

a. True
b. False

**Topic: Proactive Management**
**Skill: Conceptual**
48. Which of the following is NOT a proactive policy for managing operating exposure?

a. Matching currency of cash flow
b. Back-to-back loans
c. Cross currency swap agreements
d. All of the above are proactive management policies for operating exposure.

## Essay Questions:

1. Diversification is possibly the best technique for reducing the problems associated with international transactions. Provide one example each of international financial diversification and international operational diversification and explain how the action reduces risk.

**Answer:**
An MNE well known in the financial markets could borrow money in a country in which the firm receives foreign currency. The MNE could then use the receivables to repay the loan in the foreign currency and avoid uncertainties in exchange rates.

An MNE could establish production facilities in several countries. This could be beneficial in at least two ways. First, such diversification reduces the probability of unfavorable changes in exchange rates for one country from significantly reducing the firm's profitability. Second, an MNE with facilities in several countries is well positioned by using internal sources to recognize when a disequilibria in the market arises.

2. A British firm has a subsidiary in the U.S., and a U.S. firm, known to the British firm, has a subsidiary in Britain. Define and then provide an example for each of the following management techniques for reducing the firm's operating cash flows. The techniques to consider are:

a. matching currency cash flows
b. risk-sharing agreements
c. back-to-back or parallel loans

**Answer:**
Matching currency cash flows requires that the British firm with dollar receivables must establish an equivalent dollar payable. They could do this by borrowing dollars and repaying the loan with the proceeds from the receivables account. Or they could move all or part of their operations to the U.S. so that both receivables and payables would be in U.S. dollars.

Risk-sharing agreements are contractual clauses whereby both parties agree to an acceptable range of exchange rates at the time the international sale is made. A spot rate at time of exchange outside of the agreed upon range results in an adjustment made to the actual exchange rate that shares the difference between the spot rate and the acceptable range of exchange rates.

Back-to-back loans provide for parent-subsidiary cross border financing without incurring direct currency exposure. For example, using our British and U.S. firms, the British firm could lend pounds to the U.S. subsidiary in Britain at the same time that the U.S. firm lends an equivalent amount of dollars to the British subsidiary in the U.S. Later, the loans would be simultaneously repaid.

## Chapter 9: Operating Exposure
## Multiple Choice Answer Key:

| | | | | | | | | | |
|---|---|---|---|---|---|---|---|---|---|
| 1 | D | 11 | C | 21 | A | 31 | D | 41 | D |
| 2 | C | 12 | D | 22 | B | 32 | B | 42 | D |
| 3 | A | 13 | C | 23 | C | 33 | B | 43 | D |
| 4 | B | 14 | D | 24 | C | 34 | A | 44 | C |
| 5 | B | 15 | B | 25 | A | 35 | A | 45 | A |
| 6 | C | 16 | D | 26 | B | 36 | A | 46 | C |
| 7 | D | 17 | A | 27 | A | 37 | B | 47 | A |
| 8 | A | 18 | D | 28 | D | 38 | B | 48 | D |
| 9 | A | 19 | B | 29 | C | 39 | C | | |
| 10 | B | 20 | C | 30 | C | 40 | D | | |

# Chapter 10
# Translation Exposure

**Topic: Translation Exposure**
**Skill: Recognition**

1. Translation exposure may also be called __________ exposure.

   a. transaction
   b. operating
   c. accounting
   d. currency

**Topic: Translation Exposure**
**Skill: Recognition**

2. ____________ exposure is the potential for an increase or decrease in the parent's net worth and reported net income caused by a change in exchange rates since the last transaction.

   a. Transaction
   b. Operating
   c. Currency
   d. Translation

**Topic: Translation Exposure**
**Skill: Recognition**

3. Translation exposure measures

   a. changes in the value of outstanding financial obligations incurred prior to a change in exchange rates.
   b. the potential for an increase or decrease in the parent's net worth and reported net income caused by a change in exchange rates since the last consolidation of international operations.
   c. an unexpected change in exchange rates impact on short run expected cash flows.
   d. none of the above.

**Topic: Translation Exposure**
**Skill: Recognition**

4. According to your authors, the main purpose of translation is

   a. to prepare consolidated financial statements.
   b. to help management assess the performance of foreign subsidiaries.
   c. to act as an interpreter for managers without foreign language skills.
   d. none of the above.

**Topic: Exchange Rate Accounting**
**Skill: Conceptual**
5. It is possible to use different exchange rates for different line items on a financial statement.

a. True
b. False

**Topic: Translation Exposure**
**Skill: Conceptual**
6. If the same exchange rate were used to remeasure every line on a financial statement, then there would be no imbalances from remeasuring.

a. True
b. False

**Topic: Translation Exposure**
**Skill: Conceptual**
7. Historical exchange rates may be used for ______________, while current exchange rates may be used for ______________.

a. fixed asses and current assets; income and expense items
b. equity accounts and fixed assets; current assets and liabilities
c. current assets and liabilities; equity accounts and fixed assets
d. equity accounts and current liabilities; current assets and fixed assets

**Topic: Accounting for Translation Error**
**Skill: Conceptual**
8. If an imbalance results from the accounting method used for translation, the imbalance is taken either to __________ or __________.

a. the bank, the post office
b. depreciation, the market for foreign exchange swaps
c. current income, equity reserves
d. current liabilities, equity reserves

**Topic: Factors of Translation Method**
**Skill: Recognition**
9. Generally speaking, translation methods by country define the translation process as a function of what two factors?

a. Size; location
b. A firm's functional currency, location
c. Location, foreign subsidiary independence
d. Foreign subsidiary independence; a firm's functional currency

**Topic: Integrated Foreign Entity**
**Skill: Recognition**
10. A/an _______________ subsidiary is one in which the firm operates as an extension of the parent company with cash flows highly interrelated with the parent.

a. self-sustaining foreign
b. integrated foreign entity
c. foreign
d. none of the above

**Topic: Integrated or Self-sustaining Foreign Entities**
**Skill: Conceptual**
11. Consider two different foreign subsidiaries of Georgia-Pacific Wood Products Inc. The first subsidiary mills trees in Canada and ships its entire product to the Georgia-Pacific U.S. The second subsidiary is also owned by the parent firm but is located in Japan and retails tropical hardwood furniture that it buys from many different sources. The first subsidiary is likely a/an ___________ foreign entity with most of its cash flows in U.S. dollars, and the second subsidiary is more of a/an ___________ foreign entity.

a. domestic; integrated
b. integrated; self-sustaining
c. integrated; self-sustaining
d. self-sustaining; integrated

**Topic: Functional Currency**
**Skill: Recognition**
12. A foreign subsidiaries ____________ currency is the currency used in the firm's day-to-day operations.

a. local
b. integrated
c. notational dollar
d. functional

**Topic: FASB**
**Skill: Recognition**
13. The ____________ determines accounting policy for U.S. firms.

a. Securities and Exchange Commission (SEC)
b. Federal Reserve System (Fed)
c. Financial Accounting Standards Board (FASB)
d. General Agreement on Tariffs and Trade (GATT)

**Topic: Current Rate and Temporal Methods**
**Skill: Recognition**
14. The two basic methods for the translation of foreign subsidiary financial statements are the ____________ method and the ____________ method.

a. current rate; temporal
b. temporal; proper timing
c. current rate; future rate
d. none of the above

**Topic: Temporal vs. Current Rate Method**
**Skill: Recognition**
15. Exchange rate imbalances that are passed through the balance sheet affect a firm's reported income, but imbalances transferred to the income statement do not.

a. True
b. False

**Topic: FASB**
**Skill: Recognition**
16. Which of the following is NOT an economic indicator used by FASB for determining a subsidiary's functional currency?

a. Cash flow indicators.
b. Sales price indicators.
c. Expense indicators.
d. These are all economic indicators used by FASB.

**Topic: Current Rate**
**Skill: Recognition**
17. The current rate method is the most prevalent method today for the translation of financial statements.

a. True
b. False

**Topic: Current Rate Method**
**Skill: Recognition**
18. Gains or losses caused by translation adjustments when using the current rate method are reported separately on the ______________.

a. consolidated statement of cash flow
b. consolidated income statement
c. consolidated balance sheet
d. none of the above

**Topic: Current Rate Method**
**Skill: Recognition**
19. The biggest advantage of the current rate method of reporting translation adjustments is the fact that the gain or loss goes directly to the reserve account on the consolidated balance sheet and does not pass through the consolidated income statement.

a. True
b. False

**Topic: Temporal Method**
**Skill: Recognition**
20. Under the current rate method, specific assets and liabilities are translated at exchange rates consistent with the timing of the item's creation.

a. True
b. False

**Topic: Temporal and Current Rate Methods**
**Skill: Conceptual**
21. The basic advantage of the ___________ method of foreign currency translation is that foreign nonmonetary assets are carried at their original cost in the parent's consolidated statement while the most important advantage of the ___________ method is that the gain or loss from translation does not pass through the income statement.

a. monetary; current rate
b. temporal; current rate
c. temporal; monetary
d. current rate; temporal

**Topic: Temporal Method**
**Skill: Recognition**
22. The current rate method of foreign currency translation gains or losses resulting from remeasurement are carried directly to current consolidated income and thus introduces volatility to consolidated earnings.

a. True
b. False

**Topic: Translation Procedures**
**Skill: Conceptual**
23. Under the U.S. method of translation procedures, if the financial statements of the foreign subsidiary of a U.S. company are maintained in U.S. dollars,

a. translation is accomplished through the current rate method.
b. translation is accomplished through the temporal method.
c. translation is not required.
d. the translation method to be used is not obvious.

**Topic: Current Rate Method**
**Skill: Conceptual**
24. Under the U.S. method of translation procedures, if the financial statements of the foreign subsidiary of a U.S. company are maintained in the local currency, and the local currency is the functional currency, then

a. the translation method to be used is not obvious.
b. translation is accomplished through the temporal method.
c. translation is not required.
d. translation is accomplished through the current rate method.

**Topic: Temporal Method**
**Skill: Conceptual**
25. Under the U.S. method of translation procedures, if the financial statements of the foreign subsidiary of a U.S. company are maintained in the local currency, and the U.S. dollar is the functional currency, then

a. translation is not required.
b. translation is accomplished through the current rate method.
c. translation is accomplished through the temporal method.
d. translation is not required.

**Topic: FASB vs IASC**
**Skill: Recognition**
26. A major problem for international foreign currency transaction is that FASB and the International Accounting Standards Committee (IASC) do NOT use the same basic translation procedure.

a. True
b. False

**Topic: Balance Sheet Hedge**
**Skill: Recognition**
27. The main technique to minimize translation exposure is called a/an ________ hedge.

a. balance sheet
b. income statement
c. forward
d. translation

**Topic: Balance Sheet Hedge**
**Skill: Conceptual**
28. A balance sheet hedge requires that the amount of exposed foreign currency assets and liabilities

a. have a 2:1 ratio of assets to liabilities.
b. have a 2:1 ratio of liabilities to assets.
c. have a 2:1 ratio of liabilities to equity.
d. be equal.

**Topic: Balance Sheet Hedge**
**Skill: Conceptual**
29. If a firm's balance sheet has an equal amount of exposed foreign currency assets and liabilities and the firm translates by the temporal method, then

a. the net exposed position is called monetary balance.
b. the change is value of liabilities and assets due to a change in exchange rates will be of equal but opposite direction.
c. both b and c are true.
d. none of the above.

**Topic: Balance Sheet Hedge**
**Skill: Conceptual**
30. If a firm's subsidiary is using the local currency as the functional currency, which of the following is NOT a circumstance that could justify the use of a balance sheet hedge?

a. the foreign subsidiary is about to be liquidated, so that the value of its Cumulative Translation Adjustment (CTA) would be realized.
b. the firm has debt covenants or bank agreements that state the firm's debt/equity ratio will be maintained within specific limits.
c. the foreign subsidiary is operating is a hyperinflationary environment.
d. all of the above are appropriate reasons to use a balance sheet hedge.

**Topic: Translation ans Transaction Exposure**
**Skill: Conceptual**

31. If the parent firm and all subsidiaries denominate all exposed assets and liabilities in the parent's reporting currency this will ___________ exposure but each subsidiary would have ___________ exposure.

a. maximize translation; no transaction
b. eliminate translation; transaction
c. maximize transaction; no translation
d. eliminate transaction; translation

**Topic: Translation Loss**
**Skill: Conceptual**

32. A Canadian subsidiary of a U.S. parent firm is instructed to bill an export to the parent in U.S. dollars. The Canadian subsidiary records the accounts receivable in Canadian dollars and notes a profit on the sale of goods. Later, when the U.S. parent pays the subsidiary the contracted U.S. dollar amount, the Canadian dollar has appreciated 10% against the U.S. dollar. In this example, the Canadian subsidiary will record a

a. 10% foreign exchange loss on the U.S. dollar accounts receivable.
b. 10% foreign exchange gain on the U.S. dollar accounts receivable.
c. since the Canadian firm is a U.S. subsidiary neither a gain nor loss will be recorded.
d. any gain or loss will be recoded only by the parent firm.

**Topic: Translation vs. Transaction Exposure**
**Skill: Conceptual**

33. It is possible that efforts to decrease translation exposure may result in an increase in transaction exposure.

a. True
b. False

**Topic: Translation vs. Transaction Exposure**
**Skill: Recognition**

34. ___________ gains and losses are "realized" whereas _________ gains and losses are only "paper".

a. Translation; transaction
b. Transaction; translation
c. Translation; operating
d. None of the above

**Topic: Functional Currency**
**Skill: Recognition**
35. The dominant currency used by a subsidiary in its day-to-day operations is known as its ___________ currency.

a. operational
b. transactional
c. functional
d. foreign

**Topic: Translation vs. Operational Gains and Losses**
**Skill: Recognition**
36. Translation gains and losses can be quite different from operating gains and losses

a. in magnitude only.
b. in sign only.
c. in neither magnitude nor sign.
d. in both magnitude and sign.

**Topic: Balance Sheet Hedge**
**Skill: Recognition**
37. A balance sheet hedge is the main technique for managing ___________.

a. transaction
b. operating
c. translation
d. money market

**Topic: Hedging**
**Skill: Recognition**
38. Management can easily offset both translation and transaction exposure through

a. a passive hedging strategy.
b. an active hedging strategy.
c. either an active or passive hedging strategy.
d. It is almost impossible to offset both translation and transaction exposure simultaneously.

**Topic: Functional Currency**
**Skill: Recognition**
39. U.S. multinational firms must use ____________ as their functional currency.

a. the currency of the primary economic environment where they operate
b. the U.S. dollar
c. the local currency
d. the euro

**Topic: Translation Loss**
**Skill: Analytical**
40. If the European subsidiary of a U.S. firm has net exposed assets of €500,000, and the euro drops in value from $1/€ to $.90/€ the U.S. firm has a translation ___________.

a. gain of $50,000
b. loss of $50,000
c. gain of $450,000
d. loss of €450,000

**Topic: Translation Gain**
**Skill: Analytical**
41. If the European subsidiary of a U.S. firm has net exposed assets of €500,000, and the euro increases in value from $1/€ to $1.05/€ the U.S. firm has a translation ______________.

a. gain of $25,000
b. loss of $25,000
c. gain of $525,000
d. loss of €525,000

**Topic: Cumulative Translation Adjustment Account**
**Skill: Recognition**
42. Under the current rate method, translation gains of losses are reported in an equity reserve account called ______________________.

a. Reserve for accounting losses
b. Accounting reserve adjustment account
c. Cumulative translation adjustment account
d. None of the above; translation gains and losses flow through into the income statement

**Topic: Current Rate Method**
**Skill: Conceptual**
43. Under the current rate method, when management anticipates appreciation of a foreign currency it:

a. may move funds from cash to savings.
b. may move funds from cash into plant and equipment.
c. may try to decrease net exposed assets in that country.
d. may try to increase net exposed assets in that country.

**Topic: Translation Loss**
**Skill: Analytical**
44. If the British subsidiary of a European firm has net exposed assets of £250,000, and the pound increases in value from €1.60/£ to €1.65/£, the European firm has a translation ___________.

a. gain of €25,000
b. loss of €25,000
c. gain of £25,000
d. loss of £25,000

**Topic: Translation Gain**
**Skill: Analytical**
45. If the British subsidiary of a European firm has net exposed assets of £250,000, and the pound drops in value from €1.60/£ to €1.50/£, the European firm has a translation ___________.

a. gain of €12,500
b. loss of €12,500
c. loss of £12,500
d. gain of £12,500

**Topic: FASB-52**
**Skill: Recognition**
46. As required by FASB-52, which exchange rate is required to be used to translate assets and liabilities of a foreign entity from its functional currency to the reporting currency?

a. Forward
b. Current
c. Historical
d. The exchange rate to be used varies with the situation.

**Topic: Taxable Gains and Losses**
**Skill: Recognition**
47. Gains from forward contracts to hedge translation exposure are taxable whereas losses from hedging translation exposure are not.

a. True
b. False

**Topic: MNE Hedging Practices**
**Skill: Conceptual**
48. Multinational enterprises always completely hedge translation exposure.

a. True
b. False

**Topic: FASB-52**
**Skill: Recognition**
49. When using FASB-52, translated gains and losses due to changes in foreign currency values are usually reported as ________________.

a. gains (losses) due to foreign exchange
b. net income (loss)
c. stockholder equity
d. none of the above

**Topic: Translation Exposure**
**Skill: Conceptual**
50. Which of the following firms would NOT bear risk caused by translation exposure?

a. A U.S based manufacturing firm with a fully owned subsidiary that generates earnings in Japan. The subsidiary always keeps and reinvests the earnings.
b. A U.S. based retailer with a fully owned subsidiary in Canada that generates losses in Canada that the parent firm occasionally covers.
c. A U.S. based firm with a subsidiary in Britain that occasionally remits earnings to the parent firm.
d. All of the above are subject to translation exposure.

## Essay Questions:

1. The two methods for the translation of foreign subsidiary financial statements are the current rate and temporal methods. Briefly, describe how each of these methods translates the foreign subsidiary financial statements into the parent company's consolidated statements. Identify when each technique should be used and the major advantage(s) of each.

**Answer**

The current rate method translates almost all line items from the foreign subsidiary to the parent consolidated statements at the current exchange rate. This is the most commonly used method in the world today. Assets and liabilities are translated at current exchange rate and items found on the income statement are translated at the actual exchange rate on the date of transaction, or as an average over the statement period where appropriate. Equity accounts are translated at historical costs.

Any gains or loses caused by translation adjustments are typically placed into a special reserve account (such as a CTA). Thus, gains or losses do not go through the income statement and do not increase the volatility of net income. This is perhaps the biggest advantage to using the current rate method.

By contrast, the temporal method assumes that several individual financial statement items are periodically restated to reflect their market value. The temporal method translates individual line items based on monetary/nonmonetary criteria where monetary assets such as cash and marketable securities are translated at current exchange rates, but nonmonetary assets such as fixed assets are translated at historical rates. The gains or losses that result from translation remeasurement are recorded on the consolidated income statement and impact upon the volatility of net income. The temporal method of using historical costs may be more consistent with the practice of carrying domestic items at cost on the financial statements.

2. Describe a balance sheet hedge and give at least two examples of when such a hedge could be justified.

**Answer**

A balance sheet hedge attempts to equalize the amount of assets and liabilities of a foreign subsidiary exposed to translation risk. Thus, the gain to the firm from a change in exchange rates will be perfectly offset by an equal and opposite loss. Firms may engage in balance sheet hedges under conditions of hyperinflation, or when the subsidiary is about to be liquidated and the value of the CTA account would be realized. The author on page 16 lists other examples.

## Chapter 10: Translation Exposure
## Multiple Choice Answer Key:

| | | | | | | | | | |
|---|---|---|---|---|---|---|---|---|---|
| 1 | C | 11 | C | 21 | D | 31 | B | 41 | A |
| 2 | D | 12 | D | 22 | B | 32 | A | 42 | C |
| 3 | B | 13 | C | 23 | C | 33 | A | 43 | D |
| 4 | A | 14 | A | 24 | D | 34 | B | 44 | B |
| 5 | A | 15 | B | 25 | C | 35 | C | 45 | A |
| 6 | A | 16 | D | 26 | B | 36 | D | 46 | B |
| 7 | B | 17 | A | 27 | A | 37 | C | 47 | A |
| 8 | C | 18 | C | 28 | D | 38 | D | 48 | B |
| 9 | D | 19 | A | 29 | C | 39 | A | 49 | C |
| 10 | B | 20 | B | 30 | D | 40 | B | 50 | D |

# Chapter 11
# Global Cost and Availability of Capital

**Topic: Illiquid and Segmented Markets**
**Skill: Recognition**

1. If a firm lies within a country with ________ or __________ domestic capital markets, it can achieve lower global cost and greater availability of capital with a properly designed and implemented strategy to participate in international capital markets.

    a. liquid; segmented
    b. liquid; large
    c. illiquid; segmented
    d. large; illiquid

**Topic: Cost of Capital**
**Skill: Recognition**

2. Other things equal, a firm that must obtain its long-term debt and equity in a highly illiquid domestic securities market will probably have a _____________.

    a. relatively low cost of capital
    b. relatively high cost of capital
    c. relatively average cost of capital
    d. cost of capital that we cannot estimate from this question

**Topic: Cost of Capital**
**Skill: Recognition**

3. Relatively high costs of capital are more likely to occur in ___________.

    a. highly illiquid domestic securities markets
    b. highly liquid domestic securities markets
    c. unsegmented domestic securities markets
    d. none of the above

**Topic: Reasons for a High Cost of Capital**
**Skill: Recognition**

4. Reasons that firms that find themselves with relatively high costs of capital include:

    a. The firms reside in emerging countries with undeveloped capital markets.
    b. The firms are too small to easily gain access to their own national securities market.
    c. The firms are family owned and they choose not to access public markets and lose control of the firm.
    d. All of the above.

**Topic: Segmented Markets**
**Skill: Recognition**
5. A national securities market is segmented if the required rate of return on securities in that market differs from comparable securities traded in other, unsegmented markets.

a. True
b. False

**Topic: Factors of Segmented Markets**
**Skill: Recognition**
6. Which of the following is NOT a contributing factor to the segmentation of capital markets?

a. Excessive regulatory control
b. Perceived political risk
c. Anticipated foreign exchange risk
d. All of the above are contributing factors

**Topic: Factors of Segmented Markets**
**Skill: Recognition**
7. Which of the following is NOT a contributing factor to the segmentation of capital markets?

a. Lack of transparency
b. Asymmetric availability of information
c. Insider trading
d. All of the above are contributing factors

**Topic: WACC**
**Skill: Recognition**
8. Which of the following is NOT a key variable in the weighted average cost of capital (WACC) equation?

a. The market value of equity.
b. The market value of debt.
c. The risk-free rate of return.
d. The marginal tax rate.

**Topic: WACC**
**Skill: Recognition**
9. The weighted average cost of capital (WACC) is

a. the required rate of return for all of a firm's capital investment projects.
b. the required rate of return for a firm's average risk projects.
c. not applicable for use by MNE.
d. equal to13%.

**Topic: WACC**
**Skill: Recognition**
10. Which of the following is NOT a key variable in the weighted average cost of capital (WACC) equation?

a. The before tax cost of debt.
b. The risk-adjusted cost of equity.
c. The beta of the market portfolio.
d. The total market value of the firm's securities.

**Topic: WACC**
**Skill: Conceptual**
11. Other things equal, an increase in the firm's tax rate will increase the WACC for a firm that has both debt and equity financing.

a. True
b. False

**Topic: CAPM**
**Skill: Conceptual**
12. The capital asset pricing model (CAPM) is an approach

a. to determine the price of equity capital.
b. used by marketers to determine the price of saleable product.
c. can be applied only to domestic markets.
d. none of the above.

**Topic: CAPM**
**Skill: Recognition**
13. Which of the following is NOT a key variable in the equation for the capital asset pricing model?

a. The risk-free rate of interest.
b. The expected rate of return on the market portfolio.
c. The marginal tax rate.
d. All are important components of the CAPM.

**Topic: Systematic Risk**
**Skill: Recognition**

14. _______________ risk is a function of the variability of expected returns of the firm's stock relative to the market index and the measure of correlation between the expected returns of the firm and the market.

a. Systematic
b. Unsystematic
c. Total
d. Diversifiable

**Topic: Systematic Risk**
**Skill: Recognition**

15. Systematic risk

a. is the standard deviation of a securities returns.
b. is measured with beta.
c. is measured with standard deviation.
d. none of the above.

**Topic: Beta**
**Skill: Conceptual**

16. If a firm's expected returns are more volatile than the market, it will have a beta less than 1.0.

a. True
b. False

**Topic: Cost of Debt**
**Skill: Recognition**

17. Which of the following is generally unnecessary in measuring the cost of debt?

a. A forecast of future interest rates.
b. The proportions of the various classes of debt a firm proposes to use.
c. The corporate income tax rate.
d. All of the above are necessary for measuring the coast of debt.

**Topic: Cost of Debt**
**Skill: Conceptual**

18. The after-tax cost of debt is found by

a. dividing the before-tax cost of debt by (1 – the corporate tax rate).
b. subtracting (1 – the corporate tax rate) from the before-tax cost of debt.
c. multiplying the before-tax cost of debt by (1 – the corporate tax rate).
d. subtracting the corporate tax rate from the before-tax cost of debt.

**Topic: WACC**
**Skill: Conceptual**
19. The WACC is usually used as the risk-adjusted required rate of return for new projects that are of the same average risk as the firm's existing projects.

a. True
b. False

**Topic: Beta**
**Skill: Conceptual**
20. A firm whose equity has a beta of 1.0

a. has greater systematic risk than the market portfolio.
b. stands little chance of surviving in the international financial market place.
c. has less systematic risk than the market portfolio.
d. None of the above is true.

**Topic: Market Risk Premium**
**Skill: Recognition**
21. One of the elegant beauties of the international equity markets is that over the last 100 or so years, the average market risk premium is almost identical across major industrial countries.

a. True
b. False

**Topic: The Market Risk Premium**
**Skill: Recognition**
22. The difference between the expected (or required) return for the market portfolio and the risk-free rate of return is referred to as _______________.

a. beta
b. the geometric mean
c. the market risk premium
d. the arithmetic mean

**Topic: Geometric and Arithmetic Mean**
**Skill: Recognition**
23. In general the geometric mean will be _________ the arithmetic mean for a series of returns.

a. less than
b. greater than
c. equal to
d. greater than or equal to

**Topic: Arithmetic and Geometric Average Returns**
**Skill: Analytical**
24. The beginning share price for a security over a three-year period was $50. Subsequent year-end prices were $62, $$58 and $64. The arithmetic average annual rate of return and the geometric average annual rate of return for this stock was

a. 9.30% and 8.78% respectively.
b. 9.30% and 7.89% respectively.
c. 9.30% and 7.03% respectively.
d. 9.30% and 6.37% respectively.

**Topic: Cost of Equity**
**Skill: Conceptual**
25. If a company fails to accurately predict it's cost of equity, then

a. the firm's wacc will also be inaccurate.
b. the firm may not be using the proper interest rate to estimate NPV.
c. the firm my incorrectly accept or reject projects based on decisions made using the cost of capital computed with an incorrect cost of equity.
d. all of the above are true.

**Topic: Investment Objectives**
**Skill: Conceptual**
26. The primary goal of both domestic and international portfolio managers is

a. to maximize return for a given level of risk, or minimize risk for a given level of return.
b. minimize the number of unique securities held in their portfolio.
c. maximize their wacc.
d. all of the above.

**Topic: Portfolio Diversification**
**Skill: Conceptual**
27. Internationally diversified portfolios often have a lower rate of return and almost always have a higher level of portfolio risk than their domestic counterparts.

a. True
b. False

**Topic: Portfolio Diversification**
**Skill: Recognition**
28. Which of the following is NOT a portfolio diversification technique used by portfolio managers?

a. Diversify by type of security.
b. Diversify by the size of capitalization of the securities held.
c. Diversify by country.
d. All of the above are diversification techniques.

**Topic: Market Segmentation**
**Skill: Recognition**
29. If all capital markets are fully integrated, securities of comparable expected return and risk should have the same required rate of return in each national market after adjusting for ______________________.

a. time of day and language requirements
b. political risk and time lags
c. foreign exchange risk and political risk
d. foreign exchange risk and the spot rate

**Topic: Market Segmentation**
**Skill: Recognition**
30. Capital market segmentation is a financial market imperfection caused mainly by

a. government constraints
b. institutional practices
c. investor perceptions
d. all of the above

**Topic: Market Segmentation**
**Skill: Recognition**
31. Capital market imperfections leading to financial market segmentation include:

a. Asymmetric information between domestic and foreign-based investors.
b. High securities transaction costs.
c. Foreign exchange risks.
d. All of the above.

**Topic: Market Segmentation**
**Skill: Recognition**
32. Capital market imperfections leading to financial market segmentation include:

a. Political risks.
b. Corporate governance differences.
c. Regulatory barriers.
d. All of the above.

**Topic: Market Efficiency**
**Skill: Conceptual**
33. Efficient capital markets

a. are an academic myth.
b. adjust prices slowly but surely to the arrival of new information.
c. reflect all available information in security prices and adjust quickly and accurately to the arrival of new information.
d. none of the above.

**Topic: Market Efficiency**
**Skill: Recognition**
34. Empirical test of market efficiency fail to show that most major national markets are reasonable efficient.

a. True
b. False

**Topic: MNEs**
**Skill: Recognition**
35. The authors refer to companies that have access to a __________ as MNEs, and firms without such access are identified as ________________.

a. global cost and availability of capital; domestic firms
b. large domestic capital market; geographically challenged
c. world financial markets; antiquated
d. none of the above

**Topic: Market Segmentation**
**Skill: Recognition**
36. The MNE can ___________ its _____________ by gaining access to markets that are more liquid and/or less segmented than its own.

a. increase; MCC
b. decrease; MCC
c. maintain; MRR
d. none of the above

**Topic: Market Segmentation**
**Skill: Recognition**
37. Several years ago the Danish equity market prohibited ownership of foreign securities thus few institutional analysts outside of Denmark bothered to follow Danish equity securities. This particular fact led to market segmentation due to __________.

a. taxation
b. political risk
c. asymmetric information
d. financial risk

**Topic: Market Segmentation**
**Skill: Recognition**
38. Until 1981 Danish equity securities were taxed at a capital gains rate of 50% for securities held for over two years, and at a speculative gains rate of 75% for securities held for under two years. This led to market segmentation caused by ________.

a. taxation
b. political risk
c. asymmetric information
d. financial risk

**Topic: MCC**
**Skill: Conceptual**
39. A MNEs marginal cost of capital is constant for considerable ranges in its capital budget, but this statement cannot be made for most domestic firms.

a. True
b. False

**Topic: Debt Ratios**
**Skill: Conceptual**
40. Theoretically, most MNEs should be in a position to support higher ________ than their domestic counterparts because their cash flows are diversified internationally.

a. equity ratios
b. debt ratios
c. temperatures
d. none of the above

**Topic: International Diversification**
**Skill: Recognition**
41. According to your authors, diversifying cash flows internationally may help MNEs reduce the variability of cash flows because

a. of a lack of competition among international firms.
b. of an offset to cash flow variability caused by exchange rate variability.
c. returns are not perfectly correlated between countries.
d. none of the above.

**Topic: MNE Bankruptcy**
**Skill: Recognition**
42. Because of the international diversification of cash flows, the risk of bankruptcy for MNEs is significantly lower than that for purely domestic firms.

a. True
b. False

**Topic: MNE Versus Domestic Firms**
**Skill: Conceptual**
43. Which of the following statements is NOT true regarding MNEs when compared to purely domestic firms?

a. MNEs tend to rely more on short and intermediate term debt.
b. MNEs have greater foreign exchange risk.
c. MNEs have greater costs of asymmetric information.
d. MNEs have higher agency costs.

**Topic: Systematic Risk**
**Skill: Conceptual**
44. Empirical research has found that systematic risk for MNEs is greater than that for their domestic counterparts. This could be due to

a. the fact that the increase in the correlation of returns between the market and the firm is less than the increase in the standard deviation of returns of the firm.
b. the fact that the decrease in the correlation of returns between the market and the firm is greater than the increase in the standard deviation of returns of the firm.
c. the reduction in the correlation of returns between the firm and the market is less than the increase in the variability of returns caused by factors such as asymmetric information, foreign exchange risk, and the like.
d. none of the above. Systematic risk is less for MNEs than for their domestic counterparts.

**Topic: Optimal Capital Budget**
**Skill: Recognition**
45. The optimal capital budget

a. occurs where the marginal cost of capital equals the marginal rate of return of he opportunity set of projects.
b. is typically larger for purely domestic firms than for MNEs.
c. is an illusion found only in international finance textbooks.
d. none of the above.

**Topic: Investment Opportunities**
**Skill: Recognition**
46. The opportunity set of projects is typically smaller for MNEs than for purely domestic firms because international markets are typically specialized niches.

a. True
b. False

**Topic: Cost of Capital**
**Skill: Recognition**
47. Empirical studies indicate that MNEs have higher costs of capital than purely domestic firms. This could be due to higher levels of ____________.

a. political risk
b. political risk
c. agency costs
d. all of he above

**Topic: Optimal Capital Structure**
**Skill: Recognition**
48. The optimal financial structure of multinational firms could differ from that of domestic firms because of:

a. political pressures on the host country.
b. the greater availability of capital to multinational firms.
c. the ability of multinational firms to diversify their cash flows internationally.
d. all of the above.

**Topic: International Capitalization**
**Skill: Conceptual**
49. The international availability of capital to MNEs

a. allows the firm to avoid income taxes.
b. allows the firm to shift tax payments to other counties.
c. allows the firm to lower their cost of equity, relative to domestic firms.
d. none of the above.

**Topic: International Diversification**
**Skill: Conceptual**
50. Which of the following does not constitute a benefit to the investor of diversifying internationally?

a. The relatively low degree of correlation between the world's stock markets.
b. The increase in the expected return from an internationally diversifies investment.
c. A lower total level of nondiversifiable risk.
d. All of the above are benefits of international diversification.

## Essay Questions:

1. What do theory and empirical evidence say about capital structure and the cost of capital for MNEs versus their domestic counterparts?

**Answer**
In theory, MNEs should be able to support greater amounts of debt due to reduced variability of cash flows brought about by diversification across countries. And, because of this reduced risk borne by MNEs, they should also have a lower cost of capital. However, empirical research finds that domestic firms tend to use greater amounts of short and intermediate debt than do MNEs and that the cost of capital is greater for MNEs due to increased agency costs, political risk, exchange rate risk, and asymmetric information.

2. What are the components of the weighted average cost of capital (WACC) and how do they differ for an MNE compared to a purely domestic firm?

**Answer**
The WACC considers the proportion of weight of assets financed with debt and the proportion financed with equity. It also looks at the costs of debt and equity financing and the firm's corporate tax rate. The difficulty of such a computation is compounded for an MNE because there are several additional sources of debt financing with different required rates of return and tax rates for an MNE than for a domestic firm. Also, equity may be sourced in several different markets and subject to several different regulations of several different countries. Adding regulatory oversight, multiple sourcing locations, and

differing investor expectations may significantly complicate the process of determining an MNE's cost of capital.

**Chapter 11: Global Cost and Availability of Capital**
**Multiple Choice Answer Key:**

| | | | | | | | | | |
|---|---|---|---|---|---|---|---|---|---|
| 1 | C | 11 | B | 21 | B | 31 | D | 41 | C |
| 2 | B | 12 | A | 22 | C | 32 | D | 42 | B |
| 3 | A | 13 | C | 23 | A | 33 | C | 43 | A |
| 4 | D | 14 | A | 24 | D | 34 | B | 44 | C |
| 5 | A | 15 | B | 25 | D | 35 | A | 45 | A |
| 6 | D | 16 | B | 26 | A | 36 | B | 46 | B |
| 7 | D | 17 | D | 27 | B | 37 | C | 47 | D |
| 8 | C | 18 | C | 28 | D | 38 | A | 48 | D |
| 9 | B | 19 | A | 29 | C | 39 | A | 49 | C |
| 10 | C | 20 | D | 30 | D | 40 | B | 50 | D |

# Chapter 12
# Sourcing Equity Globally

**Topic: Equity Sourcing**
**Skill: Recognition**

1. The choice of when and how to source equity globally is usually aided early on by the advice of

   a. an investment banker.
   b. your stock broker.
   c. a commercial banker.
   d. an underwriter.

**Topic: Investment Banking**
**Skill: Conceptual**

2. Investment banking services include WHICH of the following?

   a. Advising when a security should be cross-listed.
   b. Preparation of stock prospectuses.
   c. Help to determine the price of the issue.
   d. All of the above.

**Topic: Raising Capital**
**Skill: Conceptual**

3. Most firms raise their initial capital in foreign markets.

   a. True
   b. False

**Topic: Global Equity Sourcing**
**Skill: Conceptual**

4. Which of the following is the typical order of sourcing capital abroad?

   a. An international bond issue, then cross listing the outstanding issues on other exchanges, then an international bond issue in the target market.
   b. An international bond issue in the target market then cross listing the outstanding issues on other exchanges, then an international bond issue.
   c. An international bond issue, then an international bond issue in the target market, then cross listing the outstanding issues on other exchanges.
   d. Cross listing the outstanding issues on other exchanges, then an international bond issue, then an international bond issue in the target market.

**Topic: Depositary Receipts**
**Skill: Recognition**
5. ____________ are negotiable certificates issued by a bank to represent he underlying shares of stock, which are held in trust at a foreign custodian bank.

a. Negotiable CDs
b. International mutual funds
c. Depositary receipts
d. Eurodeposits

**Topic: Global Depositary Receipts**
**Skill: Recognition**
6. Depositary receipts traded outside the United States are called _________ depositary receipts.

a. Euro
b. Global
c. American
d. None of the above

**Topic: American Depositary Receipts**
**Skill: Recognition**
7. Each ADR represents __________ of the shares of the underlying foreign stock.

a. a multiple
b. 100
c. 1
d. ADRs have nothing to do with foreign stocks.

**Topic: American Depositary Receipts**
**Skill: Conceptual**
8. ADRs cannot be exchanged for the underlying shares of the foreign stock, therefore, there is no arbitrage cannot keep the prices in line with the foreign price of the stock.

a. True
b. False

**Topic: American Depositary Receipts**
**Skill: Recognition**

9. Which of the following is NOT an advantage of ASRs to U. S. shareholders?

a. Transfer of ownership is done in the U.S. in accordance with U.S. laws.
b. In the event of the death of the shareholder, the estate does not go through a foreign court.
c. Settlement for trading is generally faster in the United States.
d. All of the above are advantages of ADRs.

**Topic: American Depositary Receipts**
**Skill: Recognition**

10. ADRs that are created at the request of a foreign firm wanting its shares traded in the United States are _____________.

a. facilitated
b. unfacilitated
c. sponsored
d. unsponsored

**Topic: American Depositary Receipts**
**Skill: Recognition**

11. Who pays the costs of creating a sponsored ADR?

a. The foreign firm shoes stocks underlie the ADR.
b. The U.S. bank creating the ADR.
c. Both the U.S. bank and the foreign firm.
d. The SEC since they require the regulation.

**Topic: American Depositary Receipts**
**Skill: Recognition**

12. An unsponsored ADR may be initiated without the approval of the foreign firm with the underlying stock.

a. True
b. False

**Topic: American Depositary Receipts**
**Skill: Recognition**

13. Level I ADRs trade primarily

    a. on the New York Stock Exchange.
    b. on the American Stock Exchange.
    c. over the counter or pink sheets.
    d. Level I ADRs typically do not trade at all, but instead are privately issued and held until maturity.

**Topic: American Depositary Receipts**
**Skill: Conceptual**

14. Level II ADRs must meet

    a. U.S. GAAP standards.
    b. home country accounting standards.
    c. both U.S. GAAP and home country standards.
    d. none of the above.

**Topic: American Depositary Receipts**
**Skill: Recognition**

15. Level ______ is the easiest standard to satisfy for issuing ADRs.

    a. 144a
    b. III
    c. II
    d. I

**Topic: American Depositary Receipts**
**Skill: Recognition**

16. Level III ADR commitment applies to

    a. firms that want to list existing shares on the NYSE.
    b. banks issuing foreign mutual funds.
    c. ADR issues of under $25,000.
    d. the sale of a new equity issued in the United States

**Topic: Cross Listing Equity Shares**
**Skill: Conceptual**

17. By cross listing and selling its shares on a foreign stock exchange a firm typically tries to accomplish which of the following?

    a. Improve the liquidity of its existing shares.
    b. Increase its share price.
    c. Increase the firm's visibility.
    d. All of the above.

**Topic: American Depositary Receipts**
**Skill: Conceptual**
18. ADRs are considered an effective way for firms to improve the liquidity of their stock, especially if the home market is small and illiquid.

a. True
b. False

**Topic: World Equity Markets**
**Skill: Recognition**
19. In order, the largest stock exchanges in the world based on market capitalization of the securities traded there are

a. London, NYSE, Tokyo, and Nasdaq
b. NYSE, Nasdaq, Tokyo, and London
c. Nasdaq, Tokyo, NYSE, and London
d. Tokyo, NYSE, Nasdaq, and London

**Topic: World Equity Markets**
**Skill: Recognition**
20. The stock exchange with the greatest value of shares traded is _________.

a. NYSE
b. Tokyo
c. Nasdaq
d. London

**Topic: World Equity Markets**
**Skill: Recognition**
21. For the worlds largest equity markets, the concentration of market value among the largest 5% of the firms listed on each exchange is typically between

a. 5% – 20%
b. 25% - 40%
c. 45% - 60%
d. 60% - 75%

**Topic: World Equity Markets**
**Skill: Recognition**
22. The Tokyo exchange is the number one choice of firms looking to gain liquidity by cross-listing their equity securities.

a. True
b. False

**Topic: World Equity Markets**
**Skill: Recognition**
23. Transaction costs for trading equity securities as measured by the bid-ask spreads are lowest on which exchange?

a. NYSE
b. Nasdaq
c. London
d. Tokyo

**Topic: World Equity Markets**
**Skill: Recognition**
24. The number of foreign firms traded on the London exchange is _________ than the number traded on the NYSE, and the costs of listing and disclosure in London are _______ those for the NYSE.

a. less than; less than
b. less than; greater than
c. greater than; less than
d. greater than; greater than

**Topic: Market Liquidity**
**Skill: Conceptual**
25. The least liquid stock markets as identified by the authors offer little liquidity for their own domestic firms, and are of little value to foreign firms.

a. True
b. False

**Topic: Market Liquidity**
**Skill: Conceptual**
26. Which one of the following characteristics does NOT contribute to overall market liquidity?

a. significant market making activities
b. reduced transaction costs
c. effective crisis management
d. All of the above contribute to efficient markets.

**Topic: Empirical Evidence of Cross-Listing**
**Skill: Recognition**
27. Your authors note several empirical studies that have found

a. no share price effect for foreign firms that cross-list on major U.S. exchanges.
b. a positive share price effect for foreign firms that cross-list on major U.S. exchanges.
c. a negative share price effect for foreign firms that cross-list on major U.S. exchanges.
d. none of the above.

**Topic: Empirical Evidence of Cross-Listing**
**Skill: Conceptual**
28. The authors note empirical evidence that shows cross-listing foreign shares of stock on U.S. exchanges has a positive stock price effect. __________ for the listing of ADRs.

a. There is no stock price reaction
b. There is a negative stock price reaction
c. There is a positive stock price reaction
d. None of the above is true.

**Topic: Empirical Evidence of Cross-Listing**
**Skill: Conceptual**
29. Empirical evidence shows that new issues of equity by domestic firms in the U.S. market typically has a _________ stock price reaction and new equity issues in the U.S. markets by foreign firms with segmented domestic markets have a _________ stock price reaction.

a. negative; negative
b. positive; negative
c. negative; positive
d. positive; positive

**Topic: Reasons for Cross-Listing**
**Skill: Conceptual**
30. In addition to gaining liquidity, which of the following could also be considered a legitimate reason for cross-listing equity?

a. Enhance a firm's local image.
b. Become more familiar with the local financial community.
c. Get better local press coverage.
d. All of the above.

**Topic: SEC Disclosure Requirements**
**Skill: Recognition**
31. For the most part, U.S. SEC disclosure requirements are _________ stringent than other, non-U.S. equity market rules.

a. more
b. less
c. as equally
d. none of the above

**Topic: Disclosure Requirements**
**Skill: Recognition**
32. According to the U.S. school of thought, the worldwide trend toward fuller and more standardized disclosure rules should _______ the cost of equity capital.

a. increase
b. decrease
c. have no impact on
d. none of the above

**Topic: Disclosure Requirements**
**Skill: Recognition**
33. Another school of thought about the worldwide trend toward fuller and more standardized disclosure rules is that the cost of equity capital The cost of U.S. level disclosure

a. chases away potential listers of equity.
b. is an onerous costly burden.
c. leads to fewer foreign firms cross listing in U.S. equity markets.
d. all of the above.

**Topic: Alternative Equity Sources**
**Skill: Recognition**
34. Which of the following were NOT identified by the authors as an alternative instrument to source equity in global markets?

a. Sale of a directed public share issue to investors in a target market.
b. Private placements under SEC rule 144a.
c. Sale of shares to private equity funds.
d. All of the above.

**Topic: Directed Public Issue**
**Skill: Recognition**

35. A ____________________ is defined as one that is targeted at investors in a single country and underwritten in whole or part by investment institutions from that country.

a. SEC rule 144a placement
b. directed public share issue
c. Euroequity public issue
d. Strategic alliance

**Topic: Euro Equity Market**
**Skill: Recognition**

36. The term "euro" as used in the euro equity market implies

a. the issuers are located in Europe.
b. the investors are located in Europe.
c. both a and b.
d. none of the above.

**Topic: Privatizing Public Firms**
**Skill: Conceptual**

37. Empirical evidence has found that on average public firms that have been privatized by issuing public equity have

a. improved profitability.
b. higher debt levels.
c. lower real sales.
d. all of the above.

**Topic: Privatizing Public Firms**
**Skill: Conceptual**

38. Empirical evidence has found that on average public firms that have been privatized by issuing public equity have

a. lowered capital investment levels.
b. decreased efficiency.
c. expanded their employment.
d. all of the above.

**Topic: SEC Rule 144A**
**Skill: Recognition**
39. SEC rule 144A permits institutional buyers to trade privately placed securities without the previous holding periods restrictions and without requiring SEC registration.

a. True
b. False

**Topic: Private Equity Funds**
**Skill: Conceptual**
40. Private equity funds (PEF) differ from traditional venture capital (VC) funds in that

a. VC operate mainly in lesser-developed countries while PEF do not.
b. VC typically invest in family business whereas PEF do not.
c. VC is almost unavailable to emerging markets while PEF capital is available.
d. all of the above are true.

**Topic: Strategic Alliances**
**Skill: Conceptual**
41. Strategic alliances are normally formed by firms that expect to gain synergies from which of the following?

a. Economies of scale
b. Economies of scope
c. Complementary marketing
d. All of the above

**Topic: Largest Equity Market**
**Skill: Recognition**
42. The largest equity market in the world as measured by market value or annual stock turnover is in

a. Germany
b. The United States
c. Japan
d. Britain

**Topic: Disclosure Requirements**
**Skill: Conceptual**

43. The reason more foreign firms do not sell equity securities in the U.S. and list on the NYSE is because of

a. the threat of confiscation.
b. detailed U.S. disclosure rules.
c. the relative inefficiency of U.S. equity markets.
d. the foreign exchange risk of listing in U.S. dollars.

**Topic: Cross Listed Shares**
**Skill: Conceptual**

44. An MNE may cross list its shares on a foreign stock exchange so that it can

a. create a secondary market so that shares may be used to compensate top local managers.
b. create a secondary market so that shares can be used to acquire local firms.
c. increase the firm's visibility to its customers and employees.
d. accomplish all of the above.

**Topic: Equity Returns**
**Skill: Conceptual**

45. The expected return on equities is greater than the expected return on debt in part because

a. debt securities are services prior to equity securities.
b. interest payments to bondholders are generally made only if the firm makes a profit.
c. only a small portion of return to equity comes from increased capital appreciation.
d. none of the above.

**Topic: ADRs**
**Skill: Recognition**

46. Which of the following is NOT a motivation for the use of ADRs?

a. To reduce liquidity and increase the profitability of the firm.
b. To reduce a firm's visibility and avoid political scrutiny.
c. To increase share price by overcoming mis-pricing in a segmented and illiquid home market.
d. All of the above are motivations to use ADRs.

**Topic: Cross Listing Shares**
**Skill: Recognition**
47. Which of the following is NOT a barrier to cross listing shares?

a. Fixed income securities such as bonds are not traded in the subject market.
b. Investor relations
c. Disclosure requirements
d. All are barriers to cross listing shares

**Topic: Private Placement**
**Skill: Recognition**
48. The sale of a security to a small set of qualified institutional buyers is called a

a. depositary receipt.
b. private placement.
c. fixed income security.
d. none of the above.

**Topic: ADRs**
**Skill: Recognition**
49. Negotiable certificates issued by a U.S. bank in the United States to represent the underlying shares of stock, which are held in a trust at a custodian bank in a foreign country, are called __________.

a. SDRs
b. FDRs
c. ADRs
d. IOUs

**Topic: Equity Liquidity**
**Skill: Recognition**
50. Which of the following is not a contributing factor to an individual equity's liquidity?

a. Depth of capital availability.
b. Crisis management capabilities of the market itself.
c. The degree to which the company is actually known and followed in the market.
d. All of the above.

## Essay Questions:

1. ADRs are a popular investment tool for many U.S. investors. In recent years several alternatives for investing in foreign equity securities have become available for U.S. investors, yet ADRs remain popular. Define what an ADR is and provide at least three examples of the advantages they may hold over alternative foreign investment vehicles for U.S. investors.

**Answer**
Depositary receipts are negotiable certificates issued by a bank to represent the underlying shares of stock held in trust at a foreign custodian bank. Those receipts traded in the U.S. and denominated in dollars are called American depositary receipts (ADR). Because ADRs can be exchanged for the underlying foreign security, arbitrage keeps the prices in line. Even though U.S. investors can invest directly into some foreign equity markets, ADRs do offer some technical advantages. Among those advantages are that dividends are received in dollars rather than a foreign currency, ADRs are in registered form rather than bearer form, transfer of ownership is done in accordance with U.S. laws, and in the event of death, probate is in the U.S. and not abroad. Taxes are easier, trading costs are typically lower, and settlement is also faster.

2. What are the two schools of thought regarding the worldwide trend toward increased financial disclosure by publicly traded firms. Explain which school of thought you hold to and why.

**Answer**
The student must give his/her own opinion and supporting background. In either case the following should be noted: Increased disclosure should decrease uncertainty thus increasing stock price. However, increased disclosure requirements result in increased costs in the form of initial preparation of financial statements, on-going costs associated with regular development of financial statements, and the costs of gathering and distributing information about the form on an on-going basis. As the authors state, disclosure is a two-edged sword.

## Chapter 12: Sourcing Equity Globally
## Multiple Choice Answer Key:

| | | | | | | | | | |
|---|---|---|---|---|---|---|---|---|---|
| 1 | A | 11 | A | 21 | B | 31 | A | 41 | D |
| 2 | D | 12 | B | 22 | C | 32 | B | 42 | B |
| 3 | B | 13 | C | 23 | A | 33 | D | 43 | B |
| 4 | C | 14 | A | 24 | D | 34 | D | 44 | D |
| 5 | C | 15 | D | 25 | D | 35 | B | 45 | A |
| 6 | B | 16 | D | 26 | A | 36 | D | 46 | C |
| 7 | A | 17 | D | 27 | B | 37 | A | 47 | A |
| 8 | B | 18 | A | 28 | D | 38 | C | 48 | B |
| 9 | D | 19 | B | 29 | C | 39 | A | 49 | C |
| 10 | C | 20 | C | 30 | D | 40 | C | 50 | D |

# Chapter 13
# Financial Structure and International Debt

**Topic: Optimal Capital Structure**
**Skill: Recognition**
1. Which financial economists are most closely associated with the financial theory of optimal capital structure?

a. Modogliani and Miller
b. Fama, Fisher, Jensen, and Roll
c. Black and Scholes
d. Markowitz and Sharpe

**Topic: Optimal Capital Structure Theory**
**Skill: Conceptual**
2. Financial theory has at last provided us with a single optimal capital structure for domestic firms.

a. True
b. False

**Topic: Cost of Capital**
**Skill: Conceptual**
3. For most firms, the cost of capital decreases to a low point as the firm ________ debt financing. At some point beyond this optimal level, the cost of capital increases as the amount of debt ______________.

a. decreases, increases
b. decreases; decreases
c. increases; increases
d. increases; decreases

**Topic: Cost of Debt**
**Skill: Recognition**
4. One of the most important factors in making debt less expensive than equity is

a. the tax deductibility of depreciation.
b. the tax deductibility of equity.
c. the tax deductibility of dividends.
d. the tax deductibility of interest.

**Topic: Cost of Debt**
**Skill: Recognition**
5. Which of the following is NOT a factor offsetting the tax advantage of debt as a source of financing?

a. Increased agency costs
b. Increased probability of financial distress (bankruptcy) due to fixed interest payments
c. Alternative tax shields to those supplied by interest payments
d. All of the above

**Topic: Optimal Capital Structure**
**Skill: Recognition**
6. Most financial theorists believe that the optimal capital structure is a _________ with a debt to total value ratio somewhere around _____________.

a. Point; 50%
b. Point; 25%
c. Range; 30% – 60%
d. Range; 10% - 40%

**Topic: Optimal Capital Structure**
**Skill: Recognition**
7. Not all affirms have the same optimal capital structure. Factors that might influence a firm's capital structure include:

a. the industry in which it operates.
b. volatility of its sales and operating income.
c. the collateral value of its assets.
d. all of the above.

**Topic: Optimal Capital Structure**
**Skill: Recognition**
8. The domestic theory of optimal capital structure does not need to be modifies for MNEs.

a. True
b. False

**Topic: Illiquid and Segmented Markets**
**Skill: Conceptual**
9. MNEs situated in countries with small illiquid and segmented markets are most like

a. small domestic U.S. firms in that they must rely on internally generated funds and bank borrowing.
b. large U.S. MNEs in that they are all MNEs and have worldwide markets and sources of financing.
c. small domestic U.S. firms in that they have a strong niche market in the U.S.
d. none of the above is true.

**Topic: MNE Debt Ratios**
**Skill: Conceptual**
10. In theory, the MNE should support _________ debt ratios than a purely domestic firm because their cash flows are _______________.

a. lower; more stable due to international diversification
b. lower; less stable due to international diversification
c. higher; more stable due to international diversification
d. higher; less stable due to international diversification

**Topic: International Diversification**
**Skill: Conceptual**
11. Portfolio diversification of domestic firms reduces risk because cash flows are not perfectly correlated. The same reasoning is often argued for MNEs diversifying into international markets.

a. True
b. False

**Topic: Cost of Debt**
**Skill: Analytical**
12. TropiKana Inc. has just borrowed $1,000,000 to make improvements to an Italian fruit plantation and processing plant. If the interest rate is 6.00% per year, how much interest will they pay in the first year?

a. $6,000
b. $60,000
c. $600,000
d. €60,000

**Topic: Foreign Exchange Risk**
**Skill: Analytical**
13. TropiKana Inc. has just borrowed €1,000,000 to make improvements to an Italian fruit plantation and processing plant. If the interest rate is 5.50% per year and the Euro depreciates against the dollar from $1/€ at the time the loan was made to $.95/€ at the end of the first year, how much interest will TropiKana pay at the end of the first year (rounded)?

a. $55,000
b. €52,250
c. $52,250
d. $57,900

**Topic: Foreign Exchange Risk**
**Skill: Analytical**
14. TropiKana Inc. has just borrowed €1,000,000 to make improvements to an Italian fruit plantation and processing plant. If the interest rate is 5.50% per year and the Euro appreciates against the dollar from $1/€ at the time the loan was made to $1.05/€ at the end of the first year, how much interest will TropiKana pay at the end of the first year (rounded)?

a. $55,000
b. $57,750
c. $52,250
d. $57,900

**Topic: Foreign Exchange Risk**
**Skill: Analytical**
15. TropiKana Inc. has just borrowed €1,000,000 to make improvements to an Italian fruit plantation and processing plant. If the interest rate is 5.50% per year and the Euro appreciates against the dollar from $1/€ at the time the loan was made to $1.05/€ at the end of the first year, how much interest and principle will TropiKana pay at the end of the first year if they repay the entire loan plus interest (rounded)?

a. $1,107,750
b. €1,107,750
c. $1,055,000
d. $1,004,760

**Topic: Foreign Exchange Risk**
**Skill: Analytical**

16. TropiKana Inc. has just borrowed €1,000,000 to make improvements to an Italian fruit plantation and processing plant. If the interest rate is 5.50% per year and the Euro depreciates against the dollar from $1/€ at the time the loan was made to $.95/€ at the end of the first year, how much interest and principle will TropiKana pay at the end of the first year if they repay the entire loan plus interest (rounded)?

   a. $1,110,525
   b. $1,055,000
   c. €1,002,250
   d. $1,002,250

**Topic: Foreign Exchange Risk**
**Skill: Analytical**

17. TropiKana Inc. has just borrowed €1,000,000 to make improvements to an Italian fruit plantation and processing plant. If the interest rate is 5.50% per year and the Euro appreciates against the dollar from $1/€ at the time the loan was made to $1.05/€ at the end of the first year, what is the before tax cost of capital if the firm repays the entire loan plus interest (rounded)?

   a. 5.00%
   b. 5.50%
   c. 10.50%
   d. 10.78%

**Topic: Foreign Exchange Risk**
**Skill: Analytical**

18. TropiKana Inc. has just borrowed €1,000,000 to make improvements to an Italian fruit plantation and processing plant. If the interest rate is 5.50% per year and the Euro appreciates against the dollar from $1/€ at the time the loan was made to $1.05/€ at the end of the first year, what is the after-tax cost of capital if the firm repays the entire loan plus interest and has a 30% marginal tax bracket (rounded)?

   a. 7.54%
   b. 7.50%
   c. 5.50%
   d. 3.85%

**Topic: Foreign Exchange Risk**
**Skill: Conceptual**
19. A significant advantage of borrowing foreign currency-denominated bonds is that the borrower need not worry about relative changes in the value of the home currency.

a. True
b. False

**Topic: International Capital Structure Norms**
**Skill: Recognition**
20. For firms to raise capital in international markets, it is more important to adhere to capital structure ratios similar to those found in the United States and United Kingdom than to those in the firm's home country.

a. True
b. False

**Topic: Cost of Capital**
**Skill: Conceptual**
21. If we accept the MNE objective of minimizing the consolidated cost of capital then

a. the subsidiary's cost of capital is relevant only to the extent that it affects this overall goal.
b. the objective of minimizing the cost of capital for each individual subsidiary may not be appropriate.
c. the value of the MNE as a whole should be maximized.
d. all of the above.

**Topic: International Debt Ratio Factors**
**Skill: Recognition**
22. Of the following, which is NOT identified by the authors as a country-specific environmental variable key to determining debt ratios?

a. Historical development
b. Taxation
c. Corporate governance
d. All of the above are key variables identified by the authors.

**Topic: International Debt Ratio Factors**
**Skill: Recognition**
23. Of the following, which is NOT identified by the authors as a country-specific environmental variable key to determining debt ratios?

a. Agency costs
b. Government regulations
c. The existence of a viable corporate bond market
d. All of the above are key variables identified by the authors.

**Topic: Localization**
**Skill: Recognition**
24. Of the following, which is NOT considered to be an advantage to MNEs of having a financial structure adhere to local debt norms?

a. A localized financial structure reduces criticism of foreign subsidiaries that have previously used a different capital structure.
b. A localized financial structure helps management evaluate return on equity investment relative to local competitors in the same industry.
c. MNE have a competitive advantage over the locals, thus by using the local capital structure, the MNE is even stronger
d. All of the above are noted as advantages to having a localized capital structure.

**Topic: Localization**
**Skill: Recognition**
25. Of the following, which is NOT considered to be a disadvantage to MNEs of having a financial structure adhere to local debt norms?

a. Why adhere to local standards if, as an MNE, the firm has important competitive advantages relating to capital structure?
b. Adhering to local standards may push the MNEs consolidated financial ratios out of the optimal range.
c. A localized financial structure makes it difficult for management to compare operating results with those of local competitors.
d. All of the above are noted as disadvantages to having a localized capital structure.

**Topic: Capital Structure**
**Skill: Conceptual**
26. The MNE in an effort to minimize the cost of external funds should choose ________ funds to minimize __________.

a. internal; debt financing
b. internal; taxes and political risk
c. external; debt financing
d. external; taxes and political risk

**Topic: Subsidiary Sources of Internal Financing**
**Skill: Recognition**
27. Of the following, which is NOT an internal source of financing for the foreign subsidiary?

a. Equity in the form of cash from the parent firm.
b. Equity in the form of real goods from the parent?
c. Debt in the form of loans from the same commercial bank used by the parent.
d. All of the above are internal sources of financing for the foreign subsidiary.

**Topic: Subsidiary Sources of Internal Financing**
**Skill: Conceptual**
28. Internal sources of funds for a foreign subsidiary of a MNE may come from the parent company but not from a sister subsidiary. Funding from sister subsidiaries are considered external funding.

a. True
b. False

**Topic: Subsidiary Sources of External Financing**
**Skill: Recognition**
29. Of the following, which is NOT an external source of financing for the foreign subsidiary?

a. Borrowing from sister subsidiaries.
b. Borrowing from commercial banks in the parent country.
c. Selling new stock to local shareholders.
d. All of the above are external sources of financing for the foreign subsidiary.

**Topic: Subsidiary External Financing**
**Skill: Conceptual**
30. Obtaining local currency debt obligations is particularly attractive to a MNE if the subsidiary has

a. substantial accounts payable in the local currency.
b. substantial financial obligations in foreign currency units.
c. substantial accounts receivable in the local currency.
d. all of the above.

**Topic: Eurocurrencies**
**Skill: Recognition**
31. __________ are domestic currencies of one country on deposit in a second country.

a. LIBORs
b. Eurocurrencies
c. Federal funds
d. Discount window deposits

**Topic: Eurocurrencies**
**Skill: Recognition**
32. Eurocurrencies are NOT the new currency developed for the common European currency.

a. True
b. False

**Topic: Eurocurrencies**
**Skill: Recognition**
33. Of the following, which was NOT cited by the authors as a valuable function provided by the Eurocurrency market?

a. Eurocurrency deposits are an efficient and convenient money market device for holding excess corporate liquidity.
b. Eurocurrency deposits are a tool used by the Federal Reserve to regulate the money supply of countries that peg their currency against the U.S. dollar.
c. The Eurocurrency market is a major source of short-term bank loans to finance corporate working capital needs.
d. All of the above were cited by the authors.

**Topic: Eurobanks**
**Skill: Recognition**
34. Eurobanks are

a. banks where Eurocurrencies are deposited.
b. major world banks that conduct a Eurocurrency business in addition to normal banking activities.
c. financial intermediaries that simultaneously bid for time deposits in and make loans in a currency other than that of the currency of where it is located.
d. All of the above are descriptions of a Eurobank.

**Topic: Eurocurrencies**
**Skill: Recognition**
35. The modern Eurodollar market has been operating since

a. post-WWI
b. the great depression of the 1930s
c. post-WWII
d. the mid 1970s when the Bretton Woods standard of fixed currency exchange rates was eliminated.

**Topic: Eurocurrencies**
**Skill: Recognition**
36. The Eurocurrency market continues to thrive because it is a large international money market relatively free of governmental regulation and interference.

a. True
b. False

**Topic: Euronotes**
**Skill: Conceptual**
37. If a MNE needed to obtain, outside of its domestic market, medium-term credit with an established secondary market it would most likely pursue ____________.

a. international bank loans
b. syndicated credits
c. some type of euronote
d. the international bond market

**Topic: Eurocredits**
**Skill: Conceptual**
38. Eurocredits are

a. bank loans to MNEs and others denominated in a currency other than that of the country where the bank is located.
b. typically variable rate and tied to the LIBOR.
c. usually for maturities of six months or less.
d. all of the above are true.

**Topic: Syndicated Eurocredit Loan**
**Skill: Analytical**

39. General Motors has agreed to a syndicated eurocredit loan with the following terms: A revolving loan of $100,000,000 with an up-front fee of 2% of the principal and an interest rate of LIBOR plus 75 basis points. If the payments are made every six months and the current LIBOR rate is 4.00%, what is the effective annual cost of this loan?

a. 4.75%
b. 4.85%
c. 4.95%
d. 4.00%

**Topic: Euro-commerical paper**
**Skill: Recognition**

40. In general, which has the shorter maturity and more appropriate for funding short-term inventory needs?

a. Euro-commerical paper
b. Euro-Medium-Term notes (EMTNs)
c. The international bond market
d. All of the above

**Topic: EMTN**
**Skill: Conceptual**

41. Which of the following is NOT true regarding Euro-Medium-Term notes (EMTNs) when compared to typical long-term bonds?

a. The EMTN is a facility allowing continuous issuance over a short period of time.
b. EMTN coupon payments are on set calendar dates regardless of the date of issue.
c. EMTNs are relatively small, often with totals of $5 million or less.
d. All of the above are true.

**Topic: Foreign Bonds**
**Skill: Recognition**

42. Foreign bonds sold in the United States are nicknamed “Yankee bonds”, foreign bonds sold in Japan and called “Samurai bonds”. What are foreign bonds sold in the United Kingdom nicknamed?

a. “Union Jacks”
b. “Royalty”
c. “Bulldogs”
d. “Churchill’s”

**Topic: Eurobond**
**Skill: Recognition**

43. A ___________ is bond that is underwritten by an international syndicate of banks and sold exclusively in countries other than the one whose currency it is denominated.

   a. foreign bond
   b. Eurobond
   c. domestic bond
   d. none of the above

**Topic: Foreign Bond**
**Skill: Recognition**

44. A _____________ is a bond underwritten by a syndicate from a single country, sold within in that country, denominated in that country's currency, but the issuer is from outside that country.

   a. foreign bond
   b. Eurobond
   c. domestic bond
   d. none of the above

**Topic: Eurobond**
**Skill: Conceptual**

45. A large U.S. MNE is looking to raise capital in Europe. The company wishes to avoid many of the regulatory constraints found in an issue of debt in the U.S. markets, wants to attract foreign investors, but also wants the issue to be denominated in dollars. The firm should issue a _______________.

   a. foreign bond
   b. domestic bond
   c. Eurobond
   d. Eurodollar

**Topic: Eurobond Market**
**Skill: Recognition**

46. Which of the following is NOT a factor in the development and continuation of the Eurobond market?

   a. The absence of regulatory interference
   b. Less stringent disclosure requirements
   c. Favorable tax status
   d. All of the above are factors in the Eurobond market

**Topic: Moody's Bond Ratings**
**Skill: Recognition**
47. Moody's rates international bonds at the request of the issuer with the stipulation that Moody's will publish the ratings even if the ratings are unfavorable.

a. True
b. False

**Topic: Project Financing**
**Skill: Recognition**
48. Project financing is the arrangement of financing for very large individual long-term capital projects.

a. True
b. False

**Topic: Project Financing**
**Skill: Conceptual**
49. Which of the following is NOT a factor critical to the success of project financing?

a. Separability of the project from its investors
b. Long-lived and capital intensive singular projects
c. Cash flow predictability from third part commitments
d. All of the above are critical factors for project financing

**Topic: MNE Long-term Borrowing**
**Skill: Conceptual**
50. A MNE that borrows long-term in a foreign currency:

a. may obtain a lower effective cost of debt.
b. might be better off borrowing dollars at a higher interest rate.
c. may gain or lose because of transaction exposure.
d. all of the above.

**Essay Questions:**

1. There is much debate about whether an MNE should consider individual country norms, known as localization, when attempting to optimize the consolidated capital structure and minimize the firm's cost of capital. Provide arguments for the advantages and disadvantages of localization of capital structure for subsidiaries. Do you think MNEs should localize the capital structure of their subsidiaries? Why/why not?

**Answer**
The authors lay out several advantages and disadvantages to localization. The main advantages include:

- Localization deflects criticism of foreign subsidiaries that have too high a debt ratio that they are not contributing risk capital to the host country, or too low debt ratios that make the subsidiary insensitive to local monetary policy.
- Localization aids in comparisons of ROE and other financial ratios with local competitors.
- Localization is a way for managers to monitor decision-making, ROA, and other profitability ratios.

The main disadvantages include:

- An MNE is supposed to have comparative advantage over the locals, and better access to international financial markets. Therefore, why should they alter an optimal capital structure just to "fit in"?
- Capital structure optimization of the parts does not necessarily imply optimization of the whole.
- The debt ratio of each subsidiary is really a reflection of the parent firm as a whole.

At this point, the students need to decide which argument they think is stronger and explain their reasoning.

2. The Euro-medium-term-note (EMTN) has filled a substantial nitch market in global financing. What are the distinguishing characteristics of the EMTN and why is it such a popular form of financing for MNEs?

**Answer**
EMTNs have maturity between the long-lived international bonds and the short-term Euro-commercial paper, thus they have an appealing time horizon to many investors. EMTNs are like international bonds in that they pay periodic interest. The distinguishing features of an EMTN are: They are similar to a shelf registration in that the entire order for the securities does not have to be issued on the same day. Coupon payments are paid continuously, and the relatively small denominations allow for some flexibility in the market.

## Chapter 13: Financial Structure and International Debt
## Multiple Choice Answer Key:

| | | | | | | | | | |
|---|---|---|---|---|---|---|---|---|---|
| 1 | A | 11 | A | 21 | D | 31 | B | 41 | D |
| 2 | B | 12 | B | 22 | D | 32 | A | 42 | C |
| 3 | C | 13 | C | 23 | D | 33 | B | 43 | B |
| 4 | D | 14 | B | 24 | C | 34 | D | 44 | A |
| 5 | D | 15 | A | 25 | C | 35 | C | 45 | C |
| 6 | C | 16 | D | 26 | B | 36 | A | 46 | D |
| 7 | D | 17 | D | 27 | C | 37 | C | 47 | B |
| 8 | B | 18 | A | 28 | B | 38 | D | 48 | A |
| 9 | A | 19 | B | 29 | A | 39 | B | 49 | D |
| 10 | C | 20 | A | 30 | C | 40 | A | 50 | D |

# Chapter 14
# Interest Rate and Currency Swaps

**Topic: Interest Rate Risk**
**Skill: Recognition**
1. The single largest interest rate risk of a firm is ___________.

a. interest sensitive securities
b. debt service
c. dividend payments
d. accounts payable

**Topic: Reference Rate**
**Skill: Recognition**
2. A ____________ rate is the rate of interest used in a standardized quotation, loan agreement, or financial derivative valuation.

a. reference rate
b. central rate
c. benchmark rate
d. none of the above

**Topic: LIBOR**
**Skill: Recognition**
3. The most widely used reference rate for standardized quotations, loan agreements, or financial derivative valuations is the ______________.

a. Federal Reserve Discount rate
b. federal funds rate
c. LIBOR
d. one-year U.S. Treasury Bill

**Topic: LIBOR**
**Skill: Recognition**
4. LIBOR is an acronym for

a. Latest Interest Being Offered Rate
b. Large International Bank Offered Rate
c. Least Interest Bearing: Official Rate
d. London Interbank Offered Rate

**Topic: Corporate Treasury Departments**
**Skill: Recognition**

5. Corporate treasury departments have traditionally been

a. profit centers.
b. centers of aggressive profit taking.
c. service or cost centers.
d. none of the above.

**Topic: Policies and Goals**
**Skill: Conceptual**

6. As a management tool, a __________ is a rule, but a ________ is an objective.

a. policy; goal
b. goal; policy
c. FIBOR; GIBOR
d. none of the above

**Topic: Policies and Goals**
**Skill: Recognition**

7. The following would be an example of a policy, not a goal.

a. Management shall minimize the firm's overall weighted average cost of capital.
b. Management shall maximize shareholder's wealth.
c. Management will not write uncovered options.
d. Management will hire only happy employees.

**Topic: Policies and Goals**
**Skill: Conceptual**

8. Which of the following is NOT true regarding a corporate policy?

a. A policy is intended to limit or restrict management actions.
b. Policies make management decision-making more difficult in potentially harmful situations.
c. A policy is intended to restrict some subjective management decision-making.
d. A policy is intended to establish operating guidelines independently of staff.

**Topic: Interest Rate Risk**
**Skill: Recognition**

9. Historically, interest rate movements have shown less variability and greater stability than exchange rate movements.

a. True
b. False

**Topic: Interest Rate Risk**
**Skill: Conceptual**

10. Unlike the situation with exchange rate risk, there is no uncertainty on the part of management for shareholder preferences regarding interest rate risk. Shareholders prefer than managers hedge interest rate risk rather than having shareholders diversify away such risk through portfolio diversification.

a. True
b. False

**Topic: Credit and Repricing Risk**
**Skill: Recognition**

11. ___________ is the possibility that the borrower's creditworthiness is reclassified by the lender at the time of renewing credit. _____________ is the risk of changes in interest rates charged at the time a financial contract rate is set.

a. Credit risk; Interest rate risk
b. Repricing risk; Credit risk
c. Interest rate risk; Credit risk
d. Credit risk; Repricing risk

For problems number 12 – 21 consider the following three different debt strategies being considered by a corporate borrower. Each is intended to provide $1,000,000 in financing for a three-year period.

- Strategy # 1: Borrow $1,000,000 for three years a fixed rate of interest of 7%.
- Strategy # 2: Borrow $1,000,000 for three years at a floating rate of LIBOR +2%, to be reset annually. The current LIBOR rate is 3.50%
- Strategy # 3: Borrow $1,000,000 for one year at a fixed rate, and then renew the credit annually. The current one-year rate is 5%.

**Topic: Credit and Repricing Risk**
**Skill: Conceptual**

12. Choosing strategy # 1 will

a. guarantee the lowest average annual rate over the next three years.
b. eliminate credit risk but retain repricing risk.
c. maintain the possibility of lower interest costs, but maximizes the combined credit and repricing risks.
d. preclude the possibility of sharing in lower interest rates over the three-year period.

**Topic: Credit and Repricing Risk**
**Skill: Conceptual**
13. Choosing strategy # 2 will

a. guarantee the lowest average annual rate over the next three years.
b. eliminate credit risk but retain repricing risk.
c. maintain the possibility of lower interest costs, but maximizes the combined credit and repricing risks.
d. preclude the possibility of sharing in lower interest rates over the three-year period.

**Topic: Credit and Repricing Risk**
**Skill: Conceptual**
14. Choosing strategy # 3 will

a. guarantee the lowest average annual rate over the next three years.
b. eliminate credit risk but retain repricing risk.
c. maintain the possibility of lower interest costs, but maximizes the combined credit and repricing risks.
d. preclude the possibility of sharing in lower interest rates over the three-year period.

**Topic: Credit and Repricing Risk**
**Skill: Conceptual**
15. Which strategy (strategies) will eliminate credit risk?

a. Strategy #1
b. Strategy #2
c. Strategy #3
d. Strategy #1 and #2

**Topic: Credit and Repricing Risk**
**Skill: Conceptual**
16. If your firm felt very confident that interest rates would fall or, at worst, remain at current levels, and were very confident about the firm's credit rating for the next 10 years, which strategy would you likely choose? (Assume your firm is borrowing money.)

a. Strategy # 3
b. Strategy # 2
c. Strategy # 1
d. Strategy # 1, #2, or #3, you are indifferent among the choices.

**Topic: Credit and Repricing Risk**
**Skill: Conceptual**

17. The risk of strategy # 1 is that interest rates might go down or that your credit rating might improve. The risk of strategy # 2 is: (Assume your firm is borrowing money.)

a. that interest rates might go down or that your credit rating might improve.
b. that interest rates might go up or that your credit rating might improve.
c. that interest rates might go up or that your credit rating get worse.
d. none of the above.

**Topic: Credit and Repricing Risk**
**Skill: Conceptual**

18. The risk of strategy # 1 is that interest rates might go down or that your credit rating might improve. The risk of strategy # 3 is: (Assume your firm is borrowing money.)

a. that interest rates might go down or that your credit rating might improve.
b. that interest rates might go up or that your credit rating might improve.
c. that interest rates might go up or that your credit rating might get worse.
d. none of the above.

**Topic: Credit and Repricing Risk**
**Skill: Conceptual**

19. After the fact, under which set of circumstances would you prefer strategy # 1? (Assume your firm is borrowing money.)

a. Your credit rating stayed the same and interest rates went up.
b. Your credit rating stayed the same and interest rates went down.
c. Your credit rating improved and interest rates went down.
d. Not enough information to make a judgment.

**Topic: Credit and Repricing Risk**
**Skill: Conceptual**

20. After the fact, under which set of circumstances would you prefer strategy # 2? (Assume your firm is borrowing money.)

a. Your credit rating stayed the same and interest rates went up.
b. Your credit rating stayed the same and interest rates went down.
c. Your credit rating improved and interest rates went down.
d. Not enough information to make a judgment.

**Topic: Credit and Repricing Risk**
**Skill: Conceptual**
21. After the fact, under which set of circumstances would you prefer strategy # 3? (Assume your firm is borrowing money.)

a. Your credit rating stayed the same and interest rates went up.
b. Your credit rating stayed the same and interest rates went down.
c. Your credit rating improved and interest rates went down.
d. Not enough information to make a judgment.

Use the information for Polaris Corporation to answer questions 22 – 26.
Polaris is taking out a $5,000,000 two-year loan at a variable rate of LIBOR plus 1.00%. The LIBOR rate will be reset each year at an agreed upon date. The current LIBOR rate is 4.00% per year. The loan has an upfront fee of 2.00%

| Loan Interest Rates | Year 0 | Year 1 | Year 2 |
|---|---|---|---|
| LIBOR (Floating) | 4.00% | 4.00% | 4.00% |
| Spread (Fixed) | 1.00% | 1.00% | 1.00% |
| Total Interest Payable | 5.00% | 5.00% | 5.00% |
| Interest Cash Flows on Loan | | | |
| LIBOR (Floating) | | ($200,000) | ($200,000) |
| Spread (Fixed) | | ($50,000) | ($50,000) |
| Total Interest | | ($250,000) | ($250,000) |
| Loan Proceeds (Repayment) | $4,900,000 | | ($5,000,000) |
| Total Loan Cash Flows | $4,900,000 | ($250,000) | ($5,250,000) |

**Topic: All-in-Cost**
**Skill: Analytical**
22. What is the all-in-cost (i.e., the internal rate of return) of the Polaris loan including the LIBOR rate, fixed spread and upfront fee?

a. 4.00%
b. 5.00%
c. 5.53%
d. 6.09%

**Topic: Variable Rate Loan Agreements**
**Skill: Conceptual**
23. What portion of the cost of the loan is at risk of changing?

a. the LIBOR rate
b. the spread
c. the upfront fee
d. all of the above

**Topic: All-in-Cost**
**Skill: Analytical**
24. If the LIBOR rate jumps to 5.00% after the first year what will be the AIC for Polaris for the entire loan?

a. 5.25%
b. 5.50%
c. 6.09%
d. 6.58%

**Topic: All-in-Cost**
**Skill: Analytical**
25. If the LIBOR rate falls to 3.00% after the first year what will be the AIC for Polaris for the entire loan?

a. 4.00%
b. 4.50%
c. 5.25%
d. 5.60%

**Topic: Hedging**
**Skill: Recognition**
26. Polaris could have locked in the future interest rate payments by using

a. a forward rate agreement.
b. an interest rate future.
c. an interest rate swap.
d. any of the above.

**Topic: Forward Rate Agreement**
**Skill: Recognition**
27. An interbank-traded contract to buy or sell interest rae payments on a notational principal is called a/an _______________.

a. forward rate agreement
b. interest rate future
c. interest rate swap
d. none of the above

**Topic: Interest Rate Future**
**Skill: Recognition**

28. A/an ____________ is a contract to lock in today interest rates over a given period of time.

a. forward rate agreement
b. interest rate future
c. interest rate swap
d. none of the above

**Topic: Interest Rate Swap**
**Skill: Recognition**

29. An agreement to exchange interest payments based on a fixed payment for those based on a variable rate (or vice versa) is known as a/an ________________.

a. forward rate agreement
b. interest rate future
c. interest rate swap
d. none of the above

**Topic: Interest Rate Future**
**Skill: Recognition**

30. Interest rate futures are relatively unpopular among financial managers because of their relative illiquidity and their difficulty of use.

a. True
b. False

**Topic: Basis Points**
**Skill: Recognition**

31. A basis point is

a. 1.00%
b. 0.10%
c. 0.01%
d. none of the above

**Topic: Interest Rate Futures**
**Skill: Conceptual**

32. The financial manager of a firm has a variable rate loan outstanding. If she wishes to protect the firm against an unfavorable increase in interest rates she could

a. sell an interest rate futures contract of a similar maturity to the loan.
b. buy an interest rate futures contract of a similar maturity to the loan.
c. swap the adjustable rate loan for another of a different maturity.
d. none of the above.

**Topic: Interest Rate Swap**
**Skill: Recognition**
33. An agreement to swap a fixed interest payment for a floating interest payment would be considered a/an ____________.

a. currency swap
b. forward swap
c. interest rate swap
d. none of the above

**Topic: Currency Swap**
**Skill: Recognition**
34. An agreement to swap the currencies of a debt service obligation would be termed a/an ______________.

a. currency swap
b. forward swap
c. interest rate swap
d. none of the above

**Topic: Currency Swap**
**Skill: Conceptual**
35. Which of the following would be considered an example of a currency swap?

a. Exchanging a dollar interest obligation for a British pound obligation.
b. Exchanging a eurodollar interest obligation for a dollar obligation.
c. Exchanging a eurodollar interest obligation for a British pound obligation.
d. All of the above are example of a currency swap.

**Topic: Swap Agreements**
**Skill: Conceptual**
36. A swap agreement may involve currencies or interest rates, but never both.

a. True
b. False

**Topic: Swap Agreement**
**Skill: Conceptual**
37. A firm with fixed-rate debt that expects interest rates to fall may engage in a swap agreement to

a. pay fixed-rate interest and receive floating rate interest.
b. pay floating rate and receive fixed rate.
c. pay fixed rate and receive fixed rate.
d. pay floating rate and receive floating rate.

**Topic: Interest Rate Swap**
**Skill: Conceptual**
38. The interest rate swap strategy of a firm with fixed rate debt and that expects rates to go up is to

a. do nothing.
b. pay floating and receive fixed.
c. receive floating and pay fixed.
d. none of the above.

**Topic: LIBOR**
**Skill: Recognition**
39. Some of the world's largest and most financially sound firms may borrow at variable rates less than LIBOR.

a. True
b. False

**Topic: Currency Swaps**
**Skill: Conceptual**
40. Polaris Inc. has a significant amount of bonds outstanding denominated in yen because of the attractive variable rate available to the firm in yen when the loan was made. However, Polaris does not have significant receivables in yen. Options available to Polaris in reduce the risk of such a loan include which one of the following?

a. Doing nothing to offset the need for yen.
b. Developing a currency swap of paying dollars and receiving yen.
c. Developing an interest rate swap of receiving a variable rate while paying a fixed rate.
d. Polaris may engage in any of the strategies to a varying degree of effectiveness.

**Topic: Counterparty Risk**
**Skill: Recognition**
41. The potential exposure that any individual firm bears that the second party to any financial contract ill be unable to fulfill its obligations under the contract is called ____________.

a. interest rate risk
b. credit risk
c. counterparty risk
d. clearinghouse risk

**Topic: Counterparty Risk**
**Skill: Recognition**
42. Counterparty risk is

a. present only with exchange-traded options.
b. based on the notional amount of the contract.
c. the risk of loss if the other party to a financial contract fails to honor its obligation.
d. eliminated by the use of insurance funds.

**Topic: Counterparty Risk**
**Skill: Recognition**
43. Counterparty risk is a greater in exchange-traded derivatives than in over-the-counter derivatives.

a. True
b. False

**Topic: Swap Strategies**
**Skill: Conceptual**
44. Which of the following would an MNE NOT want to do?

a. Pay a very low fixed rate of interest in the long term.
b. Swap into a foreign currency payment that is falling in value.
c. Swap into a floating interest rate receivable just prior to interest rates going up.
d. Swap into a fixed interest rate receivable just prior to interest rates going up.

**Topic: Swap Strategies**
**Skill: Recognition**
45. Outright techniques of interest rate risk management do not include which of the following?

a. forward rate agreements
b. interest rate futures
c. currency swaps
d. cap, floors, and collars

**Topic: Plain Vanilla Swaps**
**Skill: Conceptual**
46. Which of the following is NOT true?

a. A plain vanilla swap allows a firm to change the currency of denomination of debt service.
b. A swap does not change the legal liabilities of existing debt obligations of MNEs.
c. The swap market does not differentiate participants on the basis of credit quality.
d. All of the above are true.

**Topic: Currency and Interest Rae Swaps**
**Skill: Recognition**

47. A combined position of selling one currency forward at one maturity while buying the same currency forward at a different maturity to lock in a future interest rate ion the foreign currency is a/an

a. forward swap.
b. forward rate agreement.
c. interest rate future.
d. currency and interest rate swap.

**Topic: Cross Currency Swaps**
**Skill: Conceptual**

48. Cross currency swaps typically have larger swings in total value than "plain vanilla" interest rate swaps because:

a. cross currency swaps exchange principal as well as interest payments.
b. interest rate movements are more volatile than currency movements.
c. interest rate swap agreements do not allow, contractually, large movements from par.
d. all of the above.

**Topic: Swap Agreement**
**Skill: Conceptual**

49. A U.S.-based firm with dollar denominated debt, but continuing sales denominated in Japanese yen, could:

a. purchase an interest rate cap agreement.
b. enter into a swap agreement to swap dollar interest for Japanese interest payments.
c. purchase a series of rolling futures contracts to buy Japanese yen forward.
d. all of the above.

**Topic: Servicing Debt Obligations**
**Skill: Recognition**

50. A firm entering into a currency or interest rate swap agreement is relieved of the ultimate responsibility for the timely servicing of its own debt obligations.

a. True
b. False

## Essay Questions:

1. Your firm is faced with paying a variable rate debt obligation with the expectation that interest rates are likely to go up. Identify two strategies using interest rate futures and interest rate swaps that could reduce the risk to the firm.

**Answer**
Sell a futures position. If rates change the payoff from the futures position offsets the gain or loss on the variable rate debt obligation. Swap a variable rate debt obligation for a fixed futures payable contract.

2. How does counterparty risk influence a firm's decision to trade exchange-traded derivatives rather than over-the-counter derivatives?

**Answer**
With exchange-traded derivatives, the exchange is the clearinghouse. Thus, firms do not need to worry about the other party making good on its obligations and it is easier to trade the derivative products.

## Chapter 14: Interest Rate and Currency Swaps
## Multiple Choice Answer Key:

| | | | | | | | | | |
|---|---|---|---|---|---|---|---|---|---|
| 1 | B | 11 | D | 21 | C | 31 | C | 41 | C |
| 2 | A | 12 | D | 22 | D | 32 | A | 42 | C |
| 3 | C | 13 | B | 23 | A | 33 | C | 43 | B |
| 4 | D | 14 | C | 24 | D | 34 | A | 44 | C |
| 5 | C | 15 | D | 25 | D | 35 | D | 45 | D |
| 6 | A | 16 | A | 26 | D | 36 | B | 46 | D |
| 7 | C | 17 | B | 27 | A | 37 | B | 47 | A |
| 8 | B | 18 | C | 28 | B | 38 | A | 48 | D |
| 9 | A | 19 | A | 29 | C | 39 | A | 49 | B |
| 10 | B | 20 | B | 30 | B | 40 | D | 50 | B |

# Chapter 15
# Foreign Direct Investment Theory and Strategy

**Topic: Comparative Advantage**
**Skill: Recognition**

1. The theory that suggests specialization by country can increase worldwide production is ______________.

   a. the theory of comparative advantage
   b. the theory of foreign direct investment
   c. the international Fisher effect
   d. the theory of working capital management

**Topic: Comparative Advantage**
**Skill: Conceptual**

2. Which of the following would NOT be a way to implement comparative advantage?

   a. IBM exports computers to Egypt.
   b. Computer hardware is designed in the United States but manufactured and assembled in Korea.
   c. Water of the greatest purity is obtained from wells in Oregon, bottled, and exported worldwide.
   d. All of the above are examples of ways to implement comparative advantage.

**Topic: Comparative Advantage**
**Skill: Recognition**

3. Which of the following would NOT be considered a feature of comparative advantage?

   a. Exporters in Country A sell goods or services to unrelated importers in Country B.
   b. Firms in Country A specialize in making products that can be produced relatively efficiently, given County A's endowment of factors of production. Firms in Country B do likewise thus maximizing the combined output of Countries A and B.
   c. Trade exists between Counties A and B because of specialized factors of production that cannot be moved among countries.
   d. All of the above are features of comparative advantage.

**Topic: Comparative Advantage**
**Skill: Recognition**
4. Of the following, which would NOT be considered a way, that government interferes with comparative advantage?

a. tariffs
b. managerial skills
c. quotas
d. other non-tariff restrictions

**Topic: Comparative Advantage**
**Skill: Recognition**
5. Comparative advantage shift over time as less developed countries become more developed and realize their latent opportunities.

a. True
b. False

**Topic: Comparative Advantage**
**Skill: Recognition**
6. Comparative advantage was once the cornerstone of international trade theory, but today it is archaic, simplistic, and irrelevant for explaining why investment choices by MNEs.

a. True
b. False

**Topic: Comparative Advantage**
**Skill: Recognition**
7. In determining why a firm becomes multinational there are many reasons. One reason is that the firm is a market seeker. Which of the following is NOT a reason shy market seeking firms produce in foreign countries?

a. Satisfaction of local demand in the foreign country.
b. Satisfaction of local demand in the domestic markets.
c. Political safely and small likelihood of government expropriation of assets.
d. All of the above are market-seeking activities.

**Topic: Comparative Advantage**
**Skill: Recognition**
8. _____________ investments are designed to promote and enhance the growth and profitability of the firm. _____________ investments are designed to deny those same opportunities to the firm's competitors.

a. conservative; aggressive
b. defensive; proactive
c. proactive; defensive
d. aggressive; proactive

**Topic: Comparative Advantage**
**Skill: Recognition**
9. Which of the following is NOT considered to be a type of competitive advantage that may be enjoyed by an MNE?

a. managerial and marketing expertise
b. superior technology due to investment in research and development
c. increased agency costs
d. differentiated products

**Topic: Comparative Advantage**
**Skill: Recognition**
10. Which of the following is NOT considered to be a type of competitive advantage that may be enjoyed by an MNE?

a. competitiveness in their home markets
b. foreign exchange risks
c. economies of scale
d. economies of scope

**Topic: Economies of Scale**
**Skill: Conceptual**
11. An example of economies of scale in financing include:

a. being able to access the Euroequity, Eurobond, and Eurocurrency markets.
b. being able to ship product in shiploads or carloads.
c. being able to use large-scale plant and equipment.
d. all of the above.

**Topic: Porter's Diamond**
**Skill: Recognition**
12. Which of the following is NOT a factor of Porter's "diamond of national advantage?

a. factor conditions
b. demand conditions
c. related and supporting industries
d. all of the above are factors of the diamond of national advantage

**Topic: OLI**
**Skill: Recognition**
13. The OLI paradigms an attempt to create a framework to explain why MNEs choose ____________ rather than some other form of international venture.

a. licensing
b. joint ventures
c. foreign direct investment
d. strategic alliances

**Topic: OLI**
**Skill: Recognition**
14. The O in OLI refers to an advantage in a firm's home market that is

a. operator independent
b. owner-specific
c. open-market
d. official designation

**Topic: OLI**
**Skill: Recognition**
15. The owner-specific advantages of OLI must be

a. firm-specific.
b. not easily copied.
c. transferable to foreign subsidiaries.
d. all of the above.

**Topic: OLI**
**Skill: Conceptual**
16. A/n __________would be an example of an owner-specific advantage for an MNE.

a. patent
b. economy of scale
c. economy of scope
d. all of the above

**Topic: OLI**
**Skill: Recognition**
17. The L in OLI refers to an advantage in a firm's home market that is a

a. liability in the domestic market
b. location-specific advantage
c. longevity in a particular market
d. none of the above.

**Topic: OLI**
**Skill: Conceptual**
18. A/n __________would be an example of a location-specific advantage for an MNE.

a. patent
b. economy of scale
c. unique source of raw materials
d. possession of proprietary information

**Topic: OLI**
**Skill: Recognition**
19. The I in OLI refers to an advantage in a firm's home market that is an

a. internalization.
b. industry-specific advantage.
c. international abnormality.
d. none of the above.

**Topic: OLI**
**Skill: Conceptual**
20. A/n __________would be an example of an internalization advantage for an MNE.

a. patent
b. economy of scale
c. unique source of raw materials
d. possession of proprietary information

**Topic: OLI**
**Skill: Conceptual**
21. Which of the following is NOT a proactive financial strategy related to the OLI paradigm in explaining FDI?

a. Strategies to gain lower global cost of capital.
b. Strategies to reduce global taxation.
c. Strategies to reduce operating and transaction exposure.
d. All of the above are proactive strategies.

**Topic: FDI**
**Skill: Recognition**
22. FDI is

a. investment in real assets in foreign countries.
b. foreign direct investment.
c. influenced by behavioral factors.
d. all of the above.

**Topic: Behavioral Observations of FDI**
**Skill: Recognition**
23. Which of the following is NOT true regarding behavioral observations of firms making a decision to invest internationally?

a. MNEs initially invest in countries with a similar "national psychic".
b. Firms eventually take greater risks in terms of the national psychic of countries in which they invest.
c. Initial investments tend to be much larger than subsequent ones.
d. All of the above have been observed.

**Topic: FDI**
**Skill: Conceptual**
24. Which of the following is NOT an advantage to exporting goods to reach international markets rather than entering into some form of FDI?

a. fewer political risks
b. greater agency costs
c. lower front-end investment
d. all of the above are advantages

**Topic: FDI**
**Skill: Conceptual**
25. Which of the following is an advantage to exporting goods to reach international markets rather than entering into some form of FDI?

a. fewer agency costs
b. fewer direct advantages from research and development
c. a greater risk of losing markets to copycat goods producers
d. an inability to exploit R&D as effectively as if also invested abroad

**Topic: Exporting**
**Skill: Recognition**
26. Which of the following is NOT a form of FDI?

a. wholly-owned affiliate
b. joint venture
c. exporting
d. greenfield investment

**Topic: Licensing**
**Skill: Conceptual**
27. Licensing is a popular form of foreign investment because it does not need a sizable commitment of funds, and political risk is often minimized.

a. True
b. False

**Topic: Licensing**
**Skill: Conceptual**
28. With licensing the _________ is likely to be lower than with FDI because of lower profits, however, the __________ is likely to be higher due to a greater return per dollar invested.

a. IRR; NPV
b. NPV; IRR
c. cost of capital; NPV
d. IRR; cost of capital

**Topic: Licensing**
**Skill: Recognition**
29. Which of the following is NOT a potential disadvantage of licensing relative to FDI?

a. Possible loss of quality control.
b. Establishment of a potential competitor in third-country markets.
c. Possible improvement of the technology by the local licensee, which then enters the original firm's home market.
d. All of the above are potential disadvantages to licensing.

**Topic: Licensing**
**Skill: Recognition**
30. Which of the following is NOT a potential disadvantage of licensing relative to FDI?

a. Possible loss of opportunity to enter the licensee's market with FDI later.
b. Risk that technology will be stolen.
c. High agency costs.
d. All of the above are potential disadvantages to licensing.

**Topic: Licensing**
**Skill: Conceptual**
31. MNEs typically used licensing with independent firms rather than with their own foreign subsidiaries.

a. True
b. False

**Topic: Joint Venture**
**Skill: Recognition**
32. A __________ is a shared ownership in a foreign business.

a. licensing agreement
b. greenfield investment
c. joint venture
d. wholly-owned affiliate

**Topic: Joint Venture**
**Skill: Recognition**
33. Which of the following is NOT an advantage to a joint venture?

a. Possible loss of opportunity to enter the foreign market with FDI later.
b. The local partner understands the customs and mores of the foreign market.
c. The local partner can provide competent management at many levels.
d. May be a realistic alternative when 100% foreign ownership is not allowed.

**Topic: Joint Venture**
**Skill: Recognition**
34. Which of the following is NOT an advantage to a joint venture?

a. The local partner's reputation enhances access to local financial markets.
b. The local partner possesses technology that is advantageous in their market and perhaps beyond.
c. Higher agency costs than with a purely domestic firm.
d. The local partner's public image may enhance local sales.

**Topic: Wholly Owned Subsidiaries**
**Skill: Recognition**
35. Joint ventures are a more common FDI than wholly owned subsidiaries.

a. True
b. False

**Topic: Joint Venture**
**Skill: Conceptual**
36. Local partners in a foreign country and in a joint venture with an MNE are likely to make decisions that maximize the value of the subsidiary. Such actions probably will not maximize the value of the entire firm.

a. True
b. False

**Topic: Greenfield Investment**
**Skill: Recognition**
37. A _____________ is establishing a production or service facility from the ground up.

a. joint venture
b. licensing agreement
c. greenfield investment
d. wholly-owned facility

**Topic: Greenfield Investment**
**Skill: Conceptual**
38. Greenfield investments are typically ___________ and __________ than cross-border acquisition.

a. slower; more uncertain
b. faster; of greater certainty
c. slower; of greater certainty
d. faster; more uncertain

**Topic: Greenfield Investment**
**Skill: Recognition**
39. Which of the following is NOT a potential advantage to a cross-border acquisition compared to a Greenfield investment?

a. Market imperfections may under-price local assets and allow the purchase of assets at significant discount.
b. Cross-border acquisitions take longer, thus allowing the firm a better understanding of the local market before attempting sales.
c. Acquisitions may be a cost-effective way of gaining competitive advantages such as technology or brand names.
d. All of the above are advantages of acquisition over green field investment.

**Topic: Cross-Border Acquisitions**
**Skill: Recognition**
40. Which of the following is NOT a potential disadvantage to cross-border acquisitions?

a. The meshing of different corporate cultures.
b. Host government intervention in the post-acquisition process.
c. Mis-pricing foreign assets and paying too much for the acquisition.
d. All of the above are potential disadvantages.

**Topic: Strategic Alliance**
**Skill: Recognition**
41. All of the following may be justification for a strategic alliance EXCEPT:

a. Takeover defense.
b. A joint venture to pool resources for research and development.
c. Joint marketing and serving agreements.
d. All of the above are legitimate reasons for strategic alliances.

**Topic: Joint Ventures**
**Skill: Conceptual**
42. Joint ventures are motivated only by takeover defenses.

a. True
b. False

**Topic: Strategic Alliance**
**Skill: Conceptual**
43. Strategic alliances that have firms exchanging stock and forming joint ventures are more important in:

a. agricultural firms where government interference is critical for firm survival.
b. old fashioned basic industry where pure economies of scale are still dominant.
c. high tech industries where research and development costs are high and innovation is critical to success
d. none of the above.

**Topic: Greenfield Investment**
**Skill: Conceptual**
44. Which of the following combinations of cost and control reflect the choice of a greenfield foreign direct investment?

a. high cost, high control
b. medium cost, high control
c. low cost, high control
d. high cost, low control

**Topic: Licensing**
**Skill: Conceptual**
45. Which of the following modes of serving foreign markets requires the least capital investment by the MNE but risks the loss of key technological or managerial expertise to the marketplace?

a. acquisition
b. licensing
c. greenfield investment
d. portfolio investment

**Topic: FDI**
**Skill: Recognition**
46. Which of the following is the motivation for making foreign direct investment?

a. knowledge seeking
b. market seeking
c. raw material seeking
d. all of the above

**Topic: OLI**
**Skill: Recognition**
47. The __________ is an attempt to create and overall framework to explain why MNEs rely on FDI rather than servicing foreign markets through alternative modes.

a. OLI paradigm
b. Internationalization paradigm
c. Theory of competitive advantage
d. none of the above

**Topic: Internalization**
**Skill: Recognition**
48. The theory of __________ is an attempt to synthesize and extend those theories of FDI that are based on market imperfections.

a. internationalization
b. externalization
c. internalization
d. diversification

**Topic: Successful MNEs**
**Skill: Recognition**
49. Which of the following are characteristics of MNEs that have successfully invested abroad?

a. economies of scale and scope
b. superior technology with heavy emphasis on research
c. demonstrated competitive advantage in their home markets
d. all of the above

**Topic: FDI**
**Skill: Recognition**
50. A MNE can choose all of the following modes of entry for FDI EXCEPT:

a. a joint venture with a local partner
b. a 100%-owned greenfield subsidiary
c. merger with or acquisition of an existing local firm
d. exporting products to a local firm

## Essay Questions:

1. List and explain three strategic motives why firms become multinationals and give an example of each.

**Answer**
On page 336 the authors provide 5 strategic motives for firms to become multinationals; market seekers, raw materials seekers, production efficiency seekers, knowledge seekers, and political safety seekers. Market seekers are looking for more consumers for their products such as automobiles, or steel. Knowledge seekers may be looking for an educated workforce similar to the way firms seeking R and D set up shop in university towns. Raw materials seekers may be after commodities such as oil or copper. Production efficiencies may occur in countries like Mexico that have capable workers and lower wages. Political safety seekers are looking for countries that will not expropriate their assets, so they may stay away from countries such as Iraq or North Korea.

2. What does the OLI Paradigm propose to explain? Define each component and provide an example of each.

**Answer**
The OLI Paradigm is an attempt to develop an overall framework to explain why MNEs choose FDI to serve foreign markets rather than alternatives such as licensing or exporting. The letters of the paradigm are O for owner-specific advantages, L for location-specific advantages, and I for internalization.

Owner-specific advantages require that the firm have a comparative advantage in its home market that it feels it can exploit internationally. To be most effective, the advantages should be difficult to copy. Location specific advantages may be due to market imperfections or genuine comparative advantages such as a source of a particularly high quality natural resource. With internalization the firm has in its possession some proprietary information or product such as software or personnel that may provide an advantage in the international marketplace.

## Chapter 15: Foreign Direct Investment Theory and Strategy
## Multiple Choice Answer Key:

| | | | | | | | | | |
|---|---|---|---|---|---|---|---|---|---|
| 1 | A | 11 | A | 21 | D | 31 | B | 41 | D |
| 2 | D | 12 | D | 22 | D | 32 | C | 42 | B |
| 3 | D | 13 | C | 23 | C | 33 | A | 43 | C |
| 4 | B | 14 | B | 24 | B | 34 | C | 44 | A |
| 5 | A | 15 | D | 25 | A | 35 | B | 45 | B |
| 6 | B | 16 | A | 26 | C | 36 | A | 46 | D |
| 7 | C | 17 | B | 27 | A | 37 | C | 47 | A |
| 8 | C | 18 | C | 28 | B | 38 | A | 48 | C |
| 9 | C | 19 | A | 29 | D | 39 | B | 49 | D |
| 10 | B | 20 | D | 30 | D | 40 | D | 50 | D |

# Chapter 16
# Multinational Capital Budgeting

**Topic: Capital Budgeting**
**Skill: Recognition**
1. The traditional financial analysis applied to projects, foreign or domestic, to determine the project's value to the firm is called _______________.

a. cost of capital analysis
b. capital budgeting
c. capital structure analysis
d. agency theory

**Topic: Capital Budgeting**
**Skill: Recognition**
2. Which of the following is NOT a basic step in the capital budgeting process?

a. Identify the initial capital invested.
b. Estimate the cash flows to be derived from the project over time.
c. Identify the appropriate interest rate at which to discount future cash flows.
d. All of the above are steps in the capital budgeting process.

**Topic: Accounting Rate of Return**
**Skill: Recognition**
3. Of the following capital budgeting decision criteria, which does NOT use discounted cash flows?

a. Net present value
b. Internal rate of return
c. Accounting rate of return
d. All of these techniques typically use discounted cash flows.

**Topic: Capital Budgeting**
**Skill: Recognition**
4. There are no important differences between domestic and international capital budgeting methods.

a. True
b. False

**Topic: Capital Budgeting for Foreign Projects**
**Skill: Recognition**
5. Which of the following is NOT a reason why capital budgeting for a foreign project is more complex than for a domestic project?

a. Parent cash flows must be distinguished from project cash flows.
b. Parent firms must specifically recognize remittance of funds due to differing rules and regulations concerning remittance of cash flows, taxes, and local norms.
c. Differing rates of inflation between the foreign and domestic economies
d. All of the above add complexity to the international capital budgeting process.

**Topic: Capital Budgeting Decision Rules**
**Skill: Recognition**
6. It is important that firms adopt a common standard for the capital budgeting process for choosing among foreign and domestic projects.

a. True
b. False

**Topic: Parents and Local Evaluation**
**Skill: Recognition**
7. Project evaluation from the ________ viewpoint serves some useful purposes and/but should ______________ the ___________ viewpoint.

a. local; be subordinated to; parent's
b. local; not be subordinated to; parent's
c. parent's; be subordinated to; local
d. none of the above

**Topic: Subsidiaries**
**Skill: Recognition**
8. For financial reporting purposes, U.S. firms must consolidate the earnings of any subsidiary that is over ______ owned.

a. 20%
b. 40%
c. 50%
d. 75%

**Topic: Affiliates**
**Skill: Recognition**
9. A foreign firm that is 20% to 49% owned by a parent is called a/an __________.

a. subsidiary
b. affiliate
c. partner
d. rival

**Topic: Affiliates**
**Skill: Recognition**
10. Affiliate firms are consolidated on the parent's financial statements on a __________ basis.

a. pro rate
b. 50%
c. 75%
d. 100%

**Topic: Relative PPP**
**Skill: Analytical**
11. Given a current spot rate of 8.10 Norwegian krone per dollar, expected inflation rates of 6% in Norway and 3% per annum in the U.S., use the formula for relative purchasing power parity estimate the one-year spot rate of krone per dollar.

a. 7.87 krone per dollar
b. 8.10 krone per dollar
c. 8.34 krone per dollar
d. There is not enough information to answer this question

**Topic: Capital Budgeting**
**Skill: Recognition**
12. When evaluating capital budgeting projects, which of the following would NOT necessarily be an indicator of an acceptable project?

a. an NPV > $0
b. an IRR > the project's required rate of return
c. an IRR > $0
d. all of the above are correct indicators

**Topic: Relative PPP**
**Skill: Analytical**

13. Given a current spot rate of 8.10 Norwegian krone per dollar, expected inflation rates of 3% in Norway and 6% per annum in the U.S., use the formula for relative purchasing power parity estimate the one-year spot rate of krone per dollar.

a. 7.87 krone per dollar
b. 8.10 krone per dollar
c. 8.34 krone per dollar
d. There is not enough information to answer this question

**Topic: WACC**
**Skill: Recognition**

14. When determining a firm's weighted average cost of capital (wacc) which of the following terms is NOT necessary?

a. the firm's tax rate
b. the firm's cost of debt
c. the firm's cost of equity
d. all of the above are necessary

**Topic: WACC**
**Skill: Recognition**

15. When determining a firm's weighted average cost of capital (wacc) which of the following terms is NOT necessary?

a. the firm's weight of equity financing
b. the risk-free rate of return
c. the firm's weight of debt financing
d. All of the above are necessary to determine a firm's wacc.

**Topic: Initial Outlay**
**Skill: Recognition**

16. Of the following, which would NOT be considered an initial outlay at time 0 (today)?

a. investment in new equipment
b. initial investment in additional net working capital
c. shipping and handling costs associated with the new investment
d. all of the above are initial outlays

**Use the following information for questions 17 – 22**
The Wheel Deal Inc., a company that produces scooters and other wheeled non-motorized recreational equipment is considering an expansion of their product line to Europe. The expansion would require a purchase of equipment with a price of €1,200,000 and additional installation of €300,000(assume that the installation costs cannot be expensed, but rather, must be depreciated over the life of the asset). Because this would be a new product, they will not be replacing existing equipment. The new product line is expected to increase revenues by €600,000 per year over current levels for the next 5 years, however; expenses will also increase by €200,000 per year. (Note: Assume the after-tax operating cash flows in years 1 – 5 are equal, and that the terminal value of the project in year 5 may change total after-tax cash flows for that year.) The equipment is multipurpose and the firm anticipates that they will sell it at the end of the five years for €500,000. The firm's required rate of return is 12% and they are in the 40% tax bracket. Depreciation is straight-line to a value of €0 over the 5-year life of the equipment, and the investment also requires an increase in NWC of €100,000 (to be recovered at the sale of the equipment at the end of five years). The current spot rate is $.95/€, and the expected inflation rate in the U.S. is 4% per year and 3% per year in Europe.

**Topic: NPV**
**Skill: Analytical**
17. In euros, what is the NPV of the Wheel Deal expansion?

a. €1,524,690
b. $1,611,317
c. €24,690
d. -€111,317

**Topic: IRR**
**Skill: Analytical**
18. What is the IRR of the Wheel Deal expansion?

a. 11.27%
b. 12.00%
c. 12.59%
d. 13.00%

**Topic: After-tax Cash Flows**
**Skill: Analytical**
19. What are the annual after-tax cash flows for the Wheel Deal project?

a. €400,000
b. €240,000
c. €120,000
d. €360,000

**Topic: Exchange Rates**
**Skill: Conceptual**
20. The European expansion would have a greater NPV in dollar terms if the euro appreciated in value over the five-year life of the project, other things equal.

a. True
b. False

**Topic: NPV**
**Skill: Analytical**
21. What is the NPV of the European expansion if Wheel Deal first computes the NPV in euros and then converts that figure to dollars using the current spot rate?

a. $1,604,937
b. $1,448,455
c. $25,990
d. $23,456

**Topic: IRR**
**Skill: Conceptual**
22. What is the IRR of the European expansion if Wheel Deal first computes the NPV in euros and then converts that figure to dollars using the current spot rate?

a. 11.27%
b. 12.00%
c. 12.59%
d. 13.00%

**Topic: NPV of Foreign Projects**
**Skill: Conceptual**
23. The only proper way to estimate the NPV of a foreign project is to discount the appropriate cash flows first and then convert them to the domestic currency at the current spot rate.

a. True
b. False

**Topic: WACC**
**Skill: Analytical**
24. Benson Manufacturing has an after-tax cost of debt of 7% and a cost of equity of 12%. If Benson is in a 30% tax bracket, and finances 40% of assets with debt, what is the firm's wacc?

a. 11.20%
b. 10.36%
c. 9.72%
d. 7.68%

**Topic: IRR**
**Skill: Recognition**
25. If a firm undertakes a project with ordinary cash flows and estimates that the firm has a positive NPV, then the IRR will be ___________.

a. less than the cost of capital
b. greater than the cost of capital
c. greater than the cost of the project
d. cannot be determined from this information

**Topic: Cost of Equity**
**Skill: Recognition**
26. Generally speaking a firm's cost of _________ capital is greater than the firm's _________.

a. debt; equity
b. debt; wacc
c. equity; wacc
d. None of the above is true.

**Topic: Cost of Equity**
**Skill: Recognition**
27. When estimating a firm's cost of equity capital using the CAPM, you need to estimate

a. the risk-free rate of return.
b. the expected return on the market portfolio.
c. the firm's beta.
d. all of the above.

**Topic: Cost of Equity**
**Skill: Analytical**
28. Calculate the cost of equity for Boston Industries using the following information: The cost of debt is 7%, the corporate tax rate is 40%, the rate on Treasury Bills is 4%, the firm has a beta of 1.1, and the expected return on the market is 12%.

a. 12.8%
b. 12.6%
c. 13.2%
d. 6.6%

**Topic: Political Risk**
**Skill: Recognition**
29. _________ is the risk that a foreign government will place restrictions such as limiting the amount of funds that can be remitted to the parent firm, or even expropriation of cash flows earned in that country.

a. Exchange risk
b. Foreign risk
c. Political risk
d. Unnecessary risk

**Topic: Political Risk**
**Skill: Recognition**
30. Which of the following is NOT an example of political risk?

a. Expropriation of cash flows by a foreign government.
b. The U.S. government restricts trade with a foreign country where your firm has investments.
c. The foreign government nationalizes all foreign owned assets.
d. All of the above are examples of political risk.

**Topic: Foreign Exchange Risk**
**Skill: Conceptual**
31. Generally speaking, a firm wants to receive cash flows from a currency that is _________ relative to their own, and pay out in currencies that are _________ relative to their home currency.

a. appreciating; depreciating
b. depreciating; depreciating
c. appreciating; appreciating
d. depreciating; appreciating

**Topic: Capital Budgeting**
**Skill: Conceptual**
32. When dealing with international capital budgeting projects, the value of the project is NOT sensitive to the firm's cost of capital.

a. True
b. False

**Topic: Traditional DCF Models**
**Skill: Recognition**
33. Projects that have _____________ are often rejected by traditional discounted cash flow models of capital budgeting.

a. long lives
b. cash flow returns in later years
c. high risk levels
d. all of the above

**Topic: Real Option Analysis**
**Skill: Recognition**
34. An alternative to traditional discounted cash flow models is ___________.

a. the capital asset pricing model
b. dividend growth model
c. real option analysis model
d. none of the above

**Topic: Real Option Analysis**
**Skill: Recognition**
35. Real option analysis allows managers to analyze all of the following EXCEPT:

a. the option to defer
b. the option to abandon
c. the option to alter capacity
d. all of the above may be analyzed using real option analysis

**Topic: Parent Cash Flows**
**Skill: Conceptual**
36. For international investments, relative to project cash flows, parent cash flows are often dependent on the form of financing.

a. True
b. False

**Topic: Relevant Cash Flows**
**Skill: Recognition**
37. Which of the following considerations is NOT important for a parent firm when considering foreign investment?

a. The form of financing
b. Remittance of funds at risk due to political considerations
c. Differing rates of national inflation
d. All of the above are important considerations

**Topic: Risk Consideration**
**Skill: Recognition**
38. Which of the following is NOT a method for considering additional risk with international projects?

a. Adding an additional risk premium to the discount factor used.
b. Decreasing expected cash flows.
c. Conducting detailed sensitively and scenario analysis
d. All of the above are legitimate methods for considering additional risk.

**Topic: Current Exchange Rates**
**Skill: Analytical**
39. Your company just received a $500,000 cash remittance from your British subsidiary. If the risk-free one-year T-bill rate is 4.5% and the current exchange rate is $1.45/£, and the one-year forward rate is $1.44/£, then the present value of the remittance is ________________

a. $725,000
b. $500,000
c. $693,780
d. $478,469

**Topic: International Capital Budgeting**
**Skill: Recognition**
40. Capital budgeting analysis for a foreign project is more complex than for the domestic case for all of the following reasons EXCEPT:

a. differences in national inflation rates
b. parent cash flows must be distinguished from project cash flows
c. the possibility of unanticipated foreign exchange rate changes
d. all of the above are correct

**Topic: International Capital Budgeting**
**Skill: Conceptual**
41. When a parent corporation performs a capital budgeting analysis, the additional risks due to the foreign location of a project should generally be handled by:

a. decreasing the project's hurdle rate
b. modifying the quarterly tax payments in advance
c. adjusting the cash flows to the parent
d. informing all investors of the risk potential

**Topic: Parent vs Local**
**Skill: Recognition**
42. Cash flows the parents are ultimately the basis for dividends to stockholders, reinvestment elsewhere in the world, repayment of corporate-wide debt, and other purposed that affect the firm's many interest groups. Therefore, analysis of any foreign project should be from the viewpoint of the:

a. host country
b. parent
c. project
d. local government

**Topic: Capital Budgeting Evaluation Criteria**
**Skill: Recognition**
43. As in domestic capital budgeting, a potential international project or capital budget will be considered a net benefit to the firms if:

a. the project has a net present value greater than zero
b. the IRR on the project is less than the wacc
c. the IRR exceed the project's NPV
d. all of the above are true

**Topic: Capital Budgeting Evaluation Criteria**
**Skill: Recognition**
44. An international investment opportunity should be rejected if:

a. the project's NPV > parent viewpoint NPV
b. the IRR of the project is < 20%
c. the NPV of the project is > 0, but the NPV of the parental viewpoint is < 0
d. all of the above are true

**Topic: International Investment Risk**
**Skill: Recognition**
45. Which of the following is NOT a risk commensurate with international investments?

a. foreign exchange rate risk
b. country risk
c. political risk
d. all of the above are relevant risks

**Topic: Capital Budgeting Projects**
**Skill: Recognition**
46. Project finance is characterized by which of the following features?

a. long project life
b. high capital intensity of undertaking the investment
c. production or provision of a basic commodity or service
d. all of the above

**Use the following information to answer questions 47 – 50**
Jensen Aquatics Inc., which manufactures and sells scuba gear worldwide, is considering an investment in either Europe or Great Britain. Consider the following cash flows for each project, assume a 12% wacc, and consider these to be average risk projects for the firm. Answer the questions that follow.

| Britain | Year 0 (Today) | Year 1 | Year 2 | Year 3 |
|---|---|---|---|---|
| Total cash inflows (£) | 0 | 8000 | 8000 | 8000 |
| Total cash outflows (£) | 15,000 | 1000 | 1000 | 1000 |
| Additional dollar cash inflows ($) | 0 | 500 | 500 | 500 |
| Forecast exchange rate ($/£) | 1.50 | 1.46 | 1.45 | 1.44 |

| Europe | Year 0 (Today) | Year 1 | Year 2 | Year 3 |
|---|---|---|---|---|
| Total cash inflows (€) | 0 | 12,000 | 12,000 | 12,000 |
| Total cash outflows (€) | 20,000 | 1500 | 1500 | 1500 |
| Additional dollar cash inflows ($) | 0 | 500 | 500 | 500 |
| Forecast exchange rate ($/€) | 1.00 | .96 | .94 | .92 |

**Topic: International Capital Budgeting**
**Skill: Analytical**

47. The NPV for the British investment is estimated at ___________.

a. $3,092
b. $6,420
c. £3,092
d. $0

**Topic: International Capital Budgeting**
**Skill: Analytical**

48. The NPV for the European investment is estimated at ___________.

a. €4,945
b. $4,945
c. $6,420
d. €6,420

**Topic: International Capital Budgeting**
**Skill: Conceptual**

49. Which of the following best summarizes the preliminary results of the investment analysis for the two prospective investments?

a. The British investment should be accepted, the European investment rejected
b. The British investment is superior to the European investment
c. Both investments are acceptable
d. None of the above is true

**Topic: International Capital Budgeting**
**Skill: Analytical**

50. If the euro was forecast to remain constant at $1.00/€ throughout the investment period, how would the investment decision now be characterized?

a. The project would be even better than forecast
b. The European investment should be chosen over the British investment
c. The NPV is $6,420
d. All of the above are true

## Essay Questions:

1. The authors highlight a strong theoretical argument in favor of analyzing any foreign project from the viewpoint of the parent. Provide at least three reasons why the parent's viewpoint is superior to the local viewpoint and give an example of when the local viewpoint fails to maximize the value of the firm.

**Answer**
A project might have a positive NPV from the local viewpoint, but fail to consider relevant cash flows from the parent viewpoint. For example, a positive NPV project in one country may result from the erosion of revenues in another. A local manager would not necessarily be expected to be aware of such erosion. It may not be possible to remit all or part of the local cash flows to the parent company and reinvestment opportunities in the local economy may be inferior to what the parent could do elsewhere, thus, a less than maximum use of funds. Political and exchange rate risk add to the uncertainly of cash flows and thus increase the required rate of return by stockholders. Cash flows may be more difficult to estimate especially long-term cash flows in lesser-developed countries.

2. Explain how political risk and exchange rate risk increase the uncertainty of international projects for the purpose of capital budgeting.

**Answer**
The evaluation of foreign projects must consider several risks that are either nonexistent or much less important in domestic capital budgeting. First, if revenues and expenses are in a foreign currency, then the parent firm must estimate the exchange rate at which the foreign currency will be converted into the domestic currency. To estimate future exchange rates, the parent firm must estimate expected rates of inflation and interest rates in both countries, economic growth in each country, as well as consumer preferences and tastes in more than one country. Then, aspects of political risk must be considered. What is the likelihood that all or part of the cash flows accruing to the parent firm will be restricted through some political act? The firm must now consider the possibility of changing tax rates, new taxes, and additional restrictions on the flow of funds. Furthermore, local norms may differ from usual firm practice in terms of financing or dividend policy. Domestic capital budgeting may seem quite easy in comparison.

## Chapter 16: Multinational Capital Budgeting
## Multiple Choice Answer Key:

| | | | | | | | | | |
|---|---|---|---|---|---|---|---|---|---|
| 1 | B | 11 | C | 21 | D | 31 | A | 41 | C |
| 2 | D | 12 | C | 22 | C | 32 | B | 42 | B |
| 3 | C | 13 | A | 23 | B | 33 | D | 43 | A |
| 4 | B | 14 | D | 24 | A | 34 | C | 44 | C |
| 5 | D | 15 | B | 25 | B | 35 | D | 45 | D |
| 6 | A | 16 | D | 26 | C | 36 | A | 46 | D |
| 7 | A | 17 | C | 27 | D | 37 | D | 47 | A |
| 8 | C | 18 | B | 28 | A | 38 | D | 48 | B |
| 9 | B | 19 | D | 29 | C | 39 | B | 49 | C |
| 10 | A | 20 | A | 30 | D | 40 | D | 50 | A |

# Chapter 17
# Adjusting for Risk in Foreign Investment

**Topic: Risk**
**Skill: Recognition**
1. The possibility of suffering harm or loss, or a course involving uncertain danger or hazard is a definition of __________.

a. risk
b. standard deviation
c. beta
d. variance

**Topic: One-sided Risk**
**Skill: Recognition**
2. Which of the following is NOT an example of one-sided risk?

a. The risk of expropriation of assets by the local government
b. The risk of blocked funds by the local government
c. The risk of changing exchange rates
d. All are examples of one-sided risk

**Topic: One-sided Risk**
**Skill: Recognition**
3. Which of the following is NOT an example of one-sided risk?

a. The risk of changing exchange rates
b. The risk of blocked funds by the local government
c. General economic cycles in the foreign country
d. Government policies on tariffs

**Topic: Two-sided Risk**
**Skill: Conceptual**
4. In general, it is easier to quantify one-sided risks than it is to quantify two-sided risks.

a. True
b. False

**Topic: Marketplace Data**
**Skill: Conceptual**
5. ____________ data lends itself better to objective rather than subjective quantification. This type of data is generally ____________ in the countries MNEs are most likely to invest.

a. Institutional; less available
b. Institutional; readily available
c. Marketplace; readily available
d. Marketplace; less available

**Topic: Subjective Measures of International Risk**
**Skill: Recognition**
6. Which of the following is NOT an example of a subjective measure gathered by institutional researchers?

a. A local country's ranking for political stability.
b. A local country's ranking for economic stability.
c. A local country's unemployment rate.
d. All of the above are subjective measures.

**Topic: Firm-specific Risk**
**Skill: Recognition**
7. Of the following, which would NOT be considered a firm-specific risk?

a. The risk of getting new management.
b. Management policies toward hedging foreign exchange risk.
c. Parent company policy toward management of local subsidiaries.
d. All could be considered firm-specific risk.

**Topic: Country-specific Risk**
**Skill: Recognition**
8. ____________ risks are those that affect the MNE at the local or project level, but originate at the country level.

a. Country-specific
b. Firm-specific
c. Global-specific
d. None of the above

**Topic: Country-specific Risk**
**Skill: Recognition**

9. Which of the following is NOT an example of a country-specific risk?

 a. Transfer risk
 b. War and ethnic strife
 c. Cultural and religious heritage
 d. All of the above are examples of country-specific risk.

**Topic: Traditional Measures of International Risk**
**Skill: Recognition**

10. A more traditional risk classification system for international risk than the one used by your authors would use each of the following EXCEPT:

 a. Academic economic theories
 b. Academic political science
 c. Academic health and p.e. theories
 d. Academic finance theories

**Topic: Sensitivity Analysis**
**Skill: Recognition**

11. Which of the following is NOT a type of sensitivity analysis used for managing foreign investment risk?

 a. Plant location
 b. Adjusting discount rates
 c. Adjusting cash flows
 d. Simulating business plans

**Topic: Foreign Investment Risk**
**Skill: Recognition**

12. Which of the following is NOT a strategy to measure and manage foreign investment risks?

 a. Sensitivity analysis
 b. Diversification
 c. Insurance
 d. All are strategies to measure and manage foreign investment risk

**Topic: Business Risk**
**Skill: Conceptual**
13. Your firm is experiencing a form of business risk due to forecasting errors. This result occurs because

a. of a diversified portfolio of assets.
b. of faulty marketing, production, or finance assumptions.
c. local sourcing of production.
d. all of the above.

**Topic: Risk-adjusted Cash Flows**
**Skill: Conceptual**
14. When faced with additional risk from a foreign investment, firms typically account for the additional risk by adjusting the discount rates or by adjusting cash flows.

a. True
b. False

**Topic: Risk-adjusted Discount Rates**
**Skill: Conceptual**
15. Which of the following would be a shortcoming of adjusting discount rates to account for the increased risk of foreign investments?

a. The actual size of the cash inflows may vary from the expected values.
b. The timing of the cash flows are unknown.
c. Treating the uncertain cash flows as if they were one-sided risks rather than two-sided risks.
d. None of the above.

**Topic: Risk-adjusted Discount Rates**
**Skill: Conceptual**
16. Adjusting the discount rate to account for increased political risk is almost always the best possible way to account for risk.

a. True
b. False

**Topic: Risk Adjusted Cash Flows**
**Skill: Conceptual**
17. Surveys of MNEs show that adjusting cash flows is CLEARLY the preferred method of choice for dealing with the uncertainly of foreign investment.

a. True
b. False

**Topic: Market and Production Seeking FDI**
**Skill: Conceptual**
18. The goals of FDI tend to fall into one of the following two categories:

a. market seeking and employment seeking
b. employment seeking and production seeking
c. market seeking and production seeking
d. employment seeking and capital seeking

**Topic: Market-seeking FDI**
**Skill: Conceptual**
19. Which of the following is NOT an example of a market-seeking FDI?

a. Investing in a bauxite mine to ship the raw materials back to the home country.
b. Opening a paper mill in Brazil to sell materials in South America
c. Opening a plant in Germany to sell automobiles in Europe
d. All of these examples are market-seeking FDI.

**Topic: Governance Risk**
**Skill: Recognition**
20. _______________ is the ability to exercise effective control over a foreign subsidiary within a country's legal and political environment.

a. Political risk
b. Portfolio risk
c. Interest rate risk
d. Governance risk

**Topic: Pre-investment Negotiations**
**Skill: Conceptual**
21. Of the following, which would NOT be considered an issue for an investment agreement prior to investing in a foreign country?

a. The basis for setting transfer prices.
b. The right to export to third-country markets.
c. Provision for arbitration of disputes.
d. All of the above could be negotiated prior to investing.

**Topic: OPIC**
**Skill: Recognition**
22. OPIC stands for:

a. Organization for the Prevention of Insufficient Capitalization
b. Organization of Petroleum Importing Countries
c. Overseas Private Investment Corporation
d. Overseas Public Insurance Commission

**Topic: OPIC**
**Skill: Recognition**
23. Which of the following types of political risk does OPIC NOT cover?

a. Inconvertibility
b. Expropriation
c. War
d. OPIC covers all of the above

**Topic: Inconvertibility**
**Skill: Recognition**
24. _______________ is the risk that the investor will not be able to convert profits, royalties, or fees into dollars.

a. Inconvertibility
b. Expropriation
c. Business income risk
d. None of the above

**Topic: Expropriation**
**Skill: Recognition**
25. _______________ is the risk that the host government will take specific steps that prevents the foreign affiliate from exercising control over the firm's assets.

a. Inconvertibility
b. Expropriation
c. Business income risk
d. None of the above

**Topic: FDI Flexibility**
**Skill: Conceptual**
26. FDI may require firms to be flexible in how they do business. Which of the following is NOT a potential problem associated with a firm adapting to a government requirement of local sourcing?

a. A lack of local economies of scale to produce needed raw materials
b. Unreliable delivery schedules on the part of local firms
c. Uncertain quality control
d. All of the above are potential forced local sourcing problems

**Topic: Country-Specific Risks**
**Skill: Recognition**
27. Which of the following is NOT one of the three main country-specific risks as outlined by your authors?

a. Transfer risk
b. Cultural differences
c. Thin equity base
d. Protectionism

**Topic: Blocked Funds**
**Skill: Conceptual**
28. A country can react to the potential for blocked funds prior to making an investment, during operations, or by investing in the local country in assets than maintain their value.

a. True
b. False

**Topic: Two-sided Risk**
**Skill: Conceptual**
29. The risk that exchange rate movements may affect the returns to an investor is an example of:

a. country risk
b. two-sided risk
c. transfer risk
d. political risk

**Topic: Production-seeking Behavior**
**Skill: Conceptual**
30. An FDI project that enters a country for the purpose of constructing an assembly facility for products that is to be re-exported is an example of:

a. resource seeking behavior
b. market seeking behavior
c. production seeking behavior
d. labor seeking behavior

**Topic: Blocked Funds**
**Skill: Recognition**
31. Blocked funds are cash flows that

a. come in regular intervals in standardized amounts or blocks.
b. have been restricted in transfer out of a local country.
c. come from a certain sector or region of the world.
d. none of the above.

**Topic: Fronting Loans**
**Skill: Recognition**
32. A ____________ loan, also known as ____________ is a parent-to-affiliate loan channeled through a financial intermediary such as a large commercial bank.

a. fronting; link financing
b. parallel; a back-to-back loan
c. fronting; a back-to-back loan
d. link financing; parallel loan

**Topic: Fronting Loans**
**Skill: Recognition**
33. Which of the following is NOT a typical characteristic of a fronting loan made to an international subsidiary?

a. The parent makes a deposit equal to the size of the desired loan into a large commercial bank.
b. The bank lends to the subsidiary firm an amount equal to the parent deposit at a slightly higher interest rate.
c. The lending bank is located in the subsidiary's country.
d. All of the above are typical characteristics of a fronting loan.

**Topic: Fronting Loans**
**Skill: Conceptual**
34. Banks are very hesitant engage in fronting loans because of the low probability of repayment and thus their risk exposure up to a 100% loss.

a. True
b. False

**Topic: Fronting Loans**
**Skill: Recognition**
35. Government authorities are more likely to allow subsidiary repayment of a loan to a large international bank than to a parent firm because:

a. Stopping payment to an international bank would have a negative impact on the credit image of the country.
b. The government is also borrowing money from that bank and wants a larger loan before they choose to default.
c. Corrupt government officials have accounts at the bank and they have made an under-the-table agreement not to withhold funds from that bank.
d. None of the above are true.

**Topic: Blocked Funds**
**Skill: Recognition**
36. Which of the following is NOT a technique for moving blocked funds out of a country?

a. Use fronting loans
b. Create unrelated exports
c. Obtain a special dispensation
d. All of the above are techniques for moving blocked funds

**Topic: Blocked Funds**
**Skill: Conceptual**
37. Which of the following could be considered an example of forced reinvestment if the blockage of funds was expected to be temporary?

a. Vertical reinvestment by an automobile manufacturer to buy parts suppliers and showrooms.
b. A lumber cutting company subsequently builds a paper mill with blocked funds
c. Purchase of local money market instruments and short-term loans.
d. All of the above.

**Topic: Sovereign Risk**
**Skill: Recognition**
38. Sovereign risk

a. is the danger that the country's royalty will be overthrown in a military coup.
b. is the danger that a country will need to pay a risk premium to investors in order to raise funds at home or abroad.
c. is the danger that country's royal family is unfit to rule.
d. none of the above.

**Topic: Cultural Differences**
**Skill: Recognition**
39. Of the following, which was NOT identified by the authors as a type of cultural difference that MNEs must consider when expanding to foreign countries?

a. Differences in human resource norms
b. Differences in religious heritage
c. Differences in allowable ownership structures
d. All of the above must be considered

**Topic: Corruption Levels**
**Skill: Recognition**
40. The Scandinavian countries such as Denmark, Finland, and Sweden, are perceived as having the lowest level of corruption in the world.

a. True
b. False

**Topic: Investment Portfolio**
**Skill: Conceptual**
41. A foreign investment undertaken by a MNE that is considered risky from a political and currency perspective may still be undertaken because:

a. the investor is forming a strategic alliance with a domestic partner.
b. the MNE is basing its foreign investment decisions on a portfolio basis.
c. the MNEs management does not believe that risk can be measured or predicted.
d. the investor knows that they will be more than adequately compensate for accepting higher risk.

**Topic: Methods of Risk Adjustment**
**Skill: Conceptual**
42. Which of the following is an acceptable method of adjusting for risk when analyzing the prospects of a foreign investment?

a. adjusting the discount rate
b. adjusting the cash flows
c. conducting sensitively and scenarios analysis
d. all of the above

**Topic: Risk-free Return**
**Skill: Conceptual**

43. The U. S. Treasury bond is considered to be a "risk-free" security because the payment of principal and interest

a. will be adjusted for inflation.
b. will be adjusted for changes in the U.S. dollar's yield curve.
c. will be paid because the U.S. government has the ability to create money to repay bondholders.
d. all of the above are true.

**Topic: Bribery**
**Skill: Recognition**

44. An alternative strategy to engaging in bribery in international investments include:

a. Refuse bribery outright
b. Retain local advisors to diffuse requests for bribes
c. Educate management and local employees about the firm's bribery policy
d. All of the above

**Topic: Protectionism**
**Skill: Recognition**

45. Which of the following industries is NOT typically "protected" by government policy?

a. textiles
b. defense
c. agriculture
d. "infant" industries

**Topic: International Trade Organizations**
**Skill: Recognition**

46. Forming regional alliances is one way to help mitigate the practice of government protectionism. Which of the following is NOT a regional trade organization formed by government treaty?

a. EU
b. NAFTA
c. NATO
d. MERCOSUR

**Topic: Anti-globalization Movements**
**Skill: Recognition**
47. Which of the following is NOT among the leaders in the world's anti-globalization movement?

a. MNEs
b. Environmentalists
c. Unions whose workers lose jobs as a result of trade pacts such as NAFTA
d. Those opposed to the loss of cultural identity due to combinations such as the European Union

**Topic: Anti-pollution Treaties**
**Skill: Conceptual**
48. The United States government has been a willing participant and co-sponsor of international treaties to reduce pollution worldwide.

a. True
b. False

**Topic: Social Issues**
**Skill: Conceptual**
49. Many problems such as poverty, environmental concerns, and cyber attacks are beyond the capabilities of MNEs alone to correct and require government participation as well.

a. True
b. False

**Topic: Business Risk**
**Skill: Conceptual**
50. Business risk can be measured through sensitivity analysis but from only the project viewpoint.

a. True
b. False

## Essay Questions:

1. Generally, firms adjust for the additional risk from investing in foreign locations using one of two techniques. List and explain the two techniques, cite advantages and disadvantages of each, and provide an example of when each might be most appropriate.

**Answer:**
Risk is generally accounted for by developing risk-adjusted cash flows, or by using a risk-adjusted discount rate. Risk-adjusted cash flows would consider the techniques we use in domestic capital budgeting, but then also consider the variability that could be brought on by changing exchange rates, temporary blockage of funds, uncertain demand in foreign markets that consume your service or products, and other various forms of political risk.

A risk-adjusted discount rate attempts to account for the additional risks just mentioned above, but it adjusts the expected cash flows by increasing the discount rate for greater risk, and lowering the discount rate for less risk according to requirements in the market.

Both techniques have fault. As the authors state, adjusting expected cash flows or the rate at which they are discounted may be appropriate for those cash flows, but do not account for the entire risk to the firm implied by political risk and expropriation of the firm itself instead of just a few cash flows. Furthermore, adjusting the discount rate may be appropriate for only a portion of the time period under consideration.

2. What are blocked funds? List and explain two of the three methods the authors list in this chapter for dealing with blocked funds.

**Answer**
Blocked funds are those that have been restricted from foreign exchange in some fashion by the government of the host country. If this is a potential problems firms take a number of steps to reduce or minimize the impact of such a governmental action. In this chapter the authors identify three techniques for dealing with the problem of blocked funds. First, using fronting loans. Here the firm deposits money into a large financial institution, typically in a neutral third country, and then has the bank loan the same amount to the foreign subsidiary. There are several reasons why governments are more likely to allow repayments of such loans as opposed to repayment to the parent.

Second, the local firm may create new exports thus increasing the flow of currency into the country and achieving the goals of the government. Third, the authors also mention a special dispensation whereby firms in highly desirable and specialized industries such as telecommunications or pharmaceuticals are contractually guaranteed repatriation of funds at a greater rate than normal.

## Chapter 17: Adjusting for Risk in Foreign Investment
## Multiple Choice Answer Key:

| | | | | | | | | | |
|---|---|---|---|---|---|---|---|---|---|
| 1 | A | 11 | A | 21 | D | 31 | B | 41 | B |
| 2 | C | 12 | D | 22 | C | 32 | A | 42 | D |
| 3 | B | 13 | B | 23 | D | 33 | C | 43 | C |
| 4 | B | 14 | A | 24 | A | 34 | B | 44 | D |
| 5 | D | 15 | C | 25 | B | 35 | A | 45 | A |
| 6 | C | 16 | B | 26 | D | 36 | D | 46 | C |
| 7 | D | 17 | B | 27 | C | 37 | C | 47 | A |
| 8 | A | 18 | C | 28 | A | 38 | B | 48 | B |
| 9 | D | 19 | A | 29 | B | 39 | D | 49 | A |
| 10 | C | 20 | D | 30 | C | 40 | A | 50 | B |

# Chapter 18
# Cross-Border Mergers, Acquisitions and Valuation

**Topic: Cross-border M&A Activity**
**Skill: Recognition**

1. The bulk of the world's cross-border merger and acquisition activity includes

a. the United States and Japan.
b. the United States and the European Union.
c. Japan and Great Britain.
d. Great Britain and the European Union.

**Topic: Cross-border M&A Activity**
**Skill: Recognition**

2. Cross-border M&A activity among the developing regions of the world accounted for ___________ of worldwide M&A activity in the year 2000.

a. 25% - 35%
b. 15% - 24%
c. 5% - 14%
d. under 5%

**Topic: Cross-border M&A Motivation**
**Skill: Conceptual**

3. The one true motivation for cross-border mergers is to build shareholder value.

a. True
b. False

**Topic: The Global Competitive Environment**
**Skill: Recognition**

4. Which of the following is NOT one of the primary forces of change in the global competitive environment?

a. technological change
b. regulatory change
c. capital market change
d. all of the above are forces of change

**Topic: Cross-border Acquisition Advantages**
**Skill: Recognition**

5. An advantage of a cross-border acquisition over greenfield investments is

a. acquisitions are, on average, quicker.
b. acquisitions may be more competitive if they acquire such assets as industry leading technology.
c. acquisition may be saving a local firm from bankruptcy or take over by an undesirable suitor.
d. all of the above.

**Topic: White Knight**
**Skill: Recognition**

6. Another firm that provides needed capital to stave off bankruptcy or acquisition by an undesirable suitor is sometimes called a

a. corporate raider.
b. greenmail profiteer.
c. white knight.
d. none of the above.

**Topic: Cross-border Acquisition Advantages**
**Skill: Conceptual**

7. The best thing about cross-border acquisitions is that foreign assets are almost always undervalued, so acquisitions are relatively inexpensive.

a. True
b. False

**Topic: Cross-border Acquisition Strategic Planning**
**Skill: Recognition**

8. Which of the following is NOT a strategy and management element of the cross-border acquisition process?

a. financial settlement and compensation
b. identification and valuation of the target
c. completion of the ownership change transaction
d. management of the post-acquisition transition

**Topic: Cross-border Acquisition Strategic Planning**
**Skill: Recognition**

9. Which of the following is NOT a financial analysis and strategy element of the cross-border acquisition process?

a. valuation and negotiation
b. financial settlement and compensation
c. completion of the tender offer
d. rationalization of operations, and integration of financial goals

**Topic: Cross-border Acquisition Problems**
**Skill: Conceptual**

10. ___________ is a problem more often found in ______ markets rather than _____markets.

a. A lack of publicly traded firms; emerging; well-defined
b. Scant financial data; well-defined; emerging
c. A wide choice of publicly traded firms emerging; well-defined
d. None of the above

**Topic: Valuation**
**Skill: Recognition**

11. Valuing target firms for cross-border merger may include which of the following?

a. The basic discounted cash flow model.
b. The multiples of earnings models (earnings or cash flow).
c. Industry specific models.
d. Any of the above.

**Topic: Valuation**
**Skill: Conceptual**

12. Having several valuation techniques available to finance departments for the purpose of valuation is generally more costly than beneficial.

a. True
b. False

**Topic: Hostile Takeover**
**Skill: Recognition**

13. A __________ is in effect when the target's management does not support the acquisition process.

a. hostile takeover
b. greenmail fight
c. Bonnie and Clyde maneuver
d. green knight

**Topic: Regulatory Approval of Mergers**
**Skill: Recognition**
14. To gain approval of a merger, the MNEs involved must gain regulatory approval in their home countries but not in any of the countries in which their subsidiaries may operate.

a. True
b. False

**Topic: Target Shareholder Compensation**
**Skill: Conceptual**
15. Shareholders of target companies are typically paid in

a. government bonds from the target country.
b. government bonds from the acquiring country.
c. cash and/or shares of the acquiring firm..
d. none of the above.

**Topic: Cash Acquisitions**
**Skill: Conceptual**
16. Cash acquisitions

a. have immediate tax consequences for target shareholders.
b. remove the choice of target shareholders of when to realize the tax consequences of the acquisition.
c. reduce uncertainty about the true value of the acquisition.
d. all of the above.

**Topic: Regulatory Delay**
**Skill: Recognition**
17. A destructive force in the settlement process of an acquisition is

a. the size of the acquisition.
b. friendly parties.
c. regulatory delay.
d. the acquiring party is significantly larger than the target firm.

**Topic: Impediments to the Acquisition process**
**Skill: Conceptual**
18. Which would you expect to provide the greatest degree of difficulty in completing the compensation settlement stage of a cross-border acquisition?

a. The parties to the acquisition are all in agreement about the price.
b. Government regulators offer no resistance to the purchase.
c. Major block holders have approved the acquisition
d. None of these appear to be major impediments to the acquisition process

**Topic: Post-acquisition Management**
**Skill: Conceptual**
19. The biggest problem in post-acquisition management is almost always melding corporate cultures.

a. True
b. False

**Topic: The Market for Corporate Control**
**Skill: Recognition**
20. The competitive market for the ownership of corporate assets is collectively known as____________.

a. the stock market
b. the market for corporate control
c. corporate raiding
d. arena football

**Topic: Tender Offers**
**Skill: Recognition**
21. An individual or firm that is buying shares of stock on the open market for the purpose of control of the firm must tender an offer to all shareholders when the purchaser

a. owns the largest block of shares in the firm.
b. has majority control.
c. owns all of the shares outright.
d. may be any of the above, depending on the country of location.

**Topic: Creeping Tender Offers**
**Skill: Conceptual**
22. Creeping tenders for the acquisition of a firm are popular with bidders because

a. they are illegal.
b. they allow secret accumulation of stock ownership prior to making a public offer.
c. they protect against market manipulation by other parties.
d. all of the above.

**Topic: Mandatory Tender Offers**
**Skill: Recognition**
23. ____________ require that the bidder make a full public tender offer to all shareholders once a certain threshold of ownership is reached.

a. Mandatory offers
b. Creeping offers
c. Unlimited offers
d. Regulatory offers

**Topic: Anti-takeover Defenses**
**Skill: Conceptual**
24. Some courts have ruled that target managers in potential acquisitions are limited in the extent that they may enact anti-takeover defenses. Such limitations are designed primarily to protect _____________.

a. bidder bondholders
b. bidder shareholders
c. target shareholders
d. target bondholders

**Topic: Tender Offers**
**Skill: Recognition**
25. Some countries do not allow a bid to be made for less than all of the shares of the target firm once the mandatory offer percentage is reached.

a. True
b. False

**Topic: Cross-border Acquisitions**
**Skill: Conceptual**
26. Which of he following is NOT a potential factor in making cross-border acquisition preferable over greenfield investment?

a. Country risk factors may result in the firm being undervalues.
b. Acquisition may be more cost effective when acquiring rate and valuable assets not openly available on the market.
c. Domestic enterprises in emerging markets wish to be acquired by major MNEs to increase their market power.
d. Currency volatility may result in the target firm being undervalued by foreign country based investors.

**Topic: Cross-border Acquisitions**
**Skill: Conceptual**
27. Emerging markets pose particularly difficult problems for cross-border valuation and acquisition because:

a. the competition to acquire those asserts by MNEs is greater than in well-developed markets.
b. governments often place many restrictions and barriers to foreign investors.
c. the more valuable asserts in emerging markets have generally already migrated to developed markets.
d. all of the above.

**Topic: DCF Valuation**
**Skill: Conceptual**

28. The process of conducting a discounted cash flow valuation of a target company:

a. free cash flows for the future must be estimated.
b. all cash flows must be estimated on an after-tax basis.
c. the future free cash flows must be discounted back to the present.
d. all of the above are true.

**Topic: Chinese Boxes**
**Skill: Recognition**

29. Investor X has 50% ownership in Company A, which in turn has controlling ownership (but less than 100%) in Company B, which in turn has controlling ownership in Company C (but less than 100%), thus giving investor X relative control of Company C. This process of controlling several companies with a relatively small capital investment is known as

a. a pyramid scheme.
b. Japanese Sampan.
c. Chinese Boxes.
d. the trickle down effect.

**Topic: Cross-border Acquisitions**
**Skill: Conceptual**

30. Fortunately, the volume of cross-border acquisitions has taken a relatively complex process and turned it into a simple and mundane exercise.

a. True
b. False

**Topic: Acquisition Process**
**Skill: Recognition**

31. When considering a takeover target the bidder must work its way through three phases in the following order:

a. Identification of the target, Valuation of the target's shares, Prospects for post-acquisition operations
b. Valuation of the target's shares, Identification of the target, Prospects for post-acquisition operations
c. Identification of the target, Prospects for post-acquisition operations, Valuation of the target's shares
d. Prospects for post-acquisition operations, Identification of the target, Valuation of the target's shares

**Topic: Amortization**
**Skill: Recognition**
32. _____________ is a non-cash charge for investments made in other companies over and above the value of the assets purchased.

a. Depreciation
b. Net working capital
c. Statement of cash flows
d. Amortization

**Topic: Net Working Capital**
**Skill: Recognition**
33. Net working capital is calculated as:

a. accounts receivable + accounts payable - inventory
b. inventory + accounts payable – accounts receivable
c. accounts receivable + inventory – accounts payable
d. accounts receivable – inventory – accounts payable

**Topic: Net Operating Profit**
**Skill: Recognition**
34. Which of the following is a method used to calculate net operating profit after taxes (NOPAT)?

a. operating profit – taxes
b. earnings before interest, taxes, depreciation and amortization – taxes
c. earnings before taxes + depreciation + amortization + interest – taxes
d. any of the above

**Topic: Free Cash Flow**
**Skill: Recognition**
35. Free cash flow equals:

a. NOPAT – changes in NWC – capital expenditures
b. NOPAT + changes in NWC – capital expenditures
c. NOPAT – changes in NWC + capital expenditures
d. NOPAT– capital expenditures

**Topic: Free Cash Flow**
**Skill: Recognition**
36. Free cash flow is

a. the desired cash flow for valuation purposes.
b. NOPAT + changes in NWC – capital expenditures.
c. EBITDA – taxes – capital expenditures + changes in NWC.
d. all of the above.

**Topic: Terminal Value**
**Skill: Recognition**

37. For discounted cash flow valuation models __________ captures all free cash flows indefinitely into the future,

a. initial outlay
b. operating free cash flows
c. terminal value
d. shipping and handling

**Topic: WACC**
**Skill: Conceptual**

38. The weighted average cost of capital (wacc) should increase as

a. the risk of the average project undertaken by the firm increases.
b. the firm substitutes equity for debt financing.
c. as the tax rate increases (assuming the firm has debt financing).
d. all of the above.

**Topic: Enterprise Value**
**Skill: Recognition**

39. Enterprise value is equal to

a. the sum of the present value of all future expected cash flows.
b. the sum of the present value of all future expected equity cash flows.
c. the sum of the present value of all future expected debt cash flows.
d. none of the above.

**Topic: Valuation Multiples**
**Skill: Recognition**

40. Which of the following is NOT a common multiple used for valuing firms?

a. market-to-book ratio
b. marked-to-market ratio
c. P/E ratio
d. Price/sales ratio

**Topic: Market Valuation**
**Skill: Recognition**

41. Markets do not pay for past or present earnings.

a. True
b. False

**Topic: Market-to-Book Value**
**Skill: Conceptual**
42. A market-to-book value ratio of 1.00

a. means the firm has a positive NPV.
b. typically indicates that the firm is undervalued in the market place.
c. means the expected value of future cash flows is less than the value of the assets when first purchased.
d. all of the above.

**Topic: Consistency of Valuation Methods**
**Skill: Recognition**
43. The DCF method of firm valuation is consistent with the use of multiples in valuation in that if one technique shows the firm to be undervalued, they all will.

a. True
b. False

**Topic: P/E and M/B Ratios**
**Skill: Recognition**
44. The P/E ratio is a widely used multiple for valuation purposes. The Market-to-book ratio is also widely used.

a. True
b. False

**Topic: Terminal Value**
**Skill: Recognition**
45. The approximation of what a target firm may create in value into the distant future, in a single term, is called:

a. free cash flow
b. amortization
c. terminal value
d. cumulative depreciation

**Topic: Liquidation Value**
**Skill: Recognition**
46. Which of the following is NOT a commonly used measure for valuing an operating acquisition target?

a. discounted cash flow
b. price to earnings ratio
c. liquidation value
d. market to book ratio

**Topic: Book Value**
**Skill: Conceptual**
47. Which of the following is NOT true regarding book value?

a. It represents historical values.
b. As it applies to equity, it is defined as common stock plus paid in capital in excess of par value, plus retained earnings
c. If the M/B ratio exceeds 1, implies that the firm's equity is currently values in excess of what the stockholders invested in the firm.
d. All of the above are true

**Topic: Real Options**
**Skill: Recognition**
48. Which of the following is NOT a real option analysis?

a. the option to defer
b. the option to expand capacity
c. the option to abandon
d. all are real options

**Topic: Price to Earnings Ratio**
**Skill: Recognition**
49. Which of the following is often used as an indicator of the market's assessment of the quality and sustainability of a company's earnings?

a. market to book ratio
b. price to earnings ratio
c. free cash flow to book ratio
d. none of the above

**Topic: Multiples**
**Skill: Recognition**
50. The use of a ratio for the subject firm is compared to comparable ratios for competitors or recent acquisitions is termed:

a. multiples
b. discounted cash flow
c. price to earnings per share
d. market to book

## Essay Questions:

1. There are several alternative methods for valuing potential acquisition targets in the international arena. The authors identify and explain at least three methods of valuation. Identify and explain two of these methods.

**Answer**
The first technique is the discounted cash flow (DCF) technique that is commonly used for domestic projects as well. Here the firm is valued as the present value of all future free cash flows. The P/E ratio demonstrates what the market is willingly to pay per dollar of current earnings (or projected earnings). Higher ratios are usually indicative of higher expected growth rates. The ratio also reflects expectations about risk. A third technique is the market-to-book ratio that may be interpreted as demonstrating what the market is willing to pay above and beyond what the shareholders have already invested in the form of original capital plus subsequent retained earnings.

2. The authors identify three levels of accumulation of shares of stock as part of the market for corporate control. Those levels are 1) accumulating the single largest block ownership of stock, 2) majority control, and 3) owning all of the shares outright. Describe each of these ownership possibilities and provide advantages and disadvantages of each. Be sure to consider the viewpoint of multiple stakeholders in your answer.

**Answer**
Creeping tender offers, or the secret accumulation of stock in a single firm, allows investors to gain control of a portion of a company without announcing their intentions and without having to make an offer of a higher than market stock price to gain shares. That works well for the bidder, but some sellers are left without the opportunity to gain from the higher prices.

Majority control gives the owners the ability to control the assets of the firm without having to pay for all of the assets. Of course, they do not get all of the benefits of their decision making because they have only partial ownership.

Complete ownership eliminates any conflict of interest among shareholders and usually makes it easier for owners to reduce agency costs. However, it also requires the greatest investment in the firm.

## Chapter 18: Cross-Border Mergers, Acquisitions and Valuation
## Multiple Choice Answer Key:

| | | | | | | | | | |
|---|---|---|---|---|---|---|---|---|---|
| 1 | B | 11 | D | 21 | D | 31 | A | 41 | A |
| 2 | C | 12 | B | 22 | B | 32 | D | 42 | B |
| 3 | A | 13 | A | 23 | A | 33 | C | 43 | B |
| 4 | D | 14 | B | 24 | C | 34 | D | 44 | A |
| 5 | D | 15 | C | 25 | A | 35 | B | 45 | C |
| 6 | C | 16 | D | 26 | C | 36 | D | 46 | C |
| 7 | B | 17 | C | 27 | B | 37 | C | 47 | D |
| 8 | A | 18 | D | 28 | D | 38 | A | 48 | D |
| 9 | C | 19 | A | 29 | C | 39 | A | 49 | B |
| 10 | A | 20 | B | 30 | B | 40 | B | 50 | A |

# Chapter 19
# International Portfolio Theory and Diversification

**Topic: Beta**
**Skill: Recognition**
1. Beta may be defined as

a. the measure of systematic risk.
b. a risk measure of a portfolio.
c. the ratio of the variance of the portfolio to the variance of the market.
d. all of the above.

**Topic: Beta**
**Skill: Recognition**
2. _____________ risk is measured with beta.

a. Systematic
b. Unsystematic
c. International
d. Domestic

**Topic: Beta**
**Skill: Conceptual**
3. A fully diversified domestic portfolio has a beta of

a. 0.0.
b. 1.0.
c. –1.0.
d. Not enough information to answer this question.

**Topic: Portfolio Diversification**
**Skill: Conceptual**
4. Portfolio diversification can eliminate 100% of risk.

a. True
b. False

**Topic: Unsystematic Risk**
**Skill: Recognition**
5. Unsystematic risk is

a. the remaining risk in a well-diversified portfolio.
b. measured with beta.
c. can be diversified away.
d. all of the above.

**Topic: Portfolio Diversification**
**Skill: Recognition**
6. A well-diversified portfolio is only about ________ as risky as the typical individual stock.

a. 8%
b. 19%
c. 27%
d. 52%

**Topic: Portfolio Diversification**
**Skill: Conceptual**
7. Increasing the number of securities in a portfolio reduces the unsystematic risk but not the systematic risk.

a. True
b. False

**Topic: International Portfolio Diversification**
**Skill: Conceptual**
8. An internationally diversified portfolio

a. should result in a portfolio with a lower beta than a purely domestic portfolio.
b. has the same overall risk shape as a purely domestic portfolio.
c. is only about 12% as risky as the typical individual stock.
d. all of the above.

**Topic: International Portfolio Diversification**
**Skill: Conceptual**
9. In some respects, internationally diversified portfolios are the same in principle as a domestic portfolio because

a. the investor is attempting to combine assets that are perfectly correlated.
b. investors are tying to reduce systematic risk.
c. investors are trying to reduce the total risk of the portfolio.
d. all of the above.

**Topic: International Portfolio Diversification**
**Skill: Conceptual**

10. In some respects, internationally diversified portfolios are the different from a domestic portfolio because

a. investors may also acquire foreign exchange risk.
b. international portfolio diversification increases expected return but does not decrease risk.
c. investors must leave the country to acquire foreign securities.
d. all of the above.

**Use the following information to answer questions 11 – 14.**
In September 2002 a U.S. investor chooses to invest $500,000 in German equity securities at a then current spot rate of $0.95/€. At the end of one year the spot rate is $1.00/€.

**Topic: International Investment Returns**
**Skill: Analytical**

11. How many euros will the U.S. investor acquire with his initial $500,000 investment?

a. €475,000
b. €477,371
c. €525,000
d. €526,316

**Topic: International Investment Returns**
**Skill: Analytical**

12. At an average price of €60/share, how many shares of stock will the investor be able to purchase?

a. 8750 shares
b. 8772 shares
c. 7917 shares
d. 7956 shares

**Topic: International Investment Returns**
**Skill: Analytical**

13. At the end of the year the investor sells his stock that now has an average price per share of €57. What is the investor's average rate of return before converting the stock back into dollars?

a. 5.0%
b. –3.0%
c. –5.0%
d. 3.0%

**Topic: International Investment Returns**
**Skill: Analytical**
14. At the end of the year the investor sells his stock that now has an average price per share of €57. What is the investor's average rate of return after converting the stock back into dollars?

a. 0.0%
b. 5.0%
c. –5.0%
d. –2.0%

**Topic: International Investment Returns**
**Skill: Analytical**
15. A U.S. investor make an investment in Britain and earns 14% on the investment while the British pound appreciates against the U.S. dollar by 8%. What is the investor's total return?

a. 22.00%
b. 23.14%
c. 6.00%
d. 4.88%

**Topic: International Portfolio Diversification**
**Skill: Conceptual**
16. Which of he following statements is NOT true?

a. International diversification benefits induce investors to demand foreign securities.
b. An international security adds value to a portfolio if it reduces risk without reducing return.
c. Investors will demand a security that adds value.
d. All of the above are true.

**Topic: Risk Aversion**
**Skill: Conceptual**
17. Portfolio theory assumes that investors are risk-averse. This means that investors

a. cannot be induced to make risky investments.
b. prefer more risk to less for a given return.
c. will accept some risk, but not unnecessary risk.
d. all of the above are true.

**Topic: The Efficient Frontier**
**Skill: Recognition**
18. The efficient frontier of the domestic portfolio opportunity set

a. runs along the extreme left edge of the opportunity set.
b. represents optimal portfolios of securities that represent minimum risk for a given level of expected portfolio return.
c. contains the portfolio of risky securities that the logical investor would choose to hold.
d. all of the above.

**Topic: The Efficient Frontier**
**Skill: Recognition**
19. The graph for the efficient frontier has beta on the vertical axis and standard deviation of the horizontal axis.

a. True
b. False

**Topic: Minimum Risk Domestic Portfolio**
**Skill: Recognition**
20. The portfolio with the least risk among all those possible in the domestic portfolio opportunity set is called the minimum risk domestic portfolio.

a. True
b. False

**Topic: The Efficient Frontier**
**Skill: Conceptual**
21. The addition of foreign securities to the domestic portfolio opportunity set shifts the efficient frontier

a. down and to the left.
b. up and to the right.
c. up and to the left.
d. down and to the right.

**Topic: The Efficient Frontier**
**Skill: Conceptual**
22. Relative to the efficient frontier of risky portfolios, it is impossible to hold a portfolio that is located ________________ the efficient frontier.

a. to the left of
b. to the right of
c. on
d. to the right or left of

**Topic: The Optimal Domestic Portfolio**
**Skill: Recognition**
23. The optimal domestic portfolio of risky securities is the portfolio of minimum risk.

a. True
b. False

**Topic: Capital Market Line**
**Skill: Recognition**
24. The ______________ connects the risk-free security with the optimal domestic portfolio.

a. security market line
b. capital asset pricing model
c. capital market line
d. none of the above

**Topic: The Efficient Frontier**
**Skill: Conceptual**
25. Which of the following portfolios could not possibly be located on the efficient frontier of risky portfolios?

a. Portfolio 1 with an expected return of 6% and a standard deviation of 6%.
b. Portfolio 2 with an expected return of 10% and a standard deviation of 12%.
c. Portfolio 3 with an expected return of 10% and a standard deviation of 8%.
d. Portfolio 4 with an expected return of 12% and a standard deviation of 20%.

**Topic: Risk-free Security**
**Skill: Conceptual**
26. The standard deviation of the risk-free security is

a. less than the standard deviation of the optimal risky domestic portfolio.
b. less than the standard deviation of the optimal international portfolio.
c. is equal to zero.
d. all of the above.

**Use the following information to answer questions 27 - 28**
A U.S. investor is considering a portfolio consisting of 60% invested in the U.S. equity index fund and 40% invested in the British equity index fund. The expected returns for the funds are 10% for the U.S. and 8% for the British, standard deviations of 20% for the U.S. and 18% for the British, and a correlation coefficient of .15 between the U.S. and British equity funds.

**Topic: Portfolio Expected Return**
**Skill: Analytical**
27. What is the expected return of the proposed portfolio?

a. 9.2%
b. 9.0%
c. 19.2%
d. 19%

**Topic: Portfolio Standard Deviation**
**Skill: Analytical**
28. What is standard deviation of the proposed portfolio?

a. 38.00
b. 19.20
c. 19.00
d. 14.89

**Topic: Correlation Coefficient**
**Skill: Recognition**
29. The correlation coefficient has a range of

a. 0 to 1
b. 1 to 10
c. –1 to 1
d. –1 to 0

**Topic: Portfolio Standard Deviation**
**Skill: Recognition**
30. The standard deviation of a portfolio is the weighted average risks of the individual assets.

a. True
b. False

**Topic: Correlation Coefficient**
**Skill: Recognition**
31. The correlation of returns of the U.S. equity market index with the indexes of equity markets in seventeen other countries over the period 1977 – 1996 is between

a. –1 and -.50.
b. 1 and .50.
c. -.50 and 0.0.
d. 0.0 and .50.

**Topic: Sharpe and Treynor Measures**
**Skill: Recognition**

32. The Sharpe and Treynor measures are each measures of return per unit of risk.

a. True
b. False

**Topic: Sharpe and Treynor Measures**
**Skill: Recognition**

33. The Sharpe measure uses __________ as the measure of risk and the Treynor measure uses ____________ as the measure of risk.

a. standard deviation; variance
b. beta; variance
c. standard deviation; beta
d. beta; standard deviation

**Use the following information to answer questions 34 - 36**

| Country | Risk-free Mean Return (Monthly %) | Mean Return (Monthly %) | Standard Deviation | Beta |
|---|---|---|---|---|
| Austria | .42 | 0.77 | 6.52 | 1.02 |
| France | .42 | 1.18 | 6.76 | 1.08 |
| Japan | .42 | 1.08 | 6.66 | 1.21 |
| Netherlands | .42 | 1.39 | 4.93 | 0.89 |
| United States | .42 | 1.01 | 4.16 | 0.82 |

**Topic: Sharpe Measure**
**Skill: Analytical**

34. What is the value of the Sharpe Measure for France?

a. 0.113
b. .0071
c. either a or b
d. neither a nor b

**Topic: Treynor Measure**
**Skill: Analytical**

35. What is the value of the Treynor Measure for the Netherlands?

a. .197
b. .0109
c. either a or b
d. neither a nor b

**Topic: Sharpe Measure and Standard Deviation**
**Skill: Recognition**
36. ____________ appears to have the greatest amount of risk as measured by monthly standard deviation, but ________________ has the best return per unit of risk according to the Sharpe Measure.

a. United States; Austria
b. France; Austria
c. United States; Netherlands
d. France; Netherlands

**Topic: Sharpe and Treynor Measures**
**Skill: Conceptual**
37. The Sharpe and Treynor Measures tend to be consistent in their ranking of portfolios when the portfolio

a. is poorly diversified.
b. is properly diversified.
c. contains only U.S. equity investments.
d. none of the above.

**Topic: Capital Market Integration**
**Skill: Recognition**
38. Capital markets around the world are on average less integrated today than they were 20 years ago.

a. True
b. False

**Topic: CAPM**
**Skill: Conceptual**
39. Which of the following is NOT an important question regarding the validity of a global version of the capital asset pricing model (CAPM)?

a. Barriers to the free and open movement of capital across boundaries.
b. Difficulties in estimating a global portfolio. I.e., trading limitations, illiquid markets, and incomplete information.
c. The lack of a single true worldwide risk-free security.
d. All of the above

**Topic: CAPM**
**Skill: Recognition**

40. According to the capital asset pricing model (CAPM), which of the following is true?

a. The expected return on an asset is equal to the risk-free rate plus the amount of risk, beta, multiplied by the market risk premium.
b. The expected return on an asset is equal to the market rate plus the amount of risk, beta, multiplied by the market risk premium.
c. The expected return on an asset is equal to the risk-free rate plus the amount of risk, standard deviation, multiplied by the market risk premium.
d. None of the above.

**Topic: International Portfolio Diversification**
**Skill: Conceptual**

41. The international diversification of a portfolio

a. results in lower diversifiable risk of the portfolio.
b. decreases the currency risk component of the portfolio.
c. reduces the systematic risk component of the portfolio.
d. none of the above.

**Topic: International Portfolio Diversification**
**Skill: Conceptual**

42. Portfolio diversification is beneficial to the investor because it

a. reduces expected returns and increases risk.
b. increases expected returns.
c. reduces risk for given levels of return.
d. none of the above.

**Topic: International Investment Returns**
**Skill: Analytical**

43. A Canadian-based investor purchases a Standard & Poors 500 index (SPY) and the American Stock Exchange, in U.S. dollars. Over the course of the year the U. S. dollar appreciates 8% against the Canadian dollar, and the S&P Index rises 22%. The total return to the Canadian investor in Canadian dollar terms is approximately ________.

a. 8%
b. 14%
c. 22%
d. 30%

**Topic: International Portfolio Diversification**
**Skill: Conceptual**
44. The construction of an internationally diversified portfolio combines

a. currency and asset risk and return.
b. country risk with currency return.
c. credit risk with inflation risk.
d. asset risk with sovereign risk.

**Topic: Portfolio Diversification**
**Skill: Conceptual**
45. If a portfolio is constructed with only two assets, of equal weights, and the correlation coefficient between the two assets is exactly 1.0, which of the following is true?

a. The portfolio risk reduction is maximized
b. The return of the two assets over time are seen to follow different cycles or paths
c. Risk is not reduced significantly because of the positive correlation
d. None of the above are true

**Topic: Correlation Coefficient**
**Skill: Conceptual**
46. The maximum benefits of portfolio construction are obtained when the correlation between assets is _________.

a. -1.0
b. 0.0
c. +1.0
d. none of the above

**Topic: International Efficient Frontier**
**Skill: Conceptual**
47. The efficient frontier for an international investor is

a. not capable of being compared to that of a domestic investor unless currency risk has been eliminated.
b. greater than for a domestic investor.
c. maximized at the expected risk and return of the emerging market assets in the portfolio.
d. all of the above.

**Topic: Sharpe Measure**
**Skill: Recognition**

48. The Sharpe Measure of portfolio performance calculates the average return of the portfolio above that of the

a. market, per unit of portfolio risk.
b. market, per unit of beta risk.
c. risk-free rate, per unit of beta.
d. market, per unit of portfolio risk.

**Topic: Treynor Measure**
**Skill: Recognition**

49. The Treynor Measure of portfolio performance calculates the average return of the portfolio above that of the

a. market, per unit of portfolio risk.
b. risk-free rate, per unit of beta.
c. market, per unit of portfolio risk.
d. none of the above.

**Topic: International Portfolio Diversification**
**Skill: Recognition**

50. Which of the following is a potential obstacle to international diversification of portfolios?

a. high transaction costs
b. higher information costs
c. both a and b
d. none of the above

## Essay Questions:

1. Draw the curve representing the Optimal Domestic Efficient Frontier. Be sure to draw and label the following: The vertical axis and the horizontal axis, the risk-free security, the minimum risk portfolio, the domestic portfolio opportunity set, the optimal domestic portfolio, and the capital market line. Choose a point along the domestic portfolio opportunity set between the optimal domestic portfolio and the minimum risk domestic portfolio and explain why that point is not the optimal risky domestic portfolio for investors to hold.

**Answer**
The graph should look like that found on page 19 – 5. To answer the second part of the question, the student should draw a straight-line beginning at the point of the risk-free rate of return on the vertical axis and running through the point he/she just put on the opportunity set between the minimum risk portfolio and the optimal domestic portfolio. This graphical representation clearly shows that at any point other than holding 100% in the risk-free security, the expected risk and risk characteristics of the capital market line clearly dominate the new line just drawn.

2. If an investor is able to determine a global beta for his portfolio and holds a portfolio that is well-diversified with international investments, which performance measure is more appropriate, the Sharpe Measure or the Treynor Measure? Why? Explain each performance measure.

**Answer**
The Sharpe Measure is the ratio of excess returns above the risk-free rate of return to the standard deviation of the portfolio. The Treynor Measure substitutes the beta of the portfolio for the denominator. Thus Sharpe measures reward per unit of portfolio risk while Treynor measures reward per unit of systematic risk. In this example, the portfolio risk and systematic risk are equivalent so either measure is appropriate.

### Chapter 19: International Portfolio Theory and Diversification
### Multiple Choice Answer Key:

| | | | | | | | | | |
|---|---|---|---|---|---|---|---|---|---|
| 1 | D | 11 | D | 21 | C | 31 | D | 41 | C |
| 2 | A | 12 | B | 22 | A | 32 | A | 42 | C |
| 3 | B | 13 | C | 23 | B | 33 | C | 43 | D |
| 4 | B | 14 | A | 24 | C | 34 | A | 44 | A |
| 5 | C | 15 | B | 25 | B | 35 | B | 45 | C |
| 6 | C | 16 | D | 26 | D | 36 | D | 46 | A |
| 7 | A | 17 | C | 27 | A | 37 | B | 47 | B |
| 8 | D | 18 | D | 28 | D | 38 | B | 48 | D |
| 9 | C | 19 | B | 29 | C | 39 | D | 49 | B |
| 10 | A | 20 | A | 30 | B | 40 | A | 50 | C |

# Chapter 20
# Multinational Tax Management

**Topic: Tax Planning Objectives**
**Skill: Recognition**
1. The primary objective of multinational tax planning is to minimize the firm's worldwide tax burden.

a. True
b. False

**Topic: Taxation Ethics**
**Skill: Conceptual**
2. The issue of ethics in the reporting of income and the payment of taxes is a considerable one. The authors state that most MNEs operating in foreign countries tend to follow the general principle of

a. "when in Rome, do as the Romans do".
b. full disclosure to the tax authorities.
c. maintain a competitive playing field by cheating as much as the local competition, no more, no less.
d. none of the above.

**Topic: Tax Policy Objectives**
**Skill: Recognition**
3. Which of the following is an unlikely objective of U.S. government policy for the taxation of foreign MNEs?

a. To raise revenues.
b. To provide an incentive for U.S. private investment in developing countries.
c. To improve the U.S. balance of payments.
d. All of the above are objectives.

**Topic: Tax Policy**
**Skill: Conceptual**
4. A _________tax policy is one that has no impact on private decision-making, while a ______________ policy is designed to encourage specific behavior.

a. flat; tax incentive
b. neutral; flat
c. neutral; tax incentive
d. none of the above

**Topic: Tax Incentive Policy**
**Skill: Conceptual**

5. Which of the following is NOT an example of a tax incentive policy.

   a. The federal government gives a tax credit to MNEs that make domestic capital improvements but not foreign capital improvements.
   b. Corporations are allowed to take a direct tax credit for each dollar of matching donations they make to institutions of higher education.
   c. A tax law is passed that makes interest on property non tax-deductible, but interest payments on durable goods are.
   d. All are examples of a tax incentive policy.

**Topic: Foreign Neutrality Tax Policy**
**Skill: Recognition**

6. General Motors operates in many different countries and pays taxes at many different rates. However, they always pay the same rate as their local competitors. General Motors is operating in an environment of _________ tax policy.

   a. domestic neutrality
   b. foreign neutrality
   c. territorial approach
   d. none of the above

**Topic: Worldwide Tax Approach**
**Skill: Recognition**

7. The United States taxes the domestic and remitted foreign earnings of U.S. based MNEs no matter where the earnings occurred. This is an example of a __________ approach to levying taxes.

   a. worldwide
   b. territorial
   c. neutral
   d. equitable

**Topic: Territorial Tax Approach**
**Skill: Conceptual**

8. The United States taxes all earnings on U.S. soil by both domestic and foreign firms. This is an example of a ___________ approach to levying taxes.

   a. worldwide
   b. neutral
   c. territorial
   d. none of the above

**Topic: Worldwide and Territorial Tax Approach**
**Skill: Conceptual**
9. A country CANNOT have both a territorial and a worldwide approach as a national tax policy.

a. True
b. False

**Topic: Worldwide and Territorial Tax Approach**
**Skill: Analytical**
10. Jensen Optimetrics Inc. is based in a country with a territorial approach to taxation but generates 100% of its income in a country with a worldwide approach to taxation. The tax rate in the country of incorporation is 25%, and the tax rate in the country where they earn their income is 50%. In theory, and barring any special provisions in the tax codes of either country, Jensen should pay taxes at a rate of __________.

a. 75%
b. 62.5%
c. 0%
d. 50%

**Topic: Territorial Approach**
**Skill: Recognition**
11. The *territorial* approach to taxation policy is also termed the _______approach.

a. source
b. ethical
c. greedy
d. location

**Topic: Tax Treaties**
**Skill: Conceptual**
12. Tax treaties generally have the effect of increasing the withholding taxes between the countries that are negotiating the treaties.

a. True
b. False

**Topic: Indirect and Direct Taxes**
**Skill: Recognition**
13. _______ taxes are applied to income and ________ taxes are applied to some other measurable performance characteristic of the firm.

a. income; direct
b. indirect; income
c. indirect; direct
d. direct; indirect

**Topic: International Corporate Tax Rates**
**Skill: Recognition**
14. Depending on the host country, corporate income taxes worldwide may be as low as _________.

a. 0%
b. 5%
c. 10%
d. 15%

**Topic: Foreign Withholding Taxes**
**Skill: Conceptual**
15. The basic idea behind withholding taxes for foreign investors is

a. to receive taxes on passively earned income.
b. a recognition that most foreign investors are unlikely to file taxes in the host country.
c. to ensure that income earned is taxed by the host country.
d. all of the above.

**Topic: Value-added Tax**
**Skill: Recognition**
16. A value-added tax has gained widespread usage in Western Europe Canada and part so of Latin America.

a. True
b. False

**Topic: Value-added Tax**
**Skill: Recognition**

17. A tax that is effectively a sales tax at each stage of production is defined as a/an __________ tax.

   a. flat
   b. equitable
   c. value-added tax
   d. none of the above

**Topic: International Taxation**
**Skill: Analytical**

18. What is the total value of taxes paid in the following example if the value added tax is 10%? A farmer raises wheat that he sells for $1.50 to the grain company. The grain company sells to the processor for $2.00 per bushel. The processor turns the wheat into a breakfast cereal and wholesales it for $3.00 per bushel. The retailer sells the cereal for $4.00 per bushel.

   a. $.15
   b. $.20
   c. $.30
   d. $.40

**Topic: Transfer Tax**
**Skill: Recognition**

19. A tax that is a form of social redistribution of income is defined as a/an ________ tax.

   a. un-American
   b. transfer
   c. flat
   d. none of the above

**Topic: Tax Credits and Tax Deductions**
**Skill: Recognition**

20. A ________ is a direct reduction of taxes whereas a __________ reduces the taxable income before taxes.

   a. foreign tax credit; domestic tax credit
   b. tax deduction; tax credit
   c. tax credit; tax deduction
   d. none of the above

**Topic: Tax Credits and Tax Deductions**
**Skill: Conceptual**
21. Tax credits are less valuable on a dollar-for-dollar basis than are tax-deductible expenses.

a. True
b. False

**Use the following information to answer questions 22 - 25**
Rogue River Exporters USA has $100,000 of before tax foreign income. The host country has a corporate income tax rate of 25% and the U.S. has a corporate income tax rate of 35%.

**Topic:**
**Skill: Analytical**
22. If the U.S. has no bilateral trade agreement with the host country, what is the total amount of income taxes Rogue River Exporters will pay?

a. $25,000
b. $35,000
c. $51,250
d. $60,000

**Topic: International Taxation**
**Skill: Analytical**
23. If the U.S. has a bilateral trade agreement with the host country that calls for the total tax paid to be equal to the maximum amount that could be paid in the highest taxing country, what is the total amount of income taxes Rogue River Exporters will pay to the host country, and how much will they pay in U.S income taxes on the foreign earned income?

a. $25,000; $10,000
b. $25,000; $26,250
c. $35,000; $0
d. none of the above

**Topic: International Taxation**
**Skill: Analytical**
24. If the U.S treated the taxes paid on income earned in the host country as a tax-deductible expense, then Rogue River's total U.S. corporate tax on the foreign earnings would be _____________.

a. $10,000
b. $26,250
c. $35,000
d. $51,250

**Topic: International Taxation**
**Skill: Analytical**
25. If the U.S treated the taxes paid on income earned in the host country as a tax-credit, then Rogue River's total U.S. corporate tax on the foreign earnings would be _____________.

a. $51,250
b. $35,000
c. $26,250
d. $10,000

**Topic: International Taxation**
**Skill: Recognition**
26. Which of the following factors is not important for U.S. corporations for determining the amount of foreign tax credit allowed for direct taxes paid on income in a foreign country?

a. The Foreign corporate income tax rate
b. The U.S. corporate income tax rate
c. The foreign corporate dividend withholding tax rate
d. All of the above are important factors

**Topic: Tax Treaties**
**Skill: Recognition**
27. Tax treaties typically result in ________ between the two countries in question.

a. lower property taxes for U.S. citizens overseas
b. elimination of differential tax rates
c. increased double taxation
d. reduced withholding tax rates

**Topic: Value–added Tax**
**Skill: Recognition**
28. The value-added tax is

a. similar to an ad valorem tax on imports
b. a form of direct taxation on corporate income
c. a form of national sales tax
d. none of the above

**Topic: Tax Neutrality**
**Skill: Conceptual**
29. Domestic tax neutrality means that

a. a dollar earned anywhere in the world by a U.S. corporation is taxed the same as if earned in the U.S.
b. tax rates are neither regressive nor progressive.
c. foreign affiliates must neutralize their income by subtraction of foreign investment credits.
d. all of the above.

**Topic: International Tax Rates**
**Skill: Conceptual**
30. Some countries assess extremely low corporate income tax rates on foreign source income in order to:

a. attract tax haven affiliates of foreign multinationals.
b. boost the value of their domestic currency.
c. support higher taxes of their domestic companies.
d. none of the above.

**Topic: Foreign Tax Credits**
**Skill: Conceptual**
31. Foreign tax credits for a taxpayer

a. may be used to reduce taxes levied on domestic income.
b. are unlimited in any single year.
c. are limited to the U.S. tax on that foreign income.
d. none of the above.

**Topic: Foreign Tax Credits**
**Skill: Conceptual**
32. Foreign tax credits, unlike domestic tax credits may NOT be carried forward or backward.

a. True
b. False

**Topic: Foreign Tax Averaging**
**Skill: Conceptual**
33. Foreign tax averaging

a. may allow a firm to offset tax credits on income from a high tax nation against tax deficits from a low tax nation.
b. apply to like sources of income only (e.g., active income vs. active income).
c. is not allowable for a firm trying to offset credits on active income vs. a deficit on passive income.
d. all of the above.

Topic: Regulation Subpart F
Skill: Recognition
34. Subpart F income includes

a. passive income such as dividends.
b. income from insurance payouts.
c. financial services income.
d. all of the above.

**Topic: Foreign Taxes**
**Skill: Recognition**
35. Foreign branch offices are included in consolidated statements for tax purposes but local corporate subsidiaries are not.

a. True
b. False

**Topic: Tax Havens**
**Skill: Recognition**
36. Which of the following is NOT a characteristic of "international offshore financial centers" also known as tax havens.

a. A low tax on foreign investment.
b. An unstable currency to discourage investment in the local economy.
c. Infrastructure and workforce to support financial services.
d. Government stability.

**Topic: Foreign Sales Corporations**
**Skill: Recognition**
37. These were introduced in the Tax Reform Act of 1984 as a device to provide tax-exempt income for U.S. persons or corporations having export-oriented activities.

a. offshore banks
b. import/export firms
c. foreign sales corporations
d. none of the above

**Topic: Foreign Sales Corporations**
**Skill: Recognition**
38. A foreign sales corporation total trade income must be derived from the import of goods and services.

a. True
b. False

**Topic: Foreign-source Tax Credits and Deficits**
**Skill: Conceptual**
39. Tax credits or deficits from foreign-source income cannot be applied to net tax positions in domestic-source income and vice versa.

a. True
b. False

**Topic: Foreign-source Tax Credits and Deficits**
**Skill: Recognition**
40. Foreign-source income can be classified as active or passive. ________ income is taxed as it is remitted to the U.S. parent, while _______ income is taxed _________.

a. Passive; active; as it is earned
b. Passive; active; only in the country of origin
c. Active; passive; as it is earned
d. Active; passive; only in the country of origin

**Topic: Foreign-source Tax Credits and Deficits**
**Skill: Conceptual**
41. If foreign-derived incomes come from the same "basket" under U.S. law, then one subsidiary's foreign tax deficit can offset another subsidiaries foreign tax credit.

a. True
b. False

**Topic: Shareholder Value**
**Skill: Conceptual**
42. Developing foreign markets can create shareholder value. Manipulating global tax payments does not create shareholder value.

a. True
b. False

**Topic: Excess Foreign Tax Credit**
**Skill: Recognition**
43. Poland has a corporate income tax rate that is higher than that in the United States by the amount of 40% in Poland and 35% in the U.S. This differential mean that a U.S. parent operating with a subsidiary in Poland can realize an

a. excess profit on their Polish investment.
b. excess foreign tax deficit.
c. excess foreign tax credit.
d. none of the above.

**Topic: Value-added Tax**
**Skill: Conceptual**
44. Which of the following is NOT a disadvantage of the value-added tax?

a. The tax may have an inflationary impact
b. It is a regressive tax
c. It increases the total tax burden
d. All are disadvantages

**Topic: Withholding Tax**
**Skill: Conceptual**
45. The purpose of a withholding tax on dividend income is to:

a. raise the effective as rate of the local host country.
b. provide an incentive for MNEs to pay higher dividends to their parent companies.
c. obtain a minimum tax payment on the incomes of dividend income receipts.
d. encourage MNEs to reposition profits outside of their countries.

**Uses the following information to answer questions 46 – 50.**
MetroCity Designs Inc., located in Northern California, has two international subsidiaries, one located in the Ukraine, the other in Korea. Consider the information below to answer the next several questions.

| | Ukraine | Korea | United States |
|---|---|---|---|
| Earnings Before Taxes | $2,000,000 | $2,500,000 | |
| Corporate Income Tax Rate | 40% | 26% | 35% |
| Dividend withholding Tax Rate | 10% | 5% | 0% |

**Topic: Foreign-source Taxes**
**Skill: Analytical**
46. If MetroCity pays out 50% of its earnings from each subsidiary, what are the additional U.S. taxes due on the foreign sourced income from the Ukraine and Korea respectively.

a. Ukraine = $0; Korea = ($30,000)
b. Ukraine = $100,000; Korea = $0
c. Ukriane$0; Korea = $66,250
d. None of the above

**Topic: Foreign-source Taxes**
**Skill: Analytical**
47. The additional U.S. taxes due on the repatriation of income from the Ukraine to the United States, alone, assuming a 50% payout rate, is:

a. excess foreign tax credits of $110,000
b. additional U.S. taxes due of $97,000
c. additional U.S. taxes due of $36,500
d. excess foreign tax credits of $18,500

**Topic: Foreign-source Taxes**
**Skill: Analytical**
48. How much in additional U.S. taxes would be due if MetroCity averaged the tax credits and liabilities of the two foreign units, assuming a 50% payout rate from each?

a. $3,750
b. $13,750
c. $2,500
d. $0

**Topic: Foreign-source Taxes**
**Skill: Analytical**
49. If MetroCity set the payout rate from the Ukraine subsidiary at 25%, how should MetroCity set the payout rate of the Korean subsidiary (approxiamtely) to more efficiently manage its total foreign tax bill?

a. 28.5%
b. 24.5%
c. 42.6%
d. 82.3%

**Topic: Foreign-source Taxes**
**Skill: Recognition**
50. What is the minimum effective tax rate that MetroCity can achieve on its foreign-sourced income?

a. 26%
b. 35%
c. 40%
d. 0%

## Essay Questions:

1. Explain the worldwide and territorial approaches of national taxation. The authors state that the United States uses both approaches. How can this be? Give an example of each taxation approach.

**Answer**
The worldwide approach taxes the income of firms based on their place of residence rather than on where the income was earned. Thus, a U.S. based MNE will owe U.S. taxes on income earned in, say, Britain. The territorial approach to taxation taxes all of the income earned within the borders of the country by both domestic and foreign-based firms. Thus, a British-based firm making sales in New York will owe taxes in the U.S.

Through a series of bilateral tax agreements the U.S. and several trading partners have tried to workout tax issues. Generally, the taxes a U.S. based MNE pays abroad will help offset any required taxes the firm might have on funds remitted to the United States.

2. What is a value-added tax? Where is this type of tax in side use? Why do you suppose this form of taxation has not been widely accepted in the United States?

**Answer**
A value-added tax (VAT) is a form of national sales tax, where goods are taxed at each step of extraction, production, wholesale, and retail. A VAT tax is considered regressive because those with lower incomes pay the same taxes on a particular commodity as those with more money. Americans have never taken to this type of national tax because the most similar type of state and local tax is the sales tax, and that has always been the domain of the states. Plus the fact that it is regressive make the tax a tough sell for tax payers.

## Chapter 20: Multinational Tax Management
## Multiple Choice Answer Key:

| | | | | | | | | | |
|---|---|---|---|---|---|---|---|---|---|
| 1 | A | 11 | A | 21 | B | 31 | C | 41 | A |
| 2 | B | 12 | B | 22 | C | 32 | B | 42 | B |
| 3 | D | 13 | D | 23 | A | 33 | D | 43 | C |
| 4 | C | 14 | A | 24 | B | 34 | D | 44 | D |
| 5 | D | 15 | D | 25 | D | 35 | A | 45 | C |
| 6 | B | 16 | A | 26 | D | 36 | B | 46 | D |
| 7 | A | 17 | C | 27 | D | 37 | C | 47 | A |
| 8 | C | 18 | D | 28 | C | 38 | B | 48 | C |
| 9 | B | 19 | B | 29 | A | 39 | A | 49 | B |
| 10 | C | 20 | C | 30 | A | 40 | C | 50 | B |

# Chapter 21
# Repositioning Funds

**Topic: Political Constraints**
**Skill: Conceptual**

1. Dividends remitted from a foreign subsidiary may be severely limited excessively delayed pending government approval. This is an example of

a. a political constraint.
b. heavy transaction costs.
c. foreign exchange risks.
d. none of the above.

**Topic: Excess Transaction Costs**
**Skill: Recognition**

2. Excess transaction costs may occur when

a. foreign subsidiaries remit dividends to the parents and the parent firm simultaneously pays for goods from the subsidiary.
b. parent firms provide capital financing to foreign subsidiaries while the subsidiary is paying for goods purchased from the parent.
c. the parent firm send a check to the foreign subsidiary for finished goods while the subsidiary is sending funds to the parent for raw materials purchased.
d. all of the above are examples of excess transaction costs.

**Topic: Unbundling of Remitted Funds**
**Skill: Conceptual**

3. Unbundling of fund transfers from foreign subsidiaries to the parent may result because

a. subsidiaries prefer to transfer smaller sums of money at any given time.
b. parents prefer several separate smaller receipts of funds for accounting purposes.
c. the parent may want to avoid the appearance of excessive cash drains from a much smaller host country.
d. none of the above.

**Topic: Remitted Funds**
**Skill: Conceptual**

4. Because funds are being remitted anyway, it makes little difference to the foreign or parent taxing authority nor to the parent or local firm, if a cash remittance is for a before-tax or after-tax item.

a. True
b. False

**Topic: Unbundling of Remitted Funds**
**Skill: Conceptual**
5. Which of the following is NOT a good reason for unbundling the remittance of foreign cash flows?

a. Unbundling allows each party to see the remittance and independently judge its acceptability.
b. Unbundling facilitates the allocation of overhead between parent and subsidiaries based on a predetermined formula.
c. Each government may be able to charge extra taxes based on the definition of the stated cash flows.
d. None of the above.

**Topic: Unbundling of Remitted Funds**
**Skill: Recognition**
6. Which of the following potential conduits for moving funds from the subsidiary to the parent is NOT an example of a before-tax expense in the host country?

a. costs of goods sold
b. dividends distributed to the parent
c. payments for management services
d. all of the above are before-tax expenses

**Topic: Transfer Pricing**
**Skill: Recognition**
7. Transfer pricing is the pricing of goods and services transferred to a foreign subsidiary from an affiliated company.

a. True
b. False

**Topic: Transfer Pricing**
**Skill: Conceptual**
8. A parent wishing to transfer funds _____ a particular country can charge _____ prices on goods sold to its subsidiary.

a. out of; lower
b. out of; higher
c. into; higher
d. none of the above

**Topic: Transfer Pricing**
**Skill: Conceptual**

9. A MNE wishing to ________ its worldwide tax liabilities would likely set transfer prices ________ in high income tax countries to minimize the taxable income there.

a. maximize; higher
b. minimize; lower
c. minimize; higher
d. none of the above

**Use the following information to answer questions 10 – 15**

Jasper Industries Inc. is based in Montana, USA and has a foreign subsidiary operating in Canada. The parent firm is about to make a sale to the Canadian subsidiary and is trying to determine the appropriate transfer pricing policy to maximize after-tax net income for the combined firm. Use the information below to answer the questions that follow.

| **Low-markup Policy** | | **Jasper (USA)** | | **Jasper (Canada)** | **Jasper (Combined)** |
|---|---|---|---|---|---|
| Sales | | $2,000 | | $3,000 | $3,000 |
| Less COGS | | (1,500) | | (2,000) | (1,500) |
| Gross Profit | | $500 | | $1,000 | |
| Less Operating Exp. | | 100 | | 200 | 300 |
| Taxable Income | | | | $800 | |
| Less Income Tax | (35%) | ____ | (40%) | 320 | |
| Net Income | | | | $480 | |
| | | | | | |
| **High-markup Policy** | | | | | |
| Sales | | $2,500 | | $3,000 | $3,000 |
| Less COGS | | (1,500) | | ____ | ____ |
| Gross Profit | | $1,000 | | | |
| Less Operating Exp. | | 100 | | 200 | 300 |
| Taxable Income | | $900 | | $300 | $1,200 |
| Less Income Tax | (35%) | 315 | (40%) | ____ | 435 |
| Net Income | | $585 | | | $765 |

**Topic: Transfer Pricing**
**Skill: Conceptual**

10. Other things equal, it is better to have a high-markup policy when the sale to a subsidiary goes from a low-tax country to a high-tax country.

a. True
b. False

**Topic: Transfer Pricing**
**Skill: Analytical**
11. What is the net income for Jasper USA under the low-markup policy?

a. $585
b. $480
c. $320
d. $260

**Topic: Transfer Pricing**
**Skill: Analytical**
12. What is the taxable income for the combined firms under a low-markup policy?

a. $460
b. $800
c. $1,200
d. $1,520

**Topic: Transfer Pricing**
**Skill: Analytical**
13. What is the cost of goods sold (COGS) for the Canadian subsidiary under the high-markup policy?

a. $4,000
b. $1,500
c. $2,000
d. $2,500

**Topic: Transfer Pricing**
**Skill: Analytical**
14. What is the net income for the Canadian subsidiary under the high-markup policy?

a. $180
b. $120
c. $480
d. $260

**Topic: Transfer Pricing**
**Skill: Analytical**
15. What is the cost of goods sold (COGS) for the combined firm under the high-markup policy?

a. $4,000
b. $2,500
c. $1,000
d. $1,500

**Topic: Transfer Pricing**
**Skill: Conceptual**
16. Which of the following is true?

a. The combined net income under the low-markup policy is greater than that for the high-markup policy.
b. The combined net income under the high-markup policy is greater than that for the low-markup policy.
c. The combined net incomes are the same under low- and high-markup policies.
d. None of the above is true.

**Topic: Arm's Length Transaction**
**Skill: Recognition**
17. The correct price for transfer prices, according to taxing authorities, is that which the firm would charge for goods or services to comparable unrelated customers, or to put it into the vernacular, a/an ___________ price.

a. free market
b. caveat emptor
c. arm's length
d. everyday

**Topic: Arm's Length Transaction**
**Skill: Recognition**
18. Which of the following is NOT an IRS approved method of determining an arm's length transaction?

a. comparable uncontrolled prices
b. resale prices
c. cost-plus calculations
d. all are approved IRS methods

**Topic: Arm's Length Transaction**
**Skill: Recognition**
19. Which of the following is regarded as the best evidence of arm's length pricing?

a. comparable uncontrolled price
b. resale price
c. cost-plus calculations
d. wholesale times two

**Topic: Arm's Length Transaction**
**Skill: Recognition**
20. Comparable uncontrolled price as a determinant of an arm's length transaction is the easiest method to use due to standardization of quality, quantity, and proprietary trademarks in international trade.

a. True
b. False

**Topic: Arm's Length Transaction**
**Skill: Recognition**
21. The __________ method of determining an appropriate transfer price starts with the final selling price to an independent purchaser and subtracts an appropriate markup for the subsidiary.

a. cost-plus
b. comparable uncontrolled price
c. resale price
d. bottom-up

**Topic: Transfer Pricing**
**Skill: Recognition**
22. The __________ method of determining an appropriate transfer price adds an appropriate markup to the seller full cost.

a. resale price
b. cost-plus
c. top down
d. comparable uncontrolled price

**Topic: Advance Pricing Agreements**
**Skill: Recognition**
23. Advance pricing agreements (APA) are negotiated with BOTH the home and host country tax authorities to assure that transfer pricing policies are acceptable before they are implemented.

a. True
b. False

**Topic: Centralized Vs. Decentralized Profit Centers**
**Skill: Conceptual**
24. Domestic firms and MNEs each debate the issue of centralized vs. decentralized profit centers. The issue is more difficult for domestic firms because they do not have the luxury of seeking out the lowest international tax rates.

a. True
b. False

**Topic: Centralized Vs. Decentralized Profit Centers**
**Skill: Recognition**
25. In the MNE debate over centralized vs. decentralized profit centers, coordination is hindered by all but which of the following?

a. longer and less-efficient channels of communication
b. unique variable that influence international pricing
c. separate taxation
d. all of the above

**Topic: Centralized Vs. Decentralized Profit Centers**
**Skill: Recognition**
26. When a high-tax subsidiary sacrifices income for the benefit of the whole firm, which of the following factors or conditions might be changed?

a. Import tariffs paid by the importer and hence profit levels
b. Income tax payments
c. Profitability, as measured by the ratio net income to ether sales or capital invested
d. All of the above

**Topic: Arm's Length Transactions**
**Skill: Conceptual**
27. MNEs may be able to price transfer prices away from that of an arm's length market price if

a. local critics take the host country government to task for allowing such blatant mispricing.
b. the host government has soured favoring foreign based MNEs.
c. the host country government recognizes they need of the MNE to obtain a profit of their own standards even if that seems unreasonable by local standards.
d. none of the above.

**Topic: Accelerated Repositioning of Funds**
**Skill: Conceptual**
28. Accelerated repositioning of funds from affiliate to parent may occur because:

a. the parent has no need for cash to make dividend payments.
b. the parent needs to pay for imports from its affiliate.
c. the affiliate fears its local currency will depreciate in value.
d. the quality of bank services in the home country has deteriorated.

**Topic: Unbundling**
**Skill: Recognition**
29. The identification of funds flows from foreign affiliated to their parent companies on the basis of cash remittances for very specific, identifiable, purposes is known as:

a. unbundling.
b. segregation.
c. reinvoicing.
d. desegregation.

**Topic: Repositioning of Funds**
**Skill: Conceptual**
30. Repositioning of funds from affiliate to parent is easier if:

a. the parent owns only half of the equity in the affiliate.
b. the parent owns 100% of the equity in the affiliate.
c. the affiliate is organized as a corporate subsidiary instead of as a branch.
d. the affiliate is owned individually through a holding company in the tax-haven country.

**Topic: License Fees**
**Skill: Recognition**
31. __________ are remuneration paid to the owners of technology, patents, trade names, and copyrighted material.

a. License fees
b. Royalty fees
c. Shared Service fees
d. None of the above

**Topic: Royalty Fees**
**Skill: Recognition**
32. Royalty fees are similar to licensing fees except that royalty fees are generally for intellectual property.

a. True
b. False

**Topic: Licensing Fees**
**Skill: Recognition**
33. For intra-firm transactions within a MNE, licensing fees may be subdivided into

a. technical assistance fees and management fees.
b. management fees and license fees.
c. license fees and technical assistance fees.
d. all of the above.

**Topic: Shared Service Fees**
**Skill: Recognition**
34. A charge to compensate the parent for costs incurred in the general management of international operations and for other corporate services provided to foreign subsidiaries is a

a. shared service fee.
b. distributed charge.
c. distributed overheads.
d. all of the above.

**Topic: Licensing**
**Skill: Recognition**
35. Which of the following is NOT a typical provision placed in a licensing contract?

a. A definition of sales price
b. The time and currency of payment
c. Who pays for costs associated with required monitoring of parties
d. All of the above is a typical provision in a licensing contract

**Topic: Dividend Payments**
**Skill: Recognition**

36. Firms need only current earnings to declare and pay dividends

a. True
b. False

**Topic: Stakeholders Priority**
**Skill: Recognition**

37. The concerns of local stakeholders or joint-venture partners must always take a backseat to the desires of MNE shareholders.

a. True
b. False

**Topic: Operating and Transaction Exposure**
**Skill: Conceptual**

38. Firms looking to reduce operating and/or transaction exposure could accelerate payments made with soft or depreciating currency or lag or slow down payment made with hard or appreciating currencies.

a. lag or slow down payment made with hard or appreciating currencies; accelerate payments made with hard or appreciating currencies.
b. lag or slow down payment made with hard or appreciating currencies; accelerate payments made with hard or appreciating currencies.
c. accelerate payments made with soft or depreciating currency; lag or slow down payment made with hard or appreciating currencies.
d. none of the above.

**Topic: Leading and Lagging**
**Skill: Conceptual**

39. The parent of a foreign affiliate will most likely decelerate the rate at which it transfers earnings and cash flows from affiliate to the parent if:

a. it believes the foreign host government is becoming more political stable.
b. intra-firm payables are in the host country's currency, which is currently appreciating.
c. the income tax rate in the home country is higher than that in the host country.
d. all of the above.

**Topic: Blocked Funds**
**Skill: Recognition**
40. Which of the following is NOT one of the strategies employed to cope with blocked funds?

a. transfer pricing
b. creating unrelated exports
c. syndicated loans
d. fronting loans

**Topic: Moving Funds From Affiliate to Parent**
**Skill: Conceptual**
41. Which of the following are appropriate conduits for moving funds from affiliate to parent?

a. payment of dividends
b. payment of interest on intracompany loans
c. payment of principal on intracompany loans
d. all of the above

**Topic: Blocked Funds**
**Skill: Conceptual**
42. The primary reason for the blocking of funds by the host country is:

a. the country's persistent inability to earn hard currencies.
b. the country's dependence on price-inelastic natural resource exports.
c. anti-imperialism policies of the host government.
d. the country's surplus in its balance of payments account.

**Topic:**
**Skill: Conceptual**
43. A parent might want to reposition funds from itself to an overseas affiliate because:

a. the parent needs to pay for a capital expansion with an Internal rate of return (IRR) greater than the weighted average cost of capital (WACC).
b. the parent needs to pay for a capital expansion with an Internal rate of return (IRR) less than the weighted average cost of capital (WACC).
c. the parent needs to pay for parent exports to the affiliate.
d. the parent needs to pay a dividend to its wholly owned subsidiary.

**Topic: Arms-length Transfers**
**Skill: Conceptual**
44. Arms-length transfer pricing is especially difficult to define and follow when the products involved:

a. are sold to less developed countries.
b. are finished and highly standardized products.
c. have no ready market outside of the multinational firm itself.
d. can be purchased from an unrelated supplier.

**Topic: Leading and Lagging**
**Skill: Conceptual**
45. A firm in Thailand has an account payable denominated in the Thai bhat. Their U.S. supplier has asked the Thai firm to pay the accounts payable earlier than currently scheduled, and has offered the Thai company a discount to do so. The Thai firm is unwilling to pay early. In this circumstance, it most likely that

a. both the Thai firm and the U.S. firm expect the Thai bhat to appreciate.
b. both the Thai firm and the U.S. firm expect the Thai bhat to depreciate.
c. the U.S. firm expects the bhat to appreciate and the Thai firm expects the bhat to depreciate.
d. none of the above.

**Topic: Reinvoicing Center**
**Skill: Recognition**
46. A reinvoicing center is a separate corporate subsidiary that serves as a type of middleman between parent and in one location and all foreign subsidiaries.

a. True
b. False

**Topic: Bundling of Remitted Funds**
**Skill: Conceptual**
47. Bundling of fund remittances to the parent is used

a. to facilitate allocation of parent overhead to an affiliate.
b. to keep the structure of affiliate profitability confidential and thus way from competitors and the foreign host government.
c. to avoid home country income taxes.
d. to minimize the income tax liability of affiliates.

**Topic: Transfer Pricing**
**Skill: Conceptual**
48. Transfer pricing is needed

a. when new management takes over an affiliate.
b. when the affiliate's cash balances become excessive.
c. whenever one unit of a multinational business sells to another unit of the same business.
d. none of the above.

**Topic: Reinvoicing Center**
**Skill: Recognition**
49. Which of the following is NOT an advantage of using a reinvoicing center?

a. managing foreign exchange exposure
b. guaranteeing the exchange rate for future orders
c. managing intra-subsidiary cash flow
d. all of the above are advantages

**Topic: Reinvoicing Center**
**Skill: Recognition**
50. The main disadvantage of a reinvoicing center is that the costs may exceed the benefits.

a. True
b. False

## Essay Questions:

1. What does it mean when affiliates "unbundle" the funds remitted to parents? What are the advantages and disadvantages to remitting funds in this manner?

**Answer**
Affiliates sometimes unbundle the cash flows they send to parents and identify the specific purpose of each dollar remitted. Firms do this because it clearly spells out the purpose of each dollar remitted and that may be advantageous for both political and tax purposes. If the parent firm can show that a payment has already been taxed in the foreign country that should reduce taxes payable on that cash flow in the home country. If a firm can clearly identify where a cash flow came from and why it is being remitted, that can be politically expedient as well. For instance, it may be easier to justify receipt of a cash flow to pay a cost of goods sold, than a single large chunk of money for which there is no explanation except apparent profit to the parent firm. Of course unbundling may also increase accounting costs caused by the required explanations. Furthermore, such specific details may reveal proprietary costs to governments or competitors.

2. The retiming of the transfer of funds among international firms can be an important determinant of profitability. Explain the concepts of leading and lagging. What is an important distinction between the practices of leads and lags between affiliated firms and between completely independent firms?

**Answer**
To lead is to pay early; to lag is to pay late. When the currency of record for an account payable is depreciating, a firm should delay paying as long as possible because the longer they wait, the less valuable the currency with which they are paying. The opposite is true if the currency is appreciating. This general rule however, may well be applied differently if the parties are independent or affiliated. Lead/lag is a zero-sum game, i.e., the gain of one party is exactly offset by the loss of the other. Of course this is fine between independent firms, but for affiliates, the reason for the practice is almost certainly for tax purposes, or remittance of funds, needed liquidity, or some other financial management reason other than simple profitability.

## Chapter 21: Repositioning Funds
## Multiple Choice Answer Key:

| | | | | | | | | | |
|---|---|---|---|---|---|---|---|---|---|
| 1 | A | 11 | D | 21 | C | 31 | A | 41 | D |
| 2 | D | 12 | C | 22 | B | 32 | A | 42 | A |
| 3 | C | 13 | D | 23 | A | 33 | D | 43 | A |
| 4 | B | 14 | A | 24 | B | 34 | D | 44 | C |
| 5 | C | 15 | D | 25 | D | 35 | D | 45 | B |
| 6 | B | 16 | B | 26 | D | 36 | B | 46 | A |
| 7 | A | 17 | C | 27 | C | 37 | B | 47 | B |
| 8 | B | 18 | D | 28 | C | 38 | C | 48 | C |
| 9 | C | 19 | A | 29 | A | 39 | D | 49 | D |
| 10 | A | 20 | B | 30 | B | 40 | C | 50 | A |

# Chapter 22
# Working Capital Management in the MNE

**Topic: Working Capital Management**
**Skill: Recognition**
1. Working capital management involves the management of

a. current and long-term assets.
b. current assets and current liabilities.
c. current liabilities and long-term assets.
d. current liabilities and long-term debt and equity.

**Topic: Cash Conversion Cycle**
**Skill: Recognition**
2. The cash conversion cycle

a. is a subset of the operating cycle.
b. occurs in the latter stages of the operating cycle.
c. is a subset of the accounts receivable period.
d. all of the above.

**Topic: Operating Cycle**
**Skill: Recognition**
3. The proper order of events for the operating cycle is:

a. input serving period, accounts receivable period, inventory period, quotation period.
b. quotation period, accounts receivable period, inventory period, input servicing period.
c. quotation period, input servicing period, inventory period, accounts receivable period.
d. accounts receivable period, input servicing period, quotation period, inventory period.

**Topic: Quotation Period**
**Skill: Conceptual**
4. Polaris Corporation (US) has bid a price on a project for a Korean firm, but the Korean firm has not yet placed an order. This portion of the operating cycle is best described as the

a. quotation period.
b. input sourcing period.
c. cash conversion cycle.
d. accounts payable cycle.

**Topic: Input Sourcing Period**
**Skill: Recognition**

5. The period in the cash cycle where the customer places the order, and the firm determines what materials for manufacture are not in inventory is called the ________ period.

a. quotation
b. input sourcing
c. accounts payable
d. accounts receivable

**Topic: Accounts Payable Period**
**Skill: Recognition**

6. The accounts payable period of the operating cycle

a. is equal to the inventory period.
b. may run concurrently but shorter than the inventory period.
c. may run concurrently but longer than the inventory period.
d. any one of the above may be true.

**Topic: Transaction Exposure**
**Skill: Conceptual**

7. According to GAAP, goods shipped with a foreign currency-denominated invoice use the ________ to record the value of the sale in the local currency.

a. beginning of the year exchange rate
b. average year-to-date exchange rate
c. spot rate on the day of the transaction
d. actual spot rate at time of future payment

**Topic: NWC**
**Skill: Recognition**

8. One possible definition of net working capital (NWC) provided by your authors is

a. NWC = A/R + inventory – A/P
b. NWC = cash +A/P – inventory
c. NWC = A/P + A/R – short-term loans
d. NWC = A/R + inventory – long-term debt

**Topic: NWC**
**Skill: Conceptual**
9. Which of the following actions will result in an increase in NWC?

a. An increase in A/P that exceeds an increase in A/R.
b. A reduction in inventory.
c. A reduction in A/P plus a smaller reduction in A/R.
d. An increase in A/P and a smaller reduction in inventory.

**Topic: NWC**
**Skill: Conceptual**
10. Which of the following statements is true?

a. A/R provide part of the funding for inventory.
b. A/P provide part of the funding for A/R and inventory.
c. Inventory pays for A/R and A/P.
d. None of the above is true.

**Topic: NWC**
**Skill: Recognition**
11. In principle, the firm tries to minimize its NWC balance.

a. True
b. False

**Use the following information to answer questions 12 – 14.**

| Polaris Corporation Balance Sheet December 31, 20xx | | | |
|---|---|---|---|
| Assets | | Liabilities and Equity | |
| A/R | $50,000 | A/P | $35,000 |
| Inventory | 30,000 | | |
| Total Current Assets | $80,000 | Long-term Debt | 265,000 |
| | | Total Liabilities | $300,000 |
| Equipment | $200,000 | | |
| Other Fixed Assets | 400,000 | Common Stock | $380,000 |
| Total Assets | $680,000 | Total Liabilities and Equity | $680,000 |

**Topic: NWC**
**Skill: Analytical**
12. The NWC for Polaris is __________.

a. $80,000
b. $680,000
c. $35,000
d. $45,000

**Topic: NWC**
**Skill: Analytical**
13. If Polaris increases inventory by $10,000 and A/P also by $10,000, the net change in NWC is ___________.

a. $20,000
b. $10,000
c. $0
d. none of the above

**Topic: NWC**
**Skill: Analytical**
14. NWC currently makes up what percentage of total firm value for Polaris?

a. 6.6%
b. 5.1%
c. 11.8%
d. 9.2%

**Use the following information to answer questions 15 – 17.**

SureDrip Irrigation Systems Inc. is supplied with plastic chips for their plastic injection molding manufacturing process. Their supplier, Sun Chemical, Inc. offers financing terms of a 2% discount if the accounts payable are paid in 10 days or less with the full balance due in 45 days. Short-term financing available to SureDrip is available at an annual rate of 9.6%. SureDrip has just purchased $400,000 of plastic chips from Sun Chemical.

**Topic: Discounts**
**Skill: Analytical**
15. What is the amount of money SureDrip will save on accounts payable if they accept the discount?

a. $400,000
b. $8,000
c. $33,333
d. $20,000

**Topic: Interest Cost of Supplier Financing**
**Skill: Analytical**
16. What is the effective annual interest cost of supplier financing offered by Sun Chemical?

a. 7.3%
b. 9.5%
c. 10.4%
d. 22.9%

**Topic: Interest Cost of Supplier Financing**
**Skill: Analytical**
17. Should SureDrip take the discount offered by Sun Chemical?

a. Yes, SureDrip will get to use their raw materials 35 days earlier than if they waited to pay at the end of the 45 days.
b. No, SureDrip will not have to pay any interest if they just pay in 45 days.
c. Yes, SureDrip's short term borrowing rate of 9.6% is less than Sun's offered cost of carry of 22.9%.
d. No, it costs SureDrip 22.9% to accept the discount and they are better off paying the full amount in 45 days.

**Topic: Days Working Capital**
**Skill: Analytical**
18. Days working capital is equal to

a. days payables + days receivables - days inventory.
b. days inventory + days receivables – days payables.
c. days payables + days inventory + days receivables.
d. none of the above.

**Topic: Days Working Capital**
**Skill: Conceptual**
19. Other things equal, managers prefer a lower "days working capital" to a higher one.

a. True
b. False

**Topic: Days Working Capital**
**Skill: Conceptual**
20. Amundsen of Norway receives raw materials from their corporate parent in the U.S. with payment terms of net 60 days. Most of their sales are to firms in Norway where normal payment terms are net 30 days. This causes a problem for the subsidiary with working capital management because

a. accounts receivable are so much longer than accounts payable.
b. accounts payable are so much longer than accounts receivable.
c. accounts receivable and accounts payable are equal.
d. this doesn't really cause a problem; in fact it is to the benefit of the Norwegian subsidiary.

**Topic: Currency-denomination of Sales**
**Skill: Recognition**
21. Domestic sales are almost always denominated in the local currency, but international sales may be denominated in

a. the exporter's currency.
b. the importer's currency.
c. a third country currency.
d. any of the above.

**Topic: Currency-denomination of Sales**
**Skill: Recognition**
22. Which of the following may determine the currency used for transactions in international sales?

a. custom
b. competition
c. bargaining and negotiation
d. any of the above

**Topic: Cash Management Strategies**
**Skill: Conceptual**
23. Other things equal, a firm would rather have _________ in a depreciating currency, and ____________ in an appreciating currency.

a. accounts receivable; accounts payable
b. accounts receivable; accounts receivable
c. accounts payable; accounts receivable
d. none of the above

**Topic: Inflation**
**Skill: Conceptual**
24. In an inflationary economy, demand for credit usually exceeds supply.

a. True
b. False

**Topic: Self-liquidating Bills**
**Skill: Recognition**
25. The Europeans have a popular liquid discountable, bill originating with the Code Napoleon and backed by accounts receivable called

a. banker's acceptances.
b. self-liquidating bills.
c. commercial paper.
d. negotiable certificates of deposit.

**Topic: Japanese Credit Terms**
**Skill: Recognition**
26. Japanese markets are noted for their short maturity payment terms (less than 20 days), and the general reluctance of the manufacturer to supply any type of credit to customers.

a. True
b. False

**Topic: Home Currency Devaluation**
**Skill: Conceptual**
27. Firms might be tempted to order _________ inventory from foreign sources if they thought their currency was about to be ____________.

a. less; devalued
b. extra; revalued
c. extra; devalued
d. none of the above

**Topic: Home Currency Devaluation**
**Skill: Conceptual**

28. Firms whose currency is prime for devaluation may choose to purchase extra inventory from foreign sources before the devaluation occurs. Which of the following is NOT a potential problem associated with such a practice.

a. As a result of holding extra inventory the firm now has extra sales.
b. As a result of devaluation, the local government may freeze the price at which the firm can sell its inventory.
c. The devaluation doesn't occur and the firm now experiences additional storage costs.
d. All of the above are potential problems.

**Topic: Free-trade Zones**
**Skill: Recognition**

29. Free-trade zones may take the form of

a. warehouses for imported goods.
b. assembly plants for imported parts.
c. manufacturing plants for re-export.
d. all of the above.

**Topic: Cash Management**
**Skill: Conceptual**

30. Which of the following is NOT a precautionary motive for holding cash?

a. Anticipated funds to be remitted from several Middle East countries are in question due to unrest in the region.
b. The firm has several short-term obligations in unhedged foreign currency-denominated contracts.
c. The firm must pay ordinary wages in two days.
d. All are precautionary motives.

**Topic: Cash Management**
**Skill: Recognition**

31. Increases to cash flows can be anticipated if which of the following occurs?

a. A receivables contract is denominated in an appreciating foreign currency.
b. Sales are less than anticipated.
c. Days in accounts receivable increase by 15 days.
d. None of the above.

**Topic: Cash Management**
**Skill: Recognition**
32. For disbursement purposes, it is to the benefit of the firm to minimize float.

a. True
b. False

**Topic: Cash Management**
**Skill: Conceptual**
33. Which of the following is NOT a function covered by international cash management?

a. maximizing interest earned on idle international cash balances
b. manipulating transfer prices
c. repositioning of funds within the multinational firm
d. investing surplus cash held within the system

**Topic: Centralized Depository**
**Skill: Recognition**
34. A centralized depository benefits the firm primarily by

a. reducing the cost of repatriating funds.
b. positioning profits where taxes are lowest.
c. reducing the total amount of capital employed within the total firm.
d. earning a higher rate of return than in domestic banking deposits.

**Topic: Fund Transfer Volume**
**Skill: Recognition**
35. The volume of fund transfers averages about 1.2 trillion dollars per year.

a. True
b. False

**Topic: CHIPS**
**Skill: Recognition**
36. The Clearing House Interbank Payment System (CHIPS) is

a. the largest publicly operated payments system in the world.
b. is owned and operated by the worlds seven largest central banks.
c. a computerized network that connects banks globally.
d. none of the above.

**Topic: SWIFT**
**Skill: Recognition**
37. The Society for Worldwide Financial Telecommunications (SWIFT) is an interbank communications system that carries approximately 1.2 billion messages per year.

a. True
b. False

**Topic: Central Depository**
**Skill: Recognition**
38. Which of the following is NOT an advantage provided to MNEs by a central depository?

a. obtaining information
b. holding precautionary cash balances
c. reducing interest rate costs
d. all are advantages

**Topic: Central Depository**
**Skill: Recognition**
39. An organizational structure employed by an MNE to reduce its use of bank lending for the support of operations is

a. a centralized depository.
b. a reinvoicing center.
c. a cost center.
d. a syndicated bank.

**Topic: Free-trade Zone**
**Skill: Conceptual**
40. A free-trade zone allows the user to

a. avoid paying import duties.
b. reduce net cash flow exposed due to netting of funds between affiliates.
c. reduce tax and tariff bills because of reinvoicing.
d. postpone import duties.

**Topic: Multilateral Netting**
**Skill: Recognition**
41. ____________ is the process that cancels via offset all, or part, of the debt owed by one entity to another related entity.

a. Syndicated banking
b. Centralized depositing
c. Multilateral netting
d. Debt cancellation

**Topic: Correspondent Banking**
**Skill: Recognition**
42. Which of the following is NOT a correspondent banking service?

a. accepting bank drafts
b. honoring letters of credit
c. furnishing credit informational
d. all of the above are correspondent bank activities

**Topic: Sources of Currency**
**Skill: Conceptual**
43. In a two-country, two-currency international operation, an affiliate in country "A" needing more of its own currency can

a. borrow locally.
b. export to an affiliate and receive funds from that affiliate.
c. obtain funds from a central pool, which in turn might borrow any of several currencies and exchange them for currency "A".
d. all of the above.

**Topic: Precautionary Cash Balance**
**Skill: Conceptual**
44. A precautionary cash balance

a. is used to replace spoiled or damaged inventory.
b. is held to facilitate cash disbursements when receipts slow down.
c. is used for normal day-to-day operations.
d. is held for the benefit of a sister affiliate.

**Topic: Cash Pool**
**Skill: Recognition**
45. A cash pool is

a. excess cash held centrally for a set of affiliates, in order to be invested on more favorable terms.
b. cash held in a pooling-of-interest bank account.
c. the currency used for functional reporting.
d. cash routed through two or more affiliates to avoid taxes.

**Topic: Branch Banking**
**Skill: Recognition**
46. Which of the following is NOT true about branch banking for U.S. commercial banks?

a. Branch banking has been the most important way for U.S. banks to conduct their foreign activities.
b. Assets held are declining in Latin America.
c. Japan is the most important location of U.S. branches.
d. Branch banks account for about one-half of all international banking assets held by U.S. firms.

**Topic: Banking Affiliate**
**Skill: Recognition**
47. A/An _________ is a locally incorporated bank owned in part but not necessarily controlled by a foreign parent.

a. banking affiliate
b. Edge Act Corporation
c. international branch bank
d. bank subsidiary

**Topic: Edge Act Corporation**
**Skill: Recognition**
48. An Edge Act corporation is a subsidiary of a U.S. bank located outside of the U.S. and incorporated to engage in international banking and financing operations.

a. True
b. False

**Topic: In-house Bank**
**Skill: Conceptual**
49. An in-house bank

a. is a separate bank chartered to operate within a business firm.
b. is in fact a set of functions performed by the existing treasury department.
c. assesses the credit standing of the bank's customers.
d. provides banking services for employees.

**Topic: Bank Subsidiary**
**Skill: Recognition**
50. A foreign banking office that is separately incorporated in the host country is

a. a correspondent bank.
b. a representative office.
c. a bank subsidiary.
d. an Edge Act corporation.

## Essay Questions:

1. What is a free-trade zone? Identify three techniques and provide examples of how firms and countries can benefit from having free trade zones.

**Answer**
Free-trade zones are locations within a country where foreign firms can store, assemble, or manufacture goods without paying an import duty until the goods are actually distributed. The authors provide the example of Toyota Motor Corporation exporting cars to the United States and storing them at a facility in Los Angeles. This allows Toyota to collect an inventory of cars in the states and to be more readily able to meet consumer demand for specific models. However, they do not pay any import duty until the cars are moved from the free-trade zone.

A second example provided by the authors is that of Mercedes assembling automobiles in Alabama. Again, the parts are shipped to Alabama without being assessed an import duty until the assembled cars are distributed. And then, even though the cars are a finished products, the duty is assessed at a lower rate on the parts only. This also benefits the state of Alabama who now has a major employer in town.

Finally, a manufacturing center is placed in a free-trade or industrial zone. Here, several companies can set up shop in an area designated for foreign manufacture. Most of the items produced will be exported out of that country and not have to pay any sort of import duty. However, the country will benefit from employment, the resulting tax revenues, and perhaps being able to supply some of the parts used in the manufacturing process.

2. Central depositories are used for international cash management. What is a central depository? Identify and provide examples of at least three advantages to MNEs of having a central depository.

**Answer**
A central depository for cash management allows the parent firm to manage cash in a manner that maximizes the benefit to the entire firm rather than specific affiliates. Typically, a firm will order each affiliate to maintain only those cash balances necessary for its own transactions and to forward the balance to a centralized location.

The central depository is typically located in a world money center where it has ready and inexpensive access to information. Central depositories can reduce the size of total precautionary funds for the MNE. If the need for precautionary funds by the affiliates is not perfectly correlated, a central pool of funds will be smaller than if each of the affiliates independently held their desired precautionary balances.

Managers of a central pool of funds can seek out the lowest costs for borrowing required funds, and the highest rates for parking excess cash more efficiently than can affiliate managers who may be limited by local laws as to where they can put their funds. Finally, location is important for either cost purposes, such as low taxes or a physically central presence, or for access to information.

## Chapter 22: Working Capital Management in the MNE
## Multiple Choice Answer Key:

| | | | | | | | | | |
|---|---|---|---|---|---|---|---|---|---|
| 1 | B | 11 | A | 21 | D | 31 | A | 41 | C |
| 2 | D | 12 | D | 22 | D | 32 | B | 42 | D |
| 3 | C | 13 | C | 23 | C | 33 | B | 43 | D |
| 4 | A | 14 | A | 24 | A | 34 | C | 44 | B |
| 5 | B | 15 | B | 25 | B | 35 | B | 45 | A |
| 6 | D | 16 | D | 26 | B | 36 | C | 46 | C |
| 7 | C | 17 | C | 27 | C | 37 | A | 47 | A |
| 8 | A | 18 | B | 28 | A | 38 | D | 48 | B |
| 9 | C | 19 | A | 29 | D | 39 | A | 49 | B |
| 10 | B | 20 | D | 30 | C | 40 | D | 50 | C |

# Chapter 23
# International Trade Finance

**Topic: Unaffiliated Unknown Party**
**Skill: Recognition**
1. The exporter-importer relationship to a corporation of a foreign importer that has not previously conducted business with the firm would be an

a. unaffiliated unknown.
b. affiliated party.
c. unaffiliated unknown.
d. any of the above.

**Topic: Unaffiliated Unknown Party**
**Skill: Recognition**
2. Which of the following relationships between importing and exporting parties would require the least detailed contract to conduct business?

a. affiliated party
b. unaffiliated unknown party
c. known unaffiliated party
d. domestic supplier

**Topic: Affiliated Party Transaction**
**Skill: Conceptual**
3. Polaris Corporation has made an agreement to ship goods to a foreign firm with whom they have not entered into a contract for three years. However the firms have communicated regularly since the last sale three years ago. This is an example of an

a. unaffiliated known party transaction.
b. unaffiliated unknown party transaction.
c. affiliated party transaction.
d. none of the above.

**Topic: International Trade**
**Skill: Recognition**
4. Today, international trade is dominated by transactions between unaffiliated parties (known or unknown).

a. True
b. False

**Topic: International Trade**
**Skill: Recognition**

5. Because most international transactions are between affiliated parties, international transaction contracts are less complex, but the management of the total value of the MNE is more complex.

a. True
b. False

**Topic: Bill of Lading**
**Skill: Recognition**

6. A _________ is issued to the exported by a common carrier transporting the merchandise.

a. commercial invoice
b. banker's acceptance
c. packing list
d. bill of lading

**Topic: Commercial Invoice**
**Skill: Recognition**

7. A signed ____________ is issued by the exporter and contains a precise description of the merchandise.

a. packing list
b. bill of lading
c. commercial invoice
d. banker's acceptance

**Topic: Packing Lists**
**Skill: Recognition**

8. _____________ may be required so that the contents of containers can be identified, either for customs purposes of for importer identification of the contents of separate containers.

a. Banker's acceptances
b. Commercial invoces
c. Consular invoices
d. Packing lists

**Topic: Certificates of Analysis**
**Skill: Recognition**
9. _______________ are documents included in a contract to ensure that specific quality, purity, or weight specifications are met.

a. Consular invoices
b. Insurance documents
c. Certificates of analysis
d. None of the above

**Topic: Timing of Default Risk**
**Skill: Recognition**
10. The risk of default on the part of the importer is present as soon as

a. a price quote is requested.
b. goods are shipped.
c. the export contract is signed.
d. goods are received.

**Topic: Currency Risk**
**Skill: Recognition**
11. ____________ is the risk that interest rates will change between signing the contract and payment for goods services.

a. Currency risk
b. Risk of non-completion
c. Default risk
d. Portfolio risk

**Topic: Draft**
**Skill: Recognition**
12. Which of the following document is NOT part of a system designed to protect both the importer and exporter from non-completion of trade?

a. letter of credit
b. draft
c. bill of lading
d. all of the above are important protective documents

**Topic: Letter of Credit**
**Skill: Recognition**
13. A letter of credit is an agreement by the bank to pay against documents rather than the actual merchandise.

a. True
b. False

**Topic: Letter of Credit**
**Skill: Recognition**

14. Which of the following is NOT true regarding a letter of credit?

a. The importer and exporter agree on a transaction.
b. The importer applies to it local bank for the issuance of a letter of credit.
c. The exporter applies to its local bank for the issuance of a letter of credit.
d. The importer's bank cuts a sales contract based on its assessment of the creditworthiness of the importer.

**Topic: Letter of Credit**
**Skill: Recognition**

15. Which of the following is NOT necessary to constitute a true letter of credit (L/C) transaction?

a. The bank's commitment must have a stated maximum amount of money.
b. The bank's L/C must contain a specified expiration date or a definite maturity.
c. The issuing bank must receive a fee or other valid business consideration for issuing the L/C.
d. All of the above are necessary.

**Topic: Revocable Letter of Credit**
**Skill: Recognition**

16. A/An ____________ letter of credit is intended to serve as a means of arranging payment, but not as a guarantee of payment.

a. irrevocable
b. revocable
c. confirmed
d. unconfirmed

**Topic: Unconfirmed and Confirmed Letters of Credit**
**Skill: Recognition**

17. A/An__________ letter of credit is an obligation only of the issuing bank whereas other banks honor a/an __________ letter of credit.

a. irrevocable; unconfirmed
b. revocable; confirmed
c. confirmed; irrevocable
d. unconfirmed; confirmed

**Topic: Letter of Credit**
**Skill: Conceptual**

18. The primary advantage of a letter of credit is that it reduces risk.

a. True
b. False

**Topic: Letter of Credit**
**Skill: Recognition**
19. A letter of credit that is confirmed in the __________ country has the additional advantage of eliminating the problem of ____________.

a. exporter's; portfolio risk
b. importer's; blocked foreign exchange
c. exporter's; blocked foreign exchange
d. none of the above

**Topic: Letter of Credit**
**Skill: Recognition**
20. The major advantage to the exporter of a letter of credit is that the exporter does not receive any funds until the documents have arrived at a local port or airfield.

a. True
b. False

**Topic: International Trade**
**Skill: Recognition**
21. The three main documents in international trade are

a. letter of credit, draft, and bill of lading.
b. letter of credit, loan guarantee, and draft.
c. draft, banker's acceptance, and consular invoice.
d. packing list, draft, and export declaration.

**Topic: Draft**
**Skill: Recognition**
22. The draft is the instrument normally used in international commerce to

a. transfer title.
b. prove ownership.
c. transfer title.
d. initiate the sale.

**Topic: Letter of Credit**
**Skill: Recognition**
23. The letter of credit is designed to

a. allow the buyer to obtain title to the goods before they are received.
b. free the seller from concerns over the payment abilities of the buyer.
c. free the seller from any merchandise guarantees.
d. is issued by the bank at the request of an exporter.

**Topic: International Trade**
**Skill: Recognition**
24. A fundamental problem of international trade is

a. authorities in the importing country may disallow the consular invoice.
b. authorities in the exporting country may refuse to issue a consular invoice.
c. buyer and seller may act in collusion.
d. buyer and seller may not completely trust each other.

**Topic: Letter of Credit**
**Skill: Recognition**
25. Which are NOT types of letter of credit?

a. insurable vs. noninsurable
b. confirmed vs. unconfirmed
c. revocable vs. irrevocable
d. none are letters of credit

**Topic: Letter of Credit**
**Skill: Recognition**
26. An instrument issued by a bank, at the request of an importer, in which the bank promises to pay a beneficiary upon presentation of specified documents is a

a. time certificate of deposit.
b. time draft.
c. sight draft.
d. letter of credit.

**Topic: Letter of Credit**
**Skill: Recognition**
27. The disadvantages of a letter of credit to the importer include:

a. the exporter's reduced line of credit as a result of the letter of credit.
b. the fee charged by the exporter's bank for accepting the letter of credit.
c. the fee charged by the importer's bank for issuing the letter of credit.
d. all of the above.

**Topic: Bill of Exchange**
**Skill: Recognition**
28. The ____________ is the instrument normally used to actually effect payment in international commerce.

a. banker's acceptance
b. bill of exchange
c. bill of lading
d. letter of credit

**Topic: Maker**
**Skill: Recognition**
29. The person or company initiating the draft or bill of exchange is known as the

a. maker.
b. drawer.
c. originator.
d. any of the above.

**Topic: Drawee**
**Skill: Recognition**
30. The person or company to whom the draft or bill of exchange is addressed is the

a. drawee.
b. drawer.
c. maker.
d. originator.

**Topic: Draft**
**Skill: Recognition**
31. Which of the following is NOT a requirement for a draft to become a negotiable instrument?

a. It must be payable to order or to bearer.
b. It must be payable on demand or at a fixed or determinable future date.
c. It must be in writing and signed by the maker or drawer.
d. All of the above.

**Topic: Sight and Time Drafts**
**Skill: Recognition**
32. A sight draft is payable on presentation to the drawee; a time draft allows a delay in payment.

a. True
b. False

**Topic: Clean Drafts**
**Skill: Recognition**
33. __________ drafts are unaccompanied by any other documents, and are usually used between MNEs and ____________.

a. Clean; new trading partners
b. Documentary; their own affiliates
c. Clean; their own affiliates
d. None of the above

**Topic: Clean Drafts**
**Skill: Recognition**
34. Most drafts in international trade are "clean".

a. True
b. False

**Topic: Banker's Acceptances**
**Skill: Recognition**
35. Drafts that have been accepted by banks become

a. clean drafts.
b. nonmarketable.
c. banker's acceptances.
d. none of the above.

**Topic: Banker's Acceptances**
**Skill: Recognition**
36. A bill of exchange or draft drawn on a bank and commonly used to guarantee exporters that they will receive payment on goods delivered to importers is a/an

a. banker's acceptance.
b. clean draft.
c. bill of lading.
d. letter of credit.

**Topic: Banker's Acceptances**
**Skill: Analytical**
37. An exporter has just received a banker's acceptance created by an international transaction. If the banker's acceptance has a face value of $250,000 and the bank charges a commission of 1% per annum, how much will the exporter receive from the banker if the acceptance is held until maturity six months from today?

a. $250,000
b. $247,500
c. $248,750
d. $1,250

**Topic: Banker's Acceptances**
**Skill: Analytical**
38. An exporter has just received a banker's acceptance created by an international transaction. If the banker's acceptance has a face value of $250,000, current rates on banker's acceptances are 6%, and the bank charges a commission of 1% per annum, how much will the exporter receive if he sells the acceptance in the secondary market six months prior to maturity?

a. $250,000
b. $244,000
c. $242,500
d. $241,250

**Topic: Bill of Lading**
**Skill: Recognition**
39. Which of the following purposed is NOT served by the bill of lading?

a. It acts as a receipt.
b. It acts as a contract.
c. It acts as a document of title.
d. It acts as all of the above.

**Topic: Bill of Lading**
**Skill: Recognition**
40. The ________ is issued to the exporter by a common carrier transporting the merchandise.

a. bill of lading
b. draft
c. banker's acceptance
d. line of credit

**Topic: Securitized Receivables**
**Skill: Recognition**
41. Which of the following is NOT a factor in the discounting of a securitized export receivable?

a. The cost of credit insurance
b. The historic collection risk of the importer
c. The historic collection risk of the exporter
d. The size of the financing and service fees

**Topic: Straight Bill of Lading**
**Skill: Conceptual**

42. A straight bill of lading is most likely to be used under which of the following circumstances?

a. When the merchandize has not been paid for in advance
b. When the transaction is being financed by a bank
c. When the shipment is to an affiliate
d. None of the above

**Topic: Credit Terms**
**Skill: Conceptual**

43. An exporter who insists on cash or a letter of credit for foreign shipments is likely to lose orders to competitors from other countries that provide more favorable credit terms.

a. True
b. False

**Topic: The Foreign Credit Insurance Association**
**Skill: Recognition**

44. The Foreign Credit Insurance Association is a branch of the U.S. federal government.

a. True
b. False

**Topic: Letter of Credit**
**Skill: Recognition**

45. The three parties to a letter of credit are:

a. issuing bank, seller, and applicant.
b. importer, exporter, and shipping company.
c. notary public, importer, and importer's bank.
d. Ex-Im bank, commercial bank, and importer.

**Topic: Banker's Acceptances**
**Skill: Recognition**

46. A banker's acceptance is a ____________ that has been accepted by a bank.

a. credit certificate
b. time draft
c. line of credit
d. bill of lading

**Topic: Letter of Credit**
**Skill: Conceptual**
47. When a confirmed letter of credit is used, the exporting firm gains because

a. the government in effect subsidizes shipping costs.
b. the time involved in shipping is generally reduced.
c. the firm can sell against the promise of a local bank rather than a firm.
d. the exporting firm is considered of higher risk.

**Topic: The Export-Import Bank**
**Skill: Recognition**
48. The Export-Import Bank is an independent agency of the U.S. government established in 1934 to

a. ship money abroad.
b. import agricultural products during the recession.
c. facilitate and stimulate foreign trade of the United States.
d. none of the above.

**Topic: The Foreign Credit Insurance Corporation**
**Skill: Recognition**
49. In the United States, the Foreign Credit Insurance Corporation

a. is a subsidiary of the Export-Import Bank.
b. provides letters of credit for U.S. importers.
c. provides letters of credit for U.S. exporters.
d. provides policies that protect U.S. exporters against default by foreign importers.

**Topic: Letter of Credit**
**Skill: Recognition**
50. In a letter of credit, the bank substitutes its credit for that of the importer and promises to pay if certain documents are submitted to the bank.

a. True
b. False

## Essay Questions:

1. Explain what a letter of credit (L/C) is, who the principle parties are, what the principle advantage is, and how the L/C facilitates international trade.

**Answer**
A letter of credit (L/C) is a bank's conditional promise to pay issued by a bank at the request of an importer. The primary advantage of an L/C is the reduction in risk. This reduction in risk makes it easier for the exporter to sell goods to the importer because it

no longer need rely on the ability of the importing firm to pay for the goods, but rather it can rely on the bank.

There are three primary parties involved with a letter of credit. Party number one is the exporter, who makes a sale to the importer in exchange for the bank's L/C. Party number two is the importer who receives the goods and promises to pay the bank. And third, the bank that contracts with the importer and agrees to pay the exporter upon presentation of documents as specified in the L/C.

The advantage to an exporter is the increased likelihood of receiving payment because funds are due from a known international commercial bank as opposed to a relatively unknown importer. Furthermore, an exporter with a good reputation for delivery may be able to sell the L/C at a discount in the secondary market prior to shipping and speed up cash flow.

The importer benefits because it doesn't need to pay for goods purchased until they actually reach port. The bank benefits from the fees they charge.

2. What is a banker's acceptance? How are they initiated? Why are they desirable for the exporter?

**Answer**
A draft, or bill of exchange, is a written order from the exporter telling the importer when and how much to pay. When properly contracted, a draft can become a negotiable instrument and trade in the secondary market. If the draft provides a specific payment date and is presented to the importer's bank, it becomes a banker's acceptance (BA) and the bank makes an unconditional promise to make payment upon maturity. A BA may sell in the secondary market like any other marketable security and the holder need not wait until maturity to liquidate. Thus, BAs facilitate trade by reducing risk and potentially speeding cash flows to the exporter.

## Chapter 23: International Trade Finance
## Multiple Choice Answer Key:

| | | | | | | | | | |
|---|---|---|---|---|---|---|---|---|---|
| 1 | C | 11 | A | 21 | A | 31 | D | 41 | B |
| 2 | B | 12 | D | 22 | C | 32 | B | 42 | C |
| 3 | A | 13 | A | 23 | B | 33 | C | 43 | A |
| 4 | B | 14 | C | 24 | D | 34 | B | 44 | B |
| 5 | A | 15 | D | 25 | A | 35 | C | 45 | A |
| 6 | D | 16 | B | 26 | D | 36 | A | 46 | B |
| 7 | C | 17 | D | 27 | C | 37 | C | 47 | C |
| 8 | D | 18 | A | 28 | B | 38 | D | 48 | C |
| 9 | C | 19 | C | 29 | D | 39 | D | 49 | D |
| 10 | B | 20 | B | 30 | A | 40 | A | 50 | A |